D0430003

THE
ZIONIST
IDEA

THE
ZIONIST
IDEA

A Historical Analysis and Reader

EDITED AND WITH AN INTRODUCTION

AND BIOGRAPHICAL NOTES

by Arthur Hertzberg

FOREWORD BY EMANUEL NEUMANN

A TEMPLE BOOK

ATHENEUM

NEW YORK

For Phyllis, Linda, and Susan

Reprinted by arrangement with
The Jewish Publication Society of America
Copyright © 1959 by Arthur Hertzberg

All rights reserved. No part of this book may be reproduced or
transmitted in any form or by any means, electronic or mechanical,
including photocopying, recording, or by any information storage
and retrieval system, without permission in writing from the Publisher.

Atheneum
Macmillan Publishing Company
866 Third Avenue, New York, NY 10022
Collier Macmillan Canada, Inc.

Library of Congress catalog card number 77-90073
ISBN *0-689-70093-8*

Macmillan books are available at special discounts for bulk purchases
for sales promotions, premiums, fund-raising, or educational use.
For details, contact:

> *Special Sales Director*
> *Macmillan Publishing Company*
> *866 Third Avenue*
> *New York, NY 10022*

23 22 21 20 19
Printed in the United States of America

CONTENTS

Part 4:   The Agnostic Rabbi—Ahad Ha-Am   247

Part 7: *Religious Nationalists, Old and New* 397

FOREWORD

THE ZIONIST REVOLUTION—its triumphant consummation in a sovereign Israel—has given rise to an extensive literature. The mounting stream of books dealing with the subject attests the wide impact of the event, unparalleled in history, upon the mind of our generation.

With few exceptions the books which have appeared thus far deal almost exclusively with what may be termed the external factors. The massacre of European Jewry by the Nazis and the acute problem of the surviving remnants; the insoluble conflict between Jews and Arabs in Palestine and the breakdown of the British Mandate; the mutual rivalries of the Western powers in the Middle East and the East-West conflict in the world scene—these are some of the tangible historic forces which accelerated the birth of the Jewish State. But it is rather characteristic of our times that comparatively little attention has been given to another and deeper aspect: the internal moral and intellectual forces in Jewish life, which are at least as important and which constitute the ultimately decisive factor. Behind the miracle of the Restoration lies more than a century of spiritual and intellectual ferment which produced a crystallized Zionist philosophy and a powerful Zionist movement, the progenitor of the Jewish State.

The present volume offers an opportunity to study the genesis of an idea which galvanized a people, forged a nation, and made history. The essential source material is presented as it came from the hands and minds of its authors, constituting an intellectual history of the Zionist Revolution. The editor's illuminating and brilliantly written introduction—a book in itself—is the first important account of Zionist ideology in English. Both as author and editor, he has rendered an invaluable service to all students of this subject.

Emanuel Neumann

PREFACE

THE INITIAL IMPULSE for this volume came four years ago from Dr. Emanuel Neumann, in his capacity as head of the Theodor Herzl Foundation. It was his notion that the time had come—indeed, it was long overdue—for a presentation of the whole range of Zionist thought in English. Despite his many duties in the intervening years, he has been both a goad and a guide.

In the course of my work I have benefited greatly from the help and advice of the editors for the Herzl Press—Ben Halpern, Moshe Kohn, and Raphael Patai—and of the editor for Doubleday—Clement Alexandre. Thanks are due to the Hebrew Union College Library in Cincinnati (Herbert C. Zafren, Administrative Secretary) and to the Zionist Library and Archives in New York City (Mrs. Sylvia Landress, Director) for their co-operation in acting as the major sources of the books I required; to Itzhak Ivry, Murray Silberman, Pearl Silver, and Mrs. Minerva Kraut for technical aid; and to Evelyn Kossoff for her painstaking labors in copy editing the manuscript.

Various friends and colleagues have been generous with their time and special knowledge on specific points or sections of this book, but the list is too long to permit individual acknowledgments. I must, however, add that the responsibility for the entire manuscript, including not only the signed introduction and the choice of the readings, but also the original translations, the biographies, and the annotations, is mine.

It remains to acknowledge larger debts. In the first place, whatever interest I may have in the affairs of the spirit, I learned from my parents, Rabbi and Mrs. Zvi Elimelech Hertzberg. How much I owe to the outlook of my teacher, Dr. Salo Baron, will be evident to the reader not only from the important matters on which I have followed his lead but also even in those questions where my emphases are different. My wife's labors on this manuscript approached collaboration; the dedication of this book to her, and to our daughters, is but a small symbol of what she means to the author's work—and to the author.

Arthur Hertzberg

Englewood, New Jersey

INTRODUCTION

ZIONISM EXISTS, and it has had important consequences, but historical theory does not really know what to do with it. Though modern Zionism arose within the milieu of European nationalism in the nineteenth century, the historians of that era usually content themselves with briefly noticing the movement, for the sake of "completeness." The root cause of their difficulty (the relatively few members involved and the partial inaccessibility of the source material are quite secondary reasons) is that Zionism cannot be typed, and therefore easily explained, as a "normal" kind of national *risorgimento*. To mention only one important difference, all of the other nineteenth-century nationalisms based their struggle for political sovereignty on an already existing national land or language (generally, there were both). Zionism alone proposed to acquire both of these usual preconditions of national identity by the *élan* of its nationalist will. It is, therefore, a maverick in the history of modern nationalism, and it simplifies the task of general historians to regard it, at least by implication, as belonging only on the more parochial stage of the inner history of the Jewish community.

For Jewish historians Zionism is, of course, one of the pre-eminent facts—for most, it is the crucial issue—of Jewish life in the modern age, and it therefore engages their complete attention. Nonetheless, how to place it in some larger frame is still the most debated, and least solved, problem of Jewish historiography. In part, the difficulty stems from the very nature of the Zionist phenomenon. As the historian attempts to assimilate Zionism within his larger understanding of the Jewish past, he is confronted by a movement for which the meaning and validity of that past are a central concern. The earliest forerunners of Zionism, pious rabbis like Alkalai and Kalischer, who insisted on standing within the tradition, had to prove before the bar of the classical religious heritage that self-help was a necessary preamble to the miraculous days of the Messiah rather than a rebellion against heaven.[1] Pinsker and Herzl, who appeared several decades later to preach the total evacuation of the land of the gentiles, could make their case only by interpreting the whole of postexilic history as an otherwise insoluble struggle with anti-Semitism. Nor was the past less of a problem to the extremist versions of Zionism which crystallized in the early years of the twentieth century. Their program of total revolution, of a complete break with the entire earlier career of the Jew in favor of purely secular national life ("let us be like all the gentiles"), required the assumption that the eighteen centuries of life in exile had been a barren waste. In sum, therefore, the past was, in two senses, a crucial issue for Zionist theory: on the one hand, history was invoked to legitimize and prove the need for the Zionist revolution; in another dimension, as it followed the pattern of all revolutions in imagining the outlines of its promised land, the mainstream of Zionism sought a "usable past," to act as guideline for the great days to come. The inevitable differences about the meaning of Jewish history thus are the stuff out of which the warring Zionist theories have been fashioned. Precisely because these discussions have been complex, passionate, and often brilliant, the analysts of the career of Zionism have tended to be swept into the debate, so that most have written as partisans of, or in conscious opposition to, one or the other of these Zionist doctrines.

But there is a more fundamental difficulty. From the Jewish perspective messianism, and not nationalism, is the primary element in Zionism. The very name of the movement evoked the dream of an end of days, of an ultimate release from the exile and a coming to rest in the land of Jewry's heroic age. Jewish historians have, therefore, attempted to understand Zionism as part of the career of the age-old messianic impulse in Judaism. Writers too numerous to mention have characterized the modern movement as "secular messianism," to indicate at once what is classical in Zionism—its eschatological purpose; and what is modern—the necessarily contemporary tools of political effort, colonization, and the definition of Jewry as a nation, thereby laying claim to an inalienable right to self-determination.

The great virtue of this estimate of Zionism is that it seems to succeed in providing the modern movement with a long history of which it is the heir. Zionism is made to stand in an unending line of messianic stirrings and rebellions against an evil destiny which began,

[1]See text, Part 1.

right after the destruction of the Temple by the Romans, with the Bar Kokba revolt in the next century. This theory highlights the story of frequent "ascents" of small groups of pietists from the Diaspora to the Holy Land, occurring in every century of the medieval and pre-modern age, as expressions of a main theme—indeed, of *the* main theme—of "return," which gave meaning to Jewish experience in the exile. The bond between the people and its land, which it never gave up hope of resettling, was thus never broken, and Zionism is, therefore, the consummation of Jewish history under the long-awaited propitious circumstances afforded by the age of liberalism and nationalism.

Despite its neatness and appeal, this construction, which is chiefly identified with the name of the distinguished Israeli historian, Ben-Zion Dinur, must be subjected to serious criticism. In the first place, it is really a kind of synthetic Zionist ideology presented as history. The assumption that we are in the midst of an "end of days," of a final resolution of the tension between the Jew and the world, is as yet unprovable. To date, even after the creation of the state of Israel, Zionism has neither failed nor succeeded. The position of the Jew is still unique in the world, and only those who are certain that their theories foretell the future can be convinced that, for example, the Diaspora will soon be dissolved. This may, indeed, be true, but an interpretation of the meaning of Zionism in Jewish history which boldly asserts that it must come to pass—as this theory does—is suspect of being doctrinaire.

Much more could be said in detail about the implications of this theory, but we must pass on to its essential premise, that Zionism is Jewish messianism in process of realizing itself through this-worldly means. This description fits that stream of Zionist thought which re-mained orthodox in religious outlook, and therefore limited its tinker-ing with the classical messianic conception of the Jewish religion to the question of means; but this thesis pretends to apply to the main body of the movement, and, as such, it is artificial and evasive. What is being obscured is the crucial problem of modern Zionist ideology, the tension between the inherited messianic concept and the radically new meaning that Zionism, at its most modern, was proposing to give it.

Religious messianism had always imagined the Redemption as a confrontation between the Jew and God. The gentile played a variety of roles in this drama—as chastising rod in the divine hand, as the enemy to be discomfited, or, at very least, as the spectator to pay homage at the end of the play—but none of these parts are indispensable to the plot. In the cutting edge of Zionism, in its most revolutionary expression, the essential dialogue is now between the Jew and the nations of the earth. What marks modern Zionism as a fresh beginning in Jewish history is that its ultimate values derive from the general milieu. The Messiah is now identified with the dream of an age of individual liberty, national freedom, and economic and social justice— i.e., with the progressive faith of the nineteenth century.

This is the true Copernican revolution which modern Zionism announced—and it patently represents a fundamental change not merely in the concept of the means to the Redemption but in end values. Every aspect of Jewish messianism has been completely transmuted by this new absolute. So, classical Judaism had, for the most part, imagined that at some propitious moment an inner turning by the Chosen People would be the preamble to evoking the saving grace of God. Zionism, too, knows that the Jewish people must be remade in order to be redeemed—indeed, its sweeping and passionate demands lent themselves to being spoken in language reminiscent of the prophets (thus providing one of the several bridges between the old and the new)—but it is supremely aware that its millennium is out of reach without the assent and co-operation of the dominant political powers. In the movement's heroic age, therefore, Theodor Herzl made the international scene his primary arena and spent his career, often in pathos and tragedy, in searching for a likely ally in the ante-chambers of the potentates. Having embarked on the quest for a Jewish kingdom of this world, Zionism perforce had to address itself to the keeper of the keys to that kingdom, the gentile. Or, to state the point from a wider perspective, the scheme of Jewish religion had seen the messianic problem as one of resolving the tension between the Jew and his Maker—the Exile is punishment and atonement for sin; for the new doctrine, at its newest, the essential issue is the end of the millennia of struggle between the Jew and the world.

The secularization of the messianic ideal called into question another of the basic concepts of Judaism, the notion of the "chosen people." Modern Zionism agreed with the classical faith that the Jews had once been chosen to lead the world, and, in this connection, it was not important whether it was believed that the choosing had been done by God or by the unique Jewish national genius. However, one question, that of the place of the Jew in the postmessianic era, could not be avoided. Despite some occasional remarks to the contrary, the weight of learned opinion in the authoritative religious writings and the whole of popular Jewish feeling had always been certain that the election of the Jew would persist to all eternity.[2] This idea has been no problem to those who combined the older pieties with their Zionism, who have therefore simply accepted it, or to the unflinching secularists and humanists, who have completely discarded it. But the mainstream of the movement has not really known what to do with the idea of the "chosen people." If the new messianism meant the normalization of the place of the Jew in the world, what unique destiny was ultimately reserved for him? If his "end of days" is to be an honorable and secure share in the larger liberal society of the future, what remains of his "chosenness?"

This dilemma is already present in the writings of Moses Hess, the first Zionist thinker who was completely a man of the nineteenth century. His solution, the only apparently logical resolution to this tension between the heart and the head, was to try to define some grand "modern" and "progressive" role that Jewry alone was destined to play in fashioning the world of tomorrow. With characteristic lack of systematic exactness, he speaks mystically of new transcendent values which are to issue from a restored Zion (an idea in the older religious key) and of a new Jewish nation to act as the guardian of the crossroads of three continents and to be the teacher of the somnolent peoples of the East—i.e., he imagines a distinguished, *but not a determinant*, part for the Jew to play in the general *mission civilisatrice* of an expanding West. This last conception is quite close to Herzl's dream of a Jewish Switzerland which was to be a model creation of the aristocratic liberalism that was his political faith. The same essential doctrine was preached by Ben-Yehudah, as he labored to transform Hebrew from the "Holy Tongue" to a significant modern language, and by Borochov, for whom Zionism is a state-building preamble necessary to the creation of the arena in which the Jewish sector of the international class struggle is to take place.

To aspire to the role of the mentor of the Middle East, or the most blessedly modern small state, or the richest of the reviving national languages, or the most ideologically correct socialism—this kind of thinking is an outlet for the older emotions about the metaphysical "otherness" of the Jew from the rest of humanity, but it is no more than an outlet. This passion required a much broader *pied-à-terre*. The problem therefore came to a head in the work of Ahad Ha-Am (Asher Ginsberg), the greatest figure in the "spiritual" school of Zionism. He knew much more clearly than Hess that it was not enough to claim

[2]See George Foot Moore, *Judaism*, Cambridge, 1932, Vol. II, pp. 323–76, for a full discussion of this subject.

that which the world would easily grant, that the biblical past was the source of western morality; it was clear to him that a restored Zion would surely mean more to humanity than a sovereign Albania, but that this was still a far cry from the old concept of the "chosen people." To succeed in the apparently impossible task of asserting the continuing chosenness of the Jew in this-worldly terms, he had to claim much more, that the moral categories of the Jewish national genius would always remain uniquely sublime among all the creations of man. The messianic era, in this version, is an age in which the Jewish ethic comes to full flower in a national community in Palestine living as a moral priesthood whose authority is accepted by all mankind.

Enough has been said to prove the point that modern Zionism represents a crisis not solely in the means but in the essential meaning of Jewish messianism. Once this is understood, it becomes possible to place Zionism in its proper historical frame. It is, indeed, the heir of the messianic impulse and emotions of the Jewish tradition, but it is much more than that; it is the most radical attempt in Jewish history to break out of the parochial molds of Jewish life in order to become part of the general history of man in the modern world. Hence, we are face to face with a paradoxical truth: for the general historian, Zionism is not easy to deal with because it is too "Jewish"; the Jewish historian finds it hard to define because it is too general.

Zionism's attempt to enter the world scene was braked down by several difficulties, of which its own remaining loyalties to the older religious vision were not necessarily the most important. The world without offered only grudging and fitful co-operation in the working out of the Zionist scheme, though its real partnership, based on complete mutual understanding, was indispensable to a messianic success. Even in the midst of the realization of some of Zionism's direst predictions, like the destruction of European Jewry, and greatest hopes, in the establishment of the state of Israel, it remained apparent that the Jew and the world had not yet—if they ever would—fully come to terms. The tangible successes of Zionism as a movement have not, therefore, been widely and unquestioningly accepted as proof of the validity of Zionism as secular messianism. On the contrary, the last half century of Zionist thought has been marked by increased wrestling with the meaning of the Messiah ideal and by an ever-growing trend toward some kind of marriage between the religious vision and the need for Jewry to become, as best it can, an easily understandable part of the contemporary world.

Zionism came into the world announcing a break with the preceding century of Jewish thought, for it was the archenemy of assimilation and religious Reform, the two Jewish philosophies which dominated the first half of the nineteenth century. And yet, like them, its basic problem is the tension between the internal life of Jewry and the wider life of society as a whole. Indeed, it is within Zionism that this conflict is formulated in the sharpest and most complex terms and the most radical solutions are proposed. In order to understand Zionism we must therefore investigate its immediate roots in the total history and situation of post-Emancipation Jewry. Zionism is the heir of immediate predecessors as surely as it is their foe; it is the attempt to achieve the consummation of the freedom the modern world promised the Jew as clearly as it is the symbol of the blasting of that hope; it is the drive of Jewry to be part of society in general as much as, or even more than, it is the call to retreat; and it is the demand for a more complete involvement in modern culture, at least as much as it is a reassertion of the claim of older, more traditional loyalties.

To sum up, the issue at stake in this discussion is not merely the correct understanding of Zionism, though that alone is a matter of prime importance. It involves the fundamental question of the total meaning of Jewish history. The crucial test case is the modern period, which began with the dawn of the Emancipation of the Jews as a result of the French Revolution. Dinur argues that the Jews were always, from the beginning of their history, a nation in the modern sense—indeed the first such nation (an idea first propounded by Hess). The ghetto and the concentration of Jewish life in the exile on the religious factor were merely an expression of the national will-to-live, which used religion, then as always, as one of its several instruments. Modern developments are therefore a natural outgrowth of the national past, for they represent the story of the challenge of assimilation to the nation's survival and the logical response through Zionism. What underlies the conception that I am advancing is an insistence that the era of the Emancipation has represented a radical break with the entire past of Jewry. Until the beginning of the new age the Jew conceived of himself as part of a holy community, a divine priesthood and the elected of God, in an attitude of waiting for the Messiah. Since the Emancipation, Jewish thought has been attempting to rebuild a definition of Jewish identity, even with some—or many—bricks borrowed from the old building, but for a different need and from a different perspective: in order to make Jewish existence analogous to the categories by which western man has been defining himself. Modern Zionism, therefore, is in essence unprecedented because it is, both in time and in thought, a post-Emancipation phenomenon. But once the internal world of the Jew had become, at least in part, modern, he began to labor to come to terms with his larger past and his continuing "Jewish"—i.e., unparalleled—destiny.

II

The modern chapter of Jewish history began with the grant of full citizenship to the Jews in France as a result of the Revolution of 1789. By accepting equality, and by making his chief political policy in the next century the striving to attain it everywhere, the Jew had to do more than remake himself as an individual in the image of a proper westerner. Napoleon I may have called a new Sanhedrin to Paris in 1807, in a characteristically theatrical gesture, for reasons of domestic policy, to appease anti-Semitism in the eastern provinces of France, and perhaps even in a not too well-defined hope of becoming the new Cyrus in the mind of all Jewry, which might therefore rally to his imperialist ambitions. Nonetheless, what happened in this comic-opera setting was profoundly important. The bourgeois revolution and the nation-state, within fifteen years of coming to power, ordered the Jews to appear for a religious disputation. In the Middle Ages, the accuser in such all too frequent debates had been Christianity; it was now the monolithic state. The rather undistinguished assemblage of rabbis and Jewish notables who gathered to Paris from France and Italy (largely under police pressure) to accept the challenge did, indeed, shout themselves hoarse in protestation of loyalty to the Emperor and of their indissoluble unity of spirit with all other citizens of the two major kingdoms of their master's realm. They formally took the historically inevitable step of proclaiming that the civil law of the state, and its military needs, were to override all contrary prescriptions of Jewish religious law and ritual. But the Sanhedrin insisted that it was granting away only the political laws of Judaism, "which were intended to rule the people of Israel in Palestine when it possessed its own kings, priests, and judges." The religious laws, however, "are, by their nature, absolute and independent of circumstance and time."[3] In the here and now, the Jew is to allow nothing to stand between him and his full duty and devotion to the state which has emancipated him, but in the realm of faith he will maintain the concept of his chosenness and his dream of the Messiah.

[3]*Décisions doctrinales du Grand Sanhedrin*, Paris, 1812, p. 8.

This defensive distinction between civic duty and religion, which means the severing of the religious and national elements of Judaism, was to have a long career in the nineteenth century. In its Orthodox form—which was what the majority of the rabbinic leaders of the Sanhedrin had undoubtedly intended—it meant a marriage between punctilious observance of the Law and maintaining the hope of the Prophets for a miraculous "end of days," on the one hand, and outward assimilation to the surrounding secular life and culture, on the other. This was the version of the idea that was given currency by Samson Raphael Hirsch, the dominant voice of west European neo-Orthodoxy in religion in the middle of the nineteenth century. Reform Judaism, the important new movement that arose in that era, denied that such absolute obedience to the commandments of the tradition was either possible, in the light of the obligations imposed by equal citizenship, or intellectually defensible before the bar of rational criticism of the religious heritage. It, therefore, defined the religion of the Jew as an ethical creed, the moral heritage of the Bible. The traditional hope for the return to Zion could not be allowed to remain in the liturgy as even a pious dream, for its presence might call into question the unqualified loyalty of the Jew to the state. It was replaced by the doctrine of the "mission of Israel," the belief that the Jews had been dispersed in the world by a beneficent Providence to act as its teachers and its guides toward the ideals of justice and righteousness revealed in the Bible. Nay more, the Messiah was now to be identified with the vision of an age of individual liberty and universal peace— i.e., with the progressive faith of the first half of the nineteenth century.[4] Israel retained its mission and its divine election because it had long ago been given by revelation perfect knowledge of the values which human reason and the unfolding of the historic process were just beginning to approximate.[5]

The most radical expressions of the Reform rabbinic conferences in Germany in the 1840's had, thus, stretched the category of religion to the utmost; it had been burdened with the entire weight of acting as the guarantor of the survival of the Jew as a separate entity. In pure logic it was equally possible to do the same with the category of

[4]The difference between this modernist version of Jewish messianism and the Zionist formulation, which is obviously related to it, will be discussed later in this essay.

[5]See David Philipson, *The Reform Movement in Judaism*, New York, 1931, pp. 174–80, *in re* the three rabbinical conferences between 1846 and 1848 which defined these doctrines.

nationhood, and to do it with much less shock to Jewish mass sensitivity. The question bluntly posed by Napoleon, whether the Jew, once emancipated, would be unreservedly loyal to the state, could still be answered affirmatively. It could be maintained that Jewish nationality was not a political affair, the identity of a nation in exile in practical search of its restoration, but that of a unique spiritual community. Whatever concessions needed to be made from the ancient way of life as the price of civic and intellectual entry into the modern world could be validated by the principle of the organic unity of the national spirit beneath forms that change from age to age. This was the view of Zechariah Frankel, who walked out of one of the founding conferences of German Reform Judaism in protest against the over-sharp theological rationalism of the majority. Its best-known exponent was Heinrich Graetz, who wrote his great history of the Jews to illustrate this thesis.

Such a solution had several virtues. In the first place, it removed the problem of how to make Judaism live in the modern world from the realm of theological dispute, for the actually existing community rather than some creed yet to be defined was made into the absolute. Both conservatism and liberalism in religion, or even the substitution of folk culture for religion, could be harmonized with the principle of nationhood. But, beyond these theoretical virtues, the national definition of the modern Jew began to come to the foreground in the 1840's because it was consonant with the atmosphere of the times. This was the springtime of romantic nationalism, the age of the Revolution of 1848 and its aftermath, during which Germany and Italy were unified and all the other nationalities of Europe were struggling, with varying degrees of success, for their freedom. A national definition of Judaism was now necessary; it had to be claimed that, in his classical period before the exile, the Jew had already created a society which was the prefiguring, the advance revelation by the Spirit of History, of the age now laboring to be born. Modern Jewish nationalism, too, thus begins with the problem of redefinition that had been posed by the Emancipation; it shares with its greatest immediate enemy—religious Reform—in being essentially defensive, in the need that is common to both to save some rarefied "island within" for Jewish life outside the storms of contemporary history.

What is here being argued is that Reform and early Jewish nationalism, the first stage of modern Zionism, new and radical though they were, did not really break the inherited molds of Jewish history. The pattern had already been laid down two millennia before, when Philo of Alexandria, the first great apologist for Judaism, answered the challenge of Hellenistic philosophy and religion. The world to which he felt it necessary to respond was not the official polytheism or the popular mystery religions, but the highest expression of non-Jewish culture, the thought of the neo-Platonists. His answer was in two parts: he affirmed a deeper, hidden and allegorical, sense to Scripture than could be perceived by the traditionalists, and he then found that this essential meaning of the Revelation contained exactly those doctrines which the philosophers were laboriously discovering by the use of reason.[6] This basic solution, to reformulate Judaism in modern terms and then set it up as the valid ancestor and superior of modernity, is exactly what Maimonides, in his turn, did in the twelfth century, with Aristotelian philosophy.[7] It is the typical pattern of medieval Jewish—and Christian and Moslem—apologetics, the well-trod path on which the various initial responses to the Emancipation could walk with some confidence.

Nonetheless, despite the best efforts of the first two generations of Jewish thinkers after the dawn of the era of Emancipation, their several varieties of apologetics could not really meet in full either the political or the intellectual challenge of the new age. To discuss politics first: In the past, Jewry had always dealt with changes in its relationship to its rulers by viewing the new, which was usually the worse, as a *gezerah*, a destiny to be accepted with resignation. It even knew that certain infringements on its inner life were the price of survival. There are examples in medieval Jewish history of communities which had to march to church week after week for centuries to hear sermons against their faith. The ghetto knew that its representatives before the powers that be (the *shtadlanim*) would sometimes, and perhaps even often, have to conduct themselves in personal disregard of the Laws of the Torah. Nonetheless, despite such exceptions, the inner quality of the life of the Jewish masses prior to the Emancipation was of one piece; Israel, at once a universal religion and the destiny of a particular folk, was serving out in faithfulness the divinely appointed term of the exile.

Post-Emancipation Jewish thought did indeed attempt to deal with the new legal equality and its corollary, the entry of the Jew into western society, as a *gezerah*. Yehudah Leib Gordon, the greatest fig-

[6]See Harry A. Wolfson, *Philo*, Cambridge, 1947, p. 19.

[7]See Isaac Husik, *A History of Medieval Jewish Philosophy*, Philadelphia, 1916, p. 240.

ure and the summation of the Russian Jewish Haskalah (Enlightenment), reflects it in his version of the answer: "Be a Jew in your home, and a man outside"—and, in his slogan, he represented the essential meaning of the theories both of Reform and of cultural nationalism, which were the immediate sources of his thought. In fact, there is considerable evidence (which I hope to present in another context) that such a reaction to the mode of *gezerah* was the first, almost instinctive feeling of the Jewish masses when first confronted by the new equality after 1789. In this attitude we can find the underlying reason why all the stresses of the last century and a half have not produced a schism in Jewry. So long as it could be imagined that the new theories about Judaism and the newly secularized patterns of living were essentially defensive, that they were retreats before the outside world and not a real inner turning to an heretical ideal, Jewish feeling could ultimately allow them a considerably increased amount of the kind of latitude it had always reserved for its contacts with the non-Jewish world.

But it was unmistakably evident that history was denying Gordon's formula the kind of meaning he intended. The "outside" was no longer a place for more or less regular sojourns by a few and enforced short visits by the many. It was, wherever emancipation was in process, the most of life, affecting the entire mass of Jewry, and all that could be hoped for was that the "home" would not be completely forgotten. So radical a reversal in the ratio between the specifically Jewish and the general experience of even those "good Jews" who wished to be modern men could not really be understood in terms of political categories which were rooted in the past.

The intellectual challenge was equally unprecedented. From the beginning of the modern age, there were significant segments of the intellegentsia which did not content themselves with any of the newly fashioned apologies for Judaism. They accepted the ideals of the "outside"—liberalism, nationalism, and, later, socialism—not because they had supposedly originated in Judaism but because they had not. What made these values attractive was that they promised to fashion a new secular world which would transcend and destroy all aspects of "medievalism." The assimilationists, those Jews who consciously strove to give up their own identity entirely in order to become undifferentiated individuals in the modern world, were thus truly messianic. The very completeness and unconditionality of their surrender to the dominant values of the majority were a program for the final solution of the Jewish question: let the Jew become like everybody else, yielding up his claim to chosenness and being relieved of his role as scape-goat. Let society run on its universal and immutable principles, rooted in reason and natural law, which know neither positive nor negative exceptions for the Jew. Above all, let him disappear from the center of the stage, his own and the world's, to be one among many equally important small incidents in the history of mankind.

This was a kind of messianism that could have arisen only out of the eighteenth-century Enlightenment, for it was fundamentally at variance with both the Jewish and the Christian concepts of such an age. The centrality of the Jew to the messianic vision of Judaism has been described earlier in this essay. What needs to be added here is that, in reality, he is equally important to the traditional Christian version of the "end of days": he is not chosen but damned, but that is negative chosenness; he is doomed to wandering and suffering, be-cause he once rejected Jesus, but the indispensable preamble to the Second Coming and the "end of days" is his conversion.

It is beyond doubt that the long-standing Christian desire to con-vert the Jews was a significant aspect of the climate of opinion toward the end of the eighteenth century which prepared the ground for their emancipation. Liberal Christians believed that this would be a short cut to the devoutly desired result. So the Abbé Grégoire, the leader of this school of thought in revolutionary France, argued in a famous essay written in 1787 and published two years later, as the delegates were gathering to the meeting of the Estates-General in Paris, that "the granting of religious liberty to the Jews would be a great step forward in reforming and, I even dare say, in converting them, for truth is most persuasive when it is gentle."[8] What is even more ap-parent is that many of the *philosophies* of the Enlightenment, despite the ethical universalism and the vague deism or atheism in religion with which they were consciously subverting Christianity, were most reluctant to part with "old-fashioned" anti-Semitism. In fear of censor-ship and the Bastille, they may, indeed, have had to shoot their arrows of ridicule at Moses instead of the Apostles, in order to conduct their war against the Church in Aesopian language; but there is an edge and a nastiness to Voltaire's comments on the Jews, an insistence that it is hardly conceivable that even reason can reform them,[9] which sets

[8]M. Grégoire, *Essai sur la régénération physique, morale et politique des Juifs*, Metz, 1789, p. 123.

[9]The most recent study of this subject is the essay of Isaac E. Barzilay, "The Jew in the Literature of the Enlightenment," *Jewish Social Studies*, XVIII (1956), pp. 243–61.

one of the patterns for modern anti-Semitism: to uphold a universal and secular ideal—e.g., liberalism, nationalism, or socialism—but to exclude the Jews from its purview and effect.

Nonetheless, at its most ideologically consistent, the Enlightenment proposed full acceptance of the Jew in the new society of which it dreamed. His faults—which even pro-Jewish writers like Dohm, Mirabeau, and Grégoire waxed eloquent in describing—were, they maintained, not innate but caused by his unfortunate estate, and his claims to chosenness could be disregarded as a psychological defense the Jew found it necessary to cultivate to relieve the misery of his enslavement. All this would disappear, transmuted into good *civisme* even among this, the most difficult group to usher into the life of the modern world, once all of society is reformed. It is therefore true, as Nordau once observed, that the Emancipation came to the Jews not out of humanitarian fervor, not as a reconciliation of age-old conflicts, but for the sake of the abstractions, reason and natural law.[10] But the Jewish enthusiasts of assimilation chose to overlook that the Emancipation was not essentially conceived out of tender regard for the Jews: they preferred to accept it with passion as the totally messianic era that it purported to be.

Most of the reasons why the Jewish intelligentsia and higher bourgeoisie accepted the Emancipation as an ultimate fulfillment are well known ("the career open to talent," the opening of the door of society, etc.); but one, less obvious, consideration needs to be added. For the first time anti-Semitism could be thought of in a rationalist framework. Now, at last, its "cause" was known and its "cure," self-evident. It had existed (so the new theory ran) in the late, "medieval" era because of religious fanaticism. That age was now at an end, and in the new day of reason and progress it must entirely disappear. In order really to believe in the Emancipation, the Jew could not allow himself to imagine that anti-Semitism was a constant, beyond the dissolving power of the new ideas of the Enlightenment, or, worse still, that it might find ways of legitimizing itself in every theoretically universalist movement. And yet, Jew-hatred continued to exist, and it was not merely a leftover from the past. Everyone, including especially those Jews whose intellectual gods were Voltaire and the Encyclopedists, knew that many of the makers of the new faith were themselves no lovers of the seed of Abraham. Modern anti-Semitism, therefore, was described as a new, reasonable, and even acceptable antipathy: it was chastisement

[10]See text, Part 3.

for the sin of imperfect assimilation and the goad toward the messianic day when the Jews, by completely refashioning themselves in the image of proper westerners, would have won the acceptance that they then would merit.

As the nineteenth century wore on, as the early universalism of the Enlightenment was being replaced by the idea of a world which should be the peaceful concert of liberated nations, it became possible intellectually, and historically necessary, for a new version—a nationalist one—of this kind of thought to arise. Its immediate cause was to be the obvious inadequacy of the assimilationist view of anti-Semitism, the fact that bitter Jew-hatred persisted even where its objects were most completely de-Judaized in life and spirit. And its answer would be to substitute Jewish nation for Jewish individual in the messianic scheme above: the nation is to become like all others, for its sin is that it is a national anomaly, and anti-Semitism is its chastisement. The first statement of this theory is to be found not, as is usually imagined, in the writings of its greatest exponents, Pinsker and Herzl. Its crucial point, the nationalist redefinition of sin, occurs much earlier, in the 1840's, in the work of Alkalai, the half-forgotten Serbian rabbi and cabbalist of the old school, who was affected by the Balkan nationalist struggles which surrounded him. He took the bold step of equating the sin spoken of by the prophets not with the rebellion of the Jews against God but with their lack of zeal for their national return to Zion.[11]

What has been said thus far, therefore, can be summarized into a basic typology of Jewish responses to the Emancipation: they separate into the defensive and the messianic. The first, the traditionalist, means the attempt to have the Jew live at once in two worlds, his own, which continues the past as best it can, and the general life of society. The second is the attempt to step outside his past into a really new age in which that past is essentially irrelevant to him and is soon forgotten or ignored by the majority which receives him. Each of these attitudes enters, in turn, into combination with the two dominant ideas which came to the foreground in the French Revolution: individualism and nationalism. As the nineteenth century continued its development and brought forth such notions as socialism, in its several varieties, and the doctrine of race, they were either assimilated or rejected by the various subgroups within this typology to form more complex theories reflecting the reaction of the Jew to the changing world around him.

[11]See text, Part 1.

The scheme that I am positing is, of course, not to be found represented with mathematical precision by individual thinkers who can be quickly categorized in one or the other of its cubbyholes, but it is, I believe, a description of the inherent logic of the historic situation within which they were operating and a guide to understanding it. A more important, indeed a crucial, qualification is that, by the very nature of such a construction, its biases are intellectualist, for it deals more with ideas than directly with life itself. Since the ultimate source of the turn into this thought-world is the Enlightenment, we must remember the caution of the greatest modern student of the intellectual roots of the French Revolution, Daniel Mornet: the protest which made that explosion "aspired to social and political reforms for social and political, and not for philososphic reasons; it expressed specific woes and needs, and not ideas."[12] Visibly, society was being refashioned by radical ideals and revolutionary events; beneath the surface, the old life, and the old attitudes and prejudices, went on.

What Mornet says of French society, the cradle of the modern European world, is true, in large measure, of post-Emancipation Jewry—its mass attitudes, too, changed much more slowly than those of its "official" thinkers—but with two important qualifications. The historical tempests of the last century and a half have made and destroyed many classes and nations, often with great rapidity, but no entire community was refashioned as quickly and as radically, wherever it was emancipated, as the Jewish. The attainment of legal equality affected the destiny of every individual Jew directly and immediately, so that the time lag between the older attitudes that had felt most at home in the ghetto and the newer ones that seemed in harmony with his new status was considerably lessened. More important, no real base remained for a Jewish "counterrevolution" against the Emancipation. If Mornet is right in maintaining that revolutions are made by the hope of satisfying tangible needs, counterrevolutions, despite their diffused appeal to conservative emotions, are ultimately based on the real deprivations experienced by the losers in the struggle. In this sense, the Emancipation was not a true revolt within Jewry, for it came from the outside, and not as the result of an internal conflict, and it promised some benefit to every segment of Jewish society. It is true that the degree to which the Jew integrated himself into the world of the gentiles was directly related to the class structure,

[12]Daniel Mornet, *Les origines intellectuelles de la révolution française*, Paris, 1947, p. 465.

for the upper socioeconomic echelons, the greatest immediate beneficiaries of the new opportunities, were the most assimilationist, and
the petty bourgeoisie, who were the last to gain anything, were the
most persistently loyal to the values of the past. This is why the
traditionalist "defensive" theories of modern Jewish survival, in my
use of the term, tended to originate in the middle class, and the more
radical, "messianic" schools of thought were most often based on the
experience of the newly educated, westernized intelligentsia and the
upper social echelons. But, in essence, all of these doctrines accepted
the Emancipation; the time lag in Jewish sentiment had no historical
base in a conviction held by any class that it had been better off, in
this world's goods, in the ghetto. It was entirely a psychological matter,
a reluctance to part with older values and a way of life which had
been most at home within the now fallen protective, though con-
fining, walls of the ghetto.

There is another, perhaps even more important, observation that
needs to be added in assessing the role of the time lag of older
attitudes, both their own and those of society in general, in modern
Jewish thought. The philosophical doctrines and political changes
which created a new age for the Jew were all movements at the top
of society, the cutting edge of its advance beyond the world that had
been before. But, in the upheavals of the modern age, the struggle
for power has used many weapons, among which ideas have been the
most visible but not necessarily the most important. So, for example,
liberalism began as a vision of freedom for all humanity, but as soon
as the bourgeoisie, which was its bearer, came to power, it had no
further use for this revolutionary doctrine; humanitarianism persisted
among its more ideologically minded elements, the "reformers,"
but the propulsion for further social change and the extension of
equality no longer came from the first paladins of liberalism. Nationalism underwent a comparable process, as individual nations
achieved, or came within hailing distance, of their objectives; it, too,
soon forgot any universalist pretensions of the sort represented by
Mazzini, when the unification of Italy was but a dream, in favor of
the conservative *raison d'état* of Cavour, as soon as it became a
reality. Victorious revolutions made it their first order of business to
come to terms with what had persisted—at least, on the plane of
emotion and belief—of the old order; for it seems to be a "law" of
history: after Robespierre comes the Thermidor, and the religion of
reason is succeeded by a concordat with the church. Modern Jewish
thought, however, could operate only by accepting the new ideas and

political experiments at their face value, for the old order had a long history of anti-Semitism. As a result, after the various revolutions lost their initial *élan*, a conflict of interest ensued between the makers of the revolution and those Jews who accepted or followed it. It was useful to the newly powerful to discard the label of subverters of society and become legitimized as true heirs of the past (e.g., Stalin's invoking of the shades of the great warrior tsars in World War II); emancipated Jewry, on the other hand, especially in its "messianic" segment, needed a utopia based on reason, i.e., it required a true revolutionary break by all of society with its past.

Here we stand at the threshold of the ultimate paradox in the relationship between the Jew and modernity. His defensive schools of thought have found themselves coming to terms with ideas and social structures which were outrunning them, and the more messianic doctrines soon acquired a certain shrillness, for they inevitably assumed the unwanted role of keepers of the conscience of the main modern movements. The last doctrinaires of the Enlightenment and what followed after, the epigones of the true faiths as opposed to their sullying compromises with the world, are to be found in modern Jewish thought.

Enough has been said, so far, to suggest the historical matrix within which modern Zionism was fashioned. It is time now to turn to a specific account of the story of the Zionist idea.

III

Alkalai, Kalischer, and Hess are an overture to the history of Zionism, for most of the main themes of the later, often discordant, symphony are already present in their writings. In its time, the middle of the nineteenth century, their work had little influence; they were so quickly forgotten that the Zionism which arose again in the 1880's and 1890's, the beginning of the continuous history of the movement, had no sense of indebtedness or linkage to these earlier figures. It is only in our own century that they have been rediscovered and Hess, in particular, is ever more greatly admired. The early career of modern Zionism is, therefore, extraordinary—it is the tale of a twice-born movement—and an explanation is required.

The question is more complex than may appear on the surface. Its least difficult aspect is the abortiveness of the earliest stirrings of Zionism. It was stillborn in the middle of the nineteenth century because the advanced thought of the Jewish world was then still dominated by assimilation and religious Reform. The Emancipation had begun in France in 1791, but it was not completed even in western Europe for another two generations. The 1850's and 1860's, precisely the time in which the first theoreticians of Zionism appeared, marked the removal of the last remaining bars to full equality for the Jew from the laws of England, Germany, Italy, and Austria-Hungary. The struggle for personal equality in the western image was then equally in the foreground of modernist Jewish thought in eastern Europe. Railroad building and the beginnings of industrialization had already produced a small group of Jewish magnates of the western kind and, despite all obstacles, an intelligentsia was beginning to form which had been schooled in, or considerably influenced by, secular culture. On the Russian scene in general this was the only period when tsarist reaction was occasionally relieved by gestures of liberalization, including the easing of some of the worst features of the oppression of the Jews. Culturally, it was the age of the maximum prestige of the West, especially of France, as the model and example for a Russian national art and literature. The small, but historically significant, modernist element of Russian Jewry could therefore hope, with the Russian liberals, for a constitutional regime of progress and equality. It seemed obvious and reasonable to prepare for it by becoming the Jewish sector of "westernization" in Russia, by trying to remake the mass of their brethren in the image of the already emancipated and secularized Jews of Germany and France.

Both in the East and the West it was, therefore, almost inevitable that assimilation and Reform (the eastern version of this doctrine was a variation attuned to the local scene which called itself the Haskalah—"Enlightenment"), as the seemingly self-evident concomitants of emancipation, should continue to dominate modern Jewish thought. In that age Rothschild was the great name of European finance; a converted Jew who gloried in his origins, Disraeli, was prime minister of imperial Britain; Crémieux, the first practicing Jew to be chosen as a minister in a modern government, was still a central figure in French politics; and Lasalle was in the midst of his meteoric career as the leader of German socialism, the largest such party in Europe. Any version of Zionist theory must necessarily imply some sense of a loss of hope in the future total acceptance of the Jew as an individual by the majority society. In the heyday of his success, the middle of the nineteenth century, the modern Jew could not allow even the nose of the camel of such pessimism inside his tent.

These considerations may begin to explain why Moses Hess, the first assimilated Jew to turn to Zionism, was roundly ignored (research has, so far, discovered very few contemporary reviews of his *Rome and Jerusalem*—and almost all of these were unfavorable) by the men of his type to whom he addressed himself, but an important question still remains without answer. Why were Alkalai and Kalischer equally without influence? The nature and style of their writing, in the inherited rabbinic mold, should have caused some reaction among their colleagues in Russia, especially since Kalischer, in particular, was highly regarded both for his learning and his saintliness. Their proposals aspired to relieving the misery of the orthodox masses by a vastly increased concern for the religious commandment of dwelling in the Holy Land (Kalischer started a fund for colonization and Alkalai was constantly imagining new schemes as bold as those of the later Herzl). One would expect a certain vogue for their words and efforts in the circles of those who stood to benefit, and yet they were greeted with silence which betokened the desire to ignore a potentially dangerous aberration from the true faith.

What is involved in the failure of Alkalai and Kalischer is revealing of another aspect of the meaning of modern Zionism. Hess came too soon in the history of Jewish emancipation to lead a post-assimilation recoil back to Jewish group solidarity; Alkalai and Kalischer were equally ineffectual because they appeared before the mass of east European religious Jewry, their own specific audience, had been seriously affected by modernity. As has been said above, the instinctive reaction to the Emancipation on the part of orthodoxy was to resist change and the threat of disappearance. In western Europe, where the modern state was, at least in theory, a post-Christian phenomenon—i.e., the doctrine of liberalism spoke of a state to which the religion of its citizens, the majority included, was a matter of indifference—this sentiment could not defend itself strongly. In the East, however, even the most generous acts of the tsar were obviously thinly veiled efforts at conversionism. The modernists chose to believe that the government was moving toward a liberal dawn, but orthodoxy fought against the Russification of Jewish education, for example, which the state attempted to enforce without any accompanying grant of substantial freedom, as but another, and more dangerous, expression of official Jew-hatred. The defections of many of the educated youth from Jewry, a large proportion through baptism, added substance to the resistance of the religious masses to anything which implied acceptance of modernity. It must also be remembered that the emancipation of west European Jewry involved communities which were few in number and most of which, even those which had to wait to the middle of the century to win their fight in its entirety, had once been freed by a stroke of the pen, by order of the advancing armies of France in the revolutionary era. Russian Jewry was massive, more than half of all the Jews of the world in the mid-nineteenth century, and no decree of full emancipation existed in its earlier history to give it the confidence of battling for a freedom that it had once already attained. What Russian Jewry as a whole, exclusive of its small modernist segment, was really hoping for in that era was not a doctrinaire political equality but an easing of the worst burdens of oppression.

Even the pious proto-Zionism of Alkalai and Kalischer implied some amount of entry by the Jew into the mainstream of modernity. Both appealed to the rising nationalisms of Europe as the reason for a Jewish policy to be based on a comparable desire for national self-determination. Kalischer ends a passage in which he attempts to show that the Redemption requires a beginning in man's own efforts by pleading: "Let us take to heart the examples of the Italians, Poles, and Hungarians . . . All the other peoples have striven only for the sake of their own national honor; how much more should we exert ourselves, for our duty is to labor not only for the glory of our ancestors but for the glory of God who chose Zion!"[13] Alkalai is particularly aware of the new political possibilities that the Emancipation had opened to the Jew. The prominence of individual Jews in European society and the later formation in 1860 of the Alliance Israelite Universelle to conduct the political defense of Jewish rights all over the world were used by him as arguments for Zionism: the Jew has now learned to deal as an equal on the international scene; let him act, with all the political and economic power he has achieved in freedom, for the restoration of his people.

In their own views of themselves, Kalischer was undoubtedly a pietist concerned with the widest extension of religious observance, with special emphasis on the neglected duty of dwelling in the Holy Land, and Alkalai was a cabbalist preparing the ground for the "end of days." (Alkalai kept imagining dates prophesied in the holy writings—his favorite was 1840—which would mark the beginning of the

[13]See text, Part 1.

Redemption.) It would be wrong to attribute to them—as has been done, particularly to Alkalai, by taking remarks out of the total context of their writing—a full-blown Zionist theory. What was new in their work represented an unsystematic and almost unconscious reaction to modernity, a picking of catch phrases from the air of their day for the "defensive" purpose of strengthening the position of Jewry and the orthodox faith in a world they knew was changing. Implicit in their appeal to the Jewish hidalgos of the emancipated West were the first glimmerings of the notion that a national effort toward Zion was a platform on which non- and anti-religious Jews could stand together with the pious. A conscious expression of this idea, however, had to wait until Rabbi Samuel Mohilever, who refounded religious Zionism after 1881, required it to justify his cooperation with newly appeared Jewish secular nationalists. Nor were Alkalai and Kalischer very much concerned with a philosophical defense of the faith against the inroads of the modern ideas, for, from their vantage point in both time and place (the border between eastern and central Europe, where the old faith still reigned supreme), this was not yet a real problem. At the very beginning of "defensive" Zionism, its entry into the new world of the nineteenth century meant primarily tactics and techniques, the hope of exploiting the contemporary colonial expansion and national stirrings of Europe to create a new-old home for the old values unchanged.

Having dealt with the problem of the failure of the earliest stirrings of modern Zionism to have any impact, the question still remains: Why did they appear at all? In particular, what motivated Hess, after an important career as one of the founders of European socialism (Arnold Ruge had once dubbed him "the communist Rabbi Moses"), to write a book in 1862 in which almost every nuance of the next century of Zionist thought was prefigured?

The essence of the answer is that the nineteenth century to which Hess was reacting was much more complicated than the relatively simple intellectual world of the assimilationists and religious reformers. He knew that cosmopolitanism, progress, and individualism had not been the only children of the French Revolution; an equally immediate result had been to set into motion the incalculable force of nationalism. At the dawn of the history of the modern state, when the constitutions of the new French and American republics had been written by advanced thinkers of the eighteenth century, the political structure of the nation was, in theory, a social compact, a convenient device constructed by individuals for the sake of reasonable self-interest. It was not an end-value (Thomas Jefferson contemplated a political revolution in every generation), for the ultimates were the individual (the Rights of Man) and the international society of men of reason (the City of Man). By the middle of the nineteenth century the heyday of romanticism had intervened, with its emphasis on the organic character of the national soul as developed through the slow processes of the history of the folk. Though Herder, Rousseau, and the other ancestors of romantic nationalism had not preached the doctrine that the political nation needed to be identical with the organic folk, this connection was soon made, especially in Germany, where it first acted as a rallying cry against the advancing armies of Napoleon and then as a call to unifying that much-divided country. At its most conservative, romantic nationalism was a conscious counter-revolution against the Enlightenment in favor of new key values, blood and soil. By the time Hegel had transmuted them into the abstruse language of his philosophy, his own nation, Germany, had become the Absolute, the incarnation of the Idea. Even liberal romantic nationalism of the school of Mazzini, though in theory it was accepting of the equal rights of all nations, was more than casually aware that the various racial and folk strains had differing histories, destinies, and missions.

As has been said above, the early versions of post-Emancipation Jewish thought had been grounded in the Enlightenment. They could react to the new romantic nationalism only defensively, by narrowing the focus of their claim to acceptance in society. The modern Jew no longer needed to prove, primarily, that he had become a man of the West, but that he was indeed a participant in the mystical essence of the German, or the French, etc., national soul. We therefore find the leaders of German Reform Judaism asserting with ever greater vehemence by the 1840's that Berlin was their new Jerusalem, "the fatherland to which we cling with all the bonds of love."[14] But acceptance on these terms was much harder to achieve. Jewish apologetics could create a convincing case for the historic right of the Jew to regard himself as one of the cofounders of European civilization as a whole, but it could not really claim, with any effectiveness, any share in the folk-soul fashioned in the Teutonic forests or in the glory of Charlemagne's martial exploits. In the eyes of conservative and reactionary nationalism the Jew might indeed be regarded as truly westernized, but he was a cosmopolitan, debarred

[14]See Philipson, op. cit., p. 233.

by his history and race from ever acquiring true roots in the sacred national past. The only hope he had was in the victory of liberal nationalism, to which the past was less important than the future of the nation. That is why the French and American revolutions remained almost the sacred symbols of modern Jewish thought, even in the age of nationalism. America embarked in 1789 on a new national history which had no past for reaction to look to, and France had radically broken with its earlier history in its great convulsion. Liberal French nationalism looked forward from 1789, and, when powerful forces of reaction looked back to earlier ages in the Dreyfus affair, the last ally of the policy of Jewish assimilation was shaken and the stage was set for Herzl and the continuous history of Zionism —but we are running ahead of our story.

Neither anti-Semitism nor nationalism, as such, were the preconditions for modern Zionism. The situation within which it arose was the split within nationalism, the crystallization of its warring conservative-reactionary and liberal varieties. So individual outbreaks of anti-Semitism, like the notorious blood libel in Damascus in 1840 rippled the surface of Hess's composure, but, as he tells us, it did no more than that.[15] By 1853, however, modern racism had already published its classic, Gobineau's *Essai sur l'inégalité des races humaines*, which argued that the Aryan was inherently superior. It was soon followed by an active and full-blown racial anti-Semitism represented, in the next two decades, by Richard Wagner in art and by Georg von Schoenerer, the founder of Pan-Germanism, in politics. Hess was the first Jewish thinker to take this new doctrine seriously: not that he foresaw its full implications in terror and genocide that were to appear in the twentieth century, but that he recognized that racism would be more than strong enough to prohibit the integration of the Jew as individual into the various national societies.

Conservative nationalism, in its most contemporary (in the 1850's and 1860's) racist manifestations, provided Hess with the answer to assimilationism—but he still had to reckon with the policy of religious Reform. His counter to its basic notion, that Judaism be made into a purely universal religion stripped of all particularism, derives from one of the fathers of nationalism, from Herder. Its essence is a conception of religion which is rooted in Herder's well-known question: "Do not nations differ in everything, in poetry, physiognomy and tastes, customs and languages? Must not religion, which partakes of

[15]See text, Part 1.

all these, also differ among nations?" There is, therefore, no such thing as a valid universal religion; there is only a universal morality (on this point, Hess regards himself as a follower of Spinoza). This ethic, based on universal reason, is variously reflected in the true ultimate units of society, the nations which unite in their essences all of the categories of blood, history, faith, and sovereignty. Ancient Judaism was the first group in human history to create such an identity, and the new era laboring to be born "can look only to Judaism as its pattern and spiritual example . . . for, in reality, the spirit of the age is approaching ever closer to the essential Jewish emphasis on real life."[16] The attempt to define Judaism as a universal religious cult is, therefore, hopeless, and not only because it does violence to the past; it is a misconception of the meaning of religion and stands against the wave of the future, the day in which a world of regenerated nations, Jewry included, will live in a higher harmony as "religions based on nationality and national history."[17]

These assertions made it possible for Hess to construct a kind of syllogism which is the main axis of his Zionist thought: the Jews are a nation; reactionary nationalism, which he identified with Germany, makes it certain that they cannot assimilate as individuals; liberal nationalism, of which France is the torchbearer, will therefore, help them to recreate their own national life.

As is readily apparent, this construction is the main outline of what was later to become, with many variations, the mainstream of Zionist theory. Its first two assumptions, that Jewish identity is essentially national and that assimilation is impossible, were indeed never questioned within Zionism. The third, that the liberal world be moved to act in behalf of Jewish restoration, later became the ground for many disagreements.

Hess's own faith in this proposition is more optimistic than that of the theorists who arose a generation later. He is closer, in time and spirit, to the Promethean faith in progress which ushered in the nineteenth century. Though his reason foresaw difficulties for the Jew, his eyes had not witnessed a major debacle like the Russian pogroms of 1881. He could still believe without question that the future belonged to humanitarianism and that political changes would be determined by the moral sense professed by liberal nationalism. In short, as the very title of his book reveals, Hess was very much under

16Ibid.

17Ibid.

the spell of Mazzini and the Young Europe movement which he led. Mazzini, as an Italian nationalist, dreamed of Rome as the center of the new world. The Eternal City had once been the hub of a great pagan empire; it had become the seat of the medieval attempt to create a supranational theocratic world; was it not right, so Mazzini rhapsodized, to look to it for leadership in the new nationalist age? Hess agreed with the underlying premise of this argument, that a post-Christian era of nationalism was being born which would be the messianic consummation of all history—but Jerusalem, not Rome, would be the world center. In this reaction to Mazzini's thought Hess almost succeeded in the difficult task of translating the classical Jewish idea of the Messiah into modern parlance—but the job became ever harder for other thinkers as the century wore on.

IV

That Alkalai, Kalischer, and Hess appeared when they did shows that, as an intellectual construction, Zionism was possible as an outgrowth of the *Zeitgeist*, with a "routine" collection of Jewish woes and fears in immediate view. So, by the late 1860's and within Russian Jewry, Smolenskin proposed anew the definition of the Jews as a spiritual nation, in order to make it possible for the newly educated nonbelievers in religion to maintain allegiance to their people. The young Ben-Yehudah countered that only a secular nation like all others could interest and retain the loyalty of the modern-minded.[18] All this, however, was theory, with little relation to real life. It took two major shocks, the Russian pogroms of 1881 and the Dreyfus affair in 1895, to transform Zionism from closet philosophy into a mass movement and a maker of history.

In modern Jewish history the year 1881 is a great turning point, as important as 1789. Visibly, the pogroms were an unparalleled disaster for the Jewish subjects of the tsar which set a mass exodus of millions into motion. Beneath the surface, and in the logic of the career of Jewry after the Emancipation, the events of that year announced the beginning of the end of the century of leadership of the west European Jewish communities—the very end was to come with Herzl.

Until 1881 Russian Jewry, though it comprised more than half of the Jewish population in the world, was, historically speaking, in an

[18]See text, Part 2.

attitude of waiting. It was generally assumed, especially by their brethren in the already emancipated communities, that, in due course, the tsarist regime would transform itself into a constitutional monarchy of the western type, and that Jewish experience in the liberal Russia of the future would repeat the processes that had consistently typified the entry of the Jew into modern society. This hope came to an end in 1881, with the assassination of Alexander II and the two years of nationwide pogroms that followed. Henceforth, the terrified and increasingly impoverished mass of Russian Jewry could no longer trust the ultimate good will of the government. Elsewhere and earlier, in the usual pattern of the Emancipation, the state had been the granter and guarantor of Jewish equality, often in the face of considerable popular resistance such as had appeared, even at the very beginning, in revolutionary France. After 1881 very few could make themselves believe that the Russian state was anything else than the unequivocal and permanent enemy of the Jew. In the mass the Jew had no alternative but to seek radical new solutions in large-scale migration, mostly to America, or by joining the various revolutionary movements, as the young, in particular, were doing in ever-growing numbers.

These new policies made western Jews acutely uncomfortable. Patriotism was at once their religion and their support, and the sight of the largest Jewish community in despair of the state ran counter to a major verity on which the life of the modern Jew was founded. The executives and relief committees of the indigenous western communities, including the then small American Jewish group, were, in their majorities, eager to persuade the fleeing Russian Jews to stay home and await a happier day. The well-known, and soon notorious, participation of Jews in preparing for a revolution in Russia was, if anything, even more frightening to the western Jewish bourgeoisie, for their increasingly vociferous enemies were using it to "prove" that the "international Jew" was everywhere, by nature, the enemy of order and the subverter of society. Meanwhile, the stream of emigrants was swamping Germany, England, France, and the United States with tens of thousands of strange and foreign types, who, by their very presence, were helping to raise the "Jewish problem" again in countries in which it had been hoped that it would never again be mentioned. At least this is what the Jew of the West chose to believe; else he would have been driven to Hess's conclusion two decades earlier, that the Jew as such, himself included, and not merely the *Ostjude*, was the target of the racial anti-Semite.

As Jews and as humanitarians, the western communities could not but respond initially to the pogroms and the consistent persecution in Russia by protesting themselves and by arousing general opinion against the tsarist regime. On the surface of events there was heartening worldwide support from liberal opinion, but the western governments were more hesitant. Prompted by this campaign, some official representations were made to Russia, but *raison d'état* made it a hard and prolonged battle before the notables of American Jewry could get President Taft, almost two decades after the problem entered its acute stage, to cancel a commercial treaty with Russia. In the post-1881 events there were the seeds of an inner conflict for the western Jew which is not yet resolved: on an issue involving other Jews, those of Russia, his Jewish and liberal emotions ranged him against a wicked state, whereas his need to be an inconspicuous, uncomplicated patriot ("my country right or wrong") asked of him that he stand for nothing that might momentarily embarrass the foreign office of his native land.

It was in the intellectual realm, however, in the inner history of modern Jewish thought, that the year 1881 had its most fateful consequences. In actuality, none of the other forces mentioned above really began in that year. Mass migration from Russia and the prominence of Jews in the revolutionist parties, with all their by-products, were accelerated by the pogroms, but their origins were a decade or two earlier. The one sharp change that is datable in that year is to be seen in the emotions and outlook of the Russian Jewish intelligentsia. Before the pogroms it was under the willing tutelage of west European Jewry; in that year it consciously kicked over the traces and struck out on its own.

In addition to faith in the state, the other axiom of the western Jew was belief in education, the certainty that it was not only his passport into a wider world but also that the educated classes were his unshakable allies. He had chosen to believe this, despite the growing Jew-hatred among the intelligentsia in the second half of the nineteenth century, and before 1881 the intellectuals of Russian Jewry followed after him in that faith. But university students had joined in the making of pogroms and the outbursts of violence had been defended in respectable newspapers as valid expressions of popular discontent. Even the *Narodnaya Volya*, the organ of the respected Narodnik (Back to the People) movement, had viewed them as a praiseworthy revolt of the peasants against their oppressors, and Tolstoy and Turgenev, the greatest living Russian writers, had remained silent. This, as many contemporary Jewish intellectuals have attested, was, for them, the most searing feature of the pogroms, because it shook the last pillar of their trust in the gentile world.[19] Moshe Leib Lilienblum's reactions were, therefore, at once typical and symbolic. Before 1881 he was a leading paladin of the Haskalah, a sworn enemy of religion, a socialist, and, though already in his thirties, a student preparing himself for a diploma in secular studies. After spending several days cowering in hiding as the mobs raged, he wrote that "all the old ideals left me in a flash. Disdainfully I forsook my studies . . ."[20] He was inspired by a new ideal, the national identity of his people, which he was to serve for the rest of his days as a radical exponent of the policy of total evacuation of the western world.

The most significant reaction to the events of 1881 was the pamphlet *Auto-Emancipation* by Leo Pinsker. Like Lilienblum, he could not avoid the knowledge that the persecution of the Jew in Russia "is . . . not a result of the low cultural status of the Russian people; we have found our bitterest opponents, indeed, in a large part of the press, which ought to be intelligent."[21] Pinsker, therefore, did not pretend to himself that Jew-hatred was merely a hang-over from the medieval past. On the contrary, the historic importance of his essay is in its assertion that anti-Semitism is a thoroughly modern phenomenon, beyond the reach of any future triumphs of "humanity and enlightenment" in society as a whole. Pinsker defined three causes of anti-Semitism: the Jews are a "ghost people," unlike any other in the world, and therefore feared as a thing apart; they are everywhere foreigners and nowhere hosts in their own national right; and they are in economic competition with every majority within which they live. To hope for better days in Russia, or wherever else the Jews were under serious attack, was, therefore, a delusion, and piecemeal emigration to a variety of underdeveloped lands which might be hospitable for a moment meant merely to export and to exacerbate the problem. There was only one workable solution: the Jews must organize all their strength and, with whatever help they could muster from the world as a whole, they must find a country of their own (if possible, their ancestral home in the Holy Land) where the bulk of Jewry would at last come to rest.

In the next decade Herzl was to arrive at the same analysis in-

[19]See Louis Greenberg, *The Jews in Russia*, New Haven, 1951, Vol. II, pp. 57–58.

[20]See text, Part 2.

[21]See text, Part 2.

dependently, for he did not know of the existence of Pinsker's work when he wrote *The Jewish State*. In his diary, and on several public occasions, Herzl, indeed, made the *beau geste* of saying that he would not have written his book had he been aware of Pinsker. On the other hand, Ahad Ha-Am, Herzl's great antagonist, devoted a lengthy essay to analyzing Pinsker (whose pamphlet he translated into Hebrew) in order to deny that Pinsker was a political Zionist of Herzl's stripe.[22] Obviously neither Herzl nor his opponent Ahad Ha-Am was engaged in self-delusion. Pinsker's thesis, that anti-Semitism must henceforth be the determining consideration of a modern Jewish policy, indeed is central to Herzl's thought and, even though less apparent, it is equally at the core of Ahad Ha-Am's philosophizing. Nonetheless, the intent and direction of Pinsker's construction are significantly different from those of both his successors, and the definition of that difference is of great importance.

Pinsker's analysis of anti-Semitism, despite its surface rationalism, is, in reality, far more pessimistic than Herzl's. He mentions the Christ-killer accusation with greater emphasis as a symptom of the basic malaise, which is national conflict, and his terminology, in which anti-Semitism is called a "psychic aberration—demonopathy—the fear of ghosts," shows an intuitive awareness of its unplumbable and unmanageable depths that is not equally evident in Herzl's work. The most important difference between the two, however, appears in their conceptions of the role of the gentile world in the founding of the Jewish state. The most that Pinsker hopes for is its grudging assent to an effort that really depends, in his view, on the summoning up of the last desperate energies of the Jew.[23] Almost every page of Herzl's volume contains some reference to his confidence that the western nations will collaborate in creating the state he envisaged and some further proof of the great benefits his plan would confer not only on the Jew but on society as a whole. As a west European who had grown up in relative freedom, Herzl could assume even at the end of the century that a world of liberal nationalism (Hess's vision of nations which are "noble rivals and faithful allies") is attainable, and he imagined Zionism's solution of the Jewish problem as a

[22]See Leon Simon, *Ahad Ha-Am*, Oxford, 1946, pp. 183–201.

[23]"Our 'friends' will see us leave with the same pleasure with which we turn our backs upon them . . . Of course, the establishment of a Jewish refuge cannot come about without the support of the governments. In order to obtain such support . . . the creators of our national regeneration will have to proceed with patience and care." (Part 2.)

major contribution to such a future of international social peace and tranquillity. For Pinsker, writing in Odessa in the midst of pogroms, the focus was almost entirely on the woes of the Jew, on removing him from the recurring and inevitable nightmare.

Pinsker's generation had far less stake in the political and social structure of Europe than did Herzl's, even at its most disenchanted, but there is one level on which it was indissolubly involved in modernity. These Russian Jews had, indeed, never lived even a day as equal citizens of their native land, but, nonetheless, they had been schooled by western culture and were creations of its spirit. Pinsker writes: "The great ideas of the eighteenth century have not passed by our people without leaving a trace. We feel not only as Jews; we feel as men. As men, we, too, would fain live and be a nation like all others."[24] Though the Jew must evacuate the terribly hostile world those values have created, Pinsker can imagine no alternate to modern civilization. Ahad Ha-Am is, therefore, wrong in attempting to make Pinsker a forerunner of his own basic notion of a cultural renaissance, a reinterpretation of the old values of Judaism in terms of modernity. What Pinsker reflects is the "rent in the heart," the torment of a man who cannot believe in the good will of the general society whose faiths he shares. As the horizons of the Jew kept darkening in recent decades, this complete loss of trust in society, which began in 1881, was to lead to serious and fundamental questioning of the very foundations of western culture. Pinsker, and not Herzl, is the ultimate ancestor of the profoundly pessimistic strain in Zionism. With him there begins a new age in modern Jewish thought, the era of recoil from the values of the eighteenth and nineteenth centuries.

v

We come now to Theodor Herzl, the central and seminal figure in the history of Zionism. Particularly in the light of Nazism and the holocaust of World War II, Herzl has been read in recent years as if he had been Pinsker. This misreading has made it more difficult to account for the startling impact that he had in his day. It is certainly true that there is no accounting for the force of genius, and yet too much can be attributed to the power of even this majestic and compelling personality. There are other reasons of considerable importance. That he was a man of the West, a successful journalist with a

[24] Ibid.

European reputation, helped lend him stature among the Jews of the East, who still instinctively looked to those of their brethren who were recognized and valued by the wider world. By drawing Zionist consequences from the Dreyfus affair, the crucial political event of Europe at the end of the nineteenth century, he, in effect, affirmed for his willing listeners in Russia that the proud Jews of western Europe actually shared their historical situation, and by projecting Zionism as a movement into the international political arena he gave his followers a dignity that no organized body of Jews had recently possessed in quite the same way. Nonetheless, despite the truth of these considerations, they tend to overvalue Herzl as leader and man of action at the expense of his profound originality and importance as theoretician. The central idea of the book was at least as important as the compulsion of the man, for what he offered was Zionism as optimism, as the most complex of modern Jewish reconciliations with the world. Messianism is the essence of his stance, because he proclaimed the *historical inevitability* of a Jewish state in a world of peaceful nations.

Underlying the whole of Herzl's theory is an implicit syllogism which is more Hegelian than Aristotelian: All men, even Jew-haters, are reasonable, and they will do what is to their interest, once they understand it. Anti-Semitism disturbs the public peace and stability of Europe. Therefore, the gentile nations will be induced to purchase the social place they must desire by reasonable action in regard to the Jews—and what is reasonable and modern is sketched out by Zionism.

As is immediately apparent, this reasoning is a reincarnation of Hess's theory. Nonetheless, there are vital differences, for it was now almost forty years later in both European and Jewish history. First of all, nationalism had changed meaning by Herzl's time. Hess could still imagine that the struggle between liberal and conservative nationalism had a geographic base, that the Teutonic soul was predisposed to racism and reaction but that France, which had given birth to the Revolution, was the unshakable bastion and beacon of liberalism. With French society splitting into two warring camps over Dreyfus before his very eyes (he was then the Paris correspondent of the leading Viennese daily), Herzl was constrained to view the conflict between liberal and reactionary nationalism as international, with a line of cleavage that ran through every country of Europe. More important still, by the end of the century the forces of reaction had completely pre-empted the mystique and religion of nationalism.

Liberals were becoming ever more gingerly in thinking of individual national communities as endowed with an historical mission or in deifying the spirit of the folk, for these notions were the stock in trade of the Pan-Germans, the Pan-Slavs, and the French integral nationalists of the school of Maurice Barrès and Charles Maurras. In defense, liberalism had no choice but to insist that the modern nation was a secular community and a secular state. (It is no accident that France disestablished the church, to which the reactionaries appealed as the guardian of the mystic essence of the nation, in 1905, on the heels of the Dreyfus convulsion.) A generation earlier Hess's Jewish messianism, which was the faith of an advanced liberal of that period, expressed itself in a religio-national quarrel with Mazzini as to whether the Jew or the Italian possessed the greatest and the historically most significant national soul; Herzl, thinking in terms of the liberalism of his day, perforce conceived his messianism in terms that were entirely secular and political. This distinction between their outlooks, be it added, is related also to their differing positions in Jewish history. Hess's childhood, which came at the beginning of the century, was spent in a Jewish environment that still retained most of the old religious values (he personally read Hebrew fluently and had some knowledge of the Talmud); it is not surprising that he found Jewish nationalism and religion to be indivisible. Herzl, a child of the mid-century out of, roughly, the same milieu, was affected by one more generation of assimilation that had intervened. It is obvious, on the face of his writings, that he had much less direct and first-hand involvement in the religious tradition.

The most significant difference between the two, however, is in their implicit assumptions about what is the ultimate dynamic of history. Hess had no doubt that it was the indwelling Moral Spirit; he therefore rested his hope for a Jewish restoration on the certain triumph of humanitarianism. Herzl, in his turn, paid considerable attention to garnering support from men of good will for his proposals, but his assurance that history would vindicate him came from two sources: the iron law of self-interest and the power of will. One senses, standing over his shoulder as he wrote, the presence of the two gods of the *fin de siècle* advanced intellectuals, Marx and Nietzsche. Though Herzl was certainly not a follower of either, the seething discussions of the Marxists had made it almost mandatory for a man who wished to avoid the label "utopian" to prove that his vision was grounded in real (i.e., tangible and amoral) factors and that its victory was historically inevitable. The Nietzschean strain in Herzl is more personal; it is to be found in the Promethean overtones of his conception of his mission, in his willing acceptance and conscious use of the legend which quickly grew around him. It became his tool with which to inspire the masses with his own sense of purpose— and, often, his support for acting alone, over the objections of his associates. As a "Nietzschean," Herzl came to Zionism in order to change history; as an historical determinist, he buttressed himself with a theory in which anti-Semitism appeared, for the first time, not merely as the eternal problem of the Jew but as the major unsolved problem of the western world.

In his *Jewish State* Herzl therefore insisted, correctly proclaiming this notion to be his central idea, that the Jewish question is a "national question, and to solve it we must *first of all* establish it as an international political problem to be discussed and settled by the civilized nations of the world in council." Two years later, in the most important speech of his life, the address to the First Zionist Congress, he went further, to add his own commentary to this argument. After expatiating on the advantages to the world, and to Turkey in particular, of a restored Zion, he added: "But it is not solely from this aspect that Zionism may count upon the sympathy of the nations. You know that in some lands the Jewish problem has come to mean calamity for the government. If it sides with the Jews, it is confronted by the ire of the masses; if it sides against the Jews, it may call considerable consequences down upon its head because of the peculiar influence of the Jews upon the business affairs of the world. Examples of the latter may be found in Russia. But if the government maintains a neutral attitude, the Jews find themselves unprotected by the established regime and rush into the arms of the revolutionaries. Zionism, or self-help for the Jews, points to a way out of these numerous and extraordinary difficulties. Zionism is simply a peacemaker." This was no casual utterance unrelated to the basic thesis of political Zionism; Nordau, his closest associate, ended a lengthy pamphlet on the meaning of Zionism with the same thought as the clincher.[25]

Despite the shock of many of his devoted followers, especially in Russia, Herzl therefore had ample theoretical justification for visiting the Russian Minister of the Interior, von Plehwe, right after the Kishinev pogrom of 1903, even though that arch anti-Semite was known to be implicated in those atrocities. Herzl could imagine a

[25]See text, Part 3.

von Plehwe who was "a sensible anti-Semite," who could be convinced that it was to his country's advantage to use its influence with the Sultan of Turkey on behalf of Zionism, for it would thereby be relieved of its indigestible Jews. In the era between the two world wars, Vladimir Jabotinsky, who claimed with some justice to be the valid heir to unadulterated political Zionism (Nordau supported him in this self-definition), is to be found negotiating with Pilsudski of Poland along the same lines: Poland is troubled by a "surplus of Jews," which arouses anti-Semitic outbursts; it is, therefore, to Poland's interest, for the sake of its own internal stability, to follow a radically pro-Zionist policy in the League of Nations.

The assumption that anti-Semitism "makes sense" and that it can be put to constructive uses—this is at once the subtlest, most daring, and most optimistic conception to be found in political Zionism. Here Herzl stands as both the heir and the transcender of post-Emancipation Jewish thought. He is an heir of the preceding century, for the notion that anti-Semitism has a reasonable use was first propounded by the assimilationists. As was said earlier in this essay, they had explained the persistence of Jew-hatred as a punishment for the sin of imperfect individual assimilation to western norms. This idea, however, like all pre-Herzlian modern Jewish thought (Hess's theories excepted), was inner-directed, toward convincing the Jew to do something within his power, which would save him pain or elevate his status in the world. What is new in Herzl is that, assuming, as the heir of assimilation, that anti-Semitism is rational, he boldly turned this idea outward into the international arena.

Herzl inherited, as well, most of the other certainties of that Jewish modernity against which he was rebelling. Though of course he denied the possibility of the Jew's personal assimilation in Europe ("we shall not be let alone"), he assumes as beyond doubt that which Pinsker had mentioned with evident pain, that the Jew is, and ought to be, culturally and spiritually a man of the secular West. With pride, Herzl speaks of transferring into the renascent state the most advanced values that the Jew can bring with him from his former homes. Despite the pressure of his own east European followers, Herzl never really came to regard the modern Hebrew revival as more than a semiprivate affair, which certain circles could be permitted to foster within the broad framework of his political nationalism. Even when he spoke, at his most romantic and visionary, of restoring the Temple in Jerusalem, the separation of church and state was never in question; his Jerusalem was a more refined Paris and the Temple a more imposing version of the great cathedral synagogues which had been built in the second half of the nineteenth century by the Jewish bourgeoisie in the capital cities of Europe. But these issues, important though they are as guides to the total tone of his thought, are not matters of prime importance. They have been mentioned here as a useful preamble to understanding Herzl's position on the really fundamental issue of the Emancipation.

Pinsker had already argued, as cogently as Herzl, that Jew-hatred would persist as long as the mass of Jewry lived within non-Jewish majorities. To go beyond, to establish that the gentile keepers of the keys to the kingdom of Jewish desire had no choice but to turn them in the lock, Herzl had to make one more basic assumption about western society—that the emancipation of the Jew in Europe is irreversible! "At the same time, the equal rights of Jews before the law cannot be rescinded where they have once been granted. Not only because their recision would be contrary to the spirit of our age, but also because it would immediately drive all Jews, rich and poor alike, into the ranks of the revolutionary parties. No serious harm can really be done us."

This is perhaps the most overlooked idea in the whole arsenal of Herzl's thought, because it seems so paradoxical in the light of his insistence on the great force of anti-Semitism; and yet, it is not a parenthetical lapse from logic—it is of the very essence of his position. Herzl is a dialectical thinker, in the mold into which most European intellectuals of his generation were cast. The thesis is anti-Semitism, omnipresent and everywhere troubling public order; the antithesis is the world of liberal nationalism, which must continue to be disturbed by anti-Semitism because it is inconceivable that it should forever ignore the problem, merely temporize, or attempt a solution for itself by forcing the Jews back into the ghetto (or, horror of horrors, by fostering pogroms and extermination as a consistent policy). Therefore, the inevitable synthesis, Zionism. Let it be noted in passing that that complex figure, Herzl, is thus also the unrecognized ancestor of the much more consciously dialectic Marxist school of Zionism. Borochov, who is generally presumed to be the source of the idea that Jewish mass emigration to Palestine is a historical inevitability (his phrase, famous in its day, is that it is a "stychic process"), proceeded from premises expressed in consciously proletarian, socialist terminology, but he really adds up to the same thing. It is, to sum up, an assessment of anti-Semitism as guaranteed to be at a certain temperature: it will be hot enough to push the Jews out, but, in a basically liberal world, it can never break the ultimate bonds of decency. Its influence, therefore, will not ever serve to unite individual nations against the Jews, but to divide them in moral crisis (e.g., France in the Dreyfus affair) or to embarrass and hinder the most vicious in their intercourse with the liberal segments of humanity (e.g., Russia in the aftermath of the various pogroms). Perforce, the world will have to answer its own problem in the only conceivable way, the territorial concentration of the Jews.

Political Zionism's theory of anti-Semitism is, therefore, neither as simple nor as negative as may seem at first glance. Its explanation of Jew-hatred as a mixture of national antipathy and economic struggle made anti-Semitism the visa to the Jew's passport into the world of modernity; seen as the engine driving the train toward Zion, it is, paradox of paradoxes, one of the great acts of faith in liberalism that was produced by the nineteenth century; as an offer on the part of the Jew to assure the peace of western society by abandoning it for a state of his own, it is the ultimate sacrifice on the altar of his love for the modern world.

VI

The great counterattack on Herzl was made, as is well-known, by Ahad Ha-Am. A connected statement of his position should, no doubt, proceed according to his own order of priorities, by placing at the center what Ahad Ha-Am regarded as the real national problem of Jewry, the guaranteeing of the survival of the Jewish spirit and culture in the modern world. In his view it is not "the need of the Jews," the term Ahad Ha-Am uses to define the content of Herzlian concern but "the need of Judaism" that is the only proper subject for the labors of a Jewish national movement. Because they stood on such different ground, it is understandable why Herzl and Ahad Ha-Am, when they met at the First Zionist Congress in Basel in 1897, really could not talk to one another in any meaningful sense and parted in frustration. The inherent difficulty in communication between these two positions is symbolized even more sharply by an interchange that is reported to have taken place between Ahad Ha-Am and Nordau. Nordau, the colleague and disciple of Herzl, asked Ahad Ha-Am: "But are you a Zionist?" His answer was proudly self-conscious: "I am a Zionist," implying, by his inflection on the pronoun, that his was the true Zionism. This sense of his operating in a framework completely other than that of political Zionism is most clearly expressed in an important speech that Ahad Ha-Am gave in Minsk in 1902 before a conference of the Russian Zionist Organization. After unusually lengthy analysis and discussion, he concluded by proposing that "there are 'political' Zionists for whom the spiritual aspect of the movement is of no importance; at the other extreme, there are 'spiritual' Zionists, who are dissatisfied with political work in its present form . . . This being so, we must establish a special organization for this purpose to embrace all those, whether professed Zionists or not, who realize the importance of Jewish culture and desire its free growth and development. This organization should concentrate exclusively on its own specific problem, and should neither subserve nor be dependent on the companion political organization."[26]

Certainly Ahad Ha-Am spent his major energies on "the need of Judaism" and rather evidently, as I shall attempt to show later in this discussion, cast himself for the role of a latterday Maimonides, i.e., as the reconciler, in his own time, of the values of Judaism and secular culture. "Proof texts" can be cited to show—indeed, they were quoted with relish and vehemence by his enemies—that he had little intellectual concern with the overwhelming misery of Jewry in his day, but this is to misread him and to identify his frequent polemical exaggerations with the real mood and intent of his thought. It is inconceivable—and it is, in fact, not true—that a Russian Jew like Ahad Ha-Am, whose experience of Jewish suffering was much more immediate and personal than Herzl's, should have been less pained by the travail of his people. The key to Ahad Ha-Am, no less than to Herzl, is in his estimate of the world of the gentiles. The vital difference between them is that, at bottom, Herzl trusted this world and Ahad Ha-Am, even more than Pinsker, did not.

This deep distrust was compounded out of several factors. Underlying it all was the attitude of the ghetto within which Ahad Ha-Am had been nurtured till early manhood, which held that the surrounding world was the unchanging and hereditary enemy. His intellectual emancipation, the period in his life when this autodidact was entering "the palace of general culture," coincided with the pogroms of the 1880's, in the aftermath of which his own economic future (he was born into a family of considerable wealth) was undermined by a new ukase of the government forbidding Jews to act as factors of country estates. At the very outset of his career as a modern man Ahad Ha-Am

[26]Simon, op. cit., pp. 100–1.

was, therefore, predisposed to distinguish between the real world of the gentiles, which offered a man of his time and place no feeling of glowing dawn, and the highest intellectual culture of the age. He was constrained to adjust to the second, for his own religious faith had been shaken by his secular studies, and he could reformulate his Jewish loyalty only by defining and defending it in terms borrowed from his intellectual gods, Darwin, Spencer, and the positivist sociologists. This secularist substitute for theology, on which he spent his major efforts, could not, however, spill over into any expansive faith in a better world soon to come for all mankind.

In a significant way his experience of Pan-Slavism set the final seal upon his pessimism and colored the whole of even his theory of Jewish nationalism. By the last decade of the nineteenth century Pan-Slavism had become the faith of the great majority of the Russian intelligentsia. This doctrine owed much to the medievalism and reactionary nationalism which had made the pogroms of 1881, but its ambitions were far greater. Gobineau had once tried to prove the claim of the Aryan to racial superiority in a "reasonable" way, by listing his supposed higher qualities and achievements; Pan-Slavism did not even need to invoke history and God, i.e., the oft-repeated argument of the more orthodox reactionary Russian nationalism that the tsar was the lineal and legitimate heir of Rome, by way of Byzantium. The tribe was, for it, inherently a "chosen people" and all its members, wherever they might be, were by birth the true breed of supermen, beyond the ken and law of lesser folk. Anti-Semitism, as Georg von Schoenerer, the founder of Pan-Germanism (which Pan-Slavism imitated) maintained, was therefore part of the ideological essence of such tribalism. The Jew was not merely one—even though the most enduring—of the many outsiders to be crushed (the primary expression of the anti-Semitism which Pinsker had analyzed as "xenophobia"). His religion asserted a counterclaim to its own chosenness, and it was the source of the concept of a divinely ordained morality which all men were commanded to obey.[27] The Jew was therefore the enemy par excellence in a religious war which could know no quarter, in which not even a refuge outside of society (Pinsker's idea) could be offered the foe, and certainly no co-operation in establishing himself solidly anywhere in the world (Herzl's thesis).

Herzl could not help being aware of the Pan movements, but his

[27]See Hannah Arendt, *The Origins of Totalitarianism*, New York, 1951, pp. 222–49.

implicit estimate of their importance is to take them much less seriously than Ahad Ha-Am. In his native Austro-Hungarian empire, Pan-Germanism was both a minority party and an enemy of the multinational state, which its theories threatened with revolution and decomposition. When French integral nationalism, the local counterpart of the Pan movements, shocked him with its power and virulence, he could nonetheless reassure himself that this force, too, was an enemy of the state, of the Republic founded on the values of the French Revolution. Herzl could, therefore, regard this newest and fanciest version of anti-Semitism as but another subspecies of the genus "national antipathy." Order and legitimacy were on the side of the Jew. Ahad Ha-Am, however, as a Russian Jew, mistrusted the state, and not merely for historical reasons. There was ever less of a state to trust in a period in which the power of the tsarist regime was obviously decomposing. As the revolution-to-come kept smoldering, the court and government found an uneasy but increasingly necessary ally in Pan-Slavism, for this was the only faith held within the educated classes which could be harmonized, at least in the short run, with support for the autocracy. Of all the Pan movements it was, therefore, the most successful and respectable.

During his most creative period (1889–1907), Ahad Ha-Am could not avoid confronting the religion of Pan-Slavism as a fundamental challenge both to the safety of the Jew and, even more seriously, to the Jewish idea. True enough, the very term is not even to be found in the index of his collected essays, but it must be remembered that all of his published work appeared in journals that had to be approved by the Russian censor. Under such restrictions it was not possible to argue directly against the then dominant and almost official ideology. There was, however, a way of dealing with its basic assertions by debating not with Dostoyevsky but with Nietzsche, not with the immediate expressions of Pan-Slavism but with the sources of and parallels to its ideas about the superman and the superior race.

In announcing its claim to chosenness, modern racism had denied that progress and liberalism, the key values of the nineteenth century, had given new meaning to history. For Nietzsche, too, the essential issue in the arena of human affairs remained what it had always been, the struggle of the strong against the fetters put upon them by morality, which he called the invention of the weak. Ahad Ha-Am reacted by maintaining that this was a topsy-turvy version of Judaism; all he needed to do was to reverse its ultimate judgment, that power is superior to spirit, and he could then accept all of its premises.

Thus, in his essay on Nietzsche he does not argue against the idea of the superman; he prefers to deny only that the highest human type is necessarily identical with the Aryan "blond beast." The superman exists in a Jewish version, as the *Tsaddik*, the moral hero; indeed, if the superman is "to be a permanent feature of human life and not just a freak, there must be a suitable environment." There is such a people, the Jewish, "whose inherent characteristics make it better fitted than the others for moral development and whose scheme of life is governed by a moral law superior to the common type of morality."[28]

In their context these remarks appear to be nothing more than a literary tour de force in which the writer wants to demonstrate that he can reach his favorite conclusions about the unique spiritual vocation of the Jews from even the unlikeliest premises—but we find Ahad Ha-Am, at his most serious, proposing an explanation of nationalism that is really an expansion of this commentary on Nietzsche. All national identities are fashioned and sustained, he asserts (following in the footsteps of Herbert Spencer), by a quasi-biological will to live, but he adds that it makes a vast—indeed, an essential—difference, whether the dynamism of a nation expresses itself in the quest for power or in the service of the moral ideal. Gentile nationalism is rooted in power, but "the secret of our people's persistence is . . . that at a very early period the Prophets taught it to respect only the power of the spirit and not to worship material power."[29] What Ahad Ha-Am is thus, in effect, proposing is a dual explanation of nationalism: there is nationalism in general, that of power, which is a genus comprising many species and individuals—i.e., all the nations of the world; counterposed to it there is the nationalism of the spirit, a unique genus of which there is only one species, the Jewish. It necessarily follows that the main axis of history is, indeed, as defined by Nietzsche (and the Pan-Slavs), the hatred of the sword for the book.

Having pridefully chosen his side, Ahad Ha-Am, as the supremely self-conscious modern spokesman for the spirit of the book, could only proceed to devise a strategy that would answer the contemporary situation. He defined it in two parts: to continue the miracle of makeshifts by which the Jew had preserved himself for many centuries in the face of power and to put his best energies into refreshing and reformulating his spiritual tradition.

28Simon, op. cit., pp. 76–82.

29See text, Part 4.

Let it be noted here (more will be said about this point later in the discussion) that Ahad Ha-Am is, in theory, as much a secularist as Nietzsche—but, in the unbelieving Ahad Ha-Am modern Jewish thought came almost full circle. The ideas that he derived from the congruence of his Jewish traditionalist emotions and his rationalist reflections, which operated in a framework set for him by the newest, and most radical, enemies of his people, represent a much more thoroughgoing break with the modern world than is to be found even in Pinsker. Anti-Semitism is no longer imagined to be an extreme case of an omnipresent phenomenon, national hatred, comparable in kind, if not in degree, to the tension between the Russians and Poles, or the French and the Germans. It is all the more inconceivable that it is, as Herzl imagined, a tool of some Hegelian "cunning of reason" in history, being used for the fashioning of a better world soon to come. Ahad Ha-Am is as counterrevolutionary as the racists in asserting that the nineteenth century is either dead, or was never even born—i.e., that it represented no fundamental change in human history. He sees within it no unprecedented opportunity for ending the millennial tension between the Jew and the world. On the contrary, the messianic age is still far off, hidden in the infinite mists of the future, and it will come only when the world as a whole will be prepared to bow to the values first conceived in Zion, as reinterpreted by the descendants of the prophets. Because anti-Semitism is the central line of cleavage in history, the front on which power and spirit forever do battle, it is completely insoluble within the political world—hence Ahad Ha-Am's profound pessimism about the world of the here and now. Its persistence is, however, the somber reason for his mystic certainty that the Jews are still suffering in a transcendent cause that is, at least potentially, incarnate in their folk and tradition.

This assertion, that the Jew is, by essence, alien to the political world, had other important consequences. It made him doubt not only the possibility of attaining a normal Jewish political state; he goes farther still, to be the first Zionist thinker to deny that such a state could ever really be "normal." Immediately on the heels of the First Zionist Congress in 1897 he aroused much passion by declaring that even a total concentration of Jewry in Palestine could not solve the Jewish problem. "A political ideal which is not grounded in our national culture is apt to seduce us from loyalty to our own inner spirit and to beget in us a tendency to find the path of glory in the attainment of material power and political dominion, thus breaking the thread that unites us with the past and undermining our historical

foundation."[30] And, he adds in the same essay, "the geographical position of Palestine and its religious importance for all the world" would
act to deny it forever the status of a normal, small state, for it would
always be a football in the game of "interests" played by the great
powers.

For comparable reasons he denied the theories of his close friend
and contemporary, the distinguished historian Simon Dubnov, that
the Jew should look for a future status of political and cultural autonomy as one of many national minorities of such multinational states
as Russia and Austria-Hungary. In part, his recoil is related to his
aristocratic unwillingness to follow Dubnov in accepting the upstart
Yiddish in place of Hebrew as the national language of the Jew. Behind this feeling, however, there stands his argument that national
autonomy may be enough for those whose "national ideal is to reach
the level of nations like the Letts or the Slovaks," but "there are those
who cannot be satisfied with a future which would put the greatness of
our past to shame."[31] And he ends his critique with a variation on
the theme of his basic distrust of the political world: the nations can
have no respect for a Jewish nationality that apes their own kind of
identity; they will not recognize it but merely "hire it out to work for
others." Whatever regard the Jew can get for himself will come only
for the bearer of his great and unique past—i.e., whatever future there
is for the Jew in a gentile world can come only from the respect power
will sometimes, out of bad conscience, pay to spirit.

Therefore, in his responses to the unfolding course of the Zionist
movement in his lifetime, Ahad Ha-Am consistently maintained
that individual opportunities must be carefully used to their utmost
because they may never recur in an immoral world. Much of Ahad Ha-
Am's early career was spent in arguing that Jewish colonization in
Palestine should proceed in an orderly way, with the maxium of legal
safeguards for the settlers that could be obtained from a disintegrating
Turkey. As intimate adviser to Chaim Weizmann during the negotiations that led to the Balfour Declaration of 1917, and throughout the
discussions at Versailles and later, he kept pressing for the broadest
and most unmistakable definitions of the Jewish right to Palestine.
Even this, however, was rooted not in his desire to operate in the
political world but in his distrust of it. Despite the high emotions of
Zionism's first great political success, he could not imagine for even

[30]See text, Part 4.

[31]Simon, op. cit., p. 218.

an instant that this was the beginning of the messianic chapter in Jewish-gentile relationships. He could only continue the *Realpolitik* of one who had no faith in power and little belief that even its most generous and moral moods could last.

Having dealt at some length with Ahad Ha-Am's relationship to the gentile world, we must now turn to the more obviously dominant area of his concern, the inner scene of Jewry. Here, too, his stance is marked by lack of trust. History, as he saw it, had been not merely the struggle of the Jew to maintain himself in a hostile world; internally, too, Jewry had always lived in tension between the values of its true elite, the "men of the spirit," and the myriad forces which threatened to disintegrate the people, petrify its culture, or send it chasing after the winds of false values. Vis-à-vis the world as a whole, Ahad Ha-Am could, as was said above, solve the problem quite neatly: he could suggest that his people, as a corporate elite, await an "end of days" while living permanently outside of society. The second question, that of the proper posture of the personal elite within the Jewish community, was much harder to answer. Here, in this inner context, Ahad Ha-Am could not follow in the footsteps of Nietzsche, for the weight of the normative Jewish past deterred him, even at his most aristocratic and disdainful, from abandoning the mass, as a rabble unworthy of notice, for the sake of an isolated higher spirituality of the few.

Such a conception is, indeed, understandable in an ex-Christian like Nietzsche, whose superman is none other than an atheist monk. From its beginnings, Christianity had canonized pillar saints as a valid—perhaps even the highest—form of human perfection; bound only by their obedience to God, the true hermits have gloried in their utter rejection of society (including even the society of other monastics) and in their heedlessness of its needs and values. Let such a monk turn atheist—let him, therefore, substitute the mystique of his own will for the quest for communion with God—and the superman now stands before us, predisposed to run amuck precisely because he has retained, from his pious past, a disgust with mankind. For Judaism, on the other hand, the saint had always been the hero of piety who lives and acts within the world. When, in Ahad Ha-Am's agnosticism, the "man of the spirit of God" became simply "the man of the spirit," he retained the need to wrestle with his own immediate society for respect for and obedience to his values. He had no choice but to "prove" to others, in the face of all challengers, that he was the true aristocrat.

If the ultimate source of Ahad Ha-Am's outlook was in the thought

of the Pharisees, its immediate roots were both in his personal temperament and, more significantly, in his class position within the ghetto
he knew to be dying. As an intellectual who felt himself predestined
to fail in practical affairs, it was not strange that he conceived his
utopia as a quiescent Jewish society organized to admire the "men of
the spirit." His distrust of the masses belongs to the same cast of mind
because, like Plato before him, he knew all too well that philosopher-
kings can almost never win an election. But Ahad Ha-Am was not
merely romanticizing himself into a new elite by leaping across the
centuries to claim that, after a lapse of fifteen hundred years, he was
the harbinger of a resurrected breed of Pharisees. The more recent
inner history of the ghetto had largely turned on the conflict between
the dominant minority of the well-born and the scholars of the religious tradition, whom the rich generally obeyed, and the masses. (Let
it be added, parenthetically, that this too little studied class war is a
root cause of much of modern Jewish history and that the tensions
that resulted from it have not yet vanished, but detailed discussion of
this question is not immediately relevant in the present context.) In
ghetto terms, Ahad Ha-Am ranked as a hidalgo and he remained predisposed to believe that Jewish history had always been and would
remain the story of his class. As we shall soon see, the intellectual
content of his theory of Jewish spiritual nationalism is, on basic matters, evasive or self-contradictory. What lent unity to his position on
the inner affairs of Jewry was something he never quite acknowledged;
it was his attempt, amidst all the new turbulences of the nineteenth
century, to defend the pre-eminence of his class.

In western Europe the battle had been lost at least a half century
earlier, when the recently emancipated Jewish communities began to
look, as a matter of course, to new men as their mentors and spokesmen. The nineteenth-century age of revolution had announced the
end of the pre-eminence of the nobility and the clergy within European society as a whole; the Jewish counterpart of this event was a
rebellion against the old elite headed by the scholars of the synagogue.
The older hero of piety, who could be chosen only by the in-group,
was displaced by the new hero of secular achievement, who was inevitably (for a minority group not in control of its own political and
economic life) a creation of real or imagined gentile regard. One effect
of this new standard was to release the wealthy, for the first time in
Jewish history, from any remaining restraints imposed on their will by
rabbis; they could now be checked, as Herzl knew pre-eminently well,
only by organizing the masses against them. Another and equally im-

portant result was the arising, again for the first time in Jewish history, of an intellectual class which was highly regarded within Jewry precisely because its concerns were those of the general scene. Indeed, even the "official" Jewish scholarship of the nineteenth century was pitched in this key, for the dominant desire of the new "science of Judaism" was to prove that the subject matter of the Jewish past could be dealt with as a western and modern discipline, i.e., that it was as fit a subject for scholars as Latin and Greek. Here, too, Herzl, coming at the end of the century, is a significant part of the story; no small part of his initial success was due to his general prominence as a younger star of some magnitude in Austrian journalism.

These two elements created by the emancipation, the newly enriched Jewish bourgeoisie and the new intelligentsia, were not necessarily in alliance; quite on the contrary, the magnates usually distrusted and feared the secular intellectuals as dangerous radicals. It took but a moment for Herzl to realize, when he went in 1896 to attempt to convert the Belgian millionaire, Baron de Hirsch, to his schemes, that he and that magnate had nothing in common. For Ahad Ha-Am, however, these antagonists shared, a priori, the same fatal flaw—the brand of the parvenu. Together they were the enemy of the class for which he spoke, and their credentials to leadership had to be destroyed. He reacted like an outraged Maccabee in the face of Hellenizing Jews disporting in the Greek games, but he couched his ire in the language of modern nationalism. A real individual, he argued, is not one who stands outside any group or goes over to one in which he was not born; to possess human dignity a man must stand within and reflect the values of his own nation. Ahad Ha-Am reached crescendo, in this counterattack on the elite that had been crowding out his own, in his denunciation of a conscious and convinced assimilationist in the person of the French Jewish professor, Salomon Reinach; here he could let himself go completely, and the result was the coining of a memorable epithet for the new men, "slaves in the midst of freedom."

In re-echo of larger changes within European society as a whole, the second half of the nineteenth century produced an even newer, and perhaps more dangerous, enemy to the class for which Ahad Ha-Am spoke. Especially after the revolutions of 1848, the masses were increasingly mounting the stage of history. Their pressure expressed itself in the liberal West in ever more successful demands for broadening of the franchise and, therefore, for their direct control of the state through parliamentary government. More violently, the masses were the propelling force of the revolutions carried out in the name of the suppressed nationalisms or, abortively until 1917, on behalf of the have-not class. Certainly, all of these warring forces cannot be lumped together, and yet, there is one thing that they did share: an ultimate descent from the theory proclaimed by the French Revolution that society should be organized for the sake of the many. The necessary corollary of this assertion was the notion that true leaders were not the well-born or even the intellectuals (had not Robespierre sent Lavoisier to the guillotine and justified his act by announcing that the revolution had no need of scientists?) but the "men of the people." This political role was thus open to anybody who could seize it, and, especially in the socialist movements, it was not barred even to Jews.

Those Jews, like the German, Lassalle, who rose to public notice through the general political movements, had important effects on the Jewish community, at very least because the mythmakers of anti-Semitism used their prominence to "prove" that the "international Jew" was plotting against society. They were not, however, true contestants for leadership in Jewry's inner affairs, for, with the exception of Moses Hess in the later phases of his life, they had no such interests. On the other hand, after 1881 internal mass movements, in the image of the wider forces of democracy, nationalism, and socialism, began to appear within east European Jewry. What was happening is perhaps best illustrated by the genesis of the Jewish Socialist Bund in the 1890's. This party was launched as the enemy of Jewish nationalism and looked forward to the coming socialist revolution, which would achieve a classless society and thus end the Jewish problem. Since the respectable leaders of the existing Jewish community were opposed to such a consummation, the Bund proposed, in the immediate present, to wrest inner control from the rabbis of the religious tradition(the purveyors of "the opiate of the masses") and the Jewish rich (their "capitalist oppressors") for the sake of hastening the day of effective rebellion against the tsar. The Bund did not, of course, go unchallenged; the political Zionism which appeared at the same time, especially in its socialist formulation, was its most redoubtable enemy, and it was not the only one. This period, the three decades after 1881, was the age of political seething in Russia as a whole; on the Jewish scene, the production of political parties, suitably launched with ringing manifestos, seems to have been the main contemporary pursuit of the young intellectuals. Inevitably, such doctrinaire groups engaged in passionate conflicts (a legacy they have deeded on to the half century of Jewish thought that has followed) but, in historical perspective, they shared at least one basic position—together they represented the politicization of Jewish life. Their leaders were the enemy not only of the spiritual elite of the ghetto but also of those who had achieved personal prominence after the emancipation. The newest of the nineteenth century's new elites were, thus, the men of the parties and movements, who were sustained in their struggle to conquer the Jewish community by their claim to "speak for the masses."

Ahad Ha-Am's consistent response to this phenomenon was complete negation. The Bund was quite easy to polish off, for it could simply be denounced as just another version of assimilationism. The task became more difficult as he confronted Zionism, the movement of his own allegiance—and yet, it was here that he had to fight hardest, precisely because he believed that his kind of elite could perpetuate itself only in a nationalist context. He entered the lists with his debut in Hebrew letters, the famous essay, "This Is Not the Way," which is at the head of his collected works. Its burden was a critique of Hibbat Zion, insisting that its future was not in a program for the many but in carefully nurturing a few colonies in Palestine to be peopled by men and women of the highest spiritual quality. He followed out this thought (which the ex-socialist Lilienblum immediately recognized for what it was and vehemently opposed) by soon engaging in the most "practical" effort of his public life: he organized, with others, a secret ethical order, the "Sons of Moses," to consist of a small group of the spiritually elect, which he hoped would act as the "leaven in the dough"—i.e., as the true and unchallengeable leaders—of the national revival.

Both in his early days, and especially after the appearance of Herzl, Ahad Ha-Am was occasionally willing to imagine that Zionism would perhaps create, and should even strive to create, a Jewish settlement in Palestine of considerable size, but the very fact that he could be quoted against himself on this point in his own lifetime, and that his disciples and critics are still today debating his real meaning, indicates that this was, for him, not a matter of essence. Whenever this thought of a mass Zionist community was before him, he countered with a favorite phrase, "the preparation of the hearts," by which he meant the prior education of the national movement in the proper attitudes and scale of values, headed by respect for "spirit" and the "men of the spirit." A small and, therefore, more easily disciplined net of colonies as preferable, but much more—even a state—could be countenanced and, indeed, encouraged, provided the process of its creation was not so quick that the mass would sweep away the few.

It is now evident why Herzl's political Zionism represented a crisis not only for Ahad Ha-Am's intellect but also for his emotions. In 1896, after failing to convert the magnates, Herzl had consciously turned to the masses. The organization of the Zionist Congress in the form of a Jewish "parliament," with the corollary emphasis on so conducting its business as to attract maximal public attention and on undergirding its strength with the enrollment of millions, meant that Herzl was casting himself for the role of tribune and "president-in-exile" of all the people—hence the oft-quoted phrases from his diary about being "the man of the poor" and his glorying in a feeling of instinctive rapport, despite great cultural barriers, with the mass of his east European followers. There was indeed, as I have said earlier, a Promethean element in Herzl's inner relationship to the people, but, as a political fact, his bid for support to a large and undifferentiated following opened a new chapter in modern Jewish history. By basing his right to lead on the will of the people, he gave birth to modern Jewish statesmanship,[32] to the notion of an elite which, whatever it might personally owe to the national past, would be created solely by the choice of the new nationalist movement. Herzl thus raised himself to a plane beyond all the other new men who were concurrently arising in eastern Europe. They spoke, at most, for a class or a theory; his assertion that "we are one people" was an attempt at the Jewish equivalent of the French Revolution—i.e., the sweeping away of all "medievalism," of all encrusted distinctions within the nation (and, as well, of all future claim for special consideration), in favor of the equal rights of men and citizens, united only by their common national identity.

If Herzl was the Mirabeau of the Jewish revolution, Ahad Ha-Am was its Edmund Burke. He knew that there had been many abuses in the old Jewish life, both those forced upon it by the exile and those that could have been avoided, but he could not conceive of entirely sweeping them away. Within the framework of the old order, he was, like Burke, a liberal. The great Englishman had spoken out for the revolution made by the American colonies not in the name of natural law and a new order (the *novus ordo saeculorum*, the motto which the United States was soon to borrow from French ideologues) but because he saw them as the true defenders of continuing values, the inherited "rights of Englishmen." So Ahad Ha-Am had done battle, and never really made peace, with the standpattism of the religious

---

[32] I owe the phrase to Emanuel Neumann.

orthodox, for he too was sure that he was the true defender of conservatism, of the "law in the heart" and of the people not "of the Book, but of books"—i.e., of the organically developing creative impulse within Judaism, which had once, before it had become cribbed and confined within the ghetto of his immediate ancestors, been much freer and bolder. It is thus more than understandable why Ahad Ha-Am always felt an affinity for the English and continued to read widely in the political theorists in that language. Was not his announced purpose of "pouring new wine into old bottles" the equivalent, *mutatis mutandis,* of Tory liberalism? Out of such perspective he could only recoil from Herzl and call him un-Jewish; he could only cry out that the salvation of the Jews will come not from diplomats but from prophets.[33]

This left Ahad Ha-Am with the question with which he was forever wrestling: What, therefore, is truly Jewish? For the orthodox believers, who, because they understood him better, opposed him even more vehemently than they fought Herzl, this was no problem: Judaism meant absolute obedience to the revealed Law and patient waiting for the Messiah; but what could it mean to a socially and culturally conservative agnostic? "Spirit," undefined, was not enough of an answer, for that word could have many meanings. Perhaps it signified, as diverse programs of complete revolt have been claiming for at least a century, the spirit of the prophets, reinterpreted as the archetypical rebels against an established order. Perhaps, as the younger opponents of Ahad Ha-Am were shouting in the first decade of the present century,[34] the true and classical Jewish spirit predated the prophets and had been evident only in the golden age of the biblical kingdom, when the natural man of the plow and the sword had not yet been confined and spoiled by the Law of the Book. Was it perhaps thinkable that the Pharisees and their descendants, the rabbis of the ghetto, had been not the continuers of the Jewish spirit but its subverters? Could it be possible that the last two millennia of Jewish experience had been not only a political disaster but a moral error the memory of which needed to be blotted out—in the name of the spirit?

Or perhaps, in the fairer view of the past held by another opponent, Jacob Klatzkin, the millennial career of the Jew, the recent ghetto centuries included, had indeed been grandiose because it had represented a heroic clinging to religion; but religion was finished, since

[33]See text, Part 4.

[34]See text, Part 5, especially the writings of Berdichevski and Brenner.

modernity meant agnosticism. The true Jewish revolution, Klatzkin went on to argue, had been ushered in not by the political emancipation, which was of secondary importance, but by the loss of faith. This could not be covered over by substituting "moral spirit" for God and pretending, like Ahad Ha-Am, that nothing had changed. Only he who believes that his own values are divinely revealed can claim that upholding them makes him a member of a chosen people—and give himself leave to sit in judgment on others. The agnostic must see that "what is really new in Zionism is its territorial-political definition of Jewish nationalism. . . . In longing for our land we do not desire to create there a base for the spiritual values of Judaism. To regain our land is for us an end in itself—the attaining of a free national life . . . [Zionism's] basic intention, whether consciously or unconsciously, is to deny any conception of Jewish identity based on spiritual criteria."[35]

Ahad Ha-Am had no doubt that these notions were horrifying heresies, but, in his own terms, he could not really refute them. It was not hard for him to defend the most recent two millennia of Jewish life, the age of the exile, against the charge that they lacked moral and cultural stature, for ages which had produced the Talmud and Maimonides, and saints and martyrs without number, could not fairly be accused of spiritual insignificance—but all this Klatzkin, his most incisive critic, was willing to grant and yet the question still remained: How could one deny God and affirm chosenness?

As I hinted in the early pages of this essay, hard as Ahad Ha-Am tried, the task was insuperable.[36] He appealed to common knowledge, that "it is admitted by everyone—not excluding Nietzsche—that the Jewish people is unique in its genius for morality," but that still leaves the questions: Why this endowment limited, for all eternity, to one people? and, Is Jewish morality still superior? He could avoid the first issue only by weakly adding, in the next sentence after the passage just quoted, "no matter how it happened or by what process this particular gift developed."[37] Occasionally, as Ahad Ha-Am perforce

[35]See text, Part 5.

[36]It is instructive that the American religious naturalist, Mordecai Kaplan, who has followed Ahad Ha-Am in most major matters, had to break with him over this very matter. Kaplan has maintained that, in all logic, the "chosen people" concept must be abandoned, for, without the orthodox God to do the choosing, even the most moral of national traditions cannot claim to be the metaphysical hub of the universe.

[37]Simon, op. cit., p. 80.

returned to this issue, he almost asserted an innate racially superior moral talent of the Jew, but he immediately recoiled from such a thought. To use the idea of race to buttress his position was an inconceivable surrender to the enemy, to the theorists of modern anti-Semitism as headed by the Pan-Slavs. The Jewish moral genius were better left unexplained than based on the outlook it was meant to conquer.

Ahad Ha-Am's responses to the second question were equally inconclusive. He knew that, at very least, he would have to prove that Jewish morality continued to be higher than the Christian; and yet, some of his least convincing writing is in the pages that he devoted to this subject. It is no accident, to be explained merely by side causes, that he never brought himself to write the book that was to be his magnum opus, a definition of Jewish ethics. As the capstone of his system, such a volume needed to demonstrate, on the basis of reason, that this ethic, devised by man (i.e., by the Jewish national culture,) was unattainable in any other context. A man of faith could assert this a priori; a rationalist, as Klatzkin argued unanswerably, could only regard an ethic as an intangible standard which was, or could easily become, equally incarnate in any other culture and hence equally available to all men. Hence, said Klatzkin, the crisis of faith that had begun in the nineteenth century left the Jew, as a nationalist, only one answer: "Let us be like all the nations."

This debate, which came to a head in the first decade of the twentieth century (and which still continues),[38] had occurred, as one could guess, at least once before, in a major way, in the early decades of the nineteenth century. Then, in the first generation after the Emancipation, the call had been not for the entry of Jewry as secular nation but for that of the Jew as secularized individual into western society. The basic counter-arguments had already been advanced in the 1830's by two of the founders of "defensive" Jewish thought, S. D. Luzzatto in Italy and Nachman Krochmal in Galicia. Luzzatto told the assimilationists of his day that they were rushing toward a secular world founded on Hellenic (his term was Attic), i.e., on aesthetic and, therefore, inevitably libertine, values; Judaism, he asserted, was the sole bearer of a civilization worthy of the name, for it enshrined the only ultimate by which men could live, the biblical morality of mercy. Krochmal agreed with the enemies of the ghetto that its culture

[38]See text, Part 7, the selections from Judah Magnes, and Part 10, David Ben-Gurion.

was at the nadir of decline, but he denied that this was reason either for abandoning Judaism or even for contemning the recent past. History was cyclical, with periods of birth, maturity, and death following one another. All other nations were but partial incarnations of Spirit, and their life cycles were both irreversible and one-time affairs. Only the Jews, as the complete bearers of the Absolute, had a history consisting of several such cycles following upon each other. What, therefore, if the ghetto is moribund? It was inevitable for such a period to come occasionally, but it was preordained that Jewry would soon rise again, phoenixlike, from the ashes of decline, especially if it were reawakened to life by the light and air of a correct philosophy.

But Luzzatto could maintain this sharp distinction because he was a religious believer and, indeed, a mystic. Even the rationalist Krochmal meant more than "moral spirit" when he said the Absolute; he was imagining the philosopher's God, too austere and metaphysical to perform vulgar miracles and to intervene directly in human affairs, but nonetheless at once transcendent and immanent in history. In His name it could still be said, especially in the heyday of Hegel's philosophy of history, which cast Prussia as the incarnation of the Absolute,[39] that there was divine purpose in human affairs and that the Jews exemplified it. Though both were undoubtedly driven to philosophizing by what was to them the unhappy present state of their people, they could nonetheless rest secure in the faith that God assured the survival of its values. Herzl, too, for that matter, could take equal heart from his historical determinism and write in his diary, a month after the First Zionist Congress in August 1897, "at Basel I founded the Jewish State." Ahad Ha-Am, however, no matter how hard he tried to reassure himself, was sustained by no comparable certainty. Since the day of Luzzatto and Krochmal, another half century or more of spiritual attrition, now further complicated by mass migrations westward, had disastrously weakened the inner fiber of the Jewish community. To far graver problems than those faced by his predecessors, he brought neither Herzl's "messianic" faith in the inevitable triumph of progress and liberalism nor a refurbished version of the older Jewish religious verities. He could not help but know in his bones that his agnostic's call for loyalty to "spirit" could not, alone, guarantee the future.

[39]Despite the weight of scholarly opinion to the contrary, I am convinced by Joseph Klausner, *History of Modern Hebrew Literature* (in Hebrew), 2nd ed., Jerusalem, 1952, Vol. II, pp. 211–14, that Krochmal was a Hegelian.

But was it not possible to turn tables on this dilemma? His certainties—his distrust of the nations of the world and his disbelief in the strength and values of the Jewish masses—had been the carefully reasoned premises on which he had built his one truly original idea, the notion of a "spiritual center" in Palestine. By their light he had argued, negatively, that only a small-scale community of no political importance could hope to be left alone by the powers of the world and that anything more was beyond the creative resources of the right-minded few, the national elite. Could not his very confusions—his difficulties in defining his ultimate, the "moral spirit," and his pronounced failure to convince his intellectual enemies—be pressed into service and made the positive and clinching proof of how right he was?

As a humanist, Ahad Ha-Am believed that ideas are not pre-existing essences or divine revelations but the highest expressions of the spirit of a society. His unrivaled analysis of the contemporary ills of Jewry had shown that a true Jewish society no longer existed, for its twin foundations, the ghetto and the inherited tradition, were irretrievably gone. Hence, within so debased a milieu, how could even he do more than dimly outline the form of the Judaism of the future? In a community bereft of all cohesiveness or restraint, how could one expect more than the few to make the right choices? So the more pained Ahad Ha-Am was by the successes of the men and movements he abhorred, and the less his rational arguments could withstand their attacks, the more obvious it became to him that he was losing because the battle was being waged in the wrong arena. The task of creating and clearly defining a modern version of the superior Jewish morality had to be postponed, for only a "spiritual center" could provide the soil for sure and elemental creativity. Only within its confines would the right choices be made; only there would his values come into their own.

History, too, could be invoked to support this solution by postponement. Two millennia ago the exile had begun with the destruction of the Second Temple in Jerusalem and the scattering of the majority of the Jewish people. At the end of that war the Roman conqueror Titus had summoned the Pharisees, in the person of their leader, Rabbi Johanan ben Zakkai, to offer some political autonomy for those who remained in Palestine and perhaps even the chance to rebuild the Temple. The Pharisees had chosen, instead, to ask for the right to create an intellectual center in a town of no political or military importance, in Jamnia.[40] As Ahad Ha-Am analyzed the reasons for this choice (which means, of course, as he projected his own estimate of the present into the past), he convinced himself evermore that only a recreated Jamnia could counter the equally grave threat to unity in his own day. In his view, the Pharisees had removed Jewish life from the political realm because they had witnessed the utter defeat of their people by Rome, the symbol of power. They had seen their internal foes, the young rebels who inspired the revolt, lead the masses to disaster, and hence they were making sure, through Jamnia, that their own standards, the rule of the "spirit," would prevail in the future. True, as a physical entity, this Pharisaic seat of authority in the Holy Land had lasted only a few centuries, but the values fashioned within it had dominated and sustained a dispersed Jewish community almost to the present. What could be more pat than this archetype out of the past? What was more obvious than that a Jamnia was the need of the hour?

It must be added that this attempt at an intellectual coup is not as artificial and evasive as it may seem on the surface. In its own way, it is a restatement of the classical solutions to the basic dilemma of modern liberalism, the balancing of freedom and authority, the defining of the boundary between liberty and license. Rousseau had counterposed the "general will," the responsible, long-range purposes of society, to the momentary aberrations of the "will of all." The makers of the French Revolution had declared that the citizen had duties as well as rights, and Thomas Jefferson had preached the need of an educated yeomanry as the necessary foundation of a stable democracy. In sum, the mainstream of modern liberalism knew that to survive and succeed it required a responsible society that had already made its basic choices; hence, it was wedded to the writing of constitutions, in the image of John Locke's "social compact," and to public education, which would fashion true patriots—i.e., basically like-minded people who shared a secular faith. Otherwise, freedom could easily degenerate into anarchy and mobocracy and, as has often

[40]This time-honored interpretation of that fateful incident has recently been questioned, on scholarly grounds, by Gedaliahu Alon, who maintains—I believe, quite convincingly—that the Center in Jamnia was created not by the free choice of Johanan ben Zakkai but rather by the Roman conquerors' use of this town as a prison camp for Jewish notables. See his Studies in Jewish History (in Hebrew), Tel-Aviv, 1957, Vol. 1, pp. 219–52. But this is irrelevant to the argument above, for the notion that a free and conscious choice took place was doubted by no one until Alon.

happened throughout the modern age, the Man on Horseback would be voted in by the people.

Nonetheless, how could Ahad Ha-Am be sure that the "spiritual center" would soon acquire an unquestioned authority? Small groups of scholars and pietists of the old school had always lived in the Holy Land, supported by the contributions of the faithful in the Diaspora, but Ahad Ha-Am's righteous contempt for this system (known as Halukah) and all its works was proof that they represented no central authority which could sustain the Jewish people. Why would the role of his modernist scholars be more widely accepted—and acceptable? Was it not equally, if not much more, likely that his "spiritual center" might become but another phalanstery, another incident among the many modern examples of groups defeated by the age, retiring in impotence to be ignored in their private utopias?

Indeed, as Ahad Ha-Am knew, his were not the only values being exported to the renascent Jewish community in Palestine, for the majority of the colonists who were going there, especially in the first decade of the present century (the famous Second Aliyah,[41] which is today still the "old guard" leadership of the state of Israel) regarded his traditionalism as passé. These idealists envisaged a homeland not as the "defensive" support for the inherited Jewish life but as its "messianic" antithesis. Their voice was not Ahad Ha-Am but that bitter enemy of the recent Jewish past, Joseph Hayyim Brenner.[42]

To be sure, the passage of a stormy fifty years has tempered the early radicalism of Ben-Gurion's generation,[43] but what assured Ahad Ha-Am, a priori, that he would inevitably win the as yet undecided *Kulturkampf* for the soul of the "spiritual center"? More pointedly still, even if his version of Jewish nationalism would prevail in the homeland, why would it necessarily make the "center" into the life-giving sun around which the diverse communities of the Diaspora would revolve? Most difficult of all, why was he so certain that a revived "center" would inevitably produce a new formulation of first-rate moral ideas? Perhaps it would be a "normal" small community and, hence, give birth to second—and even third-rate ideas—or to no ideas at all?

In the face of all these objections none of Ahad Ha-Am's reasonable

[41]Aliyah is a Hebrew word meaning "ascent."

[42]See text, Part 5.

[43]See text, Part 10, where the older Ben-Gurion attempts to combine both emphases.

notions could help him. There was only one refuge, his nationalist mystique of the elite. Beginning with the Bible itself, Jewish religion had never been able to find an explanation for its ultimate mystery: Why had God made this peculiar people, the Jews? Ahad Ha-Am, as agnostic, merely replaced this question with a secular mystery: the "fact," as he insisted, that, peculiar and chosen as the Jews were, they were self-created, or, more precisely, that the Jewish people had been the matrix within which its elite, the "men of the spirit" had fashioned important and unique values for this community and, ultimately, for all humanity. For Providence he substituted the national "will-to-live," and the land hallowed by God became the only soil within which the seminal deeds of the people and its elite— like biblical prophesy and the Pharasaic erection of the "fence around the law"—could take place. A comparable miracle of the spirit was required in the present, and those who were on the side of the angels were, therefore, commanded to create its necessary precondition, the "spiritual center." What matter that he could not "prove" the inevitability of the miracle? He had faith that the "will-to-live," using the elite as its agent, would rise again to the test; indeed, whether one shared that belief (note the unconscious echoes of the Calvinist doctrine of the elect) was almost proof of whether he belonged to the elite.

These remarks can best be concluded by quoting from a statement of Ahad Ha-Am's in 1910, toward the end of his literary career (though he lived another seventeen years) and hence reflective of his most mature views. He summarized most of his main themes by ending the essay to which I alluded above on the difference between Jewish and Christian ethics with this unusual outburst of passion:

A Jew may be a liberal of liberals without forgetting that Judaism was born in a corner and has always lived in a corner, aloof from the great world, which has never understood it and therefore hates it. So it was before the rise of Christianity, and so it has remained ever since. History has not yet satisfactorily explained how it came about that a tiny nation in a corner of Asia produced a unique religious and ethical outlook, which, though it has had so profound an influence on the rest of the world, has yet remained so foreign to the rest of the world, and to this day has been unable either to master it or to be mastered by it. This is a historical phenomenon to which, despite many attempted answers, we must still attach a note of interrogation. But every true Jew, be he orthodox or liberal, feels in the

*depths of his being that there is something in the spirit of our people—
though we do not know what it is—which has prevented us from following the rest of the world along the beaten path, has led to our
producing this Judaism of ours, and has kept us and our Judaism "in
a corner" to this day, because we cannot abandon the distinctive outlook on which Judaism is based. Let those who still have this feeling
remain within the fold: let those who have lost it go elsewhere. There
is no room here for compromise.*[44]

VII

Zionist thought, whether "messianic" or "defensive," was rooted in
late nineteenth-century ideas and senses of situation, but the effective
history of the movement has unfolded within a different age. Both for
the world as a whole and for the Jew, the political and social upheavals
of the twentieth century have been far more devastating than Zionism,
even at its most pessimistic, imagined a priori.[45]

From the day of his appearance on the Jewish scene Theodor Herzl
was, as he remained for fifty years, the dominant figure of Zionism, for
he announced the beginning of the boldest attempt of the Jew to
become part of the general history of the West. A century after the
French Revolution, he confronted the still unrealized Emancipation
and announced that he alone could effect it, both for the Jew and the
world, through political Zionism. Ahad Ha-Am, at his most profound,
answered not in terms of his own peculiar, and basically indefensible,
secular metaphysics, but out of his deep sense of the uniqueness of the
situation of the Jew. He asserted that the tension between the Jew
and the world was not merely a situation, a deep-seated malaise (Herzl
defined it as landlessness) which ought to be subject to some cure
(like perhaps, the political restoration of Jewish nationhood), but a
basic category of all human history. Hence, no matter what a modern
"messianism" might attempt, Ahad Ha-Am was certain that the meaning of its work would be transformed, despite itself, by this ultimate
reality. His doctrine is thus essentially passive; it can provide, at most,
a way of living with history rather than a call to remake it. The thrust
of Zionism came from Herzl, and this impulse has, indeed, altered the
relationship between the Jew and the world. But did Herzl's ideas

[44]Simon, op. cit., pp. 127–28.

[45]See above, Section I of this Introduction, for fuller general remarks on this point.

really prevail, insofar as any ideas prevail in human life, where any consummation is far different from the vision? Or, in the last analysis, was it Herzl, the legend and the myth, who was used by the very history he came to end? We can find some clues to an answer by assessing the impact of Herzl's doctrine and the various uses to which it was put.

Eastern Europe furnished Herzl the overwhelming mass of his followers and, especially, the vanguard which created the modern Zionist settlement in Palestine. And yet, there was a vast difference between what Herzl taught and what these disciples made out of his "messianism." He had set modern Zionism into motion by proclaiming a total ingathering into the Jewish state as its aim, and political action as the tool, by which this purpose was to be achieved; his followers, and not Herzl himself, added all the other well-known values of this doctrine—Zion, practical efforts in colonization, socialism, and revolt against the spirit and culture of the ghetto. This is obviously a richer and more complex program than that of Herzl, who had occasion during his brief career to do battle against aspects of this expanded "neomessianism." It arose not by deduction from his premises but for other reasons: it was the way—with historic hindsight we can add, the only way—that "messianism" could be assimilated into the situation of the young in Russo-Jewish history at the turn of the century.

Perhaps the best summary of the mood out of which their Zionism arose is to be found in the lines addressed by Bialik to Ahad Ha-Am. He wrote in 1903: "We were born under some unknown star, at dusk, among piles of rubble, as the sons of the old age of our hoary people. . . . It was a time of primeval chaos, of erased boundaries, of end and beginning, of destruction and building, of age and youth. And we, the children of transition, were both wittingly and unwittingly bowing before and worshiping both these realms. . . . Suspended between these two magnets, all the silent feelings of our heart then looked for a *prophet*."[46] The rebels in this generation could not, however, follow Bialik in finding their hero in Ahad Ha-Am. The loss of the orthodox religious faith of their childhoods was not their only problem. Their personal prospects within Russia were of the blackest and their native ghetto was economically and—at least in their eyes—culturally stagnant. In the face of all this, mere intellectual revision of Judaism seemed far too narrow and uncongenial a task, so they rallied to Herzl—but he, too, did not answer all their needs.

[46]Hayyim Nahman Bialik, Collected Works (in Hebrew), Tel Aviv, 1935, Vol. 1, p. 117.

Their outlook drew on both older and newer sources than Herzl had used, or, indeed, had regarded as relevant. For example, in the pure logic of Herzl's theories—and of Pinsker's before him—the Jews required a land of their own to end their abnormality as a nation, but this territory did not have to be Palestine.[47] Even at its most hard-headedly secular, the Zionist movement has never countenanced such logic, for it is unimaginable without its profound mystique about Zion —and these emotions derive not from any modernist philosophizing but from the Bible. On the other hand, the very tenuousness of Herzl's relationship to the religious tradition permitted him to regard it quite dispassionately with an aristocratic sense of formal respect and *noblesse oblige*. In eastern Europe, however, "messianism" almost invariably meant an active battle against religion, for the young Zionists used "messianism" for their program of revolt against their pious parents. Herzl's own economic views were under the impress of technology and social justice and amounted to a *fin-de-siècle*, west European, progressive liberalism. To the east, in the tsarist Russia of that day, this was too mild, for the advanced faith of the younger generation was socialism. Herzl at first opposed and later never gave more than grudging assent to the efforts initiated by his east European followers to develop Zionist colonization in Palestine. In his timetable a "charter" to the land, resulting from an international political decision, was the indispensable prerequisite, but amidst the pogroms of Russia and Poland the Zionist in those countries, and especially the "messianists" among them, had no time to wait for an eventual diplomatic triumph by their leader. For Herzl, in sum, Zionism was addressed outward to only one problem, anti-Semitism; his truest followers in eastern Europe turned it inward as well, and they made "messianism" the resolution of their war with themselves and the banner under which they fought against both the older values of the ghetto and against all of the many other competing "isms" of their day.

This explanation of east European "neo-messianism" is adequate as far as it goes, but it cannot account for one remaining—and crucial— difficulty. The question of religion should put us on guard: Herzl, the purely political, post-religious man, was consistent in having neither a mystical bond to Zion nor a doctrinaire quarrel with the orthodox pieties, but what made it possible for the "neo-messianists" vehe-

[47]See text, Part 2, the concluding passages of Pinsker's *Auto-Emancipation*; and Part 3, Herzl's *Jewish State*. See also the biographical sketch of Herzl, *loc. cit.*, for the Uganda controversy of 1903.

mently to deny God and yet insist that they could rebuild the Jewish nation only on the land He had promised to Abraham? To be sure, various attempts were made to answer this question in a "respectable" way by denying that involvement in the religious tradition had anything to do with the centrality of Zion to Zionism. Ber Borochov, the leading Marxist theoretician of Zionism, had invoked an elaborate dialectic to "prove" that this land was so miserably poor that it alone, of all the countries of the world, held no attraction for predatory capitalism; therefore, it would be left to the Jews.[48] But toward the end of his short years even Borochov ceased believing that this was the true reason for bending all Jewish efforts toward Zion. He no longer took care to use only the unbiblical noun "Palestine" and began to speak of the spiritual imponderables which linked the Jew to the "Land of Israel." Borochov thus gained in wisdom, but he did lose in intellectual consistency. Remaining no less an agnostic than before, he had fallen, as Zionist, into the paradox I described just above.

Indeed, this is not the only inconsistency in the doctrine of "neo-messianism." Its socialism, too, was of a peculiar, self-contradicting kind. In the essay which was the first expression of Socialist-Zionism, Nahman Syrkin wrote this glowing hymn to the world of the morrow: "Socialism will do away with wars, tariffs, and the conflict of economic interests among civilized peoples . . . This will pave the way for the uniting of their separate histories, which will weld them into one humanity. Socialism, with its basic principles of peace, co-operation, and cultural progress, bears the seed out of which pure internationalism, that is, cosmopolitanism, will develop."[49] Such hopes seemed to be leading Syrkin to the orthodox, universalist socialist view that the Jewish problem would be solved by the victory of the international proletariat—but he said precisely the reverse. Within a few pages he was bitterly attacking the existing socialist parties of Germany, France, and Russia for opportunistic silence, or worse, in the face of anti-Semitism, and denouncing their Jewish members for being the worst kind of anti-Zionists. More fundamentally, he asserted that "socialism will solve the Jewish problem only in the remote future. . . . Socialism, whether in its daily struggle or its ultimate realization, aids all the oppressed. . . . It is altogether different with the Jews. The economic structure of the Jewish people, its lack of political rights, and its peculiar position in society combine to place it in a singular situation which

[48]See text, Part 6.

[49]See text, Part 6.

cannot be improved, at present, through the socialist struggle."[50] Syrkin's conclusion was to insist on Zionism, i.e., the formation of a Jewish state, as the only way to solve the Jewish problem but to plead that the inner life of that state had to be based on socialism. What Syrkin said thus amounted to a very interesting argument: Socialism is, in theory, a post-nationalist movement, but in immediate practice, it is in varying degrees anti-Jewish, anti-Zionist, and actually incapable of solving the Jewish problem; nonetheless, this is a noble dream of a united mankind in which men will not exploit each other; therefore, let the particular life required to solve the specific needs of the Jew be an incarnation of the socialist vision.

Despite these paradoxes (and they are not the only ones that could be cited) there is an inner consistency to "neo-messianism": behind several disguises (not the least of which was the areligious nature of its hero, Herzl), which partly obscure its true character even today, this doctrine served the same basic functions in east European Jewish experience as the roughly contemporary "social gospel" served in Christianity, i.e., it offered a humanist faith and a program of reformist action as a substitute for the classic supernatural religion. It was, however, a peculiar version of the "social gospel" and to understand it we must return to the problem which occupied us in the first part of this essay, the typology of Jewish responses to the Emancipation.

That analysis, it will be remembered, posited two main kinds of modern Jewish thought, the "messianic" and the "defensive." In essence, each of them was both a program and an estimate of the situation of the Jew in the gentile world. "Messianism" believed not only that the Jew ought to be like everybody else but also that this would happen by the agency of a benevolent liberalism, nationalism, or socialism. The "defensive" schools not only believed that the Jewish spirit was unique but they also tended to argue, or they assumed without question, that, try as he would, the Jew would never be completely accepted in the world of the majority. The major representatives of these outlooks in the successive phases of nineteenth-century Jewish thought, through Herzl and Ahad Ha-Am, remained true to type by affirming doctrines which were in every case in harmony with their own estimate of the Jew-gentile relationship. It is, however, imaginable that doctrine and sense of situation should not go hand in hand. A Jew might feel in his bones a continuing alienation from society, yet affirm the content of its modern thought as the necessary values of the

[50] Ibid.

existence which he must live in apartness. It is equally conceivable for a Jew to have no shred of such a sense of alienation, or at least hopefully to imagine that any remnants of it will soon cease to exist, and yet find reasons for his standing apart, by choice, in the inner realm of culture and emotion.

These suggested permutations represent no mere game of chess, with intellectual abstractions for pawns. They are the concrete reality of Zionism in the present century. In western Europe, modern history as a whole went through the stage of a realized bourgeois revolution, with the legal emancipation of the Jew as one of its results wherever the liberal state came into being. To be sure, anti-Semitism was always present even in this milieu, but modern society in the West was dangerously infected by it only later in the century. Herzl could still believe that Jew-hatred was as much a challenge to liberalism as it was to the Jew, that the two were still natural partners in dealing with it, and hence he could offer Zionism as a "peacemaker." The history of eastern Europe was radically different. Russian experience as a whole has been deeply affected by the fact that that country has skipped the stage of liberalism, for it went directly from tsarist autocracy to Communist dictatorship. During a half century or more of struggle for revolution in Russia, both liberalism (as Lilienblum and Pinsker knew) and socialism (as Syrkin asserted, above) became compromised by tactical alliances—or worse—with anti-Semitism, and, in east European Jewish eyes, they had accrued no prior moral credit by having had the opportunity to confer the benefit of emancipation. Under these circumstances parts of two generations entered intellectually into the temple of modernity, but their situation remained Jewish—indeed, searingly and tragically Jewish—for the gods they were following had never helped them and were even willing to accept their people as a human sacrifice. A man of classical religious faith can live with his forsakenness by explaining it as the unknowable will of God, by declaring, with Job, "though He slay me, I will yet hope in Him," but a this-worldly program of reform requires a society within which it can hope to see some fruit of its labor. This was the element provided by Zionism. It offered the east European Jew his own people as the proper object of his labors.

Vis-à-vis society as a whole eastern "neo-messianic" Zionism was, unlike Herzl's, not a "peacemaker" but a challenge. It inevitably confronted the modern movements of its time and place as the reminder of their moral failures. The young men who left Russia for Palestine in the first decade of the century banged the door shut on Europe with far greater emotion and with different intent than had motivated Herzl's "messianism." For him the realization of Zionism meant that the last problem on the docket of liberalism would have been removed; for these east European children of an aborted modernity the true revolution for mankind was yet entirely in the future. In their eyes liberalism and socialism had yet to discover their own true souls, and so their secular messianism became, very early, more than a way of living in the world as a nation among the nations. It acquired a kind of defiant hope that the new society they intended to build in Zion would take the lead in realizing the values that Russian (and all other) liberals and socialists merely talked about—and often betrayed. Here, too, Nahman Syrkin is instructive: "Because the Jews are placed in an unusual situation, that they are forced to find a homeland and establish a state, they therefore have been presented with the opportunity to be the first to realize the socialist vision. This is the tragic element of their historic fate, but it is also a unique historic mission. What is generally the vision of a few will become a great national movement among the Jews; what is utopian in other contexts is a necessity for the Jews. The Jews were historically the nation which caused division and strife; it will now become the most revolutionary of all nations."

Hence, the determining theme of the image of the Jew in the Bible, that he is the "suffering servant" of all humanity, was arising in hyper-modern garb in "neo-messianism." Those who accepted such a burden might indeed—as they did—hate the ghetto and all that could be identified with it, but, precisely because they were revolting against the ghetto, they were certain that they, and they alone, spoke for the true meaning of Jewish history. To share in the building of this new society was the proper and sufficient content of Jewish life, its great contemporary commandment for all Jews. Extending help from afar, no matter in how great a spirit of identification, was not enough; the ultimate imperative was an insistence that every Jew had, by personal choice, to come and share in the life of Zion—otherwise he would surely be punished by history for the sin of his disobedience by eventually having to run there for his life.

The twentieth century has been witness to the fantastic energies and devotion that these views have generated within Jewry. They found bitter confirmation in the modern age of political and social upheaval. Toward the end of the First World War and immediately thereafter, Herzlian dreams of an uncomplicated destiny for the Jew within a liberal world order did revive for a moment, but they were soon to fade again. Great Britain administered Palestine between the two wars by the light of a policy of retreat by stages from its solemn promise in the Balfour Declaration[51] and the rest of the liberal West was not much firmer in its support of the Zionist aims to which it gave frequent lip service. The new states of the Middle East were friendly for a moment—there was, for example, good understanding between Weizmann and Emir Feisal during the period of the Versailles Peace Conference—but the rising nationalism of the Arabs soon made a violent anti-Zionism into its cardinal principle and its lowest common denominator of unity. In Palestine, where it mattered most, the dream of co-operation with other national movements for the creating of a better life for all was to be exploded by pogroms, guerrilla wars, and unreasoning hatred. Above all, despite notable and never to be forgotten exceptions, society as a whole, in its states, movements, and even churches, exchanged morality for expediency during the Hitler years. Within Zionism as a whole, and especially in Palestine, the somber sense of standing alone could only be deepened by these events.

Nonetheless, "neo-messianism" is not really a pessimistic doctrine. Though it grew out of the same soil as the theories of Pinsker and Ahad Ha-Am, its view of Jewish life is not (like theirs) tragic but (even more than Herzl's) heroic. There was enough of the blacker mood—and, alas, more than enough in the recent career of Jewry—to have given rise to moments of distrust and despair of the world, but "neo-messianism" was essentially a hopeful, nineteenth-century faith in progress and in man, re-inforced and more than lightly colored by being spoken and conceived in the language of the Bible. It is not accidental that its greatest survivor, David Ben-Gurion, speaks today in the accents of an agnostic prophet, a cross between Isaiah and the hero of *Invictus*.

As a complex of emotions and of ideas, "neo-messianism" has had a unique career in this century, for it provided the *élan* for the building of Zion. Nonetheless, its doctrine was not of one piece, and the seams which bound its various parts have become more than a little frayed after fifty years. "Neo-messianism" has, in particular, found great difficulty in addressing itself to the new situation of Jewry after the historic turning point represented by the creation of the state of Israel. To deal with these questions intelligently, we must first return to the other possible permutation of "defensive" and "messianic" thought,

[51]A balanced, though far from exhaustive summary of the events in Palestine between the two world wars is to be found in Ismar Elbogen's A *Century of Jewish Life*, Philadelphia, 1944, pp. 589–635.

i.e., the alliance of a Jew's sense of real at-homeness in the gentile world with a desire to stand to some degree apart in spirit and emotion, for this is the context within which Herzlian Zionism was accepted and refashioned among the Jewish communities within the western democracies and especially in America.

VIII

From the day that Herzl appeared on the Jewish scene, the black-and-white of his "messianic" vision spoke more movingly and directly than Ahad Ha-Am's yes-buts even to the Zionists in the free, western lands. On the surface, they might have been expected to find Ahad Ha-Am more congenial—as they did, to some degree—because, of all the major Zionist thinkers, he alone had denied that the "ingathering" was either a near possibility or the cardinal aim of Zionism. Nonetheless, even these westerners, who were certain that they themselves would never go to Palestine, chose to follow Herzl. Nor can this be interpreted as a kind of ideological hollowness, in which a major wing of the movement formally held an ideal while the mass of its individuals permitted themselves so many exceptions that the principle was made meaningless. I have argued, just above, that "neo-messianic" Zionism was a "social gospel" evolved out of Herzl's main themes within the context of east European experience. Western Jews, too, faced the need for modern content in their inner spiritual lives; for them, too, Zionism served the function of being the vital element of their own "social gospel"; and here, too, a transmuting of the purely secular outlook of Herzl was more useful in answering the need for a faith than the metaphysics of Ahad Ha-Am.

In part, the problem posed by the notion of the "ingathering" could, indeed, be avoided and driven underground, for the Turks, and later the British, had their *raisons d'état* for never opening the doors wide and thus, in effect, challenging many Zionists to pay the implied promissory note of their "messianic" theories. As any sensible man could see, such a day was so far in the future that it did not need to engage him in any important way. For the present, he could best show his regard for the Yishuv, the always sore beset thin line of heroes in the homeland, by speaking the language of their dreams, by political effort in their support, and by providing the always insufficient financial help which the Zionist movement could scrape together. In practice, therefore, a rough partnership in "messianism" evolved between the few in

Palestine and the many outside; the former represented its "home office" and the latter conducted its "foreign affairs" and "ministry of supply." This arrangement had its difficulties, which often erupted into towering battles, but it worked reasonably well—it, at least, avoided a major ideological war—throughout the decades of exertion and struggle which preceded the emergence of the state of Israel.

There was an even deeper reason, however, for the ascendance of Herzl and the eclipse of Ahad Ha-Am during the first half of this century. The Zionist movement lived through this turbulent era in an atmosphere of successive life-and-death crises. Hence, Herzl's vision of "taking arms against a sea of troubles and, by opposing, end them" was the almost indispensable source of morale. He had spoken of the Jewish state as a command of history, of the rightful place of the Jew in the arena of international politics, and of the need for many levels of mass action by this people in order to steer through the dangerous rapids of the present toward a happier future. In a revolutionary age this political language seemed much more realistic than Ahad Ha-Am's insistence on carefully nurtured colonization, on delicate balancing between tradition and change, and on the pre-eminence of the Jewish spirit. In occasional moments of reflection, such as the traditional "cultural debates" at the various Zionist Congresses, the movement indeed reaffirmed its emotional commitment to the nobility of these values, but its pressing concerns were such "Herzlian" matters as the Mufti of Jerusalem, Hitler, and Ernest Bevin.

This seeming unity in "messianism" broke down, visibly, only in recent years, after the state of Israel came into being. It was no longer possible to avoid the doctrine of the "ingathering," for the customs sheds of Israel were now staffed by men who were looking, with ever more aggressive eagerness, for those who would come, by choice, out of the free lands. This demand was uttered at the very beginning of the hectic decade of statehood, even in the midst of the almost overwhelming flood of refugees from Europe and the Arab lands. At first, practical reasons were advanced—that Israel needed such fresh energies and talent to help it bear its grave burdens and that the new state would otherwise be in danger of losing its western character—but, real and important though they were, these were secondary considerations. Ultimately, this call to be "ingathered" was rooted in the faith by which Israel's leaders had lived and in which they had raised their children, the sabras—that the creation of the state was the last way station on the road to a Herzlian end to the peculiar history of the ghetto and Diaspora.

Almost before these words were spoken, it was evident that they would not be heeded.[52] Diaspora Zionism, despite its long-standing apparent devotion to the outlook of Herzl, began to defend itself in terms mostly borrowed from Ahad Ha-Am. A large and growing literature of speeches, articles, and, by now, even books has been devoted to asserting that America is not "exile" (something, be it said, to which Ahad Ha-Am would not have assented); that Zionism means a special set of emotional, spiritual, and cultural relations to Israel by Jews who intend to remain in the homes they love; and that, in sum, the state is not the instrument of a "messianic ingathering" but a tool forged by the Jewish people for the defense of its inner integrity and survival, which are envisaged as continuing in pretty much their present modes. From this perspective, indeed, counterdemands have been made of the new state: its spiritual life has been criticized as too secular and as insufficient to provide the sustenance expected of a "spiritual center" for world Jewry; to the outrage of many in Israel and especially of its greatest figure, Ben-Gurion, a succession of Zionist leaders in the Diaspora (Abba Hillel Silver, Emanuel Neumann, and, recently, Nahum Goldmann) have pressed for something paralleled by no other existing political arrangement, i.e., for a considerable direct voice for the Zionist movement in those matters before the state of Israel which are of concern to all Jews.[53]

[52]To my knowledge, the first connected analysis of these themes appeared in two articles of mine in the magazine *Commentary:* "American Zionism at Impasse," October 1949, and "Israel Looks at the American Jew," January 1950.

[53]Most of the current discussion is to be found in two significant small books: Mordecai M. Kaplan, *A New Zionism,* New York, 1955; and Ben Halpern, *The American Jew,* New York, 1956. In addition there are two articles that strikingly illustrate the contrasting passions of this debate; I therefore add two excerpts from these articles published in *Forum,* the occasional journal created by the World Zionist Organization in 1953 for the discussion of these issues. In Number 2 (April 1956) the American Zionist leader, Irving Miller, wrote: "The original principles of the movement have been forgotten, to the point where it is hardly believed today that to the founders of Zionism a Jewish state was not an end in itself, but merely an indispensable means for the rejuvenation of the Jewish spirit, of Jewish life and culture. The early Zionists never ceased to emphasize what the State would do for world Jewry—not the reverse . . . Israel's too ready scorn for Zionists and the World Zionist Organization illustrates the poorest means for cementing the solidarity of all Jewry." As if to leave no doubt that these comments were addressed to him, Ben-Gurion wrote a few months later (Number 3, August 1957) from his temporary retreat in Sde Boker: "It is doubtful whether there is any remedy for the old generation of Zionists in the Diaspora . . . This does not mean that there is no hope for a movement of personal implementation in the Diaspora

These notions have been uniformly rejected by the leaders of the state of Israel. In their view this "new Zionism" is indeed "new," but it is not "Zionism," and they explain it away in a neat and simple way: most Zionists were "messianists" until the state was declared; since the "messianism" of those in the free countries, especially in America, was merely a talking faith, it could not move its devotees to the proper works—i.e., emigration to Zion when the day of decision came; hence, they are presently searching for a reason for not doing what they ought to do, and they have therefore revived an Ahad Ha-Amism they have never believed and perhaps do not even believe today. Nonetheless, though such a conception of the course of Zionist intellectual history is useful in debate—David Ben-Gurion has often voiced it in the recent debates within Zionism—it is far too black-and-white to be correct. The contrary is much nearer to the truth: the "new Zionism" is not "new" at all; it is a restatement of what Zionism has meant in western Europe and America from its very beginnings.

In actual practice, even during the brief days of Herzl (and even, to some degree, in his own activities, especially toward the end of his life) the very slogans which derived from his theories acquired a paradoxical meaning; they were used in the Diaspora, especially in western Europe and America, not really as a call to break with the past and to rebel against the present but as the neatest way of adjusting to the immediate situation within which these western Jews found themselves. Zionism, as believed in the lands of freedom, has always been "defensive," and, most of all, when it seemed utterly committed to "messianism." We must, therefore, define the point of divergence, the fork in the road between the "neo-messianism" evolved by the builders of the Yishuv in Palestine out of Herzl's main themes and the variant uses to which these ideas were put by the unideological bulk of the Zionist movement.

As early as 1897 Ahad Ha-Am, as diagnostician, responded to the First Zionist Congress by foreseeing that the followers of Herzl would find other values in political Zionism which would be more to their taste than its version of the "end of days." Ahad Ha-Am overstated and oversimplified in too barbed a way as he foretold what would

---

. . . But these [younger elements] will neither be discovered nor activated by the 'Zionist' Organization, which has lost its meaning: the Return to Zion and the Ingathering of the Exiles. The center of gravity of Jewish people has now passed to the State of Israel, and it alone has the power to arouse the latent forces in the Diaspora as well."

happen, but he was basically correct in his analysis of the emotional satisfactions which the average Zionist (he spoke specifically of the west Europeans in the lands of freedom) would derive from his new involvement in the international scene: "[Zionism] provides an opportunity for communal work and political excitement; his emotions find an outlet in a field of activity which is not subservient to non-Jews; and he feels that, thanks to this ideal, he stands once more spiritually erect and has regained his personal dignity, without overmuch trouble and purely by his own efforts. . . . For it is not the attainment of the ideal that he needs; its pursuit alone is sufficient to cure him of his spiritual disease, which is that of an inferiority complex, and the loftier and more distant the ideal, the greater its power to exalt."[54]

The commentary on this estimate is writ large in the history of Zionism, both in Europe and in America. Men of the kind to whom Herzl first addressed himself, westernized intellectuals like the Franco-Swiss Edmond Fleg and the American Ludwig Lewisohn, come to Zionism not as potential emigrants but in search of inner dignity and secure personal roots in their people and its history.[55] This theme is especially prominent in American Zionism. It is to be found in the very first pamphlet ever published by the American Zionist Federation (1898). Its president, Richard J. H. Gottheil, was very emphatic in insisting that Zionism "does not mean that all Jews must return to Palestine." He therefore asked: What does Zionism offer the not ingathered? The answer was: "It wishes to give back to the Jew that nobleness of spirit, that confidence in himself, that belief in his own powers which only perfect freedom can give. . . . He will nowhere hide his own peculiarities . . . He will feel that he belongs somewhere and not everywhere."[56]

Seventeen years later Louis D. Brandeis expanded on this point before a gathering of Reform rabbis whom he was trying to convert to his views. Brandeis did not simply content himself with defending Zionism as consistent with American patriotism. He argued to the contrary that "loyalty to America demands rather that each American Jew become a Zionist. For only through the ennobling effect of its strivings can we develop the best that is in us and give to this country

[54]See text, Part 4.

[55]See text, Part 8.

[56]See text, Part 9.

the full benefit of our great inheritance." With obvious mindfulness of the sweatshops and the disturbed social conditions of the Jewish "East Sides" of that day, he went on to propose that the Zionist ideal was alone capable of protecting "America and ourselves from demoralization, which has to some extent already set in among American Jews." It alone was equal to the "task of inculcating self-respect, a task which can be accomplished only by restoring the ties of the Jew to the noble past of his race, and by making him realize the possibilities of a no less glorious future. The sole bulwark against demoralization is to develop in each new generation of Jews in America the sense of *noblesse oblige.*"[57]

The second key idea of "messianism," the call for a complete "ingathering," also changed its meaning very early. So, Gottheil, in the speech quoted above (I re-emphasize that it was published as the first official pamphlet of the newly organized American Zionist Federation), left no doubt that Zionism neither predicted nor required that American Jews should emigrate to Palestine.[58] By his calculations, however, fully three-fourths of world Jewry, i.e., those who were residing in eastern Europe, needed to move. "Whatever our own personal consideration may be, whether we like it or not, we dare not leave these unfortunates to their fate. Every fiber in our body cries 'shame' to the very suggestion that we adopt such a course as that. What then? Where are they to go in Europe? Certainly not to Austria, certainly not to Germany, to France, to Spain, or to Portugal." Gottheil surveyed the world, including his own country, to prove that room could be found nowhere for many more Jews. Hence this shattering problem could be solved in only one way, by building an ultimate haven in a Jewish homeland in Palestine.

Schechter in the next decade and Brandeis in the one thereafter followed Gottheil on this point as a matter of course. Writing later, they were naturally aware—and proudly so—of the "neo-messianic" idealists who were founding the earliest modern Zionist colonies in Palestine. The young Ben-Gurions and Ben Zvis were then, as I have

[57]See text, Part 9.

[58]The concluding paragraph of his exposition is: "And we hold that this does not mean that all Jews must return to Palestine." Indeed, he is perhaps the first to face the question of the proper political relations between American Jewry and the future state in Palestine: "I can only answer, exactly the same as is the relation of people of other nationalities all the world over to their parent home. . . . Is the Irish-American less of an American because he gathers money to help his struggling brethren in the Green Isle?" (*loc. cit.*)

said above, absolutely certain that they were the vanguard of all Jewry which was to follow; Schechter, and especially Brandeis, added another nuance to popular unideological Zionism by suggesting a counteridea. They assigned to these pioneers a creative task, by envisaging a homeland which this vanguard would lead, lovingly supported by the free and wealthy Jews, but consisting in its mass largely of refugees. In sum, Schechter and Brandeis cast the very "messianists" for a great "defensive" role—and they were thus enabled both to share with them in the immediate work of ingathering and state building and to stand apart from them in theory and, especially, to disregard their estimate of the future of the Jew in America.

Gottheil, Schechter, and Brandeis in effect announced that America was different. Both implicitly and explicitly they were willing to concede the correctness of the "neo-messianic" estimate of anti-Semitism, that gentile society would inevitably drive the Jew out, but they were certain that this analysis did not apply to their own country. This idea was concurrently being denied by Ber Borochov, one of the socialist cofounders of "neo-messianism," who lived in America before and during the First World War. He had applied his Marxist analysis to the same "East Sides" of which Brandeis was mindful and had seen only the reproduction of east European patterns of Jewish economic activity. Borochov had no doubt that the immigrant masses were doomed to suffer in those unimportant and insecure pursuits which the gentile majority contemned, like the clothing industry; he was sure that the future would bring an ever-sharpening national struggle between the gentile majority and the Jewish minority in America. That, and the additional tensions of inevitable and grievous class struggle within the Jewish community itself, would force mass re-emigration from America to Palestine.[59]

But these estimates did not remain completely unchallenged even in the very circles which had fashioned them. Their rigidity was called into question as early as 1929 by Chaim Arlosoroff, the brightest young star of Palestinian Socialist-Zionism, when he was confronted by American Jewry. He doubted that Jewish reality in the entire Diaspora really fitted into what were, by then, the conventional "messianic" formulas and he insisted, in specific, that American Jewish experience

[59]See text, Part 6. The discussion there is an excerpt from the platform he wrote for his Marxist wing of Labor-Zionism. It dates from before his migration to the United States, but it is the theory on which he based his later studies and observations.

needed to be seen with different eyes: ". . . One must judge the new Jewry in America as a different kind of historical phenomenon, a unicum, which has no precedent in the history of our people . . . for it lives and is developing under unique conditions which have never existed before and which cannot recur. Consequently, new forces and forms of life are arising, the likes of which have never existed and will never again exist, and which are, therefore, not to be compared with any others. These are forces and forms in which a new Jewish life is coming to bloom . . . The result of this transition period is the creation of a spiritual climate which, judged by our standards, is calculated to evoke an impression of primal chaos. Every American Jew of our time—if one describes him in the parlance of our own exaggerated and grotesque terms—is a free-orthodox-cosmopolitan-assimilationist-na-tionalist-Zionist thinker. The dividing lines, which the previous generations have so laboriously marked out, are erased in the mind of this Jew; the magic circle has been broken into and now already belongs to the past."[60]

For our immediate purpose it is not important to decide whether Arlosoroff's impressions of the American Jewish community were correct and clairvoyant (be it mentioned that they were largely ignored in the Palestinian circles to which they were addressed). However, he was certainly right on one point, that American Zionist thought was ideologically eclectic. So in 1944, under the impact of Hitler's murder of the Jews of Europe, Abba Hillel Silver, the most classical political Zionist among the Americans, went very far in applying the categories of Herzl to the immediate scene he was surveying. He argued, in orthodox fashion, that anti-Semitism would be a constant even in America: "The New World, for a time, made possible a pleasant sense of almost complete identification. That is no longer the case and in all probability will never be again. . . . This is realism, not defeatism. . . . Our lives as American Jews have now fallen into the well-known pattern of Israel's millennial experience in Diaspora."[61] On this premise he might have arrived at Borochov's conclusions, and it is very revealing that he did not. Even in this darkest year of contemporary Jewish history Silver continued to maintain that America is different. He saw its anti-Semitism as troubling but not disastrous. It would act to remind the American Jew of his oneness in destiny with his fellows

[60]Chaim Arlosoroff, *Leben und Werk*, Berlin 1934, p. 70.

[61]See text, Part 10.

the world over and, therefore, make it all the more evident to him that a homeland, as refuge, was necessary, not for himself but for those who had lost the battle with far fiercer Hitlerian variety of Jew-hatred.[62]

The evidence cited so far supports the thesis that there are strong reasons why western Zionism has always used the political language of Herzl and spoken of the "ingathering" while being clear, if only to itself, that it meant something far different. But what of the spiritual and cultural aspects of its Zionism? The masses of the movement were certainly aware that its Palestinian elite were passionately committed to creating an heroic new life by radically breaking with the older patterns. Here, too, the language that flowed from this demand was freely used by western Zionists, and yet it was not, and could not ever be, its real faith. To be sure, most western Jews looked to Palestine—and to Israel today—for the heroic and the new, but they never really believed those who told them that these glories would be the antithesis of the older Jewish life. This attitude is, of course, the underlying conviction on which Ahad Ha-Am had based the structure of his thought, but what we are describing here represents not his conscious followers, of whom there were few, but the many who shared his sense of situation.

Edmond Fleg is an instructive case in point. His account of his own conversion to Zionism by Herzl's call for the Jewish state speaks for many: "Was this the solution for which I was looking? It explained so many things. If the Jews really formed but a single nation, one began to understand why they were considered Jews even when they ceased to practice their religion . . . Then the Zionist idea moved me by its sublimity; I admired in these Jews, and would have wished to be able to admire in myself, this fidelity to the ancestral soil which still lived after two thousand years, and I trembled with emotion as I pictured the universal exodus which would bring them home, from their many exiles, to the unity that they had reconquered." But, as he goes on to relate, he went to Basel for the Third Zionist Congress (in 1899) not to be utterly convinced by this doctrine but to experience and be almost overwhelmed by the romantic image of that gathering as the symbol of a restored Jewish unity. "And, in the presence of all these strange faces, the inevitable happened; I felt myself a Jew, very much a Jew, but also very French, a Frenchman of Geneva, but French nonetheless." His Zionism, therefore became an admiration of the

[62]See text, Part 10.

Hebrew revival and a personal return to the history and moral imperatives of his people.[63]

This theme runs like a thread through American Zionism. It is already present in the significant earliest declaration, quoted above, by Gottheil, and it was voiced, among a host of others, even by a complete cultural outsider, by Brandeis: "But the effect of the renaissance of the Hebrew tongue is far greater than that of unifying the Jews. It is a potent factor in reviving the essentially Jewish *spirit*."[64]

The bulk of the growing Zionist body in the West, and especially in America, were not, however, true westerners; they were, as Weizmann remarked in another connection,[65] east Europeans, kneaded from the same dough as himself, who brought their Zionist emotions with them as they joined the stream of migration. Solomon Schechter, a Romanian Jew who had come, by way of a faculty post at Cambridge, to head the Jewish Theological Seminary in New York, understood these people best of all. His announcement in 1906 that he adhered to Zionism was an event of major import, in part because everyone knew that this national movement was strongly opposed by the very men from "uptown" (Jacob Schiff and Felix Warburg, among others) who had called him to the United States. The essay in which Schechter defined his views is more important still, however, because he produced the formulas by which the newcomers, who were even then the great majority of American Jews, could harmonize their two most cherished desires, to become part of America and still retain their deep Jewish sentiments.[66]

It is instructive that Schechter avoided and refused to accept any of the clashing ideological definitions of Zionism, even those of Ahad Ha-Am, whom he much admired (though Schechter did identify himself as primarily in sympathy with the religio-cultural aspect of the movement). He found it enough, in practice, that one principle could be defined on which all Zionists agreed: an independent national life in Palestine "is not only desirable, but absolutely necessary" for a part of the Jewish people. No matter how long that labor might take, he saw Zionism as already a great success in achieving two of his most cherished objectives: in balancing the necessary and desirable processes of Americanization with "reviving Jewish consciousness,"

[63]See text, Part 8.

[64]See text, Part 9.

[65]See text, Part 10.

[66]See text, Part 9.

and therefore acting as the great and indispensable contemporary bulwark against assimilation. He made no doctrinaire distinctions, even against those tendencies he disliked, as he hailed all signs of life in Zionism—whether it was practical effort, the revival of Hebrew, the renewed interest in Jewish history, or simply the reassertion of pride in one's identity—as a great gain, a necessary preparation for the ultimate days of the Messiah long awaited by religion. Schechter thus became a Zionist because he saw in the movement the tool for realizing "a true and healthy life, with a policy of its own, a religion wholly its own, invigorated by sacred memories and sacred environments, and proving a tower of strength and of unity not only for the remnant gathered within the borders of the Holy Land, but also for those who shall, by choice or necessity, prefer what now constitutes the Galut."[67]

It can be said, without too great exaggeration, that, even to the present, the cultural aspects of American Zionist thought have been, essentially, a further elucidation of this essay of Schechter's. Horace Kallen's[68] theories of secularist cultural pluralism and Judah Magnes's[69] more reformed religious outlook (deeply affected by his pacifist convictions, as well), both of which came shortly thereafter, are but variants of his basic stance. Mordecai Kaplan, the most important of American Zionist thinkers, must be read as a commentary on Schechter by a man who had been deeply affected, in religion, by the social gospel and by John Dewey's pragmatic philosophy. His *Judaism as a Civilization* which appeared in 1934, was widely read, and not only in America. Even as he deplored the anti-religious stand of the Palestinian socialist collectives (*the kibbutzim*), which he otherwise much admired, he found their example and creativity eminently usable in refreshing the spiritual life of Jewry. Here we are again in the realm of an increasingly familiar paradox, for he added the work of these enemies of the tradition to what he called Torah (the Law)[70]—i.e., he cast the very culture of the "neo-messianists" for a "defensive" role.

[67]See text, Part 9.

[68]See text, Part 9.

[69]See text, Part 7.

[70]The radical secularism and antipathy to the Jewish tradition of the Zionist settlers in Palestine was questioned even there by one of their own respected leaders, Berl Katzenelson, as early as the 1930's. Hitler's coming to power too had shaken all of world Jewry and created a pervasive mood of return to one's own folk and heritage. It helped precipitate doubts even among "neo-messianists" as to whether they had gone too far in casting aside the heritage of the tradition and

There is one new emphasis, the necessary capstone of an American "defensive" Zionism, to be found in Kaplan. In that book, and increasingly later on, up to the present, he has continued to deny, root and branch, the notion that a significant Jewish life is impossible outside of the homeland. Kaplan admits that "such a synthesis [between loyalty to the Jewish group and the democratic process] would undoubtedly constitute a new development"; he believes, nevertheless, that "given the will, the intelligence, and the devotion, it is feasible to relive and re-embody, within the frame of a democratic American civilization, the vital and thrilling experience of our people in Eretz Israel that, in the long run, we might achieve in our way as great and lasting a contribution to human values as they are achieving in theirs."[71]

All the evidence given above proves that not a single idea of the "new Zionism" is a new invention; these attitudes are all inherent in the "defensive" modes of thought of the Jew in the post-Emancipation Diaspora, which has made him want logically contradictory things —to be, at once (in Schechter's version) Americanized but not assimilated; politically, economically, and, to a great degree, culturally at home in his native land, but emotionally, religiously, and spiritually apart or, indeed, to some degree in exile—in a word, to be unique.[72]

We must now consider what these realities, which long ago forced

---

cutting loose emotionally from the embattled Jews of the Diaspora. Berl Katzenelson posed the problem in the very next year, as follows: "There are many who think of our revolution in a much too simple and primitive manner. Let us destroy the old world entirely, let us burn all the treasures that it accumulated throughout the ages, and let us start anew—like newborn babes! There is daring and force of protest in this approach. . . . But it is doubtful whether this conception, which proceeds in utter innocence to renounce the heritage of the ages and proposes to start building the world from the ground up, really is revolutionary and progressive . . . If a people possesses something old and profound, which can educate man and train him for his future tasks, is it truly revolutionary to despise it and become estranged from it? . . . The Jewish year is studded with days which, in depth of meaning, are unparalleled among other peoples. Is it advantageous—is it a goal—for the Jewish labor movement to waste the potential value stored within them?" (See text, Part 6.) At the time this was very much a minority opinion in the circles to which these remarks were addressed.

[71]See text, Part 9.

[72]These specific conclusions agree with the reasoning of Ben Halpern in his article "The Idea of a Spiritual Home," *Forum*, No. 2, April 1956, pp. 59–70. There are differences in emphasis and my general outlook (*vide* what follows) is not the same as his, but a statement of the issues between us does not belong here.

Diaspora Zionism into the arms of such pragmatic illogic, are doing today to the still passionate "neo-messianists" of Israel. The paradox is as yet largely unrecognized that they, too, are being driven into the arms of Ahad Ha-Am.

Until shortly after the creation of the state, it was possible for them to believe that everything would eventually happen "according to plan," i.e., that once all external hindrances would disappear, the "ingathering" would really begin. Herzl, and especially Nordau, had predicted this in a quite mechanical fashion: the real Jews would go home to the country and the rest, a small minority, consisting of the wealthy and highly assimilated, would quickly disappear. Klatzkin had presumed that this would not happen in haste, but that for quite a while there would be two Jewish nations, the Hebrew one in Palestine and a Yiddish-speaking one (he was thinking of pre-Hitler Europe) outside. In either view, the "ingathering" meant the severing of ties between the new nation and those Jews who were not its immediate citizens, so that the state itself would be freed of "Jewish" burdens, meaning that, at last, the main body of this people would no longer have to live out any unique dualities.

This is precisely what is not happening. In the short run, the state of Israel is still heavily dependent on political, moral, and financial support from world Jewry, and therefore unusually involved in its "irredenta"—but it is long-run considerations which are more significant. The very "neo-messianists" who are now still calling for the "ingathering" know, no matter what they may be saying, that this is (at its likeliest) "far in the mists of the future" (to use Ahad Ha-Am's counter-comment to the First Zionist Congress). What they fear most of all, and rightly so, is what Herzl predicted and almost hoped for: that the not-ingathered may go off by themselves to live or die as Jews by their own devices. Justified though such a consummation may be by "proof-texts" from the best doctrinal authorities, this threat correctly fills the responsible leaders of Israel with horror. It might be countenanced if it involved a minority of world Jewry, but how can one write of its vast majority? Nor does it help again to warn the Americans that anti-Semitism will eventually toll their doom in turn. Perhaps, as the Zionists of America have always believed, this estimate of Jew-hatred really does not fit their case, for it was constructed on the basis of east European experience; perhaps America, which alone of modern states has no prehistory of legal exclusion of the Jew, is really different. But let us assume that it may not be so; still, as David Ben-Gurion has clearly understood, in the here and now, one cannot move those who regard themselves as secure and free by frightening them with interpretations of their own situation which they either challenge or ignore.

Other motifs are certainly in play among the Israelis, headed by the deep and almost instinctive Jewish emotion which cannot imagine this people as just another group of the usual kind. The hope of being "like all the nations" seemed glorious when even that was far off; there is evidence in some of the youngest writers of modern Israel that statehood and national patriotism are already not enough for them, in great measure because of their re-encounter with the classic values of the religious tradition. It cannot be doubted, however, that the immediate cause for these renewed assertions that Israel must mean something grand and universal is the problem of both maintaining the life of the Jewish Diaspora and of centralizing its energies around Israel. Life has, therefore, led back to Ahad Ha-Am, and it is not too much to say that the true heir of that master's secular metaphysics and of his doctrine of the elite is David Ben-Gurion.

There is one major idea out of the orthodox arsenal of the east European Zionism of his youth that still remains in Ben-Gurion's present thought. He continues to dislike and rebel against that whole period in Jewish history between the beginning of the exile and the labors which created modern Israel: "The distant past is closer to us than the recent past of the last two thousand years, and not only of the sixty years in which the term 'Zionism' has been in existence." Even this idea has, however, subtly changed its meaning in the context in which he is using it at present. Its intent is twofold: In the first place, it establishes a claim for the life of modern Israel as deriving directly from and, hence, reincarnating the great days of the Bible: "We are sons of the Homeland, disciples of the Bible, and bearers of the vision of the great redemption of the Jewish people and of humanity—and the expression of that idea in the original, in the ancient original which has been renewed and rejuvenated in our time, is to be found in the prophets of Israel."

Secondly, it enables him to assert ever more forcefully the moral and spiritual superiority of Israeli Jewry. Ben-Gurion faces the danger that Israel "may be cut off from Diaspora Jewry" and he suggests a defense, "the intensification of the Jewish consciousness, the realization of our common destiny." These terms may mean many things, so he hastens to provide his own commentary. The propulsion to Zion, even in the era of modern Zionism, has not been anti-Semitism or even the modernist ideologies of Pinsker and Herzl, which flowed from it; it has been in the ancient vision of redemption that was kept alive in the Bible and prayer book, "in the attachment to the heritage of the past (which means first and foremost the Bible)." These very values, Ben-Gurion declares, are exemplified today by the youth of Israel; as proof, he adduces their interest in archaeology, which betokens their desire to rediscover the biblical past, and the emotions of living out a contemporary equivalent of the biblical sages, which were evoked in them by the heroic campaign in the desert of Sinai. Conversely, he adds that these virtues are least in evidence among those who are not being moved personally to share this life.

Having asserted all this, Ben-Gurion is left with an even sharper version of the problem that plagued Ahad Ha-Am—and that was inherent in "neo-messianism" from its very beginning: How can he, the much more forthright agnostic, claim to be the true heir of the messianic ideal of religion and of the chosenness of the Jew as the instrument of Redemption? His answers are exactly those of Ahad Ha-Am, i.e., a secular metaphysics: "My concept of the Messianic ideal and vision is not a metaphysical one, but a social-cultural-moral one . . . I believe in our moral and intellectual superiority, in our capacity to serve as a model for the redemption of the human race. This belief of mine is based on my knowledge of the Jewish people, and not, on some mystic faith; 'the glory of the Divine Presence' is within us, in our hearts, and not outside us."[73]

This Ahad Ha-Amism has led Ben-Gurion into precisely the same controversies that were aroused by the theories of his predecessor. The orthodox religionists are no more ready to concede to him spiritual leadership as a modern Isaiah than they were to respect Ahad Ha-Am as a reincarnation of Johanan ben Zakkai. His own long-time associates in Socialist-Zionism murmur against this transcendence of their accustomed theories, and it is obvious that were these thoughts being presented by a lesser man, they would be attacked much more vehemently.[74] Indeed, even the newest aspect of the present debate, the battle for moral authority within Jewry between Israel and the Zionists of the Diaspora, was foreshadowed in Ahad Ha-Am; it is the living commentary on the question he never faced, of how the "spiritual center" would influence and dominate its periphery.

[73]All the quotations of Ben-Gurion in these paragraphs are from *Forum*, No. 3, August 1957, pp. 20–38 (a correspondence with Nathan Rotenstreich).

[74]Ben-Gurion's earlier position, when he spoke in the expected "neo-messianic" vein, needs to be read in this connection. See his essay of 1944 in Part 10.

And so, we are again the realm of paradox. On the one hand, the state of Israel continues to insist on its political sovereignty and inner cultural freedom, both conceived on the model of nineteenth-century liberal ideals; on the other, it proposes this sovereignty as the clinching argument for its unparalleled right to command the Jewish Diaspora and offers this very secular life, at its highest, as the modern religion to unite and invigorate a scattered world community. Intellectually, Ben-Gurion's formulations come no nearer than Ahad Ha-Am's to solving the crucial riddle—how to deny God and affirm chosenness, how to be a nineteenth-century liberal in practice and yet find support for the unique life and self-image of the Jew.

IX

But perhaps the trouble is with the categories that have been applied in this discussion. The pure theory of "messianic" Zionism—"let us be like all the nations"—was intellectually consistent and made logical sense. Despite its great successes (e.g., the state of Israel), in the ultimate sense it has clearly not succeeded. We must ask the inevitable question: Why? No partial explanations will help us, for here we must go back to first principles, to the almost immemorial encounter between the Jew and the world around him.[75]

Philo in the first century and Maimonides in the twelfth each had no doubt what gentile modernity was and, more important still, would continue to be; for the former it was neo-Platonic thought and for the latter it was Aristotelian philosophy, as he knew it. Except as paradigm, neither could help a Jewish thinker today to define his identity and tradition vis-à-vis, let us say, Kierkegaard or Sartre—or in confrontation with Buddhism—for the assumption of a different universe of discourse makes the unchanged use of what has gone before appear curiously old-fashioned.

In its turn, Zionism (Herzl's brand, explicitly, and Ahad Ha-Am's version, implicitly) assumed that the power of the modern West would dominate the world. Politically, this meant that all future political entities would enter modernity under its tutelage, as further species of its only genus, the sovereign nation-state; spiritually and culturally, it was assumed that any society would regard itself as backward until it re-

[75]The reader will note that we are now applying the notions advanced at the end of the second section of this essay to our immediate concern, the analysis of Zionism.

thought its values as variants of nineteenth-century liberal human- ism. The lonely Moses Hess, in the 1860's, was the only major Zionist figure who had a right to believe this uncritically. By the turn of the century, evidence had begun to mount that the West would not in- evitably dominate the world. Within its own polity, there was increas- ing revulsion to its dominant culture, and its usual concomitant (along with popular fears of the "yellow peril"), a rise in respect for and interest in the culture of the East. The whole of the twentieth century has been marked by a retreat by the West from any messianic desires to refashion the world in its own image to the more modest search for accommodations with the unlike, both in politics and in affairs of the spirit. Indeed, the very upheavals which propelled the practical state- building cause of Zionism forward in our time were, ironically, way stations on the road of the decline of the West into which the state was to fit as a normal part. Therefore, the polity into which the state of Israel was born was no longer (if it, indeed, ever was or could have been) the one of its theories: the state came to be not as part of the ongoing process of creating a liberal world order but as the result of complex forces which made this unusual act possible; it was, in reality, a singular accommodation to peculiar circumstances at a juncture of the moment. To mention just two facts, the resolution of the United Nations in 1947, which is the legal basis of Israel, could not have been passed without the agreement (never since repeated, in this area of concern) of the ideological enemy and cultural halfway house be- tween West and East, Soviet Russia; the very geographic situation of Israel locates it on the edge of the western sphere of influence, in the midst of a region which channelizes much of its growing revolt against western power and culture into hatred of its new neighbor. There is, to conclude this aspect of the argument, real doubt whether the simple notions of national sovereignty as propounded by the classical political theorists will outlast our generation. Quite apart from the obvious dominance, in varying degrees, of the two super-powers of our era over their respective blocs, there is an increasing tendency for all kinds of unprecedented *ad hoc* arrangements (e.g., the various plans for the future of Cyprus) which are inconceivable in the usual modes of west- ern political thought.

Spiritually and culturally, too (though the problem is somewhat harder to define), Zionism, the Ahad Ha-Amist variety included, as- sumed something about the future in general. It arose in the heyday of the warfare of science and religion, when modernity meant the abandonment of the traditional faiths. The emphasis of the late nineteenth century was on community. Values were conceived as the highest goods of the group and religion was redefined as the "social gospel." The mainstream of Zionist cultural thought belongs to this universe of discourse, and it was, therefore, consonant with the spirit of the age for it to conceive of its labors as a practicing modern religion. The very intellectual impasse into which Ahad Ha-Am and Ben-Gurion have each in turn fallen, comes from the impossibility to define the unique (both have insisted that Jewish identity is, and ought to be, *sui generis*) in these terms—but it is revealing that their attempted answers have not stepped out of that framework. They have both invoked history, the evidence of the past life of the group, and the future, the standards the community sets before itself—both of which are the basic categories of the ethic of liberal nationalism and its religious counterpart, the "social gospel."

We must note here, as Hess correctly asserted, that the identification of religion and culture is congruent with the Jewish tradition, with its classical assumption that the universal God is particularly present in its own community and code of life. Within Christianity, such an identity with any culture is much less thinkable;[76] the "social gospel" involved, to be sure, more implicitly than explicitly, a profound heresy —that God had really become manifest on earth primarily in one culture, the western. Now that the prestige of that society is lessening, Christianity has been in full retreat from any such idea. Its major energies are now being devoted to two of its more traditional themes: the purely personal imperative of faith (e.g., existentialist theology) and the attempt to lessen its ties to its traditional habitat, the West, in order to free itself, as a pure religion, for a missionary future in the rising eastern societies. There are, be it added, non-Christian counterparts of these religious trends, like the syncretism, both religious and cultural, of Arnold Toynbee, and the vogue of completely secular philosophies of personal will and choice.

These tendencies cannot yet be said to constitute a dominant trend, but they are certainly indications that a different age is coming into being. Post-liberal thought is now sufficiently crystallized to have given birth to what has, alas, been one of the characteristic vices of western outlooks and, one might almost dare say, an early sign that a new outlook has really arisen—to a new version of intellectual anti-Semitism, which, to a great degree, makes Zionism its immediate target. A cen-

[76]The reader is referred to the account of this question in Helmut Richard Niebuhr's *Christ and Culture*, New York, 1951.

tury ago the chief cry of "modern" anti-Semitism was the charge that the Jew belonged to no nation, neither to the ones that had emancipated him nor to his own. Christian neo-orthodoxy is returning to a reformulated concern with converting the Jew, who is now criticized for being too this-worldly and nationalist—i.e., too much like the recent western past which much of advanced Christian theology would like to forget. Toynbee uses contemporary Israel as the vile example of that hyper-nationalist obduracy which stands in the way of a world culture. And against such attacks it does not help to reassert that, both as state and faith, Zionism is a high example of the best of the nineteenth century for, tragically, this leaves the movement as one of the last serious defenders in the West of the liberal tradition. Therefore the very devotion with which the Jew continues to affirm the universal values of liberalism has become the brand-mark of his own particularism, the sign of the uniqueness of his own position both as an individual in the western Diaspora and even as a nation among the nations. Others can choose antithetical values, but not the Jew.

What I have been describing here is, of course, what Jean-Paul Sartre has called "the situation of the Jew,"[77] but Sartre's analysis is only half of the truth. The Jew is not almost solely, as Sartre would have it, a creation of anti-Semitism; it is at least as significant (I believe it is basic) that the Jew creates himself, by his choice of his own identity.

There are no "pure experiments," as if in laboratory, in history, but the two great facts of contemporary Jewish experience—Zionism and the rise of the American Jewish community—are near proofs of the assertion that the Jew creates himself. The Emancipation, which was never achieved in Europe, has come closest to realization in the New World and in the ancestral home of the Jew. In both places the Jew began de novo, though, to be sure, more than a little of his "situation" tended to pursue him, but there were numerous possibilities for him to slough off the burden of his inner experience and become a new man. Nonetheless, these opportunities were not utilized. In America, under the most favorable conditions that have ever arisen for the assimilation of the Jew into a melting pot of peoples and traditions, he has changed radically—and yet, the majority of this Jewish community has obviously chosen to be itself, as the heir of its past; and the Jew in Israel, where the drive to create a new identity for himself took the most doctrinaire forms, is certainly far

[77]See his brilliant short book, written after the liberation of France from the Nazis, Anti-Semite and Jew, New York, 1948.

different from his immediate ancestors in the ghetto—but there too he is ever more the conscious scion of his millennial culture. Indeed, whenever the Jew affirms his own identity and the right to a life created by his own will, it does not matter what values he may hold, in theory. This affirmation—and not his rationalizations of it—are the primary fact; once it is made, the Jew inevitably rediscovers, in his bones, a metaphysic of his "chosenness," even though, like Ahad Ha-Am and Ben-Gurion, he cannot explain it by his reason, or, even though, like Brenner and Borochov, he would deny it on principle.

This is the essential insight of the greatest religious mystic of modern Zionist and Jewish thought, Rabbi Abraham Isaac Kook: "It is a grave error to be insensitive to the distinctive unity of the Jewish spirit . . . This error is the source of the attempt to sever the national from the religious element of Judaism. Such a division would falsify both our nationalism and our religion . . . No matter what they [i.e., the secular nationalists] may think, the particular element of the Jewish spirit that they may make their own, being rooted in the total life of our people, must inevitably contain every aspect of its ethos. . . . Once this truth is established, our opponents will ultimately have to realize that they were wasting their efforts. The values they attempted to banish were nonetheless present, if only in an attenuated and distorted form, in their theories . . ."[78]

Kook is echoed in this view by the unorthodox religious philosopher, Martin Buber: "There is no re-establishing of Israel, there is no security for it save one: It must assume the burden of its own uniqueness; it must assume the yoke of the kingdom of God. Since this can be accomplished only in the rounded life of a community, we must reassemble, we must again root in the soil, we must govern ourselves. But these are mere prerequisites! Only when the community recognizes and realizes them as such in its own life will they serve as the cornerstones of its salvation."[79] And a comparable conviction suffuses the outlook of the agnostic mystic of nature and labor, A. D. Gordon: "What, then, is that elusive, unique, and persistent force that will not die and will not let us die . . . ? There is a primal force within every one of us, which is fighting for its own life, which seeks its own realization . . . The living moment seems to call on us: You must be the pathfinders . . . Here [i.e., in Palestine] something is beginning to flower which has greater human significance and far wider

[78]See text, Part 7.

[79]Ibid.

ramifications than our history-makers envisage, but it is growing in every dimension deep within, like a tree growing out of its own seed, and what is happening is therefore not immediately obvious."[80]

It is not the task of the historian to argue for, or against, the truth of these assertions. His function is more modest, to describe the existence of such a state of mind and to place it in that framework which seems to him to define the truth about it as a phenomenon. Pat explanations, though they are partial truths, will not help us; Kook cannot merely be classified, and therefore forgotten, as an anachronistic medieval mystic; Gordon cannot be understood as simply a Tolstoyan Jew; and Buber is something more than a turn-of-the-century central European intellectual who was part of a school of thought which romanticized the "spirit of the Orient" as a counterfaith to the aridities and immoralities of a power-mad Europe. These men arose out of Zionism itself, by the necessary logic that is inherent in any revolution. Self-definition in terms of uniqueness and chosenness, of living in tension between being part of the here and now and waiting for the Messiah yet to come, of being at once analogous to other identities and yet utterly different—these notions are more than the *ancien régime* of the Jew. They are the lasting impulse of his life. From the beginning, even during its most revolutionary period, Zionism felt the force of these ideas licking at the edges of its thought. Long before the movement achieved its great contemporary political success in the creation of the state of Israel, the question of the future quality and content of Jewish existence had already come to a conscious crystallization within Zionism in terms of these age-old ultimates.

Predictions about the future are obviously dangerous. Yet I cannot doubt that as it confronts the far more complicated world of the next century Jewish thought will evolve both "messianic" and "defensive" theories. It is even more certain that Israel and the Diaspora will continue to wrestle with the demon, the "situation," and the angel, the sense of "chosenness," of the Jew.

[80]See text, Part 6.

Part 1

Precursors

RABBI YEHUDAH ALKALAI 1798-1878

YEHUDAH ALKALAI was born in 1798 in Sarajevo to Rabbi Shlomo Alkalai, the spiritual leader of the local Jewish community. We know very little about his early years, but it is established that he spent his boyhood in Jerusalem. There Alkalai came under the influence of the cabbalists, who were then a significant element in the spiritual life of its Jewish community. In 1825 he was called to serve as rabbi in Semlin, the capital of Serbia. Not far away the Greeks had recently won their national war of independence, and the other nationalities of the Balkans, including the Serbs among whom he lived, were each beginning their efforts to rise against their Turkish overlord. Hence ideas of national freedom and restoration came easily to Alkalai's mind from the atmosphere of his time and place.

The notion of commencing a serious effort to effect a Jewish Redemption appears in his writing as early as 1834, in a booklet entitled *Shema Yisrael* (*Hear, O Israel*). He proposed the creation of Jewish colonies in the Holy Land, by man's own effort, as the necessary preamble to the Redemption. This idea was, of course, at variance with the usual pious notion that the Messiah would come by miraculous acts of divine grace. Alkalai argued, both here and later, that self-redemption was justified by "proof texts" from the tradition. As cabbalist, he invoked an ancient Jewish myth, which had been much embroidered by the mystics, that the days of the Messiah were to be ushered in by a forerunner of the true miraculous Redeemer. This first Messiah, the son of Joseph, would lead the Jews in the wars of Gog and Magog; under him, they would conquer the Holy Land by the might of their sword.

The real turning point in Alkalai's life was the year 1840. The Jews of Damascus were confronted in that year by the Blood Accusation, the charge that had often been repeated throughout the Middle Ages that they annually slaughtered a gentile and used his blood in the preparation of their unleavened bread for Passover. This affair quickly became a *cause célèbre* throughout the Jewish and, indeed, the European world. It convinced Alkalai (as it half-convinced his younger contemporary, Moses Hess) that for security and freedom the Jewish people must look to a life of its own, within its ancestral home. After 1840 a succession of books and pamphlets poured from Alkalai's pen in explanation of his program of self-redemption. Much of his pleading was addressed to the Jewish notables of the Western world, men like the English financier Moses Montefiore and the French politician Adolph Crémieux, for he knew that his schemes could not succeed without the support of their money and political influence. Alkalai imagined that it would be possible to buy the Holy Land from the Turks, as in biblical times Abraham had bought the field of Machpelah from Ephron, the Hittite. The schemes which Alkalai conceived for carrying out this great work included the convocation of a "Great Assembly," the creation of a national fund for the purchase of land and another fund to receive tithes, and the floating of a national loan. Such ideas were to reappear later in Herzl and actually to be realized through the Zionist movement.

Alkalai was not merely a writer and propagandist; he journeyed frequently to the capitals of Europe to attempt to inspire practical efforts for the redemption of the Holy Land. He succeeded in organizing a few small circles, including one even in London, to support his ideas, but their careers were brief. However, Simon Loeb Herzl, Theodor Herzl's grandfather, was a disciple and admirer—one of the very few—of Alkalai. One of Alkalai's granddaughters was among the delegates to the First Zionist Congress. In a memoir that appeared in 1922, in honor of the twenty-fifth anniversary of that event, she wrote: "I thought about my grandfather, Rabbi Yehudah Hai Alkalai, who spent his life preaching the return to the Land of Israel and I remembered my grandmother—his wife—who, in joyous dedication, had sold her jewels to enable my grandfather to publish his books in which he broadcast his idea of the return to the Land of Israel."

Alkalai ended his days in the city of his visions, in Jerusalem, in 1878. Regarded among the pietists and the modernists alike as a strange being, he was half forgotten. Recent scholarship has rediscovered his writings, and in 1945 a literary epitaph in the form of a major novel in Hebrew, Judah Burla's *Kissufim* (*Longings*), helped do delayed justice to an intriguing personality.

The excerpts below are largely from one of his early works, and his first in Hebrew, *Minhat Yehudah* (*The Offering of Yehudah*), which was published in 1845.

THE THIRD REDEMPTION (1843)

IT IS WRITTEN in the Bible: "Return, O Lord, unto the tens and thousands of the families of Israel."[1] On this verse the rabbis commented in the Talmud[2] as follows: it proves that the Divine Presence can be felt only if there are at least two thousands and two tens of thousands of Israelites together. Yet we pray every day: "Let our eyes behold Thy return in mercy unto Zion."[3] Upon whom should the Divine Presence rest? On sticks and stones? Therefore, as the first step in the redemption of our souls, we must cause at least twenty-two thousand to return to the Holy Land. This is the necessary preparation for a descent of the Divine Presence among us; afterward, He will grant us and all Israel further signs of His favor.

"And Jacob came in peace to the city of Shechem . . . and he bought the parcel of ground where he had spread his tent."[4] We must ask: Why did Jacob buy this land, since, being on his way to his father, Isaac, he had no intention of living there? Obviously, he performed this act to teach his descendants that the soil of the Holy Land must be purchased from its non-Jewish owners.

We, as a people, are properly called Israel only in the land of Israel.

In the first conquest, under Joshua, the Almighty brought the children of Israel into a land that was prepared: its houses were then full of useful things, its wells were giving water, and its vineyards and olive groves were laden with fruit. This new Redemption will—alas, because of our sins—be different: our land is waste and desolate, and we shall have to build houses, dig wells, and plant vines and olive trees. We are, therefore, commanded not to attempt to go at once and all together to the Holy Land. In the first place, it is necessary for many Jews to remain for a time in the lands of dispersion, so that they can help the first settlers in Palestine, who will undoubtedly come from among the poor. Secondly, the Lord desires that we be redeemed in dignity; we cannot, therefore, migrate in a mass, for we should then have to live like Bedouins, scattered in tents all over the fields of the Holy Land. Redemption must come slowly. The land must, by degrees, be built up and prepared.

There are two kinds of return: individual and collective. Individual return means that each man should turn away from his evil personal ways and repent; the way of such repentance has been prescribed in the devotional books of our religious tradition. This kind of repentance is called individual, because it is relative to the particular needs of each man. Collective return means that all Israel should return to the land which is the inheritance of our fathers, to receive the Divine command and to accept the yoke of Heaven. This collective return was foretold by all the prophets; even though we are unworthy, Heaven will help us, for the sake of our holy ancestors.

Undoubtedly our greatest wish is to gather our exiles from the four corners of the earth to become one bond. We are, alas, so scattered and divided today, because each Jewish community speaks a different language and has different customs. These divisions are an obstacle to the Redemption.

I wish to attest to the pain I have always felt at the error of our ancestors, that they allowed our Holy Tongue to be so forgotten. Because of this our people was divided into seventy peoples; our one language was replaced by the seventy languages of the lands of exile.

If the Almighty should indeed show us His miraculous favor and gather us into our land, we would not be able to speak to each other and such a divided community could not succeed. Let no one "solve" this problem by saying that, at the time of Redemption, God will send an angel to teach us all the seventy languages of mankind, for such a notion is false. This sort of thing is not accomplished by a miracle, and it is almost impossible to imagine a true revival of our Hebrew tongue by natural means. But we must have faith that it will come, for Joel prophesied: "I will pour out My spirit upon all flesh, and your sons and your daughters shall prophesy."[5] If the prophet foretold that the sons and daughters of the era of the Redemption will prophesy in a common language which they would know and be able to use, we must not despair. We must redouble our efforts to maintain Hebrew and to strengthen its position. It must be the basis of our educational work.

The Redemption will begin with efforts by the Jews themselves; they must organize and unite, choose leaders, and leave the lands of exile. Since no community can exist without a governing body, the very first new ordinance must be the appointment of the elders of each district, men of piety and wisdom, to oversee all the affairs of the community. I humbly suggest that this chosen assembly—the assembly of the elders—is what is meant by the promise to us of the Messiah, the son of Joseph.

These elders should be chosen by our greatest magnates, upon whose influence we all depend. The organization of an international Jewish body is in itself the first step to the Redemption, for out of this organization there will come a fully authorized assembly of elders, and from the elders, the Messiah, son of Joseph, will appear. It is fundamental to the success both of an international Jewish organization and of an assemblage of elders that the elders be men of high caliber, who will command respect and obedience, so that the people of the Lord cease being like sheep without a shepherd. Redemption depends on this.

We have certain bad habits among us and there are forces which are weakening our religion. Our faith will not regain its strength until these elders are appointed. Even before we re-enter the Holy Land, as, with God's help, we assuredly will, we must first name elders to arrange for the observance of those commandments which apply, in particular, in the Holy Land, like the law of letting the soil be fallow on the seventh year, for the blessings to come to us from the land depend on the faithfulness with which we will adhere to these laws.

It is not impossible for us to carry out the commandment to return to the Holy Land. The Sultan will not object, for His Majesty knows that the Jews are his loyal subjects. Difference of religion should not be an obstacle, for each nation will worship its own god and we will forever obey the Lord, our God.

I ask of our brethren that they organize a company, on the mode of the fire insurance companies and of the railroad companies. Let this company appeal to the Sultan to give us back the land of our ancestors in return for an annual rent. Once the name of Israel is again applied to our land, all Jews will be inspired to help this company with all the means at their disposal. Though this venture will begin modestly, its future will be very great.

RABBI ZVI HIRSCH KALISCHER

1795-1874

KALISCHER, LIKE ALKALAI, was born in a buffer area—not in the Balkans but in Posen. This province was the western part of Poland, which Prussia had acquired in the second partition of that country in 1793. In Jewish life this region was the border between the older Jewish ghetto culture of the traditional pieties and learning, which Kalischer represented in his person with great distinction, and the newer milieu of western European Jewry, which was rapidly entering modern secular life. Nationalism was the major force of European history during the whole of Kalischer's adult life, but he was particularly aware of it because of his geographic position. In 1830–1831 and again in 1863 unsuccessful revolts occurred across the border in the Russian part of Poland in attempts to re-establish the independence of the Poles. Jewish population in this region was numerically significant, and in some places, including Warsaw during the two Polish revolutions, it was of political, and even military, importance whether the Jews would regard themselves as Poles, Russians, or as a separate nationality.

Kalischer's early career coincided with the rise of the Reform movement in Judaism, which was calling for the abandonment of many of the inherited beliefs and rituals. He participated in these controversies as a convinced defender of the inherited tradition and especially of the commandments prescribing the faith in the Messiah and emphasizing the special relationship of the Jew to the Holy Land. Though most of his literary activity was in the genre of talmudic legalism, of which he was an acknowledged master, he published a philosophical work and even produced one article in defense of Maimonides (it appeared in German translation in 1846).

His first expression of Zionism is to be found in a letter that he wrote in 1836 to the head of the Berlin branch of the Rothschild family. There he explained that "the beginning of the Redemption will come through natural causes by human effort and by the will of the governments to gather the scattered of Israel into the Holy Land." These notions, however, did not engage him seriously until 1860, when an otherwise unknown doctor, Hayyim Lurie, organized a society in Frankfort on the Oder to foster Jewish settlement in the Holy Land. Kalischer joined this group, and though the organization was short-lived and had no practical achievements to its credit, it provided him with the impulse to write his important Zionist work, *Derishat Zion (Seeking Zion)*, which appeared in 1862. This volume, the major ideas of which are represented in the excerpts below, was relatively well received by some of the reviewers in the renascent Hebrew literature of eastern Europe and it was quoted in Hess's *Rome and Jerusalem*, which appeared that same year.

Kalischer's professional career was undramatic. After completing his education in the conventional modes of the ghetto, he settled in Thorn, where he served as the rabbi of the community for forty years. Financially independent in his own right, he was able to engage after 1860 in innumerable journeys, meetings, and myriad literary and practical activities in behalf of the ideal to which he was henceforth devoted. Some tangible results flowed from his efforts, for he was instrumental in getting a group to buy land for colonization on the outskirts of Jaffa in 1866. His prodding finally moved the Alliance Israelite Universelle, the organization that had been created in France in 1860 for the international defense of Jewish rights, to found an agricultural school in Jaffa, Palestine, in 1870.

Even more than Alkalai, Kalischer was aware of the growing misery of the Jews of eastern Europe and he preached his Zionism as a solution to their problem. Nonetheless the pietists of these communities, who respected Kalischer as a master of the Talmud, would not follow him in these radical notions of self-redemption. There were even denunciations of his views in Jerusalem, issued by the beneficiaries of the traditional collections of alms for the pious poor of the Holy Land. In their eyes the creation of agricultural settlements, in which Jews would labor with their own hands, would lead people away from the study of the Torah and open the door to dangerous heresies.

Though far better remembered than Alkalai, Kalischer too died with his vision apparently stillborn.

SEEKING ZION (1862)

THE REDEMPTION OF ISRAEL, for which we long, is not to be imagined as a sudden miracle. The Almighty, blessed be His Name, will not suddenly descend from on high and command His people to go forth. He will not send the Messiah from heaven in a twinkling of an eye, to sound the great trumpet for the scattered of Israel and gather them into Jerusalem. He will not surround the Holy City with a wall of fire or cause the Holy Temple to descend from the heavens. The bliss and the miracles that were promised by His servants, the prophets, will certainly come to pass—everything will be fulfilled—but we will not run in terror and flight, for the Redemption of Israel will come by slow degrees and the ray of deliverance will shine forth gradually.

My dear reader! Cast aside the conventional view that the Messiah will suddenly sound a blast on the great trumpet and cause all the inhabitants of the earth to tremble. On the contrary, the Redemption will begin by awakening support among the philanthropists and by gaining the consent of the nations to the gathering of some of the scattered of Israel into the Holy Land.

The prophet Isaiah (27:6 and 12–13) expressed this thought as follows: "In the days to come shall Jacob take root, Israel shall blossom and bud; and the face of the world shall be filled with fruitage. And it shall come to pass in that day, that the Lord will beat off his fruit from the flood of the River unto the Brook of Egypt, and ye shall be gathered one by one, O ye children of Israel. And it shall come to pass in that day, that a great horn shall be blown; and they that were lost in the land of Assyria, and they that were dispersed in the land of Egypt; and they shall worship the Lord in the holy mountain at Jerusalem." He thus revealed that all of Israel would not return from exile at one time, but would be gathered by degrees, as the grain is slowly gathered from the beaten corn. The meaning of, "In the days to come Jacob shall take root," in the first verse above, is that the Almighty would make those who came first—at the beginning of the Redemption—the root planted in the earth to produce many sprigs. Afterward Israel will blossom forth in the Holy Land, for the root will yield buds which will increase and multiply until they cover the face of the earth with fruit. This conception of the Redemption is also implied in the statement (Isaiah 11:11): "And it shall come to pass in that day, that the Lord will set His hand again the second time to recover the remnant of His people, that shall remain from Assyria and from Egypt . . ." It is evident that both a first and a second ingathering are intended: the function of the first will be to pioneer the land, after which Israel will blossom forth to a most exalted degree.

Can we logically explain why the Redemption will begin in a natural manner and why the Lord, in His love for His people, will not immediately send the Messiah in an obvious miracle? Yes, we can. We know that all our worship of God is in the form of trials by which He tests us. When God created man and placed him in the Garden of Eden, He also planted the Tree of Knowledge and then commanded man not to eat of it. Why did he put the Tree in the Garden, if not as a trial? Why did He allow the Snake to enter the Garden, to tempt man, if not to test whether man would observe God's command? When Israel went forth from Egypt, God again tested man's faith with hunger and thirst along the way. The laws given us in the Torah[1] about unclean animals which are forbidden us as food are also a continuous trial—else why did the Almighty make them so tempting and succulent? Throughout the days of our dispersion we have suffered martyrdom for the sanctity of God's Name; we have been dragged from land to land and have borne the yoke of exile through the ages, all for the sake of His holy Torah and as a further stage of the testing of our faith.

If the Almighty would suddenly appear, one day in the future, through undeniable miracles, this would be no trial. What straining of our faith would there be in the face of the miracles and wonders attending a clear heavenly command to go up and inherit the land and enjoy its good fruit? Under such circumstances what fool would not go there, not because of his love of God, but for his own selfish sake? Only a natural beginning of the Redemption is a true test of those who initiate it. To concentrate all one's energy on this holy work and to renounce home and fortune for the sake of living in Zion before "the voice of gladness" and "the voice of joy" are heard—there is no greater merit or trial than this.

I have found support for this view in *The Paths of Faith*:[2] "When many Jews, pious and learned in the Torah, will volunteer to go to the

Land of Israel and settle in Jerusalem, motivated by a desire to serve, by purity of spirit, and by love of holiness; when they will come, by ones and twos, from all four corners of the world; and when many will settle there and their prayers will increase at the holy mountain in Jerusalem—the Creator will then heed them and hasten the Day of Redemption." For all this to come about there must first be Jewish settlement in the Land; without such settlement, how can the ingathering begin?

THE HOLINESS OF LABOR ON THE LAND

THERE ARE MANY who will refuse to support the poor of the Holy Land by saying: "Why should we support people who choose idleness, who are lazy and not interested in working, and who prefer to depend upon the Jews of the Diaspora[3] to support them?" To be sure, this is an argument put forth by Satan, for the people of Palestine are students of the Torah, unaccustomed from the time of their youth to physical labor. Most of them came from distant shores, risking their very lives for the privilege of living in the Holy Land. In this country, which is strange to them, how could they go about finding a business or an occupation, when they had never in their lives done anything of this kind? Their eyes can only turn to their philanthropic brethren, of whom they ask only enough to keep body and soul together, so that they can dwell in that Land which is God's portion on earth.

Yet, in order to silence this argument once and for all, I would suggest that an organization be established to encourage settlement in the Holy Land, for the purpose of purchasing and cultivating farms and vineyards. Such a program would appear as a ray of deliverance to those now living in the Land in poverty and famine. The pittance that is gathered from the entire Jewish world for their support is not enough to satisfy their hunger; indeed, in Jerusalem, the city which should be a source of blessing and well-being, many pious and saintly people are fainting of hunger in the streets.

The situation would be different if we were inspired by the fervor of working the land with our own hands. Surely, God would bless our labor and there would be no need to import grain from Egypt and other neighboring countries, for our harvest would prosper greatly. Once the Jews in the Holy Land began to eat of their own produce the financial aid of the Diaspora would suffice.

Another great advantage of agricultural settlement is that we would have the privilege of observing the religious commandments that attach to working the soil of the Holy Land.[4] The Jews who supervised the actual laborers would be aiding in the working of the land and would therefore have the same status as if they had personally fulfilled these commandments.

But, beyond all this, Jewish farming would be a spur to the ultimate Messianic Redemption. As we bring redemption to the land in a "this-worldly" way, the rays of heavenly deliverance will gradually appear.

Let no stubborn opponent of these thoughts maintain that those who labor day and night will be taken away from the study of the Torah and from spiritual to secular concerns. This counterargument is shortsighted. On the contrary, the policy we propose will add dignity to the Torah. "If there is no bread, there can be no study"; if there will be bread in the land, people will then be able to study with peace of mind. In addition, we are sure that there are many in the Holy Land who are not students of the Torah and who long to work the land. These will support the physically infirm scholars to whom no man would dare say: Work the land! but to whom all would say that they should devote themselves entirely to serving the Lord.

Such a policy would also raise our dignity among the nations, for they would say that the children of Israel, too, have the will to redeem the land of their ancestors, which is now so barren and forsaken.

Why do the people of Italy and of other countries sacrifice their lives for the land of their fathers, while we, like men bereft of strength and courage, do nothing? Are we inferior to all other peoples, who have no regard for life and fortune as compared with love of their land and nation? Let us take to heart the examples of the Italians, Poles, and Hungarians, who laid down their lives and possessions in the struggle for national independence, while we, the children of Israel, who have the most glorious and holiest of lands as our inheritance, are spiritless and silent. We should be ashamed of ourselves! All the other peoples have striven only for the sake of their own national honor; how much more should we exert ourselves, for our duty is to labor not only for the glory of our ancestors but for the glory of God who chose Zion!

MOSES HESS   1812-1875

WITH HESS we enter a different world, into the very midst of the intellectual ferment and political turmoil of the nineteenth century. Though almost entirely self-educated, Hess belongs to the generation of Heinrich Heine and a host of others almost equally famous in their day, to the first generation of German Jews who grew up as men of western culture. By temperament he was an outsider, an enemy not only of the established order but also of many of the values of the very political left with which he was associated.

Hess was born in Bonn, Germany. When his parents left that city for Cologne in 1821 the nine-year-old Moses was left behind. (His parents regarded the opportunities for Jewish education then available in Cologne as insufficient). He therefore remained in charge of his grandfather, a rabbi by training though not by profession, who taught him enough Hebrew so that, when he returned to Jewish interests after thirty years of neglect, Hess was able to tap strong emotional and intellectual roots in the tradition. As he entered maturity, however, Hess abandoned his Jewish concerns. His earliest interests were in philosophy. The 1830's were the zenith of the dominance of Hegel and of the vogue of historical philosophy in general. Hess's first book, published in 1837, grew out of this atmosphere; though it was entitled *The Holy History of Mankind, by a young Spinozist* (and Hess indeed regarded Spinoza as his master to the end of his days) the volume shows considerable traces of more current influences.

Like other advanced intellectuals of the milieu, among whom Karl Marx and Friedrich Engels were to become the most famous, Hess went on from philosophy to ideological politics. By 1840, after some wanderings, he turned up in Paris, where he was active in socialist circles. As Paris correspondent in 1842–1843, he was involved in the most radical of contemporary German newspapers, the *Rheinische Zeitung*, which Karl Marx edited, and even collaborated with both the founders of "Scientific Socialism" in two books of critical analysis of the contemporary scene. However, even though Hess was sufficiently active in the German revolution of 1848 to earn the sentence of death, the *Communist Manifesto* of that year sealed the break that had been implicit for a number of years between him and Marx and Engels. Hess was never in agreement with materialistic determinism, for his own socialism was of the ethical variety, the expression of a romantic love for man. That Karl Marx knew this and disapproved is evident in the *Communist Manifesto* itself, for he takes pains to mock Hess in that historic essay.

Hess's early Paris years were marked by the most bizarre aspect of his personal life. Evidently out of the desire to make personal atonement for the sins of man which drove poor women into the "oldest profession," he married a lady of the streets—and, somewhat surprisingly, lived happily ever after. It is not surprising, however, that this completed his personal breach with his father and family in Cologne.

By 1853 Hess was back in Paris, where he remained for the rest of his days. Though he did not abandon socialism, he devoted himself to scientific studies. As he delved into anthropology he became firmly convinced that the future world order needed to be organized as a harmonious symphony of national cultures, each expressing in its own way the ethical socialism which remained his quasi-religious faith. A rekindled interest in the faith and fate of his own people brought him back to Jewish studies and the result was the publication in 1862 of his *Rome and Jerusalem*. This diffuse short volume contains echoes of all of his ideas, including his general theory of national socialism for all peoples and his vitalistic views of science (these were published in full posthumously in 1877 by his wife under the title *Dynamic Matter*). Its major importance is, of course, in his statement of Jewish nationalism. Though Hess's later years were productive of many other essays on Jewish questions, *Rome and Jerusalem* is his classic, and the excerpts below are all from that volume.

ROME AND JERUSALEM (1862)

MY WAY OF RETURN

AFTER TWENTY YEARS of estrangement I have returned to my people. Once again I am sharing in its festivals of joy and days of sorrow, in its hopes and memories. I am taking part in the spiritual and intellectual struggles of our day, both within the House of Israel and between our people and the gentile world. The Jews have lived and labored among the nations for almost two thousand years, but nonetheless they cannot become rooted organically within them.

A sentiment which I believed I had suppressed beyond recall is alive once again. It is the thought of my nationality, which is inseparably connected with my ancestral heritage, with the Holy Land and the Eternal City, the birthplace of the belief in the divine unity of life and of the hope for the ultimate brotherhood of all men.

For years this half-strangled emotion has been stirring in my breast and clamoring for expression, but I had not the strength to swerve from my own path, which seemed so far from the road of Judaism, to a new one which I could envisage only vaguely in the hazy distance.

Twenty years ago, when news came to Europe from Damascus of an absurd accusation against the Jews,[1] a feeling of agony, as bitter as it was justified, was evoked in the hearts of all Jews. Once again we were face to face with the ignorance and credulity of the mobs of Asia and Europe, which are as ready today as they have been for the past two thousand years to believe any calumny directed against the Jews. I was painfully reminded, for the first time in many years, that I belong to an unfortunate, maligned, despised, and dispersed people—but one that the world has not succeeded in destroying. At that time, though I was still greatly estranged from Judaism, I wanted to cry out in anguish in expression of my Jewish patriotism, but this emotion was immediately superseded by the greater pain which was evoked in me by the suffering of the proletariat of Europe.

THE "PURE HUMAN NATURE" of the Germans is, in reality, the nature of the pure German race, which can rise to the concept of humanity in theory only, but in practice it has not yet transcended its innate racial sympathies and antipathies. German antagonism to our Jewish national aspirations has two sources, reflecting the dual nature of man, his spiritual and natural aspects, his theoretical and practical sides, which are nowhere so sharply defined—and opposed to one another—as among the Germans.

National aspirations as a whole are contrary to the theoretical internationalism of the Germans. However, in addition to this, the Germans oppose *Jewish* national aspirations because of racial antipathy, which even their noblest spirits have not yet overcome. The same German,[2] whose "pure human nature" revolted against publishing a book advocating the revival of the Jewish nationality, had no objection to publishing books against Jews and Judaism, though the purpose of such works is basically opposed to "pure human nature." This contradiction can be explained only on the basis of inborn racial antagonism. But the German, it seems, has no clear awareness of his racial prejudices; he makes no distinction between his egoistic and his spiritual endeavors and regards both as strivings toward values which are not merely Teutonic but really "humanistic"; he does not know that he follows the latter only in theory, while in practice he clings to his egoistic ideas.

Progressive German Jews, also, seem to think that they have sufficient reason for recoiling from any Jewish national expression. My dear old friend, Berthold Auerbach,[3] is just as disappointed with me as my former publisher is, though not on the grounds of "pure human nature." He complains bitterly about my attitude and finally exclaims: "Who appointed you as a prince and judge over us?"

Because of the hatred that surrounds him on all sides, the German Jew is determined to cast off all signs of his Jewishness and to deny his race. No reform of the Jewish religion, however extreme, is radical enough for the educated German Jews. But even an act of conversion cannot relieve the Jew of the enormous pressure of German anti-Semitism. The Germans hate the religion of the Jews less than they hate their race—they hate the peculiar faith of the Jews less than their peculiar noses. Reform, conversion, education, and emancipation—none of these open the gates of society to the German Jew; hence his desire to deny his racial origin. (Moleschott, in his *Physiological Sketches*, p. 257, tells how the son of a converted Jew used to spend hours every morning at the looking glass, comb in hand, endeavoring to straighten his curly hair, so as to give it a more Teutonic appearance.) The "radical" Reform movement[4]—an appelation which characterizes it very well, because it puts the ax to the root of Judaism, to the national and historical character of its religion—has little chance of success, and the tendency of some Jews to deny their racial descent is equally foredoomed to failure. Jewish noses cannot be reformed, and the black, wavy hair of the Jews will not be changed into blond by conversion or straightened out by constant combing. The Jewish race is one of the primary races of mankind, and it has retained its integrity despite the influence of changing climatic environments. The Jewish type has conserved its purity through the centuries.

THE REAWAKENING OF THE NATIONS

A S L O N G A S the Jew denies his nationality, as long as he lacks the character to acknowledge that he belongs to that unfortunate, persecuted, and maligned people, his false position must become ever more intolerable. What purpose does this deception serve? The nations of Europe have always regarded the existence of the Jews in their midst as an anomaly. We shall always remain strangers among the nations. They may even be moved by a sense of humanity and justice to emancipate us, but they will never *respect* us as long as we make *ubi bene ibi patria*[5] our guiding principle, indeed almost a religion, and place it above our own great national memories. Religious fanaticism may cease to cause hatred of the Jews in the more culturally advanced countries; but despite enlightenment and emancipation, the Jew in exile who denies his nationality will never earn the respect of the nations among whom he dwells. He may become a naturalized citizen, but he will never be able to convince the gentiles of his total separation from his own nationality.

The really dishonorable Jew is not the old-type, pious one, who would rather have his tongue cut out than utter a word in denial of his nationality, but the modern kind, who, like the German outcasts in foreign countries, is ashamed of his nationality because the hand of fate is pressing heavily upon his people. The beautiful phrases about humanity and enlightenment which he uses so freely to cloak his treason, his fear of being identified with his unfortunate brethren, will ultimately not protect him from the judgment of public opinion. These modern Jews hide in vain behind their geographical and philosophical alibis. You may mask yourself a thousand times over; you may change your name, religion, and character; you may travel through the world incognito, so that people may not recognize the Jew in you; yet every insult to the Jewish name will strike you even more than the honest man who admits his Jewish loyalties and who fights for the honor of the Jewish name.

Such were my thoughts in an earlier period of my life, when I was actively engaged in working for the European proletariat. My messianic belief was then the same that I hold today, namely, the belief in the regeneration of those nations which are the bearers of history and civilization by raising the lower to the level of the higher. Now, as at the time when I published my earlier works, I still believe that Christianity was a step forward on the road toward that great goal which the prophets called the "Messianic Age." Today, as before, I still believe that this final epoch in universal history first became manifest in the spiritual life of man with the appearance of Spinoza. However, I never believed, and I have never asserted, that Christianity is the ultimate stage of the sacred history of humanity, or that this sacred history found its consummation in Spinoza. It is certain (I, for one, have never doubted it) that our present yearning is for a Redemption of far broader outline than any that Christianity ever imagined, or could ever have imagined. Christianity was a star in the darkness, which provided consolation and hope for the peoples after the sun of ancient culture had set; it shed its light over the graves of the nations of antiquity. Since it is a religion of death, its mission is ended the moment the nations reawaken into life.

The history of the nations of Europe in the last three hundred years amply illustrates the truth of this assertion, but I will restrict myself to calling your attention to the events now transpiring in Italy.[6] On the ruins of Christian Rome a regenerated Italian people is arising. Like Christianity in the West, Islam in the East has also taught the supreme virtue of resignation and submission, and Turkey therefore follows the same policy with regard to Palestine that Austria exercises in Italy. Christianity and Islam are both only inscriptions on the tombstones which barbaric oppression erected upon the graves of the nations. . . . But the soldiers of modern civilization, the French, are breaking the power of the barbarians and, with Herculean arms, are rolling the tombstones from the graves of those slumbering in the dust. The nations will reawaken once more.

In those countries which form the dividing line between the Occident and the Orient, namely, Russia, Poland, Prussia, Austria, and Turkey, there live millions of our brethren who pray fervently every day to the God of their fathers for the restoration of the Jewish kingdom. These Jews have preserved the living kernel of Judaism, the sense of Jewish nationality, more faithfully than our occidental brethren. The western Jews would breathe new life into the whole of our religion, but they ignore the great hope which created our faith and has preserved it through all the tempests of history—the hope of the restoration of the Jewish nation. I turn to the faithful millions of my brethren and exclaim: "Carry thy standard high, my people! It is in you that the living kernel is preserved, which, like the grains of corn found in the graves of Egyptian mummies, retains its reproductive power after thousands of years of suspended animation. As soon as the rigid encasing form is shattered, the seed, placed in the fertile soil of the present and given air and light and rain, will strike root and bring forth life!"

The rigid forms of orthodoxy, which were entirely justified before this century of rebirth, can relax and become creative again. To be valid, such creativity must come from within, from the seminal power of the living idea of the Jewish nationality and of our historical religion. Only a national renaissance can endow the religious genius of the Jews, like the legendary giant when he touches mother earth, with new strength, and raise its soul once again to the level of prophetic inspiration. The "enlighteners" have attempted to open the Jewish scene to the light of modern culture by piercing the hard shell with which rabbinism had armored Judaism. None of them, not even the great Mendelssohn,[7] could succeed in doing this without inevitably destroying the innermost essence of Judaism, its historical national religion, and thus doing a sacred life to death.

WHAT IS JUDAISM?

THE THREATENING DANGER to Judaism comes only from those religious reformers (a breed that has by now, happily, vanished almost completely) who, with their newly invented ceremonies and empty eloquence, have sucked the marrow out of Judaism and have left only a shadowy skeleton of this most magnificent of all historical phenomena. It was not enough for them to work toward the development of a Jewish learning on modern scientific lines and to satisfy the need for an orderly and aesthetic form of our ancient Jewish religious practice. They cultivated a religious reform that was not in keeping with the spirit of the age, that was fashioned in imitation of Christian models, and that was, therefore, a stillborn notion; it has not the slightest basis either in the general situation of the modern world or in the essentially national character of Judaism.

I do not deny the validity of the Christian Reformation at the time of Luther, nor of the Jewish Reform movement at the time of Mendelssohn. The latter, however, was more of an aesthetic than a religious or ideological reform. Those reformers never dreamed of tampering with the historical basis of religion, for they well knew that the old basis cannot arbitrarily be replaced by a new one. But our contemporary reformers proposed the reform of this fundamental principle itself. Their reforms have only a negative purpose—if they have any aim at all—to proclaim *unbelief* in our nationality as the foundation of the Jewish religion. No wonder that these reforms only fostered indifference to Judaism and conversions to Christianity.

Judaism, like Christianity, would really have to disappear in the face of intellectual progress, if it were not more than a dogmatic religion, if it were not a national cult. The Jewish reformers, however—those who are still present in some German communities, and are maintaining, to the best of their ability, the theatrical show of religious reform—have so little respect for the essentially national character of Judaism that they are at great pains to erase every echo and memory of it from their creed and worship. They imagine that a recently manufactured prayer book or a hymnal which contains a philosophical theism put into rhyme and accompanied by music, is more elevating and soul-stirring than the moving prayers in the Hebrew language which express the pain of our people at the loss of its fatherland—these prayers which created and preserved the unity of our religion and which are still the tie that binds all Jews all over the world.

The efforts of our German Jewish religious reformers were directed toward making Judaism, which is both national and universal, into a second Christianity cut after a rationalistic pattern. This imitation was particularly superfluous at a time when the original itself was already mortally ill. Christianity, which came into existence on the graves of the ancient nations, had to withdraw from participation in national life. It must therefore continue to suffer from the irreconcilable opposition between the specific and the general, the material and the spiritual, until it is finally replaced among the newly regenerated nations by a religion based on nationality and national history. Such a future age can look only to Judaism as its pattern and spiritual example. This "religion of the future," of which some eighteenth-century philosophers, as well as their recent followers, dreamed, will be neither an imitation of the ancient pagan cult of Nature nor anything like that shadowy skeleton of a neo-Christianity and a neo-Judaism which exists, ghostlike, only in the minds of our religious reformers. Each nation will have to create its own historical cult; each people must become, like the Jewish people, a people of God.

Judaism is not threatened, like Christianity, with danger from the nationalistic and humanistic aspirations of our time, for, in reality, the spirit of the age is approaching ever closer to the essential Jewish emphasis on real life. The still very prevalent error, that an entire view of life can be compressed into a single dogma, is a hand-me-down from Christianity. I do not agree with Mendelssohn that Judaism has no dogmas. I claim that the divine teaching of Judaism was never, at any time, completed and finished. It has always kept on developing, always representing the typically Jewish process of harmonizing the sacred unity of life with the spirit of the Jewish people and of humanity. The free development of the knowledge of God, through untiring study and conscientious research, is the holiest religious obligation in Judaism. This is the reason why Judaism has never excluded or excommunicated philosophical thought, and why it has never occurred to any real Jew to "reform" Judaism on the basis of any philosophical system. Hence no real sects ever appeared in Judaism. Even recently, when there was no lack of passionate orthodox and heterodox dogmatists in Jewry, no sects could arise, for the dogmatic basis of Judaism is so wide as to admit every free creation of the spirit. There have always been differences of opinion with regard to metaphysical conceptions among the Jews. But Judaism has known only apostates, i.e., those who severed themselves from its community. "And even they have not been forsaken by Judaism," added a learned rabbi, in whose presence I expressed this opinion.

There are two epochs that mark the development of Jewish law: the first, after the liberation from Egypt; the second, after the return from Babylonia. The third is yet to come, with redemption from the third exile. The significance of the second legislative epoch is more misunderstood by our reformers (who have no conception of the creative genius of the Jewish nation), than by our rabbis, who place the lawgivers of this period even higher than Moses, for they say: "Ezra would have deserved that the Torah be given to Israel through him, had not Moses preceded him." In the form in which we possess it today, the Torah was handed down to us directly through the men of that second epoch. These same men, living at the same time, utilizing the same traditions, and in the same spirit, collected both the written and the oral law, which they handed down to later generations. There is no justification for ascribing a holier origin to the written law than to the oral. On the contrary, from the time of the return from the Babylonian exile the living development of the oral law was always considered of greater importance than the mere clinging to the written law. The reason for this is quite evident. The national legislative genius would have been extinguished, had the sages not occupied themselves with the living development of the law. It was to this activity that Judaism owed its national renaissance after the Babylonian exile, as well as its continuing existence in the Diaspora of that day. It was through this that the great Jewish heroes arose, who fought so bravely against the Greek and Roman enemies of their nation. And, finally, it is to this oral development of the law that Judaism owes its existence during the two thousand years of exile; and to it the Jewish people will also owe its future national regeneration.

The rabbis were justified in their long struggle against writing down the oral law. Had they kept on teaching and developing the law orally in the schools, Judaism would never have been threatened with the loss of its national legislative genius. But they were compelled to reduce the law to writing in order to avoid a still greater danger, namely, its being entirely forgotten because of the dispersion of the Jews. Today, we have no reason to fear the latter danger. But we can escape the former only if we revive the critical spirit to counteract barren formalism, and if we reawaken in our hearts and souls the holy, patriotic spirit of our prophets and sages, as an antidote to destructive rationalism. Our people must once again steep itself in its history, which has been grossly neglected by our rationalists, and rekindle in the hearts of our younger generation that spirit which was the ultimate source of wisdom and inspiration for both our prophets and our rabbis. If we begin once again to draw our inspiration from the ultimate sources of Judaism, our doctors of the law will regain among us the authority which they justly forfeited from the moment when, prompted by motives other than patriotism, they estranged themselves from Judaism and attempted to reform Jewish law. We will then again become participators in the holy spirit which alone has the right to develop Jewish law and refashion it according to the needs of the people. And then, when the third exile will finally have come to an end, the restoration of the Jewish state will find us ready for it in the right spirit.

THE MISSION OF ISRAEL

J E W I S H   R A T I O N A L I S T S , who have as little reason to remain within the fold of Judaism as have the Christian rationalists for clinging to Christianity, are as inventive as their Christian friends in discovering new pretexts for the existence of a religion which, by the logic of their position, no longer has any *raison d'être*. According to them, the dispersion of the Jews was their vocation and mission. All hail to the really splendiferous list of great tasks that our "friends of light" have compiled for the Jews to accomplish in the dispersion! First of all, they are to represent "pure" theism, in contradistinction to Christianity. In the next place, "tolerant" Judaism is to teach intolerant Christianity the principles of humanitarianism. Furthermore, it is the concern of Judaism in its dispersion that morality and life, which are severed from each other in the Christian world, should again become one. Is this all? No, through their industrial and commercial endeavors the Jews have become necessary to the civilized nations in whose midst they live, and they are an indispensable leaven to the future development of these peoples. I have even heard it said quite seriously that the Indo-Germanic race improve its quality by mingling with the Jewish race!

But, mark you, the restoration of the Jewish state will not deprive the world of even a single one of all these benefits, both real and imaginary, which the Jews in the dispersion confer upon it. At the time of the return from the Babylonian exile, not all the Jews were settled in Palestine by a messianic miracle, but the majority remained in the lands of exile, where there had been Jewish settlements since the dispersion of Israel and Judah; we, therefore, need not expect such a miracle as a feature of a future restoration. Besides, it seems to me that the benefits which the Jews in exile supposedly confer upon the world have been exaggerated, "for the sake of the cause." I consider it an anachronism to assign to the Jews those missions which they performed in antiquity, particularly at the end of that epoch, and to some extent also in medieval times, but which, at present, no longer belong peculiarly to them. As to effecting the unity of morality and life, this can be done only by a nation which is politically organized—which can embody such unity in its social institutions.

To continue the discussion further, what section of world-Jewry is to teach the Christians of today tolerance and humanity? You will surely say the westernized, "enlightened" Jews. But is not the enlightened Christian entitled to repeat to the enlightened Jew the words which Lessing,[8] in his *Nathan the Wise*, puts into the mouth of the liberal Christian in his answer to the liberal Jew: "What makes me a Christian in your eyes, makes you a Jew in mine."

Or, on the other hand, should the liberal Jew say to the orthodox Christian, "Your beliefs are mere superstitions and your religion, only fanaticism?" Cannot the liberal Christian make similar remarks about the orthodox Jew? Our cultured Jews, who accuse Christians of possessing a drive to persecute others, reason as fallaciously as does Bethmann-Hollweg[9] when he charges the Jews with the same trait. Such recriminations can neither explain nor change the course of history.

From the viewpoint of enlightenment, I see no tenable reason for the continued existence of either Judaism or Christianity. The Jew who does not believe in the national regeneration of his people has only one task—to labor, like the enlightened Christian, for the dissolution of his religion. I understand how one can hold such an opinion. But what I do not understand is how it is possible to believe simultaneously in "enlightenment" and in "the mission of the Jews in the dispersion"—in other words, how it is possible to believe at once in the ultimate dissolution and in the continued existence of Judaism.

THE NATION AS PART OF HUMANITY

I BELIEVE that the national character of Judaism does not exclude universalism and modern civilization; on the contrary, these values are the logical effect of our national character. If I nonetheless emphasize the national root of Judaism rather than its universalist blooms that is because in our time people are all too prone to gather and deck themselves out with the pretty flowers of the cultural heritage rather than to cultivate them in the soil in which they can grow. Judaism is the root of our whole contemporary universalist view of life. There is nothing in the moral teaching of Christianity, in the scholastic philosophy of the Middle Ages, or in modern humanitarianism—and, if we add the latest manifestation of Judaism, Spinozism—

there is nothing even in modern philosophy, which does not stem from Judaism. Until the French Revolution, the Jewish people was the only people in the world whose religion was at once national and universalist. It is through Judaism that the history of humanity became a sacred history, by which I mean that history became a unified, organic development which has its origin in the love of the family. This process will not be completed until the whole of humanity becomes one family, the members of which will be united by the holy spirit, the creative genius of history, as strongly as the organs of a body are united by the equally holy creative force of nature. As long as no other people possessed such a religion combining national, universal, and historical elements, the Jews alone were the people of God. Since the French Revolution, the French, as well as the other peoples which followed them, have become our noble rivals and faithful allies.

With the final victory of these nations over medieval reaction, universalist aspirations, which I fully respect, so long as they do not express themselves merely in hypocritical, flowery words, will be realized and bear fruit. Anti-national universalism is just as unfruitful as the anti-universalist nationalism of medieval reaction. In theoretical anti-national universalism I can see—to express myself as gently as I can—more idealistic dreaming than reality. We are so saturated with the perfume of spiritual love and the chloroform of humanitarianism that we have become entirely unresponsive to the real misery that is caused by the antagonisms which still exist among the various members of the great human family. Such antagonism will not be eradicated by sermons in praise of enlightenment but only by a process of historical development based on laws as unchangeable as the laws of nature.

Nature does not produce flowers and fruits or plants and animals which are all exactly alike because they represent some generalized form; on the contrary, nature produces specific and unique plant and animal types. By the same token the creative power in history produces only folk types. The plan of the plant and animal kingdoms finds its consummation in man; but the life of man has the unique dimension of independence—it is the sphere of social life—and it is therefore still in the process of development. The life of man in society begins with a primal differentiation of folk types, which at first, plantlike, existed side by side; then, animal-like, fought each other and destroyed or absorbed one another; but which will finally, in order to attain absolute freedom, live together in friendship and *each for the other,* without surrendering their particular and typical identities.

The contemporary movements for national self-realization do not only not exclude a concern for all humanity but strongly assert it. These movements are a wholesome reaction, not against universalism but against the things that would encroach upon it and cause its degeneration, against the leveling tendencies of modern industry and civilization which are threatening to deaden every primal, organic life force, by the mechanizing of life. As long as these tendencies were directed against the moribund institutions of an antiquated past, their existence was justified. Nor can there be any objection to universalist tendencies insofar as they endeavor to establish closer relations among the various nations of the world. But, unfortunately, this universalism has gone too far: both in life and in science, the typical and the creative are being denied, and, as a result, modern life is being blighted by the vapor of idealism and science, by the dust of atomism; these are resting like mildew on red corn and stifling the germinating life in the bud. It is against these encroachments on the most sacred principles of creative life that the national tendencies of our time are reacting, and it is only against these destructive forces that I appeal to the primal power of Jewish nationalism.

THE SABBATH OF HISTORY

IT SEEMS UNDENIABLE that truth is indivisible, that scientific truth cannot be of a different nature than philosophic or religious truth. However, as long as these various spheres of knowledge remain in conflict, it is a difficult matter, in a few hasty lines, for me even to make it plausible that science, philosophy, and religion do not exclude one another; that, at worst, they will continue to ignore one another for some time; and that, ultimately, they must support one another and unite into one realm of truth.

Let us, then, first make clear to ourselves the meaning of the oft-misunderstood concepts of "Freedom" and "Progress," which are used much too carelessly.

The belief in a rational, and therefore knowable, divine law, as revealed to humanity in the teaching and history of Judaism—this belief in a divine Providence, in a rational order of creation—is no blind, fatalistic belief in a destiny that is beyond being affected by man, even though even such a conception still excludes any notion of an arbitrary and lawless divine will. I do not assert, with the materialists, that the organic and spiritual world is subjected to the same external mechanical laws as the inorganic world. I affirm the contrary: the seemingly mechanical phenomena of the cosmos have the same plan, the same purposiveness, and have their source in the same sacred life as organic and spiritual phenomena. Nature and humanity are subordinate to the same divine law. The difference is that Nature follows this law blindly, while man, when perfectly developed, obeys it consciously and voluntarily. Another important difference, the ignoring of which gives rise to a misunderstanding of the concepts of "Freedom" and "Progress," lies in this, that while, in both the organic and cosmic worlds, which are the basis of our social, human sphere of life, Nature has already completed its development, humanity is still in the midst of its life-creating process. As long as human society is still occupied with creating its organic order, man, the agent of this creation, appears to be an irresponsible and unfettered being, although he is in his own creative sphere as subject as Nature is in its sphere to the eternal divine laws. The false conception of human freedom as arbitrariness arises mainly from the fact that we do not yet know the law that regulates the development of social life, i.e., its ultimate goal, for we cannot know this law from experience so long as we are still in the midst of the stream of development.

But though science is still silent concerning the law governing the development of social life, our religious genius discovered it long ago. We Jews have always, from the beginning of our history, been the bearers of the faith in a future messianic epoch. This belief is expressed symbolically in our historical religion by the Sabbath festival. The celebration of the Sabbath is the embodiment of the great idea which has always animated us, namely, that the future will bring about the realization of the historical Sabbath, just as the past gave us the natural Sabbath—in other words, that History, like Nature, will finally attain its epoch of harmonious perfection.

The biblical story of the Creation is told only for the sake of the Sabbath ideal. It tells us, in symbolic language, that when the creation of the world of Nature was completed, with the calling into life of the highest organic being of the earth—man—and the Creator celebrated his natural Sabbath, there at once began the workdays of History. Then, also, began the history of creation of the social world, which will celebrate *its* Sabbath, after the completion of the task of world history, by ushering in the messianic epoch. Here, in this conception, you can see the high moral value of the Mosaic story of

Creation, which is a symbolic story and not, as narrow supernaturalists would have it, a system of science. The very biblical Sabbath-law itself, therefore, inspires us with a feeling of certainty that a uniform, eternal, divine law governs alike both the world of Nature and the world of History. It is only in the minds of those people who do not understand the revelations vouchsafed by the religious genius of the Jews, that the historical development of humanity appears as lawless, indeterminate, infinite "Progress"; the life of Nature which they contrast History with, because it has reached the end of its development, appears as a closed world, the laws of which are calculable. It is now clear, however, that this apparent difference between the laws of Nature and those of History is merely the result of a subjective conception which cannot rise to an understanding of the great universal divine laws. The freedom that is an attribute of the creative activity of History is not to be conceived as a mere arbitrary act of will, and, by the same token, is not infinite.

Every being is free, in the natural sense, which can develop its own destiny, according to its inner calling or its natural inclinations, without any external restraint. In the moral sense, however, that being is free which decides its destiny with consciousness and will, whose will coincides with the divine law or will. Every other form of will is only arbitrariness, which does not partake of the holy, overarching, and divine act of willing, but owes its existence to an egoistic impulse. Man possesses this propensity to follow desires and passion, which lead him astray from the path of reason and morality only so long as his inner being is not sufficiently developed. Man certainly cannot be proud of this negative capacity, which is no more than a disease, indicating a lack of development. This attribute does not raise him above the animal, but, on the contrary, puts him below it; for animal life, as well as plant life, has already attained its fullest possible development.

TOWARD THE JEWISH RESTORATION

HAVE YOU NEVER READ the words of the prophet Isaiah? "Comfort ye, comfort ye My people, saith your God. Bid Jerusalem take heart, and proclaim unto her, that her time of service is accomplished, that her guilt is paid off; that she hath received of the Lord's hand double for all her sins . . . Clear ye in the wilderness the way of the Lord, make plain in the desert a highway for our God.

Every valley shall be lifted up, and every mountain and hill shall be made low; and the rugged shall be made level, and the rough places a plain. And the glory of the Lord shall be revealed, and all flesh shall see it together; for the mouth of the Lord hath spoken it."[10]

Do you not believe that in these opening words of the prophecies of Second Isaiah, as well as in the closing verse of the book of Obadiah (1:21),[11] the conditions of our day are depicted? Is not everything being made even and prepared; is not the road of civilization being laid in the desert by the digging of the Suez Canal, and by the work on a railroad which will connect Europe and Asia? To be sure, none of this reflects any intention to re-establish our nation, but you know the proverb: Man proposes and God disposes.

What we have to do at present for the regeneration of the Jewish nation is, first, to keep alive the hope of the political rebirth of our people, and, next, to reawaken that hope where it slumbers. When political conditions in the Orient shape themselves so as to permit the organization of a beginning of the restoration of a Jewish state, this beginning will express itself in the founding of Jewish colonies in the land of their ancestors, to which enterprise France will undoubtedly lend a hand. France, beloved friend, is the savior who will restore our people to its place in universal history.

Just as we once searched in the West for a road to India, and incidentally discovered a new world, so will our lost fatherland be rediscovered on the road to India and China that is now being built in the Orient. Do you still doubt that France will help the Jews to found colonies which may extend from Suez to Jerusalem and from the banks of the Jordan to the coast of the Mediterranean? Then pray read the work which appeared shortly after the massacres in Syria[12] written by Laharanne and published by the famous publisher, Dentu, under the title *The New Eastern Question*. The author hardly wrote it at the request of the French Government but he acted in accordance with the spirit of the French nation when he urged our brethren, not on religious grounds but from purely political and humanitarian motives, to restore their ancient State.

I may, therefore, recommend this work, written not by a Jew but by a French patriot, to the attention of our modern Jews, who plume themselves on an attachment to all humanity, a sentiment they borrowed from the French people. I will quote here a few pages of this work, *The New Eastern Question*, by Ernst Laharanne.[13]

"No member of the Jewish race can renounce the incontestable and fundamental right of his people to its ancestral land without thereby denying his past and his ancestors. Such an act is especially unseemly at a time when political conditions in Europe will not only not obstruct the restoration of a Jewish State but will rather facilitate its realization. What European power would today oppose the plan that the Jews, united through a Congress, should buy back their ancient fatherland? Who would object if the Jews flung a handful of gold to decrepit old Turkey and said to her: 'Give me back my home and use this money to consolidate the other parts of your tottering empire?'

"A great calling is reserved for the Jews: to be a living channel of communication between three continents. You shall be the bearers of civilization to peoples who are still inexperienced and their teachers in the European sciences, to which your race has contributed so much. You shall be the mediators between Europe and far Asia, opening the roads that lead to India and China—those unknown regions which must ultimately be thrown open to civilization. You will come to the land of your fathers decorated with the crown of age-long martyrdom, and there, finally, you will be completely healed from all your ills! Your capital will again bring the wide stretches of barren land under cultivation; your labor and industry will once more turn the ancient soil into fruitful valleys, reclaiming it from the encroaching sands of the desert, and the world will again pay its homage to the oldest of peoples."

COMMENTS

1. Jewish Creativity

It is "only after the extinction of the national life of the people, which molded the religious norms as greatly as it was molded by them," that these norms have assumed a rigid form, but this rigidity will disappear as soon as the extinct national life will reawaken, when the free current of a national, historical development will again penetrate the hard and rigid religious forms.

The holy spirit, the creative genius of the people, out of which Jewish life and teaching arose, deserted Israel when its children began to feel ashamed of their nationality. But this spirit will again animate our people when it awakens to a new life; it will create new things which we cannot at present even imagine. No one can foretell what form and shape the newborn life and spirit of the regenerated nations will assume. As regards their religious expressions, and especially with respect to the Jewish religion, they will certainly be equally different both from present-day and from ancient religion.

2. *Prejudice and Dogma and the Restoration*

You think that the Christian nations will certainly not object to the restoration of the Jewish state, for they will thereby rid their respective countries of a foreign population which has always been a thorn in their side. These sentiments, however, seem to be, according to you, only a milder form of the desire which expressed itself in past ages more brutally, in frequent expulsions of the Jews; you maintain that this modern "mildness" will be of scant comfort to our brethren. On the other hand, you see in such projects only a piece of folly which, in the final analysis, leads either to religious or secular insanity, and which should therefore be discarded immediately. Moreover, if any such suggestion were to come from pious Christians, it would be opposed by all Jews; if, on the other hand, pious Jews were to propose a Jewish restoration, all Christians would be opposed. Just as orthodox Jews would consent to a return to Palestine only on condition that the ancient sacrificial cult[14] be reintroduced in the New Jerusalem, so the Christians would give their assistance to such a project only on condition that we Jews bring our national religion as a sacrifice to Christianity at the Holy Sepulchre. And thus, you conclude, all the national aspirations of the Jews must inevitably founder on the rock of these religious differences.

I agree that if rigid Christian dogma and inflexible Jewish orthodoxy could never be revived by the living current of history, they would certainly create an insurmountable obstacle to the realization of our patriotic aspirations. The thought of repossessing our ancient fatherland can, therefore, be taken under serious consideration only when this rigidity will have been broken. And such is really the case today, not only among liberal but even among orthodox Jews and Christians.

3. *A Change of Spirit*

The main problem of the Jewish national movement is not of a religious nature but centers around one point, namely, on how to awaken the patriotic sentiment in the hearts of our progressive Jews, and how to liberate the Jewish masses, by means of this reawakened patriotism, from a spirit-deadening formalism. If we succeed in this beginning, then, no matter how difficult the practical realization of our plan may be, the difficulties will be overcome by experience itself. It is only if the Jewish heart is dead, if the Jews are no longer capable of patriotic inspiration, that we should have to despair of our hope, which, like every great historical ideal, cannot be realized without a tremendous struggle.

The objections of progressive Jews to the restoration of the Jewish state do not have their ultimate basis in that kind of spiritual education which does not shrink from the difficulties lying in the path of a great work or calculate beforehand the amount of sacrifice that may be required in its realization. On the contrary, they rest in moral and intellectual narrow-mindedness, which is unable to rise to that high humanitarian standpoint from which one can see the depth of the misfortune of our people, as well as the means of its salvation.

The Jewish religion has indeed been, as Heine thought—and with him all the "enlightened" Jews—more of a misfortune than a religion for the last two thousand years. But our "progressive" Jews are deluding themselves if they think that they can escape this misfortune through enlightenment or conversion. Every Jew is, whether he wishes it or not, bound unbreakably to the entire nation. Only when the Jewish people will be freed from the burden which it has borne so heroically for thousands of years will the burden of Judaism be removed from the shoulders of these "progressive" Jews, who will always form only a small and vanishing minority.

It is the duty of all of us to carry "the yoke of the Kingdom of Heaven" until the end.

4. Social Regeneration

The masses are never moved to progress by mere abstract conceptions; the springs of action lie far deeper than even the socialist revolutionaries imagine. With the Jews, more than with other nations which, though oppressed, yet live on their own soil, all political and social progress must necessarily be preceded by national independence. A common, native soil is a precondition for introducing healthier relations between capital and labor among the Jews. The social man, just like the social plant and animal, needs a wide, free soil for his growth and development; without it, he sinks to the status of a parasite, which feeds at the expense of others. The parasitic way of existence has played an important role in the process of human history to date and it is by no means restricted to the Jews. As long as science and industry were not sufficiently developed, the land in the possession of any nation was never large enough to maintain the entire population; the nations were therefore forced either to make war and enslave one another or to allow their own populations to divide into ruling and servile classes. But this social order of dog-eat-dog, based upon the exploitation of men, collapsed as soon as modern science and industry began to dominate the world.

The civilized nations are at present preparing for a common exploitation of Nature. This will be carried on by means of labor based on the discoveries of science, and social parasites will no longer have any function or be allowed to exist. They are preparing themselves for this new era (which is not to be confused with the Prussian new era)[15] through struggles for free national soils, by attempts at abolishing all internal and external race and class oppression, through organizing a free association of all forces of production in which the antagonism between capitalistic speculation and productive labor will disappear simultaneously with the conflict between philosophic speculation and scientific research.

I know well that the need of wholesome and just labor conditions, which should be based solely on the exploitation of Nature by man, is also strongly felt in Jewry. I know of the great efforts which are being exerted on the part of the Jews to train our younger generation as useful laborers. But I know also that the Jews in exile, at least the majority of them, cannot devote themselves successfully to productive labor: in the first place, because they lack the most necessary condition —an ancestral soil; and, secondly, because they cannot assimilate with the peoples among whom they live without being untrue to their national religion and tradition. Those commendable efforts to improve the condition of Jewish labor, because they will in effect cause the destruction of the Jewish cult, will, therefore, be as fruitless, on the whole, as the endeavors of the Reform movement, which lead directly to the same results. In exile, the Jewish people cannot be regenerated; reforms and philanthropic endeavors can, at most, bring it only to apostasy—but in this no reformer, and not even any tyrant, will ever succeed.

The Jewish people will participate in the great historical movement of present-day humanity only when it will have its own fatherland. As long as the great Jewish masses remain in their position of inequality, even the relatively few Jews who have entirely surrendered their Jewish identity in the vain attempt to escape individually from the fate of the

Jewish people, will be more painfully affected by the position of the Jews than the masses, who feel themselves only unfortunate but not degraded. Hence, no Jew, whether orthodox or not, can refrain from co-operating with the rest in the task of elevating all Jewry. Every Jew, even the converted, should cling to the cause and labor for the regeneration of Israel.

5. A Spiritual Center

It is well understood that when we speak of a Jewish settlement in the Orient, we do not mean to imply a total emigration of the occidental Jews to Palestine. Even after the establishment of a Jewish State the majority of the Jews who live at present in the civilized countries of the Occident will undoubtedly remain where they are.

The occidental Jews, who have only recently, by dint of strenuous effort, broken their way through to western culture and achieved a respected civic position, would not abandon these valuable acquisitions so quickly, even if the restoration of Judaea were more than a pious wish. Such a sacrifice of a barely acquired prize is contrary to human nature and is hardly to be expected even from patriotic Jews, let alone from the majority of our "educated" parvenus, who have succeeded in breaking off all relations with their old Jewish family and their unfortunate brethren, and who are proud of the fact that they have turned their back on the misery of their people. Yet this will not prevent the nobler natures among them from interesting themselves again in the Jewish people, which they really do not know any more, and from supporting it in its historical mission, when it will have the courage to dare claim its ancient fatherland, not only from God in its prayers, as hitherto, but also from men.

There has been a central unity among the Jews at all times, even among those who were scattered to the very confines of the earth. Jews have maintained a relation with their spiritual centers, wherever these have been. No nation has ever felt as keenly, to the furthest extremities of its national organism, any movement occurring in its spiritual nerve center as have the Jews. Even in antiquity, the dispersion to the very ends of the world did not hinder the scattered members of this remarkable people from participating in every national undertaking, from sharing the fortunes and misfortunes of fate. Today, when distance is no longer an obstacle, it is of little consequence to a Jewish state how much of the Jewish race may dwell within, or outside, its borders. Even at the time of the existence of the ancient Jewish state many Jews lived in foreign countries. At the time of the Second Temple the Jew-hater Haman could already utter the words which even today the enemies of the Jews constantly repeat: "There is a nation scattered abroad and dispersed among the people." However, there is hardly any civilized nation today members of which are not found in foreign lands, either as foreigners or as naturalized citizens. As long as an independent Jewish state does not exist and is not recognized in international law as a member of the family of civilized nations, the Jews who live in exile must necessarily strive to obtain naturalization and "emancipation," even though they are by no means abandoning the hope of the ultimate restoration of the Jewish state. It will not occur to the nations of the world, even for a moment, now that they are no longer subject to their medieval Christian war lords, to deny the Jews equal rights because they are remaining faithful to their national religion, or to refuse them the respect they so richly deserve for this unexampled fidelity.

*Part 2
Outcry in Russia—
the 1870's
and
1880's*

PERETZ SMOLENSKIN 1842-1885

THE WANDERER IN LIFE'S WAYS (*Ha-Toeh Be-Dareche Ha-Hayim*) is the title of Smolenskin's longest work, an autobiographical novel describing the adventures of an orphan who wanders through all of contemporary Jewish life, both in eastern and western Europe, until he dies defending his people in a Russian pogrom. This title and theme summarized not only Smolenskin's own life but also that of an entire generation; it was the most widely read book of modern Hebrew letters in the 1870's, because it spoke for and to many who were living in a painful halfway house between the ghetto and the world of modernity.

Like his hero in the novel, Smolenskin was born in the Russian Pale of Settlement, the western provinces of the tsarist empire which were alone open to the Jewish population. As a child he saw his oldest brother "snatched" for military service in the Russian army. These were the days of the Cantonist system, under which young Jewish boys were forced into a minimum of twenty-five years in the army and subjected to conversionist pressure. He lost his father at the age of ten, and in the next year he followed the usual pious custom of going to study at the yeshivah (talmudic academy) of Shklov. While at yeshivah he cultivated an already existing interest in "enlightenment" by studying Russian and reading secular books. Since this was regarded as a mortal sin in pious circles, he was persecuted for heresy.

Smolenskin had no alternative but to run away, and thus his wander years began. Still in his teens, he lived in various places in the Pale of Settlement and supported himself by singing in choirs and by occasional preaching in various synagogues (he could do this only as long as the congregations were not aware that the young talmudist was, in secret, one of the "enlightened"). At the age of twenty he migrated to Odessa, the great Black Sea port which contained the most modern Jewish community in Russia, and spent five years studying music and languages while earning his keep by teaching Hebrew. His Odessa days were the beginning of his literary career.

The last period of Smolenskin's life was spent primarily in Vienna, where he settled in 1868. Though he came intending to enter the university, his poverty did not permit him the luxury of a formal education. A small job as proofreader in a printing house, and later, after his marriage in 1875, as its manager, provided meagerly for his needs. His major energies were devoted to a monthly, *Hashahar* (*The Dawn*), which he founded with a collaborator in 1868 and continued to publish and write for until his death from tuberculosis in Meran, Austria, in 1885.

In his novels and especially in his essays Smolenskin is the transition figure in modern Hebrew literature between the period of the "Enlightenment," which came to an end with the Russian pogroms of 1881, and the age of return to nationalist moorings, which followed after. Until his very last, "Zionist" novel, which was written in the 1880's in the wake of the pogroms, his work in belles-lettres expressed primarily the usual notions that modernizing Jewish life was both desirable and inevitable; even then, however, he was no uncritical admirer of modernity, for his novels emphasized a countertheme, that the assimilation of the Jew would not necessarily lead him either to acceptance by society or to personal happiness. However, as essayist Smolenskin sketched out the beginnings of his cultural nationalism as early as 1869. By the 1870's, even before the debacle of the great pogroms, he had already produced a lengthy account of his nationalist counterposition to the Haskalah. On the heels of the pogroms Smolenskin abandoned his theorizing about Jewish national culture and the definition of Jewry as a spiritual notion, to call for the complete evacuation of eastern Europe; he asked its Jews not to repeat the woeful cycles of their history by emigrating to America or to any other of the lands of exile. There was only one answer, Zionism.

The excerpts which follow are from the volume mentioned above, which he published as a series of articles in his own *Hashahar* in the years 1857–1877 under the title *It Is Time To Plant;* from an essay in immediate reaction to the pogroms of 1881, which expressed his later Zionism of complete exodus; and from a late piece continuing his critique of Reform Judaism and the Haskalah, which, from the perspective of both his versions of Jewish nationalism, he regarded as the immediate enemies. Smolenskin was a diffuse writer, and the selections below, therefore, have been considerably compressed.

IT IS TIME TO PLANT (1875–1877)

THE JEWISH PEOPLE has outlived all others because it has always regarded itself as a people—a spiritual nation. Without exception its sages and writers, its prophets and the authors of its prayers, have always called it a people. Clearly, therefore, this one term has sufficient power to unite those who are dispersed all over the world. Jews of different countries regard and love one another as members of the same people because they remember that the tie that binds them did not begin yesterday; it is four thousand years old. Four thousand years! This sense of history alone is a great and uplifting thought, an inspiration to respect this bond and hold it dear. Any sensitive person must feel: For four thousand years we have been brothers and children of one people; how can I sin against hundreds of generations and betray this brotherhood? How can I fold my hands and fail to help as the cup of wrath is poured over my people?

Every sorrow and every joy will renew the covenant and strengthen the tie of Jews to their people. In a time of trouble each will remember that the afflicted are his brothers and that he must help them bear their burdens. In happier times he will rejoice that his brother's estate has been uplifted. By helping one another in difficult days, by retaining a sense of closeness even though dispersed in various lands, by not being separated in spirit despite the barriers of the various languages they acquired, the Jews have succeeded in withstanding every storm and tumult. Even in their frequent exiles, Jews were not lonely, for everywhere they found brothers—the sons of their people—in whose homes they were welcome.

Thinking people understand that this unity is the secret of our strength and vitality. But such unity can come only from a fraternal feeling, from a national sentiment which makes everyone born a Jew declare: I am a son of this people. As long as this emotion persists, our sense of brotherhood will not be weakened, and the strength of the people as a whole will be maintained. Those who may abandon some, or even many, of our religious practices will nonetheless keep a share in the inheritance of Israel. Whatever their sin, it is a sin against God and not against their people. If national sentiment is made the basis of our existence, there will no longer be cause for controversy over foolish laws and customs of religion. The superpious and the hypocrites will no longer dare to exclude from our people any Jew tainted with religious liberalism.

No matter what his sins against religion, every Jew belongs to his people so long as he does not betray it—this is the principle which we must succeed in establishing. It is the logical conclusion to be derived from the proposition that we are a people.

For the sake of argument, let us assume that we are merely children of the same faith and are united only by the laws of religion. This proposition does not stand up under analysis. If laws alone make us one community, why do we bear love in our hearts for all Jews? Is it that we obey the same laws—if so, should we not love all men equally, because all men obey the same moral laws? Should I especially love another because he too, like me, does not steal, rob, or oppress? What, then, would inspire me to help my brothers? How would we know that we are brethren? It is true that there are laws which unite us, like the Sabbath, circumcision, Yom Kippur, and the like, but all these are effective only if they are themselves based on a firm foundation, on a high sentiment. Taken in their own right, and not as expressions of some fundamental emotional loyalty, these laws are as dead as corpses.

If many begin to disobey the laws of religion, how is the sense of Jewish unity to be maintained? These unorthodox will simply declare that the tie between them and the rest of the children of Israel has been severed. Having thrown off the yoke of religious discipline, they will regard themselves as excluded from a community which is united by it alone. This is indeed the case in many countries, where significant numbers of Jews now no longer observe the laws and customs (there is precedent for such nonobservance in the Jewish past of four hundred years ago).[1] Are we to exclude these people from the community? How many Jews will we have left if these are discarded as dross? There is reason to fear that ultimately the yoke of the Law will be cast off in favor of modern life, for we see it happening before our very eyes. If we are honest, we must admit that the younger generation is far less observant than its parents. It is therefore not unlikely that in a generation or two the breakdown of religious observance will cause the name and memory of Israel to disappear.

I am aware that there is a counterargument: There is enough force in the name Israel alone to maintain us as one community. But this argument is specious. Is the name Israel based on religion, law, observance, or custom? This name exists because of national sentiment.

As long as Israel regarded itself as a people among the peoples, this name had magical power on the lips of its sons. It reminded them that they belonged to this people. If this sentiment vanishes, this name too will lose all vitality and force.

Yes, we are a people. We have been a people from our beginnings until today. We have never ceased being a people, even after our kingdom was destroyed and we were exiled from our land, and whatever may yet come over us will not eradicate our national character. But we are not today a people like all others, just as we were not a people like the others even when we dwelt in our own land. The foundation of our national identity was never the soil of the Holy Land, and we did not lose the basis of our nationality when we were exiled. We have always been a spiritual nation, one whose Torah was the foundation of its statehood. From the start our people has believed that its Torah took precedence over its land and over its political identity. We are a people because in spirit and thought we regard ourselves bound to one another by ties of fraternity. Our unity has been conserved in a different way, through forms different from those of all other peoples, but does this make us any the less a people?

We have always looked upon ourselves as a people, even though we knew that the Torah was the sole tie that bound us together. We have therefore, to this day, not ceased being a people, a spiritual nation, to which individuals belong in the dimension of spirit and thought and not in material terms. In practical reality every Jew is a citizen of the land in which he dwells, and it is his duty to be a good citizen, who accepts all the obligations of citizenship like all other nationals of the country. The land in which we dwell is our country. We once had a land of our own, but it was not the tie that united us. Our Torah is the native land which makes us a people, a nation only in the spiritual sense, but in the normal business of life we are like all other men.

We are a spiritual nation—this is the correct doctrine which we must proclaim.

LET US SEARCH OUR WAYS (1881)

CALAMITY AFTER CALAMITY and disaster after disaster have afflicted the Jews of Russia. In many communities not a stone has been left standing. The shops of our brethren have been pillaged and looted, and whatever the mob could not carry off, it has utterly destroyed. Many Jews have been murdered and the wounded are without number. The mob, a ravenous wolf in search of prey, has stalked the Jews with a cruelty unheard of since the Middle Ages. Perhaps most shocking of all, many supposedly decent people appeared among the makers of the pogroms. There is no end to the affliction that has already struck so many tens of thousands.

Even before, Russian Jewry had not been able to establish itself securely; even before, its life was one of trouble, want, and deprivation. Even in those cities where Jews were permitted to settle, they were in effect imprisoned and consigned to starvation; not even the artisans were able to eke out more than a miserable living. Nonetheless, Jews toiled without rest, existing as best they could. Now that the hand of the enemy is upon them, their homes are destroyed, their clothing is gone, and there is not even food for the babes and sucklings, who are wandering in the streets. Fear is pervasive—the pogroms[2] may start again—so even those who do have something left are afraid to begin over again in their businesses or crafts. This horrible outbreak has frightened even those who were not personally attacked: Some are brokenhearted for their brethren and others live in unrelieved terror that the calamity may afflict them too. Who knows how long it will be before confidence is restored among these frightened souls? Everything happened so suddenly and seemingly without warning.

But were there really no thunderclouds in the sky before? Did tens of thousands become Jew-haters overnight and join quite spontaneously in a lynch mob? Every sensible person knows that it did not happen that way—such an attack could not have come to pass without considerable and prolonged preparation. Everyone must ask: Why were the Jews so blind as not to see the evil coming? Why were they so complacent when the sword was being brandished before their faces? But the fact is that for many years our "prophets" so lulled us that we no longer saw reality and failed to anticipate the evil. If anyone had told the Jews of Russia of the impending disaster even a month before it came, he would have been mocked as a madman. Nonetheless any intelligent person could have foreseen that it would not be long in coming. (I regret to say that my frequent written and verbal predictions about the imminence of the evil have come true. Three months before the pogroms I said in the editorial offices of the periodicals *Raswiet* and *Russki Yevrei*, and elsewhere, that it would not be long before they started persecuting the Jews with a vengeance. And I stated unequivocally: Before you start dealing with the question of Jewish rights, first see about securing your life and property. Their answer was: Oh, we won't worry about that. Such a thing will never happen in our country. The government won't even allow the vandals to lift their heads. And so on. But sad events have proved who was right.)

The actual attack on the Jews has only just begun, but it has been in preparation for many years. The real source of all this is the anti-Jewish venom which has filled most of the Russian press and periodicals for the last twenty years. Every sort of invective has been flung at us; the whole gamut of imaginable sins, deceits, and wickednesses has been ascribed to us. The blood libel was revived and blown up to major proportions, for articles and books were written to prove that Jews drink the blood of Christian children. Is it any wonder that after twenty years of incitement to plunder, to pillage, and even to kill, these words gradually bore fruit?

During all this time the Jewish philanthropists in Russia were pre-occupied with *Haskalah*,[3] in imitation of the German Jews. They, too, were foolish enough to believe that the way of enlightenment would bring them success and honor. If they would only reach a high level of enlightenment, the gentiles would accept them with respect and brotherly love, and troublemakers would no longer attack them. Those few whose money had brought them position, and for whom all doors were open, no longer suffered like their brethren; they imagined that they were really secure and that they had no reason for fear. They repeated aloud with the anti-Semites: Yes, Jews are lending money at interest, plundering the land, and are estranged from its people. It is up to us to mend our ways and then we will enjoy peace. Every charge made by the Jew-haters has thus been repeated without change by some of our own brethren. Is it any surprise, therefore, that these uncircumcised of heart did not attempt to prevent the disaster and were not aroused to come to the rescue of their people in its time of trouble? On the contrary, we can be sure that their ilk have been, and always will be, a stumbling block and a plague to the whole House of Israel.

II

TO OUR SHAME and sorrow we must admit that there is no peace and unity among us. We were weak within—therefore our strength was little in the day of evil. Would this have happened had we believed in our hearts that the ten million Jewish souls belonged to one nation? Every person in his right senses would reply: No! Why are we treated like this? Because we have sunk so low that our self-respect has died—because we have come to like charity flung at us in disgrace and contempt.

We have no sense of national honor; our standards are those of second-class people. We find ourselves rejoicing when we are granted a favor and exulting when we are tolerated and befriended. Jewish writers sing aloud for joy when a Jew happens to be honored. They do not tire of praising the graciousness of this or that gentile who overcomes his pride and makes some slight gesture toward a Jew. Alas for such kindness and tolerance and alas for our writers, poets, and speakers who praise them. What is the real sadness of our estate? It is not the woes inflicted on us by our enemies but the wounds caused by our own brethren. If we really want to help the victims of the pogroms, we must first proclaim unceasingly that we ourselves are responsible for our own inner weakness. We must turn from the path of disaster we once chose, for we can still be saved. Even at this late hour perhaps light can still come.

III

AT PRESENT our enemies in Russia are venting their rage by demanding that the Jews leave the country.[4] This horrifies our brethren even more than all the disasters that have befallen us. But is it so wrong even for a Jew to say: Why should we not emigrate, if the government allows it? An individual may have valid reason for fearing emigration, but why should the community as a whole resent the very idea?

A policy of reducing the number of Jews in the countries where they are hated can be successful only if substantial segments of the Jewish communities emigrate. Those who leave will certainly be improving their lot, and those who remain, having become a smaller group, would be less liable to persecution. We can be sure that money will not be lacking for so important a project. Some years ago, when it was believed that the future of the Jews in Russia lay in establishing themselves in farming settlements, people donated generously to those projects.[5] It is all the more likely that everyone will contribute as much as possible to the great enterprise of emigration, which is now clearly the only hopeful policy.

There is no doubt that it would be best for people who are leaving one country to migrate together to the same new land, for they could then understand and help one another. If the wave of emigration is to direct itself to one place, surely no other country in the world is conceivable except Eretz Israel.[6]

IV

ERETZ ISRAEL! Just a few short years ago this word was derided by almost all Jews except those who wished to be buried there. In recent years, however, the idea of establishing agricultural settlements in that country occurred to some individuals who were concerned with the welfare of their people. They wished to demonstrate that the land could be made prosperous, and they hoped that gradually the eyes of those living in poverty in the lands of dispersion would be opened to the life-giving possibilities of the Land of Israel. But this important project was practically without result. In the first place, only very few believed in it, while the heart of the Jewish people remained untouched, and even the few believers had to contend with an array of enemies. Their most bitter opponents were those people in the Holy Land who oppressed and ruled over their brethren by controlling the distribution of alms. These were afraid of losing their power if any success were to come to a plan of helping Jewish farmers to earn their bread. They feared that idleness and dependence on the alms they controlled would come to an end, thus breaking their power.

A number of years therefore passed and nothing was achieved. The enemies of Zion were able to assert that there could be no hope of getting bread out of the land which God had cursed, making it barren and unproductive till the end of days. However, even though no practical results were achieved, the idea of Jewish settlement in Eretz Israel did not disappear, for it has at last evoked much interest and reflection. There is hope that it will yet develop into something more than a pious wish. The number is not small, at present, of those who understand the implicit advantages of Jewish settlement in Eretz Israel.

It is useless to try to convince those Jews who hate Zion and Jerusalem, and whose sole wish is to make us forget the memory of our ancestors, our beliefs, and our sense of kinship. Having destroyed our traditions and mocked and derided the whole heritage of Israel, why should they spare the Land from their venom? It is also useless to argue with those who wait for a day of miraculous Redemption and who are afraid to approach the Holy Land until that day, lest they appear to be blasphemous. We can only say to such people that we intend neither to attempt to force the arrival of the Messiah, nor to establish our Kingdom now. We seek only to provide bread, in a land in which there is hope that those who labor on it will find rest.

We will address ourselves to the sensible people who do not belong to either of these extremes—to those who feel for their brethren and are willing to make sacrifices on the altar of love for their people. Such people will listen, understand, act, and succeed. We shall tell them that there is no other land that will lovingly accept the exiles save the Land of Israel, and that only there can they find truth and lasting peace.

Many experts—non-Jews—have investigated this land and distinguished English explorers have been sent to travel in the country and study it. They have established that the land is very good and that, if cultivated with skill and diligence, it could support fourteen million people. Even if we assume some exaggeration (though in truth there is none) and that there is room for only half that number, Eretz Israel can nonetheless contain all those who might wish to take refuge there. Not all Jews will go there—only those who are destitute or persecuted will look for a place to which to emigrate. It would be enough if only one million of our brethren would go, for it would be a relief both to them and to those remaining in the lands of the dispersion.

Eretz Israel has considerable advantages for our purposes over other countries, such as North or South America:

1. *Those who cherish the memory of their ancestors will gladly go there, if they can be assured that they will make a living.*

2. *The country is not too distant from their former homes.*

3. All the emigrants could live together in the manner of their accustomed traditions.

4. Those who now live in idleness in the Land of Israel will gradually acquire a new spirit, which will lead them to a life of productive labor. Thousands will therefore be saved from all the evils which such idleness creates.

5. Not everyone will have to work on the land, for if some turn to agriculture, the others can successfully devote themselves to commerce. Every sensible person would agree that had Eretz Israel remained in the hands of the Jews it would long since have become a center of commerce linking Europe with Asia and Africa.

6. Settlers could prosper by establishing factories for glass and allied products, for the sand of the country is of high quality.

In a country in which it is possible to make a living from farming, commerce, and industry, there is reason to hope that those who settle there will succeed. In the course of time no propaganda will be required to induce people to go there, for many will wish to avail themselves of the possibility of a peaceful and dignified existence.

Our Jewish philanthropists should therefore not tarry, if they really want to help their less fortunate brethren. They should hasten to buy land and let Jews settle on it to begin a new life. We can be sure that money will not be lacking, if only men of sufficient vision can be found to initiate this project in the right spirit, with a desire to help their people. In all countries there exist such Jews, many more than we know of, who strive to help their people with all their might and main. Only one thing is lacking—a united purpose. As soon as we succeed in achieving unity for this great work, fruition will not be long in coming.

The idea of Jewish settlement in the Land of Israel must now become the chief topic of conversation among all those who love their people. They must arouse their friends and propagandize the entire Jewish community. It is now too early to tell what steps may be necessary to realize this project and what will be its ultimate results. Now is the time to spread this idea, and to raise funds to help settle those who will go to Eretz Israel. And now for the sake of resettlement in Zion, let us neither be still nor quiet until the light dawns and causes our healing to begin.

THE HASKALAH OF BERLIN (1883)

IN SPEAKING of the *Haskalah* of Berlin, I am referring to the vicious and corrupt doctrine that emanated from that city. Its aim was not to cultivate knowledge for its own sake but to cast off Judaism and replace it with "enlightenment." The example was set by the exponents and high priests of this doctrine—men without wisdom, who understood neither the past nor the future and did not comprehend the present either. They advanced the strange and preposterous theory that the cause of all our suffering and travail is our rejection of enlightenment; we need only to accept and cherish western civilization for the sun of righteousness to dawn upon us. What the "enlighteners" failed to see is that the Jews had not fled into caves and catacombs at the sight of hands of friendship; on the contrary, whenever a hand had been stretched out toward the Jews, it had always betokened attack, disaster, prison, and dungeon. The Jews had never refused to till, reap, and plant—they had been prevented by force from doing so. Hatred had never originated with the Jews—they had always been its targets.

The program of this Haskalah was not simply to awaken a desire for learning and knowledge among our people. Its basic intention, which was presented as the very word of God, was quite different and quite simple: "Imitate the gentiles." The Haskalah of Berlin rested on this keystone: to imitate the gentiles, to abandon our own traditions, to disdain our own manners and ideas, and to conduct ourselves both at home and without—in the synagogue, within our families, everywhere—in imitation of others. As a reward for such a great achievement, so these upright and wise teachers assured us, our children, or our children's children, or their children, would be accepted as equals.

The consequences of this doctrine were: first, the destruction of the sentiment which is the unifying principle and strongest foundation of the House of Israel—that *we are a nation*; and, second, the abandonment of the hope of redemption. For the exponents of the Haskalah of Berlin our nationhood was a serious stumbling block; an existing Jewish national patriotism would be a bar to assimilation, and the memory of the land and sovereignty that once were ours, together with a continuing hope that they be restored, make us a nation. As long as the memory of the past and the hope for the future were still alive, how could they say to the Jews: Abandon your own traditions and follow blindly in the paths of the gentiles? It was therefore necessary to cut every root of this tree of life.

They succeeded in denationalizing Jewry and in teaching it to mimic, apelike, the life around it, but nonetheless their dream did not materialize. These prophets of Haskalah had the audacity to assert over and over again that the contempt in which they continued to be held as Jews was caused by their brethren in nearby lands, through their persistent rejection of the way of Haskalah. Such assertions fanned flames of hatred among German Jews against their brethren; the Jews of Germany were utterly convinced that they were suffering for the sins of the east European Jews.

The two strong pillars which supported the House of Israel, the hope of redemption and the love of Jews for one another, were thus toppled. A false doctrine, that religion is the keystone of the House of Israel, was substituted. But this stone, too, crumbled into dust; the very people who paid all this lip service to religion contemned it and spurned all religious customs and laws because they were different from the ways of the gentiles. Yes indeed, our "enlighteners" performed miracles! They remind one of the great miracle that was performed by a wonder-working rebbe:[7] A cripple came to him and begged for help. "Throw away your right crutch!" the wonder-worker commanded. The poor man did so, and with great difficulty supported himself on the other crutch. "Throw away the other crutch!" the wonder-worker ordered. The cripple complied, and the crowd was amazed to see that, upon discarding his crutches—he fell and could not arise. This was exactly, in every detail, the miracle worked by the exponents of this Haskalah. They first commanded us to throw away any vestige of the love of our people. The House of Israel then struggled with all its might to support itself on the pillar of religion. But they proceeded to destroy it too and the House of Israel collapsed completely. Its spirit fell to the ground because nothing remained of any of the distinguishing features for the sake of which it is called Israel. When the spirit failed, the body also gradually disintegrated. In their haste to catch up with the gentiles so as to embrace and imitate them, the Jews failed to see that the enemy would attack them from the rear and rain death down upon them.

LET IT BE UNDERSTOOD that we must declare war not against the Haskalah in general, for it is a good thing which the leading spirits of our people accepted wholeheartedly even before the exponents of the Haskalah of Berlin arose, and which intelligent people still accept. Our quarrel is with this particular Haskalah. Let us define this Haskalah clearly so that we do not confuse it with anything else. These are its teachings: (1) to adopt the ways of the gentiles; (2) to transform beyond recognition all that we have inherited from our ancestors; (3) to cast off all bonds of love and group solidarity, so that we may become assimilated; (4) to abandon all hope of return to a life of dignity in our own land, the way in which all other nations live, and go on being wretched and rootless wanderers for all eternity; (5) utterly to eradicate the Hebrew language, the tongue which unites us and enables us to hear one another's cries of woe to the ends of our dispersion; (6) only to seek the favor of the other nations and shy away from whatever does not please them, even if by so doing we will fragmentize Jewry into sects and parties; (7) to be assured that by acceptance of the Haskalah we will gain the love of the gentiles and that through the Haskalah we will rise to new heights and enjoy equality; (8) to delude ourselves with false hope and speak of peace when there is no peace; (9) to accept on our heads all the sins ever ascribed to us by our enemies, to justify our persecutors, and, instead of seeking ways of saving ourselves, to seek only to "mend our ways" and to redress wrongs we have not committed; (10) not to dare speak of our virtues, lest our enemies accuse us of boasting of qualities we do not really possess. These are the "ten commandments" issued to us by the Haskalah of Berlin in place of the Torah and the wisdom of which it has robbed us; these are the characteristics by which the Haskalah may be recognized by all who wish to turn away from it and remove the stumbling blocks it has put in our path. . . .

Some ask the nonsensical question: What will we do after we have turned our backs on the Haskalah? Will we go back to the old ghetto education and to letting our youth rot in the academies of the Talmud?[8] These questioners do not really understand the subject we are discussing: We are not fighting the Haskalah, which is only an abstract term, but the corrupt doctrine its high priests have propagated in its name. . . .

They have taught that it is our duty to adopt the ways of the gentiles.

We will utterly ignore this notion, for we will choose what is best for us: the ways leading to unity and group solidarity. If we are united, our strength will grow; divided, we will fall away one by one and never rise again.

They have striven to remove all the bonds of love and solidarity which unite our people so that it should become assimilated among the gentiles. We know that this is nonsense, for assimilation is impossible without conversion. Therefore let all who refuse to become assimilated desist from a foolish policy, which can only serve to estrange our people from its spirit and which will not win us acceptance among the gentiles.

In assuring us that, as a reward for "enlightenment," we would be able to establish our homes wherever we happened to be, they have told us to abandon all hope of returning to our own land and living there in dignity, as all peoples do. And we, having seen that all this did not get us anywhere, and that it did not even help us secure the love we sought—*we* declare: Only a dog neither has nor wants a home. A man who chooses to live his whole life as a transient, without a thought for the establishment of a permanent home for his children, will forever be regarded as a dog. And we must seek a home with all our hearts, our spirit, our soul. If we succeed in reviving this desire in the heart of every one of us, then we may hope that in time men of action will arise among the desirers who will realize this dream. We must raise our hope of redemption on high as a banner—only those who hold fast to it belong to Israel—to those who would establish its house.

ELIEZER BEN-YEHUDAH   1858-1923

ELIEZER BEN-YEHUDAH will be remembered longest for his crucial role in the revival of modern Hebrew as a language of everyday speech. His purely literary legacy is small and, except for his very earliest essays, of little importance. Nonetheless, he was the first to state, and to incarnate in a significant career, a main "messianic" theme of Zionism—the notion that the Jews must end their peculiar history by becoming a modern, secular nation.

Ben-Yehudah was born as Eliezer Perlman (he Hebraized his name in 1879 in the signature to his first published essay and so it remained) in Lushki, in the Lithuanian province of the Russian empire, and received the traditional ghetto education, including some adolescent years at the yeshivah in Polotsk. At the age of fifteen he took the important step of leaving the yeshivah to enter a scientific high school in Dvinsk. In these days the schools of intermediate and higher education in Russia were hotbeds of various kinds of revolutionary thought, and the young Perlman was therefore not unusual in accepting, in turn, the programs of the *Narodniki* (the Russian back-to-the-people movement) and of the bomb-throwing Nihilists. Nonetheless, despite this radical break with his past, he continued to have sufficient interest in Hebrew letters to read *Hashahar*, Smolenskin's journal, and to react to the theories of cultural nationalism that were being formulated by the editor.

The late 1870's brought a change in the temper of Russian public life and popular literature. The Bulgarians had revolted against Turkey and were supported by the Russians, who regarded it as a holy war in aid of their Slavic brothers. Russian nationalism and Pan-Slavism therefore came to the forefront, and this new atmosphere evoked thoughts of Jewish secular, political nationalism in Ben-Yehudah. He decided to migrate to Paris to study medicine and then establish himself in Palestine. From there he sent his first essay to *Hashahar*; this piece started a debate between him and Smolenskin (the excerpt be-

low represents Ben-Yehudah's second rejoinder in this interchange).
Ben-Yehudah fell ill of tuberculosis in Paris and his hopes of a career
as a physician came to naught. After a period in the warmer climate of
Algiers he did succeed in moving to Jerusalem in 1881, where he lived,
except for four years in America during the First World War, until his
death in 1923.

Upon arrival in Jerusalem, he and his wife established the first
household in which only modern Hebrew was spoken. This resolve,
from which neither abuse nor abject poverty could swerve him, led
naturally to Ben-Yehudah's greatest work, the publication of his
Hebrew dictionary in many volumes. (Five appeared during his lifetime, three more within several years after his death, and the rest—
based in part on his incomplete manuscript—are presently being completed.) He was constrained to search the classic literature in Hebrew
for terms to be used in everyday life, especially in the light of modern
technology, and to invent what he could not find. As natural corollary
of these labors, he was cofounder, and the first president, of the Academy for the Hebrew Language (*Vaad Ha-Lashon*).

Ben-Yehudah was uncompromising in his hatred of Yiddish and all
other substitutes for Hebrew as the only language of the Jew. Intellectually he is an important ancestor of Zionism as secular messianism;
his career in Jerusalem, marked by many squabbles with the orthodox,
prefigured the still simmering *Kulturkampf* of our day between religion and secularism in Israel.

A LETTER OF BEN-YEHUDAH (1880)

29 Kislev, 5641, Algazir

TO THE PUBLISHER OF *Hashahar:*[1] Greetings!

May I, sir, submit some comments to you relative to your essay,
"The Jewish Question—A Question of Life." I have no idea, sir, what
you may add on this subject in the coming issues of *Hashahar*, but
your basic thesis seems clear from the introductory section that I have
read. I have, therefore, presumed to analyze your essay and to send you

my critical comments, in the certainty that you would not take my counterarguments amiss and would publish them in *Hashahar*.

In this article, sir, you have yourself destroyed all that you have laboriously created in the past decade. Until today, sir, you have been true to the doctrine of redemption, which has been the recurring principal theme of all your writings—so much so, that in one of your books you expressed the conviction that whoever abandons this hope, thereby ceases to be a Jew; you have striven to rebuild the ruins of our people, and you have inveighed against the "Enlightenment of Berlin" and its progenitors for having banished the hope of their people's redemption from the hearts of all their followers. For the last ten years you, sir, have dedicated yourself to this task and you have remained unmoved by the most violent attacks; and yet, now, in this latest essay, you sound like a man whose horizon is bounded entirely by the present, who has despaired of the redemption of his people, and who has no faith in its future.

For, if we may indeed still hope for redemption, if we have not yet despaired of becoming a "living nation," our thinking must be guided by the vision of what this people will become, once its renaissance is achieved. Today we may be moribund, but tomorrow we will surely awaken to life; today we may be in a strange land, but tomorrow we will dwell in the land of our fathers; today we may be speaking alien tongues, but tomorrow we shall speak Hebrew. This is the meaning of the hope of redemption, and I know no other; our hope is for redemption, in its clear and literal sense, not for some veiled and oversubtle substitute. If the hope for such a redemption inspires you, as well—if you, too, envisage such a future for our people—why did you come to the conclusion that the Hebrew language is dead, unusable for all the arts and sciences, and suitable only for "matters pertaining to Israel's heritage?"

Were I not a believer in the redemption of the Jewish people, I would have discarded Hebrew as a useless impediment. I would then agree that the *Maskilim*[2] of Berlin were right in saying that the Hebrew language has purpose only as a bridge to enlightenment. Having despaired of redemption, they could see no other use for this language. For—permit me, sir, to ask you—what is the Hebrew language to a man who is no more a Hebrew? Is it more to him than Latin or Greek? Why should he learn the Hebrew language or read its renascent literature? Why, indeed, must the "Science of Judaism" be expressed only in Hebrew? Of what value, in fact, is such a science? How can a science which can be discussed only in its original language be worthy of being called knowledge? Where is there a people whose learning and wisdom can be expressed only in its own language?

I am aware that your motives, sir, in adopting such a position are of the highest. You saw our youth abandoning the tongue of their ancestors, so you quickly developed arguments calculated to put an end to this evil. You therefore struck out on a new path and asserted a new theory—that we are a *spiritual* nation and that our life is different from the lives of all other peoples, for Israel's life is only in its spirit, this spirit is only in its Torah, and this Torah can be expressed only in the people's own language; and, therefore, if we forsake our language, we forsake our spirit—and, by so doing, we would be doomed to death!

However, for your theory to stand, all these assumptions must be true: that we are a spiritual people, that our spirit is only in our Torah, and that our Torah can be expressed only in our tongue. But on what, sir, do you base all your assumptions?

In your desire to save your nation from the deadly bite of the Maskilim of Berlin, you created these assumptions in your own keen mind. You heard the Maskilim of Berlin say: No people can survive without a land of its own; we dwell on foreign soil, therefore we are no people. You hastened to counter by crying out: That is a lie! The Jewish people is different from all other peoples. The political realm is indispensable to the lives of all other nations, but the Jewish people lives in the realm of the spirit. Its spirit, as expressed in its Torah, is its kingdom. Despite exile from its homeland, the Jewish people will survive, for its spirit and Torah remain with it; it will live as long as the spirit itself. You supported your thesis with a further argument: If I am wrong, we should brand the prophet Jeremiah a traitor and a renegade, for he undermined the morale of the army and even wanted to be taken by the enemy. After Nebuchadnezzar destroyed the prophet's fatherland, he wrote to the people in exile: "Build houses and dwell in them, plant gardens and eat their fruit . . . for you will not soon be redeemed . . ."[3] You have maintained, however, that the prophet's actions can be considered correct only if Israel is a people of the spirit, with a national life depending not on its land but on its spirit, for Jeremiah knew that this spirit would be strengthened in exile, that the heart of the people would be purified, and that it would no longer worship strange gods.

But, sir, only such a keen mind as yours could have conceived such wondrous theories. Even if we were to admit that all your arguments are true, do you really think that they would help your people? Is it not evident to you, sir, that if your opinions were to prevail among the entire Jewish people, they would harm it more than all the evil that has heretofore beset it? Were I not convinced that many causes brought about the destruction of our land, I would not hesitate to declare unequivocally that it was Jeremiah who destroyed his native land and handed it over to strangers! He did it unwittingly, for perhaps he really did think as you do, but are we any better off for his having done this unwittingly rather than willfully? Was there any difference in the degree of catastrophe when Nebuchadnezzar entered the gates of Jerusalem because of the *error* of Jeremiah than when Titus entered its gates because of the *treason* of Josephus Flavius? Did Isaiah I and II also think as Jeremiah? Did Zerubbabel and Nehemiah share his opinions? Did the sages of the Talmud follow Jeremiah's lead when they asserted: Whoever lives outside of Eretz Israel is like a man without a God?[4]

Let me, however, lay aside those very far-off days, as it is extremely difficult for a man to assess the events of some twenty-five hundred years ago, especially since only the words of Jeremiah remain from those times, while the words of the other prophets, such as Shemayahu Hanahlami, Ahab ben Kuliah, and Zidkiahu ben Maasiah, were lost without a trace.

In creating your theories your purpose was to help your people and to rekindle the loyalty of our youth to their mother nation—but will you succeed? Are opinions and arguments potent enough to contain the waters raging around us and prevent them from sweeping us away? Whether we are the people of the spirit or not makes no difference. No matter what our theoretic conclusion may be, world events will continue to develop in their own way without regard to our opinions. Can't we see that our people's end is approaching? Is the Berlin Enlightenment alone the cause bringing all this evil down upon us? Actually, even in countries where the Jews never heard of the name Moses Mendelssohn or of his teachings, Jewish youth is repeating the pattern of the Jews in Germany by turning away from its people and from the language of its forefathers. The Maskilim of Berlin wrote many books and created elaborate theories to prove that we are not a people; the Jews of all other countries, in every land where the sun of enlightenment has shone upon them, are thinking the same way, with only the difference that they do not find it necessary to waste many words in justifying themselves.

So what use is there, sir, in all this theorizing?

It is plain for all to see, sir, that our youth is abandoning our language—but why? Because in their eyes it is a dead and useless tongue.

All our efforts to make them appreciate the importance of the language to us, the Hebrews, will be of no avail. Only a Hebrew with a Hebrew heart will understand this, and such a man will understand even without our urging. Let us therefore make the language really live again! Let us teach our young to speak it, and then they will never betray it!

But we will be able to revive the Hebrew tongue only in a country in which the number of Hebrew inhabitants exceeds the number of gentiles. Therefore, let us increase the number of Jews in our desolate land; let the remnants of our people return to the land of their fathers; *let us revive the nation and its tongue will be revived, too!*

Only such an approach and position can solve all the "questions" and put an end to all the debates. Such an appeal will even compel the attention of many of those Jews who now laugh at us and think us deranged. The heart of man is moved not by reason but by emotion. We may argue all day and cry aloud that we are a people, even though we are bereft of a homeland, but all this will be futile and meaningless. We can, however, appeal to people's feelings and address ourselves to the hearts of the Jews, saying: The land of our fathers is waiting for us; let us colonize it, and, by becoming its masters, we shall again be a people like all others. Such words will be listened to attentively, for the human heart, sir, even the heart of a *Maskil*, is tender, and it is easily conquered by such an emotion.

True, the Jewish nation and its language died together. But it was not a death by natural causes, not a death of exhaustion, like the death of the Roman nation, which therefore died forever! The Jewish nation was murdered twice, both times when it was in full bloom and youthful vigor. Just as it revived after the first exile from its land, after the death of the nation that had murdered it, and rose to even higher spiritual and material estate, so now, too, after the death of the Roman nation which murdered it, it will rise even beyond what it had become before the second exile! The Hebrew language, too, did not die of exhaustion; it died together with the nation, and when the nation is revived, it will live again! But, sir, we cannot revive it with translations; we must make it the tongue of our children, on the soil on which it once blossomed and bore ripe fruit!

This people has unlimited potential! From the day it came into the world to this very day its career has been a succession of miracles; its history, its Torah and religion, and, indeed, the people as a whole are all marvels. It will therefore not be beyond the power of this people again, as once before in the days of King Cyrus, to effect the miracle of awakening to life even after its death and to revive the language that died with it!

True, sir, this is a great and difficult task, one that cannot be accomplished in a day or two, but it would be even more difficult, under modern conditions, for our people to remain alive for long on alien soil. If we have existed till now without our own land, language, and political sovereignty, it was because our religion and our whole way of life were radically different from those of all the other peoples and that difference served as a mighty fortress to preserve us. Within this circle we lived the life of a self-contained people. In those days we had a truly *Hebrew Enlightenment,* and we even possessed a national language, for our entire intellectual life was conducted in Hebrew. The present is, however, totally different. We have divested ourselves entirely of our national ornaments and we now deck ourselves in alien finery. All our arguments and efforts are foredoomed to futility, for nobody will listen to us!

I therefore contend, sir, that we have strayed from the right path. It is senseless to cry out: Let us cherish the Hebrew tongue, lest we perish! The Hebrew language can live only if we revive the nation and return it to its fatherland. In the last analysis, this is the only way to achieve our lasting redemption; short of such a solution, we are lost, lost forever! Do you, sir, think otherwise? The Jewish religion will, no doubt, be able to endure even in alien lands; it will adjust its forms to the spirit of the place and the age, and its destiny will parallel that of all religions! But the nation? The nation cannot live except on its own soil; only on this soil can it revive and bear magnificent fruit, as in days of old!

Therefore, we must turn our attention to what this people will be in "the end of days," lest the miraculous day that I envisage come and find us unprepared.

With this remark, sir, I will bring my letter to a close. In all that I have said, sir, it was your spirit speaking in me, for you were the first of the Maskilim to raise the banner of hope for redemption and to preach this doctrine courageously to all of our Maskilim. You did not fear that you might be called insane or fanatical, and your efforts have not been in vain. Your words have borne fruit, implanting in the hearts of many of our youth a holy plant, the plant of national feeling. This letter of mine is really the fruit of your labor, and I therefore hope that you, sir, will find it not unpleasing.

MOSHE LEIB LILIENBLUM   1843-1910

GHETTO CULTURE and talmudic piety, religious reform, secularization, the revolutionary movements struggling against the tsar, and the new nationalism—these were the major clashing values of Jewish life in Russia in the turbulent years between 1860 and 1900. Except for spiritual nationalism, which he opposed in the versions of both Smolenskin and Ahad Ha-Am, Lilienblum ran the gamut of these ideas in a career which, more than any other, exemplifies the history of this seminal age.

Born in Keidany in 1843, he became a sufficient scholar of the Talmud to spend five years (1864–1869) teaching in the yeshivah in Vilkomir. During this period he read considerably in the current literature of the Haskalah, which was heavily opposed to the rigors of talmudic legalism. Lilienblum became convinced that moderate religious reforms were necessary in order to harmonize religion with the spirit of the age. The publication of these views brought down upon him the inevitable anger of the orthodox, who could not allow their children to be influenced by such heresies. His friends avoided him and his family was little help. His only moral support came from an "enlightened" young woman in Vilkomir, in whom he became romantically involved, but that merely complicated his situation, for, as was the custom of the ghetto, he had been married since the age of sixteen.

Like Smolenskin a few years earlier, in 1869 he fled to Odessa, the mecca of the modernists, in the hopes of acquiring a thorough secular education. He soon came under the influence of the Russian positivists, D. I. Pisarev and G. G. Chernyshevsky, and completely lost his religious faith and all interest in abstract ideas. Nothing mattered now except the destiny of the individual in the most practical terms. The transition from such ideas to socialism was not a great step, and so, by the end of the 1870's, Lilienblum had passed from complete despair of the Jewish people to utter devotion to his secular studies in the high school, in which he was preparing himself for entrance into the university, and to a belief in the class struggle as the only hope of a better future for all mankind.

The determining break in Lilienblum's life came with the pogroms of 1881. Lilienblum devoted the rest of his life to the Zionist movement. He was a significant figure in the practical labors of the Hibbat Zion organization, the group which came into being under the impact of the events of 1881 to foster Jewish colonization in Palestine. When political Zionism arose with the appearance of Theodor Herzl, Lilienblum became one of his most active supporters in Russia.

It is regrettable that Lilienblum is almost entirely unknown in English. Within the framework of this volume, we could include selections representing only his last thirty years, i.e., his Zionist phase. Lilienblum appears here in quotations from his diary of 1881, under the shock of the pogroms which led to his nationalist resolve; in the broad-guaged views which asked all shades of opinion and belief to compromise in order to join in the labor of creating a nation in Palestine; and in his analysis of anti-Semitism, which convinced Lilienblum that outside his own land the Jew would have no future even in any liberal new world order of the morrow.

THE WAY OF RETURN (1881)

MARCH 20. The local periodical reported that the masses are ready to attack the Jews during the approaching Easter holiday. Apparently the anti-Semites are not satisfied with the famine that is ravaging the Jews in their Pale of Settlement[1] and are inciting the masses to loot and pillage. But why do they labor in vain to bring back their beloved Middle Ages, for that age will never return!

April 10. The disturbing rumors about anti-Jewish outbreaks are growing stronger, and the governor has seen fit to post notices throughout the city to the effect that if any one tries to disturb the peace and order of the city, he, the governor himself, will immediately cut off all services and have the agitators court-martialed.

April 17. Shocking reports from the city of Elizabethgrad. Riots, pillaging—the heart fails. What is this?

April 28. Reports as shocking as those from Elizabethgrad now come from Kiev and other cities.

May 5. Terrible! The situation is terrible and frightening! We are virtually under siege. The courtyards are barred up, and we keep peering through the grillwork of the court gates to see if the mob is coming to swoop down on us. All the furniture is stored in cellars, we all sleep in our clothes and without any bedding (also stored in the cellars), so that if we are attacked we will immediately be able to take the small children, who also sleep in their clothes, and flee. But will they let us flee? What does the future have in store for us? Will they have mercy on the youngsters—who don't even know yet that they are Jews, that they are wretches—and not harm them? Terrible, terrible! How long, O God of Israel? . . .

May 7. I am glad I have suffered. The rioters approached the house I am staying in. The women shrieked and wailed, hugging the children to their breasts, and didn't know where to turn. The men stood by dumfounded. We all imagined that in a few moments it would be all over with us. . . . But, thank God, they were frightened away by the soldiers and we were not harmed. I am glad I have suffered. At least once in my life I have had the opportunity of feeling what my ancestors felt every day of their lives. Their lives were one long terror, so why should I experience nothing of that fright which they felt all their lives? I am their son, their sufferings are dear to me, and I am exalted by their glory.

Undated. In September I discontinued my studies at the Gymnasium.[2]

Those intoxicated with *haskalah*, of whom there are still many among us, will taunt me with my letter of August 4, 1877, in which I said: "I solemnly swear . . . to the last drop of blood in me that I must complete some course of studies. Even if the doctors tell me that because of all the work involved I will come down with tuberculosis, and that within two days after completing my studies I will die—I still will not stop." *And now I have abandoned the cause*—for no apparent reason, out of what the "enlighteners" would regard as womanish timidity. But I say to them: In 1877 I thought: "My life is meaningless; for I cannot live like a human being if I lack high culture and formal education." At the end of 1881 I was inspired by a sublime ideal, and I became a different man, full of a sense of purpose and spiritual satisfaction, even without secular schooling.

When I became convinced that it was not a lack of high culture that was the cause of our tragedy—for aliens we are and aliens we shall remain even if we become full to the brim with culture; when my eyes were opened by the new ideal, and my spirit rose to a new task, in which, if all goes well, lies our eternal salvation—all the old ideals left me in a flash. Disdainfully I forsook my studies and threw myself completely into preparing myself to serve this new lofty ideal, though I did not yet know how I would serve it. For, basically, I could not then consider any other métier than writing articles, and the well from which articles are drawn does, after all, run dry. But how sweet and dear this idea became to me! All my life I had grieved over the decline of Jewish nationality and the thought that Jewry's existence as a nation was doomed. And now there lies before me a straight and sure path to the everlasting salvation of our people and its nationhood, a path to which the imperatives of life have brought me; and the salvation—I did not know whence and how it could come to us—stands before me in all its glory!

LET US NOT CONFUSE THE ISSUES (1882)

THE AUTHOR of the essay "Our Redemption,"[3] whose words are followed avidly by all who know him, was in this case beside the point. In speaking of the ingathering of the exiles and the settlement of Eretz Israel, which is our only haven in this time of trouble, he confused this issue—which is plainly and simply a matter of life and without whose solution we are doomed as a people—with a relatively minor side issue, that of religious reform. For all the importance of this question, I cannot for one moment regard its solution an indispensable condition for settling the question of Eretz Israel, which, in other words, is: Are the Jews to be a living people or not? In face of this question all the others pale into insignificance.

The nation as a whole is dearer to all of us than all the divisions over rigid orthodoxy or liberalism in religious observance put together. Where the nation is concerned there are no sects or denominations, there are neither modern nor old-fashioned men, no devout or heretics, but all are Children of Abraham, Isaac, and Jacob! Any one of Jewish seed who does not forsake his people is a Jew in every sense of the word. It has been well said that just as people do not have identical faces so are they not of one mind. There is no logic in any desire for all the future Jewish settlers in the ancestral land to belong to the exact same sect. Let each man there follow the dictates of his conscience; let the *Hasidim*[4] there put on two sets of *tephillin*,[5] and let the more liberal recite the *Shema*[6] and say the prayers where they will without *tephillin*; let the orthodox send their children to the *hadarim* they will establish there in the image of the *hadarim*[7] of Lithuania and Poland, and let the *Maskilim*[8] set up schools patterned after the secular schools of Europe. But let no man oppress his fellow. *Within our autonomous political life everything will find its place.*

Yes, let no man oppress his fellow. Let the orthodox know that *we are all holy*, every one of us—unbelievers and orthodox alike, we have been laying down our lives for the Sanctification of the Name for a whole year now, we are likely to continue laying down our lives for a long time to come, and we cannot see an end to it in the land in which we now live. For about a year now we have been as fish in the sea: our property has been freely looted, our homes have been booty, our honor held cheap, our wives and children put to shame, and our lives have been at the mercy of the oppressor. Every Sunday, on every Christian holiday, dread fills us. We always ask: What will tomorrow bring? Day and night we live in mortal terror. . . . All this has befallen us all, orthodox and freethinkers alike, and we have not betrayed our origins nor lost our courage; nor will we, in the days to come, swerve from the path of the God of Israel. God is in our hearts and our people is as a seal on our right arm—we will not renounce them when peace is restored. Is this not self-sacrifice for the Sanctification of the Name? Is not our entire community holy? Let the orthodox know that we are one with them in travail. All the plans and schemes that keep coming up for the salvation of our people originate with the Maskilim and the freethinkers. For brothers we have been and brothers we will remain for all eternity. Let each man conduct his private affairs as he sees fit, but let our national unity not be impaired.

But I must also caution our brethren the Maskilim and freethinkers against dividing Jewry into two camps by introducing the forbidden foods[9] or doing away with the ritual bath,[10] for the orthodox will refuse to eat in their homes or to marry among them. There is no doubt that if the liberals practice restraint, our orthodox brethren will be tolerant, and there will be peace among the Jews at this critical time. What reason cannot achieve, time will. Let all Jewry know that the true way of the Torah is not contention and civil war, and what

God favors ultimately emerges victorious. It has always been thus. There was a bitter battle between the worshipers of Baal and the worshipers of the one God, and in the end truth overcame falsehood and idolatry was wiped out in Israel. There was a long-drawn quarrel between the Sadducees and the Pharisees,[11] in which much blood was shed—to no avail. Finally, without any internal war, truth overcame falsehood and the Sadducees vanished. The Karaites[12] renounced the authority of the rabbis—and achieved nothing, for more than a thousand years later only an infinitesimal number remains, those whom the enemy did not kill off along with our own. Now the orthodox have a quarrel with the Maskilim. Let each and every one of them be assured that quarrel and hatred do not help truth overcome falsehood. Falsity vanishes of its own and truth is destined to win the day.

Let all special questions, whether religious or economic in nature, take second place to the general question, to the sole and simple aim that Israel be "saved by the Lord with an everlasting salvation." Unite and join forces; let us gather our dispersed from eastern Europe and go up to our land with rejoicing; whoever is on the side of God and His people, let him say: I am for Zion. To be sure, it is a great and complicated task, but is a nation born all at once? We must work for the development of our land, and we have no right to shirk this divine task. Let our men of great wealth immediately acquire property there with at least a small part of their fortunes. Since they themselves do not wish to leave their lands of residence, let each one of them at least invest a given sum in property in Eretz Israel, on which Jews who will cultivate the soil may settle, on terms agreeable to the investor. Let smaller capitalists, who are worth no less than ten thousand rubles, divide their money in half, half to remain here until the appropriate time and half to go into the purchase of land in Eretz Israel for themselves and for others, according to set terms. Let those with a minimum of one thousand rubles go to Eretz Israel now and buy land for themselves. All these people will be followed by masses who have nothing, and by numerous artisans and craftsmen. In due course, when conditions will have improved through agriculture, trade, and industry, prosperity will make it possible for the rest of our destitute to come there. So let us begin our labor. Our God, Who has sustained us and has not left us to the mercy of the lions among whom we have dwelt these thousands of years, will give us strength for our efforts to find rest.

Let us pay no heed to the renegades trying to lead us away from our fatherland. Let us not divide into *Mitnagdim*,[13] *Hasidim*, and

Maskilim. This is the land in which our fathers have found rest since time immemorial—and as they lived, so will we live. Let us go now to the only land in which we will find respite for our souls that have been harried by murderers for these thousands of years. Our beginnings will be small, but in the end we will flourish.

THE FUTURE OF OUR PEOPLE (1883)

THE OPPONENTS of nationalism see us as uncompromising nationalists, with a nationalist God and a nationalist Torah; the nationalists see us as cosmopolitans, whose homeland is wherever we happen to be well off. Religious gentiles say that we are devoid of any faith, and the freethinkers among them say that we are orthodox and believe in all kinds of nonsense; the liberals say we are conservative and the conservatives call us liberal. Some bureaucrats and writers see us as the root of anarchy, insurrection, and revolt, and the anarchists say we are capitalists, the bearers of the biblical civilization, which is, in their view, based on slavery and parasitism. Officialdom accuses us of circumventing the laws of the land—that is, of course, the laws directed specifically against us. Indeed, the latter charge has some basis in our very Torah. Yocheved, Moses' mother, did not obey Pharaoh's law; she did not cast her son into the river but hid him from the Egyptian police in the bulrushes on the river bank, so that she could bring him back home after the search for Hebrew boys was over. We are also accused of crimes against art and music. Musicians like Richard Wagner charge us with destroying the beauty and purity of music. Even our merits are turned into shortcomings: "Few Jews are murderers," they say, "because the Jews are cowards." This, however, does not prevent them from accusing us of murdering Christian children.

Civilization, which could virtually deliver us from those persecutions which have a religious basis, can do nothing at all for us against the persecutions with a nationalistic basis. Civilization demands the right for each man to follow his conscience, thus doing away with religious hatred, but no civilization in the world has the power to demand that an alien be accepted by a strange family as if he were a natural-born child of that family. Since all the work that an alien does and any job that he takes is no longer available to the members of the family, the latter can always say to the outsider: "You are causing me harm and I have no room for you, for you deprive me of my livelihood."

Indeed, there is, as yet, one community, the proletariat, which knows neither children nor aliens—only workers. But if this community should at some time and place gain power—then God protect us from such a day! We may be sure that when the mob is aroused—and evildoers are always trying to incite the mob—almost all of us will be put to the sword. We will be regarded as capitalists, and, as always, we will fill the role of the scapegoat, together with another role that has been bestowed upon us, that of a lightning rod. The self-appointed saviors of humanity among our youth, as well as the complacent who oppose the settlement of Eretz Israel, should take note of this.

Furthermore, not only can civilization and progress do nothing to eradicate anti-Semitic views, but indirectly they even help them along.

So that these words of mine should not appear to the reader as so much nonsense, I will clarify them.

It is evident that the over-all trend toward nationalism is not a regression, despite the assertions of the students of Roman cosmopolitanism; it represents progress which must ultimately do away with war and direct humanity, with all its nations, to the way of true unity. But this true civilization, i.e., the drive for national self-determination, is the very soil in which anti-Semitism flourishes—as nettles flourish in a green field, for there is no rose without thorns and no good without evil. Anti-Semitism is the shadow of our new and fine contemporary civilization; it will no more do away with anti-Semitism than the light will destroy the shadows it casts. That is why anti-Semitism is making such great strides.

We remember how, three years ago, when Marr[14] came out with his anti-Semitic doctrine, we all jeered at him, made fun of his schemes, dubbed them an "anachronism," and said that they were about four centuries behind the times. But hardly four years have passed and the anti-Semitic trend has already swept almost all of Europe. It has shaken the world with petitions, riots, arson, congresses, speeches in parliaments, and so on. What now? In Vienna the public prosecutor asked one of the anti-Semites whether he thought it would be possible to pass a law in Austria restricting the residence of Jews and imposing a sufferance tax on them, etc. The latter replied: "In another ten years it will be possible!" And it seems that he has some basis for his opinion.

Needless to say, although the old barbarism has been polished and given a new gloss in our time, our situation is today more precarious than ever before. In the Middle Ages the Jews were, for the most part, persecuted at a given time and place. When they were persecuted in one place, they were quickly able to find refuge elsewhere; when, after a while, the oppressions began in the new country, they returned to their original home, for its inhabitants had already begun to feel the loss caused by the absence of the Jews, who were virtually the only merchants. Now it is different. Communication is rapid. The nations of Europe are just as adept in all branches of commerce as the Jews, so that they no longer need us. They are therefore able to apply pressure on us wherever and whenever they will—while we, where are we to flee? Is there a single European nation, France and England included, that has during the past year accepted any appreciable number of our wretched wanderers? And France and England are countries where anti-Semitism has not yet begun to flourish, for, at present, there is no place there for a nationalist movement. If those countries were truly opposed to cosmopolitanism, then France would have to renounce completely its claims to Alsace-Lorraine, and England would have to withdraw from Ireland, Egypt, etc. But cosmopolitanism is not long for this world, even in those countries. And what are our prospects in the days to come? That is too terrible even to think about.

But what is to be done? What remedy can we find so that the Jews will once and for all cease to be material for questions, debates, accusations, and degrading defenses. How can we make them feel completely secure about the future?

We must make a visible effort, and if we do not succeed now, which seems unlikely, then we will have to try again at the first opportunity. The main thing is that we ourselves, Jews the world over, recognize beyond doubt the need for this sacred task. Let us but begin to carry it out, and success is assured. There will be no lack of funds. I have already said that a nation of eight million people can raise ten million rubles to get the work under way. It is possible, in addition, to suggest a kopek[15] collection. Whoever wants to support the national idea will contribute a kopek a week, to be saved for a given period in special boxes placed in every home, for the settlement of Eretz Israel. In a year this will add up to thousands of rubles. It is also possible to earmark given percentages of the sums donated in the synagogues, at weddings, at funerals of the rich, etc. Perhaps, too, a Jewish lottery

can be set up, so that there will be no more need for talk about
the sale of shares in stock companies and the like. In a word, it
is possible in some way or other to collect, with the permission of
the government, huge sums to buy many large holdings in Eretz Israel
from the Turkish government. The sums spent on the purchase of
large holdings will be recovered from the money paid by individuals
purchasing small lots and from the rent paid by the colonists. This,
in turn, will make possible the purchase of additional large holdings,
the building of roads, improvement of the irrigation systems, afforesta-
tion, etc.

If these ideas are not viable, there is nothing to prevent others from
presenting better plans for the settlement of Eretz Israel.

We must make a beginning, and life and experience will teach us
how to continue. This is certainly not a task for one year, or even for
one generation. We can, however, rest assured that as we increase our
efforts our strength will increase as well.

The enlightened segment of our people has become estranged from
us only because our life lacks ideals of immediate appeal to them. The
one modern ideal which we have had until now was petty and negative: to fight against our legal inequality. Let us only acquire high
positive ideals and the best of the westernized and enlightened Jews
will return to us. The masses, too, will hasten to join us. Man holds
dear whatever others attempt to steal from him: In the Middle Ages
our religion was attacked, so we held on to it with all our might; today,
when our national identity is under attack, it will again become our
most prized possession and we will shield it with the same devotion
with which our ancestors defended our faith.

Work! Lay the foundation for a normal and healthy national life
for the Jewish people, which has been persecuted in every time and
place, but has never surrendered. Give it back its home, something
which no people lacks, except the gypsies. Do not boast of stupid
notions about the mission which is ascribed to us by all the sophists.
Behold, we are scorned and derided, our blood is being let, we are
dying of hunger, we are persecuted everywhere with unbounded barbarity, the whole world contemns us—and we are offered the consolation of a mission. We are cast in the role of teachers of all mankind—the very mankind which has been beating on us so long and
so mercilessly! We have not been able to teach mankind, in more
than three thousand years, not to beat poor wanderers who are bereft
of a home and of protection—shall we teach mankind love, brotherhood, peace, etc?

Pay no heed to the desire for assimilation of our plutocrats in Paris, Berlin, St. Petersburg, and elsewhere, and to the "enlightened" among us who follow after them. Do not expect them to take the lead in this holy task. When Antiochus condemned the Jewish people to death, its salvation did not come from Jerusalem, but from the Hasmonean village of Modin. The wealthy assimilationists of that capital, together with the proud Sadducees, submitted shamefully to the insolence of the Greek hangmen. It took the true sons of the people, the unbelievably courageous Hasmonean priests, to rescue Israel, and only afterward did Jerusalem, too, join with them. The eternal glory remained, however, to the vanguard of the redemption of Israel!

There are three paths open to us:

1. *To remain in our present state, to be oppressed forever, to be gypsies, to face the prospect of various pogroms and not be safe even against a major holocaust.*

2. *To assimilate, not merely externally but completely within the nations among whom we dwell: to forsake Judaism for the religions of the gentiles, but nonetheless to be despised for many, many years, until some far-off day when descendants of ours who no longer retain any trace of their Jewish origin will be entirely assimilated among the Aryans.*

3. *To initiate our efforts for the renaissance of Israel in the land of its forefathers, where the next few generations may attain, to the fullest extent, a normal national life.*

Make your choice!

LEO PINSKER 1821-1891

PINSKER was the most assimilated among the Russian Jews who turned Zionist under the impact of the events of 1881. A passionate patriot with a career of service to prove it, he had truly believed that the Russian regime would liberalize itself into a constitutional monarchy in which all people would be equals. Because he had staked the most on his faith in Russia, and had relatively little Jewish knowledge and emotion of the traditional kind to draw on, he was even more disillusioned by the pogroms than most of his contemporaries.

The first half century of Pinsker's life, between his birth in Tomashov, in Russian Poland, in 1821 and the turning point of 1881, was unusual in the Russia of that day. There were no early years of ghetto education in his background, to be followed by a period of storm and stress as he strove toward intellectual emancipation. His father before him, the distinguished Hebrew scholar Simchah Pinsker, was already "enlightened" and he provided his son with the kind of education that was then a rarity for a young Russian Jewish boy. Leo Pinsker attended a Russian high school and, after some years of studying law in Odessa, he entered the University of Moscow, where he received a medical degree. Upon returning to Odessa, Pinsker was appointed to the staff of the local city hospital, soon became one of the leading physicians of the community, and was even honored by Tsar Nicholas I for his signal services to typhus-stricken soldiers of the Crimean War.

Parallel with his medical career, after 1860 Pinsker took a considerable interest in Jewish affairs. He wrote for the two earliest Jewish weeklies in the Russian language and was active in the affairs of the Society for the Spread of Culture among the Jews of Russia, which was founded in 1863. In that period of his life he went beyond the "enlighteners" who wrote in Hebrew by insisting that the Russian language and culture should be completely dominant in the inner life, and even the religion, of the Jew. Though these convictions were shaken by violent pogroms which broke out in Odessa during the Easter days of 1871, he nevertheless soon returned to his labors for the assimilation of Jewry within a liberal Russia.

As we have just seen, outbreaks of violence directed against them were no new phenomena in the life of Russian Jews when they occurred again in 1881. We must therefore ask the question: Why were the latter pogroms so far greater in their impact as to constitute an emotional crisis for many, Pinsker among them, and a break in modern Jewish history? There are two major reasons: their extent, and the composition of the mobs. Violence was triggered by the assassination of Tsar Alexander II in March of 1881 (ironically as he was about to grant a liberal constitution to his country). Within a few months at least 160 cities and villages were the scenes of such outrages that the American Ambassador in St. Petersburg, John W. Foster, reported to the State Department that "the acts which have been committed are more worthy of the Dark Ages than of the present century." It was all the more impossible to believe that these were only lynchings, carried out by an illiterate rabble, because leading newspapers had whipped up the frenzy, men of education and position participated in the attacks, and the government more than tacitly abetted pogromists.

On the morrow of these events Pinsker formally left the Society for the Spread of Culture, declaring that "new remedies, new ways" would have to be found. He went to central and western Europe to advocate his newly formed ideas about concentrating the bulk of Jewry in a national state, but he found no adherents. Adolph Jellinek, the Chief Rabbi of Vienna and a close friend of his father, told him, at a meeting in the spring of 1882, that he was in emotional shock and needed medical attention. Nonetheless Pinsker persisted. Upon his return to Russia he published his views anonymously in German in a pamphlet entitled *Auto-Emancipation*, the bulk of which is reprinted below. Like Herzl fifteen years later, Pinsker was sufficiently outside the influence of the traditional emotions centering around the Holy Land not to argue that a Jewish state necessarily had to be only in Zion. He regarded it as preferable if Palestine could be secured for the Jews, but the logic of his argument was that anti-Semitism had made the status of a minority untenable for the Jew anywhere and that, in order to save himself, any land suitable for a national establishment would do.

Pinsker's pamphlet was greeted with vociferous indignation in many circles. The orthodox regarded the author, who did not remain anonymous for very long, as lacking in religion, and the liberals, especially those who were outside Russia, attacked him as a traitor to the faith in the ultimate victory of humanity over prejudice and hatred. To be sure, some in the west, like the American Jewish poetess, Emma Lazarus, did greet him with approval, but his natural audience consisted of semi-modernized Russian Jews, ex-partisans of "enlightenment" like Lilienblum, whose nationalism, even in its modern guise, was nourished by the Bible and prayer book.

The personal prestige of the man and the intellectual impact of the pamphlet immediately propelled Pinsker to the foreground of the ferment toward creating a Jewish nationalist organization. Having been "Zionized" by his adherents, Pinsker became the leader of the new Hibbat Zion movement and convened its founding conference in 1884. In the decade that remained until his death in 1891 he was involved in wrangling with the orthodox within the movement over his lack of piety and in struggling to keep an organization alive for which only paltry financial support was forthcoming. Even so, a few colonies were established in Palestine and the educational impact of the movement prepared the ground for the later flowering of Zionist thought and action in eastern Europe.

The primary importance of Pinsker is not in the practical but in the intellectual realm. *Auto-Emancipation* is the first great statement of the torment of the Jew driven to assert his own nationalism because the wider world had rejected him. The theme was to recur in Theodor Herzl.

AUTO-EMANCIPATION: AN APPEAL TO HIS PEOPLE BY A RUSSIAN JEW (1882)

"If I am not for myself, who will be for me? And if not now, when?"
—Hillel

The misery caused by bloody deeds of violence has been followed by a moment of repose, and baiter and baited can breathe more easily for a time. Meanwhile the Jewish refugees are being "repatriated" with the very money that was collected to assist emigration. The Jews in the West have again learned to endure the cry of "Hep, Hep"[1] as their fathers did in days gone by. The flaming outburst of burning indignation at the disgrace endured has turned into a rain of ashes which is gradually covering the glowing soil. Close your eyes and hide your heads ostrich-fashion as you will; if you do not take advantage of the fleeting moments of repose, and devise remedies more fundamental than those palliatives with which the incompetent have for centuries vainly tried to relieve our unhappy nation, lasting peace is impossible for you.

September, 1882

I

THE ETERNAL PROBLEM presented by the Jewish question stirs men today as it did ages ago. It remains unsolved, like the squaring of the circle, but unlike it, it is still a burning question. This is due to the fact that it is not merely a problem of theoretic interest, but one of practical interest, which renews its youth from day to day, as it were, and presses more and more urgently for a solution.

The essence of the problem, as we see it, lies in the fact that, in the midst of the nations among whom the Jews reside, they form a distinctive element which cannot be assimilated, which cannot be readily digested by any nation. Hence the problem is to find means of so adjusting the relations of this exclusive element to the whole body of the nations that there shall never be any further basis for the Jewish question.

We cannot, of course, think of establishing perfect harmony. Such harmony has probably never existed, even among other nations. The millennium in which national differences will disappear, and the nations will merge into humanity, is still invisible in the distance. Until it is realized, the desires and ideals of the nations must be limited to establishing a tolerable modus vivendi.

Long will the world have to await universal peace; but in the interim the relations of the nations to one another may be adjusted fairly well by explicit understandings, by arrangements based upon international law, treaties, and especially upon a certain equality in rank and mutually admitted rights, as well as upon mutual regard.

No such equality in rank appears in the intercourse of the nations with the Jews. In the latter case the basis is lacking for that mutual regard which is generally regulated and secured by international law or by treaties. Only when this basis is established, when the equality of the Jews with the other nations becomes a fact, can the problem presented by the Jewish question be considered solved. Unfortunately, although such equality indeed existed in a long forgotten past, we can hope to see it restored only in the very remote future, for under present conditions any dream of the admission of the Jewish people into the ranks of the other nations seems illusory. It lacks most of those attributes which are the hallmark of a nation. It lacks that characteristic national life which is inconceivable without a common language, common customs, and a common land. The Jewish people has no fatherland of its own, though many motherlands; it has no rallying point, no center of gravity, no government of its own, no accredited representatives. It is everywhere a guest, and nowhere *at home*.

The nations *never* have to deal with a Jewish *nation* but always with mere *Jews*. The Jews are not a nation because they lack a certain distinctive national character, possessed by every other nation, a character which is determined by living together in one country, under one rule. It was clearly impossible for this national character to be developed in the Diaspora; the Jews seem rather to have lost all remembrance of their former home. Thanks to their ready adaptability, they have all the more easily acquired the alien traits of the peoples among whom they have been cast by fate. Moreover, to please their protectors, they often divested themselves of their traditional individuality. They acquired, or persuaded themselves that they had acquired, certain cosmopolitan tendencies which could no more appeal to others than they could bring satisfaction to the Jews themselves.

In seeking to fuse with other peoples, they deliberately renounced, to a certain extent, their own nationality. Nowhere, however, did they succeed in obtaining recognition from their neighbors as native-born citizens of equal rank.

The strongest factor, however, operating to prevent the Jews from striving after an independent national existence is the fact that they do not feel the need for such an existence. Not only do they feel no need for it, but they go so far as to deny the reasonableness of such a need.

In a sick man, the absence of desire for food and drink is a very serious symptom. It is not always possible to cure him of this ominous loss of appetite. And even if his appetite can be restored, it is still a question whether he will be able to digest food, even though he desires it.

The Jews are in the unhappy condition of such a patient. We must discuss this most important point with all possible precision. We must prove that the misfortunes of the Jews are due, above all, to their lack of desire for national independence; and that this desire must be aroused and maintained in them if they do not wish to exist forever in a disgraceful state—in a word, we must prove that *they must become a nation.*

This one apparently insignificant fact, that the Jews are not considered a separate nation by the other nations, is, to a great extent the hidden cause of their anomalous position and of their endless misery. The mere fact of belonging to this people is a mark of Cain on one's forehead, an indelible stigma which repels non-Jews and is painful to the Jews themselves. Nevertheless, for all its strangeness, this phenomenon has deep roots in human nature.

II

AMONG the living nations of the earth the Jews occupy the position of a nation long since dead. With the loss of their fatherland, the Jews lost their independence and fell into a state of decay which is incompatible with the existence of a whole and vital organism. The state was crushed by the Roman conquerors and vanished from the world's view. But after the Jewish people had yielded up its existence as an actual state, as a political entity, it could nevertheless not submit to total destruction—it did not cease to exist as a spiritual nation. Thus, the world saw in this people the frightening form of one of the dead walking among the living. This ghostlike apparition of a people without unity or organization, without land or other bond of union, no longer alive, and yet moving about among the living—this eerie form scarcely paralleled in history, unlike anything that preceded or followed it, could not fail to make a strange and peculiar impression upon the imagination of the nations. And if the fear of ghosts is something inborn, and has a certain justification in the psychic life of humanity, is it any wonder that it asserted itself powerfully at the sight of this dead and yet living nation?

Fear of the Jewish ghost has been handed down and strengthened for generations and centuries. It led to a prejudice which, in its turn, in connection with other forces to be discussed later, paved the way for Judeophobia.

Along with a number of other subconscious and superstitious ideas, instincts, and idiosyncrasies, Judeophobia, too, has become rooted and naturalized among all the peoples of the earth with whom the Jews have had intercourse. Judeophobia is a form of demonopathy, with the distinction that the Jewish ghost has become known to the whole race of mankind, not merely to certain races, and that it is not disembodied, like other ghosts, but is a being of flesh and blood, and suffers the most excruciating pain from the wounds inflicted upon it by the fearful mob who imagine it threatens them.

Judeophobia is a psychic aberration. As a psychic aberration, it is hereditary; as a disease transmitted for two thousand years, it is incurable.

It is the fear of ghosts, the mother of Judeophobia, which has evoked that abstract—I might call it Platonic—hatred because of which the whole Jewish nation is held responsible for the real or supposed misdeeds of its individual members, is libeled in so many ways, and is buffeted about so disgracefully.

Friend and foe alike have tried to explain or to justify this hatred of the Jews by bringing all sorts of charges against them. They are said to have crucified Jesus, to have drunk blood of Christians, to have poisoned wells, to have taken usury, to have exploited the peasant, and so on. These charges—and a thousand and one others of like nature— against an entire people have been proved groundless. Their falseness has been demonstrated by the very fact that they had to be trumped up wholesale in order to quiet the evil conscience of the Jew-baiters, to justify the condemnation of an entire nation, to demonstrate the necessity of burning the Jew, or rather the Jewish ghost, at the stake. He who tries to prove too much proves nothing at all. Though the Jews may justly be charged with many shortcomings, those shortcomings are, at all events, not such great vices, not such capital crimes, as to justify the condemnation of the entire people. In individual cases, indeed, we find these accusations contradicted by the fact that the Jews get along fairly well in close intercourse with their gentile neighbors. This is the reason that the charges preferred are usually of the most general character, made up out of whole cloth, based to a certain extent on *a priori* reasoning, and true, at most, in individual cases, but untrue as regards the whole people.

Thus have Judaism and anti-Semitism passed for centuries through history as inseparable companions. Like the Jewish people, it seems, the real "Wandering Jew," anti-Semitism, too, can never die. He must be blind indeed who will assert that the Jews are not *the chosen people*, the people chosen for universal hatred. No matter how much the nations are at variance with one another, no matter how diverse in their instincts and aims, they join hands in their hatred of the Jews; on this one matter all are agreed. The extent and manner in which this antipathy is shown depends, of course, upon the cultural level of each people. The antipathy as such, however, exists in all places and at all times, no matter whether it appears in the form of deeds of violence, as envious jealousy, or under the guise of tolerance and protection. To be robbed as a Jew or to require protection as a Jew is equally humiliating, equally hurtful to the self-respect of the Jews.

Having analyzed Judeophobia as an hereditary form of demonopathy, peculiar to the human race, and having represented anti-Semitism as based upon an inherited aberration of the human mind, we must draw the important conclusion: the fight against this hatred, like any fight against inherited predispositions, can only be in vain. This view is all the more important because it shows that we should at last abstain from polemics as a waste of time and energy, for against superstition even the gods fight vainly. Prejudice or instinctive ill will can be satisfied by no reasoning, however forceful and clear. These sinister powers must either be kept within bounds by material coercion, like every other blind natural force, or simply ignored.

III

IN THE PSYCHOLOGY of the peoples, then, we find the basis of the prejudice against the Jewish nation; but we must also consider other, no less important factors, which render impossible the fusion or equalization of the Jews with the other peoples.

No people, generally speaking, has any predilection for foreigners. This fact has its ethnological basis and cannot be brought as a reproach against any people. Now, is the Jew subject to *this* general law only to the same extent as the other nationalities? Not at all! The aversion which meets the foreigner in a strange land can be repaid in equal coin in his home country. The non-Jew pursues his own interest in a foreign country openly and without giving offence. It is everywhere considered natural that he should fight for these interests, alone or in conjunction with others. The foreigner has no need to *be*, or to *seem to be*, a patriot. But as for the Jew, he is not a native in his own home country, but he is also not a foreigner; he is, in very truth, the stranger par excellence. He is regarded as neither friend nor foe, but as an alien, of whom the only thing known is that he has no home. People do not care to *confide* in the foreigner, or to *trust* the Jew. The foreigner claims hospitality, which he can repay in the same coin in his own country. The Jew can make no such return; consequently he can make no claim to hospitality. He is not a guest, much less a welcome guest. He is more like a beggar; and what beggar is welcome? He is rather a refugee; and where is the refugee to whom a refuge may not be refused? The Jews are aliens who can have no representatives because they have no fatherland. Because they have none, because their home has no boundaries behind which they can entrench themselves, their misery also has no bounds. The *general law* does not apply to the Jews, as strangers in the true sense of the word. On the other hand, there are everywhere *laws for the Jews*, and if the general law is to apply to them, this fact must first be determined by a *special law*. Like the Negroes, like women, and unlike all free peoples, they must be *emancipated*. It is all the worse for them if, unlike the Negroes, they belong to an advanced race, and if, unlike women, they can show not only women of distinction, but also men, even great men.

Since the Jew is nowhere at home, nowhere regarded as a native, he remains an alien everywhere. That he himself and his forefathers as well were born in the country does not alter this fact in the least. Generally, he is treated as an adopted child whose rights may be questioned; *never* is he considered a legitimate child of the fatherland. The German, proud of his Teutonic character, the Slav, the Celt—not one of them admits that the Semitic Jew is his equal by birth; and even if he be ready, as a man of culture, to admit him to all civil rights, he will never go as far as to forget the Jew in this, his fellow citizen. The *legal emancipation* of the Jews is the crowning achievement of our century. But *legal emancipation* is not *social* emancipation, and with the proclamation of the former the Jews are still far from being emancipated from their exceptional *social position*.

The emancipation of the Jews naturally finds its justification in the fact that it will always be considered to have been a postulate of *logic*, of *law*, and of *enlightened self-interest*. It can never be regarded as a spontaneous expression of human *feeling*. Far from owing its origin to the spontaneous *feeling* of the peoples, it is *never a matter of course*; and it has never yet taken such deep root that discussion of it becomes unnecessary. In any event, whether emancipation was undertaken from spontaneous impulse or from conscious motives, it remains a rich gift, splendid alms, willingly or unwillingly flung to the poor, humble beggars whom no one, however, cares to shelter, because a homeless, wandering beggar wins confidence or sympathy from none. The Jew is not permitted to forget that the daily bread of civil rights must be given to him. The stigma attached to this people, which forces it into an unenviable isolation among the nations, cannot be removed by any sort of official emancipation, as long as it is the nature of this people to produce vagrant nomads, as long as it cannot give a satisfactory account of whence it comes and whither it goes, as long as the Jews themselves prefer not to speak in Aryan society of their Semitic descent and prefer not to be reminded of it—as long as they are persecuted, tolerated, protected, emancipated.

This degrading dependence of the eternally alien Jew upon the non-Jew is reinforced by another factor, making a fusion of the Jews with the original inhabitants of a land absolutely impossible. In the great struggle for existence, civilized peoples readily submit to laws which help to give this struggle the worthy form of a peaceful competition. Even in this case the peoples usually make a distinction between the native and the foreigner, the first, of course, always being given the preference. Now, if this distinction is drawn even against the foreigner of equal birth, how harshly is it insisted upon with reference to the eternally alien Jew! How great must be the irritation at the beggar who dares to cast longing glances upon a land not his own—as upon a beloved woman guarded by distrustful relatives! And if he nevertheless prosper and succeed in plucking a flower here and there from its soil, woe to the ill-fated man! Let him not complain if he experiences what the Jews in Spain and Russia have experienced.

The Jews, moreover, do not suffer only when they achieve distinguished success. Wherever they are congregated in large masses, they must, by their very *numbers*, have a certain advantage in competition with the non-Jewish population. In the western provinces of Russia we behold the Jews herded together, leading a wretched existence in the most dreadful destitution. Nevertheless, there are unceasing complaints of the exploitation practiced by the Jews.

To sum up what has been said: For the living, the Jew is a dead man; for the natives, an alien and a vagrant; for property holders, a beggar; for the poor, an exploiter and a millionaire; for patriots, a man without a country; for all classes, a hated rival.

IV

T H I S *natural antagonism* is the basis of the untold number of reciprocal misunderstandings and accusations and reproaches which both parties rightfully or wrongfully hurl at each other. Thus the Jews, instead of really facing their own situation and adopting a rational line of conduct, appeal to eternal justice and fondly imagine that the appeal will have some effect. On the other hand, the non-Jews, instead of relying simply upon their superior force and holding fast to their historical and actual standpoint—the standpoint of the stronger—try to justify their negative attitude by a mass of accusations which, on closer examination, prove to be baseless or negligible. He, however, who desires to be unbiased, who does not desire to judge and interpret the affairs of this world according to the principles of an utopian Arcadia, but would merely ascertain and explain them in order to reach a conclusion of practical value, will not make either of the parties seriously responsible for the antagonism described. To the Jews, however, in whom we are chiefly interested, he will say: "You are *foolish*, because you stand awkwardly by and expect of human nature something which it has always lacked—humanity. You are contemptible, because you have no real self-love and no national self-respect."

National self-respect! Where can we obtain it? It is truly the greatest misfortune of our race that we do not constitute a nation, that we are merely Jews. We are a flock scattered over the whole face of the earth, without a shepherd to protect us and gather us together. Under the most favorable circumstances we reach the rank of those privileged goats which, according to Russian custom, are stabled among race horses. And that is the highest goal of our ambition.

It is true that our loving protectors have always taken good care that we should never catch our breath and recover our self-respect. As individual Jews, but not as a Jewish nation, we have carried on for centuries the hard and unequal struggle for existence. Single-handed each separate individual had to waste his genius and his energy for a little oxygen and a morsel of bread, moistened with tears. In this hopeless struggle we did not succumb. We waged the most glorious of all partisan struggles with all the peoples of the earth who, with one accord, desired to exterminate us. But the war we have waged—and God knows how long we shall continue to wage it—has not been for a fatherland, but for the wretched existence of millions of "Jew peddlers."

If all the peoples of the earth were not able to blot out our existence, they were nevertheless able to destroy in us the feeling of our national independence. And as for ourselves, we look on with fatalistic indifference when in many a land we are refused a recognition which would not lightly be denied to Zulus. In the dispersion we have maintained our individual life, and proved our power of resistance, but we have lost the common bond of our national consciousness. Seeking to main-

tain our material existence, we were constrained only too often to forget our moral dignity. We did not see that on account of tactics unworthy of us, which we were forced to adopt, we sank still lower in the
eyes of our opponents, that we were only the more exposed to humiliating contempt and outlawry, which have finally become our baleful
heritage. In the wide, wide world there was no place for us. We prayed
only for a little place anywhere to lay our weary heads to rest; and so, by
lessening our claims, we gradually lessened our dignity as well, which
was diminished in our own and others' eyes until it became unrecog-
nizable. We were the ball which the peoples tossed in turn to one
another. The cruel game was equally amusing whether we were caught
or thrown, and was enjoyed all the more, the more elastic and yielding
our national respect became in the hands of the peoples. Under such
circumstances, how could there be any question of national self-
determination, of a free, active development of our national force or
of our native genius?

We may note, in passing, that our enemies, in order to prove our
inferiority, have not failed to make capital of this last trait; there is
some evidence of it, but it is essentially altogether irrelevant. One
would think that men of genius were as plentiful among our opponents
as blackberries in August. The wretches! They reproach the eagle who
once soared to heaven and recognized the Divinity, because he cannot
rise high in the air after his wings have been clipped! But even with
wings clipped we have remained on a level with the great peoples of
civilization. Grant us the happiness of independence, allow us to be
sole masters of our fate, give us a bit of land, grant us only what you
granted the Serbians and Romanians, the advantage of a free national
existence, and then dare to pass a slighting judgment upon us, to
reproach us with a lack of men of genius! *At present we still live under
the oppression of the evils you have inflicted upon us. What we lack is
not genius, but self-respect, and the consciousness of human dignity,
of which you have robbed us.*

v

H A P P I L Y , affairs are now in a somewhat different state. The events
of the last few years in *enlightened* Germany, in Romania, in Hungary, and especially in Russia have effected what the far bloodier persecutions of the Middle Ages could not effect.[2] The national
consciousness, which until then had existed only in the latent state of

sterile martyrdom, burst forth before our eyes among the masses of the Russian and Romanian Jews in the form of an irresistible movement toward Palestine. Though this movement has been poor in practical results, its existence attests, nevertheless, to the correct instinct of the people, to whom it became manifest that it needed a home. The severe tests which the Jews have endured have now produced a re-action which points to something other than a fatalistic submission to a punishment inflicted by the hand of God. Even the unenlightened masses of the Russian Jews have not entirely escaped the influence of the basic outlook of modern culture. Without renouncing Judaism and their faith, they revolted most deeply at undeserved ill-treatment, which could be inflicted with impunity only because the Russian Government regards the Jews as aliens. And the other European governments—why should they concern themselves with the citizens of a state in whose internal affairs they have no right to interfere?

Nowadays, when in a small part of the earth our brethren have caught their breath and can feel more deeply for the sufferings of their brothers; nowadays, when a number of other dependent and oppressed nationalities have been allowed to regain their independence—we, too, must not sit even one moment longer with folded hands; we must not admit that we are doomed to play on in the future the hopeless role of the "Wandering Jew." This role is truly hopeless; it is enough to drive one to despair.

If an individual is unfortunate enough to see himself despised and rejected by society, no one wonders if he commits suicide. But where is the deadly weapon to give the *coup de grâce* to all the Jews scattered over the face of the earth, and what hand would offer itself for the work? Such destruction is neither possible nor desirable. Conse-quently, it is our bounden duty to devote all our remaining moral force to re-establishing ourselves as a living nation, so that we may finally assume a more fitting and dignified role.

VI

WE ARE no more justified in leaving our national fortune entirely in the hands of the other peoples than we are in making them re-sponsible for our national misfortune. The human race, and we as well, have scarcely traversed the first stage of the practice of perfect humanitarianism—if that goal is ever to be reached. Therefore we must abandon the delusive idea that we are fulfilling by our dispersion a Providential mission, a mission in which no one believes, an honorable station which we, to speak frankly, would gladly resign, if the odious epithet "Jew" could only be blotted out of the memory of man.

We must seek our honor and our salvation not in illusory self-deceptions, but in the restoration of a national bond of union. Hitherto the world has not considered us as an enterprise of standing, and consequently we have enjoyed no decent credit.

If the nationalistic endeavors of the various peoples who have risen to life before our eyes bore their own justification, can it still be questioned whether similar aspirations on the part of the Jews would not be justified? They play a more important part than those peoples in the life of the civilized nations, and they have deserved more from humanity; they have a past, a history, a common, unmixed descent, and an indestructible vigor, an unshakable faith, and an unexampled history of suffering to show; the peoples have sinned against them more grievously than against any other nation. Is not that enough to make them capable and worthy of possessing a fatherland?

The struggle of the Jews for unity and independence as an organized nation not only possesses the inherent justification that belongs to the struggle of every oppressed people, but it is also calculated to attract the sympathy of the people to whom we are rightly or wrongly obnoxious. This struggle must be entered upon in such a spirit as to exert an irresistible pressure upon the international politics of the present, and the future will assuredly bear witness to its results.

At the very outset we must be prepared for a great outcry. The first stirrings of this struggle will doubtless be ascribed by most of the Jews, who have, with reason, become timorous and skeptical, to the unconscious convulsions of an organism dangerously ill; and certainly the attainment and realization of the object of such endeavors will be fraught with the greatest difficulties, will perhaps be possible only after superhuman efforts. But consider that the Jews have no other way out of their desperate position, and that it would be cowardly not to take that way merely because it offers only slim chances of success. "Faint heart never won fair lady"—and, indeed, what have we to lose? At the worst, we shall continue to be in the future what we have been in the past, what we are too cowardly to resolve that we will be no longer: *eternally despised Jews.*

WE HAVE LATELY had very bitter experiences in Russia. That country has too many and too few of us; too many in the southwestern provinces, in which the Jews are allowed to reside, and too few in all the others, in which they are forbidden to reside. If the Russian Government, and the Russian people as well, realized that an equal distribution of the Jewish population would accrue only to the benefit of the entire country, the persecutions which we have suffered would probably not have taken place. But, alas, Russia cannot and will not realize this. That is not our fault, and it is also not a result of the low cultural status of the Russian people; we have found our bitterest opponents, indeed, in a large part of the press, which ought to be intelligent. The unfortunate situation of the Russian Jews is due, rather, purely and simply to the operation of those general forces based on human nature which we have discussed above. Accordingly, as it is not to be our task to improve the human race, we must see what *we*, ourselves, have to do under the circumstances.

Since conditions are and must remain such as we have described them, we shall forever continue to be what we have been and are, parasites, who are a burden to the rest of the population, and can never secure their favor. The fact that, as it seems, we can mix with the nations only in the smallest proportions, presents a further obstacle to the establishment of amicable relations. Therefore, we must see to it that the *surplus* of Jews, the unassimilable residue, is removed and provided for elsewhere. This duty can be incumbent upon no one but ourselves. If the Jews could be equally distributed among all the peoples of the earth, perhaps there would be no Jewish question. But this is not possible. Nay, more, there can be no doubt that even the most civilized states would emphatically decline an immigration of the Jews en masse.

We say this with a heavy heart; but we must admit the truth. And such an admission is all the more important, because a correct estimate of our situation is an indispensable precondition to finding the correct means of improving our position.

Moreover, it would be very unfortunate if we were not willing to profit by those results of our experience which have practical value. The most important of these results is the constantly growing conviction that we are nowhere at home, and that we finally must have a *home*, if not a *country* of our own.

Another result of our experience is the recognition that the lamentable outcome of the emigration from Russia and Romania is ascribable solely to the momentous fact that we were taken by it unawares; we had made no provision for the principal needs, a refuge and a systematic organization of the emigration. When thousands were seeking new homes we forgot to provide for that which no villager forgets when he desires to move—the small matter, forsooth, of a new and suitable dwelling.

If we would have a secure home, so that we may give up our endless life of wandering and rehabilitate our nation in our own eyes and in the eyes of the world, we must above all, not dream of restoring ancient Judaea. We must not attach ourselves to the place where our political life was once violently interrupted and destroyed. The goal of our present endeavors must be not the "Holy Land," but a land of our own. We need nothing but a large piece of land for our poor brothers; a piece of land which shall remain our property, from which no foreign master can expel us. Thither we shall take with us the most sacred possessions which we have saved from the shipwreck of our former fatherland, the *God-idea* and the *Bible*. It is only these which have made our old fatherland the Holy Land, and not Jerusalem of the Jordan. Perhaps the Holy Land will again become ours. If so, all the better, but *first of all*, we must determine—and this is the crucial point —what country is accessible to us, and at the same time adapted to offer the Jews of all lands who must leave their homes a secure and unquestioned refuge which is capable of being made productive.

VIII

IN THE LIFE of peoples, as in the life of individuals, there are important moments which do not often recur, and which, depending on whether they are utilized or not utilized, exercise a decisive influence upon the future of the people as upon that of the individual, whether for weal or for woe. We are now passing through such a moment. The consciousness of the people is awake. The great ideas of the eighteenth and nineteenth centuries have not passed by our people without leaving a trace. We feel not only as Jews; we feel as men. As men, we, too, wish to live like other men and be a nation like the others. And if we seriously desire that, we must first of all throw off the old yoke of oppression and rise manfully to our full height. We must first of all *desire to help ourselves. . . .* Only then will the help of others, as well, be sure to come.

Moreover the time in which we live is particularly suitable for decisive action not merely because of our own inner experience, not merely in consequence of our newly aroused self-consciousness. The *general* history of the present day seems called to be *our* ally. In a few decades we have seen rising into new life nations which at an earlier time would not have dared to dream of a resurrection. The dawn already appears amid the darkness of traditional statesmanship. The governments are already inclining their ears—first, to be sure, in those cases in which they cannot do otherwise—to the ever louder voices of national self-consciousness. It is true that those happy ones who attained their national independence were not Jews. They lived upon their own soil and spoke *one language,* and thereby they certainly had the advantage over us.

But what if our position is more difficult? That is all the more reason why we should strain every energy to the task of ending our national misery in honorable fashion. We must go to work resolved and ready for sacrifice, and God will help us. We were always ready for sacrifice, and we did not lack resolution to hold our banner fast, even if not to hold it high. But we sailed the surging ocean of universal history *without a compass,* and such a compass must be invented. Far off, very far off, is the haven for which our soul longs. As yet we do not even know where it is, whether in the East or the West. For a people wandering for thousands of years, however, no way, no matter how distant, can be too long.

IX

WE PROBABLY LACK a leader of the genius of Moses—history does not grant a people such guides repeatedly. But a clear recognition of what we need most, a recognition of the absolute necessity of a home of our own, would arouse among us a number of energetic, honorable, and distinguished friends of the people, who would undertake the leadership, and would, perhaps, be no less able than that one man to deliver us from disgrace and persecution.

What should we do first of all and how should we make a beginning? We believe that a nucleus for this beginning already exists; it consists in the *societies already in being.* It is incumbent upon them, they are called and in duty bound, to lay the foundation of that lighthouse to which our eyes will turn. If they are to be equal to their new task, these societies must, of course, be completely transformed. They must convoke a *national congress*, of which they are to form the center. If they decline this function, however, and if they think that they may not overstep the boundaries of their previous activity, they must at least form some of their numbers into a *national institute*, let us say a directorate, which will crystallize that unity which we lack, without which the success of our endeavors is unthinkable. As a representative of our national interest this institute must comprise the leaders of our people, and it must energetically take in hand the direction of our general, national affairs. Our greatest and best forces—men of finance, of science, and of affairs, statesmen and publicists—must join hands with one accord in steering toward the common destination. This institute would aim chiefly and especially at creating a secure and inviolable home for the *surplus* of those Jews who live as proletarians in the various countries and are a burden to the native citizens.

There can, of course, be no question whatever of a united emigration of the entire people. The comparatively small number of Jews in the Occident, who constitute an insignificant percentage of the population, and for this reason, perhaps, are better situated and even to a certain extent naturalized, may in the future remain where they are. The wealthy may also remain even where the Jews are not readily tolerated. But, as we have said before, there is a certain point of saturation, beyond which their numbers may not increase, if the Jews are not to be exposed to the dangers of persecution as in Russia, Romania, Morocco, and elsewhere. It is this surplus which, a burden to itself and to others, conjures up the evil fate of the entire people. It is now high time to create a refuge for this surplus. We must occupy ourselves with the foundation of such a lasting refuge, not with the purposeless collection of donations for pilgrims or fugitives who forsake, in their consternation, an inhospitable home, to perish in the abyss of a strange and unknown land.

It is to be hoped that we have now passed that stage in which the Jews of the Middle Ages wretchedly vegetated. Those among our people who are educated in modern culture esteem their dignity no less highly than our oppressors do theirs. But we shall not be able successfully to defend this dignity until we stand upon our own feet. Only when an asylum is found for our poor people, for the fugitives whom our historic and predestined fate will always create for us, shall we rise in the opinion of the peoples. We shall forthwith cease to be surprised by such tragic happenings as those in the last few years, happenings which promise, alas, to be repeated more than once not only in Russia but also in other countries. We must labor actively to complete the great work of self-liberation. We must use all means which human intellect and human experience have devised, in order that the sacred work of national regeneration may not be left to blind chance.

X

THE LAND which we are about to purchase must be productive and well located and of an area sufficient to allow the settlement of several millions. The land, as national property, must be inalienable. Its selection is, of course, of the first and highest importance, and must not be left to offhand decision or to certain preconceived sympathies of individuals, as has, alas, happened lately. This land must be uniform and continuous in extent, for it lies in the very nature of our problem that we must possess as a counterpoise to our dispersion *one single refuge*, since a *number* of refuges would merely recreate again the features of our old dispersion. Therefore, the selection of a national and permanent land, meeting all requirements, must be made with all care, and confided to one single national institute, to a commission of experts selected from our directorate. Only such a supreme tribunal will be able, after thorough and comprehensive investigation, to render an opinion and decide upon *which* of the two hemispheres and upon *which* territory in them our final choice should fall.

Only then, and not before, should the directorate, together with an associated body of capitalists, as founders of a stock company to be organized subsequently, purchase a piece of land which several million Jews could settle in the course of time. This piece of land might form a small territory in North America, or a sovereign pashalik in Asiatic Turkey recognized by the Porte and the other Powers as neutral. It would certainly be an important duty of the directorate to secure the assent of the Porte, and probably of the other European cabinets, to this plan.

Of course, the establishment of a Jewish refuge cannot come about without the support of the governments. In order to attain such support and to insure the perpetual existence of a refuge, the creators of our national regeneration will have to proceed with patience and care. What we seek is at bottom neither new nor dangerous to anyone. Instead of the *many refuges* which we have always been accustomed to seek, we would fain have *one single refuge*, the existence of which, however, would have to be politically assured.

Let "Now or never!" be our watchword. Woe to our descendants, woe to the memory of our Jewish contemporaries, if we let this moment pass by!

SUMMARY

T H E J E W S are not a living nation; they are everywhere aliens; therefore they are despised.

The civil and political emancipation of the Jews is not sufficient to raise them in the estimation of the peoples.

The proper and the only remedy would be the creation of a Jewish nationality, of a people living upon its own soil, the auto-emancipation of the Jews; their emancipation as a nation among nations by the acquisition of a home of their own.

We should not persuade ourselves that humanity and enlightenment will ever be radical remedies for the malady of our people.

The lack of national self-respect and self-confidence, of political initiative and of unity, are the enemies of our national renaissance.

In order that we may not be constrained to wander from one exile to another, we must have an extensive and productive place of refuge, a gathering place which is our own.

The present moment is more favorable than any other for realizing the plan here unfolded.

The international Jewish question must receive a national solution. Of course, our national regeneration can only proceed slowly. We must take the first step. Our *descendants* must follow us with a measured and unhurried pace.

A way must be opened for the national regeneration of the Jews by a congress of Jewish notables.

No sacrifice would be too great in order to reach the goal which will assure our people's future, everywhere endangered.

The financial accomplishment of the undertaking can, in the nature of the situation, encounter no insuperable difficulties.

Help yourselves, and God will help you!

Part 3
Headlong into the World Arena—
Theodor Herzl Appears

THEODOR HERZL 1860-1904

THEODOR HERZL was born on May 2, 1860 in Budapest, Hungary, as the only son of a rich merchant. His mother, who adored him and remained, until his death, the dominant influence on his personal life, raised him to dream of himself as meant for great things. In the milieu of his birth such ambitions implied a career devoted neither to Jewish nor even to Hungarian interests. German was the dominant culture of the Austro-Hungarian empire and of central Europe as a whole, and the young Herzl, a voracious reader and adolescent poet, was soon hoping for a literary career in that language.

Herzl received his preliminary education in a technical school and high school in Budapest. When he was eighteen the family moved to Vienna, after his sister had died of typhoid, and he enrolled in the law faculty of the university. After gaining his doctorate in 1884, Herzl practiced for a year as a minor civil servant but soon gave up the law for good to devote himself entirely to writing. With relative ease he won regard as a feuilletonist (i.e., as familiar essayist, the favorite form of central European journalism) and as a writer of light, fashionable plays. In 1892 he was appointed to the staff of the *Neue Freie Presse*, the most important Viennese newspaper, and later that year Herzl was sent to Paris as its resident correspondent.

Herzl's pre-Zionist writings were marked by a tone of brittle irony, even by cynicism. The productions of these early years contained scarcely a dozen lines of passing references to Jews. On the surface of his consciousness Herzl held the conventional view of the westernized Jewish intellectual in the late nineteenth century, that progress was on the march for all mankind and that complete assimilation was both desirable and inevitable. Nonetheless the emotional explosion that was soon to take place in his life and result in his Zionism had its roots in his earlier life and experience. His early Jewish education had indeed been skimpy, but his grandfather, Simon Loeb, a friend and congregant of Alkalai, had lived on to come to Budapest for his *bar-mitzvah*.

While still at the university he had encountered anti-Semitism in its new theoretical forms as racism in the writings of Eugen Dühring; more personally, he had withdrawn from his fraternity because it had taken part in a Wagner memorial meeting which had been transformed into an anti-Semitic demonstration. When he arrived in Paris anti-Semitism confronted him again, as a rising phenomenon of French life. Edouard Drumont, the author of *La France Juive*, the most notorious and successful of French anti-Jewish "classics," had just founded a newspaper and was attracting a noisy, though not yet influential, circle of supporters. Herzl wrote a long account for his paper and suggested in his analytic comments that hatred of the Jew was being used universally as a lightning rod to draw the revolutionary ire of the masses away from the real woes of society.

The Jewish problem was now in the forefront of his attention. The result of two years of pondering and intellectual and emotional zigzagging was a play, *The New Ghetto*. Its hero, Dr. Jacob Samuel, is Herzl himself. Samuel dies in a duel, crying out that he wants to get out, "out of the ghetto," but in the course of the play Herzl had made the point unmistakably that even the most assimilated of Jews are in an invisible ghetto in a gentile world. He still believed in the possibility of better understanding in the future between Jews and Christians, but these hopes were ended for him by the Dreyfus affair.

In 1894 Alfred Dreyfus, a Jewish captain on duty with the French General Staff, was accused of spying for Germany. It was Herzl's duty as correspondent to provide his paper in Vienna with an account of the trial of Dreyfus and its effect on the public life of France. He was present at the Ecole Militaire at the famous dramatic scene when Dreyfus was stripped of his epaulets and drummed out the gate in disgrace. For Herzl this moment was a hammer blow, and the howling of the mob outside the gates of the parade ground, shouting "*à bas les Juifs*," transformed him into the Zionist that he was to be.

In the early days of May 1895 Herzl requested an interview with Baron Maurice de Hirsch, the founder of Jewish colonization in Argentina, to interest him in his ideas of a Jewish national state. He followed up that interview by sending de Hirsch a long letter on June 3, 1895, which is the first written statement of his views. Baron de Hirsch was not receptive and Herzl was soon hoping that perhaps the Rothschilds would listen to him. In five days of feverish writing he poured into his diary a sixty-five page pamphlet—in effect an outline of his *Jewish State*—which he entitled *Address to the Rothschilds*.

There he wrote: "I have the solution to the Jewish question. I know it sounds mad; and at the beginning I shall be called mad more than once—until the truth of what I am saying is recognized in all its shattering force." Finally, after much reworking and some difficulty in finding a publisher, his *Jewish State* appeared in February 1896.

The last eight years of Herzl's life, even though he had to continue to work as literary editor of the *Neue Freie Presse* in order to support his family, were spent in feverish, superhuman Zionist activity. He founded *Die Welt*, a weekly organ for the Zionist movement, even before the first Zionist Congress convened in the summer of 1897, and called it proudly a *Judenblatt*, a Jew's sheet, the very term of derision that was being used by anti-Semites against a number of liberal European newspapers that were owned by Jews (be it added, by highly assimilated Jews, most of whom would mention Herzl in their papers only to call him a madman and an adventurer). In August 1897 more than two hundred delegates from all over the Jewish world answered his call to come to Basel, Switzerland, to found the World Zionist Organization. Here its purpose was proclaimed: "Zionism seeks to secure for the Jewish people a publicly recognized, legally secured, home in Palestine." At succeeding Congresses, of which there were six in Herzl's lifetime, all of the essential institutions and organizational forms of the movement, as they exist to this day, were fashioned.

For Herzl, the most important aspect of his work was in diplomacy —among others he negotiated with the Sultan of Turkey, Kaiser Wilhelm, the King of Italy and Pope Pius X—but, ironically, his one great success in the international arena almost wrecked the Zionist movement. In 1903 the British government offered him a large tract of land in Uganda, East Africa, for a Jewish self-governing settlement. Herzl proposed to the Congress of that year, the last one that he was to attend, that the offer be accepted, not as a substitute for Zion, but as a "temporary haven" (which seemed all the more urgently needed at the moment because this was also the year of a brutal pogrom in Kishinev, Russia). His authority won a bare victory for a vote to investigate Uganda, but the Zionists of Russia, led by the young Chaim Weizmann, among others, lined up against him. There were no practical results from this offer because it was withdrawn in a year or so by the British Government. The scenes of high drama which attended the discussion are, however, of crucial importance in the history of Zionism, for the seal was unalterably set on its devotion to a territorial state in Zion, and only in Zion.

Worn out by his exertions Herzl died not far from Vienna on July 3, 1904. Forty-five years later, on August 17, 1949, an airplane flying the blue-white flag of the new state of Israel brought his remains to the country of which he was the principal architect.

FIRST ENTRY IN HIS DIARY (1895)

Shavuot,[1] 1895

I HAVE BEEN OCCUPIED for some time past with a work which is of immeasurable greatness. I cannot tell today whether I shall bring it to a close. It has the appearance of a gigantic dream. But for days and weeks it has filled me, saturated even my subconsciousness; it accompanies me wherever I go, broods above my ordinary daily converse, looks over my shoulder and at my petty, comical journalistic work, disturbs me, and intoxicates me.

What it will lead to it is impossible to surmise as yet. But my experience tells me that it is something marvelous, even as a dream, and that I should write it down—if not as a memorial for mankind, then for my own delight or meditation in later years. And perhaps for something between both these possibilities: for the enrichment of literature. If the romance does not become a fact, at least the fact can become a romance. Title: The Promised Land!

THE JEWISH STATE (1896)

PREFACE

THE IDEA which I have developed in this pamphlet is an ancient one: It is the restoration of the Jewish State.

The world resounds with clamor against the Jews, and this has revived the dormant idea.

I claim no new discoveries; let this be noted at once and throughout my discussion. I have discovered neither the Jewish situation as it has crystallized in history, nor the means to remedy it. The materials for the structure I here sketch exist in reality, they are quite tangible; this anyone can establish to his own satisfaction. Hence, if this attempt to resolve the Jewish question is to be described by a single word, let it be labeled not a "fantasy," but at most a "construction."

I must first of all defend my sketch from being treated as "Utopian." To do this is simply to protect superficial critics from committing a foolish error. Though, indeed, it would be no disgrace to have written an idealist Utopia. And very likely I could also assure myself easier literary success while avoiding all responsibility, if I were to offer this plan in the form of romantic fiction to a public that seeks to be entertained. But this is no amiable Utopia such as have been projected in abundance before and since Sir Thomas More. And it seems to me that the situation of the Jews in various lands is grave enough to make quite superfluous any attention-getting tricks.

An interesting book, *Freiland,* by Dr. Theodor Hertzka,[2] which appeared a few years ago, may serve to illustrate the distinction I draw between my construction and a Utopia. His is the ingenious invention of a modern mind thoroughly schooled in the principles of political economy; it is as remote from actuality as the equatorial mountain on which his dream state lies. "Freiland" is a complicated mechanism with numerous cogs and wheels that even seem to mesh well; but I have no reason whatever to believe that they can be set in motion. Even if I were to see "Freiland societies" come into being, I should regard the whole thing as a joke.

The present scheme, on the other hand, involves the use of a motive force which exists in reality. In view of my own limitations, I shall do no more than suggest what cogs and wheels constitute the machinery I propose, trusting that better mechanics than myself will be found to carry the work out.

The decisive factor is our propelling force. And what is that force? The plight of the Jews.

Who would dare to deny that this exists? We shall discuss it fully in the chapter on the causes of anti-Semitism.

Now everyone knows how steam is generated by boiling water in a kettle, but such steam only rattles the lid. The current Zionist projects and other associations to check anti-Semitism are teakettle phenomena of this kind. But I say that this force, if properly harnessed, is powerful enough to propel a large engine and to move passengers and goods, let the engine have whatever form it may.

I am profoundly convinced that I am right, though I doubt whether I shall live to see myself proved so. Those who today inaugurate this movement are unlikely to live to see its glorious culmination. But the very inauguration is enough to inspire in them a high pride and the joy of an inner liberation of their existence.

To avoid all suspicion of Utopianism, I shall also be very sparing of picturesque details in my exposition. I expect, in any case, that unthinking scoffers will caricature my sketch in an attempt to vitiate the whole idea. A Jew, of excellent judgment in other respects, to whom I explained my plan, remarked that "It is the hallmark of Utopias to present facets of the future as facts in present reality." This is a mistake. Every finance minister bases his budget estimates on future figures, and not only on projections of the actual average returns of previous years, or on previous revenues in other states, but sometimes on figures for which there is no precedent whatever; as, for example, in instituting a new tax. Anyone who has examined a budget knows that this is so. But is such a financial draft considered Utopian, even when we know that the estimates will never be rigidly adhered to?

But I expect far more of my readers. I ask the cultivated men whom I address to set aside many preconceptions. I shall even go so far as to ask those Jews who have most earnestly tried to solve the Jewish question to look upon their previous attempts as mistaken and impracticable.

There is one danger I must guard against in the presentation of my idea. If I am restrained in describing all these things that lie in the future, I may appear to be doubting the possibility of their ever being realized. If, on the other hand, I speak of them quite unreservedly as realized, I may appear to be building castles in the air.

I therefore state, clearly and emphatically, that I believe in the achievement of the idea, though I do not profess to have discovered the shape it may ultimately take. The world needs the Jewish State; therefore it will arise.

The plan would seem mad enough if a single individual were to undertake it; but if many Jews simultaneously agree on it, it is entirely reasonable, and its achievement presents no difficulties worth mentioning. The idea depends only on the number of its adherents. Perhaps our ambitious young men, to whom every road of advancement is now closed, and for whom the Jewish State throws open a bright prospect of freedom, happiness, and honor—perhaps they will see to it that this idea is spread.

I feel that with the publication of this pamphlet my own task is done. I shall not again take up my pen unless the attacks of serious opponents force me to do so, or it becomes necessary to meet objections and errors not already dealt with.

Is what I am saying not yet true? Am I ahead of time? Are the sufferings of the Jews not yet acute enough? We shall see.

It depends on the Jews themselves whether this political document remains for the present a political romance. If this generation is too dull to understand it rightly, a future, finer, more advanced generation will arise to comprehend it. The Jews who will try it shall achieve their State; and they will deserve it.

CHAPTER 1. INTRODUCTION

THE UNDERSTANDING of economics among men actively engaged in business is often astonishingly slight. This seems to be the only explanation for the fact that even Jews faithfully parrot the catchword of the anti-Semites: "We live off 'Host-nations'; and if we had no 'Host-nation' to sustain us we should starve to death." This is one case in point of the undermining of our self-respect through unjust accusations. But how does this theory of "Host-nations" stand up in the light of reality? Where it does not rest on narrow physiocratic views, it reflects the childish error which assumes that there is a fixed quantity of values in continuous circulation. But it is not necessary to be Rip van Winkle, and wake from long slumber, in order to realize that the world is considerably altered by the continuous production of new values. The technical progress achieved in our own wonderful era enables even the dullest of minds with the dimmest of vision to note the appearance of new commodities all around him. The spirit of enterprise has created them.

Without enterprise, labor remains static, unaltering; typical of it is the labor of the farmer, who stands now precisely where his forebears stood a thousand years ago. All our material welfare has been brought about by men of enterprise. I feel almost ashamed of writing down so trite a remark. Even if we were a nation of entrepreneurs—such as absurdly exaggerated accounts make us out to be—we would require no "Host-nation." We are not dependent upon the circulation of old values; we produce new ones.

We now possess slave labor of unexampled productivity, whose appearance in civilization has proved fatal competition to handicrafts; these slaves are our machines. It is true that we need workmen to set our machinery in motion; but for this the Jews have manpower enough, too much, in fact. Only those who are ignorant of the condition of Jews in many countries of eastern Europe would dare assert that Jews are unfit or unwilling to perform manual labor.

But in this pamphlet I will offer no defense of the Jews. It would be useless. Everything that reason and everything that sentiment can possibly say in their defense already has been said. Obviously, arguments fit to appeal to reason and sentiment are not enough; one's audience must first of all be able to understand or one is only preaching in a vacuum. But if the audience is already so far advanced, then the sermon itself is superfluous. I believe that man is steadily advancing to a higher ethical level; but I see this ascent to be fearfully slow. Should we wait for the average man to become as generously minded as was Lessing when he wrote Nathan the Wise,[3] we would have to wait beyond our own lifetime, beyond the lifetimes of our children, of our grandchildren, and of our great-grandchildren. But destiny favors us in a different respect.

The technical achievements of our century have brought about a remarkable renaissance; but we have not yet seen this fabulous advance applied for the benefit of humanity. Distance has ceased to be an obstacle, yet we complain of the problem of congestion. Our great steamships carry us swiftly and surely over hitherto uncharted seas. Our railways carry us safely into a mountain world hitherto cautiously scaled on foot. Events occurring in countries undiscovered when Europe first confined Jews in ghettos are known to us in a matter of an hour. That is why the plight of the Jews is an anachronism—not because over a hundred years ago there was a period of enlightenment which in reality affected only the most elevated spirits.

To my mind, the electric light was certainly not invented so that the drawing rooms of a few snobs might be illuminated, but rather to enable us to solve some of the problems of humanity by its light. One of these problems, and not the least of them, is the Jewish question. In solving it we are working not only for ourselves, but also for many other downtrodden and oppressed beings.

The Jewish question still exists. It would be foolish to deny it. It is a misplaced piece of medievalism which civilized nations do not even yet seem able to shake off, try as they will. They proved they had this high-minded desire when they emancipated us. The Jewish question persists wherever Jews live in appreciable numbers. Wherever it does not exist, it is brought in together with Jewish immigrants. We are naturally drawn into those places where we are not persecuted, and our appearance there gives rise to persecution. This is the case, and will inevitably be so, everywhere, even in highly civilized countries— see, for instance, France—so long as the Jewish question is not solved on the political level. The unfortunate Jews are now carrying the seeds of anti-Semitism into England; they have already introduced it into America.

Anti-Semitism is a highly complex movement, which I think I understand. I approach this movement as a Jew, yet without fear or hatred. I believe that I can see in it the elements of cruel sport, of common commercial rivalry, of inherited prejudice, of religious intolerance—but also of a supposed need for self-defense. I consider the Jewish question neither a social nor a religious one, even though it sometimes takes these and other forms. It is a national question, and to solve it we must first of all establish it as an international political problem to be discussed and settled by the civilized nations of the world in council.

We are a people—*one* people.

We have sincerely tried everywhere to merge with the national communities in which we live, seeking only to preserve the faith of our fathers. It is not permitted us. In vain are we loyal patriots, sometimes superloyal; in vain do we make the same sacrifices of life and property as our fellow citizens; in vain do we strive to enhance the fame of our native lands in the arts and sciences, or her wealth by trade and commerce. In our native lands where we have lived for centuries we are still decried as aliens, often by men whose ancestors had not yet come at a time when Jewish sighs had long been heard in the country. The majority decide who the "alien" is; this, and all else in the relations between peoples, is a matter of power. I do not surrender any part of our prescriptive right when I make this statement merely in my own name, as an individual. In the world as it now is and will probably remain, for an indefinite period, might takes precedence over right. It is without avail, therefore, for us to be loyal patriots, as were the Huguenots, who were forced to emigrate. If we were left in peace . . .

But I think we shall not be left in peace.

Oppression and persecution cannot exterminate us. No nation on earth has endured such struggles and sufferings as we have. Jew-baiting has merely winnowed out our weaklings; the strong among us defiantly return to their own whenever persecution breaks out. This was most clearly apparent in the period immediately following the emancipation of the Jews. Those Jews who rose highest intellectually and materially entirely lost the sense of unity with their people. Wherever we remain politically secure for any length of time, we assimilate. I think this is not praiseworthy. Hence, the statesman who would wish to see a Jewish strain added to his nation must see to it that we continue politically secure. But even a Bismarck could never achieve that.

For old prejudices against us are still deeply ingrained in the folk ethos. He who would have proof of this need only listen to the people where they speak candidly and artlessly: folk wisdom and folklore both are anti-Semitic. The people is everywhere a great child, which can be readily educated; but even in the most favorable circumstances its education would be such a long-drawn-out process that we could far sooner, as already mentioned, help ourselves by other means.

Assimilation, by which I understand not only external conformity in dress, habits, customs, and speech, but also identity of attitude and deportment—assimilation of Jews could be achieved only by intermarriage. But the need for intermarriage would have to be felt by the majority; mere legislative sanction would never suffice.

The Hungarian liberals, who have just legalized intermarriage, have placed themselves in a thoroughly false position. The doctrinaire character of this legislation is well illustrated by one of the earliest cases: it was a baptized Jew who married a Jewess. At the same time the conflict which arose in the course of enacting the new form of marriage has aggravated the difference between Jews and Christians in Hungary, thus hindering rather than furthering the amalgamation of the races.

Those who really wish to see the Jews disappear through interbreeding can hope to see it come about in one way only. The Jews must first rise so far in the economic scale that old social prejudices against them would be overcome. How this might happen is shown by the example of the aristocracy, with whom the highest proportion of intermarriage occurs. The old nobility has itself refurbished with Jewish money, and in the process Jewish families are absorbed. But what form would this process take in the middle classes, where (the Jews being a bourgeois people) the Jewish question is mainly centered? The prerequisite growth in economic power might here be resented as economic domination, something which is already falsely attributed to the Jews. And if the power the Jews now possess evokes rage and indignation among the anti-Semites, to what outbursts would a further increase lead? The first step toward absorption cannot be taken, because this step would mean the subjection of the majority to a recently despised minority, which, however, would possess neither military nor administrative authority of its own. I, therefore, hold the absorption of Jews by means of their prosperity to be unlikely. In countries which now are anti-Semitic my view will be seconded. In others, where Jews are for the moment secure, it will probably be passionately challenged by my coreligionists. They will not believe me until they are again visited by Jew-baiting; and the longer anti-Semitism lies dormant, the more violently will it erupt. The infiltration of immigrating Jews attracted to a land by apparent security, and the rising class status of native Jews, combine powerfully to bring about a revolution. Nothing could be plainer than this rational conclusion.

Yet, because I have drawn this conclusion with complete indifference to everything but the truth, I shall probably be opposed and rejected by Jews who are in comfortable circumstances. Insofar as private interests alone are held by their anxious or timid possessors to be threatened, they may safely be ignored, for the concerns of the poor and oppressed are of greater importance than theirs. But I wish from the very beginning to deal with any mistaken ideas that might arise: in this case, the fear that if the present plan is realized, it could in any way damage property and interests now held by Jews. I will, therefore, thoroughly explain everything connected with property rights. If, on the other hand, my plan never becomes anything more than literature, things will merely remain as they are.

A more serious objection would be that I am giving aid and comfort to the anti-Semites when I say we are a people—*one* people. Or that I am hindering the assimilation of Jews where there are hopes of achieving it, and endangering it where it is already an accomplished fact, insofar as it is possible for a solitary writer to hinder or endanger anything.

This objection will be brought forward especially in France. It will probably also be made in other countries, but I shall first answer only the French Jews, who afford the most striking example of my point.

However much I may esteem personality—powerful individual personality in statesmen, inventors, artists, philosophers, or leaders, as well as the collective personality of a historic group of human beings, which we designate "nation"—however much I may esteem personality, I do not mourn its decline. Whoever can, will, and must perish, let him perish. But the distinctive nationality of the Jews neither can, will, nor must perish. It cannot, because external enemies consolidate it. It does not wish to; this it has proved through two millennia of appalling suffering. It need not; that, as a descendant of countless Jews who refused to despair, I am trying once more to prove in this pamphlet. Whole branches of Jewry may wither and fall away. The tree lives on.

Hence, if any or all of French Jewry protest against this scheme, because they are already "assimilated," my answer is simple: The whole thing does not concern them at all. They are Israelitic Frenchmen? Splendid! This is a private affair for Jews alone.

However, the movement for the creation of the State which I here propose would harm Israelitic Frenchmen no more than it would harm those who have "assimilated" in other countries. It would, rather, be distinctly to their advantage. For they would no longer be disturbed in their "chromatic function," as Darwin puts it, but would be able to assimilate in peace, because present-day anti-Semitism would have been stopped for all time. For it would certainly be believed that they are assimilated to the very depths of their being if they remained in their old homes, even after the new Jewish State, with its superior institutions, had become a reality.

The departure of the dedicated Jews would be even more to the advantage of the "assimilated" than of the Christian citizens; for they would be freed of the disquieting, unpredictable, and inescapable competition of a Jewish proletariat driven by poverty and political pressure from place to place, from land to land. This drifting proletariat would become stabilized. Certain Christians today—whom we call anti-Semites—feel free to offer determined resistance to the immigration of foreign Jews. Jewish citizens cannot do this, although it affects them far more severely; for it is they who first feel the competition of individuals who engage in similar fields of enterprise, and who besides give rise to anti-Semitism where it does not exist, and intensify it where it does. This is a secret grievance of the "assimilated" which finds expression in their "philanthropic" undertakings. They organize emigration societies for incoming Jews. The ambiguous character of this project would be comical if it did not involve human suffering. Some of these charity institutions are created not for but against the persecuted Jews: Remove the paupers as quickly and as far away as possible. And thus, many an apparent friend of the Jews turns out, on closer examination, to be no more than an anti-Semite of Jewish origin in philanthropist's clothing.

But the attempts at colonization made even by truly well-meaning men, interesting attempts though they were, have so far been unsuccessful. I do not think that one or another person took up the matter merely as an amusement, that they sent Jews off on their journeys in the same spirit as one races horses. The matter was too grave and too painful for that. These attempts were interesting, to the extent that they may serve on a small scale as an experiment fore-shadowing the Jewish State idea. They were even useful, for out of their mistakes we may learn how to proceed in a large-scale project. They have, of course, also done harm. The transplantation of anti-Semitism to new areas, which is the inevitable consequence of such artificial infiltration, seems to me the least of these aftereffects. Far worse is the fact that the unsatisfactory results inspire doubt among the Jews themselves as to the capacity of Jewish manpower. But the following simple argument will suffice to dispel this doubt for any intelligent person: What is impractical or impossible on a small scale need not be so on a larger one. A small enterprise may result in loss under the same conditions that would make a large one pay. A rivulet is not navigable even by boats; the river into which it flows carries stately iron vessels.

No human being is wealthy or powerful enough to transplant a people from one place of residence to another.[4] Only an idea can achieve that. The State idea surely has that power. The Jews have dreamed this princely dream throughout the long night of their history. "Next year in Jerusalem" is our age-old motto. It is now a matter of showing that the vague dream can be transformed into a clear and glowing idea.

For this, our minds must first be thoroughly cleansed of many old, outworn, muddled, and shortsighted notions. The unthinking might, for example, imagine that this exodus would have to take its way from civilization into the desert. That is not so! It will be carried out entirely in the framework of civilization. We shall not revert to a lower stage; we shall rise to a higher one. We shall not dwell in mud huts; we shall build new, more beautiful, and more modern houses, and possess them in safety. We shall not lose our acquired possessions; we shall realize them. We shall surrender our well-earned rights for better ones. We shall relinquish none of our cherished customs; we shall find them again. We shall not leave our old home until the new one is available. Those only will depart who are sure thereby to im-prove their lot; those who are now desperate will go first, after them the poor, next the well to do, and last of all the wealthy. Those who go first will raise themselves to a higher grade, on a level with that whose representatives will shortly follow. The exodus will thus at the same time be an ascent in class.

The departure of the Jews will leave no wake of economic disturbance, no crises, no persecutions; in fact, the countries of emigration will rise to a new prosperity. There will be an inner migration of Christian citizens into the positions relinquished by Jews. The outflow will be gradual, without any disturbance, and its very inception means the end of anti-Semitism. The Jews will leave as honored friends, and if some of them later return they will receive the same favorable welcome and treatment at the hands of civilized nations as is accorded all foreign visitors. Nor will their exodus in any way be a flight, but it will be a well-regulated movement under the constant check of public opinion. The movement will not only be inaugurated in absolute accordance with the law, but it can nowise be carried out without the friendly co-operation of the interested governments, who will derive substantial benefits.

To see that the idea is carried out responsibly and vigorously, the kind of guarantee is required which can be provided by the kind of corporate body which legal terminology calls a "moral" or "legal" person. I should like to distinguish clearly between these two designations, which are frequently confused. As "moral person," to deal with all but property rights, I propose to establish the "Society of Jews." As "legal person," to conduct economic activities, there will be a parallel "Jewish Company."

Only an impostor or a madman would even pretend to undertake such a monumental task on his own. The integrity of the "moral person" will be guaranteed by the character of its members. The capacity of the "legal person" will be demonstrated by its capital funds.

These prefatory remarks are intended merely as an immediate reply to the mass of objections which the very words "Jewish State" are certain to arouse. Hereafter we shall proceed more deliberately in our exposition, meeting further objections and explaining in detail what has only been outlined as yet, though we shall try, in the interest of a smoothly reading pamphlet, to avoid a ponderous tone. Succinct, pithy chapters will best serve the purpose.

If I wish to replace an old building with a new one, I must demolish before I construct. I shall therefore adhere to this natural sequence. In the first, the general, section, I shall clarify my ideas, sweep away age-old preconceptions, establish the politico-economic premises, and unfold the plan.

In the special section, which is subdivided into three principal sections, I shall describe its execution. These three sections are: The Jewish Company, Local Groups, and the Society of Jews. The Society is to be created first, the Company last; but in this exposition the reverse order is preferable, because it is the financial soundness of the enterprise which will chiefly be called into question, and doubts on this score must be removed first.

In the conclusion, I shall try to meet every further objection that could possibly be made. My Jewish readers will, I hope, follow me patiently to the end. Some will make their objections in another order than that chosen for their refutation. But whoever finds his reservations rationally overcome, let him offer himself to the cause.

Although I speak here in terms of reason, I am well aware that reason alone will not suffice. Long-term prisoners do not willingly quit their cells. We shall see whether the youth, whom we must have, is ripe; the youth—which irresistibly draws along the aged, bears them up on powerful arms, and transforms rationality into enthusiasm.

CHAPTER 2. THE JEWISH QUESTION

NO ONE CAN DENY the gravity of the Jewish situation. Wherever they live in appreciable number, Jews are persecuted in greater or lesser measure. Their equality before the law, granted by statute, has become practically a dead letter. They are debarred from filling even moderately high offices in the army, or in any public or private institutions. And attempts are being made to thrust them out of business also: "Don't buy from Jews!"

Attacks in parliaments, in assemblies, in the press, in the pulpit, in the street, on journeys—for example, their exclusion from certain hotels—even in places of recreation are increasing from day to day. The forms of persecutions vary according to country and social circle. In Russia, special taxes are levied on Jewish villages; in Romania, a few persons are put to death; in Germany, they get a good beating occasionally; in Austria, anti-Semites exercise their terrorism over all public life; in Algeria, there are traveling agitators; in Paris, the Jews are shut out of the so-called best social circles and excluded from clubs. The varieties of anti-Jewish expression are innumerable. But this is not the occasion to attempt the sorry catalogue of Jewish hardships. We shall not dwell on particular cases, however painful.

I do not aim to arouse sympathy on our behalf. All that is nonsense, as futile as it is dishonorable. I shall content myself with putting the following questions to the Jews: Is it not true that, in countries where we live in appreciable numbers, the position of Jewish lawyers, doctors, technicians, teachers, and employees of every description becomes daily more intolerable? Is it not true that the Jewish middle classes are seriously threatened? Is it not true that the passions of the mob are incited against our wealthy? Is it not true that our poor endure greater suffering than any other proletariat? I think that this pressure is everywhere present. In our upper economic classes it causes discomfort, in our middle classes utter despair.

The fact of the matter is, everything tends to one and the same conclusion, which is expressed in the classic Berlin cry: *"Juden 'raus!"* ("Out with the Jews!").

I shall now put the question in the briefest possible form: Shouldn't we "get out" at once, and if so, whither?

Or, may we remain, and if so, how long?

Let us first settle the point of remaining. Can we hope for better days, can we possess our souls in patience, can we wait in pious resignation till the princes and peoples of this earth are more mercifully disposed toward us? I say that we cannot hope for the current to shift. And why not? Even if we were as near to the hearts of princes as are their other subjects, they could not protect us. They would only incur popular hatred by showing us too much favor. And this "too much" implies less than is claimed as a right by any ordinary citizen or ethnic group. The nations in whose midst Jews live are all covertly or openly anti-Semitic.

The common people have not, and indeed cannot have, any comprehension of history. They do not know that the sins of the Middle Ages are now being visited on the nations of Europe. We are what the ghetto made us. We have without a doubt attained pre-eminence in finance because medieval conditions drove us to it. The same process in now being repeated. We are again being forced into moneylending—now named stock exchange—by being kept out of other occupations. But once on the stock exchange, we are again objects of contempt. At the same time we continue to produce an abundance of mediocre intellectuals who find no outlet, and this endangers our social position as much as does our increasing wealth. Educated Jews without means are now rapidly becoming socialists. Hence we are certain to suffer acutely in the struggle between the classes, because we stand in the most exposed position in both the capitalist and the socialist camps.

Previous Attempts at a Solution

The artificial methods heretofore employed to remedy the plight of Jews have been either too petty, such as attempts at colonization, or falsely conceived, such as attempts to convert the Jews into peasants in their present homes.

What is achieved by transporting a few thousand Jews to another country? Either they come to grief at once, or, if they prosper, their prosperity gives rise to anti-Semitism. We have already discussed these attempts to channel poor Jews to new regions. This diversion is clearly inadequate and useless, if not actually harmful, for it merely postpones and drags out if not actually hinders the solution.

But those who would attempt to convert Jews into peasants are committing a truly astonishing error. For the peasant is a creature of the past, as seen by his style of dress, which in most countries is centuries old, and by his tools, which are identical with those used by his earliest forebears. His plow is unchanged; he sows his seed from the apron, mows with the time-honored scythe, and threshes with the flail. But we know that all this can now be done by machinery. The agrarian question is only a question of machinery. America must conquer Europe, in the same way as large landed possessions absorb small ones. The peasant is, consequently, a type which is on the way to extinction. Wherever he is preserved by special measures, there are involved political interests who hope to gain his support. To create new peasants on the old pattern is an absurd and impossible undertaking. No one is wealthy or powerful enough to make civilization take a single step backward. The mere preservation of obsolete institutions is a task vast enough to strain the capacities of even an autocratic state.

Will anyone, then, suggest to Jews, who know what they are about, that they become peasants of the old cast? That would be like saying to the Jew: "Here is a crossbow; now go to war!" What? With a crossbow, while others have small arms and Krupp cannon? Under these circumstances the Jews would be perfectly right in remaining unmoved when people try to place them on the farm. The crossbow is a pretty piece of armament, which inspires a lyrical mood in me whenever I can spare the time. But its proper place is the museum.

Now, there certainly are regions where desperate Jews go out, or at any rate are willing to go out, and till the soil. And a little observation shows that these areas, such as the enclave of Hesse in Germany and some provinces in Russia—these areas are the very hotbeds of anti-Semitism.

For the do-gooders of the world who send the Jews to the plow forget a very important person, who has a great deal to say in the matter. That person is the peasant. And the peasant is absolutely in the right. For the tax on the land, the risks attached to crops, the pressure of large proprietors who produce at cheaper rates, not to mention American competition, all combine to make life difficult enough for him. Besides, the duties on corn cannot go on increasing indefinitely. For the factory worker cannot be allowed to starve, either; his political influence is, in fact, in the ascendant, and he must therefore be treated with ever-increasing respect.

All these difficulties are well known; therefore I refer to them only cursorily. I merely wanted to indicate clearly how futile have been past attempts—most of them well intentioned—to solve the Jewish question. Neither a diversion of the stream nor an artificial depression of the intellectual level of our proletariat will avail. And we have already dealt with the panacea of assimilation.

We cannot overcome anti-Semitism by any of these methods. It cannot be eliminated until its causes are eradicated. But are they eradicable?

Causes of Anti-Semitism

We now no longer discuss the irrational causes, prejudice and narrow-mindedness, but the political and economic causes. Modern anti-Semitism is not to be confused with the persecution of the Jews in former times, though it does still have a religious aspect in some countries. The main current of Jew-hatred is today a different one. In the principal centers of anti-Semitism, it is an outgrowth of the emancipation of the Jews. When civilized nations awoke to the inhumanity of discriminatory legislation and enfranchised us, our enfranchisement came too late. Legislation alone no longer sufficed to emancipate us in our old homes. For in the ghetto we had remarkably developed into a bourgeois people and we emerged from the ghetto a prodigious rival to the middle class. Thus we found ourselves thrust, upon emancipation, into this bourgeois circle, where we have a double pressure to sustain, from within and from without. The Christian bourgeoisie would indeed not be loath to cast us as a peace offering to socialism, little though that would avail them.

At the same time, the equal rights of Jews before the law cannot be rescinded where they have once been granted. Not only because their recision would be contrary to the spirit of our age, but also because it would immediately drive all Jews, rich and poor alike, into the ranks of the revolutionary parties. No serious harm can really be done us. In olden days our jewels were taken from us. How is our movable property to be seized now? It consists of printed papers which are locked up somewhere or other in the world, perhaps in the strongboxes of Christians. It is, of course, possible to get at railway shares and debentures, banks and industrial undertakings of all descriptions, by taxation; and where the progressive income tax is in force all our movable property can eventually be laid hold of. But all these efforts cannot be directed against Jews alone, and wherever they might nevertheless be made, their upshot would be immediate economic crises, which would by no means be confined to the Jews as the first affected. The very impossibility of getting at the Jews nourishes and deepens hatred of them. Anti-Semitism increases day by day and hour by hour among the nations; indeed, it is bound to increase, because the causes of its growth continue to exist and are ineradicable. Its remote cause is the loss of our assimilability during the Middle Ages; its immediate cause is our excessive production of mediocre intellectuals, who have no outlet downward or upward—or rather, no wholesome outlet in either direction. When we sink, we become a revolutionary proletariat, the corporals of every revolutionary party; and when we rise, there rises also our terrifying financial power.

Effects of Anti-Semitism

The pressure applied to us does not improve us, for we are no different from ordinary people. It is true enough that we do not love our enemies; but he alone who has quite mastered himself dares throw that up to us. Oppression naturally creates hostility against oppressors, and our hostility in turn increases the pressure. It is impossible to escape this vicious circle.

"No!" some softhearted visionaries will say. "No! It *is* possible! Possible by means of the perfectibility of man."

Is it really necessary for me, at this late stage, to show what sentimental drivel this is? He who would peg the improvement of conditions on the goodness of all mankind would indeed be writing a *Utopia!*

I referred previously to our "assimilation." I do not for a moment wish to imply that I desire such an end. Our national character is too glorious in history and, in spite of every degradation, too noble to make its annihilation desirable. Though perhaps we *could* succeed in vanishing without a trace into the surrounding peoples if they would let us be for just two generations. But they will not let us be. After brief periods of toleration, their hostility erupts again and again. When we prosper, it seems to be unbearably irritating, for the world has for many centuries been accustomed to regarding us as the most degraded of the poor. Thus out of ignorance or ill will they have failed to observe that prosperity weakens us as Jews and wipes away our differences. Only pressure drives us back to our own; only hostility stamps us ever again as strangers.

Thus we are now, and shall remain, whether we would or not, a group of unmistakable cohesiveness.

We are one people—our enemies have made us one whether we will or not, as has repeatedly happened in history. Affliction binds us together, and thus united, we suddenly discover our strength. Yes, we are strong enough to form a State, and, indeed, a model State. We possess all the requisite human and material resources.

This would, accordingly, be the appropriate place to give an account of what has been somewhat crudely termed our "human material." But it would not be appreciated till the broad outlines of the plan, on which everything depends, have first been marked out.

The Plan

The whole plan is essentially quite simple, as it must necessarily be if it is to be comprehensible to all.

Let sovereignty be granted us over a portion of the globe adequate to meet our rightful national requirements; we will attend to the rest.

To create a new State is neither ridiculous nor impossible. Haven't we witnessed the process in our own day, among nations which were not largely middle class as we are, but poorer, less educated, and consequently weaker than ourselves? The governments of all countries scourged by anti-Semitism will be keenly interested in obtaining sovereignty for us.

The plan, simple in design but complicated in execution, will be executed by two agencies: the Society of Jews and the Jewish Company.

The scientific plan and political policies which the Society of Jews will establish will be carried out by the Jewish Company.

The Jewish Company will be the liquidating agent for the business interests of departing Jews, and will organize trade and commerce in the new country.

We must not visualize the exodus of the Jews as a sudden one. It will be gradual, proceeding over a period of decades. The poorest will go first and cultivate the soil. They will construct roads, bridges, railways, and telegraph installations, regulate rivers, and provide themselves with homesteads, all according to predetermined plans. Their labor will create trade, trade will create markets, and markets will attract new settlers—for every man will go voluntarily, at his own expense and his own risk. The labor invested in the soil will enhance its value. The Jews will soon perceive that a new and permanent frontier has been opened up for that spirit of enterprise which has heretofore brought them only hatred and obloquy.

The founding of a State today is not to be accomplished in the manner that a thousand years ago would have been the only possible one. It is silly to revert to older levels of civilization, as many Zionists propose. Supposing, for example, we were obliged to clear a country of wild beasts, we should not set about it in the fashion of the fifth-century Europeans. We should not take spear and lance and go out individually in pursuit of bears; we would organize a grand and glorious hunting party, drive the animals together, and throw a melinite bomb into their midst.

If we planned to erect buildings, we should not drive a few shaky piles in a marsh like the lake dwellers, but should build as men build now. Indeed, we shall build in bolder and more stately style than has ever been done before; for we now possess means which heretofore did not exist.

The emigrants standing lowest in the economic scale will be gradually followed by those of the next grade. Those now in desperate straits will go first. They will be led by the intellectual mediocrities whom we produce so abundantly and who are oppressed everywhere.

Let this pamphlet serve as the beginning of a general discussion on the question of Jewish emigration. That does not mean to suggest, however, that the question should be called to a vote. Such an approach would ruin the cause from the outset. Whoever wishes may stay behind. The opposition of a few individuals is quite immaterial.

Who would go with us, let him fall in behind our banner and fight for the cause with word and pen and deed.

Those Jews who agree with our State idea will rally around the Society. Thereby they will give it the authority in the eyes of governments to confer and treat on behalf of our people. The Society will be recognized as, to put it in terminology of international law, a State-creating power. And this recognition will, in effect, mean the creation of the State.

Should the powers show themselves willing to grant us sovereignty over a neutral land, then the Society will enter into negotiations for the possession of this land. Here two regions come to mind: Palestine and Argentina. Significant experiments in colonization have been made in both countries, though on the mistaken principle of gradual infiltration of Jews. Infiltration is bound to end badly. For there comes the inevitable moment when the government in question, under pressure of the native populace—which feels itself threatened —puts a stop to further influx of Jews. Immigration, therefore, is futile unless it is based on our guaranteed autonomy.

The Society of Jews will treat with the present authorities in the land, under the sponsorship of the European powers, if they prove friendly to the plan. We could offer the present authorities enormous advantages, assume part of the public debt, build new thoroughfares, which we ourselves would also require, and do many other things. The very creation of the Jewish State would be beneficial to neighboring lands, since the cultivation of a strip of land increases the value of its surrounding districts.

Palestine or Argentina?

Is Palestine or Argentina preferable? The Society will take whatever it is given and whatever Jewish public opinion favors. The Society will determine both these points.

Argentina is one of the most fertile countries in the world, extends over a vast area, is sparsely populated, and has a temperate climate. It would be in its own highest interest for the Republic of Argentina to cede us a portion of its territory. The present *infiltration* of Jews has certainly produced some discontent, and it would be necessary to enlighten the Republic on the intrinsic difference of the new *immigration* of Jews.

Palestine is our unforgettable historic homeland. The very name would be a marvelously effective rallying cry. If His Majesty the Sultan were to give us Palestine, we could in return undertake the complete management of the finances of Turkey. We should there form a part of a wall of defense for Europe in Asia, an outpost of civilization against barbarism. We should as a neutral state remain in contact with all Europe, which would have to guarantee our existence.

The holy places of Christendom could be placed under some form of international exterritoriality. We should form a guard of honor about these holy places, answering for the fulfillment of this duty with our existence. The guard of honor would be the great symbol of the solution of the Jewish question after what were for us eighteen centuries of affliction.

CONCLUSION

HOW MUCH REMAINS to be elaborated, how many defects, how many harmful superficialities, and how many useless repetitions in this pamphlet which I have so long considered and so frequently revised!

But a fair-minded reader, who has sufficient understanding to grasp the spirit of my words, will not be repelled by these defects. He will rather be roused thereby to enlist his intelligence and energy in a project which is not one man's alone and improve it.

Have I not explained obvious things and overlooked important objections?

I have tried to meet some objections; but I know that there are many more, high-minded and base.

It is one of the high-minded objections that the Jews are not the only people in the world who are in a state of distress. But I should think that we might well begin by removing a little of this misery, be it only our own for the time being.

It might further be said that we ought not to create new distinctions between people; we ought not to raise fresh barriers, we should rather make the old disappear. I say that those who think in this way are amiable visionaries; and the Homeland idea will go on flourishing long after the dust of their bones will have been scattered without trace by the winds. Universal brotherhood is not even a beautiful dream. Conflict is essential to man's highest efforts.

Well, then? The Jews, in their own State, will likely have no more enemies, and in their prosperity they will decline and dwindle, so that the Jewish people will soon disappear altogether? I imagine that the Jews will always have sufficient enemies, just as every other nation. But once settled in their own land, they can never again be scattered all over the world. The Diaspora cannot be revived, unless all of civilization collapses. Only a simpleton could fear this. The civilized world of today has sufficient power to defend itself.

The base objections are innumerable, just as there are indeed more base men than noble in this world. I have tried to refute some of the narrow-minded notions. Whoever would rally behind the white flag with the seven stars must assist in this campaign of enlightenment. It may be that it is against many a malicious, narrow-minded, short-sighted Jew that the battle will first have to be joined.

Will it not be said that I am providing weapons for the anti-Semites? How so? Because I admit the truth? Because I do not maintain that there are none but excellent men among us?

Will it not be said that I am suggesting a way in which we can be injured? This I categorically deny. My proposal can be carried out only with the free consent of a majority of Jews. Action may be taken against individuals, even against groups of the most powerful Jews, but never and by no means by governments against all Jews. The equal rights of the Jew before the law once granted cannot be rescinded, for the first attempt would immediately drive all Jews, rich and poor alike, into the ranks of revolutionary parties. The very beginning of official discrimination against the Jews has invariably brought about economic crises. Very little, therefore, can effectually be done against us that will not redound to the detriment of the perpetrator. Meantime hatred grows apace. The rich do not feel it much. But our poor! Let us ask our poor, who have been more severely proletarized since the last resurgence of anti-Semitism than ever before.

Will some of our well to do say that the pressure is not yet severe enough to justify emigration, and that even the forcible expulsions that have occurred show how unwilling our people are to depart? True, because they do not know whither! Because they only pass from one trouble on to the next. But we are showing them the way to the Promised Land. And the splendid force of enthusiasm must fight against the terrible force of habit.

Persecutions are no longer as vicious as they were in the Middle Ages? True, but our sensitivity has increased, so that we feel no diminution in our suffering. Prolonged persecution has strained our nerves.

Will people say, again, that the venture is hopeless, because even if we obtain the land with sovereignty over it, the poor only will go along? It is precisely they whom we need at first! Only desperate men make good conquerors.

Will some one say: If it were feasible it would have been done long ago?

It has never yet been possible. Now it is possible. A hundred, even fifty, years ago it would have been sheer fantasy. Today it is reality. The rich, who enjoy a comprehensive acquaintance with all technical advances, know full well how much can be done for money. And this is how it will go: precisely the poor and simple, who have no idea what power man already exercises over the forces of Nature, will have the staunchest faith in the new message. For these have never lost their hope of the Promised Land.

Here you have it, Jews! Not fiction, nor yet fraud! Every man may convince himself of it, for every man will carry over with him a portion of the Promised Land—one in his head, another in his arms, another in his acquired possessions.

Now, all this may appear to be a drawn-out affair. Even in the most favorable circumstances, many years might elapse before the founding of the State is under way. In the meantime, Jews in a thousand different places will suffer insult, mortification, abuse, drubbings, depredation, and death. But no; once we begin to execute the plan, anti-Semitism will cease at once and everywhere. For it is the conclusion of peace. When the Jewish Company has been formed, the news will be carried in a single day to the utmost ends of the globe by the lightning speed of our telegraph wires.

And immediate relief will ensue. The intellectuals whom we produce so superabundantly in our middle classes will find an immediate outlet in our organizations, as our first technicians, officers, professors, officials, lawyers, physicians. And so it will continue, swiftly but smoothly.

Prayers will be offered up in the temples for the success of the project. And in the churches as well! It is the relief from the old burden, under which all have suffered.

But first the minds must be enlightened. The idea must make its way into the uttermost miserable holes where our people dwell. They will awaken from barren brooding. For into all our lives will come a new meaning. Every man need think only of himself, and the movement will become an overwhelming one.

And what glory awaits the selfless fighters for the cause!

Therefore I believe that a wondrous breed of Jews will spring up from the earth. The Maccabees will rise again.

Let me repeat once more my opening words: The Jews who will it shall achieve their State.

We shall live at last as free men on our own soil, and in our own homes peacefully die.

The world will be liberated by our freedom, enriched by our wealth, magnified by our greatness.

And whatever we attempt there for our own benefit will redound mightily and beneficially to the good of all mankind.

FIRST CONGRESS ADDRESS (1897)

Delivered at Basel, August 29, 1897

FELLOW DELEGATES: As one of those who called this Congress into being I have been granted the privilege of welcoming you. This I shall do briefly, for if we wish to serve the cause we should economize the valuable moments of the Congress. There is much to be accomplished within the space of three days. We want to lay the foundations of the edifice which is one day to house the Jewish people. The task is so great that we may treat of it in none but the simplest terms. So far as we can now foresee, a summary of the present status of the Jewish question will be submitted within the coming three days. The tremendous bulk of material on hand is being classified by the chairmen of our committees.

We shall hear reports of the Jewish situation in the various countries. You all know, even if only in a vague way, that with few exceptions the situation is not cheering. Were it otherwise we should probably not have convened. The unity of our destiny has suffered a long interruption, although the scattered fragments of the Jewish people have everywhere endured similar vicissitudes. It is only in our days that the marvels of communication have brought about mutual understanding and union between isolated groups. And in these times, so progressive in most respects, we know ourselves to be surrounded by the old, old hatred. Anti-Semitism—you know it, alas, too well!—is the up-to-date designation of the movement. The first impression which it made upon the Jews of today was one of astonishment, which gave way to pain and resentment. Perhaps our enemies are quite unaware how deeply they wounded the sensibilities of just those of us who were possibly not the primary objects of their attack. That very part of Jewry which is modern and cultured, which has outgrown the ghetto and lost the habit of petty trading, was pierced to the heart. We can assert it calmly, without laying ourselves open to the suspicion of wanting to appeal to the sentimental pity of our opponents. We have faced the situation squarely.

Since time immemorial the world has been misinformed about us. The sentiment of solidarity with which we have been reproached so frequently and so acrimoniously was in process of disintegration at the very time we were being attacked by anti-Semitism. And anti-Semitism served to strengthen it anew. We returned home, as it were. For Zionism is a return to the Jewish fold even before it becomes a return to the Jewish land. We, the children who have returned, find much to redress under the ancestral roof, for some of our brothers have sunk deep into misery. We are made welcome in the ancient house, for it is universally known that we are not actuated by an arrogant desire to undermine that which should be revered. This will be clearly demonstrated by the Zionist platform.

Zionism has already brought about something remarkable, heretofore regarded as impossible: a close union between the ultramodern and the ultraconservative elements of Jewry. The fact that this has come to pass without undignified concessions on the part of either side, without intellectual sacrifices, is further proof, if such proof is necessary, of the national entity of the Jews. A union of this kind is possible only on a national basis.

Doubtless there will be discussions on the subject of an organization the need for which is recognized by all. Organization is an evidence of the reasonableness of a movement. But there is one point which should be clearly and energetically emphasized in order to advance the solution of the Jewish question. We Zionists desire not an international league but international discussion. Needless to say this distinction is of the first importance in our eyes. It is this distinction which justifies the convening of our Congress. There will be no question of intrigues, secret interventions, and devious methods in our ranks, but only of unhampered utterances under the constant and complete check of public opinion. One of the first results of our movement, even now to be perceived in its larger outlines, will be the transformation of the Jewish question into a question of Zion.

A popular movement of such vast dimension will necessarily be attacked from many sides. Therefore the Congress will concern itself with the spiritual means to be employed for reviving and fostering the national consciousness of the Jews. Here, too, we must struggle against misconceptions. We have not the least intention of yielding a jot of the culture we have acquired. On the contrary, we are aiming toward a broader culture, such as an increase of knowledge brings with it. As a matter of fact, the Jews have always been more active mentally than physically.

It was because the practical forerunners of Zionism realized this that they inaugurated agricultural work for the Jews. We shall never be able, nor shall we desire, to speak of these attempts at colonization in Palestine and in Argentina otherwise than with genuine gratitude. But they spoke the first, not the last word of the Zionist movement. For the Zionist movement must be greater in scope if it is to be at all. A people can be helped only by its own efforts, and if it cannot help itself it is beyond succor. But we Zionists want to rouse the people to self-help. No premature, unwholesome hopes should be awakened in this direction. This is another reason why public procedure, as it is planned by our Congress, is so essential.

Those who give the matter careful consideration must surely admit that Zionism cannot gain its ends otherwise than through an unequivocal understanding with the political units involved. It is generally known that the difficulties of obtaining colonization rights were not created by Zionism in its present form. One wonders what motives actuate the narrators of these fables. The confidence of the government with which we want to negotiate regarding the settlement of Jewish masses on a large scale can be gained by plain language and upright dealing. The advantages which an entire people is able to offer in return for benefits received are so considerable that the negotiations are vested with sufficient importance a priori. It would be an idle beginning to engage in lengthy discussions today regarding the legal form which the agreement will finally assume. But one thing is to be adhered to inviolably: The agreement must be based on rights, and not on toleration. Indeed we have had enough experience of toleration and of "protection" which could be withdrawn at any time.

Consequently the only reasonable course of action which our movement can pursue is to work for publicly legalized guarantees. The results of colonization as it has been carried on hitherto were quite satisfactory within its limitations. It confirmed the much disputed fitness of the Jews for agricultural work. It established this proof for all time, as the legal phrase has it. But colonization in its present form is not, and cannot be, the solution of the Jewish question. And we must admit unreservedly that it has failed to evoke much sympathy. Why? Because the Jews know how to calculate; in fact, it has been asserted that they calculate too well. Thus, if we assume that there are nine million Jews in the world, and that it would be possible to colonize ten thousand Jews in Palestine every year, the Jewish question would require nine hundred years for its solution. This would seem impracticable.

On the other hand, you know that to count on ten thousand settlers a year under existing circumstances is nothing short of fantastic. The Turkish government would doubtless unearth the old immigration restrictions immediately, and to that we would have little objection. For if anyone thinks that the Jews can steal into the land of their fathers, he is deceiving either himself or others. Nowhere is the coming of Jews so promptly noted as in the historic home of the race, for the very reason that it is the historic home. And it would by no means be to our interest to go there prematurely. The immigration of Jews signifies an unhoped-for accession of strength for the land which is now so poor; in fact, for the whole Ottoman Empire. Besides, His Majesty the Sultan has had excellent experiences with his Jewish subjects, and he has been an indulgent monarch to them in turn. Thus, existing conditions point to a successful outcome, provided the whole matter is intelligently and felicitously treated. The financial help which the Jews can give to Turkey is by no means inconsiderable and would serve to obviate many an internal ill from which the country is now suffering. If the Near East question is partially solved together with the Jewish question, it will surely be of advantage to all civilized peoples. The advent of Jews would bring about an improvement in the situation of the Christians in the Orient.

But it is not solely from this aspect that Zionism may count upon the sympathy of the nations. You know that in some lands the Jewish problem has come to mean calamity for the government. If it sides with the Jews, it is confronted by the ire of the masses; if it sides against the Jews, it may call considerable economic consequences down upon its head because of the peculiar influence of the Jews upon the business affairs of the world. Examples of the latter may be found in Russia. But if the government maintains a neutral attitude, the Jews find themselves unprotected by the established regime and rush into the arms of the revolutionaries. Zionism, or self-help for the Jews, points to a way out of these numerous and extraordinary difficulties. Zionism is simply a peacemaker. And it suffers the usual fate of peacemakers, in being forced to fight more than anyone else. But should the accusation that we are not patriotic figure among the more or less sincere arguments directed against our movement, this equivocal objection carries its own refutation with it. Nowhere can there be a question of an exodus of all the Jews. Those who are able or who wish to be assimilated will remain behind and be absorbed. When once a satisfactory agreement is concluded with the various political units involved and a systematic Jewish migration begins, it will last only so long in each country as that country desires to be rid of its Jews. How will the current be stopped? Simply by the gradual decrease and the final cessation of anti-Semitism. Thus it is that we understand and anticipate the solution of the Jewish problem.

All this has been said time and again by my friends and by myself. We shall spare no pains to repeat it again and again until we are understood. On this solemn occasion, when Jews have come together from so many lands at the age-old summons of nationality, let our profession of faith be solemnly repeated. Should we not be stirred by a premonition of great events when we remember that at this moment the hopes of thousands upon thousands of our people depend upon our assemblage? In the coming hour the news of our deliberations and decisions will fly to distant lands, over the seven seas. Therefore enlightenment and comfort should go forth from this Congress. Let everyone find out what Zionism really is, Zionism, which was rumored to be a sort of millennial marvel—that it is a moral, lawful, humanitarian movement, directed toward the long-yearned-for goal of our people. It was possible and permissible to ignore the spoken or written utterances of individuals within our ranks. Not so with the actions of the Congress. Thus the Congress, which is henceforth to be ruler of its discussions, must govern as a wise ruler.

Finally, the Congress will provide for its own continuance, so that we do not disperse once more ineffectual and ephemeral. Through this Congress we are creating an agency for the Jewish people such as it has not possessed heretofore, an agency of which it has stood in urgent need. Our cause is too great to be left to the ambition or the whim of individuals. It must be elevated to the realm of the impersonal if it is to succeed. And our Congress shall live forever, not only until the redemption from age-long suffering is effected, but afterward as well. Today we are here in the hospitable limits of this free city— where shall we be next year?

But wherever we shall be, and however distant the accomplishment of our task, let our Congress be earnest and high-minded, a source of welfare to the unhappy, of defiance to none, of honor to all Jewry. Let it be worthy of our past, the renown of which, though remote, is eternal!

AFTER A MASS MEETING IN THE EAST END (1896)

London, July 15, 1896

ON SUNDAY, while I sat on the platform I was in a curious mood. I saw and heard the rising of my legend. The people are sentimental; the masses do not see clearly. I believe that even now they no longer have a clear idea of me. A light mist has begun to beat about me, which will perhaps deepen into a cloud in the midst of which I shall walk. But even now if they no longer see my outline clearly, at least they understand that I mean well by them, I am the man of the poor.

MAX NORDAU 1849-1923

NORDAU was Herzl's most important colleague and disciple; indeed in 1896 when he accepted Herzl's Zionist faith, Nordau was much the more famous of the two, for he already possessed a European-wide reputation as an *avant-garde* writer and critic of society.

Like Herzl, he was born in Budapest and received a comparable education under German cultural influence. Nordau began to write in his adolescence, and by 1873 his literary gifts were sufficiently well regarded to earn him the post of Viennese correspondent of the important German language newspaper of Budapest, the *Pester Lloyd*. After two years of travel, which gave him the material for his first book, *From the Kremlin to the Alhambra*, Nordau returned to Budapest in 1875 to complete his studies for a medical degree. By 1880 he was permanently domiciled in Paris, practicing as a doctor, writing for a number of newspapers in the German language, especially for the *Vossische Zeitung* of Berlin, and publishing a succession of books.

His great literary *succès de scandale* occurred in 1883, when his *Conventional Lies of Civilization* appeared. In the name of science and positivist philosophy, which were then the dominant advanced thought of Europe, he wrote an uncompromising analysis of the cultural scene and a particularly violent attack upon religion. The Catholic Church placed the book on the Index; it was banned in Austria, Russia, and England; and the ensuing publicity resulted in seventy-three editions in a variety of languages. In two later volumes, *Paradoxes* and *Degeneration*, he widened his attacks to blast such great names in literature as Ibsen and Maeterlinck. Abnormal psychology was being created as a modern discipline in the 1880's and the Italian investigator Cesare Lombroso had called attention to the intimate relationship that he saw between genius and madness. Nordau took up the argument to assail all the writers he disliked as hypocrites, neurotics, and degenerates. In a sense he was a Freudian kind of critic of literature a generation before this genre appeared.

At the zenith of his career Nordau regarded himself as a European, personally not involved in any national allegiance, who was equally concerned for the downtrodden of all nations and religions. As an old friend, he was one of the first to whom Theodor Herzl came to expound his Zionist ideas. There is even a perhaps apocryphal story that Herzl came to Nordau not only as friend but also to consult him as psychiatrist, in the fear that he was out of his mind. After several days of conversation Nordau supposedly stretched out his hand to Herzl to say: "If you are crazy, so am I." Nordau, at any rate, had also been present at the degradation of Dreyfus on the parade ground of the Ecole Militaire and had also been deeply affected emotionally by the anti-Semitic outcries which attended that scene. Nordau had even deeper roots than Herzl in the Jewish tradition, even though he had been alienated from Jewish concerns for all his adult life, because his father, who was a teacher of Hebrew by profession, had provided him with a good early education in the sacred tongue.

Nordau's adherence to Zionism gave it the stamp of approval as "advanced" thought and helped attract younger Jewish intellectuals, like Bernard Lazare and Israel Zangwill, to the new cause. A master of rhetoric, he gave an opening address on the state of Jewry at the First Zionist Congress and repeated this performance at every one until the tenth. However, within a few years after the death of Herzl, Nordau found himself estranged from the new leadership of the Zionist movement. He remained an uncompromising "messianist," contemptuous both of philanthropic and cultural Zionism. The organization was now in the hands of the "practical" Zionists, who believed that the ultimate political aim of the movement should be subordinated to the immediate work of building up the Jewish settlement in Palestine.

When World War I broke out he announced his pacifism but nonetheless, as an Austrian subject, he had to leave France for Madrid, where he spent the war years writing. Nordau returned to the Zionist scene in 1919. He was quite impatient with the careful phraseology of the Balfour Declaration, which had been issued in 1917 while he was in Madrid, for he kept demanding not merely "a Jewish National Home in Palestine" but the immediate establishment of a Jewish state. The border war among the Poles, Ukrainians, and Russians was then raging and it was attended by the murder of tens of thousands of Jews. Though Nordau knew that conditions in Palestine were not ripe to receive the immediate immigration of large numbers, he demanded that such be done, even if many would suffer and many more would be unable to remain in the land. Evacuation was better than death, and the immediate creation of a Jewish majority in Palestine which would result was more important than careful colonization. In these views he approached the position of the young Vladimir Jabotinsky, whom we shall meet later in this volume, the most uncompromising integral nationalist of the next generation of Zionist leaders.

In 1920 Nordau was permitted to return to Paris, where he died on January 23, 1923. Three years later his remains were transferred to Tel Aviv.

SPEECH TO THE FIRST ZIONIST CONGRESS (1897)

THE WESTERN JEW has bread, but man does not live by bread alone. The life of the western Jew is no longer endangered by the enmity of the mob, but bodily wounds are not the only ones that cause pain, and from which one may bleed to death. The western Jew regarded emancipation as real liberation, and hastened to draw final conclusions from it. But the nations of the world made him realize that he erred in being so thoughtlessly logical. The law magnanimously lays down the theory of equality of rights. But governments and society practice equality in a manner which makes it as much a mockery as the appointment of Sancho Panza to the splendid position of Viceroy of the Island of Barataria. The Jew says naïvely: "I am a human being and I regard nothing human as alien." The answer he meets is: "Softly, your rights as a man must be enjoyed cautiously; you lack true honor, a sense of duty, morality, patriotism, idealism. We must, therefore, keep you from all vocations which require these qualities."

No one has ever tried to justify these terrible accusations by facts. At most, now and then, an individual Jew, the scum of his race and of mankind, is triumphantly cited as an example, and, contrary to all laws of logic, bold generalizations are constructed on the basis of such an example. Psychologically this is not surprising. The human mind is accustomed to inventing seemingly reasonable causes for the prejudices which are aroused by emotion. Folk wisdom has long been intuitively acquainted with this psychological law and has expressed it in a striking way: "If you have to drown a dog," says the proverb, "you must first declare him to be mad." All kinds of vices are falsely attributed to the Jews, because people want to prove to themselves that they have a right to detest them. But the primary sentiment is the detestation of the Jews.

I must express the painful thought: The nations which emancipated the Jews have deluded themselves as to their own feelings. In order to produce its full effect, emancipation should first have been realized in sentiment before it was proclaimed by law. But this was not the case. The history of Jewish emancipation is one of the most remarkable pages in the history of European thought. The emancipation of the Jews was not the result of a conviction that grave injury had been done to a people, that it had been shockingly treated, and that it was time to atone for the injustice of a thousand years; it was solely the result of the geometrical mode of thought of French rationalism of the eighteenth century. Without reference to sentiment and emotion, this rationalism, operating with logic alone, laid down principles as axiomatic as those of mathematics; it insisted upon trying to introduce these creations of pure intellect into the world of reality. The emancipation of the Jews was an example of the automatic application of the rationalistic method. The philosophy of Rousseau and the Encyclopedists[1] has led up to the declaration of human rights. The strict logic of the men of the Great Revolution deduced Jewish emancipation from this declaration. They formulated a logically correct syllogism: Every man is born with certain rights; the Jews are human beings, consequently the Jews by nature possess the rights of man. In this manner, the emancipation of the Jews was proclaimed in France, not out of fraternal feeling for the Jews but because logic demanded it. Popular sentiment indeed rebelled, but the philosophy of the Revolution decreed that principles must be placed above sentiment. May I be permitted to say something which implies no ingratitude: The men of 1792[2] emancipated us only for the sake of logic.

In the same way that the French Revolution gave to the world the metric and the decimal systems, it also created a kind of normal spiritual scale which other countries, either willingly or unwillingly, accepted as the normal measure of their cultural level. A country which laid claim to cultural attainment had to possess several institutions created or developed by the Great Revolution, as, for instance, representative government, freedom of the press, trial by jury, division of powers, etc. Jewish emancipation was also one of these indispensable furnishings of a highly cultured state, like a piano which is a required article of furniture in a drawing room, even if not a single member of the family can play it. In this manner Jews were emancipated in western Europe not from an inner necessity, but in imitation of a political fashion, not because the nations had decided in their hearts to stretch out the hand of fraternity to the Jews, but because their intellectual leaders had accepted a certain standard, one of whose requirements was that the emancipation of the Jews should figure in the statute book.

There is only one country, England, which is an exception to what I have said above. The English people does not allow its progress to be forced upon it from without; it develops it from its inner self. In England emancipation is a reality. It is not merely on the books; it is lived. It had already long been realized in sentiment before legislation expressly confirmed it. Out of respect for tradition, there was hesitation about formally abolishing the legal restrictions on Non-Conformists in England at a time when the English had for more than a generation no longer been making any social distinction between Christians and Jews. Naturally, a great nation, with a most intense spiritual life, must be somewhat affected by every spiritual current, or even blunder, of the age, and so England, too, has its few instances of anti-Semitism, but these are important only as imitations of Continental fashion.

Emancipation has totally changed the nature of the Jew, and made him into another being. The ghetto Jew bereft of rights did not love the prescribed yellow badge on his coat, because it was an official invitation to the mob to commit brutalities which it justified in advance. But he voluntarily emphasized it much more than the yellow badge could ever do. Wherever the authorities did not shut him up in a ghetto, he built one for himself. He would dwell with his own and would have no other relations but those of business with Christians. The word "ghetto" is today associated with feelings of shame and humiliation. But students of national psychology and history know that the ghetto, whatever may have been the intentions of the peoples who created it, was for the Jew of the past not a prison, but a refuge.

It is plain historical truth to state that only the ghetto gave Jews the possibility of surviving the terrible persecutions of the Middle Ages. In the ghetto, the Jew had his own world; it was his sure refuge and it provided the spiritual and moral equivalent of a motherland. His fellow inhabitants of the ghetto were the people whose respect he both wanted and could attain. His goal and ambition was to gain its good opinion and its criticism or ill will was the punishment that he feared. In the ghetto all specifically Jewish qualities were esteemed, and by their special development one could obtain that admiration which is the greatest spur to the human spirit. What did it matter that those values which were prized within the ghetto were despised outside it? The opinion of the outside world did not matter, because it was the opinion of ignorant enemies. One tried to please one's brothers, and their respect gave honorable meaning to one's life. In the moral sense, therefore, the Jews of the ghetto lived a full life. Their external situation was insecure, often seriously endangered, but internally they achieved a complete development of their unique qualities and were not fragmentized individuals. They were fully developed human beings, who lacked none of the elements of normal social life. They also sensed instinctively the total importance of the ghetto to their inner life and, therefore, they had but one care: to make its existence secure through invisible walls which were much thicker and higher than the stone walls that surrounded it physically. All Jewish customs and practices unconsciously pursued one sole purpose, to preserve Judaism by separation from the gentiles, to maintain the Jewish community, and to keep reminding the individual Jew that he would be lost and would perish if he gave up his unique character. This impulse toward separateness was the source of most of the ritual laws, which for the average Jew were identical with his very faith. Religious sanction was also given to purely external, and often accidental, differences in attire and custom, as soon as they became acceptable Jewish practice, in order to maintain them more securely.

Such was the psychology of the ghetto Jew. Then came the Emancipation. The law assured the Jews that they were citizens of their country in every respect. In the honeymoon period of the Emancipation, under the influence of the new legal equality, Christian feelings were evoked which were warm and accepting of the new status of the Jew. Well nigh intoxicated, the Jews rushed to burn all their bridges immediately. They now had another home, so they no longer needed a ghetto; they now had other connections and were no longer forced to live only among their coreligionists. Their instinct of self-preservation adapted itself immediately and completely to the new circumstances. This instinct had formerly been directed toward maintaining the most clear-cut apartness; now it sought the closest association with and imitation of the gentiles. In place of being different, which had been the Jew's salvation, the new policy was thoroughgoing mimicry. For one or two generations the Jew was allowed to believe that he was merely a German, Frenchman, Italian, and so forth, like all the rest of his countrymen, and that his creativity as an individual was nourished by the same folk-tradition that sustained the whole of the nation within which he had become a citizen.

All at once, twenty years ago, after a slumber of thirty to sixty years, anti-Semitism once more sprang out of the innermost depths of the nations of western Europe. It revealed to a mortified Jew, who thought anti-Semitism was gone forever, the true picture of his situation. He was still allowed to vote for members of Parliament, but he saw himself excluded, with varying degrees of politeness, from the clubs and gatherings of his Christian fellow countrymen. He was allowed to go wherever he pleased, but everywhere he encountered the sign: "No Jews admitted." He still had the right of discharging all the duties of a citizen, but the nobler rights which are granted to talent and energy were absolutely denied him.

Such is the contemporary situation of the emancipated Jew in western Europe. He has abandoned his specifically Jewish character, yet the nations do not accept him as part of their national communities. He flees from his Jewish fellow, because anti-Semitism has taught him, too, to be contemptuous of them, but his gentile compatriots repulse him as he attempts to associate with them. He has lost his home in the ghetto yet the land of his birth is denied to him as his home. He has no ground under his feet and he has no community to which he belongs as a welcome and fully accepted member. He cannot count on justice from his Christian countrymen as a reward for either his character or his achievements, and still less on the basis of any existing good feeling; he has lost his connection with other Jews. Inevitably he feels that the world hates him and he sees no place where he can find the warmth for which he longs and seeks.

This is the Jewish spiritual misery, which is more painful than the physical because it affects men of higher station, who are prouder and more sensitive. The emancipated Jew is insecure in his relations with his fellow man, timid with strangers, and suspicious even of the secret feelings of his friends. His best powers are dissipated in suppressing and destroying, or at least in the difficult task of concealing his true character. He fears that this character might be recognized as Jewish, and he never has the satisfaction of revealing himself as he is in his real identity, in every thought and sentiment, in every physical gesture. He has become a cripple within, and a counterfeit person without, so that like everything unreal, he is ridiculous and hateful to all men of high standards.

All the better Jews of western Europe groan under this misery and seek for salvation and alleviation. They no longer possess the faith which might sustain them in bearing every suffering, as the will of a punishing but nonetheless loving God. They no longer hope for the advent of the Messiah, who will raise them to Glory on some miraculous day. Some try to save themselves by flight from Judaism, but racial anti-Semitism, which denies that baptism can change anything, leaves little prospect for this mode of salvation. It is of little advantage to the Jews of western Europe, who are mostly without belief (I am of course, not referring to the minority of true believers) to enter the Christian community by means of a blasphemous lie. At very best a new Marrano, who is much worse than the old, comes into being in this way. The Marranos of old had an idealistic element in their make-up—a secret longing for the truth, a heartbreaking regret and distress of conscience, and they often sought pardon and purification for themselves through martyrdom. The new Marranos[3] leave Judaism in rage and bitterness, but in their innermost heart, even if they themselves do not acknowledge it, they carry with them into Christianity their personal humiliation, their dishonesty, and their hatred for whatever has compelled them to live a lie.

I contemplate with horror the future development of this race of new Marranos, which is sustained morally by no tradition, whose soul is poisoned by hostility to both its own and to strange blood, and whose self-respect is destroyed through the ever-present consciousness of a fundamental lie. Some Jews hope for salvation from Zionism, which is for them not the fulfillment of a mystic promise of the Scripture but the way to an existence wherein the Jew will at last find the simplest and most elementary conditions of life, which are a matter of course for every non-Jew of both hemispheres: i.e., an assured place in society, a community which accepts him, the possibility of employing all his powers for the development of his real self instead of abusing them for the suppression and falsification of his personality. There are others who are also rebelling against the lie of being Marranos, but these feel themselves so intimately connected with the land of their birth that this act of renunciation that Zionism ultimately requires is too harsh and bitter for their emotions. This group has been throwing itself into the arms of the wildest revolution, with the vague afterthought that, with the destruction of everything that exists and the erection of a new world, Jew-hatred might perhaps not be one of the precious articles transferred from the debris of the old relationships into the new.

This is the picture of the Jewish people at the end of the nineteenth century. To sum up: The majority of the Jews are a race of accursed beggars. More industrious and abler than the average European, not to mention the moribund Asiatic and African, the Jew is condemned to the most extreme pauperism because he is not permitted to use his powers freely. This poverty grinds down his character and destroys his body. Feverishly thirsty for higher education, he sees himself repulsed from the places where knowledge is attainable—a real intellectual Tantalus of our nonmythical times. He dashes his head against the thick walls of hatred and contempt which have formed over his head. Being more minded toward society than perhaps any other people— even his religion teaches that it is a meritorious and God-pleasing action for meals to be taken together in groups of three and for prayer to be held in the company of ten—he is nonetheless excluded from the society of his countrymen and is condemned to tragic isolation. One complains of Jews pushing everywhere, but they strive after superiority only because they are denied equality. They are accused of a feeling of solidarity with the Jews of the whole world; quite to the contrary, it is their misfortune that, as soon as the first word of emancipation was uttered, they tried to make room for national patriotism as their exclusive loyalty by tearing out of their hearts any trace of Jewish solidarity. Stunned by the hailstorm of anti-Semitic accusations, the Jews forget who they are and often imagine that they are really the physical and spiritual horrors which their deadly enemies represent them to be. The Jew is often heard to murmur that he must learn from the enemy and try to remedy the faults ascribed to him. He forgets, however, that the anti-Semitic accusations are meaningless, because they are not a criticism of facts which exist, but are the effects of a psychological law according to which children, wild men, and malevolent fools make the persons and things they hate responsible for their sufferings.

To Jewish distress no one can remain indifferent—neither Christian nor Jew. It is a great sin to let a race, whose ability even its worst enemies do not deny, degenerate in intellectual and physical misery. It is a sin against them and it is a sin against the course of civilization, to whose progress Jews have made, and will yet make, significant contributions.

The misery of the Jew cries out for help. The finding of that help will be the great task of this Congress.

ZIONISM (1902)

THE NEW ZIONISM, which has been called political, differs from the old, religious, messianic variety in that it disavows all mysticism, no longer identifies itself with messianism, and does not expect the return to Palestine to be brought about by a miracle, but desires to prepare the way by its own efforts.

The new Zionism has grown only in part out of the inner impulses of Judaism itself, out of the enthusiasm of modern educated Jews for their history and martyrology, out of an awakened pride in their racial qualities, out of ambition to save the ancient people for a long, long future and to add new great deeds of posterity to those of their ancestors.

For the rest, Zionism is the result of two impulses which came from without: first, the principle of nationality, which dominated thought and sentiment in Europe for half a century and determined the politics of the world; second, anti-Semitism, from which the Jews of all countries suffer to some degree.

The principle of nationality has awakened a sense of their own identity in all the peoples; it has taught them to regard their unique qualities as values and has given them a passionate desire for independence. It could not, therefore, pass by the educated Jews without leaving some trace. It induced them to remember who and what they are, to feel themselves a people once again, and to demand a normal national destiny for themselves. The principle of nationality has, in its exaggerations, led to excesses. It has erred into chauvinism, stooped to idiotic hatred of the foreigner, and sunk to grotesque self-worship. Jewish nationalism is safe from the caricature of itself. The Jewish nationalist does not suffer from egotism; he feels, on the contrary, that he must make tireless efforts to render the name Jew a title of honor. He modestly recognizes the good qualities of other nations and diligently seeks to make them his own, in so far as they can be blended in with his natural capacities. He knows what terrible harm centuries of slavery or disability have done to his originally proud and upright character and he seeks to cure himself by means of intense self-discipline.

Anti-Semitism has also taught many educated Jews the way back to their people. It has had the effect of a sharp trial which the weak cannot stand, but from which the strong emerge stronger and more confident in themselves. It is incorrect to say that Zionism is but a gesture of truculence or an act of desperation against anti-Semitism. It is true that anti-Semitism alone has moved some educated Jews to throw in their lot with Jewry once again, and that they would again fall away if their Christian fellow countrymen would but receive them in a friendly way. But, in the case of most Zionists, the effect of anti-Semitism was only to force them to reflect upon their relationship to the nations of the world, and their reflection has led them to conclusions which would endure in their minds and hearts if anti-Semitism were to disappear completely.

THE ONE POINT which excludes, probably forever, the possibility of understanding between Zionist and non-Zionist Jews is the question of Jewish nationality. Whoever maintains and believes that the Jews are not a nation can indeed not be a Zionist; he cannot join a movement which has as its sole purpose the desire to normalize a people which is living and suffering under abnormal conditions. He who is convinced to the contrary that the Jews are a people must necessarily become Zionist, as only the return to their own country can save the Jewish nation which is everywhere hated, persecuted, and oppressed, from physical and intellectual destruction.

Many Jews, especially in the West, have completely broken with Judaism in their heart of hearts, and they will probably soon do so openly; if they do not break away, their children or grandchildren will. These people desire to be completely assimilated among their Christian fellow countrymen. They deeply resent it when other Jews proclaim that we are a people apart and desire to bring about an unequivocal separation between us and the other nations. Their great and constant fear is that in the land of their birth, where they are free citizens, they may be called strangers. They fear that this is all the more likely to happen if a large section of the Jewish people openly claims rights as an independent nation, and, still worse, if anywhere in the world a political and intellectual center of Jewry should really be created, in which millions of Jews would be united as a nation.

All these feelings on the part of assimilationist Jews are understandable. From their standpoint they are justified. The Jews, however, have no right to expect that Zionism should commit suicide for their sake. The Jews who are happy and contented in the lands of their birth, and who indignantly reject the suggestion of abandoning them, are about one-sixth of the Jewish people, say two million out of twelve. The other five-sixths, or ten million, have every reason for being profoundly unhappy in the countries where they live. These ten million cannot be called upon to submit forever, and without resistance, to their slavery, and to renounce every effort for redemption from their misery, merely in order not to disturb the comfort of two million happy and contented Jews.

The Zionists are, moreover, firmly convinced that the misgivings of the assimilationist Jews are unfounded. The reassembling of the Jewish people in Palestine will not have the consequences which they fear. When there is a Jewish country the Jews will have the choice of emigrating there, or of remaining in their present homes. Many will doubtless remain—they will prove by their choice that they prefer the land of their birth to their kin and their national soil. It is possible that the anti-Semites will still throw the scornful and perfidious cry "Stranger!" in their faces. But the real Christians among their fellow countrymen, those whose thoughts and emotions are guided by the teaching and examples of the Gospel, will be convinced that the Jews who remain do not regard themselves as strangers in the land of their birth. The real Christians will understand the true significance of their voluntary renunciation of a return to a land of the Jews, and of the attachment to their homes and to their Christian neighbors.

The Zionists know that they have undertaken a work of unparalleled difficulty. Never before has the effort been made to transplant several million people peacefully and in a short space of time, from various countries; never has the attempt been made to transform millions of physically degenerate proletarians, without trade or profession, into farmers and herdsmen; to bring town-bred hucksters and tradesmen, clerks and men of sedentary occupation, into contact again with the plough and with mother earth. It will be necessary to get Jews of different origins to adjust to one another, to train them practically for national unity, and at the same time to overcome the superhuman obstacles of differences of language, cultural level, ways of thought, and varying prejudices of people who will come to Palestine from all the countries of the world.

What gives Zionists the courage to begin this labor of Hercules is the conviction that they are performing a necessary and useful task, a work of love and civilization, a work of justice and wisdom. They wish to save eight to ten million of their kin from intolerable suffering. They desire to relieve the nations among whom they now vegetate of a presence which is considered disagreeable. They wish to deprive anti-

Semitism, which lowers the morals of the community everywhere and develops the very worst instincts, of its victim. They wish to make the Jews, who are nowadays reproached with being parasites, into an undeniably productive people. They desire to irrigate with their sweat and to till with their hands a country that is today a desert, until it again becomes the blooming garden it once was. Zionism will thus equally serve the unhappy Jews and the Christian peoples, civilization and the economy of the world. The services which it can render and wishes to render are great enough to justify its hope that the Christian world, too, will appreciate them and support the movement with its active sympathy.

Part 4
The Agnostic Rabbi—Ahad Ha-Am

AHAD HA-AM (ASHER ZVI GINSBERG)
1856-1927

AHAD HA-AM was born as Asher Zvi Ginsberg in Skvira, in the Russian Ukraine on August 18, 1856. His family belonged to the very highest aristocracy of the Jewish ghetto, being particularly close to the Hasidic rebbe of Sadagura. His formal education was so strictly pious that his teacher was forbidden to instruct him even in the letters of the Russian alphabet, lest this might lead to heresy (he nonetheless taught himself to read Russian at the age of eight from the signs on the store fronts of his town). By the middle of his adolescence Asher Ginsberg was already a considerable and even somewhat celebrated scholar of the Talmud and its literature, as well as of the devotional literature of the Hasidic movement.

In 1868 his family moved to an estate which his wealthy father had leased. There, locked in his room (then and later he had no interest in nature) he began on the road toward "enlightenment" by studying the works of the great medieval Jewish philosophers, especially of Maimonides. By stages he went on to the "forbidden books" of the modern Hebrew "enlightenment," and eventually, at the age of twenty, to the wider horizons of literature and philosophy in Russian and German. Soon, like his contemporary, Lilienblum, Ahad Ha-Am discovered the works of D. I. Pisarev, one of the founders of Russian positivism, and definitely lost his religious faith.

The years between 1879 and 1886 were the most painful period of his life, marked by abortive attempts to go to Vienna, Berlin, Breslau, and Leipzig to study. Personal troubles, the severe illness of his wife (as was the custom of his class, a marriage had been arranged for him at the age of twenty), and his own self-doubts and lack of resolution kept forcing him to return home after a few weeks with, as he put it, "a pained heart." The family finally moved to Odessa in 1886, not by choice but under the constraint of a new tsarist ukase forbidding Jews to lease land. Though this was a grave economic blow, Ahad Ha-Am was nonetheless relieved to be gone from a place which was associated in his memory with inner torment.

His first article, "This Is Not the Way," was published in 1889 when he was thirty-three. Not regarding himself as a writer, he signed it as Ahad Ha-Am, i.e., "one of the people," the pen name by which he was to be known henceforth. He always refused to consider himself as a man of letters, even when increasing poverty of his family forced him to take a job in 1896 as the editor of a Hebrew monthly, *Ha-Shiloah*, in order to support his wife and, by then, three children. After six years of editing this literary journal, which he intended as a platform for the discussion of the contemporary problems of Judaism, he resigned his post, feeling bitter and depressed but relieved to be free of the hateful burdens of being a public servant. He became an official of a tea concern and traveled widely on its behalf throughout Russia for four years. He moved to London in 1907, when his firm opened a branch there, and remained there for fourteen years, until 1921, when he settled in Palestine.

Ahad Ha-Am's debut in Hebrew literature occurred in the era which followed after the pogroms of 1881, in the day of the Hibbat Zion movement. In his first essay and, within several years, in long pieces of analytical reportage that he wrote from the recently founded few colonies in Palestine, he appeared as a disturber of the peace. Comparing the high-flown verbiage of this early Zionism with its paltry and often ill-conceived practical achievements, Ahad Ha-Am was uncompromising in his insistence that work in Palestine needed to be done slowly and with great care. Above all, he suggested that the true meaning of Hibbat Zion was not to be found, as leaders like Lilienblum thought, in mass action but in the cultural revival and modernization of the Jewish people through the agency of a carefully chosen few. From the very beginning these views aroused a storm and his continued reiteration of them after the appearance of Herzl simply continued the controversy. The agnostic definitions that he was proposing for a new Jewish spiritual culture involved him in another continuing argument, a debate with the orthodox. On the other hand, the conservatism of his thought, in practical application, made him the target of many of the younger and more rebellious voices in modern Hebrew literature, who found him too traditionalist in temper, a hard taskmaster as an editor, and lacking in interest in art and belles-lettres for their own sake.

With considerable self-knowledge of his lack of capacity for leadership in practical affairs, Ahad Ha-Am consistently avoided any kind of office within Zionism. However, his first essay inspired a number of men to organize the B'nai Moshe, a semi-secret elite order the purpose of which was to raise the moral and cultural tone of the Jewish national revival. Ahad Ha-Am became its reluctant leader; he failed in this task because his idealism, the deep pessimism of his nature, and his revulsion as moralist from imposing his will on others made it inconceivable that he should succeed. Indeed, a lifetime of bad health and, especially as he grew older, frequent spells of melancholy limited his literary production to the essays that have been collected in four volumes and the six volumes of his letters, which he helped edit toward the end of his life.

Though Ahad Ha-Am's views were rejected by the bulk of the Zionist movement, and he himself never attended a Zionist Congress after the very first, many of the younger east European leaders of the movement, like Chaim Weizmann, owed much to his influence. In 1917, when Weizmann was negotiating with the British Cabinet for the issuance of the Balfour Declaration, Ahad Ha-Am was among his most intimate advisers. Ahad Ha-Am's influence on modern Hebrew writing was notable not only in the realm of ideas but also for the creation of a spare, unadorned, "western" style.

When Ahad Ha-Am settled in Tel Aviv, the street on which he lived was named after him and even closed off from all traffic during his afternoon rest hours. In his sunset years this agnostic reached his apotheosis as the secular rabbi—indeed, almost the secular Hasidic rebbe—of a wide circle within the growing Jewish settlement in Palestine.

He died in the early hours of January 2, 1927, and all Tel Aviv attended his funeral.

THE LAW OF THE HEART (1894)

THE RELATION BETWEEN a normal people and its literature is one of parallel development and mutual interaction. Literature responds to the demands of life, and life reacts to the guidance of literature. The function of literature is to plant the seed of new ideas and new desires; the seed once planted, life does the rest. The tender shoot is nurtured and brought to maturity by the spontaneous action of men's minds, and its growth is shaped by their needs. In time the new idea or desire becomes an organic part of consciousness, an independent dynamic force, no more related to its literary origin than is the work of a great writer to the primer from which he learned at school.

But a "people of the book," unlike a normal people, is a slave to the book. It has surrendered its whole soul to the written word. The book ceases to be what it should be, a source of ever-new inspiration and moral strength; on the contrary, its function in life is to weaken and finally to crush all spontaneity of action and emotion, till men become wholly dependent on the written word and incapable of responding to any stimulus in nature or in human life without its permission and approval. Nor, even when that sanction is found, is the response simple and natural; it has to follow a prearranged and artificial plan. Consequently both the people and its book stand still from age to age; little or nothing changes, because the vital impulse to change is lacking on both sides. The people stagnates because heart and mind do not react directly and immediately to external events; the book stagnates because, as a result of this absence of direct reaction, heart and mind do not rise in revolt against the written word where it has ceased to be in harmony with current needs.

We Jews have been a people of the book in this sense for nearly two thousand years; but we were not always so. It goes without saying that we were not a people of the book in the era of the Prophets, from which we have traveled so far that we can no longer even understand it. But even in the period of the Second Temple heart and mind had not lost their spontaneity of action and their self-reliance. In those days it was still possible to find the source of the Law and the arbiter of the written word in the human heart, as witness the famous dictum of Hillel: "Do not unto your neighbor what you would not have him do unto you; that is the whole Law."[1] If on occasion the spontaneity of thought and emotion brought them into conflict with the written word, they did not efface themselves in obedience to its dictates; they revolted against it where it no longer met their needs, and so forced upon it a development in consonance with their new requirements. For example: The Biblical law of "an eye for an eye" was felt by the more developed moral sense of a later age to be savage and unworthy of a civilized nation; and at that time the moral judgment of the people was still the highest tribunal. Consequently it was regarded as obvious that the written word, which was also authoritative, must have meant "the value of an eye for an eye," that is to say, a penalty in money and not in kind.

But this state of things did not endure. The Oral Law (which is really the inner law, the law of the moral sense) was itself reduced to writing and fossilized; and the moral sense was left with only one clear and firm conviction—that of its own utter impotence and its eternal subservience to the written word. Conscience no longer had any authority in its own right; not conscience but the book became the arbiter in every human question. More than that: conscience had no longer the right even to approve of what the written word prescribed. So we are told that a Jew must not say he dislikes pork: to do so would be like the impudence of a slave who agrees with his master instead of unquestioningly doing his bidding. In such an atmosphere we need not be surprised that some commentators came to regard Hillel's moral interpretation of the Law as sacrilegious and found themselves compelled to explain away the finest saying in the Talmud. By "your neighbor," they said, Hillel really meant the Almighty: you are not to go against His will, because you would not like your neighbor to go against your will. And if the doctrine of "an eye for an eye" had been laid down in the Babylonian Talmud, not in the Mosaic Law, and its interpretation had consequently fallen not to the early Sages but to the Talmudic commentators, they would doubtless have accepted the doctrine in its literal meaning; Rabbis and common people alike would have forcibly silenced the protest of their own moral sense against an explicit injunction, and would have claimed credit for doing so.

The Haskalah writers of the last generation did not get down to the root cause of this tyranny of the written word. They put the blame primarily on the hardheartedness and hidebound conservatism of Rabbis who thought nothing of sacrificing the happiness of the individual on the altar of a meticulous legalism. Thus Gordon in *The Point of a Yod* depicts the Rabbi as

> *A man who sought not peace and knew no pity,*
> *For ever banning this, forbidding that,*
> *Condemning here, and penalizing there.*

These writers appealed to the moral sense of the common man against the harshness of the Law. They thought that by painting the contrast in sufficiently lurid colors they could provoke a revolt which would lead to the triumph of the moral sense over the written word. But this was a complete mistake. There was in fact no difference between the attitude of the Rabbi and that of the ordinary man. When Vofsi[2] pronounced the bill of divorce invalid, he may have been just as sorry for the victims as was the assembled congregation, who, in the poet's words,

> *Stood all atremble, as though the shadow of death*
> *Had fallen upon them.*

It was only the Rabbi who never doubted for a moment where the victory must lie in a conflict between the moral sense and the written word; the congregation did not dream of questioning the Rabbi's decision, still less of questioning the Law itself. If they "stood all atremble," it was only as one might tremble at some catastrophe due to the unalterable course of nature. A normal people would react to a tragedy of this kind by determining that such a thing should never happen again; but a "people of the book" can react only by dumb sorrow, such as would have been occasioned by the heroine's falling dead at her wedding. To blame the written word, to revolt against the rigor of the Law—that is out of the question.

Zangwill[3] is nearer the truth in his *Children of the Ghetto*. In this novel there is an incident similar to that of Gordon's poem, but the treatment is very different. The Rabbi, Reb Shmuel, is himself the girl's father, and a very affectionate father. His daughter's happiness in her love for David is his happiness too. But when he discovers by accident that David is of the priestly family, and therefore cannot marry Hannah, who is technically a divorced woman because of a young man's stupid joke, his first words, in spite of his anguish, are "Thank God I knew it in time." All David's appeals to justice and mercy are in vain. It is God's law, and must be obeyed. "Do you think," says Reb Shmuel at the end of a long and painful scene, "I would not die to make Hannah happy? But God has laid this burden upon her— and I can only help her to bear it."

No: Vofsi and all his kind are not monsters of cruelty. They are tenderhearted enough; but their natural feelings have not free scope. Every sentiment, every impulse, every desire gives in without a struggle to "the point of a yod."

Where the natural play of heart and mind is thus stifled, we cannot expect to find self-assertion or strength of purpose in any business outside the field of the written word. Logic, experience, common sense, and moral feeling are alike powerless to lead men into new paths toward a goal of their own choice. Inevitably, as our experience has shown, this general condition puts obstacles in the way of the solution of any and every one of our problems. It has long been obvious to thinking men that there is no hope for any particular measure of improvement unless the general condition is put right first of all.

The paramount question is, then, whether there is any possibility of curing this long-standing disease; whether the Jewish people can still shake off its inertia, regain direct contact with the actualities of life, and yet remain the Jewish people.

It is this last requirement that makes the question so very difficult. A generation ago the Haskalah movement showed how the process of awakening could be brought about. Leaving the older people alone, it caught hold of the young and normalized their attitude to life by introducing them to European culture through education and literature. But it could not make good its promise to bring humanism into Jewish life without disturbing the Jewish continuity: to that its products bear ample witness. Coming into Jewish life from outside, Haskalah found it easier to create an entirely new mold for its followers than to repair the defects of the Jewish mold while preserving its essential characteristics. Hence there can be no complete answer to our question until a new and compelling urge toward normalization springs up among us from within, from our own Jewish life, and is communicated to the younger generation through education and literature, so that it may fuse with the humanism of Haskalah and prevent the latter from overwhelming and obliterating the Jewish mold.

A native-born urge of this kind has recently come into play in the form of the idea which we call Hibbat Zion,[4] though that name is inadequate to express the full meaning of the idea. True Hibbat Zion is not merely a part of Judaism, nor is it something added on to Judaism; it is the whole of Judaism, but with a different focal point. Hibbat Zion neither excludes the written word nor seeks to modify it artificially by addition or subtraction. It stands for a Judaism which shall have as its focal point the ideal of our nation's unity, its renascence, and its free development through the expression of universal human values in the terms of its own distinctive spirit.

This is the conception of Judaism on which our education and our literature must be based. We must revitalize the idea of the national renascence, and use every possible means to strengthen its hold and deepen its roots, until it becomes an organic element in the Jewish consciousness and an independent dynamic force. Only in that way, as it seems to me, can the Jewish soul be freed from its shackles and regain contact with the broad stream of human life without having to pay for its freedom by the sacrifice of its individuality.

FLESH AND SPIRIT (1904)

. . . IN THE PERIOD of our early national existence—the period of the First Temple[5]—we find no trace of the conception of a duality of body and soul. Man, as a living and thinking being, is one in all his parts. The Hebrew word *nefesh* includes everything, body and soul and all that belongs to them. The *nefesh*, the individual human being, lives as a whole and dies as a whole; nothing survives. This notwithstanding, early Judaism was not perplexed by the problem of life and death. It knew nothing of the despair which begets the materialistic philosophy of the exaltation of the flesh and of sense enjoyment as a refuge from the emptiness of life; nor did it turn its gaze upward to create in Heaven an eternal habitation for the souls of men. It offered eternal life here on earth. This it did by emphasizing the sense of collectivity, by teaching the individual to regard himself not as an isolated unit, with an existence bounded by his own birth and death, but as part of a larger and more important whole, as a member of the social body. This conception shifts the center of personality not from the body to the spirit but from the individual to the community; concurrently, the problem of life is transferred from the individual to the social plane. I live for the sake of the perpetuation and the well-being of the community to which I belong; I die to make way for others, who will remold the community and save it from petrifaction and stagnation. When the individual loves the community as himself and identifies himself completely with its well-being, he has something to live for; he feels his personal hardships less keenly, because he knows the purpose for which he lives and suffers.

But obviously this will hold good only if the community itself lives for some purpose which the individual can regard as justifying every possible sacrifice on his part: Otherwise the old question recurs, but on the plane of the community. I put up with life in order that the community may live; but why does the community exist? What end does it serve, that I must bear my troubles cheerfully for its sake? Thus, having shifted the center of life from the individual to the community, Judaism was compelled to find an answer to the problem of the collective life. It had to endow the life of the community with a purpose sufficiently large and important to sustain the morale of the individual even when his personal life was a burden to him. Hence the community of Israel became "a kingdom of priests and a holy nation," destined from the very beginning to be an example to the whole of mankind through its Torah.

This solution of the problem left no room in Judaism for the two extreme views. Man is one and indivisible; all his limbs, his senses, his emotions, his thoughts constitute a single whole. But the existence of the man who is a Jew is not purposeless, because he is a member of the people of Israel, which exists for a sublime purpose. And as the community is only the sum of its members, every Israelite is entitled to regard himself as an indispensable link in the chain of his people's life and as sharing in his people's imperishability. That is why true asceticism is unknown in the early period of Jewish history. True asceticism, hatred of the flesh and the desire for its annihilation, is possible only where men, unable to find the purpose of life in this world, are compelled to look for it in another. It is true that in early Jewish life there were Nazarites, who observed certain of the outward practices of asceticism; but this was simply part of the ritual of sacrifice and had nothing to do with hatred of the flesh. It must be remembered that even so unascetic a hero as Samson was reckoned a Nazarite.

This attitude to life, which lifts the individual above the love of self and teaches him to find the purpose of his existence in the perpetuation and well-being of the community, is regarded by many non-Jewish students of religion as overmaterialistic; and on the strength of it they pronounce Judaism inferior, because it does not, like other religions, promise immortal life to everybody and a reward to the righteous after death. There could be no better example of the blindness of prejudice. . . .

In the early period of Jewish history there was a considerable party which took a materialistic view of the national life, in the sense that it had no ideal beyond that of making the State supreme at home, respected abroad, and secure against aggression. This was the aristocratic party; it embraced the entourage of the king, the military leaders, and most of the priests—all those, in a word, who in their individual lives had no experience of the suffering which demands consolation. They attached no importance to the spiritual aspect of the national life, and they were almost always prepared to desert the nation's spiritual ideals—"to serve other gods"—if they thought that there was any political advantage in doing so. The moral idealism of the Prophets waged incessant war on this political materialism, until it disappeared automatically with the destruction of the State. But it is entirely wrong to assert, as some modern historians do, that the Prophets were opposed to the State as such, that they regarded its very existence as inconsistent with the spiritual life which was their ideal, and therefore desired its overthrow. This political asceticism, this desire for the annihilation of the physical organism of the national life in order to promote its spiritual progress, is in fact entirely repugnant to the Prophetic attitude. One has only to read those passages of the Prophets in which they rejoice in the victories of the State (in the time of Sennacherib,[6] for example) and bewail its defeats, to see at once how highly they valued the political life, and how fully they realized that national independence was an essential condition of the attainment of their own ideals. But at the same time they never forgot that it is only by the spirit that life, whether individual or national, can be raised to a higher plane, and that only from the spirit can it derive meaning and purpose; consequently they insisted that the end should not be subordinated to the means, that the body should not be given empire over the spirit. Thus the Prophets simply enunciated on the national plane the principle which Judaism had laid down for the individual life: the unity of body and spirit, in the sense explained above.

It was not till the period of the Second Temple[7] that political asceticism found expression in the life of the Jewish State. The Essenes had no antipathy to the physical life so far as the individual was concerned; but on the national plane, in relation to the State, their attitude was precisely that of the ascetic. These spiritually minded men saw that from the spiritual point of view the Jewish State was going from bad to worse. Its rulers, like those of the first kingdom, worshiped only material power; its men of vision were wasting their energies in a vain struggle to arrest the corruption of the body politic, already in the grip of relentless enemies, and to breathe into it the spirit of true Judaism. In this situation the Essenes gave up the political life in despair, turned their backs on its incurable corruption, and withdrew into the wilderness, there to live out their individual lives in purity and holiness. In their hermit-like seclusion their antipathy to the State became more and more intense, and when the State was at its last gasp, hovering between life and death, some of them made no attempt to conceal their satisfaction.

However, the political asceticism of the Essenes had not much influence on the general trend of thought. It was not to them, but to the Pharisees, that the people looked for instruction and leadership, and the Pharisees represented the Prophetic conception of Judaism, with its unification of body and spirit. So far from turning away from life and ostracizing the State, they stuck to their post in the thick of the fray, and made every possible effort to save the State from moral degeneration and to shape it in conformity with the spirit of Judaism. It was clear to them that a spirit without a body could have no reality, and that the spirit of Judaism could not develop and fulfill itself without concrete expression in a political organism. Hence the Pharisees were always fighting on two fronts: against the political materialists within the State, and side by side with them against the external enemy for the preservation of the State.

It was only at the last moment, when the imminent destruction of the political organism was beyond all shadow of doubt, that the internal difference of ideals inevitably led to a split. The political materialists, for whom the preservation of the State meant everything, had no further interest in life, and fell fighting desperately among the ruins they loved; but the Pharisees remembered even in this hour of agony that they cared for the State only for the sake of the national spirit which was embodied in the State and needed its help. It could not occur to them to suppose that the end of the State meant the end of the nation and of all that made life worth living: On the contrary, it was for them imperatively necessary to find some temporary means of preserving the nation and its spirit without the political organism, until it should please the Almighty to restore His people to their land and freedom. So the alliance was broken: The political zealots remained sword in hand on the walls of Jerusalem, and the Pharisees, Torah in hand, went to Yavneh.[8]

The work of the Pharisees bore fruit. They succeeded in creating a sort of shadow body politic, with no roots in solid earth; within this shadowy framework the Hebrew national spirit has lived its own distinctive life for two thousand years. The ghetto organization, the foundations of which were laid in the period immediately following the destruction of Jerusalem, is a miracle without parallel in human history. Its root conception is that the purpose of life is spiritual perfection, but that the spirit needs a body to serve as its instrument. Until the nation could once again find a local habitation for its spirit in one complete and independent political organism, the Pharisees thought it necessary to provide an artificial stopgap. Their method was that of concentration in a number of small and scattered communities, all built to the same pattern, all living one type of life, and all united, despite geography, by consciousness of their common origin, by devotion to a single ideal, and by the hope of complete reunion in the future.

This artificial structure, built at a time when the Messianic Age was expected to dawn at any moment, was originally intended to serve only for a brief period. It has endured far too long; now at last it is in a state of advanced decay, with cracks and fissures everywhere.

So once again spiritually minded Jews have revived the political asceticism of the Essenes. They see their people exiled and dispersed, with no hope of a return to its former estate; they see the ghetto organization, which offered at least some semblance of a concrete national life, in process of dissolution. In their despair they renounce the physical element of the national life, and regard the spiritual element as its sole foundation. For them the Jewish people is a spirit without a body. The spirit is not only the purpose of life, but the whole of life; the body is not only subordinate to the spirit, it is a dangerous enemy, which ties the spirit and prevents it from entering into its kingdom.

As might have been expected, the reaction against this extreme theory has produced an equally extreme theory on the opposite side, and there has been a recrudescence of that political materialism which sees the physical organism—the Jewish State—as the be-all and end-all of Jewish life. This development is still too recent to have run its full course; but if history is any guide, we are entitled to believe that neither of these two extreme theories truly reflects the spirit of our people. Both, we may believe, will disappear, and make way for the only view that really has its roots in Judaism: the view which was that of the Prophets in the first Jewish State and of the Pharisees in the second. If, as we hope, there is to be a third, its fundamental principle, on the national as on the individual plane, will be neither the ascendancy of body over spirit, nor the suppression of the body for the spirit's sake, but the uplifting of the body by the spirit.

ON NATIONALISM AND RELIGION (1910)

Baden-Baden, September 18, 1910

TO DR. J. L. MAGNES[9] (New York)

. . . The object of your Society, you say, is "to establish Synagogues and Houses of Study." I am not sure whether you regard the Synagogue and the House of Study as two distinct institutions and mean to establish them separately from one another; but if you do, I do not think that you will achieve your object. Experience everywhere, and especially in America, has shown that the Synagogue by itself, as a House of Prayer exclusively, cannot save Judaism, which, unlike other religions, does not depend on prayer. Nor can the separate House of Study, which is intended for young people in search of knowledge, serve as an instrument of *popular* education. What we have to do is to revert to the system which our ancestors adopted in days gone by and to which we owe our survival: We have to make the Synagogue itself the House of Study, with Jewish learning as its first concern and prayer as a secondary matter. Cut the prayers as short as you like, but make your Synagogue a haven of Jewish knowledge, alike for children and adults, for the educated and the ordinary folk. The sermon on Sabbaths and Holy Days must give the congregants instruction in Torah, not phrases of unctuous piety. But the sermon alone is not enough. The Synagogue must be the center to which those who want to learn about Judaism resort every day. "Readings" on Jewish subjects can be arranged every evening, for the more and the less educated separately. That is what our ancestors did, with good results. The spirit of the teaching must be different, to suit the altered conditions; but the system itself cannot be bettered. In the old days the evening reading consisted of the *Ain Jacob*[10] with Rashi's[11] commentary, or the *Menorat Hamaor*,[12] for ordinary people, and of Talmud for the learned. In our day, of course, we must introduce readings better suited to modern requirements. But learning—learning—learning: that is the secret of Jewish survival.

Then you say you want "to propagate national religion and religious nationalism." I must confess that this formula is not altogether clear to me. "National religion"—by all means: Judaism is fundamentally national, and all the efforts of the "Reformers" to separate the Jewish religion from its national element have had no result except to ruin both the nationalism and the religion. Clearly, then, if you want to build and not to destroy, you must teach religion on the basis of nationalism, with which it is inseparably intertwined. But when you talk of propagating "religious nationalism," I do not know what you mean (unless you are simply saying the same thing in other words). Do you really think of excluding from the ranks of the nationalists all those who do not believe in the principles of religion? If that is your intention, I cannot agree. In my view our religion is national— that is to say, it is a product of our national spirit—but the reverse is not true. If it is impossible to be a Jew in the religious sense without acknowledging our nationality, it is possible to be a Jew in the national sense without accepting many things in which religion requires belief. . . .

THE JEWISH STATE
AND THE JEWISH PROBLEM (1897)

SOME MONTHS have passed since the Zionist Congress, but its echoes are still reverberating in daily life and in the press. All kinds of gatherings—small and large, local and regional—are taking place. Since the delegates returned home, they have been calling public meetings and repeatedly regaling us with tales of the wonders that were enacted before their very eyes. The wretched, hungry public is listening, becoming ecstatic, and hoping for salvation. It is inconceivable to them that "they"—the Jews of the West—can fail to succeed in what they propose. Heads grow hot and hearts beat fast, and many "leaders" who had for years—until last August—lived only for Palestinian settlement, and for whom a penny donation in aid of Jewish labor in Palestine or the Jaffa School[13] was worth the world, have now lost their bearings and ask one another: "What's the good of this sort of work? The days of the Messiah are near at hand, and we busy ourselves with trifles! The time has come for great deeds, for great men, men of the West, have enlisted in the cause and march before us."

There has been a revolution in their world, and, to emphasize it, they have given the cause itself a new name: It is no longer "Love of Zion" (Hibbat Zion), but "Zionism" (Zioniyuth). Indeed, there are even "precisionists" who, being determined to leave no loophole for error, use only the European form of the name ("Zionismus")—thus announcing to all and sundry that they are not talking about anything so antiquated as Hibbat Zion, but about a new, up-to-date movement, which comes, like its name, from the West, where people are innocent of the Hebrew language.

Nordau's address on the general condition of the Jews was a sort of introduction to the business of the Congress. It described in incisive language the sore troubles, whether material or spiritual, which beset the Jews the world over. In eastern countries their trouble is material: they must struggle without letup to satisfy the most elementary physical needs—for the crust of bread and the breath of air which are denied them because they are Jews. In the West, in lands where the Jews are legally emancipated, their material condition is not particularly bad, but their spiritual state is serious: they want to take full advantage of their legal rights, and cannot; they long to be accepted by the gentile majority and to become part of the national society, but they are kept at arm's length; they hope for love and brotherhood, but they encounter looks of hatred and contempt on all sides; they know that they are in no way inferior to their neighbors in ability or virtue, but they have it continually thrown in their faces that they are of an inferior type and that they are unfit to rise to the level of the Aryans. And more to the same effect.

Well—what then?

Nordau himself did not touch on this question, which was outside the scope of his address. But the whole Congress was the answer. Beginning as it did with Nordau's address, the Congress meant this: that in order to escape from all these troubles it is necessary to establish a Jewish State.

There is no doubt that, even when the Jewish State is established, Jewish settlement will be able to advance only by small degrees, as permitted by the resources of the people themselves and by the progress of the economic development of the country. Meanwhile the natural increase of Jewish population both within the Palestinian settlement and in the Diaspora, will continue, with the inevitable result that, on the one hand, Palestine will have less and less room for the new immigrants, and, on the other hand, despite continual emigration, the number of those remaining outside Palestine will not be appreciably diminished. In his opening speech at the Congress, Dr. Herzl, wishing to demonstrate the superiority of his State idea to the previous form of Palestinian colonization, calculated that by the latter method it would take nine hundred years before all the Jews could be settled in their land. The members of the Congress applauded this as a conclusive argument. But it was a cheap victory. The Jewish State itself, do what it will, will find no way to make a more favorable calculation.

The truth is bitter, but with all its bitterness it is better than illusion. We must admit to ourselves that the "ingathering of the exiles" is unattainable by natural means. We may, by natural means, someday establish a Jewish State; it is possible that the Jews may increase and multiply within it until the "land is filled with them"— but even then the greater part of our people will remain scattered on foreign soils. "To gather our scattered ones from the four corners of the earth" (in the words of the Prayer Book) is impossible. Only religion, with its belief in a miraculous redemption, can promise such a consummation.

But if this is so, if the Jewish State, too, means not an "ingathering of the exiles" but the settlement of a small part of our people in Palestine, then how will this solve the material problem of the Jewish masses in the lands of the Diaspora?

The material problem will not be ended by the establishment of a Jewish State, and it is, indeed, beyond our power to solve it once and for all. (Even now there are various means at our disposal to alleviate this problem to a greater or lesser degree, e.g., by increasing the proportion of farmers and artisans among our people *in all lands*, etc.) Whether or not we create a Jewish State, the material situation of the Jews will always basically depend on the economic condition and the cultural level of the various nations among which we are dispersed.

Thus we are driven to the conclusion that the real and only basis of Zionism is to be found in another problem, the spiritual one.

But the spiritual problem appears in two differing forms, one in the West and one in the East, which explains the fundamental difference between western "Zionism" and eastern "Hibbat Zion." Nordau dealt only with the western form of the problem, apparently knowing nothing about the eastern; and the Congress as a whole concentrated on the first, and paid little attention to the second.

The western Jew, having left the ghetto and having sought acceptance by the gentile majority, is unhappy because his hope of an open-armed welcome has been disappointed. Perforce he returns to his own people and tries to find within the Jewish community that life for which he yearns—but in vain. The life and horizon of the Jewish community no longer satisfy him. He has already grown accustomed to a broader social and political life, and on the intellectual side the work to be done for our Jewish national culture does not attract him, because that culture has played no part in his earliest education and is a closed book to him. In this dilemma he therefore turns to the land of his ancestors and imagines how good it would be if a Jewish State were re-established there—a State and society organized exactly after the pattern of other States. Then he could live a full, complete life within his own people, and he could find at home all that he now sees outside, dangled before his eyes but out of reach. Of course, not all the Jews will be able to take wing and go to their State; but the very existence of the Jewish State will also raise the prestige of those who remain in exile, and their fellow citizens will no longer despise them and keep them at arm's length, as though they were base slaves, dependent entirely on the hospitality of others. As he further contemplates this fascinating vision, it suddenly dawns on his inner consciousness that even now, before the Jewish State is established, the mere idea of it gives him almost complete relief. It provides an opportunity for communal work and political excitement; his emotions find an outlet in a field of activity which is not subservient to non-Jews; and he feels that, thanks to this ideal, he stands once more spiritually erect and has regained his personal dignity, without overmuch trouble and purely by his own efforts. So he devotes himself to the ideal with all the ardor of which he is capable; he gives rein to his fancy and lets it soar as it will, beyond reality and the limitations of human power. For it is not the attainment of the ideal that he needs; its pursuit alone is sufficient to cure him of his spiritual disease, which is that of an inferiority complex, and the loftier and more distant the ideal, the greater its power to exalt.

This is the basis of western Zionism and the secret of its attraction. But eastern Hibbat Zion originated and developed in a different setting. It, too, began as a political movement; but, being a result of material evils, it could not be content with an "activity" consisting only of outbursts of feeling and fine phrases, which may satisfy the heart but not the stomach. Hibbat Zion began at once to express itself in concrete activities—in the establishment of colonies in Palestine. This practical work soon clipped the wings of fancy and demonstrated conclusively that Hibbat Zion could not lessen the material woe of the Jews by one iota. One might, therefore, have thought that, when this fact became patent, the Hovevei Zion[14] would give up their effort and cease wasting time and energy on work which brought them no nearer their goal. But, no: they remained true to their flag and went on working with the old enthusiasm, though most of them did not understand, even in their own minds, why they did so. They felt instinctively that they must go on; but, as they did not clearly appreciate the nature of this feeling, the things that they did were not always effectively directed toward the true goal, to which they were unconsciously dedicated.

For at the very time when the material tragedy in the East was at its height, the heart of the eastern Jews was sensitive to another tragedy as well—a spiritual one; and when the Hovevei Zion began to work for the solution of the material problem, the national instinct of the people felt that in this work it would find the remedy for its spiritual trouble. Hence the people rallied to this effort and did not abandon it even after it had become obvious that it was an ineffective instrument for curing the material trouble of the Jews.

The eastern form of the spiritual problem is absolutely different from the western. In the West it is the problem of the Jews; in the East, the *problem of Judaism*. The first weighs on the individual; the second, on the nation. The one is felt by Jews who have had a European education; the other, by Jews whose education has been Jewish. The one is a product of anti-Semitism, and is dependent on anti-Semitism for its existence; the other is a natural product of a real link with a millennial culture, and it will remain unsolved and unaffected even if the troubled of the Jews all over the world attain comfortable economic positions, are on the best possible terms with their neighbors, and are admitted to the fullest social and political equality.

It is not only the Jews who have come out of the ghetto; Judaism has come out, too. For the Jews the exodus from the ghetto is confined to certain countries and is due to toleration; but Judaism has come out (or is coming out) of its own accord, wherever it has come into contact with modern culture. This contact with modern culture overturns the inner defences of Judaism, so that it can no longer remain isolated and live a life apart. The spirit of our people desires further development; it wants to absorb the basic elements of general culture which are reaching it from the outside world, to digest them and to make them a part of itself, as it has done before at various periods of its history. But the conditions of its life in exile are not suitable for such a task. In our time culture expresses itself everywhere through the form of the national spirit, and the stranger who would become part of culture must sink his individuality and become absorbed in the dominant environment. In exile, Judaism cannot, therefore, develop its individuality in its own way. When it leaves the ghetto walls, it is in danger of losing its essential being or—at very least—its national unity; it is in danger of being split up into as many kinds of Judaism, each with a different character and life, as there are countries of the dispersion.

Judaism is, therefore, in a quandary: It can no longer tolerate the *Galut*[15] form which it had to take on, in obedience to its will-to-live, when it was exiled from its own country; but, without that form, its life is in danger. So it seeks to return to its historic center, where it will be able to live a life developing in a natural way, to bring its powers into play in every department of human culture, to broaden and perfect those national possessions which it has acquired up to now, and thus to contribute to the common stock of humanity, in the future as it has in the past, a great national culture, the fruit of the un-hampered activity of a people living by the light of its own spirit. For this purpose Judaism can, for the present, content itself with little. It does not need an independent State, but only the creation in its native land of conditions favorable to its development: a good-sized settlement of Jews working without hindrance in every branch of civilization, from agriculture and handicrafts to science and litera-ture. This Jewish settlement, which will be a gradual growth, will be-come in course of time the center of the nation, wherein its spirit will find pure expression and develop in all its aspects to the highest degree of perfection of which it is capable. Then, from this center, the spirit of Judaism will radiate to the great circumference, to all the communities of the Diaspora, to inspire them with new life and to preserve the over-all unity of our people. When our national culture in Palestine has attained that level, we may be confident that it will produce men in the Land of Israel itself who will be able, at a favora-ble moment, to establish a State there—one which will be not merely a State of Jews but a really Jewish State.

This Hibbat Zion, which concerns itself with the preservation of Judaism at a time when Jewry is suffering so much, is something odd and unintelligible to the "political" Zionists of the West, just as the demand of R. Johanan ben Zakkai for "Yavneh" was strange and unintelligible to the comparable party of his time. And so political

Zionism cannot satisfy those Jews who care for Judaism; its growth seems to them to be fraught with danger to the object of their own aspiration.

The secret of our people's persistence is—as I have tried to show elsewhere—that at a very early period the Prophets taught it to respect only the power of the spirit and not to worship material power. Therefore, unlike the other nations of antiquity, the Jewish people never reached the point of losing its self-respect in the face of more powerful enemies. As long as we remain faithful to this principle, our existence has a secure basis, and we shall not lose our self-respect, for we are not spiritually inferior to any nation. But a political ideal which is not grounded in our national culture is apt to seduce us from loyalty to our own inner spirit and to beget in us a tendency to find the path of glory in the attainment of material power and political dominion, thus breaking the thread that unites us with the past and undermining our historical foundation. Needless to say, if the political ideal is not attained, it will have disastrous consequences, because we shall have lost the old basis without finding a new one. But even if it is attained under present conditions, when we are a scattered people not only in the physical but also in the spiritual sense—even then, Judaism will be in great danger. Almost all our great men—those, that is, whose education and social position have prepared them to be at the head of a Jewish State—are spiritually far removed from Judaism and have no true conception of its nature and its value. Such men, however loyal to their State and devoted to its interests, will necessarily envisage those interests by the standards of the foreign culture which they themselves have imbibed; and they will endeavor, by moral persuasion or even by force, to implant that culture in the Jewish State, so that in the end the Jewish State will be a State of Germans or Frenchmen of the Jewish race. We have even now a small example of this process in Palestine.

History teaches us that in the days of the Herodian house Palestine was indeed a Jewish State, but the national culture was despised and persecuted. The ruling house did everything in its power to implant Roman culture in the country and frittered away the resources of the nation in the building of heathen temples, amphitheaters, and so forth. Such a Jewish State would spell death and utter degradation for our people. Such a State would never achieve sufficient political power to deserve respect, while it would be estranged from the living inner spiritual force of Judaism. The puny State, being "tossed about like a ball between its powerful neighbors, and maintaining its existence only by diplomatic shifts and continual truckling to the favored of fortune," would not be able to give us a feeling of national glory; the national culture, in which we might have sought and found our glory, would not have been implanted in our State and would not be the principle of its life. So we should really be then—much more than we are now—"a small and insignificant nation," enslaved in spirit to "the favored of fortune," turning an envious and covetous eye on the armed force of our "powerful neighbors"; our existence in such terms, as a sovereign State would not add a glorious chapter to our national history.

Would it not be better for "an ancient people which was once a beacon to the world" to disappear than to end by reaching such a goal as this? Mr. Lilienblum[16] reminds me that there exist today small States, like Switzerland, which are safeguarded against interference by the other nations and are not forced to "continual truckling." But a comparison between Palestine and small countries like Switzerland overlooks the geographical position of Palestine and its religious importance for all the world. These two facts will make it quite impossible for its "powerful neighbors" (by which expression, of course, I did not mean, as Mr. Lilienblum interprets, "the Druses and the Persians") to leave it alone. Even after it has become a Jewish State, they will all still keep an eye on it, and each power will try to influence its policy in a direction favorable to itself, after the pattern of events in other weak states (like Turkey) in which the great European nations have "interests."

In sum: Hibbat Zion, no less than "Zionism," wants a Jewish State and believes in the possibility of the establishment of a Jewish State in the future. But while "Zionism" looks to the Jewish State to furnish a remedy for poverty and to provide complete tranquillity and national glory, Hibbat Zion knows that our State will not give us all these things until "universal Righteousness is enthroned and holds sway over nations and States"—it looks to a Jewish State to provide only a "secure refuge" for Judaism and a cultural bond to unite our nation. "Zionism," therefore, begins its work with political propaganda; Hibbat Zion begins with national culture, because only *through* the national culture and *for its sake* can a Jewish State be established in such a way as to correspond with the will and the needs of the Jewish people.

THE NEGATION OF THE DIASPORA (1909)

"A NEGATIVE ATTITUDE TOWARD THE DIASPORA" is an expression frequently heard in discussions between the Zionists, who look beyond the Diaspora for a solution of our national problem, and the Nationalists, who do not, and the latter have come to take it for granted that the attitude in question is necessarily predicable of anybody who does accept their "autonomist" doctrine. Actually, however, the expression is not so clear as it might be.

An attitude may be either subjectively or objectively negative. If we express disapproval or dislike of something or other, our negative attitude is subjective: it relates not to the thing itself, but only to our own reactions to it. But if we say that something or other cannot possibly exist, our negative attitude is objective: it results from an examination of the objective facts, without any reference to our own predilections.

In the subjective sense all Jews adopt a negative attitude toward the Diaspora. With few exceptions, they all recognize that the position of a lamb among wolves is unsatisfactory, and they would gladly put an end to this state of things if it were possible. Those who profess to regard our dispersion as a heaven-sent blessing are simply weak-kneed optimists; lacking the courage to look the evil thing in the face, they find it necessary to smile on it and call it good so long as they cannot abolish it. But if the Messiah—the true Messiah—were to appear today or tomorrow, to lead us out of our exile, even these optimists would join the throng of his followers without a moment's hesitation.

This being so, the "negative attitude toward the Diaspora" which has become a debating counter must be negative in the objective sense. To adopt a negative attitude toward the Diaspora means, for our present purpose, to believe that the Jews cannot survive as a scattered people now that our spiritual isolation is ended, because we have no longer any defence against the ocean of foreign culture, which threatens to obliterate our national characteristics and traditions, and thus gradually to put an end to our existence as a people.

There are, it is true, some Jews who are of that opinion; but they are not all of one way of thinking. They belong in fact to two different parties, which draw diametrically opposite conclusions from their common assumption. The one party argues that, as we are doomed to extinction, it is better to hasten the end by our action than to sit and wait for it to come of its own accord after a long and painful death agony. If a Jew can get rid of his Judaism here and now by assimilation, good luck to him; if he cannot, let him try to make it possible for his children. But the other party argues that, since we are threatened with extinction, we ought to put an end to our dispersion before it puts an end to us. We must secure our future by gathering the scattered members of our race together in our historical land (or, some would add, in some other country of their own), where alone we shall be able to continue to live as a people. Any Jew who is both able and willing to get rid of his Judaism by assimilation may remain where he is; those who are unable or unwilling to assimilate will betake themselves to the Jewish State.

But so far both these parties remain merely parties, and neither has succeeded in persuading the Jewish people as a whole to accept the fundamental postulate with either of its consequential policies. Both alike have come into conflict with something very deep-rooted and stubborn—the instinctive and unconquerable desire of the Jewish people to survive. This desire for survival, or will to live, obviously makes it impossible for the Jewish people as a whole to contemplate the disappearance of the Diaspora if that involves its own disappearance; but the case is no better if the argument is that the Diaspora must disappear in order that the people may survive. Survival cannot be made dependent on any condition, because the condition might not be fulfilled. The Jews as a people feel that they have the will and the strength to survive whatever may happen, without any ifs or ands. They cannot accept a theory which makes their survival conditional on their ceasing to be dispersed, because that theory implies that failure to end the dispersion would mean extinction, and extinction is an alternative that cannot be contemplated in any circumstances whatever.

Except, then, for these two extreme parties, the Jews remain true to their ancient belief: their attitude toward the Diaspora is subjectively negative, but objectively positive. Dispersion is a thoroughly evil and unpleasant thing, but we can and must live in dispersion, for all its evils and all its unpleasantness. Exodus from the dispersion will always be, as it always has been, an inspiring hope for the distant future; but the date of that consummation is the secret of a higher power, and our survival as a people is not dependent upon it.

This, however, does not settle the question of our survival in dispersion. On the contrary, it is precisely this positive attitude toward the Diaspora that gives the question its urgency. A man at death's door does not worry much about his affairs during his last days on earth; a man on the point of going abroad is not particular about the tidiness of the lodging he occupies just before his departure. But if the Jews believe that they can and must continue to live in dispersion, the question at once arises—how is it to be done? It is neither necessary nor possible for them to go on living all the time in exactly the same old way. The will to live not only persuades them to believe that it is possible to survive in dispersion; it also impels them, in the changing circumstances of successive epochs, to find always the most appropriate means of preserving and developing their national identity. Moreover, this watchful instinct is always anticipating events, always providing in advance against the future. When Titus besieged Jerusalem, we are told, the defenders always had a new rampart ready in the rear before the one in front of it was overthrown. So it is with our national survival. And now that all but the wilfully blind can see the old rampart tottering to its fall, we are bound to ask ourselves: Where is the new rampart that is to secure our existence as a people in dispersion?

The Nationalists answer: national autonomy. What they mean by this has been made reasonably clear in the literature on the subject, and there is no need to go into detail here. But it seems to me that one fundamental point has been left obscure, and that some confusion of thought has in consequence arisen.

If we are to decide how far autonomy is a satisfactory answer to our problem, we must first of all define the scope of the problem itself. To judge from the current controversy on this matter, there appear in fact to be two different schools of thought. It is common ground among the Nationalists that we must find some new means of maintaining our distinctive national life in the Diaspora; but, on close examination, we find that while some of them are looking for a pattern of national life that will be as complete and self-contained as the ghetto life of our forefathers, others are convinced, in their heart of hearts, that that is an impossible ideal. These latter ask for nothing more than the possibility of developing our national life up to the limit of what is in practice attainable, and with no more than the unavoidable minimum of truncation and circumscription. When we are told, then, that autonomy is the solution, we must ask the further question: To what extent is it a solution? Is national autonomy put forward as a final answer to our problem, holding out a promise of full and complete national life in the Diaspora? Or is it offered merely as the best that can be had in the circumstances, it being recognized that a complete national life in the Diaspora is impossible except in the ghetto which we have left forever?

The autonomists do not answer this question. Mr. Dubnov[17] himself appears sometimes to think that autonomy would be a complete solution, providing a full synthesis of the "human" and the "national" elements in our corporate life; at other times he uses qualifying phrases like "within the bounds of possibility" or "as far as possible." But it seems to me that our doubts will disappear if we remember what is really meant by "a complete national life."

A complete national life involves two things: first, full play for the creative faculties of the nation in a specific national culture of its own, and, second, a system of education whereby the individual members of the nation will be thoroughly imbued with that culture, and so molded by it that its imprint will be recognizable in all their way of life and thought, individual and social. These two aspects of a national life may not always be realized in the same degree, but broadly speaking they are interdependent. If the individuals are not imbued with the national culture, the development of the nation will be arrested, and its creative faculties will suffer atrophy or dissipation. On the other hand, if those faculties are not sufficiently employed in the service of the development of the national culture, the education of children and adults alike will become narrow, its influence will progressively decline, and many individuals will turn elsewhere for the satisfaction of their cultural needs, with the result that gradually their minds and characters will cease to bear the nation's imprint.

Moreover, if a nation is to live a complete national life, it must have both the opportunity and the will to do so. It is the environment —the complex of political, economic, social, and moral factors—that creates both the opportunity and the psychological attitude from which springs the will to take advantage of the opportunity. This psychological attitude is of the utmost importance. When Mr. Dubnov says that autonomy will solve our problem only if we have the strength of will to make proper use of our rights, I take him to mean not that it will be entirely for us to decide, as free beings in the metaphysical sense, whether to use our rights or not, but that the external and internal conditions will be such that in our case, as in that of other national groups, the will to use our opportunities will automatically develop.

To sum up, then: If national autonomy in the Diaspora is put forward as a completely satisfactory solution of our problem, it has to promise to normalize the life of the scattered and atomized Jewish people. It has to undertake to provide the Jewish people with both the opportunity and the necessary strength of will to deploy its creative faculties to the maximum extent in the development of its specific national culture. Nor is that all. It has to guarantee the possibility of educating all the individual members of the people, in every rank of society, on the lines of the national culture, so as to ensure that when they reach maturity they will find within the circle of the national life so wide a range of intellectual interests, and such ample scope for practical activity, that they will feel neither the need nor the desire to desert that sphere for another.

Now it may be that autonomists of the Yiddishist school believe that national autonomy can satisfy these requirements. For them our national culture means Yiddish literature, national education means speaking Yiddish, and the national ideal is to reach the level of nations like the Letts or the Slovaks, which have not as yet made any contribution whatever to the general stock of human culture. If "Nationalists" of this type regard autonomy in the Diaspora as the perfect solution of our problem, we can more or less understand their point of view. But it is otherwise with Nationalists who have a historical perspective—who demand that the future of our nation shall be a continuation of its past, and date the beginning of our national history from the Exodus from Egypt, not from the birth of the Yiddish novel and drama. Such Nationalists cannot be satisfied with a future that would put the greatness of our past to shame, and consequently they must see that the sort of exiguous living-space that might perhaps suffice for the infant toddlings of a nation of yesterday cannot provide elbow-room for the cultural life of the "eternal people," which has an ancient heritage of spiritual values and a fund of creative energy too large to be pent up within its own narrow confines. It is with Nationalists of this kind alone that I am here concerned, and they, I feel sure, would not subscribe to the obviously untenable view that autonomy can perform all these miracles. At any rate, pending an explicit statement on their part that they do subscribe to that view, I feel that to develop the arguments against it would be pushing an open door.

It may, then, be taken as practically certain that the autonomists admit that national autonomy in the Diaspora cannot give us the possibility of a full and complete national life; their contention is that nonetheless, if we wish to survive, we must struggle for national rights in the Diaspora, so as to broaden the basis of our national life to the greatest possible extent. It is, however, common ground that at best we cannot get all we really need, and that our national culture and education must remain fragmentary and distorted, for lack of sufficient elbow-room within the framework of the alien culture which hems us in on every side.

If the autonomist doctrine is put in this more modest form, I doubt whether any true Jew will be opposed to it, in the sense of not regarding the extension of our national rights in the Diaspora as something to be desired and to be worked for whenever possible. Any opposition to it must be based on the view that it is objectively impossible; that our position among the nations is unique, and that the rest of the world will never be induced to admit that we have national rights in the territories that belong to other nations. True, the autonomists are fond of comparing our position with that of other small nations in Russia, Austria, and elsewhere, of which some have achieved autonomy and others hope to acquire it some day. But what is the use of our forgetting the difference between ourselves and the other small nations if those with whom the decision rests will not forget it? Each of the other small nations in question has lived in its national territory for generations and was once independent. The independence has gone, but even the new overlords cannot deny the historic right of the indigenous people, or regard its nationality as a foreign growth on the very soil on which it first came to birth. And if in the course of time some branches of the national tree have spread into the neighboring fields, without losing their connection with the parent stem, that is a perfectly natural and normal historic process. But we Jews entered every one of the lands of our dispersion as a foreign people, with a national culture which had been born and developed elsewhere. Wandering beggars from a distant clime, we have been compassionately granted asylum by the nations of the earth; but there never was, and is not now, any nexus between the life into which we have been admitted and the Jewish type of life which we brought with us, already fully developed, on our arrival. For this reason it is not likely that the world will recognize "the historic right of an alien people to live a national life of its own in a country of which from the very first it has never thought (and still less has anybody else ever thought) as belonging to itself. Ownership is after all a matter of convention; so long as individual ownership is recognized, national ownership cannot be condemned."

This, however, is by the way. My object was not to argue against the autonomist doctrine, but to explain what it leaves obscure and to carry it to its logical conclusion. Hence I leave the question of practicability on one side. The point I really wish to make is this: If the autonomists agree that autonomy in the Diaspora is not a complete solution, and that we have to struggle for it merely on the principle that half a loaf is better than no bread, then they must also agree that we have to look for other and more radical ways of strengthening and enlarging our national life, on the principle that a whole loaf is better than half a loaf. The will to live, it must be remembered, will not be satisfied with the half loaf; it will give us no rest until we throw all our latent strength into the task of achieving its demands in full. But if this is so, the autonomists, like the rest of us, have still to face the question with which we started: Where is the new rampart that is to secure our existence as a people in dispersion in place of the old rampart, which is tottering before our eyes?

The autonomists know that for twenty years one Zionist school of thought has answered this question by saying that the new rampart must be built outside the Diaspora, in our historic land. This school of thought differs from those who claim to be the "real" Zionists in refusing to believe in the possibility of transferring all the Jews in the world to Palestine, and consequently in refusing to accept the proposition that we cannot survive in the Diaspora. On the contrary, it holds that dispersion must remain a permanent feature of our life, which it is beyond our power to eliminate, and therefore it insists that our national life in the Diaspora must be strengthened. But that object, it holds, can be attained only by the creation of a fixed center for our national life in the land of its birth. Isolated groups of Jews wandering about the world here, there, and everywhere can be nothing more than a sort of formless raw material until they are provided with a single permanent center, which can exert a "pull" on all of them, and so transform the scattered atoms into a single entity with a definite and self-subsistent character of its own. This answer, as I have said, has been given again and again during the last twenty years, and the arguments for and against it have been so thoroughly canvassed that there is no need to embark on a long explanation of it here. But when our autonomists argue with Zionists, they seem to recognize only one kind of Zionism—the kind that pins its faith on the transfer of all the Jews to Palestine and is therefore open to the charge that it adopts the dangerous doctrine of the impossibility of Jewish life in the Diaspora. They completely ignore the other kind of Zionism, which is not open to that criticism, and in doing so they more or less admit, as it seems to me, to a feeling at the back of their minds that their own doctrine leads them straight into the arms of this version of Zionism. For otherwise they are on the horns of a dilemma. They must either promise that Diaspora autonomy will completely solve our problem or deny that any complete solution is possible. But the first alternative is not open to them, because they do not believe in miracles, and the second is equally impossible, because it is too pessimistic—it means that our unhappy people has to look forward to an endless sick-bed existence with no hope of recovery. So in the end the autonomists, too, will be driven to look eastward and to recast their program so as to include, along with the maximum possible improvement and expansion of our national life in the Diaspora, the search for a complete solution outside the Diaspora.

HAYYIM NAHMAN BIALIK   1873-1934

THE CLASH OF CULTURES within late nineteenth-century Russian Jewry was, as we have seen, the great theme to which many essayists and novelists addressed themselves. These inner tensions, the increasing pain of a much massacred community, and the anodyne to both woes in the dawning national affirmations of Zionism gave rise, as well, to a new Hebrew poetry, the greatest since the Middle Ages. Its supreme master was Hayyim Nahman Bialik.

Bialik's early life was of the kind we know from the biographies of Smolenskin, Lilienblum, and Ahad Ha-Am. He was born in a village near Zhitomir, in the Russian province of Volhynia, as the eighth and youngest child of poor parents. Bialik tells in his fragmentary autobiography of being left very much to himself in his earliest childhood, to dream under the blue skies. Tragedy came at the age of seven with the death of his father and his mother's bitter, but unavailing struggle to support her family. The boy was soon sent to live with his strict and very pious grandfather. Bialik owed to these years his excellent education in the classical texts of the religious tradition and his taste for omnivorous reading. Among the books he devoured were the writings of the "enlighteners," and, as a result, he was soon restless under the uncompromising religious regime of his grandfather's house. At the age of seventeen he was given reluctant consent to leave for the famous yeshivah of Volozhin, where he remained for eighteen months. It was there that he began to write; at Volozhin he took a further step toward intellectual emancipation by joining a secret students' organization of Hibbat Zion.

When Bialik left the yeshivah in 1891 to strike out on his own, he made his way to Odessa, which was then graced by the presence of a whole galaxy of intellectual leaders of the national revival in Hebrew, and especially of Ahad Ha-Am. The older man encouraged him as a writer and even arranged for the publication of his first poem, thus beginning a life-long friendship between the two. Nonetheless, Bialik did not yet dream of making literature his career. He married the daughter of a lumber merchant and settled down in a small town for four years to work in his father-in-law's business. It was among the poet's foibles all his life that he imagined himself to possess a talent for business, but he lost his money in this first venture and by 1897 he turned to the traditional occupation of Hebrew writers, teaching that language to the young. His experiences as educator in a Polish provincial town were even unhappier than his career in business, and so after three years he returned to Odessa, which was to be his home until after the Bolshevik Revolution.

Bialik's intellectual emancipation from the orthodox religious faith was not as thoroughly rationalist as that of his master, Ahad Ha-Am, and his romantic love of the Jewish past included even the recent ghetto, which Ahad Ha-Am disliked. He felt as keenly—and more sentimentally—the need to preserve the treasures of classical Hebrew literature as a "usable past" for the Zionist national revival. His labors as publisher and editor, from which he made his living until his death, were largely devoted to this aim. In his essays and, especially, his speeches—he was a master of intimate causerie in both Hebrew and Yiddish—he returned many times to the theme of *kinnus*, i.e., the winnowing of the chaff from the wheat in Jewish literature in order to create a new "canon" of works accepted as indispensable classics. When the Hebrew University was projected he became one of its most enthusiastic protagonists, for here he believed the old and the new, the Jewish and the supranational, would meet to blend in a contemporary but traditional Hebrew culture. The excerpt below represents a speech he gave in the presence of Lord Balfour and a galaxy of other dignitaries at ceremonies marking the opening of the University in 1925.

Though Bialik's prose only is represented in this volume, a word must be said about his poetry. Passionately felt and intensely personal though all of Bialik's poetry was, the generation which loved him deeply was correct in regarding him as the voice of all, the Jewish national poet. Certainly he spoke both for others as well as for himself in lines like these from *Al Ha-Shehitah*, the defiant dirge he wrote in Kishinev right after the pogrom of 1903:

> *If there is justice—let it appear at once!*
> *But if justice will appear*
> *Only after I am destroyed from under heaven—*
> *Let its chair be uprooted forever!*

Under pressure from the renowned Maxim Gorky, the Communist rulers of Russia permitted Bialik to emigrate in 1921. After three years in Berlin he settled in Tel Aviv, on a street the municipality called by his name. He died in Vienna, where he had gone for an operation, in the summer of 1934 and was buried in Tel Aviv.

BIALIK ON THE HEBREW UNIVERSITY

AT THE INAUGURATION OF THE HEBREW UNIVERSITY JERUSALEM, JANUARY 4, 1925

THE SOLEMNITY AND EXALTATION of this moment can only be desecrated by any sort of exaggeration. It is therefore our duty to declare openly and honestly in the presence of this gathering that the house which has just been opened on Mount Scopus by our honored guest Lord Balfour[1] is now but the embryo of an institution, hardly more than a name. For the time being it is but a vessel that may become filled with content and its future is as yet unrevealed and in the hands of fate. Nevertheless I feel certain that the thousands assembled here, and with them tens of thousands of Israel in all corners of the world, feel, in hearts that are trembling with joy, that the festival which is being celebrated this day upon this spot is not an artificial ritual that someone has devised but a great and holy day unto our Lord and unto our People. I am sure that the eyes of tens of thousands of Israel that are lifted from all parts of the Diaspora to this hill are shining with hope and comfort; their hearts and their flesh are singing a blessing of thanksgiving unto the Living God Who hath preserved us and sustained us and let us live to see this hour. They all realize that at this moment Israel has kindled upon Mount Scopus the first candle of the renaissance of her intellectual life. This day the glad tidings will come unto all the scattered families of Israel, wherever they may be, that the first peg in the upbuilding of the Higher Jerusalem (*Yerushalayim shel Ma'lah*) has been fixed for all time.

For let people say what they may: This peculiar people called Israel has, despite all the vicissitudes which for two thousand years have daily, yea hourly, attempted to expel it from its own milieu and uproot it from its spiritual climate—this people, I assert, has accepted upon its body and soul the burden of eternal allegiance to the Kingdom of the Spirit. Within that Kingdom it recognizes itself as a creative citizen and in that eternal soil it has planted its feet with all its might for all time. All the sordidness of the accursed Galut and all the pain of our people's poverty did not disfigure its fundamental nature. Obliged to sacrifice temporal life for eternal life, it learned in the days of suffering and travail to subordinate material to spiritual needs and the requirements of the body to those of the soul. Within the boundaries of the realm of the Spirit the Jewish nation fashioned the bases of its national heritage and its principal national institutions. These preserved it through millennia of wandering, safeguarded its inner freedom amid outward bondage and have led up to this joyful event of the Inauguration of the University on Mount Scopus. The national school in all its forms—the *heder*, the *yeshivah*, the *bet-midrash*[2]—these have been our securest strongholds throughout our long, hard struggle for existence, and for the right to exist, in the world as a separate and distinct people among the peoples. In times of tempest and wrath we took refuge within the walls of these fortresses, where we polished the only weapon we had left—the Jewish mind—lest it become rusty. At this moment I cannot but recall a saying of our sages, a saying of unparalleled bitter sadness. A certain scholar, when reading in the Pentateuch (Leviticus 26:44) "Nevertheless, even when they are in the land of their enemies I shall not detest them, and I shall not abhor them . . .", remarked bitterly: "What has, then, been left to Israel in the Galut that has not been detested and abhorred? Have not all the goodly gifts been taken from them? What has been left to them? Only the Torah. For had that not been preserved for Israel, they would in no wise be different from the gentile."

The concept of "Torah" attained in the esteem of the people an infinite exaltation. For them the Torah was almost another existence, a more spiritual and loftier state, added to or even taking the place of secular existence. The Torah became the center of the nations secret and avowed aspirations and desires in its exile. The dictum "Israel and the Torah are one" was no mere phrase: the non-Jew cannot appreciate it, because the concept of "Torah," in its full national significance, cannot be rendered adequately in any other tongue. Its content and connotations embrace more than "religion" or "creed" alone, or "ethics" or "commandments" or "learning" alone, and it is not even just a combination of all these, but something far transcending all of them. It is a mystic, almost cosmic, conception. The Torah is the tool of the Creator; with it and for it He created the universe. The Torah is older than creation. It is the highest idea and the living soul of the world. Without it the world could not exist and would have no right to exist. "The study of the Torah is more important than the building of the Temple." "Knowledge of the Torah ranks higher than priesthood or kingship." "Only he is free who engages in the study of the Torah." "It is the Torah that magnifies and exalts man above all creatures." "Even a heathen who engages in the study of the Torah is as good as a High Priest." "A bastard learned in the Torah takes precedence over an ignorant High Priest."[3]

Such is the world outlook to which almost seventy generations of Jews have been educated. In accordance therewith their spiritual life was provisionally organized for the interim of the exile. For it they suffered martyrdom and by virtue of it they lived. The Jewish elementary school was established shortly before the destruction of Jerusalem and has survived to this day. As a result of such prolonged training, the nation has acquired a sort of sixth sense for everything connected with the needs of the spirit, a most delicate sense and always the first to be affected, and one possessed by almost every individual. There is not a Jew but would be filled with horror by a cruel decree "that Jews shall not engage in the Torah." Even the poorest and meanest man in Israel sacrificed for the teaching of his children, on which he spent sometimes as much as a half of his income or more. Before asking for the satisfaction of his material needs, the Jew first prays daily: "And graciously bestow upon us knowledge, understanding, and comprehension." And what was the first request of our pious mothers over the Sabbath candles? "May it be Thy will that the eyes of my children may shine with Torah." Nor do I doubt that if God had appeared to one of these mothers in a dream, as He did once to Solomon, and said, "Ask, what shall I give unto thee?" she would have replied even as Solomon did: "I ask not for myself either riches or honor, but O Lord of the Universe, may it please Thee to give unto my sons a heart to understand Torah and wisdom and to distinguish good from evil."[4]

Ladies and Gentlemen! You all know what has become of our old spiritual strongholds in the Diaspora in recent times and I need not dwell upon this theme now. For all their inner strength, and for all the energy the nation had expended upon creating and preserving these centers, they stood not firm on the day of wrath; by the decree of history they are crumbled and razed to the foundations and our people is left standing empty-handed upon their ruins. This is the very curse of the Galut, that our undertakings do not, indeed cannot, prosper. In every land and in every age we have been sowing a bushel and reaping less than a peck. The winds and hurricanes of history always begin by attacking the creation of Israel and, in a moment, uproot and utterly destroy that which hands and minds have produced over a period of generations. Through cruel and bitter trials and tribulations, through blasted hopes and despair of the soul, through innumerable humiliations, we have slowly arrived at the realization that without a tangible homeland, without private national premises that are entirely ours, we can have no sort of a life, either material or spiritual. Without Eretz Israel—Eretz means land, literally land—there is no hope for the rehabilitation of Israel anywhere, ever. Our very ideas about the material and intellectual existence of the nation have also meanwhile undergone a radical change. We no longer admit a division of the body and the spirit, or a division of the man and the Jew. We hold neither with Beth Shammai, that the heavens were created first, nor with Beth Hillel,[5] that the earth was created first, but with the sages that both were created simultaneously by one command so that neither can exist without the other. In the consciousness of the nation the comprehensive human concept of "culture" has, meanwhile, taken the place of the theological one of "Torah." We have come to the conclusion that a people that aspires to a dignified existence must create a culture; it is not enough merely to make use of a culture—a people must create its own, with its own hands and its own implements and materials, and impress it with its own seal. Of course our people in its "diasporas" is creating culture; I doubt whether any place in the world where culture is being produced is entirely devoid of Jews. But as whatever the Jew creates in the Diaspora is always absorbed in the culture of others, it loses its identity and is never accounted to the credit of the Jew. Our cultural account in the Diaspora is consequently all debit and no credit. The Jewish people is therefore in a painfully false position: Whereas its true function culturally is that of a proletariat—i.e., it produces with the materials and implements of others for others—it is regarded by others, and at times even by itself, as a cultural parasite, possessing nothing of its own. A self-respecting people will never become reconciled to such a lot; it is bound to arise one day and resolve: No more. Better a little that is undisputedly my own than much that is not definitely either mine or somebody else's. Better a dry crust in my own home and on my own table than a stall-fed ox in the home of others and on the table of others. Better one little university but entirely my own, entirely my handiwork from foundations to coping stones, than thousands of temples of learning from which I derive benefit but in which I have no recognized share. Let my food be little and bitter as the olive, if I may but taste in it the delicious flavor of a gift from myself.

It was in this frame of mind that we took refuge in this land. We are not come here to seek wealth, or dominion, or greatness. How much of these can this poor little country give us? We wish to find here only a domain of our own for our physical and intellectual labor. We have not yet achieved great things here. We have not had time to wash the dust of long wanderings from our feet and to change our patched garments. Undoubtedly many years have yet to pass until we have healed this desolate land of the leprosy of its rocks and the rot of its swamps. For the present there is only a small beginning of upbuilding; yet already the need has been felt for erecting a home for the intellectual work of the nation. Such has ever been the nature of our people: it cannot live for three consecutive days without Torah. Already at this early hour we experience cultural needs that cannot be postponed and must be satisfied at once. Besides, we are burdened with heavy cares for the cultural fate of our people in the Diaspora. Nations born only yesterday foolishly imagine that through intellectual parching, by means of a *numerus clausus*,[6] they can do to death an old nation with a past of four thousand years of Torah. We must therefore hasten to light here the first lamp of learning and science and of every sort of intellectual activity in Israel, ere the last lamp grows dark for us in foreign lands. And this we propose to do in the house whose doors have been opened this day upon Mount Scopus.

There is an ancient tradition that in the time of the Redemption the synagogues and houses of study of the Diaspora will be transported, along with their foundations, to Palestine. Naturally this legend cannot come true literally; the house of knowledge and learning that has been erected on Mount Scopus will differ greatly, not only in the materials of which it is made but in its nature and purpose, from the old *bet-midrash*. But, Ladies and Gentlemen, amid the ruins of those hallowed structures there are many sound and beautiful stones that can and ought to be foundation stones of our new edifice. Let not the builders reject these stones. At this hallowed moment I feel impelled to pray: May those stones not be forgotten! May we succeed in raising the science and learning that will issue from this house to the moral level to which our people raised its Torah! We should not be worthy of this festive day if we proposed to content ourselves with a poor imitation of other peoples. We know well that true wisdom is that which learns from all; the windows of this house will therefore be open on every side, that the fairest fruit produced by man's creative spirit in every land and every age may enter. But we ourselves are not new-comers to the Kingdom of the Spirit and while learning from everybody we also have something to teach. I feel sure that a time will come when the moral principles upon which our Houses of Torah were founded, such as those enumerated in the wonderful short *baraitha*⁷ known as "The Chapter on the Acquisition of Torah," will become the heritage of humanity at large.

Ladies and Gentlemen! Thousands of our youth, obeying the call of their hearts, are streaming from the four corners of the earth to this land for the purpose of redeeming it from desolation and ruin. They are prepared to pour all their aspirations and longings and to empty all the strength of their youth into the bosom of this wasteland in order to revive it. They are plowing rocks, draining swamps, and building roads amid singing and rejoicing. These young people know how to raise simple and crude labor—physical labor—to the level of highest sanctity, to the level of religion. It is our task to kindle such a holy fire within the walls of the house which has just been opened upon Mount Scopus. Let those youths build the Earthly Jerusalem with fire and let them who work within these walls build the Heavenly Jerusalem with fire, and between them let them build and establish our House of Life. "For Thou, O Lord, didst consume it with fire, and with fire Thou wilt rebuild it."

Let me say in conclusion a few words to the honored representative of the great British people, Lord Balfour.

"Who despises a day of small deeds?"⁸ asked the prophet. Least of all should small undertakings be despised in our small country. This country has the virtue of turning small things into great things in the fullness of time. Four thousand years ago there gathered in this land, from Ur of the Chaldees, from Aram, from Egypt, and from the Arabian Desert, some groups of wandering shepherds divided into a number of tribes. They became in time, in consequence of events of apparently no great importance, a people small and poor in its day— the people Israel. Few and unhappy were the days of this people on its land as "a people dwelling apart, not counted among the nations." But this people produced men—for the most part of humble station, shepherds, plowmen, and dressers of sycamores, like their brethren—who carried the tempest of the spirit of God in their hearts and His earthquakes and thunders in their mouths. Those men, in speaking of nations and individuals and in discoursing upon the history of their times and the apparently trivial affairs of the moment, dared to turn to eternity, to the Heavens and to the Earth. And it was they who in the end provided the foundation for the religious and moral culture of the world. Across the centuries and over the heads of nations ascending and descending the stage of history, their voice has come down to us to this day, and it is mighty and sublime and filled with the power of God even more than at first, as if it were constantly gaining in strength with increasing remoteness in time. After the proclamation of Cyrus, some tens of thousands of exiles rallied again to this poor, waste country and again formed a poor small community, even poorer and smaller than the first. After only some three hundred years, there arose again in this land a man of Israel, the son of an Israelite carpenter, who conveyed the gospel of salvation to the pagan world and cleared the way for the days of the Messiah. Since then two thousand years have elapsed, and we are all witnesses this day that idols have not yet disappeared from the face of the earth; the place of the old has been taken by new ones, no better than the former. And then came the Balfour Declaration. Israel is assembling in Eretz Israel for a third time. Why should not the miracle be repeated again this time? Providence willed that the fate of the Jewish people be associated with that of every civilized nation in the world, and this circumstance has perhaps developed in them more than in other peoples a sense of moral responsibility toward, and concern for, the future of civilization. Many years ago one of our sages gave fitting expression to this feeling: "A man should always think of himself and of the world as half righteous and half guilty. If he has committed a single transgression—woe betide him, for he has weighed down the scales of the whole world on the side of guilt." Who knows but that the task in which great nations have failed amid the tumult of wealth may be achieved by a poor people in its small country? Who knows but in the end of days this doctrine of responsibility for the fate of humanity may go forth from its house of learning and spread to all the people? Surely not for nothing has the hand of God led this people for four thousand years through the pangs of hell and now brought it back unto its land for the third time.

The Books of Chronicles, the last of the Scriptures, are not the last in the history of Israel. To its two small parts there will be added a third, perhaps more important than the first two. And if the first two Books of Chronicles begin with "Adam, Seth, Noah" and end with the

Proclamation of Cyrus, which three hundred years later brought the gospel of redemption to the heathen of old, the third will undoubtedly begin with the Proclamation of Balfour and end with a new gospel, the gospel of redemption to the whole of humanity.

Part 5
Rebels at Their Most Defiant

MICAH JOSEPH BERDICHEVSKI

1865-1921

"I LOVE AND I HATE," Catullus wrote about the lady he could neither be happy with nor abandon. In essence Berdichevski's many volumes embroider this theme, except that his was a love-hate relationship with Judaism and the Jewish tradition. He described this state of soul, correctly, as the mark of his generation, "the rent in the heart" that inevitably attended the passage from the religious faith of the ghetto to secular values of modern European civilization. But Ahad Ha-Am and Bialik found some peace in their synthesis in cultural Zionism; Berdichevski, Ahad Ha-Am's greatest adversary, denied that such a peace was real or possible. He saw only tension and affirmed only revolt. For Berdichevski tradition was an illusion, whether in Jewish history or in the history of civilization as a whole, and balance between the old and the new a figment of the imaginings of closet philosophers. True, primal values were the creations of rebels, who arose to challenge all conventional life and thought, and therefore a valid Jewish national revival was to be found not in the morality of books but in the proud human dignity of men who were not enslaved even by a great past. And yet from Berdichevski's pen we have some of the most poignant appreciations of the very tradition he professed to contemn and unsurpassed volumes opening the door for the modern reader to talmudic legend and morality, and to Hasidism.

Berdichevski, even more than Ahad Ha-Am, could have begun an autobiography exactly as Henry Adams began his *Education*, by announcing himself as, by birth, a Brahmin of Brahmins, a veritable scion of high priests, come into the world in the shadow of the Temple. He was born in Miedzyborz, Russia, in the city which had been the cradle of Hasidism in the middle of the eighteenth century, into a family of the most notable rabbinic lineage. By the age of seventeen, when a suitable match with an heiress was arranged for him, he was already well known as a phenomenal scholar of talmudic literature and of the mystical texts of Cabbala and Hasidism. In secret, however,

Berdichevski was reading in "enlightened" works; when caught in this "crime" by his pious father-in-law, he was thrown out on the street and the recent marriage was broken up. He went briefly to the yeshivah at Volozhin and began to write seriously. His earliest essays and stories were unimportant, conventional attempts to do what he later denounced as impossible, i.e., to find a compromise between the rabbinic tradition and enlightenment.

The stay at Volozhin and the years immediately thereafter were, however, a transition period. In 1890 he left for western Europe to study first at the University of Breslau and even for a while at its academy for painting. Within two years a radically different writer was revealing himself, one who spoke now of the vagueness of all the much debated great values, like Jewish tradition, culture, and nationalism, and of the neglect of the individual. Nietzsche was then one of the gods of advanced young men and, though it can be doubted whether Berdichevski was ever completely a disciple, it is beyond question that he was deeply influenced by the doctrine of the superman. A key idea of Nietzsche, the need for the "transvaluation of all values," was soon adopted by Berdichevski, who used it as the slogan for his radical attack on the Jewish tradition.

Berdichevski was a distinguished writer (though there are many lapses of style and taste) not only in Hebrew, his major language of literary expression, but also in Yiddish and German. He wrote on many, and often contradictory levels, from the seriousness of his dissertation in German devoted to the relationship of ethics and aesthetics, to light short stories and even popular philosophy in Yiddish. In the later years of his life he was concurrently producing collections of talmudic and post-talmudic legends—this with immense regard for their nobility—and preparing a major study (part appeared posthumously, entitled *Sinai und Gerisim*) in which he asserted that nature worship and idolatry, not biblical monotheism, had been the real religion of ancient Israel in its days of glory. His writings in Hebrew, collected by him in twenty volumes, were, however, the most significant aspect of Berdichevski's career.

From 1911 Berdichevski lived in Berlin, supporting himself as a dentist, in seclusion from public affairs and utterly devoted to his scholarly writings and to belles-lettres. Though he sought no disciples, his death in 1921 left a legacy which still lives on, for his thought is, even for many who do not know it, the source of a strain of humanist, Promethean *grandezza* which colors modern Israel.

WRECKING AND BUILDING (1900–1903)

THIS TIME in which we live is not like yesterday or the day before —it has no counterpart, for all the bases and conditions of our previous existence are now undermined and changed. The "long, dark night" is gone, and new days, with new circumstances, have replaced it. There is reason for the fear in our hearts—it is true that we are no longer standing on a clear road; we have come to a time of two worlds in conflict: To be or not to be! To be the last Jews or the first Hebrews.

Our people has come to its crisis, its inner and outer slavery has passed all bounds, and it now stands one step from spiritual and material annihilation. Is it any wonder that all who know in their hearts the burden, the implications, and the "dread" of such an hour should pit their whole souls on the side of life against annihilation? And this, too, such men must feel: that a new life must arise, broader in scope and different in condition from what has been. In devoting ourselves to the essential task, the resurrection of the people, we cannot even be indulgent to its tradition.

It is true that our past is that which gives us an historic claim and title to live on in the future; and as we go forward in our struggle for existence we look back to the day of Judah's bannered camp, to our heroes and ancient men of war, to our sages, the beacons of our spirit. Yet we cannot hide from ourselves that our ancestral heritage is not entirely an asset; it has also caused us great loss.

After the destruction of the Temple our political status declined and our independence came to an end. We ceased to be a people actively adding to its spiritual and material store and living in unbroken continuity with its earlier days. As our creativity diminished, the past— whatever had once been done and said among us, our legacy of thoughts and deeds—became the center of our existence, the main supports of our life. The Jews became secondary to Judaism.

All sentiments of survival, all vital desires that had swelled the hearts of Jacob's children in former times, sought an outlet through these channels. Many thought that they could satisfy the national conscience that lived in their hearts by preserving what had been handed down from their ancestors.

Apart from turning us into spiritual slaves, men whose natural forces had dried up and whose relation to life and to the world was no longer normal, this brought about the great interruption in our social and political development, an interruption that has almost led us to total decay.

Our young people were made to believe that spiritual attachment to the Jewish people necessarily meant faith in a fixed and parochial outlook, so they turned away and left us, for their souls sought another way.

We are torn to shreds: at one extreme, some leave the House of Israel to venture among foreign peoples, devoting to them the service of their hearts and spirits and offering their strength to strangers; while, at the other extreme, the pious sit in their gloomy caverns, obeying and preserving what God had commanded them. And the enlightened, standing between, are men of two faces: half Western—in their daily life and thoughts; and half Jews—in their synagogues. Our vital forces disperse while the nation crumbles.

For all the yearning for a revival which has begun to awaken in the hearts of the remaining few, we feel that such a revival must encompass both the inner and the outer life. It cannot arise other than by a total overturn, that is, by a transvaluation of the values which have been the guide lines of our lives in the past.

Our hearts, ardent for life, sense that the resurrection of Israel depends on a revolution—the Jews must come first, before Judaism—the living man, before the legacy of his ancestors.

We must cease to be Jews by virtue of an abstract Judaism and become Jews in our own right, as a living and developing nationality. The traditional "credo" is no longer enough for us.

We desire to elevate our powers of thought, to enrich our spirit, and to enlarge our capacity for action; but let us never force our spirits into set forms which prescribe for us what we may think and feel.

It is not reforms but transvaluations that we need—fundamental transvaluations in the whole course of our life, in our thoughts, in our very souls.

Jewish scholarship and religion are not the basic values—every man may be as much or as little devoted to them as he wills. But the people of Israel come before them—"Israel precedes the Torah."

The world about us, life in all its aspects, the many desires, resolves, and dispositions in our hearts—all these concern us as they would any man and affect the integrity of our soul. We can no longer solve the riddles of life in the old ways, or live and act as our ancestors did. We are the sons, and sons of sons, of older generations, but not their living monuments. . . .

We must cease to be tablets on which books are transcribed and thoughts handed down to us—always handed down.

Through a basic revision of the very foundations of Israel's inner and outer life, our whole consciousness, our predispositions, thoughts, feelings, desires, and will and aim will be transformed: and we shall live and stand fast.

Such a fundamental revision in the people's condition, the basic drive toward freedom, and the boundless urge to new life will revive our souls. Transvaluation is like a flowing spring. It revives whatever is in us, in the secret places of the soul. Our powers are filled with a new, life-giving content.

Such a choice promises us a noble future; the alternative is to remain a straying people following its erring shepherds. A great responsibility rests upon us, for everything lies in our hands! We are the last Jews —or we are the first of a new nation.

IN TWO DIRECTIONS (1900–1903)

TO THIS DAY I wonder how Israel's sages came to coin the saying, "The blade and the book descended from Heaven coupled together,"[1] when it is obvious that the two contradict and destroy each other.

Their periods are distinct. Each one has its own time, and upon the appearance of one, the other vanishes . . .

There is a time for men and nations who live by the sword, by their power and their strong arm, by vital boldness. This time is the hour of intensity, of life in its essential meaning. But the book is no more than the shade of life, life in its senescence.

The blade is not something abstracted and standing apart from life; it is the materialization of life in its boldest lines, in its essential and substantial likeness. Not so the book.

There are times when we live, and there are times when we only think about life.

The Talmud rules: " 'A man should not go out on the Sabbath bearing either a blade or a bow.' The sages commented that arms were not a mark of honor, since it is written, 'They shall beat their swords into plowshares.' "

The blade and the bow, by whose force Israel fared so nobly, through which it became a people, these are now discreditable, since it is written . . .

But a vestige of vitality still remained in Rabbi Eliezer.[2] There was a man alive at the time who had not utterly capitulated to the moral rebellion; and he said: It is permissible to go out on the Sabbath bearing a blade and a bow, for they are an ornament to a man.

Now here comes Ahad Ha-Am and calls Rabbi Eliezer to book for not rising, in his ethical conceptions, to the level of the other sages of his time, and failing to sense in his heart the dishonor that lies in the strong arm and in its implements.

Ornament or discredit, Rabbi Eliezer or Ahad Ha-Am, which of these two stands higher?

Even if it were not plain Scripture, one should have to say: In the beginning God created the Universe, and then afterward, He made man, only afterward . . . And thus we, with our thoughts and feelings and desires and destiny and all we have and are, are the drippings of the bucket, the dust in the scales, against the world and all that's in it.

The Universe telleth the glory of God, the works of His hand doth Nature relate; for Nature is the father of all life and the source of all life; Nature is the fount of all, the fount and soul of all that live . . .

And then Israel sang the song of the Universe and of Nature, the song of heaven and earth and all their host, the song of the sea and the fullness thereof, the song of the hills and high places, the song of the trees and the grass, the song of the seas and the streams. Then did the men of Israel sit each under his vine or his fig tree, the fig put forth her buds and the green hills cast their charm from afar . . .

Those days were the days of breadth and beauty.

After these things, behold! The Day of the Lord came for all the cedars of Lebanon and all the oaks of Bashan, for all the high hills and lofty mountains, and for all noble life.

Not man alone needs must bow before the glorious pride of the Cause of Being, but Nature, too, the whole Universe and all things that live. Not man alone must humble himself, become meek in all he does, but Nature too and all its doings must become lowly.

Not only upon the lowly, submissive man does the Blessed Holy One bestow His Presence, but it is Mount Horeb of all mountains on which He chose to be revealed, for it is the lowest of the hills and high places . . .

We had thought that God was power, exaltation, the loftiest of the lofty. We had thought that all that walked upon the heights became a vehicle for His Presence, but lo! a day came in which we learned otherwise . . .

Not the Universe is the source, but man alone, and in man, only his deeds. It is not man that is an incident to Creation, but quite the reverse.

Is it any wonder that men like Rabbi Isaac arose in our academies who said: The Bible should not have begun with Genesis, but with the Law? . . .[3]

Is it any wonder that there arose among us generation after generation despising Nature, who thought of all God's marvels as superfluous trivialities?

Is it surprising that we became a non-people, a non-nation—non-men, indeed?

I recall from the teaching of the sages: Whoever walks by the way and interrupts his study to remark, How fine is that tree, how fine is that field—forfeits his life![4]

But I assert that then alone will Judah and Israel be saved, when another teaching is given unto us, namely: Whoever walks by the way and sees a fine tree and a fine field and a fine sky and leaves them to think on other thoughts—that man is like one who forfeits his life!

Give us back our fine trees and fine fields! Give us back the Universe.

THE QUESTION OF CULTURE (1900–1903)

I DO NOT BELIEVE those who say that we have a living inner culture, nor do I believe those who say that a culture can be grafted upon us from without. I do not believe it is possible to transmit our ancient light to continuous generations in exile, to spin this thread further in a true and vital line.

We boast in vain of a lofty ethical culture destined to be a light unto the gentiles, while in our tents is darkness and our lives are unlit.

Our shops deny our synagogues and houses of study; our secular lives deny our holiness. Despite all the beacons we bear aloft in our hands, what are we and what is our life?

Yet, to those who go to tend alien vineyards, it must be said: Your lives, your substance, the blood that is in you, denies in some way all that you have ever said, thought, or believed. Enlightenment and knowledge will avail little, so long as they are not necessary expressions of the course of our own history. Every culture is the end of a process, not a fresh beginning induced from without.

Culture is a spiritual and historical possession, comprehending the entire spiritual life of men and involving them in a fixed national-historic-psychic form which is peculiar to a particular community. If we wish to formulate it abstractly, we might say: Culture is the residue of eternity in temporal lives, a residue transmitted from father to son, from generation to generation. Every son begins at the point where his father concluded, and so each generation inherits from its ancestors and finds its work before it—to perfect and advance its selfhood.

In every other people, nationality is the single storehouse in which are preserved human individualities, and where the individual sees his achievements secured and his gains safeguarded. Among us, the individual finds in his Jewish nationality a power hostile to what is in his heart. Every one of us feels this opposition the moment he begins to improve himself and seek for culture; whether much or little, consciously or unconsciously, it is felt.

As a general rule, nationality enriches the individual, bestowing upon him ancient wealth, and, in turn, it becomes enriched from the individual works and creations of its representatives in every generation; but among us all those who work or wish to work in the field of culture find nothing from which to begin.

Other peoples demand sacrifices of their sons only in times of war, when foreigners seek to destroy them. In peacetime, in the processes of everyday life, the price of patriotism is rarely sacrifice—that is, the individual is not aware that he lives, or should live, on behalf of his people. The normal actions of the individual are themselves of benefit to the community. But among us, every individual is required to live always on behalf of his people and to make sacrifices for it every day, every hour, every minute; we demand this of him because his own life and needs strain toward a different arena than the group life, and, in some measure, his personal goals oppose the life of the group.

We require of every Jew that he be greater than other men, while our capacity for such greatness is severely limited.

The existence of our people, the very possibility of its existence, depends on creating a harmonious framework for our individual lives within the community—it depends on our capacity to be united within a structure capable of future survival. Our people can continue to exist only if there will be created among us a spiritual atmosphere and material possibilities for artists and builders.

Give the chance to live to a single individual, and the mass will follow after of its own accord.

THE QUESTION OF OUR PAST (1900–1903)

IF I HAD OCCASION at this time to take up the question of our past and present, and the relation between them, I could no longer divide them into two realms totally opposed to each other, two realms each of which can exist only by destroying the other.

It is true that when we struggle to create a new thing, suited to our contemporary lives and our aspirations of today, when our hearts are full of dreams and, deep within, a new universe is woven, a universe fashioned by our own hands—then there arises in our hearts the urge to destroy the universes that came before us and to eliminate whatever oppresses us by its existence. For the past demands that we devote our powers to guard and to serve it by every service of body and soul, but what we need is a new spirit. We need the spirit of God, that we too may speak to Him face to face; we need a God present in the secret places of our heart and in the universe of our own imagining.

The tablets of the Law are the work of God and persist down the generations; the letters inscribed on the tablets can no more be erased than the heavenly bodies. But let us renew them as the stars are re-kindled; let us sing our song of life in our own way, and so achieve our essence, our immediacy. Let us, too, stand at the foot of God's mountain and cry out: "And God descended in the cloud . . ."[5] Let us, too, see with our own eyes visions of the Almighty.

Among us, man is crushed, living by traditional customs, laws, doctrines, and judgments—for many things were bequeathed us by our ancestors which deaden the soul and deny it freedom. But we also have the "Song of Songs"—we have paeans to life and its bounty; we have the praises of David ben Jesse for the sublime and boundless glories of nature. . . . Our soul speaks this benediction: O Lord God, how great art Thou; Thou hast robed Thyself in splendor and glory! Unto this God do we hope, to God Who covereth Himself with light as a garment, Who stretcheth out the heavens like a curtain; we hope in the Almighty God Who giveth salvation and freedom to man. . . . How mighty are the deeds of God, the whole earth is full of His creations! Bless the Lord, bless ye all His works.

When we ourselves stand in the midst of events, in the very stream of life, the past weighs upon us as a heavy load, and we reject it with wrath and fury. It is different when we regard the past as observers, not as struggling men. Our attitude changes when we see it as a completed thing, established in the final form of an historical phenomenon. Then the past often seems rich and beautiful. Nature has acquired a second sphere, the sphere of history, in which something is preserved and evolved from generation to generation.

What the individual cannot achieve for himself, he can acquire when he attaches himself to the group, and when his ear is attuned to the still voice of the whole. What a man cannot acquire in a single day, he can achieve by a bond with days gone by. The individual is not simply impoverished, but when he participates in the group he may also be enriched through the enduring wealth of the community.

Even a man of heroic spirit, laboring to attain sanctity for himself, could not—beginning on his own—devise the Sabbath which is given to the simplest man who observes it—because he was commanded, because he serves all those who ever observed it. . . .

What vast spiritual and moral labors are needed, even for the exceptional spirit, before one can reckon up his good and bad deeds and beg forgiveness for the bad. But here we have the simple, everyday Jew, far removed as he is all year long from any ethical spirit or absorption in divinity—on Yom Kippur he repairs to the synagogue, and at once the fear of the Lord falls upon him, the fear of God comes over him, and his heart is full of thoughts of repentance and the cleansing of his ways. One short prayer, not even properly understood, but with the hearts of hundreds of generations and myriads of souls poured into it, such a prayer softens the hardest heart and grants it healing. . . .

What the individual cannot achieve, that the whole can do.

The great sins we committed against life, because of which we are dying, were committed by men of perfect righteousness, by men of magnificent virtues. . . . Even in submission, in the duty to be trodden by every foot, there is a kind of grandeur; even in a man's lowliness before the Divine there is awe and fearsomeness and a kind of power. . . .

Even when we question the existence of God or deny His unity, we are overawed by the glory of those who died and were slain for the sanctity of His Name. . . .

Religion, the religion of the community, is a force that is active in us, and that enriches even while it oppresses us.

Rachel bewaileth her children. At a time when the strength of the individual is as nothing, the Synagogue raises its voice from the devastation of Mount Horeb.

That Israelite who laid down his life for a single one of the minor commandments, his blood cries out to me from the earth; and whenever I transgress that commandment, the image of that martyr, broken, shattered, blurred, and crushed though it be, confronts me as a reproof.

This is the grief that is in history; these are the pangs of memory, pangs that fill our hearts and souls, pangs that rend, tear, divide, and deliver them in turn to victories and submissions.

When we defeat the past, it is we ourselves who are defeated. But if the past conquers, it is we, and our sons, and the sons of our sons, who are conquered. . . . Elixir and poison in one and the same substance. Who shall show us the way? Who shall clear us a path?

ON SANCTITY (1899)

SCRIPTURE SAYS: Sanctify yourselves and be ye holy.[6] And this is our beacon light, even though we build new worlds and seek new ways.

Be ye holy—not only in thought and speech, not only in act and will, but in all your substance. The wholeness of heart, man's purity in all things, is the ultimate end. Thoughts alone are worthless, nor do complexes of feeling avail; wholeness is required of you, wholeness in everything.

And ye shall be a holy people; but a holy people is not a people expiring in torments. A beaten, tortured, and persecuted people is unable to be holy. If we have no national livelihood, if we do not eat the fruit of our soil, but only toil on the lands of strangers, how can we be exalted in the spirit? If we are at war with ourselves in everything we do and think and are, how shall we attain elevation of soul and find the way to purification? A holy people must surely be a living people.

JOSEPH HAYYIM BRENNER 1881-1921

BRENNER'S FIRST NOVEL, *Ba-Horef* (*In the Winter*) ends with a symbolic scene in which his autobiographical hero, Feierman, is put off a train because he has no ticket; he is left stranded beside a snow-covered road in the middle of nowhere. By other names Feicrman (i.e., Brenner) is the protagonist of every one of his succeeding novels and his destiny is always the same: abortive beginnings, unrealized strivings, and bitterness against himself and the world. Only once did Brenner permit himself a more hopeful conclusion. His first novel of Palestine, *Mi-Kaan Umi-Kaan* (*From Here and There*) contains a counter-hero, Aryeh Lapidot, who was drawn in the image of A. D. Gordon (we shall meet him in the next section). The last lines of this book depict Lapidot and his young grandson collecting thorns for a fire on which to bake some bread: "The old man and the child were both crowned with thorns, as they stood life's watch together. The sun shone; life was thorny; the account was still open."

Both in his art and in his personal life Brenner wandered between these two poles of the blackest pessimism and qualified affirmation. His childhood and youth were conventional—born in the Ukraine, educated in the usual orthodoxy, and then a break to general studies—but there seems to have been an extra dimension of poverty and personal suffering. He grew to maturity in the 1890's, during a particularly hopeless period in the life of Russia and Russian Jewry. All thought of accommodation with the tsarist regime was ended by then; there were only three alternatives—to labor for a revolution, to migrate westward, or to turn Zionist and go to Palestine. In turn, Brenner attempted each of these solutions.

Brenner was first attracted in his late teens by the *Bund*, the newly formed group of revolutionary socialists which was Jewish in membership but violently opposed to Jewish nationalism (it believed in a future world order in which the workers of all peoples would unite). He did illegal work for the party, but he drifted out of that movement after three years to reaffirm his specific Jewish loyalties through Zionism. In 1902–1903 Brenner served in the Russian army—he depicted this period of his life in a novella, *Shanah Ahat* (*One Year*)—and then escaped to London. His experiences there made him no happier than those that had gone before. The new east European immigrants were then packed tight in its Whitechapel section, London's "East Side," living in indescribable misery and eking out an existence in sweatshops. Brenner himself made the barest of livings as a typesetter. His four years in London confirmed him in the certainty that emigration from Russia meant merely that Jews were exchanging new pain for the old. In the sight of the sweatshops, he became even more of a proletarian writer, a despiser of the bosses and the respectable bourgeoisie. After a short period back in eastern Europe, this time in Lemberg, Austrian Poland, Brenner took the final journey of his odyssey. In 1909 he went to Palestine. There Brenner was a leader in the circles of the then small labor and pioneer groups, taught during the war years in Tel Aviv's first high school, and continued to edit and write. He was found murdered near Tel Aviv during the Arab outbreaks against the Jews in May 1921.

When Brenner began to write in the 1890's, Russian literature was under the influence of Dostoyevsky and Tolstoy. Brenner certainly did not assimilate the metaphysics of the first or the historical vision of the second. What he did learn from these Russian masters was their uncompromising criticism of society, the attitude they shared, for different reasons, that convention is a sham. The other source of Brenner's vision was in the writings of Mendele Moher Sefarim (Shalom Jacob Abramovitz). Mendele, the greatest of nineteenth-century novelists in both Hebrew and Yiddish, had made the disintegrating Russian ghetto his subject and had found it bad. Brenner, from a conscious proletarian perspective, repeated this social criticism with far greater vehemence.

The considerably shortened excerpt from Brenner to be found below is from a lengthy review essay he wrote entitled *Haarahat Azmenu be-Sheloshet Ha-Krahim* (*The Estimate of Ourselves in Three Volumes*), upon the appearance of a collected edition of Mendele's works in Hebrew. It is a summary of his hatred of the Jewish past, both its culture and its society, and his despairing hope that a new, sound, healthy Jew could be made to arise if he were to begin over again in Zion.

SELF-CRITICISM (1914)

THE SKEPTICS AND REBELS who have just recently appeared in our literature say: What? The Jews have survived? Yes, it's true they have survived. But, my friends, survival alone is not yet a virtue. Certainly, it is better for any man, any people, any organism to be than not to be. Better life than death, for existence in itself is pleasant —but existence in itself is no evidence of an estimable character. Such and such a man, let us say, has reached a "venerable" old age—well and good; but we shall never venerate age alone, unless it expresses traits of bodily vigor and spiritual elevation, nor shall we do homage to the old simply by virtue of their age.

The Jews are one of the peoples of antiquity who have survived and remained. How does Mendele[1] put it? "Caravans come and caravans go—but the *Luftmenschen* of Kislon and Kabtziel go on forever." However, this fact by itself proves nothing. It is not always the noblest who survive; but only the noble survive honorably. There is certainly a mystery in our extended survival; there is undoubtedly some special significance in it—for is not all of Creation full of mystery and significance?—but it is beyond our ken. We can judge only the quality of our existence, the mode of our living. And this mode is not one that does us great honor.

Yes, indeed, we have survived, we live. True, but what is our life worth? We have no inheritance. Each generation gives nothing of its own to its successor. And whatever was transmitted—the rabbinical literature—were better never handed down to us. In any case, by now it is more and more certainly passing away. Everything we know about our lives tells us that there are only masses of Jews who live biologically, like ants, but a living Jewish people in any sociological sense, a people each generation of which adds a new stratum to what preceded it and each part of which is united with the other—such a people hardly exists any longer. Everything we know about our lives suggests that if our nature had been different we should perhaps not have survived; if we had nevertheless done so, then our present existence would look quite different than it does. And when we cry nowadays: "If we do not become different—if now, the circumstances of our environment having changed, we do not really become a Chosen People—become, that is, like all other nations, each of whom is Chosen by itself—then we shall soon perish"; then what we mean is that we *shall* perish as a people—we *shall* die as a social entity. Yes, we may exist as a mass of gypsies, peddlers, traveling salesmen, and bank clerks; in this guise we may survive biologically for many years, as we have until now, even if we neither change nor are changed in the least.

Certainly we wish to live, to survive in any way, even like ants or dogs. Certainly the live dog, following the rule of self-love, adaptation, and propitiation in order to survive in the world, is better off than the dead lion, whose self-love drives him to stand against all comers, so that he perishes from the earth. A "living" people whose members have no power but for moaning and hiding a while until the storm blows over, turning away from their poorer brethren to pile up their pennies in secret, to scratch around among the *goyim*, make a living from them, and complain all day long about their ill will—no, let us not pass judgment upon such a people, for indeed it is not worth it.

Then they come and tell us: All praise to our history of martyrdom! All praise to the martyr-people who suffered everything and yet survived despite all persecution, all oppression by authorities, and all hatred of the people. But here, too, who can tell us what might have happened if not for the oppression and the hatred? Who can tell us whether, had there been no universal and understandable hatred of such a strange being, the Jew, that strange being would have survived at all? But the hatred was inevitable, and hence survival was equally inevitable! A form of survival such as befits that kind of being, survival with no struggle for worldly things (apart from those familiar livelihoods by which we live a dog's or a loan-shark's life) but, of course, full of martyrdom for the sake of the world-to-come, yes, certainly, in the name of the Kingdom of Heaven.

Then, they may say: Such hatred, universal and inevitable, is in itself evidence that there is something here, some peculiar power in that strange being.

Some power—certainly! Every living being, whatever it may be, has some power which sustains it. But the question, once more, is: What is the nature of that power? How does it express itself?

It would be a sign of steadfastness and power, of productive strength, if the Jews would go away from those who hate them and create a life for themselves. That I would call heroic sacrifice. In our own time, when the government oppressed the Russian peasant Dukhobors for religious reasons, they left everything and went to Canada to make their living any way they could. Compared with that, just see the hollowness of our own colonization, the Jewish colonies in Argentina and Palestine. Oh, certainly! Colonization is a difficult matter, some among us will say, with an air of political sophistication. Even powerful governments with all their resources, and so on and so forth, while we have no government at all. But, at the same time, they utterly forget, first, that if we have no government, that is, no concentration of our national strength in a single organization, this is simply because we never had any real national strength; second, that if any other people but ourselves had found itself in the condition (or the noncondition) we are in, then, regardless of all difficulties of colonization, nothing would have stood in its way. Among us people speak expertly of the difficulties and the tested and approved methods of facilitating colonization, when we lack the very basis: We have no colonists, no workers, no laborers; all we have are pipe dreams of speculation worthy of the heirs of Reb Leib the *Melamed*.[2] Why all the talk? If there is no great colonial-territorial movement among us today, if only a handful of young men can be found among twelve million to give their sweat with which to rinse off the horrible plague of huckstering that has infested us, and their calloused hands to roll our historic shame off our backs—then this is a sign, the sign of Cain, that the hucksters cleave to their huckstering because they lack strength for anything better.

Then come our national apologists and tell of the steadfastness of the Jews in their religious belief. But what value is there for us in our ancestors' practice of some religious customs, particularly those that cost them no money, in the hope of being rewarded in the world to come? For the language, the manners, the deeds, and all the basic patterns which reflected human creativity, even during the Middle Ages, so long as the Jews were not shut up in the ghetto, and afterward as well, were in imitation of the gentiles. Moreover, even our faith and our religious concepts were, for the most part, taken over, borrowed, and influenced in every way—and vulgarly so—by others (Q.E.D., angels, demons, hocus-pocus, and sorcery in the Talmud). Be that as it may, commercial matters surely always played a more important role in the lives of our ancestors than religious matters, and wherever the two came into conflict—religion did not emerge victorious. It is a grave error to describe our history as one long war for the sanctification of our religion when that long war was for the purpose of gaining rights for ourselves. Those hundreds of generations lived not on Sanctification of the Name, but on various schemes aimed at fulfilling, for their own benefit, the commercial functions demanded of them by the general populace; they lived to safeguard their money and increase the interest rates, and also—to guard themselves against baptism. But concessions in religious matters to the demands of the external environment were never lacking.

In their prayers, their liturgy, and sacred books the Jews complained to God for not redeeming them, for not restoring them forever to their homeland, while they were doing so much for His Great Name's sake, despite the bitter exile which prevented them from observing all the laws and commandments properly. At the same time, however, they were always quite content to remain where they were, among the wicked gentiles, so long as the latter allowed them to remain. Naturally, they paid for their lives with money, withdrew into their shells, their tortoise shells, whenever they were subjected to oppression, peered through the chinks in their cave walls, looking forward all the while to better days when they would be able to emerge, spread out over the land, and do business with it. Not a history of Sanctification of the Name, but a history of awaiting the chance to assimilate—such is our history. The expulsions and the ghettos—these assured our survival. Even the Golden Jewry of Spain[3]—who knows what would have remained of them, of those Spaniards of Mosaic Persuasion, beyond what remained of their Marranos of Christian Persuasion! It is only because they were suddenly expelled by the tens of thousands to a strange land of a lower cultural level, in which, as a result, they did not fare as well as in the land which expelled them, that we have today our Arabic-Sephardim,[4] Turco-Sephardim, Serbo-Sephardim, and the Bulgarians of Mosaic Persuasion in the Ottoman Empire and the Balkan lands.

History! History! But what has history to tell? It can tell that wherever the majority population, by some fluke, did not hate the Jews among them, the Jews immediately started aping them in everything, gave in on everything, and mustered the last of their meager strength to be like everyone else. Even when the yoke of ghetto weighed most heavily upon them—how many broke through the walls? How many lost all self-respect in the face of the culture and beautiful way of life of the others! How many envied the others! How many yearned to approach them!

It had been the consensus of our literature until recently that our forefathers, the Jews of the old ghetto, felt within their hearts a pride and a superiority to the gentile, even while kissing his hand and abasing themselves before him.

This thesis is: There was outward humiliation and servility, but inward pride and beauty.

It is possible, of course, that some Jews who were sensitive to their mortification consoled themselves with the promise to Jews of a better life in the world to come. Perhaps they assured themselves that despite all the gentile's earthly possessions of large estates, horses, carriages, minstrels, and all the pleasures of this world, he would never inherit Paradise with us. This was a consolation, but nothing more.

But whence this disdain of and sense of superiority over the gentile? Was the Jew really so insensitive, so dead to the world, as not even to realize how much more beautiful and rich was the gentile's life than his own? No, this is impossible! This we cannot believe! If there was disdain of the gentile, it was but the natural envy that the poor man has for the rich, the monk for the knight, and the weak man for the strong. Such disdain was really but a shrug of resignation of our share in this world, some sort of consolation—depending upon the mood —in hopes of the world to come, followed by a quiet gritting of the teeth and conscious or subconscious inner turmoil.

The contempt for everything that is contemptible in our life has struck ever deeper roots in our belletristic literature since Mendele. It maintains that the contempt for us through the ages has been for nought! True, our literature suffers from the unstable health of an old man; it is very pathological. Its nerves are shattered. Its environment is tottering and our very life has become pathological. Can our self-contempt escape being pathological too?

Yes, our environment is crumbling. This is nothing new, for this environment has never been stable; it has always lacked a firm foundation. We never had workers, never a real proletariat. What we had and have are idle poor. Basically nothing has changed, but now the very forms of life have dissolved.

We live now without an environment, utterly outside any environment. We have to start all over again, to lay down a new cornerstone. But who will do that? Can we do it, with our sick character? This is the question.

This is the question: In order that our character be changed as much as possible, we need our own environment; in order to create such an environment ourselves—our character must be radically changed.

We are at an impasse, but the pen is still in hand. Our literature lives with Mendele and with all who have succeeded him, and it continues to seek the way, with true self-criticism for a guide.

Our literature cries out. A true outcry—it feels—is to some extent a liberation. Our literature also evaluates. True evaluation—it feels—even a negative one, bears a positive potential. True self-realization and acceptance of even a harsh verdict will somehow help us transcend ourselves.

The literature of self-criticism since Mendele says: Our function now is to recognize and admit our meanness since the beginning of history to the present day, all the faults in our character, and then to rise and start all over again. For we are no aristocrats! But there is still room for reform and "he who confesses and makes amends will be dealt with mercifully."

And it—our poor and confused literature—knows very well that logic will argue and disprove, for how can we become that which we are not?

But let logic argue what it may. Our urge for life, which stands above logic, says otherwise. Our urge for life says: All this is possible. Our urge for life whispers hopefully in our ear: Workers' Settlements, Workers' Settlements.

Workers' Settlements—this is our revolution. The only one.

JACOB KLATZKIN 1882-1948

KLATZKIN was the most temperate stylist, and yet perhaps the most devastating antitraditionalist, of all the rebels within Zionism. Berdichevski, too, imagined a modern Jewish national culture that would break with the past, but he envisaged it in new, primal, Nietzschean grandeur. Brenner, for all his doubts, was sustained by the desperate hope for a Jewish nation which would be outstanding in its proletarian dignity; the very fire of his denunciations of the past implied that mere respectable dullness was not enough for the future. Klatzkin, who regarded himself as a professional philosopher, was, at least in public attitude, beyond such passionate hatreds, but he also did not rebound toward equally intense affirmations. In all of Zionist literature he has been known chiefly as the most radical denier of any possibility of a future Jewish life in the Diaspora. It has been less emphasized—though, I think, more significant—that he is the most important Zionist thinker to affirm that a third-rate, normal, national state and culture would be enough.

Like Berdichevski and Ahad Ha-Am, Klatzkin was born within the ghetto aristocracy of Russia. His father was a rabbi and distinguished scholar of the Talmud; Klatzkin's own first published book, in 1902 when he was but twenty, belonged to the genre of traditional rabbinic scholarship. He was, however, already attracted to secular culture and to Zionism. After a few years of study in western Europe, the transformation in his life was complete. Already a notable writer in modern Hebrew, he had become a fine stylist in German as well. From 1909 to 1911 he served the World Zionist Organization as the editor of its official organ, *Die Welt*, and then as director of the main office of the Jewish National Fund. Concurrently Klatzkin crystallized his own views in a number of essays in Hebrew which were collected in 1914 under the title *Tehumim* (*Boundaries*). He rewrote this book in German during World War I. The excerpts by which he is represented in this volume contain the main outlines of his argument, which he regarded as his chief contribution to Zionist theory.

Though Klatzkin continued to engage in Zionist work as writer and editor, there was a significant other side to his career, as pure scholar and independent philosopher. Together with Nahum Goldmann, he founded the Eschkol publishing firm in Berlin in the 1920's and projected the *Encyclopaedia Judaica*, of which ten volumes appeared in German and five in Hebrew before the work was suspended with the advent of Hitler. His four-volume dictionary of Hebrew philosophical terms is a chef-d'oeuvre of learning. His own philosophic position was that of a vitalist who found his inspiration in the flux of life and the unreasoning courage of man. In this field, too, he wrote in both Hebrew and German. One volume of aphorisms representing his personal philosophy has appeared in English translation under the title *In Praise of Wisdom* (1943).

Klatzkin's Zionist position is based on his general definition of nationalism. What makes a nation, he asserted, is land and language. Therefore, the Jews needed to reacquire their land and again speak their language, Hebrew. Let there be no talk, therefore, of spiritual uniqueness, of destiny and mission, for all this is a mark of the diseased abnormality of an un-nation. Obviously, it also follows that all Jews not only will but must, with all deliberate speed, either emigrate to Palestine or disappear by intermarriage. There could be neither a middle ground nor an alternative, so Klatzkin insisted, to these solutions.

When Hitler came to power in 1933 Klatzkin left for Switzerland, and in 1941 he came to the United States. After World War II Klatzkin returned to Europe and died in Vevey, Switzerland, in 1948.

BOUNDARIES (1914–1921)

JUDAISM IS NATIONALISM

IN THE PAST there have been two criteria of Judaism: the criterion of religion, according to which Judaism is a system of positive and negative commandments, and the criterion of the spirit, which saw

Judaism as a complex of ideas, like monotheism, messianism, absolute justice, etc. According to both these criteria, therefore, Judaism rests on a subjective basis, on the acceptance of a creed. Both define the Jewish people as a denomination: according to the first standard it is a religious denomination, and, in the second, it is a community of individuals who share in a *Weltanschauung*. It therefore follows, from the first definition, that one who does not believe in the Jewish religion excludes himself from the Jewish people. The logic of the second position makes a comparable conclusion inevitable—whoever denies the ideas and ethical values of Judaism automatically excludes himself from the community.

In opposition to these two criteria, which make of Judaism a matter of creed, a third has now arisen, the criterion of a consistent nationalism. According to it Judaism rests on an objective basis: *To be a Jew means the acceptance of neither a religious nor an ethical creed.* We are neither a denomination nor a school of thought, but members of one family, bearers of a common history. Denying the Jewish spiritual teaching does not place one outside the community, and accepting it does not make one a Jew. In short, to be part of the nation one need not believe in the Jewish religion or the Jewish spiritual outlook.

Is the content of our sense of national identity, therefore, essentially the bond of a common history, a partnership in the past? A bond can be severed and a partnership may be dissolved. Is such an objective basis for Jewish identity enough, without a subjective foundation? Is it as impossible for a man to depart from Judaism as to deny his family? The first two criteria have the advantage of allowing for the principle of freedom, since according to them to be a Jew means to choose a religious or an ethical creed; the national definition, on the other hand, seems to make being a Jew into an objective fact, into something forced on us by history.

But this is not true. The national definition, too, requires an act of will. It defines our nationalism by two criteria: partnership in the past and the conscious desire to continue such partnership in the future. There are, therefore, two bases for Jewish nationalism—the compulsion of history and a will expressed in that history. A Jew who no longer wishes to belong to the Jewish people, who betrays the covenant and deserts his fellows in their collective battle for redemption, has thereby abandoned his share in the heritage of the past and seceded from his people. By the same token, a convert cannot become a Jew merely by accepting our religious and spiritual values; he gains a share in the Jewish future by an act of will, by deciding to take part in the life of the Jewish people and by becoming absorbed within its history.

A NATION MUST HAVE ITS OWN LAND AND LANGUAGE

DOES JEWISH NATIONALISM, therefore, mean to negate the spirit of Judaism? Such a stricture would be unjust. Jewish nationalism does not deny Jewish spiritual values—it only refuses to raise them to the level of a criterion by which the nation is defined. It refuses to define being a Jew as something subjective, as a faith, but prefers to base it on something objective: on land and language. These are the basic categories of national being.

But our land is not ours and our language is not today the language of our people. Yes, these are consummations yet to be realized by our national movement. At present we validate our right to be a nation by our hope for the future, toward which we are striving, and by negating our Galut existence. The striving toward the goal of a national future for our land and language, the orientation toward a future existence which is not yet realized—these are the only possible claims of Jewry in the Diaspora to the status of a nation.

The assimilated Jews claim that we have ceased being a nation in the Diaspora. Jewish nationalists must reply: We are a nation even in the Diaspora, so long as our goal is to be redeemed from it, so long as we labor for the rebirth of our land and our language.

Diaspora nationalism maintains that we are a national entity even in the Diaspora, even though we are dwelling in foreign lands and expressing ourselves in foreign languages, if only we live and labor in the spirit of Judaism. Valid Jewish nationalism must reply: In strange lands and foreign tongues our existence is never a national one, even when we live and create in the spirit of Judaism, i.e., in the spirit of Jewish ethical teaching. Without the two future poles of a national land and a national language, nationalism in the Diaspora has no meaning and assimilation is the courageous and logical path for the Diaspora to take.

What is really new in Zionism is its territorial-political definition of Jewish nationalism. Strip Zionism of the territorial principle and you have destroyed its character and erased the distinctions between it and the preceding periods. This is its originality—that Judaism depends on form and not on content. For it the alternatives are clear: Either the Jewish people shall redeem the land and thereby continue to live, even if the spiritual content of Judaism changes radically, or we shall remain in exile and rot away, even if the spiritual tradition continues to exist.

In longing for our land we do not desire to create there a base for the spiritual values of Judaism. To regain our land is for us an end in itself—the attaining of a free national life. The content of our life will be national when its forms become national. Indeed, let it not be said that the land is a precondition for a national life; living on the land is *ipso facto* the national life.

It is no accident that the theory of Judaism as a spiritual outlook, even in its nationalist form, has fought hard against the territorialist conception of Zionism. It feared, correctly, that from such Zionism it would receive its deathblow. All the varieties of "spiritual" thought, including the nationalist, have joined in combating political Zionism in the name of the spirit of Judaism, i.e., the ethics of the prophets, and have asserted that the ultimate goal of the Jewish people is not a political state but the reign of absolute justice. All these schools of thought mocked Herzl, the hero and genius of our renaissance, by saying: We are a priest people, a nation of prophets—what does he mean coming to us talking about political action? The "spiritists" all cited the Galut as evidence that the basis for our life is the eternal content of Judaism.

Zionism stands opposed to all this. Its real beginning is *The Jewish State* and its basic intention, whether consciously or unconsciously, is to deny any conception of Jewish identity based on spiritual criteria.

Zionism began a new era, not only for the purpose of making an end to the Diaspora but also in order to establish a new definition of Jewish identity—*a secular definition*. I am certain that the builders of our land will in the future sacrifice themselves for national forms, for land and language, as our ancestors accepted martyrdom for the sake of the religious content of Judaism. But we are, as yet, standing at the crossroads and do not yet see the distinction between one period and another. The Galut figure of Ahad Ha-Am still obscures the nationalist light of Herzl.

The "spiritual" criterion is a grave danger not only to our national renaissance but, even more, to our renaissance as individuals. It binds our spirit with the chains of tradition and subordinates our life to specific doctrines, to a heritage and to the values of an ancient outlook. We are constrained by antiquated values, and, in the name of national unity and cohesiveness, our personalities are crippled, for we are denied freedom of thought. Moreover, the "spiritual" definition of what is a Jew leads to national chauvinism. National freedom is meaningless unless it fosters the freedom of the individual. There can be no national renaissance worth fighting for unless it liberates and revives human values within the national ethos.

ASSIMILATION IS POSSIBLE

THERE IS a school of thought which says: Total assimilation of the Jewish people is impossible. All efforts toward assimilation have failed and we are still identifiably a people. The Jewish problem has not been solved by these efforts even temporarily, let alone permanently. We are therefore not to be regarded as some number destined to disappear in a much greater number but as a unique essence which cannot be absorbed and to which the laws of assimilation do not apply.

This belief in the impossibility of complete assimilation is one of the basic tenets of Zionism. Lately this belief has sought support in the theory of race, which has been revived in certain scholarly circles. Even before the validity of this theory has been demonstrated, it has become the basis of many speeches on Zionism, which now use it as a quasi-scientific premise.

Another school of thought maintains: Zionism, in essence, has not come to solve the problem of the Jews but the problem of Judaism. Its purpose is an Hebraic settlement in the land of our fathers which shall become the spiritual center of our people, the national soil for the development of its culture, and the national pale for its creativity. From this center, which is envisaged as a sort of national sun, rays will stream forth to the mass of Jewry in the far reaches of the dispersion. The light and warmth shed by the national sun will protect world Jewry from wasting away. Eretz Israel cannot serve for an ingathering of the exiles, but it can be the spiritual shrine of our people and it can sustain the Galut, which will draw its energies from the roots of our people in the land.

Another feature of this school of thought is an exaggerated interest in philosophizing about the essence of Judaism. It attempts to define the Jewish national spirit in abstract terms, characterizing it as an ethical system and a unique Weltanschauung expressed in such concepts as, for example, the ideal of social justice, the messianic idea, the concept of abstraction and the like . . . In this "spiritual" school of thought, "spiritual center" means "center for the moral spirit of our people." This spirit is our unique national treasure and Eretz Israel is conceived as the temple for the spiritual essence of the nation.

These opinions have as their corollary a faith in the unique power of survival of our people. It is a position parallel to the faith of the religious: the religionists believe that the children of Israel are eternal, basing their faith on the eternity of our holy Torah; those who define Judaism in spiritual terms have faith in the everlasting power of our ethical doctrine and therefore tend to believe that it is impossible for the Jewish people to be destroyed or completely assimilated. They, too, maintain that the Jewish people can never come to an end.

In opposition to these doctrines, I assert: The total assimilation of our people is possible.

Assimilation is infecting ever greater segments of our people and its impact is becoming ever more profound. It has not yet obscured our national identity nor has it solved the Jewish problem, but this is no proof that it will not come to that. Assimilation is still in mid-career. And yet even in its earlier stages it has managed to disfigure and impoverish our people.

Our long survival in the Galut is certainly no proof of the impossibility of assimilation. The hold of the forms of our religion, which have served as barriers between us and the world for about two thousand years, has weakened and there are no longer any strong ghetto walls to protect a national entity in the Galut.

What of the spirit of Judaism, the spirit of its sublime ethic, this healthy seed which is not spoiled by the loss of its shell, religion—can it not guarantee national survival?

No, it cannot. . . . The power of the shell is greater than that of the seed. The laws of our religion represent a national base; due to them our life in Galut has had a national and almost a political character. There can be no national base in an ethical doctrine, in ideas and concepts, in a *Weltanschauung*. National apartness is inherent in the many forms and prohibitions of our religion, not in the spirit of our ethics. Only our religion, and not the spirit of our ethic, can crystallize our national identity, because religion possesses binding power and authority. Unlike the abstract spirit of ethics, our religion is rich in forms which can fashion and protect a national life. Indeed, the forms of our ethic are to be found only in the vessels of religion.

In short, an ethic is not sufficiently defined and crystallized—it does not have sufficient concreteness and form—to delimit and protect a national identity. The domain of an ethical system is a kind of "movable possession" which can be freely transported across national boundaries. Ethics came into the world for such a mission; the Jewish ethic is therefore the source of our concept of mission, which consists of a desire to spread the light of our ethic among all mankind. An ethic may originate within a national culture, but that is only a first stage, which it transcends, as it is purified, by becoming the possession of man as an individual. The very virtue of an ethic is in its capacity for development toward a universal system; if it cannot so develop, its significance is nil and it loses its right to exist.

This judgment, that the spirit and doctrine of an ethic cannot define a people, implies that we cannot pin our national hopes on the power of the ethic of Judaism. Perhaps it is strong enough always to maintain itself, but it has not the power to guarantee the survival of the people which bears it. Perhaps it generates sufficient energy to spread the spirit of Judaism in the world, but it is incapable of preserving the national character and identity of the Jewish people.

We must conclude that the assimilation of our people is not an impossibility. We cannot brush off the theory of assimilation as a solution of the Jewish problem by asserting that it is impossible for the Jewish people to assimilate. On the contrary, assimilation is very definitely possible. Now that the walls of our religion have been breached, the spirit of Judaism, its philosophy and *Weltanschauung*, is not strong enough to erect a containing wall in the Galut and guarantee our national survival within its boundaries.

THE GALUT IS UNWORTHY OF SURVIVAL

LET US ASSUME that the Galut can survive and that *total* assimilation will not inevitably follow the abandonment of religion. Nonetheless we must assert: The Judaism of the Galut is not worthy of survival.

The Galut falsifies our national character

Perhaps our people can maintain itself in the Galut, but it will not exist in its true dimensions—not in the prime of its national character. Galut can only drag out the disgrace of our people and sustain the existence of a people disfigured in both body and soul—in a word, of a horror. At the very most it can maintain us in a state of national impurity and breed some sort of outlandish creature in an environment of disintegration of cultures and of darkening spiritual horizons. The result will be something neither Jew nor gentile—in any case, not a pure national type.

Perhaps it is conceivable that, even after the disintegration of our national existence in foreign lands, there will yet remain for many generations some sort of oddity among the peoples going by the name —Jew. Indeed, both we and the nations of the world are already quite accustomed to showing our lack of respect for this designation by applying it even to ultra-assimilationists who were conceived, born, educated, and grew to maturity in denial of their Jewishness. For an individual to be identified and considered a Jew it suffices for the nations of the world, and even for ourselves, that there should still exist within him some small remnant of a buried Judaism, some little relic of its destruction, perhaps just the negative sign of a most minute difference in his relationship to individuals from other peoples. How poor is such a Judaism which is not symbolized and defined by national affirmations. Alas for people who are known as Jews by a slight intonation in their accent or by their Jewish nose—even though they have been utterly cut off from the national being of the Jewish people and have struck deep roots in an alien culture.

Does it make any sense for us to struggle to maintain this empty label? Why prolong its existence and cling to a slight difference that, possessing only a negative and not a positive national significance, has outlived its meaning?

The Galut is corrupting our human character and dignity

Such a life, even if it continues to exist, will represent no more than a rootless and restless wandering between two worlds. It will cause rent and broken human beings to persist—individuals diseased by ambivalence, consumed by contradictions, and spent by relentless inner conflict. What will survive will be a people that is depressed, bereft of the soil for healthy growth and with geographical-political foundations for real existence, but a people, on the other hand, with an exaggerated amount of worldly intellectualism living a false and perverted existence by means of surrogates for reality.

And our thousands of years of Galut—were they a total waste? Did we create no national values in the Galut? Though we were suffering the Exile, were we not among the leaders of human civilization? If it was so in the midst of distress and poverty, how much greater will be our achievement after we shall have acquired equality among the nations of the world?

Such logic, though it is often encountered in the writings of many of our best publicists, is basically erroneous. The fallacy is itself fundamental, and it is, in turn, the source of many other errors, of false hopes and of vain consolations. There is no analogy between the Galut that preceded the Haskalah and the one that came after. They were two totally different kinds of Galut. Just as we begin a new era in our calendar with the date of the destruction of the Temple, so by right we should have instituted a new calendar from the time of the destruction of our religion, our Temple in the Galut. Such a division of time would surely have been made if the destruction of our religious realm had come from without and not from within—if it had happened as a sudden disaster and not as a gradual process, which obscured the break and hid the time of the beginning of the new era.

No, the argument is not valid. So long as our religion was strong, it was a solid wall protecting us and enabling us to live a national life, almost a political life, on alien soil. In effect, even in the Galut we lived a sovereign life. The Crown of the Torah accompanied us; our Book of Laws was our companion in our wanderings.

THE GALUT MUST BE PRESERVED LONG ENOUGH TO BE TRANSCENDED

AND WHAT ABOUT THE GALUT? Will it simply wither away?

Its function will be to serve as a source of supply for the renaissance of our people in its homeland. Eretz Israel will need the Galut for many generations to come. It will draw upon the Galut for energy and vitality; it will gradually strip that Jewry, which is doomed to oblivion, and *to the extent that it will strip it, it will save it.*

Galut Jewry cannot survive and all our efforts to keep it alive can have only a temporary success. But let us by no means disparage such a success. Such a temporary life has a great function, if it serves the purpose of a lasting life, of the upbuilding of our nation in its homeland. Galut Jewry cannot survive and all our efforts to keep it alive are simply an act of coercion, the maintenance of an unnatural existence. These efforts, however, are not entirely useless, for we have no intention of building our future on the ruins of a Galut which is on the verge of collapse, nor are we attempting to make it survive by propping it up. We are simply hoping to delay its end for a short while so that we may have the time to salvage some bricks for a new structure.

The Galut does not deserve to survive—not as an end in itself. It would richly deserve survival only as it conceived of itself as a means and a transition to a new existence. *The Galut has a right to life for the sake of liberation from the Galut.* In essence, it is the vision of the homeland which validates the Galut. Without this *raison d'être*, without the goal of a homeland, the Galut is nothing more than a life of deterioration and degeneration, a disgrace to the nation and a disgrace to the individual, a life of pointless struggle and futile suffering, of ambivalence, confusion, and eternal impotence. It is not worth keeping alive.

From this point of view we affirm the importance of the national effort in the Galut, an affirmation based both on negation of the Galut and definition of its purpose. Without negation of the Galut there is no basis for such an affirmation.

We must conserve Galut Jewry to the very best of our abilities. We must cultivate a national culture despite existing conditions and inevitable trends. We must increase self-restrictions and prohibitions, for the sake of protecting our identity and apartness, and we must define boundary after boundary between ourselves and the nations among whom we are assimilating. Nonetheless, let us not be deceived. We know that such means of existence cannot long endure; we know that in the Galut a national life, bereft of a soil on which to live a natural existence, is only artificial. We know that the struggle against assimilation has no chance of victory. But this is an era of transition between an age falling into ruin and a time of building. It is our task to delay the end and to slow the process of disintegration so that, meanwhile, our people may be rebuilt. This is no meaningless procrastination, for it has a purpose. This transitional existence is of significance, precisely because it is transitional.

THE NATIONAL RENAISSANCE AND PERSONAL DIGNITY

EVEN ASSIMILATION aids the Jewish renaissance. The very culture that engulfs us so transforms our moral and aesthetic sense that we return to our own people, for we have learned to be sensitive to the crime of assimilation and its consequences.

Many are deterred from complete apostasy only by their moral and aesthetic sensibilities, but these sensibilities are not sufficiently developed to make them feel the sin and disgrace of partial apostasy.

The higher our cultural level, the better equipped we become to feel in assimilation the crippling of our individual human dignity.

It is no accident that Zionism arose in the West and not in the East. Herzl appeared among us not from the national consciousness of a Jew but from a universal human consciousness. Not the Jew but the man in him brought him back to his people. He recognized the moral collapse of assimilation and its disgrace. There is a moral-aesthetic power throbbing in every one of his Zionist speeches; it is he who said to the assimilationists: We must begin by creating decent people. He told us nothing new, but everything he said was new. A new spirit found utterance in him, the spirit of a man in his human dignity.

It is the accepted opinion that anti-Semitism was the cause of Herzl's revelation. Quite true, but this was only an external factor, not the inner motivation; it was the stimulus and not the cause, as the falling of the apple was to Newton's discovery of the law of gravity.

We find, therefore, that the national renaissance among western Jewry is nourished by a number of non-national but universal-human elements not found in the East; it is not as yet nurtured by Judaism but by civilization in general. Moral and aesthetic factors are expressing themselves within it; fighting sham and hypocrisy, it is struggling for truth, purity, and dignity. A sense of sin is disturbing it; the holiness of repentance is trembling within it. Seeking healing for crippled souls, it is striving to convert men to the good in the very process of returning them to their people. One hears in it the beating wings of a great revolution, of the revelation of a moral-aesthetic vision, the trembling of an experience. This is the rebirth of the man in the Jew.

Not so in the East. There the national renaissance draws its energies directly from the sources of Judaism. It has none of the heroism of revelation; there is within it no contrition or joy of repentance, no new upsurge within the soul. The East views Zionism as a continuation, not as a world-destroying and world-building movement. It sees it as a solution to the Jewish problem and does not sense in it the redemption of the individual; it does not feel its cultural-humanistic force or share in its moral and aesthetic soaring.

The assimilationists of the East, when they return to their people, return from a depressed culture and they do not enrich our national possessions with any of those moral and aesthetic values that paved the way for the renaissance in the West. The universal human elements—the feeling for liberty and honor, the quest for human dignity, truth, and integrity—had not developed within them to the degree required for a national renaissance. They lack depth and sensitivity of heart and mind; they have not sufficient purity and imagination. They could not even express our national anger, the cry of vengeance for the blood that has been spilt. Why? Because of the crippling of the man in the Jew.

Hence it follows that as civilization matures and the sense of morality and beauty advances, the claims of dignity, truth, integrity, and purity will increase. The Zionist vision will grow ever stronger through these values, for Zionism is an aspiration toward morality and beauty. It has come, as one of its chief purposes, to redeem the man in us.

Zionism pins its hopes, in one sense, on the general advance of civilization and its national faith is also a faith in man in general—faith in the power of the good and the beautiful.

Part 6
The Zionism of Marxist and
Utopian Socialists

NAHMAN SYRKIN   1867-1924

SOCIALISM AND NATIONALISM had been combined by the first great Zionist writer, Moses Hess, but his work was forgotten. That such a combination would be made again, when Herzlian Zionism appeared, was inevitable, for socialism was then, in the 1890's, the greatest single influence on the thought of young Jewish intellectuals. Bernard Lazare (for him, see part 8), one of Herzl's earliest associates in France, was immediately impelled to rewrite Hess, without knowing it, but he, too, founded no school of thought and is today almost unremembered. The more obvious soil for such ideas was the misery and ferment of Russian Jewry; Socialist-Zionism, which is to this day the dominant force within the state of Israel, arose in the context of Russian Jewish life, and one of its immediate ancestors is Nahman Syrkin.

He began life in a pious family in Mohilev. By temperament a rebel, he soon fought his way to secular education and entered the local high school. The young Syrkin was soon expelled for objecting to anti-Semitic remarks by a teacher, and he finished school in Minsk, where he joined a group of Hibbat Zion and also was involved in the revolutionary underground. After being jailed briefly for these activities, which sealed a personal breach with his family, Syrkin emigrated to London, where supposedly he even acted on the Yiddish stage for a few months. By 1888 he was in Berlin, starving but nonetheless studying at the university and becoming ever more expert in all varieties of contemporary economic thought and socialist theory.

At that time the major schools of learning in both Germany and Switzerland were full of Russian Jewish students like himself, who had come to the more liberal west because they were barred, as Jews, from the Russian universities. Within the milieu of these student circles all the clashing "isms" of the day were hotly debated, and Syrkin was one of the most notable of a whole galaxy of celebrated controversialists. As he was to tell later in reminiscence, it took all the inner certainty and skill in argument he could muster to stand alone, at war with the entire intelligentsia within which he moved, when he first announced his Socialist-Zionism. Syrkin first published his thesis in a pamphlet in 1898, *Die Judenfrage und der sozialistische Judenstaat,* his debut in print, of which the most important passages are in the text below.

Syrkin had attended the First Zionist Congress the year before and he remained in the organization until 1905, when it was definite that the British offer of Uganda had come to naught. For four years he was a Territorialist (i.e., one who believed that a Jewish state should be founded on any available land, not necessarily in Palestine) and then he returned to Zionism as representative of the newly formed Poale Zion (Workers of Zion) party. Throughout this decade, both as Zionist and as Territorialist, Syrkin was actively writing propaganda and editing journals in Yiddish and Hebrew in support of his views. He moved to the United States in 1907 to continue his career as official of the Labor Zionist movement and as controversialist. Unfortunately his essays are scattered in many periodicals and, despite abortive attempts, they have not yet been adequately collected. Syrkin died in New York in 1924.

Syrkin's socialism was not Marxist but ethical and utopian; it was rooted, like Hess's, in love of humanity and the ideals of biblical prophecy. The newest note in Syrkin, present also in Lazare, was the assertion that Herzl's vision of a state would be realized only by the poor. Herzl's early hopes that the men of wealth within Jewry would be converted to his Jewish nationalism and take the lead in realizing its aims had been denied by Syrkin from the very beginning. He had even less faith that the existing order of western national states would help create a new state for the Jews. Society, both Jewish and general, was, in his view, dominated by the class interests of the bourgeoisie, which ran counter to Jewish nationalism, or even to the French, German, and other nationalisms which the wielders of power professed. Nor could Syrkin have unqualified faith in a socialist new order, because he forecast that even within it the position of the Jew would still be different, for he would still be prey to exclusion as the member of a minority. Hence, the only true bearers of Jewish nationalism were the masses; the only true socialism would have to include a Zionist solution of the Jewish problem.

THE JEWISH PROBLEM AND THE
SOCIALIST-JEWISH STATE (1898)

1. JEWS AND GENTILES

FROM THE VERY BEGINNING of their encounter tension has always existed between the Jews and the world around them. In the modern age this tension has assumed the guise of anti-Semitism. Since this enmity between Jew and gentile is to be found in all places and ages, we must seek its causes in general factors which come into play whenever these two worlds come into contact: on the one hand, in the particular characteristics of the Jewish people and in its unparalleled historical situation, and, on the other hand, in the general forms of social life, both past and present, within which this hatred has found root and sustenance.

Once the Jews lost their national and political independence, they began to live a strange life, unparalleled in history—the life of a nation without a land, the life of an exiled people. In their scattering they encountered a social milieu which was completely opposite, in spirit, cast, and outlook, to their own. The places of exile to which the Jews found their way after the destruction of the Temple were, culturally, a blend of the disintegrating Greco-Roman civilization and of the spirit of Christianity which had originated in Palestine. The Jews brought with them attitudes of soul which made them react inimically and negatively to both these fundamental strains. The uncompromising subjectivism of the Jews of Palestine, which found expression in the monotheistic faith, in the quest for the absolute, and in the moral life, met utterly opposed spiritual outlooks and a fundamentally different culture in the Greco-Roman world.

Thus, perforce, two of mankind's intellectual and emotional constructions became involved in each other, and it was inevitable that they would do battle.

The naked force of secular might, the oppressiveness and barbarity of Rome and of the Christian Middle Ages, offended the sensibility of the Jew—the legacy of the prophets—which had been aroused to self-consciousness in the time of national trouble. The compromise which

Christianity had effected with the power of the state—a compromise which, in practice, gave the state control of the church—was alien and unacceptable to the Jews, a people faithful to the Torah and prophets, whose entire history was nothing else than the unending struggle of the prophetic ideal for realization. The relation of Judaism to Christianity was not made the less negative by the inner and historic nearness of the two faiths. The unmeasured arrogance with which the church had falsified the image of the Rabbi of Nazareth and depicted him as the Son of God stirred Judaism, which clung to the faith in monotheism, to anger and contempt. In the view of Jewry the Nazarene was not the Son of God, but only an errant son. The worship of the Christian deity was, to Judaism, merely a miserable form of idolatry. The cross, the holy icons, and the church were all regarded as idolatrous symbols; and the false position assigned to Jesus in Christianity so repelled Jewry that it could not even acknowledge the ethical content of this religion.

This sense of their higher religious estate, rooted in the general cast of the Jewish spirit, was the source of their morale in their war with the world. The world was full of hatred and contempt for this stranger who had come into it as an exile, who was as bitter as he was weak and as stubborn as he was powerless. The eternal antagonism between the strong and the weak, the proud and the contemned; hatred and persecution, based on inequality of power and made all the sharper by the submissiveness with which the weak were forced to hide their anger—all these became a great fire blazing against the Jews. Inequality of power and the antagonism between the Jews and their environment were, therefore, the soil from which the historic Jewish problem arose and grew to be unique in all the annals of mankind.

The religious conflict between Jew and gentile was the source of insatiable hatred. However, while Judaism harbored only covert antagonism and disguised contempt for Christianity, the latter attacked Judaism with both obloquy and the fist. The view of the Gospels, that Israel is the sinful child that rebelled against its God and is consigned to punishment, that it is the errant sheep that must yet return to the bosom of God—this gentle estimate, as expressed in practice, developed into a policy of hatred, inhumanity, mercilessness, and murder directed against an alien and poor people. A monistic faith, if it takes itself seriously, can suffer no competition and must jealously strive for undisputed mastery. Judaism was, therefore, to Christianity the incarnation of stiff-neckedness; the disgrace of Christendom and its founder; an unnatural and evil being, whose utter destruction would represent a new and glorious victory for the faith.

How did the Jews react to the world? The religious-psychological difference had already sown the seed of estrangement and hatred between Christian and Jew, and the many troubles the Jews had suffered added to their bitterness. Huddling together with his brethren in the ghetto, the Jew gritted his teeth, cursed the enemy, and dreamed of revenge, the vengeance of heaven and earth.

This negation of the world, this feeling that all mankind was its enemy, which was the basic mood of the Jews in the Middle Ages, could have turned them into a worthless, gypsy community, if this had been the only sentiment determining their outlook. But the soul of Israel contained other, higher and more humane, ideas; even in degradation, these preserved the moral loftiness of this people. If persecutions made the Jew the enemy of the world, his martyr's career raised him to the level of its suffering servant. From his crown of pain, glory emanated to the world which cursed him; out of the sensitivity born of suffering, he prayed to his God for the very mankind which cast him out. The Jew in the Middle Ages possessed two differing characters, a weekday and a Sabbath soul; if one moved him to hate the rest of the world, the second raised him beyond the world. Shylock alone is not a complete representation of the medieval Jew; to see him at his most sublime, we must also include the nobility symbolized by Nathan the Wise.[1]

On the soil of hatred and persecution, oppression and contempt, there grew and flourished the hope of redemption—the hope for the liberation of Israel in the near future and for its national rebirth. In the figure of the Messiah, the wondrous divine being who lives eternally within the Jewish people and awaits the moment of fulfillment, this marvelous hope found tangible personal expression. This hope was no vague dream, coming to the foreground only occasionally; it was a real power, ruling the hearts and determining and giving direction to the life of the ghetto.

This was the way Israel found to protect its spirit amidst the tempests of medieval history—but, what was its later destiny?

2. EMANCIPATION AND ANTI-SEMITISM

CONTEMPORARY EVENTS, which are only incidentally related to Jewish history, have propelled Jewish life in our era toward new channels.

When the bourgeoisie gained supremacy over the nobility and the bureaucracy, it identified its own class interests with objective, general truth and proclaimed the inalienable rights of man. The primary class interest of the bourgeoisie was to achieve freedom and political power, that is, to gain overt recognition of the predominance it had achieved through superior wealth and education. The basic bourgeois class interest was freedom—freedom of religion and conscience, unlimited rights of property, and untrammeled social mobility.

The proclamation of human rights emancipated the Jews, with striking suddenness, from their medieval servitude and granted them civil and political equality with scarcely any exertion on their part. Supported by no real power of their own and not even organized into an effective force in order to foster the emancipation, the Jews were accidentally liberated by the triumph of the principle of equality. The ghetto walls were broken, releasing the Jew into the world as a factor in civil life. The millennial Jewish condition of servitude came to an end; the wound that had been festering within Jewry since the fall of Jerusalem began to heal with the fall of the Bastille.

Despite the germ of progress contained within bourgeois society, no form of social organization ever came into the world vitiated by greater weakness. "Freedom" was inscribed on the bourgeois ensign, but no society was ever marked by so much dependence of man on man. "Equality" was destroyed to an unparalleled degree, by differences in wealth and property, while "fraternity," in bourgeois society, became an ironic joke. In its struggles, the bourgeoisie unfurled the banner of "humanity," but never was individualism so much an end in itself as it is today. The contradictions of the bourgeois society find their expression in the individualistic character of that society; these contradictions will lead to its breakdown. The very freedom and equality which the bourgeois society once proclaimed, but which it now denies, marshal the forces that spell its doom.

Bourgeois society, whose sole aim is the accumulation of material wealth through the medium of competition, brought about a new appraisal of Jewish values. The traditions and aspirations of the ghetto clashed with the new order of society and had to be thrust aside. While ghetto Jewry was a homogeneous, though isolated, nation, emancipated Jewry soon disposed of its nationalism in order to create for itself the theoretical basis for emancipation. This same Jewry, which but recently prayed thrice daily for its return to Jerusalem, became intoxicated with patriotic sentiments for the land in which it lived.

It appeared as though bourgeois freedom and Jewish assimilation had finally solved the old Jewish problem. But, in reality, the splendor of the solution lasted only as long as the reign of liberalism. The more the bourgeoisie, once it became the ruling class, betrayed the principles of liberalism, the shakier the ideological underpinnings of the emancipation became. The struggle for economic power, both of individual and class, became the chief characteristic of modern bourgeois society, once it had discarded the higher principles of its revolutionary era as unnecessary burdens. The emancipation of the Jew and his admission to all aspects of active citizenship could not be harmonized with the principle of egotism which is basic to bourgeois society. Jewish emancipation, therefore, began to evaporate together with the remains of liberalism. But it emphasized again that the emancipation of the Jews was, from the beginning, a result of logical conformity to the implication of a principle, rather than a real need. There is further proof of this in the fact that wherever the emancipation has depended on the state or society, it has not come to pass.

What is the basis of modern Jew-hatred? In the Middle Ages it was difference in religion: the abyss separating Judaism and Christianity. Today, the fundamental doctrine of modern anti-Semitism is the conflict of race. In other words, now that bourgeois society has come to regard religious conflict as passé, the imponderables of racial difference have been pressed into service. Contemporary Jew-hatred sails under the flag of anti-Semitism, although it is the same ship, with the same crew.

"The Jews are an incurably bad people, a people always seeking its own benefits and wanting to enslave the entire world, a people which, in spite of all its efforts to assimilate, still remains strange and hostile to the non-Jews. The Jew is the torchbearer of capitalism, exploitation, usury, and suppression. At the same time, he is also the yeast of history, upsetting and destroying all that is stable, the troublemaker incarnate. In short, the Jewish people is the curse of humanity." Such is the plaint of modern bourgeois society.

But the unbiased observer must question this outcry and ask of bourgeois society: Is not the bourgeois Jew really your alter ego, in a somewhat abler guise? Do you not find yourself reflected in him, and him in you? Does not the Jew exploit because he can, and do you not rob because you can? Are then not usury, exploitation, and swindle as characteristic of you as they are of him? Are you not both ready, twenty-four hours a day, to betray your state for your class interests, and your class for your private interests? The Jewish bourgeoisie, despite its protestations of assimilation, is really closer to its own oppressed than you are to yours, your hypocritical protestations of love and sympathy to the contrary notwithstanding. Do you not resemble each other much more than you differ?

Nonetheless, bourgeois society beats its breast and shouts dishonestly: "Jew-slave! What is right for me is not right for you, for we differ in spirit. That which I create is genuinely Germanic in spirit—you falsify and distort! Your racial character is inherently evil, and so you are outside the law! Hep! Hep!"[2]

When this filthy egotism is clothed in the dark mantle of racial superiority—a doctrine essentially false, for Semites and Aryans belong to the same Caucasian race—logic is silenced and morality becomes a laughingstock. Ahlwardt[3] has now become the philosopher, and Dühring[4] is now the teacher of ethics.

Anti-Semitism, which serves to unite the various classes in capitalist society, is not equally intense in each class. In dormant form, it pervades society, because it is a product of the class structure. However, it reaches its highest peak in declining classes: in the middle class, which is in process of being destroyed by the capitalists, and within the decaying peasant class, which is being strangled by the landowners. In modern society, these classes are the most backward and morally decayed. They are on the verge of bankruptcy and are desperately battling to maintain their vanishing positions. They belong to the propertied class, but their property consists of debts. They are owners, but they do not possess that which even the common workers have— labor power. They stand between the capitalist class and the proletariat and live in constant fear of falling into the latter. The more wretched their positions become, the fiercer their internal conflicts, the more they are driven to become vampires who suck the blood of the working class. As time passes, the middle classes sink deeper and deeper into this infernal abyss. Unlike the proletariat, they are without culture or the desire for it, without character or ideal, without self-consciousness or desire for freedom. Despite their steady economic decline, the middle classes still hold on to the tail of the ruling classes; their eyes are focused above, though their bodies are sinking into the deep; they help maintain an order whose victims they are.

These classes pretend to be revolutionary, but their struggle is egotistic and far removed from any principles. Should their own interests be satisfied, should they be granted adequate support from public funds, they would regard this as being the best of all worlds. They would then become the most loyal and devoted guardians of contemporary society. These classes address themselves to the ruling groups with the following slogan: Exploit, and let us exploit, too!

That anti-Semitism, which is dormant everywhere, has become the guiding political and social principle of these depressed classes is explained by their condition and character. While class interests in general caused the war on the Jews, the middle class was the most strongly affected because, in the general competitive struggle, it suffered most from Jewish competition. Along with the gentile capitalist, the Jewish capitalist, to be sure, delivered heavy blows to the petty bourgeoisie. The Jewish storekeeper was at dagger points with his Christian neighbor over a customer; the Jewish broker attempted to beat his Christian competitor. Competition from the Jew was all the harder to face, because natural selection had made him an especially fierce adversary in business. This is why anti-Semitism became the mainstay of the socio-political program of these classes.

Since the lower middle classes were the most vulgar elements of society, their anti-Semitism, too, was of the most vulgar type. Their opposition to the Jew was not fundamentally a result of Jewish characteristics, though, admittedly, assimilation and self-negation produced an unfortunate caricature of the Jew which might have nauseated the non-Jew. Nor was their opposition based on the national and religious misunderstanding, the prime cause of medieval Jew-hatred, for these degraded classes were not capable of such intellectualized experiences. Only egotism, the lust for Jewish money, the desire to undermine the Jewish competitor and expel him from the land—these were the sole reasons for their anti-Semitism. Hatred, jealousy, and falsehood characterized them in their fight against the Jew.

Anti-Semitism of the middle class is a revolutionary movement of a low type, the revolt of class against class and against the existing order not for the sake of higher human principles but for egotistic interests; though they clothe themselves in an ideological mantle, the debased nature of their intentions is completely apparent. This type of anti-Semitism is best reflected in its leadership. The dregs of bourgeois and proletarian society, who have lost every vestige of truth and self-respect, and creatures of the semi-underworld who can be moved only by the lowest of passions raise the banner of anti-Semitism and become its torchbearers. No party, therefore, has as many leaders whose reputation is shady as does the party of anti-Semitism. If their criminal records are such convincing evidence of their moral degeneration, it is even more evident in their insults, lies, and in blackmail. At least one part of Ludwig Börne's[5] famous saying, that the anti-Semites of the future will be candidates either for the workhouse or for the insane asylum, has been realized.

In spite of the moral degeneration of the leaders of anti-Semitism, in spite of the disgust which the average intelligent person has for this movement, it is constantly growing. The more the various classes of society are disrupted, the more unstable life becomes, the greater the danger to the middle class and the fear of the proletarian revolution (directed against the Jews, capitalism, the monarchy, and the state) —the higher the wave of anti-Semitism will rise. The classes fighting each other will unite in their common attack on the Jew. The dominant elements of capitalist society, i.e., the men of great wealth, the monarchy, the church, and the state, seek to use the religious and racial struggle as a substitute for the class struggle.

Anti-Semitism, therefore, has the tendency to permeate all of society and to undermine the existence of the Jewish people. It is a result of the unequal distribution of power in society. As long as society is based on might, and as long as the Jew is weak, anti-Semitism will exist.

3. JEWS AND SOCIALISM

A CLASSLESS SOCIETY and national sovereignty are the only means of solving the Jewish problem completely. The social revolution and cessation of the class struggle will also normalize the relationship of the Jew and his environment. The Jew must, therefore, join the ranks of the proletariat, the only element which is striving to make an end of the class struggle and to redistribute power on the basis of justice. The Jew has been the torchbearer of liberalism which emancipated him as part of its war against the old society; today, after the liberal bourgeoisie has betrayed its principles and has compromised with those classes whose power rests on force, the Jew must become the vanguard of socialism.

Jews began to join the revolutionary socialism concurrently with the birth of modern anti-Semitism. The Jewish socialists of western Europe, who sprang from the assimilationist Jewish bourgeoisie, unfortunately inherited the tradition of assimilation and displayed the same lack of self-respect and spiritual poverty, except that the moral degeneration of the socialist brand of assimilationism was more sharply apparent. To the Jewish socialists, socialism meant, first of all, the abandonment of Jewishness, just as the liberalism of the Jewish bourgeoisie led to assimilation. And yet, this tendency to deny their Jewishness was unnecessary, being prompted by neither socialism nor liberalism. It was a product of the general degeneration and demoralization of the Jews; Judaism was dropped because it conferred no benefits in the new world of free competition.

Impelled by their Judaism toward the path of revolution, the socialists committed the great intellectual and moral sin of not safeguarding the purity of their revolt. Instead of emphasizing the basic note of their revolutionary opposition to a society based on class division, the fact that they themselves belonged to the most oppressed people in the world—instead of first crying out as Jews and then raising their protest to the level of the universal—with peculiar Jewish logic, they did the contrary. They robbed the protest of its Jewish character, suppressed all reference to their Jewish origin, and thus became merely another variety of Jewish assimilationist.

The assimilated bourgeoisie turned away from Judaism because the Jewish people was weak and there was no economic advantage in being a Jew; Jewish socialists turned away from Judaism, because, for them, socialism was not the result of a moral protest against the world of the oppressors, but a last haven for the Jew whom liberalism had betrayed. Jewish assimilation clothed itself in the mantle of vicarious nationalism, of patriotic fervor for those lands in which Jews resided; Jewish socialism used internationalism as a cloak to cover its nakedness. This negation and honorless attitude toward its Jewish origin was no more justified by the truth of internationalism than by the illusion of foreign nationalism.

The term "internationalism," because of the poverty of our vocabulary, is a source of unconscious mistakes and conscious falsifications. Two quite diametrically opposed phenomena, which imply completely contrary ethical and historic-philosophical values, are denoted by the above term. We must, therefore, engage in exact criticism and analysis in order to arrive at a clear conception of its meaning.

Internationalism, not only in its attenuated modern sense but also in a cosmopolitan spirit of the Enlightenment, is undoubtedly the ideal toward which history is striving. The blending of all the nations into a higher unity, the creation of one humanity with a common language, territory, and fate—the dream which the greatest spirits of all eras have shared—this conception is undoubtedly the great victory of the human mind over the accidental and the unknown in history. Nationalism is always an accidental creation; it is not a phenomenon of historic reason. Nationalism is only a category of history, but it is not an absolute. National differences arose in certain stages of history and they will disappear at a higher stage. The characteristic symbol of nationality is neither language, religion, nor state, but the consciousness of historic unity.

Socialism will do away with wars, tariffs, and the conflict of economic interests among civilized peoples; it will eliminate the possibility of the oppression of one nation by another, and it will increase commercial and cultural intercourse, thus creating a common base of interests and purposes among the civilized nations. This will pave the way for the uniting of their separate histories, which will weld them into one humanity. Socialism, with its basic principles of peace, co-operation, and cultural progress, bears the seed out of which pure internationalism, that is, cosmopolitanism, will develop.

Socialism, which proclaimed the holiness of freedom and the right to self-determination, is both in its nature and in its practice the absolute opposite of pseudo-internationalism. Socialism is the opponent of all those conspiring to suppress or destroy the national character of a people. The socialist movement staunchly supports all attempts of suppressed peoples to free themselves. Each national emancipation movement finds its moral support in socialist ethics and in socialist concepts of freedom. The Internationale was the first to express solidarity with the Polish revolt against the Czar. The socialist masses of France and Italy hailed the rebellion of the people of Crete against Turkey. At the various national and international socialist congresses the right of every nation to self-determination has consistently been proclaimed as an ideal organically related to the ethic of socialism.

The socialists of most nations have already solved the problem of the relationship between nationalism and their socialism. There are no socialist leaders, in any national group, who deny their own nationality and preach assimilation to a dominant nationality. Only the bourgeoisie of oppressed nations deny their own nation and abandon it, unhesitatingly committing treason when it behooves them to do so for a profit. Thus, the Polish bourgeoisie betrayed Poland and Polish nationalism and was the first to join hands with the enemy. Likewise, the Jewish bourgeoisie adopted assimilation and dropped the ballast of its Jewishness so that it might swim more freely in the waters of the stock exchange.

The bearers of the idea of national emancipation among all oppressed nations are the intelligentsia, the socialists, and the proletariat. Only in the case of the Jews, among whom everything is topsy-turvy, have the socialists inherited assimilation from the bourgeoisie and made it their spiritual heritage. In such a policy we can see only a lack of seriousness in their socialism and in their devotion to liberty.

That Jewish national existence lacks content is no excuse for the alienation of Jewish socialists. It is true, this nationalism does not represent some high national ideal—that is the tragic contradiction of Jewish life. Nonetheless, the enemy has *always* considered the Jews a nation, and they have always known themselves as such. Though they were robbed of all external national characteristics—being dispersed, speaking all languages and jargons, possessing no national property or creative national forces—they were a distinct nation whose very existence was sufficient reason for its being. The existence of the Jews, who have waged a bitter struggle for long centuries against the external world, possesses perhaps a higher significance, because, by their very existence, the Jews represent freedom of conscience. If the suppression of the Jew is an affront to justice and is rooted in the rule of the fist, then his existence is a protest against injustice. The Jew symbolizes the battle for human rights, and much of that battle would be lost if he were to vanish. The destruction of the Jew would mean nothing less than the destruction of humanity.

The national suicide of the Jews would be a terrible tragedy for the Jews themselves, and that epoch would certainly be the most tragic in human history. Let us imagine the last Jew surviving, after Jewry had died, in the midst of the blossoming peoples of the world. The blood which the Jews shed in their struggle for existence, the millions of victims who had been strewn over all lands to bear eternal witness to the revolutionary struggle of Israel against all its oppressors—all these would appear to him a tragic farce, as a game that had been lost. It is the sacred duty of the Jew to live, for he represents freedom and justice. Schopenhauer[6] once stated that life is an offense, because we pay for it with the penalty of death; for the Jew, life is a duty, because to him death is an offense.

In such a time as ours, when the large mass of Jewry do not and cannot assimilate, when the Jew is surrounded by mortal enemies, when need and misery are the fate of the entire people, when the human rights of the Jew are publicly disregarded, when his honor is trodden under foot and his misfortunes are derided—it is contemptible to justify assimilation because Jewish life looks content. The motto of the better type of Jew must be not to deny our people because its life is empty but to elevate its life by giving it high meaning. Out of the need of the Jew to fight for his existence, there arises the high moral duty of endowing his life with significant national content and of removing all that hinders the unfolding of the creative genius of the Jewish people.

If Jewish socialism, which claims that it is not a result of class interests but of ideological considerations, wants to rise to the level of real moral protest, then it must acknowledge and proclaim in public that the Jewish protest is its basic motif. The socialism of the Jew must become a truly Jewish socialism.

From the sound of these words one may perhaps picture a type of reactionary socialism, because the word "Jewish" seems to parallel the terms "Christian," "German," "National," etc. However, this is not a valid inference; in logic and truth, Jewish socialism should be placed on the same level with proletarian socialism, because both have a common source in the oppression of human beings and the unjust distribution of power.

Where the Jewish proletariat has become class conscious, it has also created a true Jewish socialism, free of every servile trace of assimilation. The socialism of the Jewish proletariat contains a special Jewish protest, as well, which expresses itself along with its class consciousness. The peculiar literature, thought, and sentiment of the Jewish masses, which stamp them unmistakably with a well-defined national character, are clearly reflected in Jewish socialism. Free from assimilation and without a tendency toward self-denial, the Jewish proletariat is, both consciously and, even more, unconsciously, the bearer of the specific Jewish protest.

In so far as the Jewish proletariat was nourished, in its earliest stage, by the propaganda of the assimilated intelligentsia, the poison of assimilation penetrated within it, but the healthy self-consciousness of the proletariat, its self-confidence and self-respect, fought and checked this infection. In contrast, the class-conscious Jewish proletariat is greatly influencing the Jewish intelligentsia, which is associated with it, and is arousing the latter to personal and national self-respect.

Jewish socialism will, sooner or later, remove all assimilatory tendencies from its ranks, and will loyally and openly declare itself to be the great protest movement of Jewry. As a protest movement against Jewish suffering, socialism can become the common possession of all Jews, because Jewish suffering affects every class of Jewry—the proletariat as well as the intelligentsia, the middle class as well as the upper bourgeoisie.

4. ZIONISM

SOCIALISM WILL SOLVE the Jewish problem only in the remote future. Though Jewish suffering is the result of the general condition of society, it has a specific characteristic with which socialism cannot deal. Socialism, whether in its daily struggle or its ultimate realization, aids all the oppressed. Through the socialist struggle, they all have an opportunity to increase their political power, improve their economic lot, and raise their spiritual level.

It is altogether different with the Jews. The economic structure of the Jewish people, its lack of political rights, and its peculiar position in society combine to place it in a singular situation which cannot be improved, at present, through the socialist struggle.

The class struggle can help the Jewish middle class but little, if at all. Economic instability is its prime characteristic, and it is being ever more weakened by the advance of anti-Semitism. Not only is the class struggle unable to solve its problem, but, since anti-Semitism is nourished by the class struggle, the situation of the Jewish middle class is, indeed, made worse by a sharpened class struggle.

Nor can the insecurity of the Jewish intelligentsia be removed through the class struggle; competition is, indeed, making it worse. The social boycott which is rapidly developing against the Jewish people, in general, and against its intelligentsia in particular, cannot be broken by any form of Jewish self-defense. At best, the intelligentsia can bear economic and social hardship with an air of resignation. Even those governments which have granted civil and political rights to the Jews have policies directed against this class. With the intelligentsia of every nation steadily becoming more dependent upon its government, the Jewish intelligentsia is losing its footing. Nor can the socialist movement, because of its proletarian character and for tactical reasons actively aid any part of the middle class, and particularly not the Jewish middle class, which belongs to a despised people.

The class struggle cannot immediately aid the Jewish proletariat to the extent that it helps the general proletariat. The *lumpen-proletariat*,[7] which embraces the greater part of the Jewish workers, and which consists of small merchants, peddlers, etc., is incapable of class struggle or socialist activities. It can, at best, strive toward socialism and sympathize with the class struggle, but socialism cannot help it at all in a direct way.

The middle class cannot die. The elimination of small, independent businesses is not advancing with that tempo originally predicted by socialist theory. The objective process of evolution is slow, and those doomed by the laws of economics are somehow adapting themselves to change and postponing the fate which awaits them.

In eastern Europe, where the mass of Jewish proletariat lives in great need, economic development will not quickly change its depressed position in society. The unemployed Jewish proletariat must naturally, both as an oppressed class and as Jews, accept socialism, but socialism, as a practical movement, bears no reference to the peculiar conditions under which they, as Jews, are living.

Socialist principles and theory are opposed to any denial of Jewish rights; yet it often happens that, for tactical and opportunistic reasons, socialist parties adopt passive attitudes or even abet attacks on the Jews. No matter how diametrically opposed the Social Democratic Party of Germany is to anti-Semitism in principle, there were numerous political occasions when the party rejoiced in anti-Semitism, or, at least, failed to attack it. Recent political history offers a number of examples to illustrate the character of the socialist parties. A case in point is the attitude of the French socialists toward the "Dreyfus Affair."[8] Just as the opportunism of the German Social-Democratic Party sometimes led it in a direction opposite to the basic principles of socialism, so, too, because of opportunism, the French Party excluded the Jews from its devotion to absolute justice.

If the socialist parties of democratic lands, despite their concern for all the oppressed, are indifferent to Jewish suffering, socialism is of even lesser comfort in those lands where the Jews have not yet been emancipated. In Russia, where Jews are not emancipated, their condition will not be radically altered through an overthrow of the present political regime. No matter what new class gains control of the government, it will not be deeply interested in the emancipation of the Jews. That emancipation will come to the Jews of Russia as "manna," or as a result of idealism and humanitarian principles, is inconceivable. Russian Jewry will attain its emancipation only in the future socialist state. Till then they will have to remain in their present state of misery. Nonetheless, this realization should not restrain them from joining the most radical parties of the opposition, in order to express their healthy instinct of protest.

With respect to the Jews, we are driven to the sad and unusual conclusion that unlike all the other oppressed, he has no real, immediate weapon with which to win an easing of his lot. His only alternative, as it was centuries ago, is emigration to other countries. In western countries, the Jews seek a temporary solution in social isolation; in eastern Europe, in emigration to free lands.

How shall the Jew react to his unique tragedy? In the Middle Ages the Jews accepted their fate with resignation and as individuals fought the world for their personal survival. But modern Jewry adopted the rational means of migration. To pave a united road for all the Jews who are being forced to migrate—for the poor driven by need, for refined Jews stung by insults, and for romantic and religious Jews who bewail the deterioration of the people and the destruction of the Temple; to give a rational purpose to all those who feel the pain of the Exile; and to raise their individual protest to the level of a general moral resistance aimed at the rebuilding of Jewish life—that is the purpose of Zionism, a movement inevitably born of Jewish sufferings which has encompassed all segments of Jewry.

Zionism is a real phenomenon of Jewish life. It has its roots in the economic and social positions of the Jews, in their moral protest, in the idealistic striving to give a better content to their miserable life. It is borne by the active, creative forces of Jewish life. Only cowards and spiritual degenerates will term Zionism a utopian movement.

All non-Zionist attempts to solve the Jewish problem bear a utopian stamp. For example, when the assimilationists parade about with the hope that Jews will assimilate—it is utopian. Likewise, when some benevolent Jews believe that the Jews can turn to agriculture in the land where they reside and that their middle class and intelligentsia will lower their living standard—this, too, is utopian. Furthermore, it is utopian when German Jewish assimilationists, feeling their position weakened by Zionism, believe that Zionism will disappear and the Jews will sink to their former state of resignation. All these solutions to the Jewish problem are utopian, since they are in conflict with the striving and mood of contemporary Jewry.

It is not the utopian element that bars great masses of Jews from Zionism, but their servility and passiveness, which are the result of our thousand-year-old bondage. Opponents base their opposition to Zionism on various completely contradictory schools of thought; yet it all springs from one source—inner poverty and emptiness.

Jewish socialists dig up baseless reasons to support their anti-Zionist attitude. When the excuses of internationalism and the denial of the existence of a Jewish nationality were discarded, they found another argument—that Zionism conflicts with the class struggle. The Jewish people, too, they maintain, is divided into classes which struggle against each other, while Zionism ignores these economic differences, postulating a so-called unity of the Jewish nation. There can be no more foolish argument than to maintain that the Jewish class struggle conflicts with Zionism. Those who maintain this have invented ideological contradictions which bear no relation to reality. Why should the Jewish proletariat, which will be the first to be helped by Zionism in the material sense, reject it merely because the other classes of Jewry have also adopted Zionism for national and ideological reasons?

The class struggle does not exhaust all the expressions of social life. When a people is endangered, all parties unite to fight the outside enemy, though in normal times the classes fight each other. Likewise, within the limits of their higher principles, opposing parties unite in elections and form coalitions against internal enemies. Modern parliamentarianism is based on this procedure. In every union of men for idealistic purposes, the struggle which divides man against man disappears and higher forms of solidarity emerge to the foreground. Class struggle is the main driving force of history, but it is a misconception to explain all social life, in its manifold expressions, in terms of this alone. All defensive, creative, and ideological activities are realized not through the class struggle but despite it. Zionism is a creative work of the Jews, and it, therefore, stands not in contradiction to the class struggle but beyond it. Zionism can be accepted by each and every class of Jews.

The Jewish proletariat, the poor Jewish masses, the intelligentsia, and the middle class, can justifiably oppose a Jewish state which may be built on the principles of capitalism. True, the Jewish state, regardless of form, can greatly erase the Jewish problems, but the modern conscience is so much permeated by social and economic ideals that the Jewish masses will not accept, and rightly so, a capitalistic Jewish state.

The *form* of the Jewish state is the only debatable issue involved in Zionism. Zionism must be responsive to the opinion of the Jewish masses, for, without them, the movement will be stillborn. The wheels of the Jewish state cannot be turned without the strong arms of the Jewish workers. Zionism must take into consideration the socialist bent of the middle class and intelligentsia. Zionism must of necessity fuse with socialism, for socialism is in complete harmony with the wishes and hopes of the Jewish masses. Sociological and technical factors make any other form of Jewish state impossible.

5. THE SOCIALIST-JEWISH STATE

CONTEMPORARY POLITICAL ZIONISM is striving for a Jewish state based on the rights of private property. The exodus of the Jews from their places of exile will be effected through a recognized public body; the new life to be created is to be a replica of the old. In order to appeal to the workers, a shorter workday is promised in the future Jewish state. In essence, this does not differ from the practical attempts at colonization that have already been made in Eretz Israel and the Argentine, for these, too, were based on private property.

And yet, it is inconceivable that people will agree to the creation of an autonomous state based on social inequality, for this would amount to entering into a *social contract of servitude*. No new social contract will ever come to be unless its foundation is freedom. Primarily, social inequality is the product of the impersonal forces of history. It is the aim of conscious social action to transmute the *status quo* along rational lines and to elevate it morally. A republic born out of an act of will, which would have no rational plan for society and would merely tread the old path of free competition and class distinctions—this would be social and psychological folly.

The moment that all doors are opened to a system of *laissez faire*, the economic process will put its indelible stamp on social life. The factories will be established by the capitalists, who will thus control the means of production. Since this entire effort at colonization will be taking place in an underdeveloped country, wages will be depressed far below any level of subsistence that a European Jew could find acceptable. Most of the workers will, therefore, be recruited among the native populace, because they will work for less. Colonization will thus more and more become a pure business venture; Jewish immigrants will be forced to leave, and the groups intending to follow will be stopped by fear. The entire movement will disintegrate almost before its beginning.

A future Jewish state founded on capitalism is impossible for technological reasons, as well. Within the limits of petty capitalism, it is not possible to mechanize agriculture and to create large industries. In order to realize the maximum benefit from machinery, and the greatest productivity from labor, large-scale enterprise is a must. Nor can the law of supply and demand, with its wastefulness and the depressions which are its inevitable result, be allowed to regulate the economy. Only socialism can bring supply and demand into equilibrium.

For a Jewish state to come to be, it must, from the very beginning, avoid all the ills of modern life. To evoke the sympathetic interest of modern man, its guidelines must be justice, rational planning, and social solidarity. Once a Jewish state has been realized on such scientific social principles, the time will come for modern technology to flourish within it. The Jewish state can come about only if it is socialist; only by fusing with socialism can Zionism become the ideal of the whole Jewish people—of the proletariat, the middle class, and the intelligentsia. All Jews will be involved in the success of Zionism, and none will be indifferent. The messianic hope, which was always the greatest dream of exiled Jewry, will be transformed into political action. The Jewish people, presently living in misery, will gain lofty content.

Not only the Jews, and the countries which desire to be rid of them, will be greatly interested in the socialist Jewish state, but also all those who strive for higher forms of social life—the socialists and the social reformers.

Because the Jews are placed in an unusual situation, that they are forced to find a homeland and establish a state, they therefore have been presented with the opportunity to be the first to realize the socialist vision. This is the tragic element of their historic fate, but it is also a unique historic mission. What is generally the vision of a few will become a great national movement among the Jews; what is utopian in other contexts is a necessity for the Jews.

The Jews were historically the nation which caused division and strife; it will now become the most revolutionary of all nations. From the humblest and most oppressed of all peoples it will be transformed to the proudest and greatest. The Jews will derive their moral stature from their travail, and out of the pain of their existence will come a pattern of noble living. The Jew is small, ugly, servile, and debased when he forgets and denies his great character. He becomes distinguished and beautiful in the moral and social realms when he returns to his true nature.

Israel is to be compared to a sleeping giant, arising from the slough of despair and darkness and straightening up to his infinite height. His face is rimmed by rays of glory of the pain of the world which he has suffered on his own body. He knows his task, to do justice and proclaim truth. His tragic history has resulted in a high mission. He will redeem the world which crucified him.

Israel will once again become the chosen of the peoples!

BER BOROCHOV   1881-1917

WITHIN A DECADE after Herzl appeared in 1896 there was no major contemporary influence, from Tolstoy to Nietzsche, which had not found a re-echo in some variety of Zionist ideology. The exception was Karl Marx. For Zionism, "scientific socialism" was the most unassimilable of all outlooks, for it pronounced nationalism to be, like religion, an opiate of the masses, a force being used by the capitalists to divert the proletariat from its true interests. Both Jewish and non-Jewish Marxists had always denied with special vehemence that there was any specific Jewish problem; the socialist revolution of the future, they asserted, would put an end to anti-Semitism and the Jews would disappear into the proletariat. To be sure Syrkin had argued against these ideas, as a humanitarian and utopian socialist, but he was not effective among the Marxists. A theory of Zionism that was expressed solely in terms of dialectical materialism was still lacking, and it was provided by Ber Borochov.

We are today too remote from the mood of Russia in the last days of tsarism, when Marxist faith that revolution was inevitable so permeated the young, to appreciate the impact of Borochov. By the same token, Marx's thought is no sacred canon to us, and so we are not moved by a theory of Zionism that is evolved like a geometrical theorem from "prooftexts" in *Das Kapital*. Nonetheless, in and for that time and place, Borochov's construction was a brilliant intellectual achievement. It remains significant today, and not only historically, because an important minority element in the Israeli labor movement continues to be Marxist in its outlook and to derive, substantially, from Borochov's early theories.

Borochov was born in a small town in the Ukraine but was raised in the city of Poltava. For some reason this town had been chosen by the Russian Government as a favorite place of exile for revolutionists. Poltava had also been one of the first communities in which a branch of Hibbat Zion was founded and Borochov's father had been one of its active members. Both socialism and Zionism were therefore in the air during his childhood. His highly intellectual and "enlightened" parents provided him with a first-class formal education, to which he added considerably by his own readings. Upon graduation from the local high school Borochov resolved not to go to university; he had already encountered anti-Semitism in his teachers at high school and he knew that more would face him in a Russian school of higher learning. Devoting himself to politics, he worked for a year in the Social Democratic Party until he was expelled as a Zionist deviationist. From that point his life's work was Jewish national activity in workers' groups and the evolving of his Marxist-Zionist thought.

The next decade or so Borochov moved among the bewildering variety of splinter groups, and splinters of splinter groups, which were the scene of the nascent Zionist left. In December 1906, the Russian Poale Zion (Workers of Zion) group crystallized, and Borochov, aided by another brilliant young theoretician, Isaac Ben-Zvi (now the non-Marxist, very mildly socialist, and almost universally beloved president of Israel), wrote its platform. After 1907 difficulties with the Russian police forced him to leave and he devoted himself to travel all over Europe as party functionary and propagandist. Concurrently Borochov was doing research in Yiddish philology, to which he made some basic scholarly contributions.

With the outbreak of World War I Borochov came to America. Here too he continued his careers as ideologist, writer, editor, and party official. The rigors of his Marxism were increasingly tempered during these years. By degrees he abandoned the orthodox faith of a material determinist, but he was never to write a connected exposition of his newer, more idealist, views. After the Kerensky revolution in Russia, in March 1917, he returned to his native land and died in Kiev in December of that year, at the age of thirty-six.

Borochov appears below in two aspects of his theorizing: we present first his use of stray hints from Marx and Engels to prove that the existence of nations is rooted in "acceptable," i.e., economic, factors; the second piece, a selection from the platform he wrote in 1906 for the Poale Zion, revolves around his equally original, and in part prophetic, idea that only Palestine would remain open to large Jewish immigration and that an inevitable (he called it *stychic*) process would bring Jews there.

THE NATIONAL QUESTION AND THE
CLASS STRUGGLE (1905)

IN ORDER TO LIVE, men must produce. In order to produce, they must combine their efforts in a certain way. Man does not as an individual struggle with nature for existence. History knows man only as a unit in a social group. Since men do live socially, it follows that between them certain *relations* are developed. These relations arise because of the production. Indeed, Marx terms them: *relations of production*.

"The sum total of these relations of production constitutes the economic structure of society—the real foundation, on which rise legal and political superstructures and to which correspond definite forms of social consciousness."[1] Thus, the relations of production in China, or in France, for example, are the basis for the whole "social order" of Chinese or French society.

But when we refer to societies by different names, we imply that there are *several* societies. These societies are in some manner *differentiated* one from the other. If this were not so, we could not speak of an English bourgoisie, for example, and a German bourgeoisie, of an American proletariat and a Russian proletariat. Then we would speak only of mankind as a whole, or at least of civilized humanity, and no more. But the English and the Germans, the Americans and the Russians, are each a part of mankind, and, if you will, of civilized humanity, and yet they are differentiated from one another. We therefore see that humanity is divided into several societies.

The above is common knowledge, and it would never occur to anyone to deny it. The question is, however, how can we explain the causes which make for this division of humanity? To be sure, many explanations have already been offered. One has but to inquire of those who speak in the name of "national ideologies," of a "pure Russian spirit," of a "true German spirit," of "Judaism," and so on. The problem for us, however, is to explain this in terms of the materialistic concept, which teaches us to seek the basic causes of every social phenomenon in economic conditions.

We stated above: In order to live, men must produce. In the process of production various *relations of production* arise. But the production itself is dependent on certain *conditions*, which are *different* in *different* places.

The conditions of production vary considerably. They are geographic, anthropological, and historic. The historic conditions include both those generated within a given social entity and those imposed by the neighboring social groups.

These conditions are recognized by Engels[2] in his second letter in the *Socialist Academician.* He states therein that among the many factors which make for different economies are also the geographical environment, the race, and even the human type, which has developed *differently* in different places.

In the third volume of *Capital* Marx also states that one and the same economic base can develop in different ways because of different conditions, such as natural environment, race, and external historic influences. Therefore we see, according to the teachers of historic materialism, that one and the same process of development of productive forces can assume various forms according to the differences in the conditions of production.

Of the above-mentioned conditions of production, the natural, nonsocial factors predominated first. As society develops, however, the social and historic environment gains in importance over the nonsocial, natural conditions, just as man in general assumes mastery over nature.

In this conception of the "conditions of production" we have a sound basis for the development of a purely materialistic theory of the *national* question. For in it is contained the theory and the basis of national struggles.

We, therefore, come to the formulation and explanation of the following two sorts of human groupings: (1) the groups into which humanity is divided according to the differences in the conditions of the relatively distinct productions are called *societies*, socioeconomic organisms (tribes, families, peoples, nations); (2) the groups into which the society is divided according to their role in the system of production itself, i.e., according to their respective relations to the means of production, are called *classes* (castes, ranks, etc.).

Every social phenomenon is primarily related to the material elements of society. A struggle is waged not for "spiritual" things, but for certain economic advantages in social life. The class struggle is waged not for "spiritual" values, but for the means of production. So too, with the national struggle.

The class struggle is waged for the material possessions of the classes, i.e., for the means of production. The means of production may be material or intangible. Material wealth is for the most part something that can be expropriated, such as machines. Intangible assets, on the other hand, are those which cannot be expropriated, as for example, technical proficiency, skill, and so on. Despite the fact that the struggle between classes very often assumes the form of a conflict between cultural-spiritual ideologies, such a struggle is not waged for the possession of intangible assets, but for the control of the material means of production.

The national struggle is also waged for the material possessions of social organisms. The assets of a social body lie in its control of the *condition of production*. These, too, may be material or "spiritual," i.e., such as can and such as cannot be expropriated. The material conditions consist of the territory and all the products of the material culture which have been developed by man, particularly the tangible conditions of production. The "spiritual" conditions consist of languages, customs, mores, *Weltanschauungen*, in other words—the "historic" conditions of production. The national struggle is waged not for the preservation of cultural values but for the control of material possessions, even though it is very often conducted under the banner of spiritual slogans.

The resources of a society, in general, we have pointed out, are the conditions of its system of production. These may be material or spiritual. *The most vital of the material conditions of production is the territory. The territory is furthermore the foundation on which rise all other conditions of production,* and it serves as a base for the introduction of all external influences.

In addition, every nationality also has fashioned certain instruments for the preservation of its resources. These are its political unity and the political institutions, its language, its national education, and nationalism itself.

It is false to accept the widespread fallacy which claims that the proletariat has no relation to the national wealth and therefore also has no national feelings and interests. No class in a society is outside the conditions of production of that society. It therefore follows that the state of these conditions of production is of vital concern also to the proletariat. Let us forget the flippant and dangerous conceptions about this question usually entertained by the progressive elements. If the general base and reservoir of the conditions of production, the territory, is valuable to the landowning class for its land resources and as a base for its political power; if this territory serves the bourgeoisie as a base for the capture of the world market, and serves the middle classes of society as the consumers' market; and if the organs of preservation of the national wealth have for each of the above-mentioned classes their respective worth, then *the territory also has its value for proletariat, i.e., as a place in which to work.* The organs of preservation, too, are of special value to the proletariat.

There are also other workers' interests related thereto. These are the cultural interests of language, education, and literature. All these are valuable as media for the development of class consciousness. However, class consciousness is really nurtured not so much by the "culture" as by the processes of the class struggle itself.

But the class struggle can take place only where the worker toils, i.e., where he has already occupied a certain workplace. The weaker his status at this position, the less ground he has for a systematic struggle. As long as the worker does not occupy a definite position, he can wage no struggle. It is, therefore, in his own interests to protect his position.

From whatever angle we may approach the national question to determine the scope of its existence for the proletariat, even if we should primarily approach it only by way of his cultural needs, we must always arrive finally at its material basis, i.e., at the question of the place of employment and the strategic base of struggle which the territory represents for the proletariat.

The nationalism of oppressed nationalities assumes a more peculiar form. The system of production of oppressed nationalities is always subject to abnormal conditions. The conditions of production are abnormal when, as we stated above, a nation is deprived of its territory and its organs of national preservation (such as political independence and the freedom of language and cultural development) or when it is hindered in their fullest enjoyment. Such abnormal conditions tend to harmonize the interests of all members of a nation. This external pressure not only lessens and dissipates the influence of the conditions of production but also hinders the development of the relations of production and the class struggle, because the normal development of the mode of production is hampered. Class antagonisms are abnormally mollified while national solidarity exerts a more potent influence.

Not only are the special interests of every class affected by this external pressure, but also every individual in the nationality feels it and understands that this pressure is of national significance. It derives from a foreign nation and is directed against his own nationality as such. Under such circumstances, the mother tongue, for example, assumes greater significance than that of a mere means to preserve the local market. When the freedom of his language is curtailed, the oppressed person becomes all the more attached thereto. In other words, the national question of an oppressed people is detached from its association with the material conditions of production. The cultural aspects assume an independent significance, and all the members of the nation become interested in national *self-determination*.

In the course of the struggle for national emancipation, however, the class structure and class psychology manifest themselves. One can usually identify the middle and petty bourgeoisie, and, above all, the clerical elements and landowners, as those groups of an oppressed nation which are vitally concerned with traditions. The dabblers in national education and in national literature (teachers, writers, etc.) usually garb their traditionalism in national hues. The chief protagonists of national emancipation, however, are always the progressive elements of the masses and the intelligentsia. Where these latter elements are sufficiently developed and have already freed themselves from the bonds of traditionalism, their nationalism assumes a purer character. Fundamentally, the process of emancipation is not nationalistic but national; and among such progressive elements of oppressed nations, there develops a genuine nationalism which does not aspire to the preservation of traditions, which will not exaggerate them, which has no illusions about the ostensible oneness of the nation, which comprehends clearly the class structure of society, and which does not seek to confuse anyone's real class interests. It is the aim of this type of nationalism to achieve the real emancipation of the nation through the normalization of its conditions and relations of production.

Genuine nationalism in no way obscures class consciousness. It manifests itself only among the progressive elements of oppressed nations. The genuine nationalism of the progressive class—of the organized revolutionary proletariat of an oppressed nation—expresses itself in the strong, clearly defined demands embodied in its minimum program. It is the purpose of these demands to assure the nation normal conditions of production and to assure the proletariat of a normal base for its labor and class struggle.

Once this goal has been achieved, the purpose of genuine nationalism has been realized. Instead of the former solidarity of national interests engendered by certain emancipation processes—a forced and abnormal solidarity—there now appears, in a new and clear form, a healthy class structure and a sound class struggle.

OUR PLATFORM (1906)

. . . IN OUR ANALYSIS of the Jewish problem we must bear in mind the fact that the national struggle is closely allied with the social. There is no struggle which is equally in the interest of all classes of a nation. Every class has national interests differing from the national interests of other classes. National movements do not transcend class divisions; they merely represent the interests of one of several classes within the nation. A national conflict develops not because the development of the forces of production of the whole nation conflicts with the conditions of production, but rather because the developing needs of one or more classes clash with the conditions of production of its national group. Hence the great variety of types of nationalism and national ideologies.

Since the Jewish nation has no peasantry, our analysis of its national problem deals with urban classes: the upper, middle, and petty bourgeoisie; the masses who are being proletarized; and the proletariat.

The upper bourgeoisie, because it is not confined to the home market, is not national in any true sense, but highly cosmopolitan. The Jewish bourgeoisie finds its interests best served by assimilation; and were it not for the "poor Ostjuden," the Jewish upper bourgeoisie would not be disturbed by the Jewish problem. The continuous stream of immigration of east European Jews and frequent pogroms remind the upper bourgeoisie of western Europe only too often of the miserable lot of their brethren. The east European Jewish bourgeoisie is, of course, more directly affected by the status of Jewry. The west European upper bourgeoisie, however, considers the entire problem to be a gratuitous and unpleasant burden. And yet it cannot find a safe retreat away from our east European masses. Since the Jewish upper bourgeoisie would like above all else to lose its individuality and be assimilated completely by the native bourgeoisie, it is very much affected by anti-Semitism. It fears everything which tends to spread anti-Semitism. If anti-Semitism were the hobby of only a few psychopathic and feeble-minded individuals, it would not be dangerous. But anti-Semitism is very popular among the masses, and very frequently its propaganda is tied up closely with the social unrest of the lowest elements of the working class. This creates a dangerous cumulation of Judaeophobia.

Anti-Semitism is becoming a dangerous political movement. Anti-Semitism flourishes because of the national competition between the Jewish and non-Jewish petty bourgeoisie and between the Jewish and non-Jewish proletarized and unemployed masses. Anti-Semitism menaces both the poor helpless Jews and the all-powerful Rothschilds. The latter, however, understand very well where the source of trouble lies; the poverty-ridden Jewish masses are at fault. The Jewish plutocracy abhors these masses, but anti-Semitism reminds it of its kinship to them. Two souls reside within the breast of the Jewish upper bourgeoisie—the soul of a proud European and the soul of an unwilling guardian of his eastern coreligionists. Were there no anti-Semitism, the misery and poverty of the Jewish emigrants would be of little concern to the Jewish upper bourgeoisie. It is impossible, however, to leave them in some west European city (on their way to a place of refuge) in the care of the local governments, for that would arouse anti-Semitic ire. Therefore, in spite of themselves and despite their efforts to ignore the Jewish problem, the Jewish aristocrats must turn philanthropists. They must provide shelter for the Jewish emigrants and must make collections for pogrom-ridden Jewry. Everywhere the Jewish upper bourgeoisie is engaged in the search for a Jewish solution to the Jewish problem and a means of being delivered of the Jewish masses. This is the sole form in which the Jewish problem presents itself to the Jewish upper bourgeoisie.

The middle bourgeoisie is bound more closely to the Jewish masses. In general, the economic interests of a middle and petty bourgeoisie depend on the market which the mass of the people affords, which market is coextensive with the national language and culture institutions. Therefore, in the case of territorial nations, the middle and petty bourgeoisie is the chief supporter of all types of "cultural" nationalism. Since this section of the Jewish bourgeoisie has no territory and market, it falls under the influence of assimilatory forces. On the other hand, because of the intense national competition in which the middle and lower bourgeoisie is involved, the isolating factor of anti-Semitism is felt in every branch of activity. Anti-Semitism is at the root of all the discriminatory laws against Jews in politically backward countries and of the social boycott in the bourgeois-democratic countries. The boycott, which is becoming more organized and more intensive, overtakes the Jewish bourgeoisie everywhere; in trade, in industry, in social life, and even in the press. With the growth of capitalism, there is a corresponding growth of political democracy on the one hand, and of national competition on the other. Those who see in the growth of political democracy the elimination of discriminatory laws against the Jews and the corresponding lessening of the acute form of Judaeophobia (such as pogroms) see merely one side of the process. They fail to recognize the continual sharpening of national competition in bourgeois society, the growth of which is parallel with that of democracy. This process strengthens the hostility and makes for a stronger and more efficiently organized boycott against the Jews. The Jewish middle and petty bourgeoisie, with no territory and no market of its own, is powerless against this menace. In the white-collar class the discrimination against the Jewish physician, engineer, and journalist forces them to face the Jewish problem. Jewish misery is closer to them than to the upper bourgeoisie. Their nationalism, however, is of a specially middle and petty bourgeois character. Lacking any means of support in their struggle for a market, they tend to speak of an independent political existence and of a Jewish state where they would play a leading political role. They feel the effects of state anti-Semitism very strongly and therefore strive to protect Jewish civil and national rights. Since they are directly affected by the poverty and degeneration of the Jewish masses, they tend to advocate a Jewish national policy.

But as long as they succeed in retaining their middle-class position, as long as the boycott and the isolation brought about by anti-Semitism have not yet undermined their material well-being, the center of gravity of their political interests continues to be in the Galut. Their personal needs remain outside the Jewish national sphere, for the conflict between their economic interests and the conditions of production restricting Jewish life has not yet reached a peak. In other words, as long as the Jewish middle bourgeoisie retains its economic position, it is relatively unconcerned with the Jewish problem. True, the Jewish position is a cause of certain discomforts to the middle class, but the class is not sufficiently hard-pressed to desire a radical change in its condition. Its energy can be utilized to a certain extent on behalf of the rehabilitation of Jewish life, but the middle class as a whole can never be the base for a movement of Jewish emancipation.

For the purpose of this discussion we may consider the Jewish petty bourgeoisie and the proletarized masses as one group. As a result of historical circumstances, this group constitutes a large majority of the Jewish people. To us proletarian Zionists this class is doubly significant. In the first place, the Jewish proletariat has become socially differentiated from the larger group only recently. (To understand the Jewish proletariat it is necessary to analyze properly the petty bourgeoisie, which still serves as its reservoir of manpower.) Secondly, the heterogeneous mass of emigrating petty bourgeoisie and proletarians-to-be is the main source of the human material for the future Jewish rehabilitation . . .

The national problem of the declining Jewish petty bourgeoisie consists in a search for a market which should free it from the horrible economic isolation which characterizes it at present.

In the case of this group, the national problem is very acute. To solve it, the Jewish petty bourgeoisie is forced to abandon its native lands and to migrate to new countries, but even there it finds no satisfactory solution. Misery overtakes the bourgeoisie; poverty is its lot in the new country. It therefore enters the labor market and is transformed into a part of the working masses. In the labor market, too, it must face national competition. Consequently, the proletarized Jewish petty bourgeoisie can penetrate only the final levels of production. Thus there arises a national struggle based on need and the impossibility of satisfying the need.

The nation question of the petty bourgeoisie, then, is the quest for a national market and the conservation of the associated cultural institutions such as the language, national education, etc. Concretely the problem of the Jewish petty bourgeoisie is that of emigration: the quest of an expatriated nation for a place of economic security.

The Jewish problem migrates with the Jews. Thus a universal Jewish problem is created which involves not only Jewish philanthropists but also the political powers of the civilized nations . . .

Emigration alone does not solve the Jewish problem. It leaves the Jew helpless in a strange country. For that reason Jewish immigration and any other national immigration tend toward compact settlements. This concentration alleviates the process of adaptation to the newly found environment, but at the same time it accelerates the rise of national competition in the countries into which the Jews have recently immigrated. If so large a number of Jewish immigrants had not settled in New York, Philadelphia, and Chicago, it is doubtful whether national competition against them would have come into existence; but the existence of the Jews as such would have become impossible. The outward contradictions of Jewish immigration—the clash between the habits brought along from the old country and the conditions in the new country—necessitate concentration.

Such concentration, however, contains a double contradiction. Mass concentration aims at facilitating the process of adaptation to the new environment, but it results in the segregation of the newly arrived group and hinders the process of adaptation. Upon his arrival the immigrant seeks to enter the first levels of production. Through their concentration in the large cities, the Jews retain their former economic traditions and are condemned to the final levels of production—the manufacturing of consumers' goods. Thus the need of the Jews to develop their forces of production and to become proletarized remains unsatisfied.

The contradictions inherent in this process lead to decentralization of the concentrated mass of immigrants. Jewry settles in more or less compact masses not in one place, but in many, thus aggravating the problem. Instead of remaining localized, the contradictions appear in numerous places. The Jewish problem thus becomes more acute and evolves into a world problem.

As a result of these two fundamental contradictions, the Jewish petty bourgeoisie and working masses are confronted by two needs. The impossibility of penetrating into higher levels of production creates the need for concentrated immigration into an undeveloped country. Instead of being limited to the final levels of production, as is the case in all other countries, the Jews could in a short time assume the leading position in the economy of the new land. Jewish migration must be transformed from immigration into colonization. This means a territorial solution of the Jewish problem.

In order that the Jewish immigration may be diverted to colonization of undeveloped countries, it is not sufficient that the colonization merely should be useful to the Jews. It is also necessary that the immigration to the previous centers become more difficult. This, as a matter of fact, is taking place. Because of national competition, immigration into the well-developed capitalistic countries is being limited. At the same time, the need for Jewish emigration is steadily becoming greater; and it can no longer be satisfied by the old centers of absorption. New lands must be found, and the emigrants increasingly tend to go to semiagricultural countries.

To avoid decentralization, there is need for organizational forces which would unite the Jewish masses and which would introduce system into the spontaneous processes of migration. Left alone, Jewish migration will continue to be a confused and scattering process. A new and conscious element is required. The Jewish emigrating masses must be organized and their movements directed. That is the task of the conscious Jewish proletariat.

The scheme of the dynamics of Jewish life operates as follows: (1) emigration of the petty bourgeoisie who turn to proletarization, (2) concentration of Jewish immigration, and (3) organized regulation of this immigration. The first two factors are the products of the spontaneous processes operating in Jewish life; the last, however, is introduced by the organized Jewish proletariat.

Capitalistic economy has reached the stage where no revolutionary changes are possible without the participation of the working masses and especially of the organized sections of the proletariat. The emancipation of the Jewish people either will be brought about by Jewish labor, or will not be attained at all. But the labor movement has only one weapon at its command: the class struggle. The class struggle must assume a political character if it is to lead to a better future.

Proletarian Zionism is possible only if its aims can be achieved through the class struggle; Zionism can be realized only if proletarian Zionism can be realized.

. . . The Jewish proletariat is in need of revolution more than any other. It is hoping most ardently for the good which is expected to come with the growth of democracy in society. The terrible national oppression; the exploitation on the part of petty Jewish capitalists; and the comparatively high cultural level and restlessness of the city-bred Jewish proletarian, the son of the "people of the book"—these generate an overwhelming revolutionary energy and an exalted spirit of self-sacrifice. This revolutionary zeal, hampered by the limitations of the strategic base, very frequently assumes grotesque forms. A disease of surplus energy is the tragedy of the Jewish proletariat, and is the source of its sufferings. A chained Prometheus who in helpless rage tears the feathers of the vulture that preys on him—that is the symbol of the Jewish proletariat.

. . . Jewish immigration is slowly tending to divert itself to a country where petty Jewish capital and labor may be utilized in such forms of production as will serve as a transition from an urban to an agricultural economy and from the production of consumers' goods to more basic forms of industry. The country into which Jews will immigrate will not be highly industrial nor predominantly agricultural, but rather semiagricultural. Jews alone will migrate there, separated from the general stream of immigration. The country will have no attraction for immigrants from other nations.

This land will be the only one available to the Jews; and of all countries available for immigrants of all lands, this country will provide the line of greatest resistance. It will be a country of low cultural and political development. Big capital will hardly find use for itself there, while Jewish petty and middle capital will find a market for its products in both this country and its environs. *The land of spontaneously concentrated Jewish immigration will be Palestine . . .*

Political territorial autonomy in Palestine is the ultimate aim of Zionism. For proletarian Zionists, this is also a step toward socialism.

The broadening and consolidation of Jewish economic and cultural positions in Palestine will proceed at a rapid pace along with the above mentioned processes. Parallel with the growth of economic independence will come the growth of political independence. The ideal of political autonomy for the Jews will be consummated by *political territorial autonomy in Palestine.*

AARON DAVID GORDON 1856-1922

IF HERZL was Zionism's president-in-exile and Ahad Ha-Am its secular rabbi, Aaron David Gordon was the movement's secular mystic and saint. In 1904 he came, unknown and unannounced, to Palestine, to do physical labor by the side of the much younger handful of Zionist idealists who were already there or were soon to arrive—and almost immediately he became their central personality. Revered in his lifetime, since his death Gordon has become a legend and a saga.

The external facts about him can be told quickly. He was born in a village in the province of Podolia, in a family of notable piety and learning which was related to Baron Horace Günzburg, one of the great magnates of Russia. His childhood and youth were spent in a farming village on an estate which his father managed for the Günzburg's. After Gordon's marriage he himself soon entered the service of these wealthy relatives as an official on another of their enterprises, a large tract of land which they had rented for farming. Here he spent twenty-three years (1880–1903) until the lease ran out. His career in this period of almost complete obscurity was distinguished by uncompromising personal rectitude, by a particular interest in young people, who were drawn to him, and by adherence to the Zionist ideals of Hibbat Zion, but there was little to foreshadow the drama that was to follow.

Now forty-seven, with a wife and two almost grown children, Gordon had to find a new job. His relatives offered suggestions and opportunities in business and there was thought of emigration to America, but Gordon wanted neither alternative. After months of indecision, because he was troubled by the duty he owed his family, Gordon gave them whatever money he had—it was enough to provide for a while, until, as he hoped, he could bring them to rejoin him— and left for Palestine. Middle-aged, a white-collar worker all his days, and physically weak, he nevertheless insisted that he must be a laborer on the land. The redemption of man as a whole, and of the Jew in particular, could come, he believed, only through physical labor; he felt compelled by these principles to practice his faith. After initial difficulties he found day labor in the vineyards and wineries of Petah Tikva. Five years of work there, three more nearby after he had brought over his wife and daughter (his wife died almost immediately), and then ten years at various places in Galilee were the working career of Gordon in Palestine. His last days were spent in Degania, one of the earliest *kibbutzim* (collective farming settlements) of the Labor-Zionist movement. He fell ill in 1921, but insisted on working with his last strength. The malady was finally diagnosed as cancer and he was sent to Vienna to be treated. It was not kept from him there that he was incurable and he went home in the beginning of 1922 to die. The heroic calm with which he faced the end is expressed in the last of the several selections from Gordon's works to be found below.

The best commentary on Gordon is in his own writings, for his essays were true occasional pieces growing out of his autobiography. Nonetheless some remarks need to be made about the sources of his thought, and especially of the "religion of labor" with which his name is identified. Gordon's outlook and career remind one immediately of the later life of Leo Tolstoy, including the Russian writer's flight from his family to live among the peasants in true communion with nature and his soul. Behind them both stands the romantic idealization of the natural man, the notion that man is inherently good but is corrupted by society, of which Rousseau had been the great modern spokesman. Gordon, in particular, is related to a preceding century of criticism of the Jewish ghetto as a spiritual ruin because of its stunted economy. Let the Jews, so this argument went, cease concentrating on livelihoods earned by their wits and return to farming; let them at least acquire a "normal" economic profile, engaging in proper proportion in all levels of production, rather than figuring so overwhelmingly as the middlemen. As we have seen in Brenner, Syrkin, and Borochov, the last and most important stage of this argument was its use in Socialist-Zionist circles of every shade of opinion to plead for the creation of a new Jewish life in Palestine as the only road to economic health.

As substratum to these notions, Gordon, even though he was no longer a practicing orthodox Jew in the last period of his life, anchored his outlook in a mystique about the metaphysical bond between the Jew and the land of Israel which derives from the classical religious tradition with some cabbalistic overtones. Nations, he asserts, are cosmic phenomena, the result of the interaction of man with nature in its particular expression in one place, by which the unique soul and history of the group is formed. No matter what may happen to a nation after it is once created—even if, like the Jews, a nation is exiled—both its corporate soul and the souls of its individuals are stunted until they return to their true habitat. There they can become whole again by living the life of nature. Hence, physical labor, the renewal of the true self in reverent harmony with the cosmos, is religion.

We shall encounter some of these ideas again, in different contexts, in both Martin Buber and Rabbi Kook. Like all utopians and mystics, Gordon has been more admired than followed; and yet, he was, and is even today, a generation after his death, the greatest teacher—in the deepest sense, the heterodox Hasidic master—of the Labor-Zionist movement.

LOGIC FOR THE FUTURE (1910)

AND WHEN, O Man, you will return to Nature—on that day your eyes will open, you will gaze straight into the eyes of Nature, and in its mirror you will see your own image. You will know that you have returned to yourself, that when you hid from Nature, you hid from yourself. When you return you will see that from you, from your hands and from your feet, from your body and from your soul, heavy, hard, oppressive fragments will fall and you will begin to stand erect. You will understand that these were fragments of the shell into which you had shrunk in the bewilderment of your heart and out of which you had finally emerged. On that day you will know that your former life did not befit you, that you must renew all things: your food and your drink, your dress and your home, your manner of work and your mode of study—everything!

On that day, O Man, deep in your heart you will know that you had been wandering until you returned to Nature. For you did not know Life. A different life, a life not ready-made, a life to be experienced in preparation and creation—that life you did not know. Therefore your life was cut in two—a very small shred of existence and a huge experience of nonexistence, of work, of labor, of busy-ness—"Sabbath" and the "Eve of the Sabbath." You did not think, and it did not occur to you, that there is no life in a life ready-made. Preparation is itself Life, for Nature also lives within the preparation of Life, within the creation of Life.

PEOPLE AND LABOR (1911)

THE JEWISH PEOPLE has been completely cut off from nature and imprisoned within city walls these two thousand years. We have become accustomed to every form of life, except to a life of labor—of labor done at our own behest and for its own sake. It will require the greatest effort of will for such a people to become normal again. We lack the principal ingredient for national life. We lack the habit of labor—not labor performed out of external compulsion, but labor to which one is attached in a natural and organic way. This kind of labor binds a people to its soil and to its national culture, which in turn is an outgrowth of the people's soil and the people's labor.

Now it is true that every people has many individuals who shun physical labor and try to live off the work of others. But a normal people is like a living organism which performs its various functions naturally, and labor is one of its basic and organic functions. A normal people invariably contains a large majority of individuals for whom labor is second nature. But we Jews are different. We have developed an attitude of looking down on manual labor, so that even those who are engaged in it work out of mere compulsion and always with the hope of eventually escaping to "a better life." We must not deceive ourselves in this regard, nor shut our eyes to our grave deficiencies, not merely as individuals but as a people. The well-known talmudic saying, that when the Jews do God's will their labor is done for them by others, is characteristic of our attitude. This saying is significant. It demonstrates how far this attitude has become an instinctive feeling within us, a second nature.

Who among us thinks about this problem? Who is sensitive to it? We have no labor—and yet we are not aware that anything is missing. We take no notice of it even when we talk of our national rebirth.

Labor is not only the force which binds man to the soil and by which possession of the soil is acquired; it is also the basic energy for the creation of a national culture. This is what we do not have—but we are not aware of missing it. We are a people without a country, without a living national language, without a living culture—but that, at least, we know and it pains us, even if only vaguely, and we seek ways and means of doing what needs must be done. But we seem to think that if we have no labor it does not matter—let Ivan, or John, or Mustapha do the work, while we busy ourselves with producing a culture, with creating national values, and with enthroning absolute justice in the world.

After very prolonged and very stubborn battles, the ideal of culture has finally won a place in our national (Zionist) movement. But what kind of culture is it?

By culture we usually mean what is called in Zionist circles "the rebirth of the spirit," or "a spiritual renaissance." But the spirit which we are trying to revive is not the breath of real life which permeates the whole living organism and draws life from it, but some shadowy and abstract spirit, which can express itself only within the recesses of heart and mind. Judging by the deliberations at the Zionist Congress, culture is entirely a matter of ideas or ideology. Such being the case, culture may mean to some of us the ideology of Hermann Struck[1] and Rabbi Reines,[2] i.e., the religious orthodoxy of Mizrahi, while to others it may signify the outlook of the school of Marx and Engels.

A vital culture, far from being detached from life, embraces it in all its aspects. Culture is whatever life creates for living purposes. Farming, building, and road-making—any work, any craft, any productive activity—is part of culture and is indeed the foundation and the stuff of culture. The procedure, the pattern, the shape, the manner in which things are done—these represent the forms of culture. Whatever people feel and think both at work and at leisure, and the relations arising from these situations, combined with the natural surroundings—all that constitutes the spirit of a people's culture. It sustains the higher expressions of culture in science and art, creeds and ideologies. The things we call culture in the most restricted sense, the higher expressions of culture (which is what is usually meant when culture is discussed in our circles)—this is the butter churned out of culture in general, in its broadest sense. But can butter be produced without milk? Or can a man make butter by using his neighbors' milk and still call the butter all his own?

What are we seeking in Palestine? Is it not that which we can never find elsewhere—the fresh milk of a healthy people's culture? What we are come to create at present is not the culture of the academy, before we have anything else, but a culture of life, of which the culture of the academy is only one element. We seek to create a vital culture out of which the cream of a higher culture can easily be evolved. We intend to create creeds and ideologies, art and poetry, and ethics and religion, all growing out of a healthy life and intimately related to it; we shall therefore have created healthy human relationships and living links that bind the present to the past. What we seek to create here is life—our own life—in our own spirit and in our own way. Let me put it more bluntly: In Palestine we must do with our own hands all the things that make up the sum total of life. We must ourselves do all the work, from the least strenuous, cleanest, and most sophisticated, to the dirtiest and most difficult. In our own way, we must feel what a worker feels and think what a worker thinks —then, and only then, shall we have a culture of our own, for then we shall have a life of our own.

It all seems very clear: From now on our principal ideal must be Labor. Through no fault of our own we have been deprived of this element and we must seek a remedy. Labor is our cure. The ideal of Labor must become the pivot of all our aspirations. It is the foundation upon which our national structure is to be erected. Only by making Labor, for its own sake, our national ideal shall we be able to cure ourselves of the plague that has affected us for many generations and mend the rent between ourselves and Nature. Labor is a great human ideal. It is the ideal of the future, and a great ideal can be a healing sun. Though the purpose of history is not, to be sure, to act the teacher, still the wise can and must learn from it. We can learn from our condition in the past and in the present, for we must now set the example for the future. We must all work with our hands.

We need a new spirit for our national renaissance. That new spirit must be created here in Palestine and must be nourished by our life in Palestine. It must be vital in all its aspects, and it must be all our own.

What we need is zealots of Labor—zealots in the finest sense of the word.

Any man who devotes his life to this ideal will not need to be told how difficult it is, but he will also know that it is of immense importance.

SOME OBSERVATIONS (1911)

IT MUST BE absolutely clear to us that we have two paths to choose from in Palestine: one is the practical way of the worldly-wise, the other is the real life of national rebirth. The first means the continuation of Galut life, with all its shortsighted practical wisdom, with all the attitudes and the whole philosophy of life that goes with Galut life. The second is the way to the true and meaningful life we seek in this country. Let each man choose whichever of the two ways he will, but let him know for certain that the choice of one forever excludes the other. Galut is always Galut, in Palestine no less than in any other country. Whoever seeks national rebirth and a full life as a Jew must give up the life of the Galut. Such is the price to be paid (not, to be sure, a price in the coin of the market place) and it is not an exorbitant one.

No thing in this world can be obtained for nothing. That does not mean that whoever wishes to see a future for his people must renounce life in the here and now. Not at all. That person is precisely the one who must seek a full life, but he must seek it in a different way and he must seek a different kind of life. Let me illustrate by a concrete example, which, though seemingly platitudinous, is nonetheless true. The lover prefers a dry morsel of bread in a poor cottage in the company of his beloved to a life of luxury without her. That is what he calls life. To be sure, he too desires a life of comfort and even of luxury, but only together with his beloved. Whoever separates him from his beloved deprives him of life. There is a contemporary version of psychology which pretends to probe so deeply into the nature of human behavior that little is supposedly left of the romantic emotion. But this notion is far from proved. I should maintain that the feeling of love has evaporated in our day not because of the growth of knowledge, but because of our physical and spiritual abnormalities, and our chasing after the goods of this world, because of the lives we live in the market place which are stamped by its values. No, healthy natural sentiment has a wisdom of its own, more profound than the so-called psychological analysis. The same holds true of spiritual love. The Jew who is genuinely in search of national rebirth will strive for the kind of a life in Palestine that is stamped with the seal of a true renaissance. Whatever is stamped by that seal, whether it be a life of comfort or even that of a simple laborer, is part of real life, and one that fails to bear that stamp is sham and emptiness.

There is only one way that can lead to our renaissance—the way of manual labor, of mobilizing all our national energies, of absolute and sacrificial devotion to our ideal and our task. Not even by thousands of title deeds can national assets be acquired, for whatever title deeds we do possess to land in Palestine have so far not given us real title to our country. Truth to tell, we have as yet no national assets because our people has not yet paid the price for them. A people can acquire its land only by its own effort, by realizing the potentialities of its body and its soul, by unfolding and revealing its inner self. This is a two-sided transaction, but the people comes first—the people comes before the land. But a parasitical people is not a living people. Our people can be brought to life only if each one of us recreates himself through labor and a life close to nature. Should he fall short of achieving this self-rehabilitation, the next generation, or the one thereafter, will complete the process. This is how we can, in time, have good farmers, good laborers, good Jews, and good human beings. On the other hand, if in Palestine we continue the life of the Galut, with its petty trading and all that goes with it, the coming generations will pursue the same road even more vigorously.

This road to national rebirth is a hard one, but there is no other. After all, the road to life, to whatever life it may be, is difficult, but it is made easier by the vision of the goal. The difference is only in what one envisages as the goal. The average pious Jew of a generation or two ago saw life as including physical comfort, provided it also enabled him to carry out the precepts and commandments of his religion. He aspired to such a life and no difficulty deterred him from pursuing it. Any other kind of life had no meaning for him. The ordinary Jew of today who emigrates to America or Australia, or even to Palestine, sees the real meaning of life in economic advancement. He works hard and is ready to endure a great deal to attain such a life. This road, too, is not an easy one, but he is ready to pay the price. He is willing to make every sacrifice, without regard to what he is giving up, even of the enjoyment of life, not to speak of the higher pleasures of the spirit. The life of national renaissance in Palestine is also one that must be acquired by effort, but in the eyes of those who seek it, such a life is the one that is most worth while—the most desirable. Such a life does not exclude physical comfort or even luxuries, but only on condition that they do not interfere with the main objective. This is a way of life which requires a radical change, a complete revolution in our Galut notions and attitudes and in our Galut view of life.

This demand would be an empty phrase if it were addressed in general to the entire people. It has no meaning unless it is put to each individual Jew among us who aspires to a national renaissance and hopes for a new life in the Homeland. This demand embraces every detail of our individual lives. Every one of us is required to refashion himself so that the Galut Jew within him becomes a truly emancipated Jew; so that the unnatural, defective, splintered person within him may be changed into a natural wholesome human being who is true to himself; so that his Galut life, which has been fashioned by alien and extraneous influences, hampering his natural growth and self-realization, may give way to one that allows him to develop freely, to his fullest stature in all dimensions. This is a very difficult task. It requires climbing a steep and narrow path, strewn with thorns and stumbling blocks, but the result would be loftiness and—life! Such a life would be so rich and meaningful that I could hardly begin to describe it, or I should seem to be exaggerating.

We are told that the life we left behind us, the life we seek to escape, is catching up with us here, in Palestine, that that life is stronger than the one we are trying to build up and that in the end it is bound to prevail. Evidently those who argue this way do not appreciate just what this new life is that we are trying to build here. They do not understand—they are not capable of understanding—that such life means as much to us as, for example, religion means to a truly pious Jew. The argument may be reversed: It may be said that we, who seek a life that suits our ideas, are incapable of appreciating the life of the ordinary, worldly-wise, practical people, that there must be something wrong in our make-up, that we are not quite normal, that we fail to realize how compelling is the force of ordinary life and how enmeshed it is with the life of all individuals and all nations. But we and they belong to different worlds anyway and are pursuing different paths. If we follow the dictates of practical necessity, or as our opponents claim, of historical necessity, we shall never attain our goal in Palestine. Historical necessity, as understood by those who invoke it, is not for us, but against us. It may be possible to achieve a comfortable position in Palestine, but no more than that—no national renassiance, no release from the life and spirit of the Galut. Our fellow Jews who live in the free countries did not achieve it, nor did our Sephardic brethren, who, compared to us, enjoyed more freedom outwardly, but did not attain more inner freedom. Nor will our national culture be any less Galut-like, even if we have our fill of universities and academies. Certainly it will not be any more free in spirit than were the yeshivot of Pumbadita and Nahardea.[3] In other words, we would have no more than a Galut culture, even if it were strictly Jewish. It will be impossible for that culture to be richer and deeper than the life of Galut. Real achievements are the results of creative work, not of clever business transactions. It requires the greatest self-control to call the latter creative. Certainly such a life cannot be called creative in the national sense.

It may be said that the life I picture is good for the select few, but not for the many. Yes, only for the few, for only the select are capable of laying foundations. It is always necessary to place strong stones at the foundation of a building to make it last. The majority will follow later. After all, only the few are coming to Palestine anyway. It is better, then, that they be of the select few rather than of the poorer kind. That is something that the select few ought to know.

"Will the dead now awake? Will the dead now stir?" asked our great poet Bialik.

It is impossible for our people not to stir! So great is the pain, so deep is the pain, that even apparent death cannot keep it from stirring.

There are still great spirits among us, though they are few in number. Nothing can knock louder on the door of the heart than the hard and bitter truth, the terrible truth which evokes self-dedication and sacrifice. Let the truth be known as it is, with all its terrors. Let the terrible abyss that lies at our feet be seen—and then there will be people who, without reckoning the cost and without asking questions, will rush to save what can still be saved. They will not be deterred by all the prophets of worldly wisdom, who will try to convince them that to plunge ahead is sheer folly and quite useless. All the illustrations taken from life to prove to them that they will not be able to salvage anything, that our hopes are vain, that our national renaissance is doomed, and that all our strength is illusory, will not make them desist. For their decision will stem not from beautiful dreams, or from intellectual reflection, nor will they become aware of our strength and our hope by reading books or by psychological analysis. Their faith will spring from the depth of their being, from the depth of their Jewish pain. And if they are possessed of any frailties, defects, shortcomings, as, being human, they must be, these will not deter them. Perhaps, on the contrary, their very defects may prove to be a positive force.

It is they, the few, who will bring about the true redemption of the Jewish people, and not the many who are "practical."

It is for their sake, for the sake of these few, that one must speak the truth, one must proclaim it day in and day out, in every way and in every tongue.

OUR TASKS AHEAD (1920)

THERE IS A COSMIC ELEMENT in nationality which is its basic ingredient. That cosmic element may best be described as the blending of the natural landscape of the Homeland with the spirit of the people inhabiting it. This is the mainspring of a people's vitality and creativity, of its spiritual and cultural values. Any conglomeration of individuals may form a society in the mechanical sense, one that moves and acts, but only the presence of the cosmic element makes for an organic national entity with creative vitality.

I think that every one of us ought to retreat for a moment into his innermost self, free himself from all outside influences—both from those of the gentile world and even from the influence of our own Jewish past—and then ask himself with the utmost simplicity, seriousness, and honesty: What, essentially, is the purpose of our national movement? What do we expect to find in Palestine that no other place can give us? Why should we segregate ourselves from the nations among whom we have lived our lives? Why leave the lands of our birth, which have fashioned our personalities and so largely influenced our spirits? Why should we not share fully and unreservedly with those nations in their great work for the progress of mankind? In other words, why should we not completely assimilate ourselves among those nations? What stops us?

Surely it is not religion. In our day it is quite possible for man to live without any religion at all. As for those who still retain strong loyalties to Judaism—merely as a religion—they may confidently look forward to complete religious freedom in the not too distant future. Certainly this is a more likely prospect for the near future than the attainment of full national redemption. At any rate, the effort to achieve religious emancipation is more obviously of immediate benefit. A time would then come when any Jew, if he so wished, would be able to live as a Russian, German, Frenchman, or what not, of the Jewish faith, and at the same time feel perfectly comfortable. It is being done even today, but not very comfortably.

The argument that this is an impossibility—that the Jews cannot assimilate—is pure sophistry. History has witnessed the dissolution of nearly all ancient peoples—why not the Jews? It can happen, if we will it, if we agree to it, if we cease fighting it so stubbornly. Mere inability to die is not a valid enough basis for a people's survival. This empty and barren negation becomes absurd when it is used as a reason to stop those who wish to leave the fold. But, as a matter of fact, the process of assimilation has been gaining, at least, until very recently. Why, then, must we make such strenuous efforts to reverse the trend? Why not let the current carry us wherever it may, rather than try to swim against it?

We are told that it is national sentiment that prevents the Jews from assimilating. But what is this national sentiment? What strange kind of nationality is ours, which is not alive but yet will not die? Wherein lies its strength? We have no country of our own, we have no living national language, but instead a number of vernaculars borrowed from others. Religion? But our religion is on the wane, and it certainly cannot be the answer for those who are not religious. What, then, is that elusive, unique, and persistent force that will not die and will not let us die?

It seems to me that every one of us can answer this question if he is really himself free of all foreign influences and if he is not ashamed to face the matter squarely and be honest with himself. That answer is that there is a primal force within every one of us, which is fighting for its own life, which seeks its own realization.

This is our ethnic self, the cosmic element of which we spoke, which, combined with the historic element, forms one of the basic ingredients of the personality of each and every one of us. The ethnic self may be described as a peculiar national pattern of mental and physical forces, which affects the personality of every individual member of the ethnic group. It is like the musical scale, which every composer uses in his own way. The ethnic self, to continue the parallel, is like choral singing, in which each individual voice has its own value, but in which the total effect depends on the combination and the relative merit of each individual singer, and in which the value of each singer is enhanced by his ability to sing with the rest of the choir.

Jewish life in the Diaspora lacks this cosmic element of national identity; it is sustained by the historic element alone, which keeps us alive and will not let us die, but it cannot provide us with a full national life. What we have come to find in Palestine is the cosmic element. In the countries of the Galut we are compelled to lead an inanimate existence, lacking in national creativity (and, from the point of view of genuine personality, also lacking in individual creativity). There we are the dependents of others materially and perhaps even more spiritually. There our ethnic self is forced into a ruinously constricted and shrunken form; having no living source of spontaneous vitality, it must perforce draw on our past and become ever more desiccated, or it must tap alien sources and become blurred, dissolving in the spirit of its environment.

It is life we want, no more and no less than that, our own life feeding on our own vital sources, in the fields and under the skies of our Homeland, a life based on our own physical and mental labors; we want vital energy and spiritual richness from this living source. We come to our Homeland in order to be planted in our natural soil from which we have been uprooted, to strike our roots deep into its life-giving substances, and to stretch out our branches in the sustaining and creating air and sunlight of the Homeland. Other peoples can manage to live in any fashion, in the homelands from which they have never been uprooted, but we must first learn to know the soil and ready it for our transplantation. We must study the climate in which we are to grow and produce. We, who have been torn away from nature, who have lost the savor of natural living—if we desire life, we must establish a new relationship with nature; we must open a new account with it. We, the Jews, were the first in history to say: "For all the nations shall go each in the name of its god," and "Nation shall not lift up a sword against nation," and then we proceeded to cease being a nation ourselves.

As we now come to re-establish our path among the ways of living nations of the earth, we must make sure that we find the right path. We must create a new people, a human people whose attitude toward other peoples is informed with the sense of human brotherhood and whose attitude toward nature and all within it is inspired by noble urges of life-loving creativity. All the forces of our history, all the pain that has accumulated in our national soul, seem to impel us in that direction. The abysmal void, which has formed in our soul during all its estrangement from nature, seems to demand it. But the final, decisive urge seems to stem from a living moment, in which we feel the immense pressure of an experience struggling to be born, and sense that something of great moment is stirring in the world at large and in our own world—that both are, as it were, about to be reborn. That living moment seems to call on us: We must be the pathfinders.

We are engaged in a creative endeavor the like of which is not to be found in the whole history of mankind: the rebirth and rehabilitation of a people that has been uprooted and scattered to the winds. It is a people half dead, and the effort to recreate it demands the exclusive concentration of the creator on his work. The center of our national work, the heart of our people, is here, in Palestine, even though we are but a small community in this country, for here is the mainspring of our life. Here, in this central spot, is hidden the vital force of our cause and its potential for growth. Here something is beginning to flower which has greater human significance and far wider ramifications than our history-makers envisage, but it is growing in every dimension deep within, like a tree growing out of its own seed, and what is happening is therefore not immediately obvious. Here, in Palestine, is the force attracting all the scattered cells of the people to unite into one living national organism. The more life in this seed, the greater its power of attraction.

It is our duty, therefore, to concentrate all our strength, all our thinking, all our mind and heart, on this central spot. We must not ever, even for a moment, let our minds wander from it. We must shun political activity as destructive of our highest ideals; otherwise we become unwitting traitors to the principle of our true self, which we have come here to bring back to life. Nor must we tie ourselves to the world proletariat, to the International, whose activities and whose methods are basically opposed to ours. For, as I have already explained, in doing so we deprive our work of its soul and tear it in two disparate shreds. I believe that we should not even combine with Jewish workers in the Diaspora specifically as workers, much as we respect labor; they should be our allies as Jews, just like any other Jews in the Diaspora who share our aspirations, no more and no less. We must draw our inspiration from our land, from life on our own soil, from the labor we are engaged in, and must be on guard against allowing too many influences from outside to affect us. What we seek to establish in Palestine is a new, recreated Jewish people, not a mere colony of Diaspora Jewry, not a continuation of Diaspora Jewish life in a new form. It is our aim to make Jewish Palestine the mother country of world Jewry, with Jewish communities in the Diaspora as its colonies—and not the reverse. We seek the rebirth of our national self, the manifestation of our loftiest spirit, and for that we must give our all.

The future will tell whether there is a basis for our aspiration in the form in which I have expressed it. The test of reality will make it clear whether there is anything in the hope of creating new relationship with life and of fashioning a really human people, and whether we have it within us to make such a hope a reality. But, I think, it is our duty to do all we can, in any way.

YOM KIPPUR (1921)

I ASK MYSELF, and I wonder whether I am alone in this question: What is the Day of Atonement to us, to those who do not observe the forms of religion?

Facing me are a fact and a possibility. It is a fact that for many generations it was a day which the entire people dedicated to repentance, prayer, and the service of the heart. It presented a possibility to spiritually sensitive people to make their inner reckoning on the loftiest plane.

I ask: Is this day for us merely a heritage from the past, a remnant of antiquity? Do we not really need such a day, especially as part of the national culture we are creating? If this day ceases to be what it has been—if it becomes an ordinary day like all others—will this not represent a great national and human loss, a spiritual disaster from which none of us, neither the people as a whole, nor we, its individual children, can ever recover?

As long as we were penned within ghetto walls, ragged, and cut off from the great life of the world, from man and from his broad and abundant life, we accepted what our ancestors had bequeathed to us. We believed in it and we gave our lives for it. When the walls of the ghetto fell, when we saw the world and all that is in it at close range, when we came to know man and his life, when we added cultural values from without to all this—we realized that the traditions of our ancestors were no longer in harmony with what was growing and developing in our own spirits. But did we deeply ponder this problem? Did we analyze and examine what had really become antiquated and unsuitable, utterly useless or decayed? In the final analysis, did we ask: What has become obscured or unacceptable in form only? What needs merely a more fitting and noble form, since it is alive and fresh? What is, in essence, sound, awaiting only a higher regeneration?

During all our long exile we existed by the strength of our religion. It sustained us in our grave and prolonged suffering and inspired us to live—often to live heroically. Is it possible, can the mind entertain the possibility, that such a force is a mere figment of the imagination, of the ramblings of an ignorant soul, and that it possesses no elemental and lasting core? Has the accepted idea been sufficiently examined and analyzed critically—is it sufficiently founded in logic and in the human spirit—that with the loss of the basis for the blind faith the basis for religion has also been destroyed?

FINAL REFLECTIONS (1921)

THE ESSENCE of the personality of the "madman of the spirit," as we have seen him in his various forms from ancient times till today, is his inability to reconcile himself to the present, to ignore it, or to deceive himself about it. He can find no escape either in poetry or in song, not in culture or in literature, not in art or in embellishing his own refined, shining, but really limited ego. Even religion is no escape. He seeks life—not an end to thinking about it—human life, human life of cosmic dimensions, life in the image of God, life eternal. Therefore, in olden days, when the "madman of the spirit" was still whole in spirit, and a son of nature, he made demands in masterful voice, in the name of God; his words were full of power, of the abundance of life, and they blazed with sparks of fire. He based all things on the will of man: Did but man will it, he and his life would become worthy.

This was the way of Jews when they lived in their own land. They were a living people, at peace with God and with man, with life and with the world. It is different since we were torn from our land, since we became an uprooted and a withered people with an empty life and a petty spirit. Our condition has changed strikingly in recent times, since the crumbling of the ghetto. The limited amount of independent life that still survived inside its walls has been destroyed while we, together with all mankind, have increased in knowledge, but at the expense of the spirit and of real life.

Today, the "madman of the spirit" is no longer strong in his spirit and unshakable in his conviction, full of the zest of life and flaming with fire, like his ancestors. What he sees—the course of his own life —fills him with rancor and pain. He is full of doubts as to whether that peculiar, chaotic world called human life and that strange creature called man can be improved. More important, he doubts whether man has, or ever will have, the desire for improvement.

In one respect, however, he resembles his ancestors—he cannot make peace with the present or stop thinking about life. He finds no escape from life in poetry, or in song, in literature or in art, or in the private improvement of his limited ego. What are aesthetics, poetry, belles-lettres, literature, art, to me? For me the beauty or nobility of spirit and the exaltation of my soul is Life! Life—full, complete, great, lofty, eternal Life! Life itself must be a song! Man must be a vital creature! One must not stop thinking about life, even for a single moment. But what is literature, art, and the rest, if not a substitute for thinking about life, a way to flee from life to a world of beauty, thought, song, and artistic creation? Man is forbidden to run away—or to withdraw from life. The alternatives are life or death— there is no third choice.

This is the tragic lot of the "madman of the spirit" of today: The earth is no longer firm under his feet; he lacks the absolute faith that both life and man need to be, can be, and must be lofty. He lacks the confidence that his ancestors had, but his spirit makes demands that are as urgent and compelling as were theirs. Perhaps, indeed, out of his constant wrestling and struggling with doubts, with contradictions, with indifference, out of his standing against easy adaptability of the great majority—and of the authors, poets, artists, and all the others who justify the majority—these demands become more acute; they become a sort of *idée fixe*. Deep within him, too, there lives the absolute certainty, beyond any shadow of doubt, that everything depends on the will of man. But he looks at the majority of mankind and begins to doubt whether the majority of men are capable of an act of will—whether, in general, most men have any great tendency toward wanting what they should want. The entire structure of the contemporary "madman of the spirit" rests on doubt: Perhaps man can improve; perhaps the creation of man has not yet been completed; perhaps he must yet struggle on in a more exalted direction. The "madman" of today has no other foundation than this "perhaps"; hence he holds on to it as though it were an anchor and for this "perhaps" he gives his life.

A few more words—about necrologies, eulogies, and the like. Men wish to honor that which leaves them never to return, for they must assume that he who is gone will have no further existence. All that was the "he" has gone to the source of creation, and that "he" has entered into associations and relationships that are inconceivable to those who remain alive. The living are face to face with the secret of eternity, which they must treat as a secret. If they wish to do honor to the departed, that honor should be paid in silence. Let each one withdraw into his corner, into the seclusion of his own soul; let him meditate or weep in solitude over the fate of him who has passed on and over the fate of all mankind. Is this not enough?

This has been my custom—I have honored in silence all those who have passed on—and I would wish that custom to be followed in my case. Let those who wish to honor me do it silently. For at least one year let them not speak or write anything about me.

Whatever I have written should be discussed only if it still possesses, and only to the extent that it still may possess, living value—that is to say, not a literary or a journalistic value, but a vital value for the life that is being regenerated.

BERL KATZENELSON 1887-1944

THE GENERATION of those who were born in Russia in the 1880's and came to Palestine in their early manhood, the group known as the Second Aliyah, quickly became the leadership of the new Zionist settlement. The political activists among these young men, mostly socialists of various kinds, were but a handful. Yet the movement they fashioned has dominated the government of Israel throughout the first decade of its existence, and two of this group, David Ben-Gurion and Isaac Ben-Zvi, are today its highest officers.

Berl Katzenelson was their exact contemporary and, until his death in 1944, a central figure of Socialist-Zionism. While still an adolescent in the White Russian city of his birth (Bobruisk) he entered the whirlpool of ideologies and parties which was then the predominant concern of advanced young Russian Jews. Always a lover of the Hebrew language and emotionally a Zionist, he nonetheless wandered among the parties of the left for a few years without rooting himself deeply in any of their particular doctrines. After turning twenty he decided to go to Palestine and prepared himself in several skills, including that of a blacksmith. Illness and family concerns delayed him, but in 1909, at the age of twenty-two, he arrived in Jaffa. Like the older A. D. Gordon and his near contemporary Brenner, who became his friends, Katzenelson started his life in Palestine as a day laborer on the farm. He soon acquired a reputation as organizer and leader among the workers' groups. In these early years he led a strike, founded a traveling library for farm workers, helped create a labor exchange to find work for newcomers, and wrote frequently for the journals of the Labor-Zionist movement.

During World War I Katzenelson remained in Palestine and, when the British army conquered its southern part, he enlisted in 1918 in its newly formed battalion of Palestinian Jews. His life after 1920, when he was released from the army, was that of a front-rank official of Palestinian Jewry and the World Zionist movement. He was consistently, until his death in Jerusalem in 1944, at the center of Labor-Zionist affairs and a frequent spokesman for his group before various international bodies and in many voyages to Jewish communities abroad. Katzenelson's major importance, was, however, not in politics but in journalism and cultural affairs in general. In 1925 Katzenelson founded the Tel Aviv newspaper *Davar*, as the organ of the trade union organizations (the Histadrut), and he remained its editor until his death. *Am Oved*, the publishing house of the Histadrut, was also his creation; indeed, the entire cultural program of Palestinian labor was under his influence.

Though he was a prolific writer on ideological matters, it would be an overstatement to describe him as an original thinker. He is intellectually significant not so much for the depth and range of his arguments as for the quality of his prose and the nature of his stance. In Katzenelson there was a greater harmony between the new of Socialist-Zionism and the old of traditionalist emotion than is to be found in anyone else.

REVOLUTION AND TRADITION (1934)

WE LIKE TO call ourselves rebels—but may I ask, "What are we rebelling against?" Is it only against the "traditions of our fathers?" If so, we are carrying coals to Newcastle. Too many of our predecessors did just that. *Our rebellion is also a revolt against many rebellions that preceded ours.* We have rebelled against the worship of diplomas among our intelligentsia. We have rebelled against rootlessness and middlemanship, and not only in the forms in which they appeared in the older Jewish way of life; we have rebelled against their modern version as well, against the middlemanship and rootlessness of some of the modern Jewish nationalist and internationalist intellectuals, which we find even more disgusting than all the earlier manifestations of these diseases. We have rebelled against the assimilationist utopia of the older Jewish socialist intelligentsia. We have rebelled against the servility and cultural poverty of the Bund. We are still faced with the task of training our youth to rebel against "servility within the revolution" in all its forms—beginning with those Jews who were so much the slaves of the Russian Revolution that they even distributed proclamations calling for pogroms in the name of the revolution, and including the Palestinian Communist Party of our day, which is acting in alliance with the pogromists of Hebron and Safed.

There are many who think of our revolution in a much too simple and primitive manner. Let us destroy the old world entirely, let us burn all the treasures that it accumulated throughout the ages, and let us start anew—like newborn babes! There is daring and force of protest in this approach. Indeed, there really were many revolutionaries who thus pictured the days of the Messiah. But it is doubtful whether this conception, which proceeds in utter innocence to renounce the heritage of the ages and proposes to start building the world from the ground up, really is revolutionary and progressive, or whether there is implicit within it a deeply sinister reactionary force. History tells of more than one old world that was destroyed, but what appeared upon the ruins was not better worlds, but absolute barbarism. Greece and Rome sinned grievously and were destroyed by their sins, but in place of this ancient world, with its art and creativity, a barbaric society was established, which is today a source of inspiration and nostalgia for Hitler. Hundreds of years went by until the spirit of man rose somewhat beyond this barbarism—but another retrogression is now occurring before our very eyes.

I shall not question the realism of this conception or its feasibility. I shall not ask what would be the language of man after this "operation" destroying the total fabric of the Old World would have been completed. (One is reminded of the tragicomic hero of one of Gorky's[1] stories, who undertakes to suppress all his evil qualities and consequently remains—without qualities of any kind.) I shall approach this matter only from the viewpoint of the educational tendency involved.

Man is endowed with two faculties—memory and forgetfulness. We cannot live without both. Were only memory to exist, then we would be crushed under its burden. We would become slaves to our memories, to our ancestors. Our physiognomy would then be a mere copy of preceding generations. And were we ruled entirely by forgetfulness, what place would there be for culture, science, self-consciousness, spiritual life? Archconservatism tries to deprive us of our faculty of forgetting, and pseudorevolutionism regards each remembrance of the past as the "enemy." But had humanity not preserved the memory of its great achievements, noble aspirations, periods of bloom, heroic efforts, and strivings for liberation, then no revolutionary movement would have been possible. The human race would have stagnated in eternal poverty, ignorance, and slavery.

Primitive revolutionism, which believes that ruthless destruction is the perfect cure for all social ills, reminds one, in many of its manifestations, of the growing child who demonstrates his mastery of things and curiosity about their structure by breaking his toys. In opposition to this primitive revolutionism, our movement, by its very nature, must uphold *the principle of revolutionary constructivism*. This view is in no way resigned to the defects of the existing order; it sees the need for a thoroughgoing revolution, but, at the same time, it knows that the creative potentiality of destruction is severely limited, and it directs its efforts toward constructive action, which alone can assure the value of a revolution.

Precisely because we fully recognize the catastrophic state of the world in which we live, because we see the need for the most fundamental overturn, because we know that at the door of every new social system the sins of the old are waiting to enter—therefore we insist that revolutionary efforts (which *promise* a new structure) are worthless unless they are accompanied by renewed and improved constructive energies. Our criterion of revolutionary success is not the quantity of bloodshed (as the Revisionist prophet[2] of "revolutionary Zionism" asserts) but its constructive achievements.

Our revolutionary constructivism cannot confine itself only to the economic field; it must embrace our entire life and stamp its imprint upon our culture and our milieu.

The major prophets of the revolution were men of historical memory who were rooted in and valued their cultural heritage. Marx loved Shakespeare, admired Darwin greatly, and respected our historian Graetz.[3] No true revolution is conceivable without intense spiritual life. "Professional" revolutionaries, who measure everything with the yardstick of their "profession," impoverish the spirit of the movement. This is the bureaucratic degeneration which menaces revolution in the same way that it menaces religion. It desecrates revolution, as it desecrates religion. These "professionals" who sidle up to and exploit the revolutionary movement bear the same relationship to the men of principle, the prophets who heralded the revolution and set it in motion, as the religious functionaries who cater to the wishes of the rich have to Rabbi Akiba[4] and the Rambam.[5]

A renewing and creative generation *does not* throw the cultural heritage of ages into the dustbin. It examines and scrutinizes, accepts and rejects. At times it may keep and add to an accepted tradition. At times it descends into ruined grottoes to excavate and remove the dust from that which had lain in forgetfulness, in order to resuscitate old traditions which have the power to stimulate the spirit of the generation of renewal. If a people possesses something old and profound, which can educate man and train him for his future tasks, is it truly revolutionary to despise it and become estranged from it? If the revolt of Spartacus had been preserved in the memory of the European people, and the Church had commemorated "Spartacus Day," what should have been the attitude of a labor movement worthy of the name? Should it have despised and belittled that date or should it have redeemed it from the hands of the Church and fostered and consecrated the memory of that tragic revolt?

There are many days commemorated at present which are artificial, having some passing importance, or even none at all. Perhaps one out of a thousand will be long remembered, but the rest will wilt away after the first storm. But those days which have taken root within the soil of the nation and to which generation after generation have given of their spirit will have a different destiny.

The Jewish year is studded with days which, in depth of meaning, are unparalleled among other peoples. Is it advantageous—is it a goal —for the Jewish labor movement to waste the potential value stored within them? The assimilationists shied away from our Jewish holidays as obstacles on the road to their submergence among the majority because they were ashamed of anything which would identify them as a distinct group—but why must we carry on their tradition? Did not bourgeois assimilationism and enlightenment, and even the Jewish socialism which followed in their wake, discard many valuable elements of social uplift which are contained in our tradition? If we really are Zionist-Socialists, it does not befit us to behave like dumb animals following every stupid tradition, just because it calls itself "modern" and is not hallowed by age. We must determine the value of the present and of the past with our own eyes and examine them from the viewpoint of our vital needs, from the viewpoint of progress toward our own future.

Let us take a few examples: *Passover.* A nation has, for thousands of years, been commemorating the day of its exodus from the house of bondage. Throughout all the pain of enslavement and despotism, of inquisition, forced conversion, and massacre, the Jewish people has carried in its heart the yearning for freedom and has given this craving a folk expression which includes every soul in Israel, every single downtrodden, pauperized soul! From fathers to sons, throughout all the generations, the memory of the exodus from Egypt has been handed on as a personal experience and it has therefore retained its original luster. "In every generation every man must regard himself as if he personally had been redeemed from Egypt." There is no higher peak of historic consciousness, and history—among all the civilizations of the world and in all the ages—can find no example of a greater fusion of individual with group than is contained in this ancient pedagogic command. I know no literary creation which can evoke a greater hatred of slavery and love of freedom than the story of the bondage and the exodus from Egypt. I know of no other remembrance of the past that is so entirely a symbol of our present and future as the "memory of the exodus from Egypt."

And *Tishah b'Ab*.[6] Many nations are enslaved, and many have even experienced exile. Proud Poland, whose refugees lived in exile for only two or three generations, immediately suffered a great measure of assimilation. Masses of refugees from among the powerful Russian people were scattered abroad after the October Revolution, and they are already bewailing the assimilation and the cultural estrangement of the younger generation and are holding up as an example the Jewish nation which remains unvanquished by two thousand years of dispersion. Yes, indeed, Israel knew how to preserve the day of its mourning, the date of its loss of freedom from oblivion. On this day each generation and each person in Israel felt as if his own world had just been destroyed. On each anniversary burning tears were shed and each generation expressed its pain. National memory associated with this day of wrath many of its bitter experiences, beginning with the destruction of the First and Second Temples through the expulsion from Spain up till our own time, until the outbreak of the World War. Our national memory was able, with these very simple means, *to make every Jewish soul, all over the world, feel heavy mourning at the same day and the same hour*. Each organ that was still at all attached to the nation's body wrapped itself in gloom, immersed itself in sorrow, and let its heart be permeated by the feeling of ruin, bondage, and exile. Each creative generation added something of its own to this feeling of woe, from the mournful chants of Jeremiah, to those of Spain and Germany, to Bialik's "Scroll of Fire."

It is told of Adam Mickiewicz, the great Polish poet—who all his life bewailed Poland's subjection and drew revolutionary plans for its liberation—that on Tishah b'Ab he would go to a Jewish synagogue to join the Jews in their mourning over the loss of their motherland. This non-Jew understood the power and depth of Tishah b'Ab.

I am not setting specific rules as to the form our holidays should assume. Suitable forms will grow from a living feeling within the heart and an upright and independent spirit. However, I want to refute the opinion which asserts: "Certainly, we should not forget Tishah b'Ab, but a nation which is returning to rebuild its home now has to turn the day of mourning into a festive holiday." Our achievements in this country may multiply rapidly, and even after we shall have attained a life of dignity, we shall not say, "we are redeemed," until all of our exile has ended. As long as Israel is dispersed and is prey to persecution and hatred, to contempt and to forced conversion, as in Yemen in Asia, Algiers in Africa, and Germany in Europe—or even though they enjoy emancipation purchased through assimilation in capitalistic France and communistic Russia—I shall never forget, I shall never be able to forget, the most fearful day in our destiny—the day of our destruction.

How will our people behave after its dispersed have assembled, after its complete liberation from bondage—*including its liberation from the oppression of class by class?* Perhaps it will then celebrate this day with dance and song, or perhaps it will desire that each child born in liberty and equality, unacquainted with hunger and material oppression, shall know the sufferings of all preceding generations. This we shall discuss when that day will come.

Part 7
Religious Nationalists,
Old and New

RABBI SAMUEL MOHILEVER   1824-1898

SO FAR the selections in this reader and the biographical sketches at the head of each selection have seemed to tell the story of the Zionist idea in a straight line: it began with certain stirrings in the minds of men of religion (e.g., Alkalai and Kalischer) and went on to express itself as a secular nationalism, though Zionism always more or less assumed, and was in tension with, emotions derived from religion. This impression needs to be qualified. Religious Zionism—that is, not mere traditional piety about the Holy Land but a conscious blending of orthodoxy in religion with modern Jewish nationalism—has been an important, albeit minority, trend throughout the history of the modern movement.

The seminal figure in its development, the immediate ancestor of this tendency in its existing form, was Rabbi Samuel Mohilever. He played a central role in the development of pre-Herzlian Russian Zionism, the Hibbat Zion movement, and lived long enough to announce his adherence to Herzl and to help his newly founded organization absorb the older one.

Mohilever was born in 1824 in a village near Vilna, the intellectual center of Lithuanian Jews. He was so brilliant a student of the traditional talmudic curriculum that he was ordained a rabbi at the age of eighteen. At first Mohilever refused to practice this calling and instead was a merchant of flax for five years. Business reverses and the death of his well-to-do in-laws constrained him to accept the office of rabbi in his home village. A period of six years there was followed by successive calls to ever larger communities. In the 1870's, when he first displayed signs of an active interest in work for the Holy Land, Mohilever was the rabbi of Radom in Poland. Already notable not only as a scholar but as a communal leader, he was elected to a much larger post, also in Poland, in Bialystok, which he occupied for fifteen years until his death in 1898.

Mohilever was moved to practical Zionist labors by the pogroms of

1881. Tens of thousands of Jews had fled across the Russian border to Galicia, in the Austrian-held part of Poland. Mohilever attended a conference of western Jewish leaders that was called on the spot, in Lemberg (the capital of Galicia), to decide what to do with these refugees. He suggested, without effect, that they be diverted to Palestine. On this journey Mohilever also visited Warsaw, where he had better success; he was instrumental in organizing there the first formal section of the then nascent Hibbat Zion. While in Warsaw, he convinced two of his most distinguished rabbinic colleagues to join with him in issuing a call for emigration to Palestine, but these men soon fell away from such activities. The Hibbat Zion movement was dominated by secularists like Leo Pinsker, and Mohilever remained one of the few distinguished figures among the rabbis of the old school to be active within it.

His decision to remain in Hibbat Zion, side by side with avowed agnostics who did not live in obedience to the Law, was the crucial turn in the history of religious Zionism, for it determined not only its future as an organized "party" but also the nature of the problems it would have to face henceforth. On the one hand Mohilever, like his successors to the present, had to do battle with the ultra-orthodox; it was no small matter for an undoubted pietist to announce that all Israel was in peril and hence "would we not receive anyone gladly and with love who, though irreligious in our eyes, came to rescue us?" Even seventy years later, though this fight is now largely won, there are still those among the orthodox who do not accept the notion of a Jewish national loyalty that all should share, which is greater than religious differences. On the other hand Mohilever inevitably exercised constant pressure—and here too he has been followed by his successors —on the national movement to be more responsive, at least in practice, to the demands of orthodox religion. This note is sounded in what was in effect his testament, the message to the First Zionist Congress that he sent through his grandson (the selection below is a translation of that entire text). Earlier, in 1893, a long series of differences between him and the main office of Hibbat Zion in Odessa, which was largely secularist, had led to a decision of the movement to create another center, headed by him, to do propaganda and cultural work among orthodox Jews. This office was given the Hebrew name *Mizrahi* (an abbreviation for *merkaz ruhani*, or "spiritual center"); when the presently existing Zionist organization was refounded in 1901 by Rabbi Jacob Reines and others of Mohilever's disciples, they continued the name, the spirit, and the stance.

It should be added that Mohilever was active not only in organizational and propagandistic affairs but also in the labors in behalf of colonization in Palestine. His single greatest service in this field came early, in 1882, when he went to Paris to meet the young Baron Edmond de Rothschild. Mohilever convinced him to take an interest in the struggling settlers in the Holy Land; Rothschild remained, until his death in 1934, the greatest single benefactor of the Zionist work there.

MESSAGE TO THE FIRST ZIONIST CONGRESS (1897)

HIGHLY HONORED BRETHREN, leaders of the chosen people, beloved sons of Zion, may you be granted eternal life!

My feeble strength does not permit me to accept your invitation and come in person, so in my stead I send my grandson, Dr. Joseph Mohilever, as a token that my heart is with you. From the depths of my soul I pray to the Almighty: I beseech Thee, O Lord, do Thou inspire the utterances of the delegates of Thy people, the House of Israel. Instruct them in what they shall speak and grant them understanding to utter the right words, so they stumble not with their tongues, God forbid, to speak against our Holy Law or in opposition to the secular governments which rule over us. Grant them Thy assistance and support to enable them to realize their noble vision. Allow them to find favor in the eyes of the Kings, Princes, and Rulers before whom they may stand to plead for Thy people and Thy land. Imbue, I pray Thee, the hearts of all Israel with a new spirit of abounding love for their dispersed people and their land! Amen!

I will now, by your leave, make certain remarks regarding the matters before this honored assembly.

1. With respect to the object of your meeting, I have but to transcribe the words of the announcement by the chairman and secretary of the Organizing Committee: "The Congress will strive toward ends which are both immediate and attainable. All other reports concerning it are unfounded rumors. All acts of the Congress will be given full publicity. Neither in its debates nor in its resolutions will there be

anything contrary to the laws of any country or to our duties as citizens. We are pledged, in particular, that the total conduct of the meeting will be in a manner acceptable to the Hovevei Zion[1] and to their distinguished government." I feel certain that this expression of good faith will be observed to the full; if, nevertheless, opinions are expressed which are not in accordance with the above pledge, they will find no response. The main aim of this assembly, I wish to add, must be to intercede most forcefully and energetically with the Turkish Government to permit our people to purchase land and to build houses without let or hindrance. We must strive with all the means in our power to obtain such permission, for upon it the very existence of all our colonization work is dependent.

2. In the Congress a central body, whose seat will be outside of Russia, will undoubtedly be chosen to carry on our holy work. It is incumbent upon us to see that the members of that central body be devoted to our cause with all their heart and soul.

3. It is essential that the Congress unite all "Sons of Zion" who are true to our cause to work in complete harmony and fraternity, even if there be among them differences of opinion regarding religion. Our attitude toward those among us who do not observe the religious precepts must be, as it were, as if fire had taken hold of our homes, imperiling our persons and our property. Under such circumstances would we not receive anyone gladly and with love who, though irreligious in our eyes, came to rescue us? Is this not our present plight, my brethren? A great fire, a fearful conflagration, is raging in our midst, and we are all threatened. Our enemies have multiplied until they surpass many millions; were it not for the fear of the police, they would devour us alive. If brethren put out their hands to us in aid, doing all in their power to deliver us from our dire straits, are there such among us as would dare spurn them? If all factions will really understand this thought, this covenant of brothers will surely stand.

4. All "Sons of Zion" must be completely convinced and must believe with a perfect faith that the resettlement of our country—i.e., the purchase of land and the building of houses, the planting of orchards and the cultivation of the soil—is one of the fundamental commandments of our Torah. Some of our ancient sages even say that it is equivalent to the whole Law, for it is the foundation of the existence of our people. A true Lover of Zion is a man who believes this with all his heart and soul. Whoever assists us and does not hold this faith is comparable to one who contributes to a cause in which he does not really believe.

5. The basis of Hibbat Zion is the Torah, as it has been handed down to us from generation to generation, with neither supplement nor subtraction. I do not intend this statement as an admonition to any individual regarding his conduct, for, as our sages have said: "Verily, there are none in this generation fit to admonish." I am nevertheless stating in a general way, that the Torah, which is the Source of our life, must be the foundation of our regeneration in the land of our fathers.

6. Our task is to build and to plant and not to tear down and destroy. We must, therefore, carefully avoid injuring the "Halukah"[2] funds in Jerusalem in any way. Thousands are dependent on these funds, and, as long as they have no other source of income, we must not jeopardize their livelihood.

7. We must dispatch compelling speakers to all the lands of the Diaspora to spread our cause among our people and gain their support. We know from our experiences in Russia that such speakers are very effective. We must also publish pamphlets in Hebrew, Yiddish, and other languages spoken by the masses of our people. It is also very important that we publish a pamphlet in Russian, German, French, English, Italian, and other languages, setting forth our ideals simply, logically, and attractively, for distribution, in general, among the leading figures of the nations of the world and, in particular, among our own eminent sons in all countries of the Diaspora.

8. As for the National Trust, we must make every effort to persuade the Directors of the Jewish Colonization Association[3] to set aside a great portion of the monies under their control for the resettlement of the Holy Land. We must make similar approaches to other wealthy men among our people. It would also be wise to arrange that a percentage of all the funds collected for the work of colonization be set aside in reserve for the National Trust.

9. I think it would be fitting for the Congress to address a letter of thanks to the great philanthropist, Baron Edmond de Rothschild,[4] to express its gratitude to him for his immense efforts toward the resettlement of our land. Is he not the first, since our country was laid waste, to bestir himself on behalf of our cause? He has already expended tens of millions of francs upon this noble work, and he is doing and is prepared to do much more yet, to bring to life the waste places of our land. This exalted son of Israel is worthy of the honor and respect of this first Congress of Lovers of Zion from all lands.

In conclusion, I lift up my voice to my brethren: Behold, it is now two thousand years that we await our Messiah, to redeem us from our bitter exile and to gather our scattered brethren from all corners of the earth to our own land, where each shall dwell in security, under his vine and under his fig tree. This faith, strong within us, has been our sole comfort in the untold days of our misery and degradation. And even though in the last century some have arisen in our midst who have denied this belief, tearing it out of their hearts and even erasing it from their prayers, the masses of our people hold fast to this hope, for the fulfillment of which they pray morning, noon, and night, and in which they find balm for their suffering. Of late certain orthodox rabbis have arisen in western Europe, among whom one has even declared that the promises of future bliss and consolation made by our seers were in the form of symbols and parables. The coming of the Messiah, they say, will not be to bring Israel back to the Land of its Fathers and put an end to its long dispersion and many sorrows, but will be to establish the Kingdom of Heaven for all mankind, while Israel continues in exile as a light to the gentiles. Others of these rabbis assert, without qualification, that nationalism is contrary to our belief in the advent of the Messiah. I am therefore constrained to declare publicly that all this is not true. Our hope and faith has ever been and still is, that our Messiah will come and gather in all the scattered of Israel, and, instead of our being wanderers upon the face of the earth, ever moving from place to place, we shall dwell in our own country as a nation, in the fullest sense of the word. Instead of being the contempt and mockery of the nations, we shall be honored and respected by all the peoples of the earth. This is our faith and hope, as derived from the words of our prophets and seers of blessed memory and to this our people clings!

We are, indeed, far from being unconcerned about the good of all mankind. No less than others do we believe in the promises to all men that are made in the words of our prophets, and on the New Year and the Day of Atonement we do indeed pray: "Grant, we pray Thee, O Lord our God, Thy awe on the work of Thy hands and Thy fear on all that Thou hast created, that all Thy works behold Thee and all Thy creatures bow down to Thee, that they make a single band to do Thy will with a whole heart." But after this prayer for all men, we also ask: "Grant, O Lord, honor to Thy people, good hope to them that seek Thee, praise to them that fear Thee, and courage to those that await Thee, joy to Thy land and rejoicing to Thy city, and exaltation of the horn of David Thy servant." Truly the honor of our people, its praise and good hope, are solely bound up with our land, and our happiness depends upon the rebuilding of Jerusalem in joy. Only then "will the mouth of unrighteousness be stopped, and all evil vanish like smoke, and the reign of arrogance pass away from this earth."

May the Eternal, the Blessed, the Exalted, the Keeper and Redeemer of Israel, bring to pass the saying of His prophet (Zechariah 8 : 7–8): "Thus saith the Lord, Behold, I shall bring My people from the East and the lands of the setting of the sun, I shall bring them and they shall dwell in Jerusalem. They shall be My people and I will be their God in truth and righteousness."

YEHIEL MICHAEL PINES 1842-1912

YEHIEL MICHAEL PINES was born in Grodno, in the Russian-held part of Poland, in 1842. His education was unusual in that day for the scion of a notable, pious family, for he was taught not only Bible and Talmud but also the German language and its literature. Pines came to public notice in his twenties, through a series of articles (they appeared in book form in 1871, entitled *Yalde Ruhi, or Children of My Spirit*) in which he attacked the then fashionable notions about the need for religious reforms. This period was the height of the Russian Jewish "enlightenment," when all the great names of modern Hebrew literature were anti-orthodox. A young man who had the temerity to counterattack was a rare bird. That he did it not in the manner and language of the old school but as the possessor of a good western education, not unaware of science, and in a prose style as modern as that of the anti-traditionalists made him all the rarer.

The reputation that accrued to Pines from this debut, as that of a pietist who was not sealed off from the new age, was what won him the important appointment of his career. In 1874 a fund was created in honor of the ninetieth birthday of the Anglo-Jewish leader, Sir Moses Montefiore. Sir Moses had displayed a lifelong interest in the Jews of Palestine and the fund was therefore intended for work there. This new organization ended a long search for an agent to direct its labors on the spot by appointing Pines. He moved to Jerusalem in 1878 and henceforth his life was identified with its Jewish community.

Pines's early months in Palestine were marked by an unpleasant squabble with some leaders of the ultra-orthodox group within its Jewish community. He rebuffed a request from these circles to share in the control of the fund he had come to direct, and they replied to this affront by excommunicating him as a heretic. It is not surprising that a violent debate ensued, in which much ink was spilled both to attack and defend his reputation for piety. When this storm had abated Pines settled down to his work to become a recognized expert in land and colonization, as well as a productive writer on Zionist affairs. He was the first to collaborate with Eliezer Ben-Yehudah, after his arrival several years later, in the work of reviving Hebrew as the spoken tongue. In the 1890's he belonged briefly to the Palestinian lodge of the secret order, B'nai Moshe, which Ahad Ha-Am led. Nonetheless Pines remained severely critical of the nationalist theories of both. At the end of his life (he died in 1912) Pines was an instructor in Talmud at the Hebrew Teachers' Seminary in Jerusalem.

Perhaps the best way to define Pines's intellectual position is by contrast with Ahad Ha-Am. Pines insisted just as strongly that the Jewish national identity was unique, but he saw this uniqueness not in the national ethic but in religion. For him Jewish religion and nationhood were indivisible, so that a secular Jewish nation was completely inconceivable. On the other hand it was just as impossible for him to admit the notion held by German Jewish Reform of a denationalized Judaism as a "pure" religion. There was no Judaism that could be indifferent, even in theory, to the destiny of the Jews. His Zionism therefore envisaged a Jewish national community in Palestine whose life would be organized according to all the norms—not merely the ethical ones, as in Ahad Ha-Am's thought—of traditional religion.

In practice Pines was willing to make tactical concessions from this optimum. Indeed he was sufficiently influenced, at least indirectly, by the German historical school of the middle of the nineteenth century to admit that religion, too, had undergone historical development and that some of its forms were modified or even cast aside through the ages—though he insisted that this was permissible only as an unconscious process, not as a conscious reform. Pines' outlook was a blend of relative liberalism in theory and tactic with a religious orthodoxy which, in practice, admitted merely the faintest dash of liberalization. This has been the nature of orthodox religious Zionism since his time.

ON RELIGIOUS REFORMS (1868-1871)

J U D A I S M can never find itself in conflict with results of scientific discoveries. It may be taken for granted that the human mind will probably never attain the limit of an all-embracing scientific knowledge of the universe, which will be able to solve all its riddles. At any rate, this much we know: that no amount of scientific study and research is capable of nullifying the inner evidence of the existence of an unseen spiritual being by which the universe is sustained and contained. Judaism has very wisely contented itself with stating this general creed, while shunning all effort to represent the nature of the Supreme Being by concrete images which limit its conception. Our faith has left it to each individual to interpret for himself the eternal verities in accordance with his own judgment, by the light of the philosophy prevalent in each age, or according to his own original thinking. Judaism has affirmed the existence of the One God, leaving it to the simple man to worship Him in his own simple-minded way, to the philosopher to give the idea a philosophic explanation, to the mystic to seek in God the key to the world's riddles—all that matters in Judaism is the deeds that a man performs, deeds which serve as a vehicle for noble ideas, not always recognizable but always embodied in them, as a fruit is held in its shell. That is why it has been possible for believing and practicing Jews to adapt various intellectual, ethical, and social interpretations to their faith. To sum up: Judaism has never attempted to contain the premises of spirit and of reason within prescribed limits or to impose on them any permanent images. It has left them, as they had been, a mystery.

Nevertheless, Judaism has always found an outlet and expression for religious ardor in human conduct, in deeds. Word and deed are to the Jew what images and statues and the cross are to the pagan and the Christian. They represent the symbol of the idea and are the embodiment of faith. But yet, how vast is the difference between those two kinds of symbolism! While the images and the cross offer us the likeness of the Divinity within the limits of external delineations, the word and the deed tell us only of God's actions and of His relation to the Cosmos. Judaism has thus been enabled to survive the changes in world outlook and philosophic doctrines which have taken place from age to age and to come to terms with the contemporary philosophy of every age. Judaism has withstood Egyptian, Hellenic, Persian, and Roman influences and has emerged intact, but sharpened and polished by these encounters. Nor have the German philosophers and the school of Spinoza affected it adversely. It still lives inwardly and outwardly as it was when first given on Mount Sinai. Judaism has followed the pattern of Nature: Just as the spirit of Nature is expressed by word and deed, so the spirituality of Jewish faith is revealed by deeds and conduct. That is why Judaism's evolution has resembled the processes of Nature: The essence remains while the forms undergo change from moment to moment.

The foundations of Judaism are still firm enough to withstand the challenge of current philosophies. The foundations being unshakable, the affirmative structure built upon them will endure. Although at various times of turmoil and upheaval the Jewish people has been known to disregard the commandments of its religion, the stabilization of society is inevitably followed by a renewed and vigorous return to Judaism.

METHODS IN REFORMS

THERE IS NO ROOM for religious reform as long as the people is ready to obey religious authority and observe religious practices. This applies even to reforms this writer would consider desirable. Why should we try to make premature breaches in the present structure? We ought not outrun natural development, but be guided by it. That is the way to reach our proper goal, without falling into either of two extremes because of a desire for partisan victory. It is part of wisdom to understand that there is nothing to be accomplished by forcing an issue before the time is ripe for it. Our sages were right in their warning: "Let no man destroy a house of worship before he has built another in its place." We must heed that warning so that we may not act too hastily with our reforms, before we know for certain what is to remain and what is to be discarded. We may leave it to the Jewish people to find the proper channels for change in an orderly fashion, when such change becomes necessary. In deciding which of the religious rules and practices still retain their vitality and which have become outmoded, we ought to be guided not by the conclusions of our own theoretic thinking, but rather by the lessons of experience. A withered branch will fall off by itself, while a green one will bloom and bear fruit.

Our main task ought to be to introduce reforms in the mundane life of the Jewish masses, in their economic position, their occupations, their education, and their community organization. These reforms ought to be made in accordance with the spirit of the times and in response to immediate needs, to make them function in a useful manner. We ought to make the Jews more worldly-minded, more practical in their everyday life.

JEWISH NATIONALISM CANNOT BE
SECULAR (1895)

I HAVE NO SYMPATHY with the currently fashionable idea, with the movement to make the Jewish people a pure secular nationality in place of the combination of religion with nationality that has enabled us to survive to this day.

Whatever merit there may be to this theory, it is to be found only in its possible value as applied to the assimilated Jews, that is, to those de-Judaized individuals who have remained members of the Jewish faith in name only and are ready to drop out of the Jewish community. Such Jews may find in the idea of secular Jewish nationality a new bond to reinforce their attachment to their people. But I see a strong tendency these days, one fostered by a well-known school of thought, to impose the idea of secular nationalism on the whole Jewish people, including pious Jews, to try to separate religion from nationality, and to make the latter a self-sufficient entity upon which Jewish survival is to depend. It is against this that I rise in vigorous opposition, for in the consequences of this doctrine I can see nothing but incalculable harm. It is as if one were to try to deprive a living body of its soul in order to revive it by an electric shock, which may have value in resuscitation, but is no substitute for real vitality.

What, then, is the difference between the Jewish people and all other ethnic groups? The answer to that question is self-evident. The Jewish people did not, at its very beginning, come into the world as a separate entity in the ordinary way, as a result of the combined influences of race and soil, but as a group professing a separate faith and bound in a mutual covenant to observe that faith.

Nor has the growth and development of the Jewish people through the ages followed the ordinary pattern. Rather, it has paralleled the evolution of its religion and has been bound up with it. After the Jewish people acquired a homeland and formed a sovereign state, it still did not look upon its statehood as the essence of its peoplehood; it was generally willing to accept foreign domination with minimal protest and rose in revolt only when its religion was threatened. Conversely, when it was deprived of its homeland and was scattered abroad, and even ceased speaking its national language, the Jewish people continued to live as a national entity only by virtue of the Torah, which accompanied it in all its wanderings and lived with it in every country in which it settled.

All these facts prove that the Jews are not an ethnic group like others and cannot be defined as an ordinary, "natural" nationality, a definition which secular Zionists are attempting to impose upon them against their will. The Jewish people is a race that is not by its nature capable of absorbing such an alien implantation. Why, then, do the secularists vainly try such grafts? Though you may argue that nothing is impossible in skillful horticulture and that even a fig branch can be successfully grafted onto an olive tree, you will have to admit that certain natural conditions of growth are required for the success of such grafting. How is it possible to graft the idea of secular nationality onto the Jewish people when it lacks the two principal attributes of an ordinary nationality? The Jews do not live on one territory and do not speak one language.

RELIGION IS THE SOURCE OF JEWISH NATIONALISM (1895)

SCIENCE AND EDUCATION are no less precious to me than they are to you, secularists. I set a high value on this divine light which has been given us by our Creator at our birth. I, too, no less than you, would like to see the Jewish people advance in scientific knowledge and in worldly education, for I know how important such advance is in improving human nature, in improving manners and ethics, and in raising the cultural level. I also know how much real knowledge can contribute to the ennobling of religious feeling. But knowledge divorced from faith is not what I consider a desirable goal. That is not the enlightenment which our better leaders of the preceding generation declared to be the sister of faith, while their predecessors thought it the handmaiden of faith. But a sister or a handmaid who sets herself up as a rival to her sister or her mistress will only lure the master away from his wife, without leaving even a small corner in his heart for the affection he once bore her.

The enlightenment we seek is one that is organically integrated in faith, so that the two are inseparable. Why should we try to isolate the one from the other? Have we not been given the Torah to teach us to purify our thoughts and our sentiments as the goldsmith refines the gold? Has not reason been given us by Heaven so that we may be able to contemplate the greatness of our Creator as revealed in His work and the glory of the Law He implanted in our hearts? In the world of the spirit there are no compartments. Whatever the man thinks and feels, if it is directed toward Truth, is enveloped in holiness.

Nor have you, the secularists, any monopoly on the Zionist sentiment. I am as much a Lover of Zion as you are, not a whit less. But mine is not the Love of Zion which you have abstracted from the whole Jewish tradition to set it up in a separate existence. Any other people can perhaps have a national aspiration divorced from its religion, but we, Jews, cannot. Such nationalism is an abomination to Jews. Moreover, it cannot succeed, since it has no roots in our reality. What is Jewish nationality divorced from Jewish religion? It is an empty formula, nothing but pretty phrases. After all, what is "nationality" if not a concept, or, in other words, a thought-image. But a thought-image which has no basis in reality is an illusion. What other basis in reality can there be for the thought-image of Jewish nationality except the unity of the Jewish people with its Torah and its faith?

I know the answer you will give me: Our history and our language also form part of our national heritage. True enough, a common past is a national heritage, but it is not the begetter of nationality. It is unheard of for an effect to turn around and become the cause of its own cause! Can a man sate his hunger by eating his own flesh? And as for the Hebrew language you mention—perhaps, if we still spoke it, it might offer some slight basis for our nationality, but in view of the state of the Hebrew language today, one can hardly see why you are ready to dedicate yourself to it. Who or what forces you to bring it back to life? Is it national sentiment? Again we see the effect becoming a cause! All of the vitality of national sentiment is in the national language, but the language itself has no vitality except in so far as it is nourished by national sentiment! But this is a circular argument which can go on ad infinitum!

The nationalism I represent is the nationalism of Rabbi Yehudah Halevi[1] and of Rabbi Moshe ben-Nahman,[2] of blessed memory, a national sentiment organically integrated in faith, nationalism whose soul is the Torah and whose life is in its precepts and commandments.

JEWS WILL ACCEPT HARDSHIP ONLY IN THE HOLY LAND (1892)

THE FATE OF THIS IDEA of settling the Holy Land with Jews is like that of the fairy prince transformed by evil magic until rescued. The contemporary fairy godmothers of our people deserve our recognition and are assured of a golden page in Jewish history. Many praise the famous philanthropist who lavishly spends money to colonize Jews in Brazil. But despite all the outward advantages that American colonization seems to have, it will never be able to compete with Palestine. For the one advantage of the sanctity of tradition will, in the end, prevail, even in the practical sphere, over all the economic advantages possessed by other countries. None of these advantages can create in the settlers the spirit of determination and devotion necessary to overcome the initial hardships which are inevitable in any colonizing effort. The mere prospect of material benefits will not suffice for the Jewish settlers in America to develop those qualities. But in Palestine, as we see for ourselves, the exalted idea revitalizes its bearers and raises them above all obstacles and hardships and gives them strength to prevail and win out. I have seen many Jews who had every possibility of leaving the soil in Palestine to which they had painfully attached themselves, in order to migrate to easier conditions in America, but they refused to move. They deliberately chose a life of hardship and poverty rather than the riches of America; they made strenuous efforts to make good where they were—and succeeded.

I said they succeeded, for experience has demonstrated how strong is the prospect of ultimate success in Palestine. True enough, when the work first began the obstacles were many and great, and the results were poor enough to discourage and dishearten any believer in the idea. But their strong devotion did not allow them to give up, so that new experiments and new methods in the end pointed the more promising way to attaining the objective.

RABBI ABRAHAM ISAAC KOOK
1865-1935

MODERN ZIONIST THOUGHT is the creation of a whole gallery of passionate and extraordinary men, but even among them a few stand out as originals. Abraham Isaac Kook is one of this handful. Kook cannot be explained from the outside in—if he can be explained, at all—by a listing of the facts of his life, the influences that touched him, and the antecedents of his thought. The essence of Kook is within. He was a mystic whose entire career was determined by experiences of inner illumination; he was a religious Zionist engaged not in defending the ritual observances—though, of course, he practiced and preached them with unique fervor—against secularism but in living out an approaching "end of days." Kook's view of Zionism, and his most important acts as the first chief rabbi of Palestine after the British mandate, make sense only if we understand that he was certain that the present generation was the one foretold in prophecy as the age of the coming of the Messiah. He could therefore both seriously prepare himself for future office as priest of the restored cult in the Temple in Jerusalem and accept all builders of Palestine, heretics included, as unwitting instruments of the ever more manifest Redemption. These are both part of the same whole to use a technical term, of his "realized eschatology."

Even as a child, Kook was known for unusual endowments of mind, but this was not unprecedented or unparalleled. What did set him apart in his native Latvian small town and in the somewhat larger cities in which he studied in his adolescence was his fervor in prayer and his sense of the immediacy of God. By the time he came to the yeshivah in Volozhin at the age of nineteen it was apparent that Kook was different in another regard: he loved to speak Hebrew, then usually a sign of at least incipient heresy, but there was no evident change in his rapturous piety.

At the age of twenty-three Kook assumed the post of rabbi in the village of Zimel, where he remained for six years, until 1894. His next

call was to the much larger city of Boisk, Lithuania, and in the nine
years that he served there Kook's stature became ever more apparent.
While in Boisk he published his first essay on Zionism, in which he
accepted modern Jewish nationalism, even at its most secularist, as an
expression of the divine endowment within the Jewish soul and a
forerunner of the Messiah. His own longing to settle in the Holy
Land was growing meanwhile. Though flattering calls were coming,
offering very distinguished rabbinic posts in Lithuania, Kook chose
instead to go to Jaffa. He arrived in the summer of 1904, as chief
rabbi of that city and of the agricultural colonies nearby.

The years in Jaffa were the crucial period of his career. He increased
his scope both as a writer and a communal leader, laboring ever
more self-consciously for a renaissance of orthodox Judaism. In 1909
he was the spokesman for leniency in a controversy over the biblical law of letting the soil of the Holy Land lie fallow on the seventh
year, for he permitted a dispensation on technical grounds. To defend
his views he wrote a treatise in talmudic law on this question. While
he was in Jaffa the various wings of orthodoxy throughout the Jewish
world were splitting ever more definitely over Zionism, and Kook tried
to keep peace among them. But above all it was in Jaffa that Kook
had that initial mystical experience for which his previous life had
been a preparation and on which the years to come were largely commentary.

In the summer of 1914 he left Palestine to visit Europe, where he
was caught by the outbreak of World War I. He made his way to
Switzerland, but could get no further on the way back home. Stranded
without any means, Kook was helped by Abraham Kimche, who
invited the rabbi to be his guest in St. Gallen, Switzerland. After
more than a year there, spent mostly in writing, Kook accepted a call
to serve temporarily as rabbi in London, where he was from 1916 to
1919, i.e., throughout the time of negotiation and controversy that
attended the issuance of the Balfour Declaration (November 2, 1917).
In the summer of 1919 he returned to Palestine to serve as chief
rabbi of the Ashkenazi (occidental) Jews in Jerusalem. Two years
later the British Government of Palestine called the first national
conference of its Jewry to create their autonomous religious law
courts and institutions. Kook was elected the Ashkenazi head of the
new rabbinic court of appeals, and therefore, in effect, the Ashkenazi
chief rabbi of Palestine. He served in his office until his death in
1935.

His years as chief rabbi, despite his dislike for many of the practical matters with which he had to be concerned, were a period of great achievement. Almost immediately Kook founded his own school of higher talmudic learning, which differed from others because its language of instruction was Hebrew and because the classics of Jewish philosophy and devotion were studied there as seriously as the Law. He continued on his path of understanding and defending the irreligious against the strictures of the orthodox. Kook never faltered in his personal courage; in 1933, when emotions among Palestinian Jewry ran high over the assassination of Hayyim Arlosoroff, the political secretary of the World Zionist Organization, Kook did not hesitate to take a most unpopular stand. All the while he was writing, and much of what he left behind is still being published.

The selections below are from a posthumous volume, *Orot* (*Lights*), which first appeared in 1942. The actual dates of their composition range over the last quarter century of Rabbi Kook's life.

THE LAND OF ISRAEL (1910-1930)

ERETZ ISRAEL is not something apart from the soul of the Jewish people; it is no mere national possession, serving as a means of unifying our people and buttressing its material, or even its spiritual, survival. Eretz Israel is part of the very essence of our nationhood; it is bound organically to its very life and inner being. Human reason, even at its most sublime, cannot begin to understand the unique holiness of Eretz Israel; it cannot stir the depths of love for the land that are dormant within our people. What Eretz Israel means to the Jew can be felt only through the Spirit of the Lord which is in our people as a whole, through the spiritual cast of the Jewish soul, which radiates its characteristic influence to every healthy emotion. This higher light shines forth to the degree that the spirit of divine holiness fills the hearts of the saints and scholars of Israel with heavenly life and bliss.

To regard Eretz Israel as merely a tool for establishing our national unity—or even for sustaining our religion in the Diaspora by preserving its proper character and its faith, piety, and observances—is a sterile notion; it is unworthy of the holiness of Eretz Israel. A valid strengthening of Judaism in the Diaspora can come only from a deepened attachment to Eretz Israel. The hope for the return to the Holy Land is the continuing source of the distinctive nature of Judaism. The hope for the Redemption is the force that sustains Judaism in the Diaspora; the Judaism of Eretz Israel is the very Redemption.

JEWISH ORIGINAL CREATIVITY, whether in the realm of ideas or in the arena of daily life and action, is impossible except in Eretz Israel. On the other hand, whatever the Jewish people creates in Eretz Israel assimilates the universal into characteristic and unique Jewish form, to the great benefit of the Jewish people and of the world. The very sins which are the cause of our exile also pollute the pristine wellspring of our being, so that the water is impure at the source. Once the unique wellspring of Israel's individuality has become corrupt, its primal originality can express itself only in that area of loftiest universal creativity which belongs to the Jew—and only in the Diaspora, while the Homeland itself grows waste and desolate, atoning for its degradation by its ruin. While the life and thought of Israel is finding universal outlets and is being scattered abroad in all the world, the pristine well of the Jewish spirit stops running, the polluted streams emanating from the source are drying up, and the well is cleansing itself, until its original purity returns. When that process is completed, the exile will become a disgust to us and will be discarded. Universal Light, in all its power, will again radiate from the unique source of our being; the splendor of the Messiah who is to gather in the exiles will begin to be manifest; and the bitter lament of Rachel weeping for her children will find sweet and glorious consolation. The creativity of the Jew, in all its glory and uniqueness, will reassert itself, suffused with the all-encompassing riches of the spirit of the greatest giant of humankind, Abraham, whom the Almighty called to be a blessing to man.

A JEW CANNOT BE as devoted and true to his own ideas, sentiments, and imagination in the Diaspora as he can in Eretz Israel. Revelations of the Holy, of whatever degree, are relatively pure in Eretz Israel; outside it, they are mixed with dross and much impurity. However, the greater is one's yearning for and attachment to Eretz Israel, the purer his thoughts become, for they then live in the air of Eretz Israel, which sustains everyone who longs to behold the Land.

IN THE HOLY LAND man's imagination is lucid and clear, clean and pure, capable of receiving the revelation of Divine Truth and of expressing in life the sublime meaning of the ideal of the sovereignty of holiness; there the mind is prepared to understand the light of prophecy and to be illumined by the radiance of the Holy Spirit. In gentile lands the imagination is dim, clouded with darkness and shadowed with unholiness, and it cannot serve as the vessel for the outpouring of the Divine Light, as it raises itself beyond the lowness and narrowness of the universe. Because reason and imagination are interwoven and interact with each other, even reason cannot shine in its truest glory outside the Holy Land.

DEEP IN THE HEART of every Jew, in its purest and holiest recesses, there blazes the fire of Israel. There can be no mistaking its demands for an organic and indivisible bond between life and all of God's commandments; for the pouring of the spirit of the Lord, the spirit of Israel which completely permeates the soul of the Jew, into all the vessels which were created for this particular purpose; and for expressing the word of Israel fully and precisely in the realms of action and idea.

In the hearts of our saints, this fire is constantly blazing up with tongues of holy flame. Like the fire on the altar of the Temple, it is burning unceasingly, with a steady flame, in the collective heart of our people. Hidden away in the deepest recesses of their souls, it exists even among the backsliders and sinners of Israel. Within the Jewish people as a whole, this is the living source of its desire for freedom, of its longing for a life worthy of the name for man and community, of its hope for redemption—of the striving toward a full, uncontradictory, and unbounded Jewish life.

This is the meaning of the Jew's undying love for Eretz Israel—the Land of Holiness, the Land of God—in which all of the Divine commandments are realized in their perfect form. This urge to unfold to the world the nature of God, to raise one's head in His Name in order to proclaim His greatness in its real dimension, affects all souls, for all desire to become as one with Him and to partake of the bliss of His life. This yearning for a true life, for one that is fashioned by all the commandments of the Torah and illumined by all its uplifting splendor, is the source of the courage which moves the Jew to affirm, before all the world, his loyalty to the heritage of his people, to the preservation of its identity and values, and to the upholding of its faith and vision.

An outsider may wonder: How can seeming unbelievers be moved by this life force, not merely to nearness to the universal God but even toward authentic Jewish life—to expressing the divine commandments concretely in image and idea, in song and deed. But this is no mystery to anyone whose heart is deeply at one with the soul of the Jewish people and who knows its marvelous nature. The source of this Power is in the Power of God, in the everlasting glory of life.

THE WAR (1910–1930)

FORCES FROM WITHOUT compelled us to forsake the political arena of the world, but our withdrawal was also motivated by an inward assent, as if to say that we were awaiting the advent of a happier time, when government could be conducted without ruthlessness and barbarism. That is the day for which we hope. Of course, in order to bring it about, we must awaken all our potentialities and use all the means that the age may make available to us: Everything evolves by the will of the Creator of all worlds. But the delay is a necessary one, for our soul was disgusted by the dreadful sins that go with political rule in evil times. The day has come—it is very near— when the world will grow gentler; we can begin to prepare ourselves, for it will soon be possible for us to conduct a state of our own founded on goodness, wisdom, justice, and the clear Light of God.

It is not meet for Jacob to engage in political life at a time when statehood requires bloody ruthlessness and demands a talent for evil. At the beginning of our history we were granted only the foundation, the minimum that was necessary to establish a nation. After our race was weaned, our political sovereignty was destroyed, and we were dispersed among the peoples and sown in the depths of the soil, "till the time of singing is come, and the voice of the turtledove is heard in the land."

THE SECURING of the structure of the world, which is now tottering in the bloody tempests of war, demands the upbuilding of the Jewish nation. The building of the people and the revelation of its spirit are one and the same process; it is indispensable to the rebuilding of the shaken world, which is waiting for the supreme and unifying force that is to be found in the soul of the Holy Congregation of Israel. The soul of Israel is full of the spirit of God, the spirit of the Name, and no man who is responsive to the demands of his own soul can be silent at this great hour. He must cry out to the slumbering powers of our people: Awake and rise to your task.

The voice of God calls out mightily. His call is attested in the recesses of our soul and by the changing processes of life: Israel must tap the source of its life, and plant itself on the feet of its spiritual character. World civilization is crumbling, the human spirit is weakened, and darkness is enveloping all the nations.

The time is ripe. Everlasting light, the true Light of God, the Light of God of Israel, revealed by his wondrous people, must rise to the level of consciousness. This awareness must penetrate the inner being of our people, so that it recognizes the ultimate oneness of its own potentialities and becomes aware of the God Who dwells in it. Once it knows that God is within it, our people will also know how to draw from its own elemental source. Our nation is called to drink not from alien wells but from its own deeps. Let it fill its vessels with will from the depth of its prayers, with life from the well of its Torah, with courage from the roots of its faith, with order from the integrity of its reason, and with heroism from the might of its spirit, for all that arises under the canopy of its skies derives from the spirit of God that is hovering over the universe, from the beginning unto the end of time.

All the civilizations of the world will be renewed by the renascence of our spirit. All quarrels will be resolved, and our revival will cause all life to become luminous with the joy of fresh birth. All religions will don new and precious raiment, casting off whatever is soiled, abominable, and unclean; they will unite in imbibing of the dew of the Holy Lights, that were made ready for all mankind at the beginning of time in the well of Israel. The active power of Abraham's blessing to all the peoples of the world will become manifest, and it will serve as the basis of our renewed creativity in Eretz Israel. The destruction of our day is a preparation for a new and unique renascence of the deepest dimensions.

The Light of God's grace is shining. The name of God, "I am that I am," is ever more revealing itself. Let us attest to the greatness of our God.

THE REBIRTH OF ISRAEL (1910–1930)

THE WORLD and all that it contains is waiting for the Light of Israel, for the Exalted Light radiating from Him Whose Name is to be praised. This people was fashioned by God to speak of His Glory; it was granted the heritage of the blessing of Abraham so that it might disseminate the knowledge of God, and it was commanded to live its life apart from the nations of the world. God chose it to cleanse the whole world of all impurity and darkness; this people is endowed with a hidden treasure, with the Torah, the means by which the Heaven and the Earth were created.

The Light of Israel is not a utopian dream, or some abstract morality, or merely a pious wish and a noble vision. It does not wash its hands of the material world and all its values, abandoning the flesh, and society and government to wallow in their impurity, and forsaking the forces of nature, which fell in the Fall of Man, to remain in their low estate. It is, rather, a raising of all of life.

No people has yet grown sufficiently in mind and spirit to be able to appreciate the sacredness of the universe, the joy in God's greatness, the enthronement of Creation from its very beginning to its very end, completely enveloped, as the world is, by the infinite goodness, the mighty strength, and the perfect purity of the One God.

All the peoples, as we well know, are under the influences of their varying civilizations. We know the exact value of each; we can estimate how much of light and darkness are intermingled in their respective ideals and aspirations. In the course of our history we have conquered the most oppressive and sinister forces of paganism, and we are now engaged in overcoming lesser manifestations of the darkness.

An ancient Jewish heresy, in which pagan influence was present, announced the abolition of the specific commandments of the Torah, while it haughtily and magniloquently took over religious and ethical values from Judaism. Such darkness stems from the inability of the non-Jewish mind to grasp the full meaning of the splendor of the exalted Divine order, which unites Heaven and Earth, body and soul, creed and deed, image and action, individual and society, this world and the world to come, the beginning and the end of Creation, the grandeur of eternity and the joy of Heaven and Earth and all their hosts. But a time will come when even the lowest of the world's depths will be cleansed of its filth, even the worst of its crookednesses will be set straight, and even the slightest perversion will be corrected. Then light will shine for the righteous.

The world of the gentiles is tattered and rent. In its view the body is divided from the soul, and there is no inner bond and identity between matter and spirit, no basic unity between action and idea. At present, before the Light of Israel becomes manifest, the doctrine of Communism represents the highest spiritual ascent of gentile culture. But how poor is a world in which this black evil has raised its head and pretends to be its highest aspiration. What a treasure chest of wickedness is hidden in this most fearful lie, which has such a dangerous exterior sheen of purity! How pitiable are the spiritual streams out of the Jewish world of true holiness which are pouring into this swamp of wickedness! How much more incandescent the Light will have to become in order to redeem the rays which have fallen into darkness! But they will be redeemed, once and for all, with the redemption of the Holy People.

REDEMPTION IS CONTINUOUS. The Redemption from Egypt and the Final Redemption are part of the same process, "of the mighty hand and outstretched arm," which began in Egypt and is evident in all of history. Moses and Elijah belong to the same redemptive act; one represents its beginning and the other its culmination, so that together they fulfill its purpose. The spirit of Israel is attuned to the hum of the redemptive process, to the sound waves of its labors which will end only with the coming of the days of the Messiah.

IT IS A GRAVE ERROR to be insensitive to the distinctive unity of the Jewish spirit, to imagine that the Divine stuff which uniquely characterizes Israel is comparable to the spiritual content of all the other national civilizations. This error is the source of the attempt to sever the national from the religious element of Judaism. Such a division would falsify both our nationalism and our religion, for every element of thought, emotion, and idealism that is present in the Jewish people belongs to an indivisible entity, and all together make up its specific character.

But, mistaken as is the attempt to divide these indivisible components of the Jewish spirit, it is an even greater error to imagine that such a sundering could possibly succeed; it is, therefore, pointless to wage a bitter and ill-conceived war against those who are loyal to only one aspect of the Jewish character. If the only bar to separating the various spiritual elements that are present within the congregation of Israel were that this is prohibited by the law of the Torah, then we would indeed be duty-bound to resist this to the very end. But since such a sundering is an absolute impossibility, we can rest assured that its protagonists can err only in theory, but not in practice. No matter what they may think, the particular element of the Jewish spirit that they may make their own, being rooted in the total life of our people, must inevitably contain every aspect of its ethos.

Our quarrel with them must be directed only to the specific task of demonstrating their error and of proving to them that all their effort to fragmentize the higher unity of Israel is foredoomed to failure. We who represent the integrity of the Jewish will and spirit must react in a deeply natural way, by merely analyzing the opposing positions to show that any individual element of the Jewish spirit cannot help but include all the values that the "sunderers" hope to forget and destroy. Once this truth is established, our opponents will ultimately have to realize that they were wasting their efforts. The values they attempted to banish were nonetheless present, if only in an attenuated and distorted form, in their theories, and the result of their labors could only be spiritual hunger, narrowed horizons, and the loss of any true sense of direction. One path alone will then be open to our adversaries; to acknowledge the truth proved by experience and to cleave to the entire living and holy content of the fully manifest Light of Israel. Their souls will then no longer be tortured by nebulous and ghostlike ideas from which they could neither free themselves nor find in them clear illumination of the spirit. They will then realize that nationalism, or religion, or any other element of the spirit of Israel, can realize itself only in the context of a Jewish life that is full, stirring, and entirely true to every shade of its essence.

LIGHTS FOR REBIRTH (1910-1930)

OUR NATIONAL LIFE, both intrinsically and in its relationship to all mankind, has had a long career. We have existed for a long time, and we have, therefore, expressed ourselves in many ways. We are a great people, and our mistakes are equally great; therefore, our woes and the consolations to follow them are both on the grand scale.

It is a fundamental error to turn our backs on the only source of our high estate and to discard the concept that we are a chosen people. We are not only different from all the nations, set apart by a historical experience that is unique and unparalleled, but we are also of a much higher and greater spiritual order. Really to know ourselves, we must be conscious of our greatness. Else we shall fall very low.

Our soul encompasses the entire universe, and represents it in its highest unity. It is, therefore, whole and complete, entirely free of all the disjointedness and the contradictions which prevail among all other peoples. We are one people, one as the oneness of the universe. This is the enormous spiritual potential of our innate character, and the various processes of our historical road, the road of light that passes between the mountains of darkness and perdition, are leading us to realize the hidden essence of our nature. All the mundane sine-qua-nons of national identity are transmuted by the all-inclusiveness of the spirit of Israel.

It is impossible to lop off any branch from the great, leafy tree of our life and to give it an existence of its own. Every fiber of our being would be roused to opposition and, in total self-awareness, we would react with all the inner strength at our command. The long road of our history has been determined by the hope for complete renascence of ourselves and of everything that is ours. Nothing can be ignored—not a single line in the image of our people dare be erased.

Yes, we are stronger than all the cultures of the ages and more enduring than all the permanencies of the world. Our longing is to reawaken to life in the amplitude of our ancestors—and to be even greater and more exalted than they were. We have made great moral contributions to the world, and we are now ready to become its teacher of joyous and vibrant living. Our spirit is unafraid of the passing ages; it gives birth to these ages and puts its stamp upon them. The power of our creativity is such that it impresses the most sublime spirituality on the practical stuff of life. As life evolves toward higher forms, this creative power increases, and the process of its fashioning the world into tangible expressions of the spirit becomes ever more marvelous to behold. All this will reach its highest fulfillment when our Jewish life is renascent in all its facets.

Society today is in a state of movement and tumult; but how poor and stultifying is this age, and how vast is the void that remains in the heart, after all the high-pitched emotions of wars and rumors of wars —for all of this is bereft of ultimate purpose and represents only the passing life of one or another group of men. Nor is there much greater value even to broad social revolutions, especially when these are attended by major upheavals which inflame the heart and confuse the mind. Without an ultimate spiritual ideal which can raise the whole of man's striving to the level of the highest forms that reason and sublime emotion can conceive, no movement can be of any value, or long endure.

But let us return to the Divine purpose, which is to realize the general good through the perfection of every person and group. It is not enough to exemplify this ideal at a moment of high emotion. To approach the estate of spiritual wholeness and to be assured of survival, a society must express the ideal clearly in every aspect of its soul. That which is beyond the reach of language will be said, in all its force, by the future all-encompassing and eternal divine order.

True, in the days of our decline the sparks of spiritual light are dim, and they are present, for the most part, in the memories embodied in our traditional way of life, in all the religious commandments and rules which stem from the past and look toward the future. But these conserve enormous vitality, and the dust that spiritual callousness has allowed to collect on them will be shaken off by a really serious movement of national renascence. The fiery sparks will become visible; they will join in becoming a great divine flame, warming the world and illuminating its uttermost reaches.

Our present is but a translated shadow of our great past; it is always turned toward the lofty future, a future that is so exalted that it lights up the present and gives it dimensions of active power unwarranted by its real estate, which is one of waiting and longing for the future. Everything depends on the value of the past and the future: Some pasts and futures can give light and warmth only to the most immediate present, and others are great enough to make of the present, which lives by their power, an age that is truly alive and creative. Our past is a great one, and our future is even greater, as is evidenced by our striving for the ideals of justice that are latent in our souls. This great force inspirits our present and gives it full life. From the deep range of our memories we draw many examples, a particular kind of wisdom and creativity, a unique outlook on the world, *mitzvot*, traditions, and customs—all suffused with spiritual content, love, and gentleness, and nurtured by the dew of life, heroism, and majesty—by our own gentleness, our own heroism, and our own majesty.

APART FROM the nourishment it receives from the life-giving dew of the holiness of Eretz Israel, Jewry in the Diaspora has no real foundation and lives only by the power of a vision and by the memory of our glory, i.e., by the past and the future. But there is a limit to the power of such a vision to carry the burden of life and to give direction to the career of a people—and this limit seems already to have been reached. Diaspora Jewry is therefore disintegrating at an alarming rate, and there is no hope for it unless it replants itself by the wellspring of real life, of inherent sanctity, which can be found only in Eretz Israel. Even one spark of this real life can revive great areas of the kind of life that is but a shadow of a vision. The real and organic holiness of Jewry can become manifest only by the return of the people to its land, the only path that can lead to its renascence. Whatever is sublime in our spirit and our vision can live only to the degree that there will be a tangible life to reinvigorate the tiring dream.

As the world becomes spiritual and the spirit of man develops to higher levels, the demand becomes ever stronger in man that he live in accordance with his true nature. This call contains much truth and justice, and it is incumbent upon the moral leadership that they purify it and direct it into the right channel. Man increasingly discovers God within himself, in his correct impulses; even those inner drives which appear on the surface to stray from what is conventionally held to be the true road, man can raise to such a high level that they, too, contribute to the ultimate good.

On awakening to life, the community of Israel will rediscover its courage and dignity. The purity and holiness that it used to demonstrate in submission is ever more being displayed through the courage of the soul in deeds of national heroism. These two states will become one, and, in their uniting, heroism will become all the greater because it will have been made sweeter by holiness.

THERE IS an eternal covenant which assures the whole House of Israel that it will not ever become completely unclean. Yes, it may be partially corroded, but it can never be totally cut off from the source of divine life. Many of the adherents of the present national revival maintain that they are secularists. If a Jewish secular nationalism were really imaginable, then we would, indeed, be in danger of falling so low as to be beyond redemption.

But Jewish secular nationalism is a form of self-delusion: the spirit of Israel is so closely linked to the spirit of God that a Jewish nationalist, no matter how secularist his intention may be, must, despite himself, affirm the divine. An individual can sever the tie that binds him to life eternal, but the House of Israel as a whole cannot. All of its most cherished national possessions—its land, language, history, and customs—are vessels of the spirit of the Lord.

How should men of faith respond to an age of ideological ferment which affirms all of these values in the name of nationalism and denies their source, the rootedness of the national spirit, in God? To oppose Jewish nationalism, even in speech, and to denigrate its values is not permissible, for the spirit of God and the spirit of Israel are identical. What they must do is to work all the harder at the task of uncovering the light and holiness implicit in our national spirit, the divine element which is its core. The secularists will thus be constrained to realize that they are immersed and rooted in the life of God and bathed in the radiant sanctity that comes from above.

DESPITE THE GRAVE FAULTS of which we are aware in our life in general, and in Eretz Israel in particular, we must feel that we are being reborn and that we are being created once again as at the beginning of time. Our entire spiritual heritage is presently being absorbed within its source and is reappearing in a new guise, much reduced in material extent but qualitatively very rich and luxuriant and full of vital force. We are called to a new world suffused with the highest light, to an epoch the glory of which will surpass that of all the great ages which have preceded. All of our people believes that we are in the first stage of the Final Redemption. This deep faith is the very secret of its existence; it is the divine mystery implicit in its historical experience. This ancient tradition about the Redemption bears witness to the spiritual light by which the Jew understands him-

self and all the events of his history to the last generation, the one
that is awaiting the Redemption that is near at hand.

THE CLAIM of our flesh is great. We require a healthy body. We
have greatly occupied ourselves with the soul and have forsaken the
holiness of the body. We have neglected health and physical prowess,
forgetting that our flesh is as sacred as our spirit. We have turned our
backs on physical life, the development of our senses, and all that is
involved in the tangible reality of the flesh, because we have fallen
prey to lowly fears, and have lacked faith in the holiness of the Land.
"Faith is exemplified by the tractate *Zeraim* (*Plants*)—man proves
his faith in eternal life by planting."[1]

Our return will succeed only if it will be marked, along with its
spiritual glory, by a physical return which will create healthy flesh
and blood, strong and well-formed bodies, and a fiery spirit encased
in powerful muscles. Then the one weak soul will shine forth from
strong and holy flesh, as a symbol of the physical resurrection of the
dead.

SAMUEL HAYYIM LANDAU   1892-1928

RELIGIOUS ZIONISM, too, produced some rebels. Its second generation, men who grew to maturity toward the end of the First World War, first expressed themselves through a youth movement. They differed with their elders by becoming markedly more impatient with Jewish life in the Diaspora and more eager not to leave the task—and the honor—of colonizing Palestine to the secularists. Though these young men were no less punctiliously observant of the Law than all other religious Zionists, here, too, there was a difference. Like Kook, who was later to influence some of them directly, they too were dreaming of a new and vibrant piety which could be experienced only on the soil of the Holy Land; to this they added, under some socialist influence, that to renew itself Jewish religion needed to be freed from its usual setting in the middle classes. By the early 1920's all these ideas added up to more than a religious youth movement; not yet a "party," they had become an ideology—religio-socialist Zionism.

Samuel Hayyim Landau was not the true initiator of this school of thought (historical evidence suggests that that honor belongs to Isaac Rivkind), but he was its outstanding early personality. Landau was born in 1892 in a Polish town dominated by Hasidism, and he always retained his allegiance to the Hasidic rebbe (master) of his youth and to the emotional piety which pervaded this early environment. He suffered much during the First World War, for his native Poland was a major battlefield. The Russian army once almost shot him as a hostage; later, during the "small war" between the newly independent Poland and the Bolsheviks, the Poles suspected him of being an undercover agent for the enemy and revoked his death sentence only at the last moment.

Right after the wars Landau joined the Mizrahi (religious Zionist) movement and rose rapidly to its top leadership in Poland. He was recognized as the spokesman and ideologist of the younger group,

and many of the stirrings toward pioneering in Palestine and toward
a conscious religious socialism crystallized around him. Landau spent
the last three years of his life in Palestine, where he moved after his
election as a member of the central office of religious Zionism. He
died there in the late spring of 1928 at the age of thirty-six.

TOWARD AN EXPLANATION OF OUR
IDEOLOGY (1924)

JEWRY, and religious Jewry in particular, has always attached prime
importance to the rebuilding of Eretz Israel. The Hovevei Zion regarded it as a national duty; for the religious it was a divine commandment as well, one equal in importance to all the other precepts of the
Torah. In the religious view it was, therefore, an ultimate value, and
the sense of obligation to this task was unconditioned even by national
loyalty. "To dwell in the Holy Land is a *mitzvah*"—the commandment might be interpreted as either national or religious, but it was
essentially abstract and mystical. The role of the nation in the process
of rebuilding the land was realized solely through the obedience of its
individuals to this commandment; it bore no relationship to the national existence and character of the Jewish people. Such a viewpoint
could not inspire our people to labor for the rebuilding of the land.
Its effect was largely negative, because the commandment to dwell in
the land, understood only as a *mitzvah* incumbent upon each individual Jew, could be obeyed in many ways that were totally unrelated
to a true rebuilding.

Zionism came into the world to announce a fundamental change.
This movement emphasized that the concept of nationhood is the
primal value of our people. The entire program of Zionism, therefore,
revolves around this idea, and all other national values are significant
only to the degree that they serve as instruments of the absolute—the
nation. Even the rebuilding of the land is secondary, for the land
was created for the nation and not the nation for the land.

This approach is shared by the religious wing of the Jewish national
movement as well; even though it may derive its reason for rebuilding
Eretz Israel from the divine commandment mentioned above, this

mitzvah itself is understood as rooted in the idea of the national renaissance. Did not the Talmud teach that "the Torah was created for the sake of Israel?" It is therefore self-evident that our approach to the rebuilding of the land must be governed by the ultimate goal, the national renaissance. We can admit only such guidelines as indispensable to our labors as are logically implied by the one absolute value. Even the idea of "Torah Va-Avodah" (Torah and Labor), which we have made our fundamental blueprint for the regeneration of Eretz Israel, must be measured by this yardstick.

What do we mean by Torah?

This "Torah," the heritage of Israel, has two basic meanings: The first refers to the Torah as a code of law which is incumbent upon the individual, which every single Jew must obey; the second connotes the Torah as a totality, as the national spirit, the source of its culture and life—i.e., the national and collective aspects of the Torah. (These ideas are, of course, not new.) In its individual aspect the Torah is unrelated to the nation as nation; it relates only to the children of Israel as individuals. In this sense it is an obligation that rests on every Jew in the Diaspora, and all the more so in the Land of Israel. This, however, implies no specific and essential connection between the Torah and the process of rebirth in Eretz Israel. The second meaning of Torah, as the collective spirit of the people, implies a totally different relationship. The Torah, interpreted in this sense, permeates completely the process of the national renaissance, appearing as both cause and effect, and it is therefore as related to the essence of the renaissance as the flame is to the glowing ember. A national renaissance is inconceivable without the national spirit, "for our people is not a people except through its Torah," and the spirit of our people cannot express itself unless there be a national revival in our own Land, for "the divine spark can influence our people only in its own Land."

In this sense—but only in this sense—the Torah is more than the command which individual Jews, the national vanguard in the Holy Land included, must obey; it is the *primum mobile*, the essential element, and the efficient cause of the national revival. It is more than the signpost and mold of individual and collective life; it denotes the ultimate spiritual source of the movement.

II

WHAT WE HAVE SAID about "Torah" applies also to "Avodah" (Labor).

Seemingly, there is now general agreement that labor is an important factor in the colonization of Eretz Israel, and that all who come or intend to come must work, and indeed that only those have a right to *aliyah* who are trained and prepared to work. Nonetheless we cannot deduce from this that labor as *ideal*, as a basic and essential component of the general idea of the national renaissance, has prevailed within our national movement. To subscribe to the necessity and usefulness of labor is not necessarily to accept the concept which was born in the mind of the founders and vanguard of the labor movement in Eretz Israel, that labor as idea and value possesses the power to effect our national regeneration. Labor out of intellectual commitment, informed by the right intent and attitude of the worker, can rise to the level of an act not merely of obligation and individual compulsion but of national rebirth.

This concept requires much elucidation. What does "Avodah" mean?

If "Avodah" is intended only as solution of the economic problem, it bears no more than a temporal relation, one of day-to-day existence, to the national movement. It affects the individual members of the nation, be they few or many, and involves the community only in the quantitative sense, through the individuals that comprise it, and not the "eternal life," the quality of the people. "Avodah" determined by such "practical" considerations is bereft of any basic positive value as the premise of a movement engaged in creating a new life. To serve such a function "Avodah" must be elevated to a higher level related to the very essence of national ideology.

What is this higher level? Some identify it with the moral aspect of labor. Commerce, so they assert, is shot through with swindle and deceit; only the life of labor contains objective possibilities for ordering society on foundations of justice and righteousness. This idea can, however, be contradicted. To be sure, it supplies labor with moral significance by ascribing to it a purpose nobler than the mere filling of the stomach, but even so lofty a purpose does not make for a movement of national renaissance. Its intent is not to deal with the forms of social life but to create a basis for national existence. It is concerned with the fundamental problem, the creation of life, and all questions of economic, social, and moral order are subsidiary in rank. The desire to make "Avodah" a basic premise of the renaissance is actually an organic expression of the essence of the movement of national rebirth—this is the new word of the labor movement in Eretz Israel. Labor is important not for economic reasons, or even for the sake of social morality and righteousness (lofty though these values be), but for the sake of the renaissance. All the rest is commentary on this basic idea, that "Avodah" is identical with the national renaissance and the return of its children to a forsaken people.

III

IN EXILE Israel ceased to be a nation, or, to be more precise, a living nation. The term "nation" denotes the unique element, the collective personality, the organic and creative community which is more than the sum of its individual parts. A nation is a living entity in its own right, a collective "I," and not merely an aggregate of individuals. The nation is the agency by which the individual relates himself to the world, to the whole of creation, and becomes part of humanity and the cosmos.

A distinction must be drawn between "nation" and "people." "People" refers to spiritual factors—to characteristics of soul, race, and history—which determine the nature of the collective. "Nation" encompasses all the aspects of life, including physical needs, class and status, and economic pursuits. "People" points to the spiritual element of national life, and "nation" means the soul and body together, the soul as the force giving life to and encased in its own particular body. In exile Israel ceased to be such a "nation."

A nation which has no land, which—whether willingly or perforce—has severed itself from natural life, and which is subject to the will and whims of others—such a folk, despite all its unique spiritual qualities, genius, and abilities, is, by definition, not a nation. Conscious and unconscious parasitism, both individual and collective, has become its second nature. It knows that it is always sustained by others, and dependent upon them for its daily bread; it therefore regards itself as an adjunct of other nations and not as something existing in its own right—hence, the negative attitude toward labor and productivity, the lack of respect for the worker as a partner in the divine process of creation, and the feeling of pity tinged with contempt for anyone who "must," alas, be a workingman. In short: "When a people falls into ruin . . ."

This is the area in which the work of revival must begin.

Its object and purpose is to imbue a scattered and disintegrated conglomerate with new life, with a collective personality, and to make this conglomerate into a "nation" by restoring to it the conditions which are necessary—nay, imperative—to national being. This is the source of the desire for the return to Zion, and it is also the *mystique* of the labor movement.

Labor—this is the beginning of rebuilding the ruins of our nation. National life means total creative independence, activism, and separate existence and sovereignty. It necessitates war against all forms of parasitism—a war the weapons of which are labor and creativity. Labor is therefore the beginning and foundation of the renaissance.

There is a basic difference between a labor movement in this sense and the proletarian movements in general. The latter are concerned with the question of the economic order or, at their highest, with social justice. A precondition for such movements is an already existing life which they propose to reform. This is the obvious and natural situation among nations which are really enjoying a national life, of whatever moral stature, in their native lands. The labor movement in Eretz Israel faces a radically different problem, for its basic task is to create the very beginnings of national life.

This fundamental distinction between seemingly similar labor movements necessitates many other differences in the scope of activity and the tactics to be used to attain their respective goals. Moreover, it is beyond doubt that the more the labor movement in Eretz Israel approximates the program and tone of the general proletarian movement, to that degree it is estranging itself from its own proper form, denying the idea which gave it birth, emptying itself of national spiritual content and substituting for it values which are foreign and antithetical to the spirit which molded it at its origin. But our present subject is the idea, the spiritual essence, of the labor movement and not the aberrations of those who make it act in the real world in a way alien to its real self. What I am defining is the doctrine of "Avodah" and the way of life that properly follows from it.

IV

AFTER THESE GENERAL REMARKS about the terms "Torah" and "Avodah" I wish to dwell briefly on their interrelationship as the slogan of the Mizrahi youth movement.

As was maintained above, the national rebirth is the ultimate value of both Torah and Labor. Torah in the sense of a way of life and an outlook encompassing life in all the ramifications, from the most profane to the most sacred, from the most mundane to the most spiritual, all of which are illumined and hallowed by its light—Torah, in this sense, is both a precondition of the national renaissance and predicated upon it. For, even though it is possible for individuals, and for the community as an aggregate of individuals, to observe all the commandments of religion, including the laws applying only to those who dwell in Eretz Israel, nonetheless "Torah" in its broad and true sense—life permeated by Torah and Torah permeating life—cannot be realized except by Israel as a nation and by individuals organically related to the nation. This is the real meaning of the rebirth—the rebirth of our nation in its own land.

The same is true of "Avodah." In its broadest and most inclusive meaning, as cause of the creation of a nation and the re-establishment of its life, "Avodah" is inextricably interwoven with the national movement. These two concepts, "Torah" and "Avodah," are therefore two forms of the same essence, the *Renaissance*, which requires both of them to rise to full stature.

"Torah and Avodah" are united by their spiritual origin and their ultimate goal. They cannot be severed from each other without mortally wounding both, because a half-form and a half-renaissance are inconceivable.

Torah cannot be reborn without labor, and labor, as a creative and nation-building force, cannot be reborn without Torah—Torah which is the essence of the *Renaissance*.

This is the whole of our ideology.

JUDAH LEON MAGNES   1877-1948

MAGNES WAS AN ARISTOCRAT, conscious of his powers, who could not help being a disturber of the peace and the tribune of the masses. He began as an American Reform rabbi, and toward the end of his life he was most at home, by feeling, in a small Hasidic synagogue in Jerusalem. As Zionist, Magnes traversed the spectrum from early adherence to Herzl and closeness to socialist Zionism, through a continuing attachment to the teachings and persons of Ahad Ha-Am and Solomon Schechter, to the loneliness of his last twenty years, when he headed a small, but intellectually notable, group of more or less unqualified pacifists who were trying to find a basis for an Arab-Jewish compromise—and the people to do the compromising. Magnes, too, was an original.

He was born in San Francisco in 1877, and after graduation from high school he chose to go to Cincinnati to take the combined course leading to a rabbinic degree at its university and at the Reform rabbinical seminary, the Hebrew Union College. After his ordination in 1900 Magnes studied for two years in Europe, mostly at the universities of Berlin and Heidelberg, and then was associated for one year with the faculty of his seminary in Cincinnati. In 1904 he accepted a call to Brooklyn, to be the rabbi of its leading Reform synagogue, Temple Israel. Magnes came to this congregation not to limit himself to its immediate service but to be part of the tumultuous life of New York's Jewry.

In that day a chasm divided the "uptown," Americanized, religiously reformed, overwhelmingly anti-Zionist group to which Magnes belonged by birth and social class, from the growing masses on the "East Side," who were east Europeans, Yiddish-speaking, and adherents of orthodoxy in religion, or of the newer doctrines of socialism or Zionism, or of several of these faiths at once. Magnes was not alone in the first decade of this century in his deep concern for these immigrants. Jewish leaders of his own circle were laboring diligently to assimilate their poor brethren as rapidly as possible into American society; these years were the zenith of muckraking in American life as a whole, and men like Lincoln Steffens had written much about the economic exploitation to which these immigrants were being subjected. What set Magnes apart was his deep sense of personal identification with the east Europeans, with their more traditional modes of Jewish life and their sense of Jewish nationhood. Magnes derived these emotions from Zionism, to which he had been converted in his Berlin days. Once in New York, he became secretary of the American Zionist Federation (1905–1908), led the protest activities evoked by the pogroms in Russia in 1903 and 1905, and fought within his congregation for a revision of its reformed position toward a greater religious traditionalism.

In the further stages of his career in New York, Magnes was for two years (1908–1910) associate rabbi of the most important Reform congregation in America, Temple Emanu-El, but parted company with it over his religious traditionalism; he served for a year as the rabbi of a Conservative synagogue, B'nai Jeshurun, but its more moderate religious liberalism was equally unacceptable to him; Magnes then organized his own congregation, called the Society for the Advancement of Judaism, which he lead until 1920.

During his stay at Temple Emanu-El Magnes was the leading spirit in initiating the one great attempt in the history of New York to organize a unified Jewish community, a *kehillah*. In the war years Magnes was among the leaders of American Jewish relief efforts in Europe, helping to organize the major agency to do that work, the Joint Distribution Committee. This decade was marked by two other important developments in his life: Magnes was ever more out of step with official Zionism, and in 1915 he resigned from the American branch of the movement; neither a Jewish state nor Jewish mass political action, but his religious version of Ahad Ha-Amism—careful colonization and spiritual rebirth—seemed to him to be the meaning of Zionism. Magnes was becoming ever lonelier on another score, because he had become a pacifist, and despite bitter attacks he would not silence his convictions during the war years.

The greatest practical labor of Magnes's life was the Hebrew University in Jerusalem. He had been interested in this idea from his earliest days in Zionism, and after he moved to Palestine in 1922 he soon was heavily involved in the preliminaries to the actual opening of the new institution. When the university began classes in 1925 he became its chancellor and, in 1935, its president; he saw it through to the erection of its buildings on Mount Scopus (now still cut off behind the Jordanian border) and its rise almost to its present academic stature. He died on a trip to New York in October 1948. In Palestine Magnes's political beliefs made him a figure of great controversy. Contrary to most Zionist opinion, he doubted that a Jewish state in Palestine could be established—certainly not peaceably. The only hope that he saw for the implementation of the Jewish aims essential to him was in a binational state. The essay below, in which he first gave full public expression to his views, is in itself an historic document. There had been bloody outbreaks by the Arabs in August 1929, triggered by wild tales that the Jews intended to seize the Mosque of Omar and throw it down in order to clear its site for the rebuilding of the Temple. In the very midst of a wave of fear and anger within Palestinian Jewry, Magnes, though he knew he would be denounced, issued a pamphlet in English, Hebrew, and German of which the pages given here are the essence.

"LIKE ALL THE NATIONS?" (1930)

THE DISCUSSION concerning the future political regime in Palestine is now happily beginning to take on a more or less objective character and the searching question is being asked as to what we want here. What is our Zionism? What does Palestine mean for us?

As to what we should want here I can answer for myself in almost the same terms that I have been in the habit of using many years:

Immigration.

Settlement on the land.

Hebrew life and culture.

If you can guarantee these for me, I should be willing to yield the Jewish state, and the Jewish majority; and on the other hand I would agree to a legislative assembly together with a democratic political regime so carefully planned and worked out that the above three fundamentals could not be infringed. Indeed, I should be willing to pay almost any price for these three, especially since this price would in my opinion also secure tranquillity and mutual understanding. If the Jews really have an historical connection with Palestine, and what student of history will deny it, and if the Jewish people is to be in Palestine not on sufferance (as during the days of the Turks) but as of right—a right solemnly recognized by most governments and by the League of Nations, and also by thinking Arabs—then surely these three rights are elemental and hardly to be contested.

Whether through temperament or other circumstances I do not at all believe, and I think the facts are all against believing, that without Palestine the Jewish people is dying out or is doomed to destruction. On the contrary it is growing stronger; and what is more, it should grow stronger, for Palestine without communities in the dispersion would be bereft of much of its significance as a spiritual center for the Judaism of the world. To me it seems that there are three chief elements in Jewish life, in the following order of importance: the living Jewish people—now some sixteen million; the Torah, in the broadest sense of this term, i.e., all our literature and documents and history, as also the great religious and ethical and social ideals the Torah contains for use and development in the present and the future; and third, the Land of Israel. My view is that the people and the Torah can exist and be creative as they have existed and have been creative without the Land; that, however, the Land is one of the chief means, if not the chief means, of revivifying and deepening the people and the Torah.

The living Jewish people is primary. It is the living carrier and vessel of Judaism, the Jewish spirit. It has used even its Exile for spreading light and learning. Palestine can help this people to understand itself, to give an account of itself, to an intensification of its culture, a deepening of its philosophy, a renewal of its religion. Palestine can help this people perform its great ethical mission as a national-international entity. But this eternal and far-flung people does not need a Jewish state for the purpose of maintaining its very existence. The Jewish community throughout the world is a wondrous and paradoxical organism. It participates in the life of many nations, yet in spite of numberless predictions in the past and the present, it is not absorbed by them. It is patriotic in every land, yet it is international, cosmopolitan. Palestine cannot solve the Jewish problem of the Jewish people. Wherever there are Jews there is the Jewish problem. It is part of the Jewish destiny to face this problem and make it mean something of good for mankind.

Nor are the Jews dying out, despite their weaknesses, their mixed marriages, their ignorance of Judaism, and the deterioration that has laid hold of many a limb. I see them in America growing healthier and stronger in numbers and intellectual power. Their hearts respond generously to every Jewish call. They are multiplying their communities, their synagogues, schools, societies, libraries, unions. They are acquiring economic independence, and their sons and daughters are getting what the universities and colleges can give them. They are ignorant of Judaism. But they are asking eagerly, mostly in vain, to know what Judaism is. Perhaps it is not the fault of the teachers that the answers take so long in coming. Judaism is a complex phenomenon. It is and it is not religion, philosophy, ethics, politics, ceremonies, life. The answer as to what it is and may mean to a new generation cannot come overnight.

This is a day of ferment throughout the world, also within Judaism. The materials are there and are in the hands of the Potter. Palestine can perhaps help fashion this clay more than any one factor. But it is a living Jewish people everywhere that Palestine must serve. It is a people of useful citizens permeating the life of hundreds of communities, and yet giving evidence of the changelessness of that mystic phenomenon—their continued existence as a body set apart and separate. They are scattered, yet are one; they are unorganized, yet held together through spiritual bonds more subtle than organization. One sees this people in all the lands of its exile continuing to yield out of its body individuals of mind and spirit in the arts and sciences, and common soldiers for groups whose goal is the betterment of our human lot. The dispersion of this people, the Diaspora, is a marvelous instrumentality for the fulfillment of its function as a teacher. The dispersion is an irrevocable, historical fact, and Palestine can be a means of making this fact into an even greater blessing.

Unfortunately, one hears most of that Zionism which is not born of a positive, hopeful relationship toward the tremendous, unique fact of the Diaspora but of despair. It is a Zionism that loathes the ghetto (which it identifies with the dispersion), and that is so in despair of the future of Diaspora Judaism, and that in its own way loves Jews and Judaism so passionately that the further existence of Jews and Judaism is thought impossible if the present-day Palestine be not made ready to act as savior.

Palestine is the center of this organism, but by no means all of it. The dispersion and Palestine are both required for the fullest development of the Jewish people. This peculiar people could not be content with either, alone. This *sui generis* organism which we call the Jewish people has need of these all-embracing, complicated forms—

an intensive center and a great periphery. The complete salvation and working power of Judaism is dependent upon both together.

But if I have thus exalted the Diaspora, what is Palestine to us? It is the Land of Israel, our Holy Land. It is holy for us in a practical and a mystic sense. Its holiness attracts our old and our young, the religious and the nonreligious from faraway places, and they want to work its soil, and build up an ethical community, and thereby make the land still more sacred. Its very landscape and color help every child and simple man among us to understand our classic literature and our history. It helps us as no other means does to lay bare our very soul, to get down deep into the sources of our being, as they are recorded for us and as we feel and apprehend them among these hills and valleys and deserts, and among these peoples, wild yet related. The sources of being, history. Does history really mean so much? The individual does without it, but the community is a Bedouin camp without it. If we want to live, the more intensive must be our apprehension of our history and literature. Palestine served Israel in exile for centuries in this regard even though it was but a far-off ideal. Palestine as a reality is itself the very scroll on which our history is written and spread out for us.

Three great things this poor little land has already given Israel in two generations. Hebrew has become a living possession and has thus restored to us and our children the sources of our history and our mind, and has thus given us the medium again for classic, permanent Jewish expression. The second great thing is the return of Jews to the soil, not only for the sake of a living from the soil but also for the sake of their love of this particular soil and its indissoluble connection with the body of the Jewish people. Third, the brave attempt on the part of city-bred, school-bred young Jews—moderns of the modern—to work out in life, in the cities and on the land, a synthesis between the radicalism of their social outlook and their ancestral Judaism. It is problems of the same nature that a whole world in travail is laboring to solve; and among Jewry no more splendid attempt at a synthesis has been made than here, in everyday life and not in theory alone.

The beginnings of all this, and much more than the beginnings, were made under the Turks; and Palestine is of such moment to us that it is capable of giving us much even though our community here be poor and small. I have indicated above that I do not want it to be poor and small. But poor and small and faithful to Judaism, rather than large and powerful like all the nations.

It is in derogation of the actual importance of the living Jewish people and of Judaism to place them on one side of the scale and have it balanced by the relatively unimportant Arab community of Palestine. The true parallels and balancing forces are Jews and Judaism on the one side, and the Arab peoples and even all of Islam on the other. In this way you get a truer perspective of the whole and you increase the significance of Palestine as being that point where in this new day Judaism meets Islam again throughout all its confines, as once they met centuries back to the ultimate enrichment of human culture.

Our theories may differ as to the purposes Palestine may or may not serve. But there is no question that it is now serving as a testing ground, a dangerous frontier land for the lovers of peace in Israel. Much of the theory of Zionism has been concerned with making the Jews into a normal nation in Palestine like the gentiles of the lands and the families of the earth. The desire for power and conquest seems to be normal to many human beings and groups, and we, being the ruled everywhere, must here rule; being the minority everywhere, we must here be in the majority. There is the *Wille zur Macht*, the state, the army, the frontiers. We have been in exile; now we are to be masters in our own Home. We are to have a Fatherland, and we are to encourage the feelings of pride, honor, glory that are part of the paraphernalia of the ordinary nationalistic patriotism. In the face of such danger one thinks of the dignity and originality of that passage in the liturgy which praises the Lord of all things that our portion is not like theirs and our lot not like that of all the multitude.

We are told that when we become the majority we shall then show how just and generous a people in power can be. That is like the man who says that he will do anything and everything to get rich, so that he may do good with the money thus accumulated. Sometimes he never grows rich—he fails. And if he does grow rich under those circumstances his power of doing good has been atrophied from long lack of use. In other words, it is not only the end which for Israel must be desirable, but what is of equal importance, the means must be conceived and brought forth in cleanliness. If as a minority we insist upon keeping the other man from achieving just aims, and if we keep him from this with the aid of bayonets, we must not be surprised if we are attacked and, what is worse, if moral degeneration sets in among us.

The anti-Semite has accused us of being democrats and liberals and radicals everywhere on the ground that we are not deeply rooted in

any soil. He has charged us with having no conservative instincts because we have no real hearth and home, boundaries and property of
our ancestors to defend. We are spectators, onlookers, bystanders, he
says. We have always answered, that should we have the opportunity
of exercising statecraft on our own soil, we would as participant and
not as bystander uphold our prophetic traditions.

Now, here we are, and it seems to be harder for us as a minority
than we had pictured it as a majority. It is as though Providence
itself was putting us to the test. We, the great democrats of the world,
are trying to find every kind of reason to justify the denial of even
the beginning of democracy to ourselves and others. I am afraid of
this demoralization. For the Jewish people no high end will ever
justify low means. We have been nurtured too long in the rabbinic
tradition for that. This may be disappointing to some. It may even
excite the contempt of those two Englishmen and that Jew who told
me not so long ago that, as the history of all conquest and colonization shows, the only possible hope of success is frankly to espouse
the Joshua method. Perhaps so. At least I do not believe it, and I
know that plain Jews everywhere and the plain Jews who have come
here to live and work do not believe it. But if it be so, the Jewish
people, thank God, will never be successful conquerors and colonizers.
Neither the hostile world nor their own soul will let them.

I have no illusions about the Jews here becoming a Quaker community. That would be too good to be true. Nor do I see the possibility in Palestine or elsewhere of doing without adequate police
protection. This ought to be given everywhere by any government
worthy of the name; and if a future government be as helpless as this
one, we might have to take measures which all the world should know
about. What I am driving at is to distinguish between two policies. The
one maintains that we can establish a Jewish Home here through the
suppression of the political aspirations of the Arabs, and therefore a
Home necessarily established on bayonets over a long period—a policy
which I think bound to fail because of the violence against us it
would occasion, and because good opinion in Britain and the conscience of the Jewish people itself would revolt against it. The other
policy holds that we can establish a Home here only if we are true to
ourselves as democrats and internationalists, thus being just and help-
ful to others, and that we ask for the protection of life and property
the while we are eagerly and intelligently and sincerely at work to
find a *modus vivendi et operandi* with our neighbors. The world—not
in Palestine alone—may be bent upon violence and bloodshed. But

will not my opponent agree that there is a better chance of averting this tendency to bloodshed if we make every possible effort politically as well as in other ways to work hand in hand—as teachers, helpers, friends—with this awakening Arab world?

You ask me, Do I want to quit? No, I do not. The Jew will not abandon the Land of Israel. He cannot abandon it. I have said that Palestine is of value by and of itself—its rocks, its hills, its ruins, its beauty—and that it is of value to Judaism even if our community here be small and poor. I am afraid the first of the quitters will be those who say it is useless except we be in the majority. But I also know that we cannot establish our work as it should be established if it be against the determined will of the Arab world, and if we have not the good will of the good European world on our side. Palestine means so much in the Jewish scheme of things that I am sure that if the experiment fails, Heaven forbid, this time (due, as always, partly to our own sins) there will be another time. But I do not want it to fail, and the only way it can succeed, so it seems to me, and that success is worth having, is if we overcome all obstacles through all the weapons of civilization except bayonets: spiritual, intellectual, social, cultural, financial, economic, medical . . . brotherly, friendly weapons. The Jew may have to be prepared to face for a further period the hostility of a section of Arabs and of English and others. Provided our own attitude is just and fair we should face that opposition and not abandon the struggle. Our goal must be to have our enterprise rest upon the conviction of all concerned that it is right and just.

Palestine is holy to the Jew in that his attitude toward this Land is necessarily different from his attitude toward any other land. He may have to live in other lands upon the support of bayonets, but that may well be something which he, as a Jew, cannot help. But when he goes voluntarily as a Jew to repeople his own Jewish Homeland, it is by an act of will, of faith, of free choice, and he should not either will or believe in or want a Jewish Home that can be maintained in the long run only against the violent opposition of the Arab and Moslem peoples. The fact is that they are here in their overwhelming numbers in this part of the world, and whereas it may have been in accord with Israelitic needs in the time of Joshua to conquer the land and maintain their position in it with the sword, that is not in accord with the desire of plain Jews or with the long ethical tradition of Judaism that has not ceased developing to this day.

MARTIN BUBER   born 1878

THOUGH BORN IN VIENNA, Martin Buber was by earliest experience a Galician Jew. Until the age of fourteen he was raised in Lemberg in the "enlightened" house of his grandfather, Solomon Buber, who was a wealthy aristocrat and a distinguished figure in modern, "scientific" talmudic scholarship. Though he was not directly part of it as a boy, Martin Buber made contact with the dominant milieu of Galician Jewry, hasidism, which was later to become decisive in his development. In 1896 Buber left for the University of Vienna, and during the next four years he studied in Leipzig, Zurich, and Berlin. He became a Zionist in 1898, and in that year he was the founder of the Zionist organization in Leipzig and of the Jewish students' club at the university. In 1901 Buber worked for some months under Herzl in Vienna as editor of *Die Welt*, the official organ of Zionism. By the end of that year there was a break between him and Herzl, for Buber was ever more a cultural and spiritual, rather than a political, Zionist. He left the editorship and was instrumental, with Weizmann and others, in founding the "democratic fraction" in opposition to Herzl (for cultural reasons) at the Fifth Zionist Congress. Buber soon associated with several of this group in founding a publishing house to encourage a renascence of Jewish spiritual creativity.

Buber withdrew from public activity in 1904 to return to his studies. During this period he both began his writings on Hasidism and devoted himself to investigations in the philosophy of religion. The outlines of his independent Zionist philosophy were becoming clearer in such works as his *Three Speeches About Judaism* (1911), and his influence on central European young Jewish intellectuals was growing. Concurrently Buber was interested in mysticism, Christian and oriental as well as Jewish, and preparing himself for his crucial book in religious philosophy, *I and Thou*, which, though it appeared in 1923, existed in first draft in 1916. These parallel concerns, in developing his Zionist position and in expounding his ever more dialogic and existential philosophy, expressed themselves in the founding and editing of the journal *Der Jude* from 1916 to 1924 and in his later labors, from 1926 to 1930, as copublisher (with the Catholic theologian, Joseph Wittig, and the Protestant psychotherapist, Viktor von Weizsäcker) of *Die Kreatur*, a journal of religious discussion, with particular reference to social and pedagogical problems.

During the 1920's Buber was engaged in an important collaboration with Franz Rosenzweig. Together they completed fourteen volumes of a new German translation of the Bible, to the completion of which Buber has presently returned. Buber was involved with Rosenzweig in founding the famous school of adult Jewish studies in Frankfurt, and after 1923 he was for ten years professor of religion and ethics at the university there. With the advent of Hitler, Buber worked five years as the director of educational activities of the Frankfurt Jewish community, strengthening its inner defenses against the enemy. In 1938 Buber emigrated to Palestine, where he occupied the chair in social philosophy at the Hebrew University until his retirement in 1951. Upon his arrival in Palestine, Buber soon joined with Magnes and others, many of them his disciples from central Europe, in advocating a binational state. He is still the leading spirit of this circle, which is now organized under the name Ihud. Since his retirement Buber has lectured several times in the United States and has taught in other countries as well. He has been the object of some recent controversy in Jewish circles because of his willingness to accept the Goethe prize, tendered him by the city of Hamburg, and because of other evidences of his resuming some contact with the intellectual and cultural life of Germany.

Buber's Jewish position has been much commented upon, and many have said, correctly, that it is the basis for his larger philosophy. It is the common coin of these discussions that his notion that man's deeper self is reached ultimately only in relationship to a group descends from romantic nationalism, from Hegel, and, immediately, from the ideas about *Gemeinschaft* of his contemporary, Gustav Landauer. At first, as in his early work, *Three Speeches About Judaism*, Buber saw the Jewish striving for unity, the hallowing of the deed, and messianism as a folk and racial endowment; in the selections below these views are expressed in the context of his more recent views about the vocation of Israel as the elect of God. What needs to be added here, from the perspective of Zionist intellectual history, is that Buber is inherently related to Berdichevski (Part 5). Both are indebted to

Nietzsche's vision of a new society to be created by men of superior capacity, to his dream of a new morality and a new age. Berdichevski and Buber took the obvious step, for Jews who knew the classical tradition of Judaism and who were turning Zionist, of asserting that the land of Israel was especially and uniquely fit for greatness and that the Jewish people was by nature peculiarly capable of rising to unparalleled heights. They diverged in that Berdichevski imagined the supermen and the superculture of Zionism as perhaps toying with might, while the heroic that Buber sought was in the dimension of morality, of answering the greatest demands that God can make of man.

THE JEW IN THE WORLD (1934)

*Address Delivered at the Lehrhaus
in Frankfort on the Main in 1934*

THE CONCEPT of the "Jew in the world" in its most serious sense did not arise until a certain quite definite juncture. This juncture did not—as one might suppose—coincide with the destruction of the Jewish state by Titus, but with the collapse of the Bar Kokba[1] rebellion. When Jerusalem ceased to be a Jewish city, when the Jew was no longer permitted to be at home in his own country—it was then that he was hurled into the abyss of the world. Ever since, he has represented to the world the insecure man. Within that general insecurity which marks human existence as a whole, there has since that time lived a species of man to whom destiny has denied even the small share of dubious security other beings possess. Whether or not it is aware of it, this people is always living on ground that may at any moment give way beneath its feet. Every symbiosis it enters upon is treacherous. Every alliance in its history contains an invisible terminating clause; every union with other civilizations is informed with a secret divisive force. It is this inescapable state of insecurity which we have in mind when we designate the Jewish Diaspora as *Galut*, i.e., as exile.

What is the cause of this fate of insecurity? The Jewish group plainly cannot be fitted into any known scheme. It resists all historical categories and general concepts; it is unique. This uniqueness of Israel necessarily thwarts the nations' very natural desire for an explanation, and explanation always implies arrangement in categories. The existence of whatever cannot be cubbyholed, and hence understood, is alarming. This state of affairs provides a basis of truth for the observation that anti-Semitism is a kind of fear of ghosts. The wandering, roving, defenseless group which is different from any other and comparable to none seems to the nations among which it lives to have something spectral about it, because it does not fit into any other given group. It could not be otherwise. The Jewish people was, indeed, always a "sinister," homeless specter. This people, which resisted inclusion in any category, a resistance which the other peoples could never become quite accustomed to, was always the first victim of fanatical mass movements (the Crusades of the eleventh century, for instance). It was branded as the cause of mass misfortunes ("the Jew is responsible for the 'Black Death' "). No matter how hard it tried, it never quite succeeded in adjusting to its environment. (The Inquisition followed upon Marranism.)[2]

When I say that the nations regard us as a specter—and this myth is symbolized in the form of the wandering Jew—we must distinguish between being and appearance. We ourselves know very well that we are not specters, but a living community, and so we must ask ourselves what our nonclassifiability really signifies. Is it due merely to a lack of vision and insight on the part of the nations? Is it that we can be fitted into a system, only they are not able to do it? Is this resistance of ours to classification merely a negative phenomenon, one that is temporary? Does it simply mean that we cannot be classified until—at some future time—we are?

We have only *one* way to apprehend the positive meaning of this negative phenomenon: the way of faith. From any viewpoint other than faith, our inability to fit into a category would be intolerable, as something counter to history and counter to nature. But from the viewpoint of faith, our inability to fit into a category is the foundation and meaning of our living avowal of the uniqueness of Israel. We would differentiate this uniqueness from the general uniqueness we attribute to every group and each individual. The uniqueness of Israel signifies something which in its nature, its history, and its vocation is so individual that it cannot be classified.

Moreover, Israel will not fit into the two categories most frequently invoked in attempts at classification: "nation" and "creed." One criterion serves to distinguish a nation from a creed. Nations experience history *as nations*. With individuals as such experience is not history. In creeds, on the other hand, salient experiences are undergone by individuals, and, in their purest and sublime form, these experiences are what we call "revelation." When such individuals communicate their experiences to the masses, and their tidings cause groups to form, a creed comes into being. Thus, nations and creeds differ in the same way as history and revelation. Only in one instance do they coincide. Israel receives its decisive religious experience *as a people*; it is not the prophet alone but the community as such that is involved. The community of Israel experiences history and revelation as one phenomenon, history as revelation and revelation as history. In the hour of its experience of faith the group becomes a people. Only as a people can it hear what it is destined to hear. The unity of nationality and faith which constitutes the uniqueness of Israel is our destiny, not only in the empirical sense of the word; here humanity is touched by the divine.

Now, in order to understand our position in the world, we must realize that a twofold desire comes to the fore in the history of Diaspora Jewry: the insecure Jew strives for security; the Jewish community which cannot be classified strives to be classified. These two strivings are by no means on a par. Like all human longing for security, this search for security is in itself quite legitimate. Man cannot be condemned to spend his life in insecurity. So the striving toward security is unobjectionable, but the means taken to arrive at this desired end may well be questioned. The striving for security is familiar to us from the history of the ancient Hebrew state which presaged the insecurity of the Diaspora in a rather curious way. Wedged between Egypt and Babylonia, the two great powers of the ancient Orient, this state attempted time and again to overcome its geographic and political insecurity by employing power politics. Driven by the hope of overcoming its insecurity, it veered and compromised now with the one side, now with the other. The actual political content of the prophets is a warning against such false security. The prophets knew and predicted that in spite of all its veering and compromising Israel must perish if it intends to exist only as a political structure. It can persist—and this is the paradox in their warning and the paradox of the reality of Jewish history—if it insists *on its vocation of uniqueness*, if it translates into reality the divine words spoken during the making of the Covenant. When the prophets say that there is no security for Israel save that in God, they are not referring to something unearthly, to something "religious" in the common sense of the word; they are referring to the realization of the true communal living to which Israel was summoned by the Covenant with God, and which it is called upon to sustain in history, in the way it alone can. The prophets call upon a people which represents the *first real attempt at "community"* to enter world history as a prototype of that attempt. Israel's function is to encourage the nations to change their inner structure and their relations to one another. By maintaining such relations with the nations and being involved in the development of humanity, Israel may attain its unimperiled existence, its true security.

In the late Diaspora the need for security assumed the anomalous form of a need to be categorized. It was reasoned that if it was our nonclassification which made us seem mysterious to the others, then that characteristic must be removed. This too is presaged in our ancient history, in the wanting to be "like unto all the nations" in the crisis during Samuel's time. But then and ever since then, the inner strength of faith was and is the resisting factor. The need for inclusion does not assume actual historical shape (if only history in caricature) until a late period of the exile, until the Emancipation. The Jews, to be sure, are not primarily to blame for the inadequacy of the Emancipation, for the fact that they were accepted as individuals, but not as a community.

At the beginning of the Emancipation, the nations pondered the question whether this unclassifiable Israel could not, after all, be included in one of the usual categories, and so they asked whether the Jews were a nation or a religion. The discussions which preceded the Emancipation in France anticipate all the later differences of opinion connected with this problem. Among other statements, we find the following words of Portalis, the French minister of education, whom Napoleon had asked to report on the Jews in 1802. What he wrote was: "The Government could not but consider the eternal life of this people, which has been preserved up to the present through all the stupendous changes and all the misfortunes of the centuries, since . . . it enjoys the privilege of having God himself as its lawgiver."

These words might well have been the prelude to the legal recognition of our people as such. But not one of the nations perceived the great task of liberating and accepting the Jewish community as a community *sui generis*, and not a single Jew from out of his age-old awareness thought to exert such a claim upon the unaware nations. Jewry disintegrated into small particles, to comply with the nations' demand. The urge to conform became a cramp. Israel lost its reality by becoming a "confession." Our era attempted to counteract this by nationalization. The attempt failed. The one thing that is essential, the element of uniqueness, was ignored.

There is no re-establishing of Israel, there is no security for it save one: It must assume the burden of its own uniqueness; it must assume the yoke of the kingdom of God.

Since this can be accomplished only in the rounded life of a community, we must reassemble, we must again root in the soil, we must govern ourselves. But these are mere prerequisites! Only when the community recognizes and realizes them as such in its own life will they serve as the cornerstones of its salvation.

HEBREW HUMANISM (1942)

ZIONIST THINKING in its current forms has failed to grasp the principle that the transformation of life must spring from the return to the origin of our nature. It is true that every thoughtful Zionist realizes that our character is distorted in many ways, that we are out of joint, and expect the new life in our own land, the bond to the soil and to work, to set us straight and make us whole once more. But what a great many overlook is that the powers released by this renewed bond to the soil do not suffice to accomplish a true and complete transformation. Another factor, the factor of spiritual power, that same return to our origin, must accompany the material factor. But it cannot be achieved by any spiritual power save the primordial spirit of Israel, the spirit which made us such as we are, and to which we must continually account for the extent to which our character has remained steadfast in the face of our destiny. This spirit has not vanished. The way to it is still open; it is still possible for us to encounter it. The Book still lies before us, and the Voice speaks forth from it as on the first day. But we must not dictate what it should and what it should not tell us. If we require it to confine itself to instructing us about our great literary productions, our glorious history, and our national pride, we shall succeed only in silencing it. For that is not what it has to tell us. What it does have to tell us, and what no other voice in the world can teach us with such simple power, is that there is truth and there are lies, and that human life cannot persist or have meaning save in the decision in behalf of truth and against lies; that there is right and wrong, and that the salvation of man depends on choosing what is right and rejecting what is wrong; and that it spells the destruction of our existence to divide our life up into areas where the discrimination between truth and lies, right and wrong, holds, and others where it does not hold, so that in private life, for example, we feel obligated to be truthful, but can permit ourselves lies in public, or that we act justly in man-to-man relationships, but can and even should practice injustice in national relationships.

The *humanitas* which speaks from this Book today, as it has always done, is the unity of human life under one divine direction which divides right from wrong and truth from lies as unconditionally as the words of the Creator divided light from darkness. It is true that we are not able to live in perfect justice, and in order to preserve the community of man, we are often compelled to accept wrongs in decisions concerning the community. But what matters is that in every hour of decision we are aware of our responsibility and summon our conscience to weigh exactly how much is necessary to preserve the community, and accept just so much and no more; that we do not interpret the demands of a will-to-power as a demand made by life itself; that we do not make a practice of setting aside a certain sphere in which God's command does not hold, but regard those actions as against his command, forced on us by the exigencies of the hour as painful sacrifices; that we do not salve, or let others salve, our conscience when we make decisions concerning public life, but struggle with destiny in fear and trembling lest it burden us with greater guilt than we are compelled to assume. This trembling of the magnetic needle which points the direction notwithstanding—this is biblical *humanitas*. The men in the Bible are sinners like ourselves, but there is one sin they do not commit, our archsin: They do not dare confine God to a circumscribed space or division of life, to "religion." They have not the insolence to draw boundaries around God's commandments and say to him: "Up to this point, you are sovereign, but beyond these bounds begins the sovereignty of science or society or the state." When they are forced to obey another power, every nerve in their body bears and suffers the load which is imposed upon them; they do not act lightheartedly nor toss their heads frivolously.

He who has been reared in our Hebrew biblical humanism goes as far as he must in the hour of gravest responsibility, and not a step further. He resists patriotic bombast which clouds the gulf between the demand of life and the desire of the will-to-power. He resists the whisperings of false popularity which is the opposite of true service to the people. He is not taken in by the hoax of modern national egoism, according to which everything which can be of benefit to one's people must be true and right. He knows that a primordial decision has been made concerning right and wrong, between truth and lies, and that it confronts the existence of the people. He knows that, in the final analysis, the only thing that can help his people is what is true and right in the light of that age-old decision. But if, in an emergency, he cannot obey this recognition of "the final analysis," but responds to the nation's cry for help, he sins like the men in the Bible and, like them, prostrates himself before his Judge. That is the meaning in contemporary language of the return to the origins of our being. Let us hope that the language of tomorrow will be different, that to the best of our ability it will be the language of a positive realization of truth and right, in both the internal and external aspects of the structure of our entire community life.

I AM SETTING UP Hebrew humanism in opposition to that Jewish nationalism which regards Israel as a nation like unto other nations and recognizes no task for Israel save that of preserving and asserting itself. But no nation in the world has this as its only task, for just as an individual who wishes merely to preserve and assert himself leads an unjustified and meaningless existence, so a nation with no other aim deserves to pass away.

By opposing Hebrew humanism to a nationalism which is nothing but empty self-assertion, I wish to indicate that, at this juncture, the Zionist movement must decide either for national egoism or national humanism. If it decides in favor of national egoism, it too will suffer the fate which will soon befall all shallow nationalism, i.e., nationalism which does not set the nation a true supernational task. If it decides in favor of Hebrew humanism, it will be strong and effective long after shallow nationalism has lost all meaning and justification, for it will have something to say and to bring to mankind.

Israel is not a nation like other nations, no matter how much its representatives have wished it during certain eras. Israel is a people like no other, for it is the only people in the world which, from its earliest beginnings, has been both a nation and a religious community. In the historical hour in which its tribes grew together to form a people, it became the carrier of a revelation. The covenant which the tribes made with one another and through which they became "Israel" takes the form of a common covenant with the God of Israel. The Song of Deborah, that great document of our heroic age, expresses a fundamental reality by repeatedly alternating the name of this God with the name of Israel, like a refrain. Subsequently, when the people desire a dynasty so that they may be "like unto all the *nations*" (I Samuel 8:20), the Scriptures have the man who, a generation later, really did found a dynasty, speak words which sound as though they were uttered to counterbalance that desire: "And who is like Thy people Israel, a *nation* one in the earth" (II Samuel 7:23). And these words, regardless of what epoch they hail from, express the same profound reality as those earlier words of Deborah. Israel was and is a people and a religious community in one, and it is this unity which enabled it to survive in an exile no other nation had to suffer, an exile which lasted much longer than the period of its independence. He who severs this bond severs the life of Israel.

One defense against this recognition is to call it a "theological interpretation" and, in this way, debase it into a private affair concerning only such persons as have an interest in so unfruitful a subject as theology. But this is nothing but shrewd polemics. For we are, in reality, dealing with a fundamental historical recognition without which Israel as a historical factor and fact could not be understood. An attempt has been made[3] to refute this allegedly "theological interpretation," by a "religious interpretation," the claim being made that it has nothing whatsoever to do with the Judaism of a series of eminent men, as the last of whom Rabbi Akiba is cited, the first being none other than Moses. Remarkable, to what lengths polemic enthusiasm will go! As a matter of fact, it is just as impossible to construct a historical Moses who did not realize the uniqueness of Israel as a historical Akiba who was not aware of it. Snatch from Rabbi Akiba his phrase about "special love" which God has for Israel (*Sayings of the Fathers* III: 18), and you snatch the heart from his body. Try to delete the words: "Ye shall be Mine own treasure from among all peoples" (Exodus 19:5) from the account of the coming of Israel to the wilderness of Sinai, and the whole story collapses. If such comments as these about Moses have any foundation at all, I do not know on what hypotheses of Bible criticism they are based; they are certainly not supported by anything in the Scriptures.

There is still another popular device for evading the recognition of Israel's uniqueness. It is asserted that every great people regards itself as the chosen people; in other words, awareness of peculiarity is interpreted as a function of nationalism in general. Did not the National Socialists believe that Destiny had elected the German people to rule the entire world? According to this view, the very fact that we say, "Thou hast chosen us," would prove that we are like other nations. But the weak arguments which venture to put "It shall be said unto them: Ye are the Children of the living God" (Hosea 1:10) on a par with "The German essence will make the whole world well" are in opposition to the basic recognition we glean from history. The point is not whether we feel or do not feel that we are chosen. The point is that our role in history is actually unique. There is even more to it. The nature of our doctrine of election is entirely different from that of the theories of election of the other nations, even though these frequently depend on our doctrine. What they took over was never the essential part. Our doctrine is distinguished from their theories in that our election is completely a demand. This is not the mythical shape of a people's wishful dreams. This is not an unconditional promise of magnitude and might to a people. This is a stern demand, and the entire future existence of the people is made dependent on whether or not this demand is met. This is not a God speaking whom the people created in their own image, as their sublimation. He confronts the people and opposes them. He demands and judges. And he does so not only in the age of the prophets at a later stage of historical development, but from time immemorial; and no hypothesis of Bible criticism can ever deny this. What he demands he calls "truth" and "righteousness," and he does not demand these for certain isolated spheres of life, but for the whole life of man, for the whole life of the people. He wants the individual and the people to be "wholehearted" with him. Israel is chosen to enable it to ascend from the biological law of power, which the nations glorify in their wishful thinking, to the sphere of truth and righteousness. God wishes man whom he has created to become man in the truest sense of the word, and wishes this to happen not only in sporadic instances, as it happens among other nations, but in the life of an entire people, thus providing an order of life for a future mankind, for all the peoples combined into one people. Israel was chosen to become a true people, and that means God's people.

Biblical man is man facing and recognizing such election and such a demand. He accepts it or rejects it. He fulfills it as best he can or he rebels against it. He violates it and then repents. He fends it off, and surrenders. But there is one thing he does not do: he does not pretend that it does not exist or that its claim is limited. And classical biblical man absorbs this demand for righteousness so wholly with his flesh and blood, that, from Abraham to Job, he dares to remind God of it. And God, who knows that human mind and spirit cannot grasp the ways of his justice, takes delight in the man who calls him to account, because that man has absorbed the demand for righteousness with his very flesh and blood. He calls Job his servant and Abraham his beloved. He tempted both; both called him to account, and both resisted temptation. That is Hebrew humanity.

IT REMAINED for our time to separate the Jewish people and the Jewish religious community which were fused from earliest beginnings, and to establish each as an independent unit, a nation like unto other nations and a religion like unto other religions. Thanks to the unparalleled work in Palestine, the nation is on the rise. The religion, however, is on a steep downward fall, for it is no longer a power which determines all of life; it has been confined to the special sphere of ritual or sermons. But a Jewish nation cannot exist without religion any more than a Jewish religious community without nationality. Our only salvation is to become Israel again, to become a whole, the unique whole of a people and a religious community; a renewed people, a renewed religion, and the renewed unity of both.

According to the ideas current among Zionists today, all that is needed is to establish the conditions for a normal national life, and everything will come of itself. This is a fatal error. We do, of course, need the conditions of normal national life, but these are not enough —not enough for us, at any rate. We cannot enthrone "normalcy" in place of the eternal premise of our survival. If we want to be nothing but normal, we shall soon cease to be at all.

The great values we have produced issued from the marriage of a people and a faith. We cannot substitute a technical association of nation and religion for this original marriage, without incurring barrenness. The values of Israel cannot be reborn outside the sphere of this union and its uniqueness.

Objection will be made that this point is one that concerns intellectual and cultural problems, but not problems about actual, present-day life. No! Let us not forget we are as yet only striving to join the ranks of nations with a land and a law of their own. Tomorrow many little nations will be weighed and found wanting. But this will surely not be the fate of a people that brings great tidings to struggling mankind, and conveys them not only through the word, but through its own life, which realizes that word and represents such realization. We shall not, of course, be able to boast of possessing the Book if we betray its demand for righteousness.

FROM AN OPEN LETTER
TO MAHATMA GANDHI (1939)

YOU, MAHATMA GANDHI, who know of the connection between tradition and future, should not associate yourself with those who pass over our cause without understanding or sympathy.

But you say—and I consider it to be the most significant of all the things you tell us—that Palestine belongs to the Arabs and that it is therefore "wrong and inhuman to impose the Jews on the Arabs."

Here I must add a personal note in order to make clear to you on what premises I desire to consider your thesis.

I belong to a group of people who from the time Britain conquered Palestine have not ceased to strive for the concluding of a genuine peace between Jew and Arab.

By a genuine peace we inferred and still infer that both peoples together should develop the land without the one imposing its will on the other. In view of the international usages of our generation, this appeared to us to be very difficult but not impossible. We were and still are well aware that in this unusual—yes, unprecedented—case it is a question of seeking new ways of understanding and cordial agreement between the nations. Here again we stood and still stand under the sway of a commandment.

We considered it a fundamental point that in this case two vital claims are opposed to each other, two claims of a different nature and a different origin which cannot objectively be pitted against one another and between which no objective decision can be made as to which is just, which unjust. We considered and still consider it our duty to understand and to honor the claim which is opposed to ours and to endeavor to reconcile both claims. We could not and cannot renounce the Jewish claim; something even higher than the life of our people is bound up with this land, namely its work, its divine mission. But we have been and still are convinced that it must be possible to find some compromise between this claim and the other, for we love this land and we believe in its future; since such love and such faith are surely present on the other side as well, a union in the common service of the land must be within the range of possibility. Where there is faith and love, a solution may be found even to what appears to be a tragic opposition.

In order to carry out a task of such extreme difficulty—in the recognition of which we have had to overcome an internal resistance on the Jewish side too, as foolish as it is natural—we have been in need of the support of well-meaning persons of all nations, and have hoped to receive it. But now you come and settle the whole existential dilemma with the simple formula: "Palestine belongs to the Arabs."

What do you mean by saying a land belongs to a population? Evidently you do not intend only to describe a state of affairs by your formula, but to declare a certain right. You obviously mean to say that a people, being settled on the land, has so absolute a claim to that land that whoever settles on it without the permission of this people has committed a robbery. But by what means did the Arabs attain the right of ownership in Palestine? Surely by conquest, and in fact a conquest with intent to settle. You therefore admit that as a result their settlement gives them exclusive right of possession; whereas the subsequent conquests of the Mamelukes and the Turks, which were conquests with a view to domination, not to settlement, do not constitute such a right in your opinion, but leave the earlier conquerors in rightful ownership. Thus settlement by conquest justifies for you a right of ownership of Palestine; whereas a settlement such as the Jewish—the methods of which, it is true, though not always doing full justice to Arab ways of life, were even in the most objectionable cases far removed from those of conquest—does not justify in your opinion any participation in this right of possession. These are the consequences which result from your axiomatic statement that a land belongs to its population. In an epoch when nations are migrating you would first support the right of ownership of the nation that is threatened with dispossession or extermination; but were this once achieved, you would be compelled, not at once, but after a suitable number of generations had elapsed, to admit that the land "belongs" to the usurper. . . .

It seems to me that God does not give any one portion of the earth away, so that the owner may say as God says in the Bible: "For all the earth is Mine" (Exodus 19:5). The conquered land is, in my opinion, only lent even to the conqueror who has settled on it—and God waits to see what he will make of it.

I am told, however, I should not respect the cultivated soil and despise the desert. I am told, the desert is willing to wait for the work of her children: she no longer recognizes us, burdened with civilization, as her children. The desert inspires me with awe; but I do not believe in her absolute resistance, for I believe in the great marriage between man (*adam*) and earth (*adamah*). This land recognizes us, for it is fruitful through us: and precisely because it bears fruit for us, it recognizes us. Our settlers do not come here as do the colonists from the Occident to have natives do their work for them; they themselves set their shoulders to the plow and they spend their strength and their blood to make the land fruitful. But it is not only for ourselves that we desire its fertility. The Jewish farmers have begun to teach their brothers, the Arab farmers, to cultivate the land more intensively; we desire to teach them further: together with them we want to cultivate the land—to "serve" it, as the Hebrew has it. The more fertile this soil becomes, the more space there will be for us and for them. We have no desire to dispossess them: we want to live with them. We do not want to dominate them: we want to serve with them. . . .

Part 8
Intellectuals in Search of Roots

BERNARD LAZARE 1865-1903

BERNARD LAZARE is another of Zionism's great originals. He is perhaps best seen through the eyes of love, in the pages in his memory that were written by Charles Péguy, the famous French poet and Catholic mystic who was his best friend. (This essay is in its own right one of the great pieces of modern writing about the Jew, and it is a source of regret that it was outside the scope of this volume.) Péguy said of Lazare: "Because a man wears spectacles, because he wears eyeglasses athwart a fold on his nose, in front of two big eyes, modern man believes him to be modern, modern man is incapable of seeing, does not see, does not know how to recognize the ancientness of the prophetic look . . . He was a fellow who had the very habits of freedom. He had freedom in his skin, in his marrow and in his blood; in his spine. And not at all an intellectual and conceptual freedom, a bookish freedom, a ready-made freedom, a library freedom either. A trade-marked freedom. But a freedom, rather, of the wellspring, a wholly organic and living freedom. Never have I seen a man believe to such a degree, to such a degree be certain, to such a degree be aware that a man's conscience is something absolute, invincible, eternal, something free, that victorious and everlastingly triumphant stands firm against all the greatness of the earth."

Lazare was born in Nîmes, southern France, in 1865 in an assimilated family of Sephardic extraction. He came to Paris at the age of twenty-one, and within a few years he achieved a literary reputation of some proportions. After 1890 he contributed essays of criticism to the organ of the symbolists and published two volumes of his own poetry. In politics the decade of Lazare's maturing was the period of rising anti-Semitic agitation in France, which was to culminate in the Dreyfus affair. Unlike the rest of his *avant-garde* circle, Lazare took these currents seriously, especially since he was encountering them not only in expected places, among the reactionaries, but also among the socialists. He therefore devoted himself to a serious investigation of anti-Semitism, which appeared in two volumes (*L'Antisémitisme, son histoire et ses causes*) in 1894. Lazare diagnosed its cause as the Jews themselves, in their resistance to assimilation, though they had outlived any reason for maintaining their peculiar kind of national identity. The cure—as Lazare saw it then, while still a believer in cosmopolitanism—was in the post-national order of the future in which all subgroups would merge in one humanity.

The turning point for Lazare, as for Herzl, Nordau, and many others, was the Dreyfus affair. Lazare went to work as a legal counsel for the Dreyfus family immediately after the unfortunate captain's first trial in 1894. He was the first to see the case in perspective not only as a judicial error but as a political plot against the French Republic. The pamphlet in which he stated these views was published in 1896, and henceforth to the end of his brief years, Lazare, along with Clemenceau, Zola, Péguy, and some others, insisted that nothing less than a reversal of the original sentence—not the pardon of 1899—would do to end the controversy. Be it remembered that this was no abstract argument, for Lazare's life was endangered, in street riots and even in a duel, by the prophetic vehemence with which he advocated his convictions.

Lazare's Zionism flowed from the Dreyfus affair by the same logic as Herzl's, with two important differences. Lazare remained a social revolutionary, and despite a surface rationalism, he had a much more religious and mystical cast of soul than Herzl. He was a formally affiliated Zionist only briefly, until 1899. Lazare then wrote an open letter of resignation attacking supposed autocratic tendencies in Herzl's Zionist executive body. In truth, the deeper reason for his leaving was in himself, in the temperament of a man who could not but walk alone. During the four years that remained of his life Lazare was cut off from all of organized Jewish life, for he had previously broken with all "respectable" French Jewry, who wanted quiet at almost any cost, during the Dreyfus affair. Only Péguy's journal, the *Cahiers de Quinzaine*, printed him, and it was there that his last piece on a Jewish subject, his attack on the Romanian government for its treatment of the Jews, appeared in 1902. Lazare died in 1903, at the age of thirty-eight.

Lazare is represented in this volume by passages from two lectures that he gave, one in 1897 and the other in 1899, on the subject of Jewish nationalism and the meaning of the emancipation of the Jews.

JEWISH NATIONALISM AND EMANCIPATION (1897–1899)

IT IS BECAUSE the Jews are a nation that anti-Semitism exists. Granted—and this cannot be too much emphasized—that religious prejudice lies at the root of the hatred of Israel, yet this religious prejudice at the same time implies the existence of the Jewish people upon which for nineteen hundred years have fallen the anathemas of the Church. Assume that Christianity had never existed and yet that the Diaspora had come into existence, the Jews, a nation without territory, a people scattered among the peoples, would all the same have provoked anti-Judaism. It would probably have been less violent, and yet even that is not certain; for Judaism would with equal readiness have come into conflict with other religious principles, just as took place in Alexandria and in Rome. This conflict would have lacked the element of deicide, nothing more.

If the cause of anti-Semitism is the existence of the Jews as a nationality, its effect is to make this nationality more tangible for the Jews, to make them more aware of the fact that they are a people.

Some thirty years ago the world's Jews were divided into emancipated Jews and Jews subject to discriminatory laws. A great part of the Jews suffering under the system of persecution had as their ideal the status of the emancipated Jews, and the greater part of the emancipated Jews were inclined to cast off their Jewishness, to cut themselves off from the Jewish mass still in servitude, with which these emancipated Jews pretended to have no other bonds than those required by the claims of humanity.

This situation is already a thing of the past. A hundred years ago in France, more recently still in Germany, in Austria, and in England, the Jews of the West were freed. The material barriers which separated them from Christian society were destroyed; they were permitted to exercise their rights as men. There followed a golden age for the Jews, an age when every dream soared: all dreams, all ambitions, all appetites. What happened was that a small section, the propertied section, of the Jews impetuously rushed to the conquest of pleasures from which it had been cut off for so many centuries. It got rotten through contact with the Christian world, which had upon it the same dissolving effect as civilized man has upon the savages to whom he brings alcoholism, syphilis, and tuberculosis. It is obvious that the so-called upper class among western Jews, and especially among French Jews, is in an advanced state of decay. It is no longer Jewish, it is not Christian, and it is incapable of substituting a philosophy, even less a free morality, for the creed it no longer owns. Whereas the Christian bourgeoisie holds itself upright thanks to the corset of its dogmas, traditions, morality, and of its conventional principles, the Jewish bourgeoisie, deprived of its age-old stays, poisons the Jewish nation with its rottenness, and it will poison the other nations if it does not make up its mind—and this is something we cannot too strongly urge upon it—to adhere to the Christianity of the ruling classes, so that Judaism may get rid of it.

Now, while this category of Jews thought only of the acquisition of fortunes, dignities, honors, decorations, and high positions, while the lesser Jewish bourgeoisie developed intellectually, the ancient ghetto was already being rebuilt. According to economic and political circumstances, anti-Semitism was being born, but these circumstances were only, it should be clearly noted, the immediate causes, suited to reawaken ancient prejudices. Anti-Semitism aimed at the restoration of the old legislation against Israel; but this self-assumed purpose was an ideal purpose. What real and practical purpose has it achieved? It has not succeeded and will probably not succeed in France, Austria, and Germany, in again erecting separate dwelling quarters, or in enclosing the Jews in a special area, as is the case in Russia; but thanks to anti-Semitism a moral ghetto has very nearly been re-established. No longer are Jews cloistered in the West; no longer are chains stretched at the ends of the streets on which they dwell, but around them has been created a hostile atmosphere, an atmosphere of distrust, of latent hatreds, of unavowed—and thus all the more powerful —prejudices, a ghetto more terrible than one whence you might escape by rebellion or exile. Even when this animosity is dissembled, the intelligent Jew is aware of it; henceforward he feels a resistance, he has the impression of a wall erected between him and those in whose midst he lives.

What, at the present moment, can you show the Jew of eastern Europe, who so keenly desired to attain the position of his western brothers? You can show him the Jew pariah. Is that not a beautiful ideal for him to achieve? And what shall we say to him if he quite simply declares: "My position is abominable; I have obligations and

I have no rights; I am reduced to a frightful degree of wretchedness and degradation. What remedy do you suggest for me? Emancipation? What will your emancipation give me? It will afford me a social situation which will allow me to refine myself; thanks to this I shall acquire new capacities for feeling, and consequently I shall find it more difficult to suffer; it will develop within me a greater sensibility and withal it will not cause to disappear the things which wound that sensibility—quite the opposite. Out of a wretch sometimes benumbed by his wretchedness, it will make a sensitive being who will doubly feel every pinprick, and whose existence will consequently become a thousand times less tolerable. Out of an unconscious pariah it will make a conscious pariah. What advantages shall I gain from this changed position? None. And so I am through with your emancipation; it offers neither a guarantee, nor an assurance, nor an improvement."

This is why we must not, as do the emancipated Jews, look upon ourselves solely with an eye to anti-Semitism, this is why we must not seek what the peoples among whom we dwell might expect of us; we must seek what we can extract from ourselves, and to this end we must not Christianize Judaism but, on the contrary, Judaize the Jew, teach him to live for, and to be, himself. This is why we should answer those who tell us, "You should labor for humanity," by saying, "Yes, but our ambition is to work for mankind in other fashion than do those dungheaps which by their decay bring forth new flowers and new fruits. We are through with being eternally exploited by all peoples, a troop of cattle and of serfs, the butt of every lash, a flock to which men even deny a stable, a horde of people denying themselves the right to have a free soil or to live and die in liberty. We do not want to bow our backs, and we will gladly let our rich men—without brains, without force, without will, without brotherhood, and without pity—supplicate those around them and say: 'See how much like you we are; we have all your vices and even all your virtues, we forego our own thoughts, our own ideals, we have the same abject souls, the same fears, and the same cruelties.'" We stand up and we say to them: "We are ever the ancient stiff-necked people, the unruly and rebel nation; we want to be ourselves, and we shall know well how to conquer the right which is ours, not only to be men but also to be Jews." And who are we? We, the intellectuals, the proletarians, and the poor people of Israel. Is not this enough? When Cyrus allowed the Jews to return to Palestine, there came back to Jerusalem only forty thousand men. They were the proletarians, the wretched, the righteous of the Psalms, the revolutionary prophets; the rich remained in Babylon. They must still remain there, for it is the poor who make nations; the rich do not know how to create, they do not even know how to give. We call a nation free when it can materially, intellectually, and morally develop itself, without any external trammels whatever being placed upon that development. If one nation, by reason of conquest or in any other fashion causes another nation to become dependent upon it, there will remain of the second nation only a certain number of denationalized individuals, that is, persons no longer able to give expression to their special collective spirit, that is, persons having lost their collective freedom.

These individuals are the vanquished, the conquered, are therefore relegated to a state of inferiority, and if they are unwilling to disappear, they lose their own proper freedom. Why don't they disappear, men will ask, why do they continue to cling to ancient forms which, during one moment of time, they represented? Here are idle questions. At the very most it could be said in reply that only such human groups as are still amorphous, possessed only of ill-defined traits and a vague awareness of themselves, are capable of letting themselves be absorbed.

Firmly established and homogeneous groups, having settled traits and a clear-cut awareness of themselves, necessarily resist. It is as true of collectivities as it is of individual men that the weak yield and the strong persevere. However that may be, we are confronted here with an historic fact: the maintenance and the survival in the midst of the nations of certain individuals belonging to different nationalities, by which I mean men who have preserved forms of being different from the forms of those who surround them. These individuals, by the very fact that they have held out, suffer a constraint, since all peoples have an inevitable tendency to reduce the heterogeneous elements existing among them. Hence their freedom is diminished, and, if they continue in their stubborn refusal to yield, they will be able to keep their individual liberty only on the condition that they are able to win back the collective liberty which they have lost. In short, the rebirth of their nationality is the prerequisite of their individual freedom. The constraint under which they labor likewise prevents their contributing everything that lies within them, a portion of their energies being spent upon that resistance, upon that struggle, which alone allows them to retain the capacity for development, without that development being able to take place. Once again, it is the re-establishment of their nationality which will give them an opportunity to flower.

This is the case of the Russian or Romanian Jews who are in no position, under the present circumstances, to contribute in the measure of which they are capable. Tomorrow, western Jewry may find itself in the same situation, obliged to spend its strength in the struggle against anti-Semitism—eternal struggle, perpetual strife, built of victories and of disasters, eminently suited to exhaust the minority which wages it.

For a Jew, the word nationalism should mean freedom. A Jew who today may declare, "I am a nationalist," will not be saying in any special, precise, or clear-cut way, "I am a man who seeks to rebuild a Jewish state in Palestine and who dreams of conquering Jerusalem." He will be saying, "I want to be a man fully free, I want to enjoy the sunshine, I want to escape the oppression, to escape the outrage, to escape the scorn with which men seek to overwhelm me." At certain moments in history, nationalism is for human groups the manifestation of the spirit of freedom.

In saying this, I do not in the least deny internationalist ideas. When socialists fight nationalism, in fact they are fighting protectionism and national exclusivism; they fight that chauvinistic, narrow, and absurd patriotism which leads peoples to set themselves up against each other as rivals or as enemies determined to grant each other neither reprieve nor mercy. Such is the selfishness of nations, as hateful as the selfishness of individuals and as deserving of contempt. Internationalism obviously presupposes the existence of nations. To be an internationalist means to set up between nations bonds not of diplomatic friendship but of human brotherhood; it means to abolish the political-economic structure of our present nations, since this structure has been created only to protect the people's private interests, or rather those of their governments, at the expense of neighboring peoples. To suppress the frontiers does not mean to produce one sole amalgam of all the inhabitants of the globe. The federative concept, the concept of a fragmented humanity made up of a multitude of cellular organisms, is one of the commonplace notions of international socialism and even of revolutionary anarchism. Granted that in its ideal development this theory conceives that the cells which will thus come together will be knit by virtue of affinities not entailed by any ethnological, religious, or national tradition. But this is of little import as long as the theory allows for groups. Moreover, our task is only to deal with our own day, and our own day requires us to seek the most suitable means for assuring men their freedom. Now in our day and generation, it is by virtue of traditional principles that men wish to associate together. To this end they invoke certain identities of origin, their common past, similar ways of looking upon phenomena, beings, and things; a common philosophy, a common history. They must be allowed to band together.

But, object certain socialists, in furthering the development of nationalism, you encourage unity among classes in such fashion that the workers forget the economic struggle and link themselves to their enemies. This result, however, is not necessary. Such an alliance is generally only temporary and—be it noted—it is most frequently not the property holders who require it of the poor and of the workers, but rather the latter who force the rich to go along with them. Moreover, is it not necessary for the wretched mass of working-class Jews that, before it can escape from its proletarian wretchedness, it should possess its freedom, which means the opportunity to struggle and to conquer? That problem will certainly arise when, for instance, access to certain countries will be refused to the Jews who leave Russia.

I find nothing in nationalism which would be contrary to socialist orthodoxy, and I, who am orthodox in nothing, do not hesitate for an instant in accepting nationalism alongside internationalism. On the contrary, I believe that for internationalism to take root, it is necessary that human groups should previously have won their autonomy; it is necessary for them to be able to express themselves freely, it is necessary for them to be aware of what they are.

EDMOND FLEG   born 1874

FLEG, TOO, represents the assimilated writers and men of the spirit who recoiled from anti-Semitism to Zionism and, through it, to a reaffirmation of their roots in the Jewish people and tradition. Though Fleg's life and literary creativity have been bound up with France, his family is Alsatian in origin and he was born in Geneva, Switzerland. He came to Paris to study at the Sorbonne and was part of a circle of aesthetes when the Dreyfus affair began. In reaction to the rampant anti-Semitism which was coming to the fore, Fleg began his return to the Judaism he had discarded. Part of the record of that journey of the spirit is in the passages below, which are quoted from his autobiographical *Why I Am a Jew* (1927). Fleg has written poetry, plays, and novels, edited anthologies, and, in sum, been a typical French *homme de lettres* throughout a productive life, but his theme has generally been bound up with the history and destiny of the Jew. Fleg's writing has revolved around the tension between his deep attachment to Western culture and France, on the one hand, and the re-echoing cries of the divine imperative and of the Orient in his Jewish soul.

In the First World War Fleg, who was then not yet a French citizen, joined the Foreign Legion in order to fight for the country of his adoption. He won the *Croix de guerre* and he was honored later, in 1937, by being made an officer of the Legion of Honor. The Second World War brought him the deepest personal sorrow, for both his sons were killed fighting for France.

The best-known of Fleg's books that has appeared in English translation is his *Jewish Anthology*, which attempted, through excerpts, to present a spiritual history of the Jew.

WHY I AM A JEW (1927)

PEOPLE ASK ME why I am a Jew. It is to you that I want to answer, little unborn grandson.

When will you be old enough to listen to me? My elder son is nineteen, the younger fourteen. When will you be born? Perhaps in ten years' time, perhaps in fifteen. When will you read what I am writing? In 1950 or thereabouts? In 1960? Will anybody be reading in 1960? What will the world look like then? Will the machine have killed the soul? Will the mind have created for itself a new universe? Will the problems that trouble me today mean anything to you? Will there still be Jews?

I believe there will. They have survived the Pharaohs, Nebuchadnezzar, Constantine, Mohammed, the Inquisition, and assimilation; they will know how to survive the motorcar.

But you—will you feel yourself a Jew, my child? People say to me, "You are a Jew because you were born a Jew; you neither willed it nor can change it." Will this explanation satisfy you if, though born a Jew, you no longer feel one?

When I was twenty I too felt I had no lot nor part in Israel; I was persuaded that Israel would disappear, and that in twenty years' time people would no longer speak of her. The twenty years have passed, and another twelve, and I have become a Jew again—so obviously, that I am asked, "Why are you a Jew?"

What has happened to me can happen to you, my child. If you believe that the flame of Israel is extinguished in you, watch and wait; one day, it will burn again. This is a very old story, repeated in every generation: A thousand times Israel, it has seemed, must die, and a thousand times she has lived again. I want to tell you how she died and lived again in me, so that, if she dies in you, you in your turn can feel her born in you once more.

So I shall have brought Israel to you, and you shall bring her to others, if you will and can. And both of us, in our own way, will have preserved and handed on the divine commandment:

"Therefore shall ye lay up these my words in your heart and in your soul; and ye shall bind them for a sign upon your hand, and they shall be for frontlets between your eyes. And ye shall teach them to your children."

Since the beginning of the Dreyfus affair the Jewish question had seemed to me a reality; now it appeared tragic:

"What is Judaism? —A danger, they say, for the society to which you belong. What danger? . . . But first, am I still a Jew? . . . I have abandoned the Jewish religion. . . . You are a Jew all the same. . . . How? . . . Why? . . . What ought I to do? . . . Must I kill myself because I am a Jew?"

At moments I envied the strong and narrow faith of my ancestors. Penned in their ghettos by contempt and hatred, they at least knew why. But I knew nothing. How could I learn?

Of Israel I was entirely ignorant. And I regretted all the years I had spent in the study of philosophy, of Germanic philology, and of comparative literature. I ought to have learned Hebrew, to have studied my race, its origins, its beliefs, its role in history, its place among the human groups today; I ought to have attached myself, through my race, to something that would be myself and more than myself, and to have continued, through her, something that others had begun and that others after me would continue.

And I told myself that if I made some other use of my life, if I devoted myself to some other study, if later I founded a family without being able to bequeath to my children some ancestral ideal, I should always experience an obscure remorse, the vague feeling of having failed in a duty. And I remembered my dead father, I reproached myself with not having understood that Jewish wisdom of which he talked to me and which lived in him—and with no longer finding, by my own fault, anything in common between Israel's past and my own empty soul.

It was then that, for the first time, I heard of Zionism. You cannot imagine what a light that was, my child! Remember that, at the period of which I am writing, this word Zionism had never yet been spoken in my presence. The anti-Semites accused the Jews of forming a nation within the nations; but the Jews, or at any rate those whom I came across, denied it. And now here were the Jews declaring: "We are a people like other peoples; we have a country just as the others have. Give us back our country."

I made enquiries: The Zionist idea, it appeared, had its origins far back in the days of the ancient prophets; the Bible promised the Jews of the dispersion that they should return to the Holy Land; during the whole of the Middle Ages only their faith in this promise kept them alive; in the eighteenth and nineteenth centuries, such great spirits as Maurice de Saxe, the Prince de Ligne, and Napoleon had caught a glimpse of the philanthropic, political, economic, religious, and moral advantages which a resettlement of the Jews in Palestine might offer; since 1873 colonies had been founded there and were developing; and now a new apostle, Theodor Herzl, was calling upon the Jews of the whole world to found the Jewish state.

Was this the solution for which I was looking? It explained so many things. If the Jews really formed but a single nation, one began to understand why they were considered Jews even when they ceased to practice their religion, and it became credible, too, that a nation which had welcomed them should be able to accuse them of not always being devoted to its national interests. Then the Zionist idea moved me by its sublimity; I admired in these Jews, and would have wished to be able to admire in myself, this fidelity to the ancestral soil which still lived after two thousand years, and I trembled with emotion as I pictured the universal exodus which would bring them home, from their many exiles, to the unity that they had reconquered.

The Third Zionist Congress[1] was about to open at Basel. I decided to attend it. My knowledge of German enabled me to follow the debates pretty closely.

I listened to it all; but, with even greater interest, I looked about me. What Jewish contrasts! A pale-faced Pole with high cheekbones, a German in spectacles, a Russian looking like an angel, a bearded Persian, a clean-shaven American, an Egyptian in a fez, and, over there, that black phantom, towering up in his immense caftan, with his fur cap and pale curls falling from his temples. And, in the presence of all these strange faces, the inevitable happened; I felt myself a Jew, very much a Jew, but also very French, a Frenchman of Geneva, but French nonetheless.

I now well understood that the Zionist program in no way implies the return of all Jews to Palestine—a thing numerically impracticable: the Jewish fatherland is only for those Jews who feel they have no other. Now I was French on my mother's side, and my heart and mind had always gone out to France. At first, when I was quite small, there was the gratitude of my parents as Jews toward that country; then came my literary aspirations, then my long residence in Paris with fellow students whose camaraderie and friendship had helped me to become what I was; and finally the Dreyfus drama, which was an agony for me in an agonized France. In my thoughts I could not separate my little fatherland, Geneva, from that great spiritual fatherland to which even Geneva in so many ways belongs. When, therefore, I abandoned my dilettante egoism, and tried to find deep down in me a tradition, I found stronger and more conscious than the Jewish instincts, which were only just beginning to wake in me, the French tradition, mingled with that of Israel.

What then, for me, was Zionism? It could enthrall me, it enthralls me still, this great miracle of Israel which concerns the whole of Israel: three million Jews will speak Hebrew, will live Hebrew on Hebrew soil! But, for the twelve million Jews who will remain scattered throughout the world, for them and for me, the tragic question remained: What is Judaism? What ought a Jew to do? How be a Jew? Why be a Jew?

I am a Jew because, born of Israel and having lost her, I have felt her live again in me, more living than myself.

I am a Jew because, born of Israel and having regained her, I wish her to live after me, more living than in myself.

I am a Jew because the faith of Israel demands of me no abdication of the mind.

I am a Jew because the faith of Israel requires of me all the devotion of my heart.

I am a Jew because in every place where suffering weeps, the Jew weeps.

I am a Jew because at every time when despair cries out, the Jew hopes.

I am a Jew because the word of Israel is the oldest and the newest.

I am a Jew because the promise of Israel is the universal promise.

I am a Jew because, for Israel, the world is not yet completed; men are completing it.

I am a Jew because, above the nations and Israel, Israel places Man and his Unity.

I am a Jew because, above Man, image of the divine Unity, Israel places the divine Unity, and its divinity.

Sometimes, my child, when I wander through a museum, and stand before all the pictures and statues and furniture and armor, the faïence, the crystals, the mosaics, the garments and the finery, the coins and the jewels, gathered there, from every place and every age, to hang on the walls, to stand on the plinths, to line up behind the balustrades, to be classified, numbered, and ticketed in the glass cases, I think that one or other of my ancestors may have seen, touched, handled, or admired one or other of these things, in the very place where it was made, and at the very time when it was made, for the use, the labor, the pain, or the joy of men.

This door with the gray nails, between two poplars, in a gilded frame, this is the Geneva synagogue where my father went in to pray. And see this bridge of boats on the Rhone: my grandfather crossed the Rhine, at Hüninger. And his grandfather, where did he live? Perhaps as he dreamily calculated the mystical numbers of the cabbala he saw, through his quiet window, this sledge glide over the snow of Germany or Poland? And the grandfather of his grandfather's grandfather? Perhaps he was this money-changer, in this Amsterdam ghetto, painted by Rembrandt.

One of my ancestors may have drunk from this wine goblet, on returning home from the lesson of his master Rashi, at the school of Troyes in Champagne; one of my ancestors may have sat on this jade-incrusted armchair as he felt a sultan's pulse; one of my ancestors may have been led to the auto-da-fé by a hooded monk who carried this cross of Castile; one of my ancestors may have seen his children trampled down by the horse of the Crusader who bore this armor.

These feather headdresses, did another get them from an American savage? These African ivories, these Chinese silks, did another buy them by the banks of the Congo or the Amur, to sell them again on the shores of the Ganges or on the Venetian lagoons?

One of them drove this plow, tempered in the fire, through the plain of Sharon; one of them went up to the Temple to offer, in these plaited baskets, his tithe of figs.

When this marble Titus was in the flesh, one of my ancestors was dragged bleeding at his chariot wheels in a Roman triumph; beneath the feet of this bearded image with the fringed robe, flanked by two winged bulls of human profile, one of my ancestors smelled the dust of Babylon; at the breath of this porphyry Pharaoh, with the two flat hands on the two flat thighs, one of my ancestors bowed himself down, before girding on his girdle and taking up his staff to follow Moses across the Red Sea; and this Sumerian idol, with spherical eyes and angular jaws, is perhaps the very one that Abraham broke when he left his Chaldean home to follow the call of his invisible God.

And I say to myself: From this remote father right up to my own father, all these fathers have handed on to me a truth which flowed in their blood, which flows in mine; and shall I not hand it on, with my blood, to those of my blood?

Will you take it from me, my child? Will you hand it on? Perhaps you will wish to abandon it. If so, let it be for a greater truth, if there is one. I shall not blame you. It will be my fault; I shall have failed to hand it on as I received it.

But, whether you abandon it or whether you follow it, Israel will journey on to the end of days.

LUDWIG LEWISOHN   1883-1955

LUDWIG LEWISOHN was born in Berlin, Germany, in 1883 in a family which had been assimilated for several generations and brought to the United States, to Charleston, South Carolina, at the age of seven. As a child he was strongly influenced at home by German culture and at school by ecstatic Christian piety, for he received his early education in a school run by Baptists. At eighteen Lewisohn graduated from the College of Charleston and two years later he received his M.A. from Columbia University. Lewisohn first seriously encountered anti-Semitism when he tried to get a job teaching, but some years were to elapse before his reactions to further such experiences were to convert him to Zionism.

Until 1910 Lewisohn lived, precariously, off his pen, mostly as a free lance writer for magazines. His first novel appeared in 1908, but it was neither an artistic nor a financial success. Lewisohn did finally achieve his wish of an academic appointment in 1910, when he went to the University of Wisconsin as instructor in German; from 1911 to 1919 he served as professor at Ohio State University. During those years Lewisohn published several books which made him a considerable reputation as an expert on contemporary European writing and as a literary critic. He turned full time to criticism after he left the academic life, to serve until 1924 as the drama critic and then as member of the editorial staff of the liberal weekly, the Nation.

Lewisohn's conversion from assimilation came during this period of his life. Regarding himself then, as Lazare had a quarter century before, as a liberal man of letters, he, too, saw a connection between anti-liberalism and anti-Semitism and found the answer in an image of the Jew as the eternal defender of righteousness. In the book in which he first gave a connected account of his new faith, Israel (1925), Lewisohn surveyed the Jewish world of the day, "whether in America or in Europe or in Palestine," to prove that "the House of Jacob is remembering its necessary service to mankind—to resist unrighteousness, to break every yoke, to establish peace." This theme of personal return was also to be expressed in the best-known of his novels on a Jewish subject, *The Island Within* (1928).

A prolific writer and lecturer, Lewisohn was henceforth one of the leading literary figures associated with American Zionism. From 1943 to 1948, during the height of the battles for the creation of the state of Israel, he edited the *New Palestine*, the organ of the Zionist Organization of America, and then, until his death in 1955, he was a member of the faculty of Brandeis University. Lewisohn's Zionist thought is represented here by a piece he chose himself for an anthology he edited, entitled *Rebirth*, which appeared in 1934.

A YEAR OF CRISIS (1933)

LET US TRY the simplest approach to the inextricable coil of problems, arising from subtlest mental confusions and spiritual diseases. Wherever three or four Jews gather in the world, they will sooner or later talk about the Jewish problem; they will discuss their situation in the country in which they are or the status of the Jews in other countries; they will say, unless persecution is very active in their dwelling place, that conditions are not bad and are likely to improve more and more and that the persecutors in other lands are evidently on a lower civilizatory plane than the people among whom they live. I have heard exactly this talk in Youngstown, Ohio, and in Marienbad in Czechoslovakia, and in Constantine in the African mountains. Or else there will be, except in hours of extreme danger of woe for some part of the people, the talk of those who are trying to detach themselves from Israel. For they do not live their detachment, the vast majority of them, but talk about it. And finally there is the lowest stratum on which people tell Jewish jokes, jokes at the expense of their people, the psychical purpose of which is (among other things) to differentiate the teller of the anecdote from the subject of it and thus to establish a detachment on the part of the teller of the tale from those vices and foibles which gentiles attribute to Jews and which the anecdotes commonly illustrate.

Everywhere and every day this interminable futile talk goes on and on. It has an hundred variations, subtler and coarser, but it can always be reduced to the several kinds noted above and it always consists psychologically of an intricate system of subconscious *suppressio veri* and *suggestio falsi* by means of which millions and millions of Galut Jews try to keep themselves from facing the harsh but possibly healing weather of reality. They will not even objectify and so seek to interpret the continuousness and intensity of their preoccupation with themselves and their people and its fate. For did they do so they would be forced at once to seek to make this preoccupation a rational one by giving it the food of both reflection and knowledge. But they will practice the most agonized gestures of defense against this process, since to yield to it would destroy a thousand easy habits, shatter a thousand false conventions, and force upon them a reorganization of their whole lives. They are not particularly to be blamed. All human beings use the same system of psychical defense against some problem that is too difficult to meet, some truth that seems to them too brutal to face. But the difference between gentiles and Jews in respect to the practice of these psychological defenses is this, that for gentiles it may mean an impairment of intellectual integrity or of social functioning or of efficiency, but for Jews it has become a matter of life and death for each one and for our whole people. A matter of life and death. For the same sparks from which burst forth this year the foul and fatal German conflagration are smoldering, however hid in ashes, however swept out of sight by sincere gentile good will and by unacknowledged Jewish terror, in every land of the dispersion. In every one. In every one. There is still time to stamp them out. But it is the eleventh hour. And the stamping out of them cannot be accomplished at a smaller expense than that of the spiritual reorganization of millions of Jewish lives and the consequent reorganization, both spiritual and sociological, of the Galut communities.

(Practical suggestions? I am coming to them by and by. Have patience with me. Note first: I am advising no stampede to Palestine, which is physically impossible, for one thing, and would be futile, since it would destroy the Yishuv that we have. I am fully aware of the fact that the great majority of the Jewish people will have to continue in the dispersion. They will have to save themselves and help to save their gentile fellow men where they are. Therefore the task of the age, which is the task of saving the people, is twofold: (1) the rapid strengthening and upbuilding of the Yishuv; (2) the reorganization, both spiritual and sociological, of the communities of the dispersion.)

Now it is evident that we cannot reorganize the communities unless

the people who constitute them will inwardly consent to the reorganization, will have reached an insight so deep that it issues in necessary
action. If the majority says, "We can still get by in the old discredited
ways; never mind what befalls our children or grandchildren," then, of
course, there is no hope. Hence millions of Jews must be converted,
must achieve a *teshuvah* (repentance), each for himself, in order to
consent to the saving of their people, in order to consent to the reconstruction of the Jewish communities of the world. Nothing less than a
conversion, nothing less than a profound inner change, nothing less
than a broken and a contrite Jewish heart, and yet a heart proud in its
brokenness and its contrition, will avail. On April 1, 1933, on the day
of the boycott in Germany, the *Jüdische Rundschau* of Berlin, that
highminded and intrepid paper, which has been as a beacon and a
light in the German darkness, carried the headline: *"Tragt ihn mit
Stolz, den gelben Fleck"* ("Wear the yellow badge with pride").
We must do that everywhere and always. We must do more than
that. The yellow badge must sink from the garment upon which
hostile hands have sewn it into the heart; it must become one with the
heart and fill it wholly, so wholly, so utterly, that none knows the
difference between the yellow badge and his own heart.

We are far from that self-affirmation. We are so far from it that we
must begin at the humble level of trying to make people see how futile
and foolish is preoccupation without reflection and knowledge. Here
you are, we must say to these millions of Jews, poor and rich, learned
and simple, and every day, impelled thereto by what you unescapably
are, you talk about Jewish affairs and the Jewish problem (never
dreaming that you, you in your tepidness and ignorance and lack of
strong self-affirmation according to knowledge and feeling, constitute
the deepest Jewish problem), and you talk of the Jewish people and
grieve over its griefs and triumph in its few triumphs, and how many
Jewish books are in your houses, and how many purely Jewish acts do
you perform, and how saturated are you with the flowering into legend
and ritual and poetry and philosophy of the instincts and the being of
our people? Your contribution is defensive talk, and meanwhile your
souls harden or wither and with it the souls of the people, and so you
rob the people as a whole, of which you are a member and which in
your hidden and obscure way you love, of all pride and erectness and
power of reaction and defense, and deliver it up, bound and gagged
and blindfolded, to the implacable forces of the world. And you will
not permit yourselves to know that these forces are implacable, not
because men are equally stupid and brutal and maddened everywhere,

but because the present post-emancipatory structure of Jewish life and the consequent confrontation of gentile-Jew are built upon a theory that is false and has been proven false—false and hollow to the very crumbling and corrupted core of it, the theory, namely, that Jews can cease to be Jews in order to buy their way into gentile civilization, or that the master of the gentile civilizations will admit that the price of the de-Judaization of the Jews has ever been wholly paid. (I explained all this in Israel eight years ago, and two years later Arnold Zweig explained it with a depth and precision still unrivaled in *Caliban, oder Politik und Leidenschaft*. And our books, instead of becoming instruments toward the auto-emancipation of Jewry and the warding off of a catastrophe, were patronized by a few high-brows whose "ifs" and "buts" were stamped out in the year 1933 in blood and dirt.)

It is well to be pessimistic today in order to be able to be a little optimistic on some future day. It is, of course, not to be thought of that the Jewries of German speech will be able to continue that creative and scholarly leadership which they have held from Zunz[1] to Martin Buber and his disciples and from Herzl to the Zionist thinkers of yesterday. The Polish communities, though less catastrophically stricken, are so oppressed and burdened that leadership cannot be expected from them. The Russian Jews are lost to us in this generation by the device of Red assimilation, quite analogous to Prussian assimilation and mass baptism during certain decades of the nineteenth century, or to the processes of any polity which, in the period of consolidation, is willing temporarily to admit that assimilation can proceed to the point of paying. Hence the leadership of world-Jewry outside of Palestine devolves upon American Jewry, and American Jewry, the most populous and powerful in the world today, is also the most ignorant and the one in which the crippling sickness of preoccupation without knowledge is most prevalent . . .

It is a necessity and a duty to be brutal today. It is necessary to be brutal even at the risk of being misunderstood. For, given the precise circumstances that confront us from now on, the Jewish ignorance of American Jewry may prove a disaster of incalculable consequences to all Israel.

Am I pleading *pro domo*? I am. But the *domus*, the "house" that I am pleading for is none other than *khol beth Yisrael*, the whole House of Israel, which stands in need of salvation *b'chayeykhon u-b'yomeikhon*, within your lifetime and within your days, *ba'agala u-bizeman kariv*, now and in briefest time! Do you ever read even the Kaddish or do you just mouth and mumble it? You are Jews. Nothing will save you anywhere in the world from bearing the Jewish fate that is yours. Wherewith will you bear it and help others to bear it, how will you affirm it and consent to it and even rejoice in it, if Israel and its life and its history and its meaning and its speech and its ethos are not alive and eloquent in your hearts and minds?

Part 9
In the New World

RICHARD JAMES HORATIO GOTTHEIL
1862-1936

LIKE THE INTERNATIONAL Zionist movement as a whole, Zionism began in America under the leadership of a small group of highly intellectual "westerners," though its foot soldiers were overwhelmingly east European Jews. Hibbat Zion had echoed feebly in America and here, too, there had been abortive Zionist dreams earlier in the nineteenth century, such as those of the Jewish politician Mordecai Emanuel Noah and the Quaker convert to Judaism, Warder Cresson, among others. The appearance of Herzl evoked a Zionist organization, the Knights of Zion, which was created in Chicago in 1896, even before the First Zionist Congress in the next year. Individual groups were springing up in various cities during those years of high emotion, and there were American Zionists in Basel when the Herzlian movement was officially born. All these stirrings resulted in a national conference in New York in July 1898, at which the Federation of American Zionists was launched, as a constituent of the world body, encompassing all the Zionist societies in the United States. Its first president was Richard J. H. Gottheil.

His father, Gustav Gottheil, who was then on the verge of retirement as rabbi of the most important reformed congregation in America, Temple Emanu-El of New York, had also adhered to Zionism, to the scandal of most of his congregants. The family had come to America in 1873 from Manchester, England, where Richard had been born in 1862. The younger Gottheil attended Columbia University (A.B., 1881) and then pursued graduate studies in Semitic languages at several German universities. He became a lecturer in Syriac at Columbia in 1886 and was raised to a professorship there in the next year. Gottheil's academic life was identified entirely with Columbia and with the New York Public Library, which appointed him the head of its Oriental department in 1898. He served in both capacities until his death in 1936.

Richard Gottheil was a dignitary in scholarly circles. At various times he held such offices as president of the Society of Biblical Literature (1902–1903), director of the American School for Oriental Research in Jerusalem (1909–1910), and president of the American Oriental Society (1933–1934). Both on his account and together with his father, the coupling of the Gottheil name with Zionism gave the new movement needed prestige in the Jewish and the wider American community. Apart from organizational and political services during his six years, from 1898 to 1904, as president of the Federation of American Zionists, Gottheil did important work in behalf of Zionism as a writer. For example, his article on Zionism in *The Jewish Encyclopedia*, which was published in New York in 1904, is still the best short history of the earliest years of the movement.

More important, however, is the reworking of Herzl's main themes in consonance with American experience, which Gottheil initiated. The pages that appear below are taken from the first pamphlet to be published by the Federation he headed and they represent, therefore, the first official statement of the philosophy of American Zionism. In this essay Gottheil was already confronting the problems which were to occur and recur with particular bite in America. Here he began the debate that American Zionism would long continue with the notions, of some, that Zionism means total evacuation of the western world and, of others, that adherence to it is unpatriotic. The essence of the answers that were used then and later are in this excerpt.

THE AIMS OF ZIONISM (1898)

A PROFESSOR at the University of Vienna has recently said: "The best way to protect ourselves from the Jews is to shoot them off." I admit, this is a practical solution; I will even say, a magnanimous one in very many cases. But such stoic magnanimity is not for us who are of their flesh and of their blood. If we are to save these Jews—and mind you we are here speaking of fully three-quarters of the Jewish people —we must take them out of the places in which it has become impossible for them to live. Whatever our own personal consideration may be, whether we like it or not, we dare not leave these unfortunates to their fate. Every fiber in our body cries "shame" to the very suggestion that we adopt such a course as that. What then? Where are they to go in Europe? Certainly not to Austria, certainly not to Germany, to France, to Spain, or to Portugal. Even in England, Lord Hardwicke's Alien Immigration Bill has already passed the House of Lords;[1] and the Primrose League (a league founded to do honor to the memory of a Jewish Premier)[2] had in July last gathered no less than 23,000 signatures to a petition that the Bill be put in the Government program for the coming session. This means that England has as many Jews as she cares to have; that she desires no addition to their number. Shall they all come to America, to the greater New York? It is more than an open secret that we cannot cope with the 400,000 Jews in our city; Boston, Baltimore, Philadelphia, and Chicago will give you the same answer. Or shall they all be taken to the Argentine Republic, where millions have already been spent in the vain endeavor to colonize a few thousands? Even if the magnificent charity of Baron de Hirsch had proved a success, in a few years' time that country would have its full quota of Jews, and we should be building up there a similar state of affairs to that which we see in Russia and Galicia today.

For the fact which we must bear in mind is not so much that there are Hamans and Stöckers and Drumonts and Lügers.[3] Such men, I am afraid, there will always be; and a civilization ought not to be judged by its most abased products. The fact which ought to make us stop and think is this, that of all the popular cries, that of all the popular watchwords, the one "*à bas les Juifs*" is the most popular, the most certain of a large following. The racial and—I am sorry to say—the religious feelings upon which those fanatics play have never left the people. They are always there; and though they may slumber for a while, they are ready to break forth at the very first call. Like waves of an angry sea, they rise and fall; and the history of the Jews is but the log of a storm-tossed ship which can find no rest until it gets back again into the haven from which it started.

That haven from which it started was Palestine; and to that haven it must again come; to that haven, protected by the international guarantees which will keep the waves from once more touching our ship. And all through the Jewish Middle Ages, though the ship has been forced westward, the hearts of those who were in it have turned in secret longing and in public prayer to this place of rest. Though the Jew clothed this hope in his Messianic Prophetism, it was no less of a real hope——

And now it does seem as if there were some chance that our own nineteenth century, said to be the most prosaic and the most material of all the centuries, may see the realization of this Jewish hope.

But perhaps I am wrong, and the Jew is destined ever to remain a wanderer? Many not-yet Zionist Jews seem to answer "Yes," and to remind us at the same time of what is technically called "The Mission of the Jews," the mission to carry out among the nations of the world the truths of the Jewish Faith. You will certainly hear nothing from me which could militate against so noble an object for a people's existence. But are we not woefully deceiving ourselves? How much are we doing; how much can we do to fulfill this mission? Are the pitiful denizens of our eastern ghettos preaching actively a gospel to the world? Or are the well-fed dwellers in our golden western ghettos more actively engaged in this messianic propaganda? Mission-preaching and wealth-getting can never go hand in hand. Until we can let the last go, it is sheer folly for us to talk of being a nation of priests. And if a poor man comes to you, storm-beaten and drenched with rain; if he begs from you a morsel of bread, would you offer him a spiritual mission, a grand ideal with which to fill his stomach? Shame upon you if you did; unless you yourselves were willing to discard palace and home and work with him in poverty for the realization of this ideal. The first mission of man is to live as a decent member of society. The first mission of a people is to live its life as a member of the great family of nations the world over; and in so far as it lives that life worthily and well and contributes to the moral uplifting of society, it is fulfilling its first and primary mission. When that is accomplished, it is time enough to remind it of its higher mission. With three-fourths of Jewry in dismal penury, unwilling to remain in such condition, fighting tooth and nail against a whole world in the effort to rise above it; with the other one-fourth seeking a comfortable and easy life in well-warmed houses and at well-supplied tables, what, I ask, has become of the Mission of Israel?

Zionism has sought and has found for us a basis which is a broader one than the religious one (and on which all religious distinctions vanish), that of race and of nationality. And even though we do not know it, and even though we refuse to recognize it, there are forces which are unconsciously making for the same end, working out in spite of us the will of Almighty God. Never before has such intelligent interest been taken by the Jews in their own past history. Germany has become honeycombed with societies for the study of Jewish history. Vienna, Hamburg, and Frankfurt have associations for the preservation of Jewish art. The Société des Etudes Juives, the American Jewish

Historical Society, the Anglo-Jewish Historical Society, the Maccabeans in London, the Judaeans in New York, the Council of Jewish Women, the Chautauqua Assembly meetings—all of these and many others are working in the same direction. They are welding the people of Israel together once more. They are not religious societies, mark you. They rest upon the solid basis of common racial and national affinity.

FOR SUCH AS THESE among us Zionism also has its message. It wishes to give back to the Jew that nobleness of spirit, that confidence in himself, that belief in his own powers which only perfect freedom can give. With a home of his own, he will no longer feel himself a pariah among the nations, he will nowhere hide his own peculiarities —peculiarities to which he has a right as much as any one—but will see that those peculiarities carry with them a message which will force for them the admiration of the world. He will feel that he belongs somewhere and not everywhere. He will try to be something and not everything. The great word which Zionism preaches is conciliation of conflicting aims, of conflicting lines of action; conciliation of Jew to Jew. It means conciliation of the non-Jewish world to the Jew as well. It wishes to heal old wounds; and by frankly confessing differences which do exist, however much we try to explain them away, to work out its own salvation upon its own ground, and from these to send forth its spiritual message to a conciliated world.

But, you will ask, if Zionism is able to find a permanent home in Palestine for those Jews who are forced to go there as well as those who wish to go, what is to become of us who have entered, to such a degree, into the life around us and who feel able to continue as we have begun? What is to be our relation to the new Jewish polity? I can only answer, exactly the same as is the relation of people of other nationalities all the world over to their parent home. What becomes of the Englishman in every corner of the globe; what becomes of the German? Does the fact that the great mass of their people live in their own land prevent them from doing their whole duty toward the land in which they happen to live? Is the German-American considered less of an American because he cultivates the German language and is interested in the fate of his fellow Germans at home? Is the Irish-American less of an American because he gathers money to help his struggling brethren in the Green Isle? Or are the Scandinavian-Americans less worthy of the title Americans because they consider precious the bonds which bind them to the land of their birth, as well as those which bind them to the land of their adoption?

Nay! it would seem to me that just those who are so afraid that our action will be misinterpreted should be among the greatest helpers in the Zionist cause. For those who feel no racial and national communion with the life from which they have sprung should greet with joy the turning of Jewish immigration to some place other than the land in which they dwell. They must feel, e.g., that a continual influx of Jews who are not Americans is a continual menace to the more or less complete absorption for which they are striving.

But I must not detain you much longer. Will you permit me to sum up for you the position which we Zionists take in the following statements:

We believe that the Jews are something more than a purely religious body; that they are not only a race, but also a nation; though a nation without as yet two important requisites—a common home and a common language.

We believe that if an end is to be made to Jewish misery and to the exceptional position which the Jews occupy—which is the primary cause of Jewish misery—the Jewish nation must be placed once again in a home of its own.

We believe that such a national regeneration is the fulfillment of the hope which has been present to the Jew throughout his long and painful history.

We believe that only by means of such a national regeneration can the religious regeneration of the Jews take place, and they be put in a position to do that work in the religious world which Providence has appointed for them.

We believe that such a home can only naturally, and without violence to their whole past, be found in the land of their fathers—in Palestine.

We believe that such a return must have the guarantee of the great powers of the world, in order to secure for the Jews a stable future.

And we hold that this does not mean that all Jews must return to Palestine.

This, ladies and gentlemen, is the Zionist program.

We take hope, for has not that Jewish Zionist said, "We belong to a race that can do everything but fail."

SOLOMON SCHECHTER 1847-1915

IN THE DIRECT SENSE Schechter's career belongs more to the history of Jewish religion and scholarship than to the story of Zionism. Nonetheless, though he never took active part in the organized movement, he is a central figure in its development in America. During his fourteen years in the United States Schechter had an enormous personal influence on a number of younger leaders, like Judah Magnes, who were to understand Zionist ideas in ways that they had learned largely from him. His own credo (reprinted here), a reinterpretation of Ahad Ha-Am in the context of Schechter's own unfanatical but traditionalist religiosity, naturalized cultural Zionism in America. Above all, Schechter imparted a Zionist temper to the Conservative movement in American Judaism, of which he was the master builder, both intellectually and institutionally, so that it remained henceforth the most overwhelmingly Zionist of the three major Jewish religious groupings in America.

Solomon Schechter was born in a small town in Romania, probably in 1847; no accurate birth records were kept there in those days and he himself was in some doubt as to the exact year. After a thorough traditional education in Talmud and rabbinic texts, he went to Vienna, where he studied both at the university and under Isaac Hirsch Weiss and Meir Friedmann, two of the great modern, "scientific" talmudists. From Vienna, Schechter went to Berlin, where he came to the attention of Claude G. Montefiore, the Anglo-Jewish scholar and religious reformer. Montefiore invited Schechter in 1882 to come to England to be his tutor in rabbinics. Though Schechter arrived there knowing not a word of English, he mastered the language so quickly that he used it only three years later for his first published essay (*The Study of the Talmud*). Schechter was to continue to write in this vein all his life, becoming a notable stylist and the greatest of all interpreters of Judaism to the English-speaking world. The three volumes of these essays, under the title *Studies in Judaism*, have been often reprinted. Both in these volumes and in *Some Aspects of Jewish Theology,* a somewhat more technical volume in the same genre, Schechter expounded his religious outlook, that of a successor to Zechariah Frankel in carrying forward the idea of "positive-historical Judaism."

Schechter's spiritual physiognomy was well-formed in his years in England. In 1890 he was appointed to an academic post at Cambridge and in 1899 to a professorship of Hebrew at University College, London. Toward the end of this decade Schechter achieved international fame in scholarship. He identified a leaf of manuscript as part of the lost Hebrew original of Ecclesiasticus and in the winter of 1896 he went to Egypt, to return from Cairo with thousands of ancient manuscript pages out of the Genizah (depository of texts no longer usable) of its ancient synagogue. This find was as important in its day, for rabbinic scholarship, as the recent discoveries in the region of the Dead Sea have been to students of the Bible.

In 1902 Schechter came to America to head a reorganized Jewish Theological Seminary. In the years of his presidency he fashioned this institution to represent his liberal traditionalist religious views. By the very nature of his position, with its emphasis on the religious nationhood of the Jew, he was close to at least one form of Zionism. His essay below accepts political Zionism as the useful handmaiden of his ultimate spiritual purposes and the indispensable tool for saving Jews in need in eastern Europe. In a nonmystical and much more modern way Schechter is reminiscent of Kook's ideas, which he was developing at the same time. To both anything that is creative within Jewry is a tool, often despite itself, to the achievement of the divine aims which are inherent in the Jewish people.

Schechter died in New York in 1915.

ZIONISM: A STATEMENT (1906)

THERE IS A STORY TOLD of a German Jew of the older generation that when his friends came to him about the beginning of the eighties of the last century, and asked what he thought of the *new* attacks on the Jews, he looked rather astonished, and said, "They are not new; they are the old ones." I may say with equal justice that the attacks on Zionism which have come lately from press and pulpit are not new. They have been refuted ever so many times, and have been as often repeated. Lest, however, my ignoring direct challenges in accordance with the old rule, "Silence is tantamount to admission," be taken as a proof that I have at last become converted by the arguments of our opponents, I will state here clearly the reasons for my allegiance to Zionism. I wish only to premise that I am no official expounder of Zionism. I am not claiming or aspiring to the role of leadership in this movement. The following remarks have only the value of representing the opinion of one of the rank and file, stating clearly his attitude toward this movement, though he believes that he reflects the views of a great number of fellow Zionists. Zionism is an ideal, and as such is indefinable. It is thus subject to various interpretations and susceptive of different aspects. It may appear to one as the rebirth of national Jewish consciousness, to another as a religious revival, whilst to a third it may present itself as a path leading to the goal of Jewish culture; and to a fourth it may take the form of the last and only solution of the Jewish problem. By reason of this variety of aspects, Zionism has been able to unite on its platform the most heterogeneous elements, representing Jews of all countries, and exhibiting almost all the different types of culture and thought as only a really great and universal movement could command. That each of its representatives should emphasize the particular aspect most congenial to his way of thinking, and most suitable for his mode of action, is only natural. On one point, however, they all agree, namely, that it is not only desirable, but absolutely necessary, that Palestine, the land of our fathers, should be recovered with the purpose of forming a home for at least a portion of the Jews, who would lead there an independent national life. That the language of the leaders was sometimes ambiguous and not quite definite in the declaration of this principle is owing to the boldness of the proposition and the environments in which these leaders were brought up, where everything distinctly Jewish was in need of an apology, rather than to any doubt about the final aim of Zionism, as conceived in the minds of the great majority of Zionists. Nor was it strange that some backslidings should occur, and that in moments of despair, counsels of despair would prevail, considering the terrible crises through which we have passed during the last few years. The great majority of Zionists remain loyal to the great idea of Zion and Jerusalem, to which history and tradition, and the general Jewish sentiment, point. It is "God's country" in the fullest and truest sense of the words. It is the "Promised Land" still maintaining its place in every

Jewish heart, excepting those, perhaps, with whom Jewish history com-
mences about the year 1830, and Jewish literature is confined to the
transactions of the rabbinical synods of the last century, and the files
of Philippson's *Allgemeine Zeitung des Judentums.*[1]

To me personally, after long hesitation and careful watching,
Zionism recommended itself as the great bulwark against assimilation.
By assimilation I do not understand what is usually understood by
Americanization: namely, that every Jew should do his best to acquire
the English language; that he should study American history and
make himself acquainted with the best productions of American
literature; that he should be a law-abiding citizen, thoroughly appreciating the privilege of being a member of this great commonwealth,
and joyfully prepared to discharge the duties of American citizenship.
What I understand by assimilation is loss of identity; or that process
of disintegration which, passing through various degrees of defiance
of all Jewish thought and of disloyalty to Israel's history and its
mission, terminates variously in different lands. In Germany, for instance (where the pressure from above in favor of the dominant
religion is very strong), it ends in direct and public apostasy; in other
countries where this pressure has been removed, it results in the
severance of all affiliation with the synagogue, and is followed by
a sort of "eclectic religiosity," that coquettes with the various churches,
not neglecting even the Christian Science Temple, and is consummated by a final, though imperceptible, absorption in the great
majority. This consummation will surely be hastened by the gradual
disappearance of social disparity. What this process finally means for
Judaism will perhaps be best seen from the following quotation from
Wellhausen's *History of Israel.*[2] After giving Spinoza's oft-quoted
view regarding the possibilities of the absorption of Israel by its surroundings, the well-known Bible critic remarks: "The persistency of
the race may, of course, prove a harder thing to overcome than
Spinoza has supposed; but, nevertheless, he will be found to have
spoken truly in declaring that the so-called emancipation of the Jews
must inevitably lead to the extinction of Judaism wherever the process
is extended beyond the political to the social sphere."

The only comfort that Wellhausen leaves us is that "for the accomplishment of this, centuries may be required." We, and the few
generations that are to succeed us, are to abide cheerfully in this
intermediate condition, and to acquiesce in the tortures of a slow
death, or, as the great Alexandrian sage in his description of the
punishment awaiting the specially wicked expresses it, we are "to live

continually dying," and to endure an unceasing dissolution until death will have mercy upon us and will give us the last *coup de grâce*. It is this kind of assimilation, with the terrible consequences indicated, that I dread most; even more than pogroms. To this form of assimilation, Zionism in the sense defined will prove, and is already proving, a most wholesome check. Whatever faults may be found with its real or self-appointed leaders, Zionism as a whole forms an opposing force against the conception of the destiny of Israel and the interpretation of its mission the leading thought of which is apparently the well-known epigram, "Whosoever shall seek to gain his life shall lose it, but whosoever shall lose his life shall preserve it." Zionism declares boldly to the world that Judaism means to preserve its life by *not* losing its life. It shall be a true and healthy life, with a policy of its own, a religion wholly its own, invigorated by sacred memories and sacred environments, and proving a tower of strength and of unity not only for the remnant gathered within the borders of the Holy Land, but also for those who shall, by choice or necessity, prefer what now constitutes the Galut.

The term Galut is here loosely used, expressing, as I have often heard it, the despair and helplessness felt in the presence of a great tragedy. And the tragedy is not imaginary. It is real, and it exists everywhere. It *is* a tragedy to see a great ancient people, distinguished for its loyalty to its religion, and its devotion to its sacred law, losing thousands every day by the mere process of attrition. It *is* a tragedy to see sacred institutions as ancient as the mountains, to maintain which Israel for thousands of years shrank from no sacrifice, destroyed before our very eyes and exchanged for corresponding institutions borrowed from hostile religions. It *is* a tragedy to see the language held sacred by all the world, in which Holy Writ was composed, and which served as the depository of Israel's greatest and best thought, doomed to oblivion and forced out gradually from the synagogue. It *is* a tragedy to see the descendants of those who revealed revelation to the world and who developed the greatest religious literature in existence, so little familiar with real Jewish thought, and so utterly wanting in all sympathy with it, that they have no other interpretation to offer of Israel's scriptures, Israel's religion, and Israel's ideals and aspirations and hopes, than those suggested by their natural opponents, slavishly following their opinions, copying their phrases, repeating their catchwords, not sparing us even the taunt of tribalism and Orientalism. I am not accusing anybody. I am only stating facts that are the outcome of causes under which we all labor, but for none of which any party in particular can be made responsible, though it cannot be denied that some among us rather made too much virtue of a necessity, and indulged, and are still indulging, in experiments in euthanasia. The economic conditions under which we live; the innate desire for comfort; the inherent tendency toward imitation; the natural desire not to appear peculiar; the accessibility of theological systems, possessing all the seductions of "newness and modernity," patronized by fashion and even by potentates, and taught in ever so many universities, and condensed in dozens of encyclopedias, are sufficient and weighty enough causes to account for our tragedy. But, however natural the causes may be, they do not alter the doom. The effects are bound to be fatal. The fact thus remains that we are helpless spectators in the face of great tragedies, in other words, that we are in Galut. This may not be the Galut of the Jews, but it is the Galut of Judaism, or as certain mystics expressed it, the Galut of *Hannephesh*, the Galut of the Jewish soul, wasting away before our very eyes. With a little modification we might repeat here the words of a Jewish Hellenist of the second century who, in his grief, exclaims: "Wherefore is Israel given up as a reproach to the heathen, and for what cause is the people whom Thou best loved given unto ungodly nations, and why is the law of our forefathers brought to naught, and the written covenants come to none effect? And we pass away out of the world as grasshoppers, and our life is astonishment and fear, and we are not worthy to obtain mercy."

The foregoing remarks have made it clear that I belong to that class of Zionists that lays more stress on the religious-national aspects of Zionism than on any other feature peculiar to it. The rebirth of Israel's national consciousness, and the revival of Israel's religion, or, to use a shorter term, the revival of Judaism, are inseparable. When Israel found itself, it found its God. When Israel lost itself, or began to work at its self-effacement, it was sure to deny its God. The selection of Israel, the indestructibility of God's covenant with Israel, the immortality of Israel as a nation, and the final restoration of Israel to Palestine, where the nation will live a holy life on holy ground, with all the wide-reaching consequences of the conversion of humanity and the establishment of the Kingdom of God on earth—all these are the common ideals and the common ideas that permeate the whole of Jewish literature extending over nearly four thousand years, including the largest bulk of the Hellenistic portion of it. The universalistic passages in the Scripture usually paraded by the "prophetic Jew" as implying the final disappearance, or extinction, of Israel are in every case misquotations torn from their context, or ignoring other utterances by the same writer. Indeed, our prophetic Jew

> *Boldly pilfers from the Pentateuch:*
> *And, undisturbed by conscientious qualms,*
> *Perverts the Prophets, and purloins the Psalms.*

The interpretations smuggled into the passages are just as false and unscientific as the well-known Christological passages extracted from the Old Testament, and even from the Talmud, to be met with in missionary tracts, composed especially for the benefit of fresh converts.

The reproach that Zionism is unspiritual is meaningless. Indeed, there seems to be a notion abroad that spirituality is a negative quality. Take any ideal, and translate it into action, any sentiment of reverence, and piety, and give it expression through a symbol or ceremony, speak of the human yearning after communion with God, and try to realize it through actual prayer and you will be at once denounced as unspiritual. However, the imputation is as old as the days when the name Pharisee became a reproach, and it is not to be expected that the Zionists would be spared. In general, it is the antinominian who will tell you that he is the only heir to the rare quality of spirituality, whereas the real saint is in all his actions so spontaneous and so natural that he is entirely unconscious of possessing spirituality, and practically never mentions it.

The Zionists are no saints, but they may fairly claim that few movements are more free from the considerations of convenience and comfort, and less tainted with worldliness and other-worldliness than the one which they serve. Nothing was to be gained by joining it. All the powers that be, were, and still are, opposed to it, whether in their capacity as individuals or as wealthy corporations. The Zionists are just beginning to be tolerated, but I remember distinctly the time when adhesion to the cause of Zionism might interfere with the prospects of man's career, the cry being, "no Zionists need apply." The classes from which the Zionists were recruited were mostly the poorest among the poor. College men and university men, more blessed with enthusiasm and idealism than with the goods of this world, also furnished a fair quota. But this lack of means did not prevent them from responding most generously to every appeal made on the behalf of the cause. They taxed themselves to the utmost of their capacity, and beyond. I myself have witnessed cases in which men and women joyfully contributed their last earnings, foregoing their summer vacations, for which they had been saving a whole year.

The activity of Zionism must not be judged by what it has accomplished *in* Zion and Jerusalem—where it has to deal with political problems as yet not ripe for solution—but by what it has thus far achieved *for* Zion and Jerusalem, through the awakening of the national Jewish consciousness, notwithstanding the systematic and ruthless efforts made in the opposite direction during the greater part of the last century. Our synagogues and our homes plainly show the effect. Zion and Jerusalem have not been allowed to stand as a sad, glorious remembrance of a past, as mere objects of pious sentiment. Indeed, the astounding discovery was made that far from being considered as a day of disaster, the Ninth of Ab has to be looked upon as a day of liberation, when Judaism threw off the shackles of nationalism to congeal into a mere Church—with a ritual and a body of doctrines to be promulgated some nineteen hundred years later. Unfortunately, Israel was smitten with blindness, failing to understand its real destiny, and in the perversion of its heart, for eighteen hundred years observed the Ninth of Ab as a day of mourning and weeping, of humiliation and fasting, thus willfully delaying its redemption. I have always wondered that the Church has not yet been enterprising enough to put up a statue in gratitude to its benefactor Titus, the *delectus generis humani*, representing the goddess *Universa*, with a scribe and a priest cowering in chains at her feet.

The work, accordingly, in which Zionism had to engage first, and in which it will have to continue for many years to come, was the work of regeneration. It had to re-create the Jewish consciousness before creating the Jewish state. In this respect, Zionism has already achieved great things. There is hardly a single Jewish community in any part of the globe which is not represented by a larger or smaller number of men and women acknowledging themselves as Zionists and standing out as a living protest against the tendencies just hinted at. It has created a press, and has called into life a host of lecturers and speakers propagating its doctrines and preaching them boldly to Israel all over the world. It has given Asher Ginsberg, or as he is better known, by the pen name of Ahad Ha-Am, one of our finest intellects and most original thinkers; and he is followed by a whole host of disciples, all of them working under the stimulus of the Jewish national ideal, much as they may differ in the Zionistic aspects they happen to emphasize. It has enriched our literature with a large number of novels and lyrics, and even distinct Zionist melodies are not wanting. It has further called into existence numerous societies, whose aim it is to make the sacred tongue a living language by means of writing and even conversing in it, while in several communities special schools have been established with the same end in view. Better to advance this end, a whole series of Hebrew primers, grammars, and reading books for the young have been produced. Several translations prepared from German, French, and English works bearing on Jewish history and cognate subjects, all of them calculated to strengthen religious-national consciousness, have also appeared under the inspiration of Zionism. Foremost of all, Zionism has succeeded in bringing back into the fold many men and women, both here and in Europe, who otherwise would have been lost to Judaism. It has given them a new interest in the synagogue and everything Jewish, and put before them an ideal worthy of their love and their sacrifice. Cases have come under my notice where Jewish college men, at a comparatively advanced age, began to study the sacred language and to repair to the synagogue, sharing both in its joys and in its griefs, some among them encountering the displeasure and ridicule of their relatives, who were fanatical assimilators and who brought up their children without religious education of any kind. Of course, backslidings and relapses occur; but it is an advantage to Zionism that in its present condition, at least, it is all sacrifice and no gain. It holds out no prospect to the ambitious and to "those who exalt themselves to establish the vision" of a Jewish state without Jewish memories, without historic foundation, and without traditional principles. The undesirables and the impatient will thus, under one pretense or another, leave it soon, and indeed are dropping out already, so that its purification of all alloy and discordant elements is only a question of a very short time.

The taunt of retrogression and reaction has no terrors for us. To insist on progressing when one has come to the conclusion that a step forward means ruin is sheer obstinacy. Unless we are convinced so deeply of our infallibility that we take every utterance of ours as a divine revelation, and our every action as a precedent and as tradition, there may come a time in our lives when we may have to return. As a fact, Zionism is the natural rebound from an artificial and overstrained condition of things which could no longer last. It is the Declaration of Jewish Independence from all kinds of slavery, whether material or spiritual. It is as natural and instinctive as life itself, and no amount of scolding and abuse will prevent the reassertion of the Jewish soul, which in our unconscious Zionism is an actual present-day experience, though the expression given to it takes different shape in different minds. Moreover, Zionism thoroughly believes in progress and development; but it must be progress along Jewish lines, and the goal to be reached must be the Jewish historic ideal.

But whilst Zionism is constantly winning souls for the present, it is at the same time preparing for us the future, which will be a Jewish future. Only then, when Judaism has found itself, when the Jewish soul has been redeemed from the Galut, can Judaism hope to resume its mission to the world. Everybody whose view has not been narrowed by the blinkers imposed on him by his little wing or by party considerations knows well enough that it is not only traditional religion which is on trial. We are on a veritable volcano created by the upheavals of the newest methods of "searching research," which respects as little the new formulae, such as the categoric imperative, conscience, the notion of duty, and the concept of morality and ethics, as it does creeds and dogmas. The disruption may come at any moment unless revelation is reasserted. The declaration, *Freedom is our Messiah*, which I have so often heard, may be good Fourth of July oratory, but it is miserably bad theology, and worse philosophy, having in view the terrible woes and complicated problems besetting humanity. Now, what happened once may happen again, and Israel may another time be called upon with its mission to the nations. Under the present conditions, however, we have neither a defined mission, nor does any man take this "mission" seriously, and the talk about it is allowed to be a mere *licentia predicatorum*. But we know that the Bible, which influenced humanity so deeply and proved so largely instrumental in the partial conversion of the world, arose in Palestine or in circles which looked on Palestine as their home. Those who wrote the Bible moved and had their whole being in the religious national idea, and lived under the discipline of the Law. History may, and to my belief, will repeat itself, and Israel will be the chosen instrument of God for the new and final mission; but then Israel must first effect its own redemption and live again its own life, and be Israel again, to accomplish its universal mission. The passages in the Bible most distinguished for their universalistic tendency and grandeur are, as is well known, the verses in Isaiah and Micah, and there it is solemnly proclaimed: "Out of Zion shall go forth the law, and the word of the Lord from Jerusalem."[3]

Our sages have themselves given expression to this correspondence between the universalistic and the nationalistic elements in Judaism. A solemn declaration, thus they declare, has the Holy One, blessed be He, registered: "I will not enter the heavenly Jerusalem, until Israel shall come to the earthly Jerusalem." Not in conflict but in consonance with Israel's establishment of the divine institutions in their full integrity in God's own land will be the triumph in all its glory of the Kingdom of Heaven.

LOUIS DEMBITZ BRANDEIS   1856-1941

LOUIS DEMBITZ BRANDEIS was the most distinguished figure in American life to become a Zionist. The story of the successive stages of his public and legal career, from his days of battling the "interests" as a lawyer in Boston to the twenty-two years of his service on the Supreme Court of the United States, is too well-known to need retelling here. The opinions of Brandeis will always remain the landmark in the turning of constitutional law toward social and economic realism. Brandeis is, however, of great importance as well in the development of Zionism.

After the failure of the revolution of 1848 his parents and their families fled Prague for the New World and settled in Louisville, Kentucky. Brandeis was born there in 1856. He gave early proof of intellectual brilliance, graduating from high school at fourteen with the highest honors. From 1872 to 1875 Brandeis was in Europe, at first traveling with his family and then for two years at school in Dresden. Upon his return he entered Harvard and graduated from its law school in 1877, before his twenty-first birthday, at the head of his class. Brandeis achieved early success and financial independence at the bar in Boston and devoted himself ever more to public causes. It was one of these activities which began his involvement in Jewish affairs.

Brandeis had been brought up without any formal religion, and until he was fifty-four he had come into no appreciable contact with the Jewish community. He met its newest segment in 1910, when he was called in to help settle a strike in New York in the Jewish-dominated garment industry. Always a man to take great pains, Brandeis got to know a lot about the Jewish life of the immigrants on the "East Side" and was moved by a deep sense of kinship with the workers whom he was meeting at the arbitration table. His immediate stimulus to Zionism was a conversation with Jacob de Haas in 1912. De Haas was then the editor of a Boston Jewish weekly, but he had been part of Herzl's original entourage. As a result of this meeting Brandeis joined and became active in the Federation of American Zionists.

When the First World War broke out, the work of the Zionist movement was handicapped by the fact that its central office was in Berlin. The responsibility for support of the Jewish settlement in Palestine and for the major political work of Zionism seemed in 1914 to have devolved largely on American Jewry. A Provisional Executive Committee for General Zionist Affairs was organized in New York, and Brandeis gladly accepted unanimous election to be its head. From 1914 to 1918, the years he served in this office, Brandeis was thus the active leader of American Zionism and at the very top of international Zionist affairs. In his new role Brandeis immediately set out on a speaking tour in the fall and winter of 1914, to explain and gain support for Zionism. He felt particularly constrained to address himself to the relationship between his own affirmation of Jewish loyalties through Zionism and his American patriotism. Most of the text of this considered credo, in its final version as a speech to a conference of Reform rabbis in 1915, is given below.

Perhaps the most important service that Brandeis rendered to Zionism during those years was his significant work in Washington during the negotiations that preceded the issuing of the Balfour Declaration in 1917. The full story of his role has not yet been told, but it is at least arguable on the evidence so far available that his influence was of crucial importance, especially since after 1916 he was on the Supreme Bench and personally very close to Woodrow Wilson.

At the Pittsburgh Zionist convention in 1918 Brandeis defined a five-point code of social justice for the Jewish homeland. The intent of his approach, as he developed it there and later, was to put all of Zionist effort into the most careful and businesslike upbuilding of Palestine, for which he wanted to enlist the active aid and co-operation at the decision-making level of men not necessarily Zionist by ideology. Brandeis regarded himself as a follower of Herzl and he was impatient with anything in Zionism, like cultural work in the Diaspora, that was not directly related to the task of upbuilding Palestine. The European Zionists, as headed by Weizmann, had differing conceptions, and personal dislikes also came into play. These quarrels resulted in a formal breach at an international Zionist meeting in London in 1920 and the carrying of the fight to America. Brandeis and his followers lost at the convention in Cleveland in 1921 and he resigned office, though he retained Zionist membership.

After this breach Brandeis helped in organizing a number of corporations, ultimately merged in the Palestine Economic Corporation, to do practical work in the homeland. He remained vitally concerned with Zionism, lending advice and support during all the crises of Palestinian Jewry, to the end of his life in 1941.

THE JEWISH PROBLEM
AND HOW TO SOLVE IT (1915)

LET US BEAR clearly in mind what Zionism is, or rather what it is not. It is not a movement to remove all the Jews of the world compulsorily to Palestine. In the first place there are 14,000,000 Jews, and Palestine would not accommodate more than one-third of that number. In the second place, it is not a movement to compel anyone to go to Palestine. It is essentially a movement to give to the Jew more, not less freedom; it aims to enable the Jews to exercise the same right now exercised by practically every other people in the world: to live at their option either in the land of their fathers or in some other country; a right which members of small nations as well as of large, which Irish, Greek, Bulgarian, Serbian, or Belgian, may now exercise as fully as Germans or English.

Zionism seeks to establish in Palestine, for such Jews as choose to go and remain there, and for their descendants, a legally secured home, where they may live together and lead a Jewish life, where they may expect ultimately to constitute a majority of the population, and may look forward to what we should call home rule. The Zionists seek to establish this home in Palestine because they are convinced that the undying longing of Jews for Palestine is a fact of deepest significance; that it is a manifestation in the struggle for existence by an ancient people which has established its right to live, a people whose three thousand years of civilization has produced a faith, culture, and individuality which will enable it to contribute largely in the future, as it has in the past, to the advance of civilization; and that it is not a right merely but a duty of the Jewish nationality to survive and develop. They believe that only in Palestine can Jewish life be fully protected from the forces of disintegration; that there alone can the

Jewish spirit reach its full and natural development; and that by securing for those Jews who wish to settle there the opportunity to do so, not only those Jews, but all other Jews will be benefited, and that the long perplexing Jewish problem will, at last, find solution. They believe that, to accomplish this, it is not necessary that the Jewish population of Palestine be large as compared with the whole number of Jews in the world; for throughout centuries when the Jewish influence was greatest, during the Persian, the Greek, and the Roman empires, only a relatively small part of the Jews lived in Palestine; and only a small part of the Jews returned from Babylon when the Temple was rebuilt.

Since the destruction of the Temple, nearly two thousand years ago, the longing for Palestine has been ever present with the Jew. It was the hope of a return to the land of his fathers that buoyed up the Jew amidst persecution, and for the realization of which the devout ever prayed. Until a generation ago this was a hope merely, a wish piously prayed for, but not worked for. The Zionist movement is idealistic, but it is also essentially practical. It seeks to realize that hope; to make the dream of a Jewish life in a Jewish land come true as other great dreams of the world have been realized, by men working with devotion, intelligence, and self-sacrifice. It was thus that the dream of Italian independence and unity, after centuries of vain hope, came true through the efforts of Mazzini, Garibaldi, and Cavour; that the dream of Greek, of Bulgarian, and of Serbian independence became facts.

The rebirth of the Jewish nation is no longer a mere dream. It is in process of accomplishment in a most practical way, and the story is a wonderful one. A generation ago a few Jewish emigrants from Russia and from Romania, instead of proceeding westward to this hospitable country where they might easily have secured material prosperity, turned eastward for the purpose of settling in the land of their fathers.

To the worldly-wise these efforts at colonization appeared very foolish. Nature and man presented obstacles in Palestine which appeared almost insuperable; and the colonists were in fact ill-equipped for their task, save in their spirit of devotion and self-sacrifice. The land, harassed by centuries of misrule, was treeless and apparently sterile; and it was infested with malaria. The Government offered them no security, either as to life or property. The colonists themselves were not only unfamiliar with the character of the country, but were ignorant of the farmer's life which they proposed to lead; for the Jews of Russia and Romania had been generally denied the opportunity of owning or working land. Furthermore, these colonists were not inured to the physical hardships to which the life of a pioneer is necessarily subjected. To these hardships and to malaria many succumbed. Those who survived were long confronted with failure. But at last success came. Within a generation these Jewish Pilgrim Fathers, and those who followed them, have succeeded in establishing these two fundamental propositions:

First: That Palestine is fit for the modern Jew.

Second: That the modern Jew is fit for Palestine.

Over forty self-governing Jewish colonies attest to this remarkable achievement.

This land, treeless a generation ago, supposed to be sterile and hopelessly arid, has been shown to have been treeless and sterile because of man's misrule. It has been shown to be capable of becoming again a land "flowing with milk and honey." Oranges and grapes, olives and almonds, wheat and other cereals are now growing there in profusion.

This material development has been attended by a spiritual and social development no less extraordinary; a development in education, in health, and in social order; and in the character and habits of the population. Perhaps the most extraordinary achievement of Jewish nationalism is the revival of the Hebrew language, which has again become a language of the common intercourse of men. The Hebrew tongue, called a dead language for nearly two thousand years, has, in the Jewish colonies and in Jerusalem, become again the living mother tongue. The effect of this common language in unifying the Jew is, of course, great; for the Jews of Palestine came literally from all the lands of the earth, each speaking, excepting those who used Yiddish, the language of the country from which he came, and remaining, in the main, almost a stranger to the others. But the effect of the renaissance of the Hebrew tongue is far greater than that of unifying the Jews. It is a potent factor in reviving the essentially Jewish spirit.

Our Jewish Pilgrim Fathers have laid the foundation. It remains for us to build the superstructure.

Let no American imagine that Zionism is inconsistent with Patriotism. Multiple loyalties are objectionable only if they are inconsistent. A man is a better citizen of the United States for being also a loyal citizen of his state, and of his city; for being loyal to his family, and to his profession or trade; for being loyal to his college or his lodge. Every Irish American who contributed toward advancing home rule was a better man and a better American for the sacrifice he made.

Every American Jew who aids in advancing the Jewish settlement in Palestine, though he feels that neither he nor his descendants will ever live there, will likewise be a better man and a better American for doing so.

Note what Seton-Watson[1] says:

"America is full of nationalities which, while accepting with enthusiasm their new American citizenship, nevertheless look to some centre in the old world as the source and inspiration of their national culture and traditions. The most typical instance is the feeling of the American Jew for Palestine, which may well become a focus for his déclassé kinsmen in other parts of the world."

There is no inconsistency between loyalty to America and loyalty to Jewry. The Jewish spirit, the product of our religion and experiences, is essentially modern and essentially American. Not since the destruction of the Temple have the Jews in spirit and in ideals been so fully in harmony with the noblest aspirations of the country in which they lived.

America's fundamental law seeks to make real the brotherhood of man. That brotherhood became the Jewish fundamental law more than twenty-five hundred years ago. America's insistent demand in the twentieth century is for social justice. That also has been the Jews' striving for ages. Their affliction, as well as their religion, has prepared the Jews for effective democracy. Persecution broadened their sympathies. It trained them in patient endurance, in self-control, and in sacrifice. It made them think as well as suffer. It deepened the passion for righteousness.

Indeed, loyalty to America demands rather that each American Jew become a Zionist. For only through the ennobling effect of its strivings can we develop the best that is in us and give to this country the full benefit of our great inheritance. The Jewish spirit, so long preserved, the character developed by so many centuries of sacrifice, should be preserved and developed further, so that in America as elsewhere the sons of the race may in the future live lives and do deeds worthy of their ancestors.

But we have also an immediate and more pressing duty in the performance of which Zionism alone seems capable of affording effective aid. We must protect America and ourselves from demoralization, which has to some extent already set in among American Jews. The cause of this demoralization is clear. It results in large part from the fact that in our land of liberty all the restraints by which the Jews were protected in their ghettos were removed and a new generation left without necessary moral and spiritual support. And is it not equally clear what the only possible remedy is? It is the laborious task of inculcating self-respect, a task which can be accomplished only by restoring the ties of the Jew to the noble past of his race, and by making him realize the possibilities of a no less glorious future. The sole bulwark against demoralization is to develop in each new generation of Jews in America the sense of *noblesse oblige*. That spirit can be developed in those who regard their people as destined to live and to live with a bright future. That spirit can best be developed by actively participating in some way in furthering the ideals of the Jewish renaissance; and this can be done effectively only through furthering the Zionist movement.

In the Jewish colonies of Palestine there are no Jewish criminals; because everyone, old and young alike, is led to feel the glory of his people and his obligation to carry forward its ideals. The new Palestinian Jewry produces instead of criminals, scientists like Aaron Aaronson,[2] the discoverer of wild wheat; pedagogues like David Yellin;[3] craftsmen like Boris Schatz,[4] the founder of the Bezalel; intrepid *Shomrim*,[5] the Jewish guards of peace, who watch in the night against marauders and doers of violent deeds.

And the Zionist movement has brought like inspiration to the Jews in the Diaspora, as Steed[6] has shown in this striking passage from *The Hapsburg Monarchy*:

"To minds like these Zionism came with the force of an evangel. To be a Jew and to be proud of it; to glory in the power and pertinacity of the race, its traditions, its triumphs, its sufferings, its resistence to persecution; to look the world frankly in the face and to enjoy the luxury of moral and intellectual honesty; to feel pride in belonging to the people that gave Christendom its divinities, that taught half the world monotheism, whose ideas have permeated civilization as never the ideas of a race before it, whose genius fashioned the whole mechanism of modern commerce, and whose artists, actors, singers and writers have filled a larger place in the cultured universe than those of any other people. This, or something like this, was the train of thought fired in youthful Jewish minds by the Zionist spark. Its effect upon the Jewish students of Austrian universities was immediate and striking. Until then they had been despised and often ill-treated. They had wormed their way into appointments and into the free professions by dint of pliancy, mock humility, mental acuteness, and clandestine protection. If struck or spat upon by 'Aryan' students, they rarely ventured to return the blow or the insult. But Zionism gave them courage. They formed associations, and learned athletic drill and fencing. Insult was requited with insult, and presently the best fencers of the fighting German corps found that Zionist students could gash cheeks quite as effectually as any Teuton, and that the Jews were in a fair way to become the best swordsmen of the university. Today the purple cap of the Zionist is as respected as that of any academical association.

"This moral influence of Zionism is not confined to university students. It is quite as noticeable among the mass of the younger Jews outside, who also find in it a reason to raise their heads, and, taking their stand upon the past, to gaze straightforwardly into the future."

Since the Jewish problem is single and universal, the Jews of every country should strive for its solution. But the duty resting upon us of America is especially insistent. We number about 3,000,000, which is more than one-fifth of all the Jews in the world, a number larger than that comprised within any other country except the Russian Empire. We are representative of all the Jews in the world; for we are composed of immigrants, or descendants of immigrants, coming from every other country, or district. We include persons from every section of society, and of every shade of religious belief. We are ourselves free from civil or political disabilities, and are relatively prosperous. Our fellow Americans are infused with a high and generous spirit, which insures approval of our struggle to ennoble, liberate, and otherwise improve the condition of an important part of the human race; and their innate manliness makes them sympathize particularly with our efforts at self-help. America's detachment from the old world problem relieves us from suspicions and embarrassments frequently attending the activities of Jews of rival European countries. And a conflict between American interests or ambitions and Jewish aims is not conceivable. Our loyalty to America can never be questioned.

Let us therefore lead, earnestly, courageously, and joyously, in the struggle for liberation. Let us all recognize that we Jews are a distinctive nationality of which every Jew, whatever his country, his station, or shade of belief, is necessarily a member. Let us insist that the struggle for liberty shall not cease until equality of opportunity is accorded to nationalities as to individuals. Let us insist also that full equality of opportunity cannot be obtained by Jews until we, like members of other nationalities, shall have the option of living elsewhere or of returning to the land of our forefathers.

The fulfillment of these aspirations is clearly demanded in the interest of mankind, as well as in justice to the Jews. They cannot fail of attainment if we are united and true to ourselves. But we must be united not only in spirit but in action. To this end we must organize. Organize, in the first place, so that the world may have proof of the extent and the intensity of our desire for liberty. Organize, in the second place, so that our resources may become known and be made available. But in mobilizing our force it will not be for war. The whole world longs for the solution of the Jewish problem. We have but to lead the way, and we may be sure of ample co-operation from non-Jews. In order to lead the way, we need not arms, but men; men with those qualities for which Jews should be peculiarly fitted by reason of their religion and life; men of courage, of high intelligence, of faith and public spirit, of indomitable will and ready self-sacrifice; men who both think and do, who will devote high abilities to shaping our course, and to overcoming the many obstacles which must from time to time arise. And we need other, many, many other men, officers commissioned and noncommissioned, and common soldiers in the cause of liberty, who will give of their efforts and resources, as occasion may demand, in unfailing and ever-strengthening support of the measures which may be adopted. Organization thorough and complete can alone develop such leaders and the necessary support.

Organize, Organize, Organize, until every Jew in America must stand up and be counted, counted with us, or prove himself, wittingly or unwittingly, of the few who are against their own people.

HORACE MAYER KALLEN   born 1882

HORACE KALLEN's career has been divided between the academic life of a professor of philosophy and active participation, both as organizational leader and thinker, in Jewish affairs. These two realms of his interest are connected, for his Jewish position is a particular application of the pragmatic philosophy that Kallen formed under the influence of his teacher, William James.

Kallen was born in Germany in 1882, and brought to the United States as a child. After both undergraduate and graduate training at Harvard (Ph. D., 1908) he taught philosophy there for three years. A year at Clark College and seven more, until 1918, at the University of Wisconsin were the further preamblers to his appointment to the New School for Social Research, with which he has henceforth been identified.

Kallen has written many books on education, art, politics, and religion. What is relevant here of his general outlook are its guidelines, pluralism and secularism. Kallen has followed James in affirming that human experience cannot be reduced to conformity to one way, for it varies in different traditions and cultures, all of which have an equal right to self-expression. He has mediated the counterclaims of science and religion by insisting that religion is not revealed but man-made, the expression of the highest values of the group, and hence one of a number of factors which act to bind a tradition together. Not faith but group life therefore differentiates society into subgroups. Consequently, the basis of democratic life is secular, i.e., it is the organization of society in such a way that the absolute of no group predominates over that of another.

In the Jewish field Kallen has been especially active in educational affairs and a lifelong Zionist. He has envisaged a Jewish community in America living as one of the many cultural subgroups of a pluralistic democracy. Zionism has been important to him in two senses. As movement, it represents, in his view, an affirmation of Jewish loyalty centering around group and culture rather than religion. As state-builder Kallen has looked to it to create a secularized Jewish society in Palestine.

The first two of the pieces below are from the most important early statement of his views, a collection of papers published as a book, *Judaism at Bay* (1932). The third is from a speech given in 1933.

JEWISH LIFE IS NATIONAL AND SECULAR (1918)

THE OUTCOME OF THE HASKALAH, which is the true reform, the actual reform of Jewish life in eastern Europe, is the recovery of the idea of Jewish nationality on a secular and civil basis, as the peer of other European nationalities. Consequently, Jewish life has become for the community indefinitely more extensive than the Jewish religion; it has become an organic envelope and support for religion as the body is for the lungs or the heart. In it religion is but a part. It has remained Jewish life, but it has acquired a completely secular dimension. This is to be observed in the modern neo-Hebrew and Yiddish literature, in the development of secular theories of Jewish history, in the organization of Jewish education on a secular basis, in the rise and growth of Jewish art and music, in the complete emergence of the Jewish mind in Yiddish and Hebrew literature, in the reorganization of the community. The non-Judaistic Jew, like the Bundist or Revolutionist in Russia, is not cut off from his community by his nonadherence to Judaism. In the reformed synagogue of western Europe, inability to agree with the reform rabbis on Judaism is by rabbinic fiat self-elimination from the Jewish community. In eastern Europe, in a word, there has been a reform as complete and drastic as the reform in western Europe, but in eastern Europe the reform has been creative and renovating. It has been performed by an assimilation of the new elements to the old. In western Europe, it has cut off the old elements altogether. In consequence, Judaism among the Jews has become as Christianity among the gentiles, a subordinate part of the greater Jewish life.

The problem of Judaism is at this point not any different from the problems of any other religion. It is the problem of saving itself, of keeping going in a setting which on the whole is secular, and promises to become more and more so. It is perfectly clear that the value of religion can be determined only by its bearing on the rest of life, and so far as the survival of Judaism is concerned, if Judaism is to survive at all, it can survive only as a functional component of this larger living complex we call Hebraism. Just as the nose or the arm can go on existing only so long as it is attached to the body, so alone can a religion go on existing. If you cut off Jewish religious life from the total complex of Jewish life, you cut it off from life. It has been so cut off in the reform synagogue, and that is why the generations of the reformed do not remain Judaists. The place of religion is within, not above or around, the social complex. Elsewhere, the sap of life either melts it or leaves it. Orthodoxy hence is stiffening, and is left, as the penalty for cutting off Judaism from the larger life which Jewry shares with all mankind, dry and brittle. Reform again is jellified and melting, as the penalty for cutting off Judaism from concrete and specific sources of its particular and Jewish being, for shattering its natural channel. If orthodoxy is a rocky barren, reform is a gas-breeding swamp. As mere religious sects, there is no healthy life in either.

The Haskalah movement represents not a middle way between these two extremes, but a third and altogether different way. Its history has emerged as an assimilation of the new material to the old vision. In a word, it designates the line of growth in Jewish life. In the Haskalah movement there began a natural readjustment of the organic Jewish community, the nationality, to its new life-conditions. By virtue of this readjustment Judaism can get its proper place in the co-ordination of things which compose the Jewish national life. For survival, Judaism is dependent on the continuance of the Jewish community-complex. Unless, however, this community-complex is thought of in historic terms, in terms of the Jewish spiritual individuality, of Jewish tradition, customs, history, growth, there is no place for Judaism. The place and function of Judaism in Jewish life is like the place and function of any religion in any national life. It is an item in that life; only an item, no matter how important, in a whole which is determined by the ethnic character of the people that live it, by their history, by their collective will and intent. These three factors define the total conditions of national life. Judaism, to survive, must fit among the other social elements somewhere in a Jewish national life. If it does not, it will, in the natural course of things, die. There exists, however, much uncertainty about the will and intent of the Jewish life. And so long as this remains, Judaism remains a problem. The problem of Judaism cannot be solved by itself. It requires to be treated as a part of the solution of the problem of the Jewish people.

ZIONISM AND LIBERALISM (1919)

MR. MORRIS COHEN,[1] delivering himself on Zionism, says he attacks, not Zionism the measure of relief, but Zionism the expression of a "nationalist philosophy." Ostensibly, it is this philosophy which horrifies Mr. Cohen. Now it happens that this philosophy is as widespread as civilization, that it permeates all peoples, particularly oppressed peoples; that it utters a state of mind and feeling basic to established as well as aspiring nationalities. Nor are Americans of the ruling class unendowed with it. Of course, like other philosophies, even "liberalism," it rests upon premises in nature and in human experience and aspiration which can be used to establish conclusions of Chamberlain's[2] Teutonism and Katkov's[3] Slavism. But there is as little reason in identifying those with the normal "nationalist philosophy" of Zionism as there is in identifying Lloyd George,[4] who is one of its defenders, with William Hohenzollern, or England with Germany, or a normal man with a lunatic. The Jewish nationality is only one among very many which has a program of regeneration and freedom resting upon the common normal nationalist philosophy. That Mr. Cohen should choose to pervert that one, rather than the program of any other—say of the Poles or Greeks or Italians, as he might, with better reason, do—is an unconscious admission of the truths envisaged in "nationalist philosophy" which even liberals of Mr. Cohen's kind might profitably ponder.

To the contentions Mr. Cohen offers in support of his caricature of Zionism the facts compel a categorical denial. It is simply false that "Zionism rests on a nationalist philosophy which is a direct challenge to liberalism." The nationalist philosophy of Zionism is an extension of the assumptions of liberalism from the individual to the group. It antedated the "liberalism of the French Revolution" by a thousand years, and only changed, as Spinoza suggested that it might, from a religious to a political mode in consequence of that revolution. Of course, it is "anti-assimilationist." Pan-Germanism, Pan-Slavism, and all the other panic movements are assimilationist. They refuse to minorities the right of association in communities of speech, of custom, tradition, and culture according to their own lights and ways. They want to Germanize, Slavonize, Magyarize; and they have their echoes in America. Democracy is anti-assimilationist. It stands for the acknowledgment, the harmony, and organization of group diversities in co-operative expansion of the common life, not for the assimilation of diversities into sameness. Zionism is anti-assimilationist because it is democratic, because it has enough faith in "the progress of the slow movement known as an enlightenment," to apply its teachings to groups as well as to individuals. Had Mr. Cohen spoken from observation rather than passion, he would have known these things.

Through more than a millennium and a half the Jewish people were subject to disabilities, individual and collective, either because they were held to belong to an alien creed or because they were held to belong to a "foreign" nation or both. Liberation from these disabilities was conditional upon conversion, assimilation—both surrender of conscience and alienation from relatives, friends, and community—that is upon repudiating the essential rights of freedom of thought and of association. If enlightenment has meant anything at all, it has meant the progressive confirmation of these two rights. In the life of the peoples of Europe to assert these rights was to give concrete expression to "the cosmopolitan reason and enlightenment which overthrew medievalism." The nationalism which is only another name for them was a development of, not a reaction against, the spirit of the French Revolution. It was that spirit which all over the continent of Europe fought both the imperialism of Napoleon and the oppression of the dynasts. Democracy and nationalism made up a single engine of liberalism; they were together against the oppressor. The prophet and philosopher of this nationalism is not Chamberlain, not Katkov, but Mazzini, and the sum of his teaching might be uttered in a slight modification of the Declaration of Independence: all nationalities are created equal and endowed with certain inalienable rights; among these rights are life, liberty, and the pursuit of happiness.

This is the whole Zionist ideology. Zionists have opposed it on the one hand to the clerics of the reformed synagogue who do not in fact "fundamentally accept the ideology of Chamberlain and Katkov, but draw different conclusions," preaching the arrogant doctrine of the "chosen people" and the "mission of Israel," and on the other to the protagonists of this anti-Semitic ideology itself. To both the Zionists have said: "The Jews are a historic people among other peoples, neither better nor worse. They have their national qualities which their past attests and which afford some indication of the future. They are entitled equally with any other to express their qualities freely and autonomously as a group, making such contribution to the co-operative enterprise of civilization as their qualities as a group promise." Nobody who has read Ruppin[5] and Zollschan,[6] who have met the ethnological attack, nor the host of writers (whose dean is Ahad Ha-Am) who have met the religious and cultural attack, could have failed to know this, nor to recognize the true liberalism of which it is an extension.

For the naturalistic cosmopolitanism of the eighteenth century analyzed the living groupings of mankind into abstract individuals —"natural" men; while the economic internationalism of the nineteenth analyzed it into equally abstract individuals—"economic" men: laborers, capitalists. Both failed to see that individuality was not congenital but achieved, and that all men depend in their beginnings on a society which is a nation before it is anything else. Its power in the history of democratic times, against the appeal of all other sorts of associations, should have opened their eyes, but did not. It cannot be disposed of merely by refutation of absurd dialectic aberration or eugenic claims based on it. Whether races or nationalities are of "pure" breed or not, they exist as associations deriving from a real or credited predominant inheritance, an intimate sameness of background, tradition, custom, and aspiration. Genuine liberalism requires for them the same freedom of development and expression as for the individual. Indeed, in requiring it for the individual, it must necessarily require it for them. They are the essential reservoirs of individuality. Zionism might be described as aiming to conserve and strengthen, under far more favorable than ghetto conditions, the values of such a type of reservoir.

For the sources of cultures are in those types, and nowhere else. Thus, the language of the Roman conqueror was absorbed by the Spanish and Portuguese no less than by the French. It underlies Italian also. But what mankind prizes in the spirits and literatures of these peoples is just that diversity which comes from Latin having been used by peoples of different breeds, traditions, and habits. Perhaps Mr. Cohen's liberalism would have been satisfied with a universal Latinity. Medieval religious imperialism and scholastic pedantry did their best to enforce that. Nevertheless, true liberals do not regret that Dante's Italian, and Cervantes' Spanish, and Camoëns' Portuguese exist beside Molière's French and St. Thomas' Latin. They know that the alternative to diversity of cultures is cultural imperialism, of which, modernly, the Prussians have illustrated the possibilities both in pretension and in theory. They have their imitators, and the Jews have suffered for their rejection of such imperialism from ancient times to the present day. It is slander to attribute to the Zionists anything beyond the wish for international service through national freedom.

JEWISH UNITY (1933)

UNITY IS NECESSARY. Unity is indispensable. But its attainment must meet the conditions of modern life. The first of these conditions is an extension of the idea of "Emancipation." It is necessary for Jews to recognize that the rule, which, because of Jewish effort, has been written into the law of nations in order to safeguard for religious and cultural minorities their rights to life, liberty, and the pursuit of happiness, is infallibly, inescapably, the rule for Jews also. No individual can be emancipated through, in, and for himself. He can only be emancipated for himself in and through his group. First and foremost, he must have freedom of association with the members of his group; he must have the right to express himself through the common life of his group. The word "Jew" is a collective term, not an individual term. It designates an associative relationship. That any individual should be penalized because of this relationship is repugnant to the ideals of democracy and to the existence of free institutions. Thus, the first term of Jewish unity in freedom is the association together of Jews as Jews for self-fulfillment, for service, and for self-defense.

The basis of such an association must be wide enough to admit Albert Einstein as well as the Gerer Rebbe;[7] Benny Leonard[8] as well as Stephen Wise;[9] Leon Trotsky[10] as well as Horace Kallen. It must even have a place for Cyrus Adler.[11] It must provide a common platform for all persons who are called Jews, regardless of class, creed, or country. The least common denominator of such a platform is defensive. It is the unity of laboring together against the false and the cowardly attacks of anti-Semitism in every walk of life. Beyond defense, there is always the constructive program which so many Jews share—the upkeep and development of Hebraic culture and ideals as the Jewish contribution to the substance and purpose of our civilization. And there is the upbuilding of the Jewish Homeland.

The form of such an unification must be integrated with the conditions of modern life. The days of the ghetto are past. We are living in a world of factories, automobiles, telegraphs, telephones, airplanes, and radios. In this world no single nation can be self-sufficient and separated from any other nation either in culture, politics, or economics.

Culturally, the peoples of the world have been interdependent so long as culture has existed among men, and the recognition of this interdependence has been continuous and frank till Hitler came. Economic and political interdependence of the world is a later growth which reached slowly into the conscience of businessmen and politicians.

Because of the Germanic desire and endeavor to transform this interdependence into an imperial monopoly, the Great War was fought two decades ago. The formation of the League of Nations on the initiative and insistence of a great American president, Woodrow Wilson, was a fruit of this War, and an explicit, if weak, acknowledgment of this interdependence. Mr. Wilson's successor of today just as frankly acknowledges it, and stresses it. He speaks of establishing "order in place of the present chaos by a stabilization of currencies, by freeing the flow of world trade, and by international action to raise price levels. It (Government) must, in short, supplement individual domestic programs for economic recovery, by wise and considered international action." Indeed, today the economic interdependence of mankind is a commonplace of our thinking.

The cultural, social, spiritual, and economic interdependence of the Jewish part of mankind should be equally acknowledged, and equally a commonplace of Jewish thinking. Problems of civic status, economic security, cultural improvement make it as necessary for the Jews of the world, as for other groups, to come together to consult about their Jewish problems, and through discussion and an exchange of view to reach a consensus concerning principles and policy. Even if we wanted to be separated from one another, the conditions of modern life would not let us. For this reason, Jewish unity must embrace in the form of proper organization all the Jewish communities of the world. Proper organization can only be democratic and representative organization. Spokesmen for Jewry, for Jewish communities, must have a definite collectively executed mandate to speak. And the councils of Israel in which they speak must be as public, as open to the scrutiny and the criticism not only of their constituencies but of the enlightened public opinion of the world, as the councils of peoples, free churches, or learned societies. The world's Jewry is in a condition of anarchy and futility. Yet it is charged with a purposeful, secret international organization. Let there be an end to this fantasy. Let the Jews of the world create in fact a free open international organization. Such an organization will help restore the lost integrity of the Jewish people, will help make Jewish life centripetal, will provide an adequate instrument in the service of Jewry to its fellow communities. For the Jewish people are an organic part of the peoples of the Western world; the Jewish problem is a problem for non-Jews no less than for Jews. The efforts toward its solution in terms of humanity, justice, and freedom call for the attention and the co-operation of all mankind. Alone the open processes of democracy can make this call and win the right answer.

MORDECAI MENAHEM KAPLAN
born 1881

MORDECAI M. KAPLAN was born in Lithuania and brought to the United States at the age of eight. He received his secular education at the College of the City of New York and Columbia University, and his rabbinic degree in 1902 from the Jewish Theological Seminary of America. Solomon Schechter invited him in 1909 to be principal of the Teachers' Institute of the Seminary; in the next year Kaplan was appointed professor of homiletics in its Rabbinical School, and since then he has held a variety of other posts at that institution. Always active as a rabbi and community leader, Kaplan "invented" the idea of the synagogue-center in 1916, when he organized the Jewish Center in Manhattan. After a few years he broke with this group, which would not follow him as his religious views became more liberal, to found the Society for the Advancement of Judaism (in 1922). This synagogue was created to reflect his concept of what an institution of Jewish religion should be, and Kaplan has remained its guiding spirit as leader, and now, as leader emeritus, to the present.

Whether as teacher or, after his late thirties, as an increasingly prolific writer and lecturer, Kaplan's true career has been in the service of his philosophy of Judaism. His approach, which he named Reconstructionism, was expounded in *Judaism as a Civilization*, a book which caused a furor when it appeared in 1934. These controversies grew more heated in the next ten years, as several Reconstructionist prayer books appeared, with important deletions from the traditional texts, and as he published a succession of other volumes in exposition of his views. The passages by which he is represented here come from his most recent major book, *The Future of the American Jew*.

Kaplan's premises are essentially the same as Kallen's, though he is far more involved in religion. For Kallen it is enough to define Judaism as one of many parallel national civilizations; Kaplan regards religion as so characteristic of Jewish experience that he insists on a hyphenated adjective—religio-national—as the correct way to describe this particular civilization. Like any complex of rituals and values which make up a way of life, Judaism will survive only if it answers the real needs of men. Hence Kaplan follows Ahad Ha-Am in arguing that a homeland is necessary, where Judaism can become relevant to the modern age by refashioning itself in its own way.

Many of the specific ideas which Kaplan upholds—like his denial of the orthodox concepts of revelation and of the "chosen people," or his affirmation of a theology which is a Jewish version of the "social gospel"—can be denied, without destroying his Zionist stance. He has affirmed the importance both of the homeland and of those who choose to live outside it; he has asked of one that it be more tradition-minded and of the other, that, for the sake of its own survival, it be more open to change. Most recently, Kaplan has taken the lead in talking of Jewish creativity as bipolar, as a tension between the full national life of Israel and the life in two cultures (the American and his own in-group's) of the Jew in America; while admitting that the first is central, Kaplan has increasingly insisted that the second is of creative value, to mankind and to Jewry. In all this Kaplan has represented more than his particular philosophy of religion. He stands as the summary of American Zionism, the synthesizer of all that has preceded.

THE FUTURE OF THE AMERICAN JEW (1948)

NO JEWISH HOMELAND WITHOUT JUDAISM IN THE DIASPORA

JEWS IN THE DIASPORA will continue to owe exclusive political allegiance to the countries in which they reside. The tie that binds Diaspora Jewry to Eretz Israel is a cultural and religious one. Culture and socioeconomic life are so closely interrelated that it is difficult for Diaspora Jewry to create new Jewish cultural values, since there is no possibility in the Diaspora of an autonomous Jewish social and economic life.

American Judaism is needed, and will long continue to be needed as a force to inspire and motivate our participation in the establishment of a Jewish commonwealth. The role of American Jewry in relation to Eretz Israel is similar to the role of the American home front in relation to the battle front during the recent World War. Were it not for the backing of the home front, or for the fact that America proved to be the "arsenal of democracy," the most clever strategy and the most arduous valor on the battle line would have been of no avail. Similarly American Jewry will for a long time have to give moral, political, and economic support to the Eretz Israel enterprise, which is the deciding factor in Israel's struggle for survival in the modern world. Should the morale of the American front deteriorate, should American Jewry grow listless and disheartened, or should it lose faith in the significance of its struggle for existence, after the manner of our fainthearted escapists and assimilationists, what would become of a Jewish Eretz Israel? Would the little Yishuv alone be also to withstand British imperialism, Arab intransigence, and ubiquitous anti-Semitism? What it has already achieved with the aid and support of world Jewry is miracle enough, but to expect it to perform similar miracles in the future, without such aid, is to ask the impossible. We dare not let our home front crumble, and thus betray those who are fighting our battle and holding the line on its most crucial sector, Eretz Israel.

An attitude of distrust toward the possibility of maintaining Jewish life in the United States, is, moreover, unfair to our country. Our duties as citizens are not fully discharged by rendering obedience to its laws, or even by participating patriotically in its defense in time of war. We have a part in the social, economic, and cultural life of America, and, unless we give to the common welfare of the American people the best that is in our power to give, we are not doing our full duty to our country. But as Jews, the very best we have to give is to be found in Judaism, the distillation of centuries of Jewish spiritual experience. As convinced Jews and loyal Americans, we should seek to incorporate in American life the universal values of Judaism, and to utilize the particular sancta of Jewish religion as an inspiration for preserving these universal values. To fail to do so would mean to deprive Judaism of universal significance and to render Jewish religion a mere tribalism that has no relevance to life beyond the separate interests of the Jewish group. The attitude of Jewish isolationists or the *sholele hatefuzah* (negators of the Diaspora), which would keep American Jewry with its loins perpetually girt for a hasty departure for Eretz Israel, is not likely to inspire our neighbors with confidence in the Jew, or with respect for Judaism.

Those of our young people who possess the abilities that are needed now in Eretz Israel to build there a productive economy for the rising

Jewish Commonwealth, an economy based on the socialized exploitation of natural resources instead of on the exploitation of the weak by the strong, should by all means be encouraged to go to Eretz Israel. The colonizing and constructive effort in Eretz Israel should enlist those of our youth who possess the kind of pioneer spirit essential to nation-building. Our Jewish young men and women ought to be made to feel that their going to Eretz Israel to serve their own people would be as legitimate and noble an adventure as for other Americans to serve the various peoples in the Far East in a missionary or cultural capacity. But students who plan to go to Eretz Israel, with the expectation of engaging in some white-collar profession, would not render any specially needed service there, and only deprive American Jewish life of some needed service they might render here. We American Jews need desperately every available person who has the ability to transmute the cultural and religious values of our tradition into a living creative force.

We Jews who have come to this country bore the gifts of a great historic tradition. To tell us that Judaism can have no future here is to tell us that these gifts are worthless and that, as a group, we can be only cultural parasites. Whatever the future holds in store for us is a matter of speculation, but that there are today five million Jews in the United States is not speculation but a fact that carries with it inescapable responsibilities. We Jews have the same need as have all other Americans of belonging to a community where we are wanted and welcomed, and where we can derive the moral and spiritual values that give meaning and dignity to human life. We naturally look to the Jewish community to give us a faith to live by and to live for. Whatever deprives us of faith in the possibility of Jewish life in America not only de-Judaizes millions of our people; it demoralizes and degrades us.

The problem of how to make Jewish life a source of self-fulfillment to the American Jew is one of great complexity. Nothing less than whole-hearted and whole-minded concentration on that problem will result in a satisfactory solution. It is natural, therefore, to find excuses for evading the problem altogether, and few excuses seem as plausible as hopelessness about Diaspora Judaism. When Zionism first appeared on the scene, it came as a challenge to those who evaded the urgent task of self-emancipation by projecting the redemption of our people into the distant messianic future. Likewise, those who despair of Jewish survival in the Diaspora, by maintaining that only in Eretz Israel can Judaism survive, evade the urgent task of rendering Judaism viable in America. Long-distance building of Eretz Israel is no less important than building it on the spot, but it cannot serve as a substitute for living a Jewish life here. Until Jews realize that the Jewish problem in the Diaspora and the Jewish problem in Eretz Israel are one, they are running away from reality and defeating their own purpose. Only as we assume the responsibility for having Judaism live wherever Jews are allowed to live are we likely to succeed in any of our Jewish undertakings.

There can be no question that in the Diaspora we Jews lack the spirit of dedication that goes with our people's renascence in Eretz Israel. We are without the magic power that comes with the spoken and creative Hebrew word. We are far from the land where the Jewish spirit is being reborn. But given the will, the intelligence, and the devotion, it is feasible so to relive and to re-embody, within the frame of a democratic American civilization, the vital and thrilling experience of our people in Eretz Israel that, in the long run, we might achieve in our way as great and lasting a contribution to human values as they are achieving in theirs.

THE NEGATION OF JEWISH LIFE IN THE DIASPORA

AT THE PRESENT TIME the most vocal among the educators who subscribe to the religio-cultural conception of Judaism take a negative attitude toward any prospect of a future for Judaism outside Eretz Israel. From all that has recently happened to European Jewry they conclude that anti-Semitism is not merely a passing madness; it is a chronic disease of all Western civilization. They maintain, therefore, that it is quixotic to expect the democratic countries to give us Jews the sense of security necessary to the leading of a normal life. Whatever Jewish education is to be given to our children must, accordingly, be based on the acceptance of suffering and exile as our lot in life, from which there is only one escape, and that is migration to Eretz Israel. The principal aim of Jewish education, therefore, should consist in fostering in the child a yearning to live in Eretz Israel, and, in case that is not feasible, in fostering in him heroic resignation to a life of self-denial and sacrifice, made necessary by the sadistic tendencies of the dominant population toward all minority groups.

The foregoing view of the course of democracy is entirely unacceptable, and the conclusion drawn from such a view for Jewish education is the height of absurdity. If the future in the democratic countries is, indeed, as dark as our pessimists paint it, then they might as well advocate some kind of physical or spiritual suicide for the Jewish people. To assume that, with the democratic countries constitutionally incapable of bringing anti-Semitism under control, it is possible for Jews to achieve freedom and security in Eretz Israel is to forget that the world is one, both for good and for evil. Moreover, resigning ourselves to injustice and oppression at the hands of our fellow men may be the only course of action open to us, but it certainly cannot constitute the highest good upon which to base the purpose of educational endeavor.

It is that, in the past, Jewish education did train the child to regard himself as belonging to a people in exile, and to be prepared to suffer on that account. But it then laid the chief stress not on the present suffering, but on the future glories that awaited his people and on the ineffable bliss in the world to come that awaited those who lived in accordance with the will of God, as expressed in the Torah. That prospect more than compensated for all the suffering that his people endured in this world. Does the modern Jewish educator, who insists on having the child realize the full meaning of *Galut*, exile, hold out the same naïve faith in the advent of the Messiah and in the bliss of the world to come? If not, then he has nothing to offer the child but a sense of misery in being fated to be born a Jew. Only sheltered and cloistered pedagogues, who seek to avenge themselves upon the young for their own frustrated lives, could devise such a fantasic purpose. No one, with any love of children, and with the real desire to have them grow up to be happy, would want to turn life for them into that kind of nightmare.

Another approach to the question whether it is possible for the Jewish people to retain its identity, under the terms of the Emancipation and Enlightenment, is to point to the actual disruption of Jewish life which goes on apace, as the result of being integrated into the general population. Some Jewish educators stress that result as an inevitable consequence of the democratic process. These educators, too, consider it misleading to try to persuade Jewish children that it is possible to lead a normal Jewish life in the Diaspora. On the contrary, they claim, it is necessary to make clear to the child that, even under the best of circumstances, Jews cannot possibly retain their group identity outside Eretz Israel. They believe that the child should be saved from the illusion that Judaism is being given a fair chance to prove its potency as an influence for good in their lives. When the child grows up, he will then realize that Jewish life is not to be blamed for its shortcomings, its lack of vitality and creativity. Such Jewish educators assume that, by inculcating in the child a feeling of discontent with the odds against being a Jew in a non-Jewish environment, we can develop in him a passionate yearning for Eretz Israel as a national Jewish home.

This kind of Eretz-Israel-centered education in America is bound to have a ruinous effect on the happiness and character of the child. It holds out to him no reason why he should be condemned to lead an abnormal life all his days, since, either by migrating to Eretz Israel, or by ignoring Judaism altogether, he might lead a normal life. The assumption that it is inherently impossible for the Jew to feel at home in a non-Jewish environment, which one may reasonably expect in time to be free of anti-Semitism, is a counsel of despair, and we cannot build an educational system on despair.

THE NEED OF A TWOFOLD NORM FOR JEWISH LIFE

THERE IS AN ALTERNATIVE to either of the two preceding types of approach to the question of survival in a democratic state. Instead of judging the democratic process by the way it has worked hitherto, we should judge it by what it was intended to become. It was intended to become a means of enabling human beings to make the most out of their lives, or to achieve salvation as they view it, provided, of course, they do not interfere with the salvation of their fellows, as the latter view it. Whatever prevents people, as individuals or as a group, from achieving salvation cannot be ascribed to the democratic process. Whatever militates against the salvation of a minority group, which does not aim at aggression or domination, must in the end jeopardize the salvation of the majority population as well.

As Jews, we cannot achieve our salvation unless the democratic process permits us to retain our identity as an indivisible people. If, therefore, democracy is so interpreted that it prevents us from fostering our religio-cultural tradition and from being true to our destiny as a people, then we are presented with a very strange paradox which we must try to resolve, not only in our own interest as Jews, but also in the interest of a better world for all mankind. Only when we have come to understand this paradox fully can we be in a position to suggest a possible solution. That solution will have to be the basis of a Jewish educational system in this country.

We can best learn the nature of the paradox which complicates the status and future of Jewish life in democratic countries by asking the question: "How was democracy intended to function in relation to historical groups and religions generally?" This question has not been answered, as most people think, by the separation of church and state. That separation has by no means solved the problem of the relation of religion to the social, economic, and political interests. Actually, religion is inextricably bound up with these interests. No religion that hopes to be treated seriously can afford to take a neutral position in any matter pertaining to human welfare, and true welfare is unattainable without the benefits which good religion can confer.

Is, then, the legal separation of church and state a fiction? Not at all. Such separation affirms the very important principle that the democratic state should not monopolize the life of the citizen. It should leave place in his life for ideals and loyalties that transcend the state. The democratic state should undertake to provide for the social security of the citizen, but should not claim to be the sole source of moral and spiritual security. Even if it helps him to some extent to lead a moral and spiritual life, it encourages other agencies—especially historic groups—to make that their principal function.

This means that there must henceforth be two standards of normality for Jewish life; one standard for Eretz Israel, where Jewish life can be lived out fully as a complete civilization that provides those who live by it with all the elements of life necessary to their self-fulfillment and happiness; and a second standard for democratic countries like the United States, where they must look for economic and social security to American citizenship, which in turn expects them to find their moral and spiritual security elsewhere. That security they can for the present find mainly within their own Jewish people and its tradition. In time, however, with American democracy having achieved more self-awareness and consistency, it, too, will become for Jews, as well as for the rest of the population, a source of inner peace.

EDUCATIONAL AIM IN TERMS OF TRADITION AND SOCIAL STRUCTURE

THE POSITION ADVOCATED in this discussion may be summarized as follows: There is nothing inherently abnormal in a synthesis of the democratic process with the maintenance of Jewish group individuality, though such a synthesis in the Diaspora would undoubtedly constitute a new development of Jewish life. Secondly, by educating our children to live as Jews in an American environment, we shall not be imposing on them an abnormal kind of existence.

But the real question is whether such a synthesis is at all possible.

Jewish group individuality is articulated by means of a tradition which arose and developed under conditions very different from our own. If we expect that tradition to help us live as both Jews and Americans, we must have it speak to us in terms that are relevant to ethical and spiritual problems of our day. This calls for the following:

In the first place, it is essential to realize that our tradition, as it has come down to us, belongs to a universe of thought that was radically different from our own. We are bound to fail in our effort to revitalize that tradition if we yield to the temptation to ignore the wide gap that divides us from the ancients in the general outlook on life. We must become accustomed to the idea of growth in experience and meaning. The essence of growth is continuity in change. Before we can discover the permanent elements in tradition, we must be fully aware of the changes in knowledge of the physical world, in the conception of God, and in the ethical values which differentiate the modern man's world from the ancient man's.

Secondly, in order to render the tradition relevant to present-day ethical and spiritual concerns, it is necessary to discover the latent and permanent ethical and spiritual urges beneath such elements in the tradition as the miracle story, the obsolete law, or the primitive rite. This calls for research into the historical background of the tradition not only in Israel, but in the entire universe of thought within the scope of which Israel came. Upon the results of such research a knowledge of the human sciences should be brought to bear, in order that we may discover to what extent the Jewish tradition verifies the existence of the higher trends in human nature.

A third step is to relate these verifications of the higher trends in human nature to the social and spiritual problems that are agitating mankind today, the problems pertaining to the meaning of life and death, to the rights and duties of the individual and of society, to the prerogatives of the various loyalties and to the proper utilization of power. There is need for evolving something that will be in our day the analogue of the Talmud and Midrash in ancient times. In this development, the ancient Talmud and Midrash should constitute the greater part of the tradition to be reinterpreted and reworked.

Finally, provision must be made for dealing with the many situations that were not provided for by the ancient tradition. No tradition that ceases growing can live. But this step cannot be taken within the tradition itself. The impetus for it must come from a living body which is the carrier of the tradition, and without which no tradition can live. All this research cannot, of course, be expected of those who are engaged professionally in elementary education. We must realize, however, that unless this research is carried on to the point where the Jewish traditions can be made to function in our day, there can be no modern kind of Jewish education, no education that can generate in the young of our people the will to live as Jews.

In addition to revitalizing the tradition as a means of synthesizing Jewish life with Americanism, we have to create the kind of social structure which would set in motion the newly interpreted and evolved Jewish values. The most inspiring and wholesome teachings are likely to remain a dead letter unless they become part of the consciousness of a living, functioning community. All efforts at reinterpreting and revaluing our tradition are carried on in a vacuum so long as we are without an organic Jewish community that possesses the educational machinery to put into circulation the results of those efforts. In the past, for example, though the Torah was regarded as having been given by God to Moses, it would have remained at best esoteric doctrine, had there not been a nation to adopt it as its constitution. It was the social structure of the Jewish people which gave the Torah its potency throughout the centuries.

Before the era of Emancipation, it was impossible for Jews, whether they happened to be few or many, to live without some kind of communal structure to make them aware of their solidarity with the Jewish nation. As soon as Jews, however, were permitted to become part of the body politic of the majority, they lost the urgency for Jewish communal life. The various organizations, including congregations, do not constitute the kind of communal organism which is essential to the functioning of a tradition, any more than scientific and philanthropic societies constitute a nation. By the same token that we need to reinterpret that Jewish tradition properly if we want it to live in the modern universe of thought, we need, also, to reorganize the social structure of the Jewish people properly if we want it to have a place in the frame of modern society. Judaism cannot function in a vacuum. It has to be geared to a living community. In that community all who wish to be known as Jews should be registered, and expulsion from it should deprive one of the right to use the name Jew. The creation of such organic communities based on the spirit of democratic constitutionalism is the first and most indispensable prerequisite to Jewish survival in the Diaspora.

Part 10
Ideologists in Action

RABBI MEIR BAR-ILAN (BERLIN)
1880-1949

ZIONIST IDEOLOGY began with analyses of the contemporary problems of Jews and Judaism and proposed a variety of solutions, each of which soon became the particular doctrine of some school of thought or party. These groups fought side by side against adverse circumstances and against the often unfriendly policy of the Turks, and later the British, and the rising enmity of the Arabs. Concurrently, these Zionisms were in conflict with one another, over the temper of the life and institutions that were arising in the Yishuv and over the policies to be pursued by the World Zionist Organization. Their leaders were at once ideologists and men of affairs; together, they were the immediate architects of the state of Israel.

The commanding figure of religious Zionism for the last three decades of his life was Meir Berlin. He was born within the most eminent rabbinic family of Lithuania, the son of the old age of Rabbi Naftali Zwi Berlin, the last head of the yeshivah of Volozhin before it was closed in 1892 by the Russian Government. Two years later, after the death of his father, Meir Berlin began six years of wanderings, during which he studied at various schools of higher talmudic learning. At the age of twenty he was married; he had already come to the resolve, in that year, that his life would be devoted to religious Zionism. In part, this decision was rooted in the example of his much revered father; the older man had been less willing than his friend and contemporary, Rabbi Mohilever, to co-operate with the secularists of the old Hibbat Zion organization, but nonetheless he had himself been a notable proponent of increased Jewish effort and settlement in the Holy Land.

Berlin spent some years before the First World War in Germany. At first he absented himself from public affairs in order to further his secular studies, but he was soon again active in Zionism. Deeply impressed by the combination of uncompromising piety and modernity that he found in some German Jews, Berlin hoped that this would become the dominant type in the homeland. He was later disenchanted by the anti-Zionism that continued to prevail in many of these circles, but the image of piety harmoniously blended with worldliness remained his guiding light. As writer and editor and, soon, as official of the religious Zionist (Mizrahi) organization, Berlin fought the characteristic battles of his group both against the anti-Zionism of the ultraorthodox and the secularism of many Zionists.

After an earlier trip to the United States for propagandistic purposes, he came here in 1914 to settle. Berlin rose quickly to the national leadership of Mizrahi in America. He was active in all Zionist political concerns and paid particular attention to the upbuilding of orthodox religious education in the United States. He emigrated to Palestine in 1926, when he became the international head of Mizrahi. His life from that day to his death in the spring of 1949, less than a year after the state of Israel was declared, was coextensive with the history of Zionism and Palestine in that troubled, tragic, and heroic period. (Like many, Berlin Hebraized his name, in his case to Bar-Ilan, after the state of Israel was declared.)

As the leader of Mizrahi, he marshaled its forces for the *Kulturkampf* between religion and secularism in Israel, which is still undecided. The paper below, though written in 1921, is therefore still contemporary.

WHAT KIND OF LIFE SHOULD WE CREATE IN ERETZ ISRAEL? (1922)

THERE ARE CONCEPTS and values that are nominally alike, but altogether different in essence. Sometimes a concept, in the course of its development, loses its original meaning and takes on a new one; it sheds its inner form and acquires another. These changes are not apparent to the spiritually shortsighted, who use concepts indiscriminately and identify them by their names and not by their real meanings. They evaluate the developing concept, which has taken on a new significance, by the criterion of its former content.

Out of such a mistaken approach a "new" problem is now arising among us, the question of "church and state." To be sure, this issue has not yet become a "burning" one, but its flames are already licking at the edges of our life, and there are already partisans demanding its solution. There are those among them who predict that the church-state question will lead to a terrible struggle in our country, after the pattern of comparable conflicts elsewhere, between the political leadership and the clergy. They guess that the majority of the people will support the clergy, but that the state, supported by the "liberals," will finally emerge victorious. There are those who assert that the question will be resolved peaceably. It has been maintained as an undeniable axiom that "religion is a private matter to be left to the individual conscience." This is the manner in which people are debating this question, but what they do not realize is that they are committing a basic error by treating the question of religion in Jewish life as a question of church and state. They are confusing two separate matters which have nothing whatsoever in common.

Both our people, as a whole, and our religion, in specific, are totally different from all others. Among the nations of the world statecraft is kept separate from religion. The foundations of each derive from different realms of the spirit, and there is a wide gap between the forms in which each expresses itself. The state does not impinge upon the sphere of religion, and religion does not concern itself with the conduct of the state. Even the most devout Christian or Moslem can find no guidance for his political conduct in the dictates of his religion. To be sure, these religions do contain references to the good and the bad in politics, to what is beautiful and what is ugly in the relations between man and man and between the citizen and his country, but these religions lay down no laws and regulations for the state as such to follow. Even the most devout nations must formulate their own statutes governing political, social, and family life. These laws are set down by living people, mortals, in a natural way, and whoever takes exception to the accepted rules or who does not abide by them is not considered a "sinner" before the bar of religion. Therefore church and state are kept separate and treated as separate provinces. Clergyman and civil judge have separate duties covering different spheres, and one does not encroach upon the domain of the other.

Our case is different. Our Torah and traditions are not a man-made constitution but God's own law. If we say, "This law is good, this one is not," we negate everything. We can have no partial acceptance, for this destroys the sanctity of the Torah. An advocate of such a policy thereby excludes himself from the community of believers, either as a

Jew or as a religious person. Our Torah more than touches upon state and public life; it provides rules and regulations governing these aspects of life. These laws, indeed, are basic and essential parts of the Torah and our religious legislation. The very sections of our laws which deal with man's relation to his conscience and to his Maker also offer general and specific guidance on the conduct of the state and social life and on our relations with other countries—how to wage war on them and how to live at peace with them. Neither when we dwelt in our homeland nor during the exile have we ever had laws that were of an exclusively "secular" nature. We have no "church" that is not also concerned with matters of state, just as we have no state which is not also concerned with "church" matters—in Jewish life these are not two separate spheres.

Thus we see that although there is but one term designating this question of church and state, there is a vast difference between the forms it takes among the gentiles and among us. Moreover, among us the question is not even a real one. When we have a state, should anyone try to separate church and state, this will represent not a separation but a contradiction. Should someone say: Let the religious concern themselves with religious matters and stay out of the affairs of the state, it will be as if he were saying: Let us divide the Torah into sections; the minor portions, dealing with moral and spiritual matters, we shall accept, but the rest, dealing with custom and daily action, we shall eliminate and replace with other laws. Such an approach, whenever it may appear, has no basis in anything in the political life of the European lands or of America; its source is in our own ancient history, when "our ancestors were idol worshipers . . ."

II

THERE IS a general principle as to how society developed: Modes of behavior were not formulated a priori. People did not come to a country with a set plan of how to conduct their lives. First people migrated to a country individually and in groups. Then they organized for various activities, and out of their private and social lives they evolved customs and mores adapted to themselves and to the environment in which they lived. After that there was no need to make laws. The lawmakers merely recorded how the people lived and the scale of punishment for those who deviated from the accepted behavior. Certainly it was so in ancient times. The legal historians, especially those of Roman law, prove beyond doubt that the various laws are rooted in the conditions under which the individual nations were formed. This explains the numerous and vast differences between the laws of various nations—these originate in their differing characters and ways of life.

If this process obtained today as well, our return to our homeland would be very difficult. A serious situation would then confront us: How shall we integrate the laws of our ancestral heritage with the customs and outlooks to which we have become accustomed in the various lands of our dispersion? Since it is virtually axiomatic that laws are not formulated a priori but are a natural, spontaneous outgrowth of the life process, each one of us, every group and faction, is already set in its ways and outlook—how then shall we set about drawing up our constitution? Shall we adopt the laws and customs that we bring with us from the Diaspora, even if they are in measurable conflict with our traditions; or shall we adhere rigidly to the letter of the Law, even if we are thereby compelled to live by a book that is foreign to the modern tempo and conditions? On the other hand, we must put this question to those who feel that the laws of the Torah are purely academic, but of no practical interest, and who believe that actually we should be governed by modern law: Is it our intention to welcome to our shores only people from one land, so that we shall have a people capable of adhering to only one way of life they would be bringing with them? Since, however, it is our hope and desire that Jews from every country migrate to Eretz Israel—the Sephardim from the Oriental countries being as dear to us as the Ashkenazim of Europe; the Yemenites, primitive though they are, being no less welcome than the Americans—how, then, shall we formulate our customs, mores and laws: in the spirit of the "backward" Yemenites or in the spirit of the "civilized" Americans; to suit the Westerners or to suit the Orientals?

There will be many coming to Eretz Israel, especially from Europe and America, who, though in general sympathy with Judaism, are not at all familiar with the Torah. These will say, "What are the laws of the Jewish tradition to us? Let each man and every group live by its own customs and traditions. Later, when things are stabilized, the situation will be ready for the work of the lawmakers. They will then choose the best and worthiest practices, from among all those that will exist, and formulate them as laws. In the meantime, let us live here on a temporary basis according to the customs and traditions we brought with us from the Diaspora, which have become an integral part of our being. If our inherited laws and traditions of the Torah have elements in them which are in conflict with our ways of life—so much the worse for the laws of the Torah." In opposition to this opinion another kind of extremist may maintain that modern customs and conditions are to be ignored entirely. We must live only according to the laws of our Torah, and it is irrelevant to us that many people do not understand its laws or know their meaning. These two factions will cause dissension among us. It is possible that we shall even see "reform" and "reformers" in our country, of a new and even less admirable kind than those in the Diaspora, since these reforms will not be confined solely to the prayer book and the synagogue service but will affect law and the basic order of life.

We recommend our way, the third approach, as the solution to this conflict. It is our conviction that "there can be no substitute for the Torah," that the only means to unite all sects and factions of the Jewish people into one homogenous state is by regenerating every aspect of our life on the basis of our heritage of Torah. This does not mean that we should scoff at and ignore the values and customs of this generation. Even if these values and customs are in contradiction to the laws of our Torah, we must modify them gradually. We have to begin our task not with passing laws but by educating the young and by influencing their elders. We have to educate the people to accept our laws; we must extend our influence, even by using indirect means if necessary, through schools and textbooks, newspapers and literature, so that the inhabitants of our country will slowly change their thinking and outlook and draw near to the laws of our Torah. Such a change will result in the acceptance of the laws of the Torah for their intrinsic worth—voluntarily, from an inner recognition of their value—rather than by either moral or physical coercion.

In sum: The question of the right way of life in our homeland is a question of education and influencing the community. In the light of this conclusion, we must deal with the really basic question: How shall our schools be run? Shall we be content with teaching our children only language and literature in these schools and not be disturbed if these subjects are taught in an atmosphere inimical to religion and faith? Or shall we demand that language and literature be studied only from a religious viewpoint? If we could accept the general view that church and state are two separate spheres, then we could say that the laws of daily life and the laws of the Torah are not one and the same, and every one has the right to study whatever he wishes. Let the religious and the secularists each establish their own schools, on condition that the language and literature studied in both shall be Hebrew. However, since we have proved that, with respect to our people, even church and state are more than two separate entities that are closely interrelated but are really only one, we cannot substitute Roman law for the laws of the Torah. We must, therefore, teach the people, young and old, to respect and know the Torah, in the same way as the leaders of various social movements first condition the people to their aims. The most effective means to this end is to make all schools public, governmental institutions, so that the pupils who attend them—and through them their parents—will be educated in the spirit of religion and tradition, because to us religion and tradition are what language and literature are to the gentiles. Americans are rightly concerned that if their children are ignorant of the English language and literature, they will, in time, stop loving their people and lose the desire to defend their country; so we too must be concerned lest our children grow up devoid of religious and national feeling, lest they break the link that binds them to Jewish life and Jewish values and make the land of Israel into a country no different than those of the gentiles.

III

WHEN WE ADVOCATE that the Jewish schools in our country become public schools, we are referring only to the elementary schools. These schools are the educational foundation in every country because they are an indispensable necessity for everyone of every class. This is not true of the high schools. These are not equally necessary for everyone, and for many they are spiritual luxuries. It is, therefore, not possible to place these schools under public control. Even in those countries where all the schools, from the most elementary to the most advanced, are supported by the government, there are "private" schools that are of great value in the education and development of their inhabitants. Certainly we shall not want to hinder personal freedom, and every minority will therefore be granted complete autonomy to act as it will, provided that no harm is done to society as a whole.

We can see in advance that the question of the schools is going to be complicated and difficult. When the first foundation stones were laid for the rebuilding of our country, immediately and without delay the foundation for the Hebrew University was also laid. Even if we admit that there were overriding political reasons for founding and establishing the University, despite the opposition of many who felt that the time was not ripe for such an institution, this act nonetheless proves that there is an inner tendency on the part of Zionist leadership to interest itself in schools and education. If such be the case at this early stage, it will be all the more true later, after the Jewish state is established, and a new way of life becomes settled in our land. Therefore, even if a unitary system will prevail in the elementary schools, and these schools will be organized as Jewish public institutions, we cannot expect higher education, too, to be of "one denomination."

It is obviously not the purpose of this essay to furnish a curriculum for our schools. We are dealing with this question only in so far as it touches upon the whole temper of life. If we have schools conducted in a traditionalist-national spirit, these will influence our lives, which will then be lived in the same spirit; but if the schools be secular, life, too, will reflect this secular spirit, even if the masses of our people continue to harbor a religious spirit. There are "pious" and "observant" people in the Diaspora, who observe all the minor and major commandments of the Torah, and nonetheless their entire behavior has about it the air of assimilation to gentile culture. Nowadays we may criticize these people and show up their faults, but when the homeland itself, the center that is most Jewish in spirit, begins to produce such people, we shall no longer dare to cavil at them and their behavior, and we may even make the mistake of imagining that this is the true picture of what Judaism intends.

If we wish to continue our spiritual heritage and not create a new Judaism, we must make of our schools in our homeland places where more than language and vocations are taught; they must be real educational institutions in keeping with the nation's ideals and principles. Knowledge of talmudic law and all that this implies should play an important role in these studies. The Talmud and its literature must remain, to some degree, the heritage of the whole House of Israel and should not constitute a science and discipline only for those who are professional scholars of the Torah. Naturally, we also need experts who will devote their lives to the study of the Talmud—and these should be of the highest caliber. But the spirit of the Talmud and some knowledge of talmudic laws and literature should be part of the schooling of every educated Jew. It is customary among the gentiles that every schoolboy have some basic knowledge of physics and mathematics, and, even though he may not utilize these studies in his lifework, these basic disciplines are regarded as indispensable. Our attitude to the knowledge of talmudic law should be comparable: Every schoolboy should be required to master certain sections of the Talmud and to imbibe its spirit, even though he may not make this field of study his life's work.

This demand, which many may regard as too extreme, requires us not to be satisfied with establishing the type of yeshivot and Hebrew schools now prevalent both in the Diaspora and in Israel. We must realize that our homeland will be, and should be, a progressive and enlightened country, and that we cannot isolate ourselves. The Chinese people boasts of a culture that is older than any in Europe, and yet when one of its sons wants to become "cultured," he goes to Europe or to America. Therefore, if we want to be a modern people, we too must not allow that our entire education be reduced to those national or religious studies peculiar to us, so that when we need doctors, architects, and engineers, we shall have to import them from other countries or send our children abroad to study. Nor do we have the right to segregate the schools, so that "ours" will be devoted only to the Torah and Jewish subjects, and "theirs" (meaning the schools of those who do not accept our views) will teach general culture. If we do this, we will lower the standards of our schools and their pupils will achieve less than pupils in the secular schools. We must not permit this to happen not merely for economic but also for moral reasons. Life has taught us: "He who increases in wealth, increases his dignity."[1] If the secular schools are to produce the wealthy and enlightened class, whereas the pupils of our schools will be merely God-fearing scholars of the Torah, the influence of the secularists will predominate in everything. The same sad pattern that prevailed in the Diaspora will recur again: The yeshivah students are poor in material wealth and downtrodden in spirit, while the college students are successful and their influence, both direct and indirect, is ever greater.

If it is our wholehearted desire that all our children know the Torah and follow its teachings, we must establish schools which combine both Jewish and secular studies. The Jewish studies should consist not only of literature and language; they must include the entire religious heritage, so that our children know more than just the Bible.

These views on how we should organize the communal life now coming into being in the homeland should be the yardstick for all who deal with the rebuilding of our country, for all those who really want to see the Hebrew nation revitalized on its land and in the spirit of its Torah.

Mizrahi, which was the first, in recent times, to raise the banner of a national-religious renaissance, must now accept the further task of implementing these views with deeds.

VLADIMIR JABOTINSKY   1880-1940

VLADIMIR JABOTINSKY has been dead for almost twenty years, and yet he remains the most controversial figure in Zionism. No man in its entire history, except Herzl, was as adored by his disciples; the passion with which Jabotinsky's enemies hated him was unique. His followers rallied to him as the Garibaldi of the Jewish revolution; his foes reviled him as its would-be Mussolini. Obviously, he was an extraordinary man.

He was born in Odessa, when that great center of Jewish life on the Black Sea was at its zenith, but he belonged to a generation which was raised much more on Russian than on Jewish culture. In 1898, in his last year of high school, Jabotinsky chose not to wait to graduate but to go abroad to study. Since he had given early evidence of literary talent, one of the Odessa newspapers accepted the eighteen-year-old as its foreign correspondent, on "space rates." After a few months in Bern, Jabotinsky went to Rome, where he spent three years at the university. He had moved, as correspondent, to the staff of another Odessa daily, and the columns he wrote for it soon became so popular that he was recalled in 1901 to serve on its editorial staff.

There is evidence of his earlier assent to the Zionist ideal, but Jabotinsky became an active Zionist in 1903, when he helped organize a Jewish self-defense corps in Odessa, in the face of a threatening pogrom. He was already one of the great orators of the day, and thereafter Jabotinsky put this talent, as well as his pen, to the uses of Zionist propaganda. He continued to make a living as a journalist; in balancing both these careers he traveled widely all over Russia and Europe in the years before 1914, including two periods in Constantinople around the time of the Young Turk revolution of 1908 and a lengthy stay in Vienna. Though there was some shifting of ground in his views, Jabotinsky was coming to the certainty that Zionism could mean only a bold, Herzlian, political struggle for a state. He did not believe that either the Turks, who then ruled Palestine, or the Arabs would accommodate themselves more easily to Zionism if, as its leadership then believed, it de-emphasized its final aims or was even willing to abandon them. In his view, colonization and everything else depended on political achievements and ultimately, therefore, on power.

After the outbreak of the First World War Jabotinsky went to northern and western Europe as a roving correspondent for a liberal Moscow daily. Once Turkey joined the war in October 1914, on the side of Germany, Jabotinsky was certain that the future of Jewish aspirations in Palestine rested with the Allies. Turkey, he was sure, would be dismembered, no matter what the outcome of the war; hence, the Jews had to fight on the Allied side and share in the military effort to occupy Palestine. The feeling of most of the Zionist leadership (Chaim Weizmann, who then aided Jabotinsky, discreetly, was the one notable exception) was that neutrality was the policy to follow in the war. Almost singlehanded, Jabotinsky finally won British consent to the formation of three Jewish battalions, the first of which (the 38th Fusiliers) fought with Allenby in the campaign in Palestine in 1918. He himself enlisted as a private and was soon made a lieutenant.

When the war ended, Jabotinsky was the least hopeful of all the Zionists that there would be real support from the British or smooth relations with the Arabs during the expected period of mass immigration. During the Arab riots of 1920, he organized a self-defense corps in Jerusalem and was jailed by the British military administration and sentenced to fifteen years for the illegal possession of arms. This caused a storm, and he was soon pardoned and the conviction was subsequently revoked. Jabotinsky's reputation was now at its height. He was elected to the Zionist Executive in 1921, but almost immediately he and Chaim Weizmann were at odds. Jabotinsky believed in rapid mass immigration to Palestine and in major dependence on Jewish military and police units; Weizmann trusted the British, or at least believed that nothing could be done without their consent, and wanted a policy of careful colonization. Other issues were involved, as well, so that within two years Jabotinsky resigned, charging that the policies of his colleagues would result in the loss of Palestine.

Jabotinsky returned to Zionist work in 1925, when he organized a new Zionist party, the Revisionists. After a decade in which he was ever more out of tune with the official leadership of Zionism as too minimalist and compromising, his group left the movement entirely in 1935, to found the "New Zionist Organization." Illegal immigration into Palestine during the 1930's and the direct action of the Irgun against the British from that period until 1948 were conducted with special daring and *élan* by groups under his influence. Jabotinsky died on a trip to the United States in 1940.

The pages below represent the whole of his direct testimony before the British Royal Commission on Palestine of 1937. This group, known also as the Peel Commission, was directed to inquire into the Palestinian impasse, after the Arab riots and guerrilla warfare of 1936, and to make recommendations for its solution. It suggested a plan to partition Palestine, which was soon abandoned by the British government. Jabotinsky appeared before this body on behalf of his New Zionist Organization. What he said there stands as an instructive summary of his mature views.

EVIDENCE SUBMITTED TO THE
PALESTINE ROYAL COMMISSION (1937)

House of Lords, London
February 11, 1937

THE CONCEPTION OF ZIONISM which I have the honor to represent here is based on what I should call the humanitarian aspect. By that I do not mean to say that we do not respect the other, the purely spiritual aspects of Jewish nationalism, such as the desire for self-expression, the rebuilding of a Hebrew culture, or creating some "model community of which the Jewish people could be proud." All that, of course, is most important; but as compared with our actual needs and our real position in the world today, all that h.s rather the character of luxury. The Commission have already heard a description of the situation of world-Jewry especially in eastern Europe, and I am not going to repeat any details, but you will allow me to quote a recent reference in the New York *Times* describing the position of Jewry in eastern Europe as "a disaster of historic magnitude." I only wish to add that it would be very naïve, and although many Jews make this mistake I disapprove of it—it would be very naïve to ascribe that state of disaster, permanent disaster, only to the guilt of men, whether it be crowds and multitudes, or whether it be Governments. The thing goes much deeper than that. I am very much afraid that what I am going to

say will not be popular with many among my coreligionists, and I regret that, but the truth is the truth. We are facing an elemental calamity, a kind of social earthquake.

Three generations of Jewish thinkers and Zionists, among whom
there were many great minds—I am not going to fatigue you by quoting them—three generations have given much thought to analyzing
the Jewish position and have come to the conclusion that the cause of
our suffering is the very fact of the Diaspora, the bedrock fact that we
are everywhere a minority. It is not the anti-Semitism of men; it is,
above all, the anti-Semitism of things, the inherent xenophobia of the
body social or the body economic under which we suffer. Of course,
there are ups and downs; but there are moments, there are whole
periods in history when this "xenophobia of Life itself" takes dimensions which no people can stand, and that is what we are facing now.

I do not mean to suggest that I would recognize that all the Governments concerned have done all they ought to have done; I would be
the last man to concede that. I think many Governments, East and
West, ought to do much more to protect the Jews than they do; but
the best of Governments could perhaps only soften the calamity to
quite an insignificant extent, but the core of the calamity is an earthquake which stands and remains. I want to mention here that, since
one of those Governments (the Polish Government) has recently tried
what amounts to bringing to the notice of the League of Nations and
the whole of humanity that it is humanity's duty to provide the Jews
with an area where they could build up their own body social undis-
turbed by anyone, I think the sincerity of the Polish Government, and
of any other Governments who, I hope, will follow, should not be
suspected, but on the contrary it should be recognized and acknowledged with due gratitude.

Perhaps the greatest gap in all I am going to say and in all the
Commission have heard up to now is the impossibility of really going
to the root of the problem, really bringing before you a picture of what
that Jewish hell looks like, and I feel I cannot do it. I do hope the day
may come when some Jewish representative may be allowed to appear
at the Bar of one of these two Houses just to tell them what it really is,
and to ask the English people: "What are you going to advise us?
Where is the way out? Or, standing up and facing God, say that there
is no way out and that we Jews have just to go under." But unfortunately I cannot do it, so I will simply assume that the Royal Commission are sufficiently informed of all this situation, and then I want
you to realize this: The phenomenon called Zionism may include all

kinds of dreams—a "model community," Hebrew culture, perhaps even a second edition of the Bible—but all this longing for wonderful toys of velvet and silver is nothing in comparison with that tangible momentum of irresistible distress and need by which we are propelled and borne.

We are not free agents. We cannot "concede" anything. Whenever I hear the Zionist, most often my own Party, accused of asking for too much— Gentlemen, I really cannot understand it. Yes, we do want a State; every nation on earth, every normal nation, beginning with the smallest and the humblest who do not claim any merit, any role in humanity's development, they all have States of their own. That is the normal condition for a people. Yet, when we, the most abnormal of peoples and therefore the most unfortunate, ask only for the same condition as the Albanians enjoy, to say nothing of the French and the English, then it is called too much. I should understand it if the answer were, "It is impossible," but when the answer is, "It is too much," I cannot understand it. I would remind you (excuse me for quoting an example known to every one of you) of the commotion which was produced in that famous institution when Oliver Twist came and asked for "more." He said "more" because he did not know how to express it; what Oliver Twist really meant was this: "Will you just give me that normal portion which is necessary for a boy of my age to be able to live." I assure you that you face here today, in the Jewish people with its demands, an Oliver Twist who has, unfortunately, no concessions to make. What can be the concessions? We have got to save millions, many *millions*. I do not know whether it is a question of rehousing one-third of the Jewish race, half of the Jewish race, or a quarter of the Jewish race; I do not know; but it is a question of millions. Certainly the way out is to evacuate those portions of the Diaspora which have become no good, which hold no promise of any possibility of a livelihood, and to concentrate all those refugees in some place which should *not* be Diaspora, not a repetition of the position where the Jews are an unabsorbed minority within a foreign social, or economic, or political organism. Naturally, if that process of evacuation is allowed to develop, as it ought to be allowed to develop, there will very soon be reached a moment when the Jews will become a majority in Palestine.

I am going to make a "terrible" confession. Our demand for a Jewish majority is not our maximum—it is our minimum: it is just an inevitable stage if only we are allowed to go on salvaging our people. The point when the Jews will reach a majority in that country will not be the point of saturation yet—because with 1,000,000 more Jews in Palestine today you could already have a Jewish majority, but there are certainly 3,000,000 or 4,000,000 in the East who are virtually knocking at the door asking for admission, i.e., for salvation.

I have the profoundest feeling for the Arab case, in so far as that Arab case is not exaggerated. This Commission have already been able to make up their minds as to whether there is any individual hardship to the Arabs of Palestine as men, deriving from the Jewish colonization. We maintain unanimously that the economic position of the Palestinian Arabs, under the Jewish colonization and owing to the Jewish colonization, has become the object of envy in all the surrounding Arab countries, so that the Arabs from those countries show a clear tendency to immigrate into Palestine. I have also shown to you already that, in our submission, there is no question of ousting the Arabs. On the contrary, the idea is that Palestine on both sides of the Jordan should hold the Arabs, their progeny, *and* many millions of Jews. What I do not deny is that in that process the Arabs of Palestine will necessarily become a minority in the country of Palestine. What I do deny is that *that* is a hardship. It is not a hardship on any race, any nation, possessing so many National States now and so many more National States in the future. One fraction, one branch of that race, and not a big one, will have to live in someone else's State: Well, that is the case with all the mightiest nations of the world. I could hardly mention one of the big nations, having their States, mighty and powerful, who had not one branch living in someone else's State. That is only normal and there is no "hardship" attached to that. So when we hear the Arab claim confronted with the Jewish claim; I fully understand that any minority would prefer to be a majority, it is quite understandable that the Arabs of Palestine would also prefer Palestine to be the Arab State No. 4, No. 5, or No. 6—that I quite understand; but when the Arab claim is confronted with our Jewish demand to be saved, it is like the claims of appetite versus the claims of starvation. No tribunal has ever had the luck of trying a case where all the justice was on the side of one party and the other party had no case whatsoever. Usually in human affairs any tribunal, including this tribunal, in trying two cases, has to concede that both sides have a case on their side and, in order to do justice, they must take into consideration what should constitute the basic justification of all human demands, individual or mass demands—the decisive terrible balance of Need. I think it is clear.

I now want to establish that this condition was perfectly well known, perfectly realized, and perfectly acknowledged, by the legislators responsible for the act known as the Balfour Declaration and subsequently for the Mandate. The paramount question was Jewish distress. I was privileged myself to take part in our political negotiations with France, Italy, and England, from 1915 to 1917. I was also associated with others who conducted those negotiations. I can assure you that the main argument mentioned in every conversation with the Italian ministers, with M. Delcassé in France, with Lord Newton here, with Lord Balfour, with Mr. Lloyd George, and with everybody else, was the argument of the terrible Jewish distress, especially keen at that moment. England, France, and Italy, three Liberal countries, happened to be Allies of Tsarist Russia. I need not describe to gentlemen of your generation what it meant to any Englishman, whether Liberal or Conservative, when he read in the newspapers, especially in 1915 and 1916, certain information as to the fate of the Jews in the Russian sector of the war. It was the common talk everywhere—the feeling that something should be done to relieve that disaster, and the feeling that that disaster was only an acute expression of a deep-seated, chronic disease that was alive everywhere. And I claim that the spirit that created the Balfour Declaration was that spirit, the recognition that something should be done to save a people in that position.

My Lord and Gentlemen, here we come to the beginning of a very sad chapter. I will do my best to put it to you as moderately as I can. You will certainly use patience and perhaps more than patience with a man who has to tell you about a very great disappointment. I always thought before coming to England that if a civilized country, a civilized Government, assumed a trust, internationally, under *such* conditions, with *such* implications, dealing with a people who have so long suffered and who have so long hoped and whose hopes are, after all, sacred to every Englishman—I expected that Government to sit down and prepare a blueprint, a plan "how to do it." Under whatever interpretation of the "home" promise, there should have been a plan how to build it; what were to be the implications of "placing a country under such administrative, economic, and political conditions as might facilitate the establishment" of whatever you mean by the Jewish national home.

That was one condition—a Plan; and the second condition was letting it be clear to all that that was the trust they have accepted and "That is what we are going to do." That blueprint or planning should begin with a geological survey of both sides of the Jordan in order to ascertain what parts of the territory are really reclaimable, cultivable; a scheme for their amelioration and reclamation; a scheme of a loan which should be launched and which the Jews would have to provide, to pay for the amelioration and parcellation, and for creating a land reserve on both sides of the Jordan, out of which both Jewish and Arab applicants for agricultural settlement could be satisfied. Further, a plan of industrial development calculated to provide sustenance for large-scale immigration; a plan of what tariff laws and customs measures should be adopted in order to protect that development; a plan for a taxation system, as in every country under colonization, adapted to assisting the new settlers and newcomers.

Finally, measures for guaranteeing security. A nation with your colossal colonizing past experience surely knows that colonization never went on without certain conflicts with the population on the spot, so that the country had to be protected; and as the Jew never asked to be protected by someone else, the Plan should embody the Jewish demand that they should themselves be allowed to form a protecting body in Palestine, or at least a considerable part of it. Especially there should be a very careful selection of Civil Servants. Such a work, unparalleled, unprecedented, certainly needs Civil Servants first of all sympathetic, and secondly, acquainted with the work. There should be some special examination, some new branch of the Service. That is what everybody expected. I need not tell you how totally disappointed we were in hearing, instead of all that, the expression "muddling through"—hearing it even mentioned as something desirable and commendable as a system; on more solemn occasions it was called "empiricism" and sometimes "going by horse sense." I do not know if all this is good for the Empire; it is not for me to judge. I can only say that we have greatly suffered under this absence of system, this deliberate aversion from making plans while undertaking something very new, very important, and very responsible. We have suffered terribly. Yet, whenever we complained, we got the strange reply: "The man on the spot knows better." May I submit most respectfully that the Mandate was granted to Great Britain by fifty nations because those fifty nations believed in Britain's collective experience and conscience, and especially in the fact of their close control over the man on the spot. The idea of control by a nation over its executives is an English idea. We Continentals learned it from the English. So, in our submission, the Mandatory Government cannot discharge its Mandatory duty by selecting even a genius and appointing him as the man on the spot. But that was practically always their reply: "We have appointed a man on the spot, let him do it, and we shall wait and see." Or sometimes we got another reply—"Probably the Government is administered quite satisfactorily, because both Jews and Arabs have grievances and complaints." We never could understand this. Is my duty, for instance, with regard to my children or with regard to my two clients, sufficiently discharged if I have managed to make myself obnoxious to both of them? I do not think so.

We were terribly disappointed by the absence of a system and plan. We were even more disappointed by the absence of the second requirement: clarity. The Arabs were never told what the Balfour Declaration was meant by Lord Balfour and all the others to mean. They were never told. Here again, My Lord, I am going to limit myself, as being perhaps a sufficient illustration of that attitude to truth, to recall a little story which has been told to this Commission in Palestine: that instead of writing on coins, etc., "Eretz Israel" they just write the two Hebrew letters for E. I. Why? What is the meaning of it? If the country is to be called Eretz Israel, Land of Israel, if that is the name avowed, then print it in full; if it is something which cannot be allowed, remove it. But the "way out" adopted in this case illustrates the whole "system," which is to hint that there is the Balfour Declaration, and perhaps there is something in it, but then again perhaps there is nothing in it. That has been the "system" from the beginning to the end. If questioned, I am prepared to support this reproach by many facts, but I believe the Royal Commission have already had sufficient information to form their own judgment.

A very important factor in implementing the Mandate is looking after security. I presume the Commission have already had time to draw their own conclusions as to that, but it is my duty to remind them of a few aspects of it. In Palestine we were threatened with pogroms; we were telling so to the Government for years and years, but they went on cutting down and cutting down on the number of troops in Palestine. We said: "Remember that we have children and wives; legalize our self-defense, as you are doing in Kenya." In Kenya until recently every European was obliged to train for the Settlers Defense Force. Why should the Jews in Palestine be forced to prepare for self-defense underhand; as though committing a legal offense? You know what a pogrom means in Jewish history; we know what pogroms mean in the history of Mandatory Palestine. The Jews have never been allowed to prepare for that holy duty of self-defense, as every Englishman would have done. We had in our case to prepare by underhand methods, with insufficient equipment, with insufficient drilling, in an amateurish way. I really do not know how a Government can allow or tolerate such a state of things after three experiences, of which 1929 was a terrible one. . . . I am sorry if I am getting excited and I apologize to the Commission and hope they understand the reason for it; but I do not think I have overstepped the boundaries of logic in submitting to this Royal Commission my case.

If you cut down the troops in Palestine far beyond the limit of safety, and the explanation is that the British taxpayer does not want to give his money nor his sons, that is quite natural, but we—the Jews of all parties—have for years been demanding: "Why have you disbanded the Jewish Regiment? Why not allow the Jews to take over: our men and our money under British command and under British military law?" I do not claim a "Jewish Army" before there is a Jewish State; we want the Jewish Regiment just as it existed during the War, rendering decent service. Why should the impression be created in this country that we want Johnny, Tommy, and Bobby to defend us? We do not. If, in the building of Palestine, sweat and gold have to be employed, let us give the sweat and let us give the gold; if blood has to be shed by the defenders of Palestine, let it be our blood and not English blood. But that suggestion has always been turned down.

As I said: I know the attitude of this Commission in refusing to dwell on the actual course of the riots, and I have to bow before it. On the other hand—here again I must ask, not about this Commission, but about the Colonial Office, about the Mandatory Government: Is there a plan, is there a line of action? Mr. Eden in Geneva, most formally, in so many words, promised the League's Council that "a Royal Commission" had been appointed to investigate the prevailing unrest, that they would investigate the facts; and the Permanent Mandates Commission was persuaded to abstain from asking questions until "a Royal Commission"—I do not say *this* Royal Commission—had investigated actual events. This Royal Commission is, of course, sovereign to refuse to do so, and I can understand their motives, but My Lord, where is then that Royal Commission which *will* investigate who is guilty? Because I claim somebody is guilty, I claim that a tremendous amount of ammunition for the Arabs has been allowed to percolate into Palestine both before and during the events, I claim there was neglect of duty in examining the first victims. I claim there is something I want to understand but do not understand in the fact that while a general strike in Jaffa was in progress, there was no general strike in Haifa. I want to understand whether it is true there had been some gentlemen's agreement, a "revolt by leave" in one part of Palestine, but no revolt where it was requested by somebody in office that there should not be revolt. I want to understand why Mr. Kawkaji was allowed to depart from Palestine in state; why the bands were allowed to disband; why there was no subsequent disarmament of the population. I want to know why it is that such things can happen in a country and nobody is guilty, nobody is responsible.

With this famous theory of the man on the spot, I want the man on the spot to stand before a Royal Commission, before a Judicial Commission, and I want him to answer for his errors. Sometimes even a humble man like myself has the right to say the words "J'accuse." They are guilty. They are guilty of commission, omission, neglect of duty. If I am not mistaken, somebody has to answer to the Permanent Mandates Commission of the League of Nations who gave you the Mandate. Who is going to answer? I am informed that, instead of by this Royal Commission, a report on the events will be presented in a general way in the report of the Palestine Government to the League of Nations—the party whom we accuse will present it. I submit to this Royal Commission: Among your recommendations as to remedies (because you are requested in your terms of reference to mention remedies) the first is to find the guilty ones and to punish them. Also inquire about the Supreme Moslem Council, or whatever is the official description of that group of persons headed by His Eminence the Mufti and the other gentlemen. The Government gave them a sort of diplomatic immunity. The Government negotiated with them. I submit most respectfully and humbly that some independent Commission, independent of the Colonial Office and independent of the man on the spot, should inquire and investigate into this question of guilt. I believe it is guilt, and I believe that the person guilty should be punished, and that is what I humbly demand.

As to the remedies, the main remedy in my opinion is the Plan and the truth. Arabs and Jews should be informed what the real implications of the Mandate are. To my way of thinking there is only one way of interpreting the Mandate. And a Scheme should be prepared. We call it a Ten-Year Plan. In our opinion it should embrace agrarian reforms, taxation, and customs reforms, a reform of the Civil Service, opening up of Trans-Jordan for Jewish penetration, and assurance of public security by the establishment of a Jewish contingent and by the legalization of Jewish self-defense.

At the same time, I think on the Jewish side too, reforms are necessary, for we have also committed many errors in our own systems. In my opinion it all culminates in the reform of the Jewish Agency. I was asked by Lord Peel whether we represented a body distinct from the Jewish Agency. Yes. We claim that the Jewish Agency *de facto* does not today represent the whole or even the majority of Zionist Jewry and we think the time has come when this body should be rebuilt, with the consent of the Mandatory, on the basis of universal suffrage, because the problem of Zionism today has really become the interest of practically everybody in Jewry, no longer only of adherents of a particular political group. We think that reform is quite timely and it might put an end to many abuses which I cannot deny. One of them will be brought to the knowledge of this Commission in the report of the "Betar"—the British Trumpeldor organization—on the distribution of certificates, about which this Commission have received, to my great regret, misleading information from some other Jewish representatives.

CHAIRMAN: Are you going to tell us where it is misleading? What is the main point?

ANSWER: Yes, if you will allow me another ten minutes. There is a suggestion that when we are asking for what I am asking for, that we are trying to involve this Empire in formidable complications and obstacles. I deny it. To the best of my belief I affirm, and I am not the only one, that should Great Britain go this way and really help us to save the Jewish people as it was meant and promised in the Balfour Declaration, the course of this great experiment will be as normal as the course of any other great enterprise of social evolution. We utterly deny that it means bringing Great Britain into conflict with world Islam, we utterly deny that it means a real physical conflict with the neighboring states, we deny all this. It has been exaggerated beyond any recognition. It is not true. Given a firm resolve, made clearly known to both Jews and Arabs, all this would be performed with the normal smoothness of any other equally big colonization enterprise.

As to keeping the country quiet and avoiding disturbances: I have already submitted—try what has never been tried—try re-establishing the Jewish Regiment as part and parcel of the permanent garrison. Try legalizing Jewish self-defense. It is anyway almost inevitable. Jewish self-defense is "practically" legalized today; it is and it is not; it "should not" exist, but it does exist; it "should not" be armed, but if it is armed, well . . . and so on. Well, I think the decisive step should be made in the necessary direction.

You have, of course, heard of compromises and halfway houses which are being suggested, including cantonization, or the parity scheme, or the cultural rapprochement, or the Jews "giving in" and so on. Believe my sincerity, and it is the sincerity of the whole Movement, the sincerity of every Jew I am now trying to voice: We wish a halfway house could be possible, but it is perfectly impossible. We cannot accept cantonization, because it will be suggested by many, even among you, that even the whole of Palestine may prove too small for that humanitarian purpose we need. A corner of Palestine, a "canton," how can we promise to be satisfied with it? We cannot. We never can. Should we swear to you we would be satisfied, it would be a lie. On what other point can we "give in?" What can the "concession" be on the part of Oliver Twist? He is in such a position that he cannot concede anything; it is the workhouse people who have to concede the plateful of soup, and there is no way out of it. We do not believe in any compromise on those lines. Cantonization is a dream and parity is a lie. It will never be enforced or believed by anybody; and trying it again and again means prolonging the state of things which in my submission has led to the riots of 1920, 1921, 1929, and 1936, and it will lead again to the same result.

There is only one way of compromise. Tell the Arabs the truth, and then you will see the Arab is reasonable, the Arab is clever, the Arab is just; the Arab *can* realize that since there are three or four or five wholly Arab States, then it is a thing of justice which Great Britain is doing if Palestine is transformed into a Jewish State. Then there will be a change of mind among the Arabs, then there will be room for compromise, and there will be peace.

It is my very unpleasant duty to wind up by taking into consideration a melancholy pessimistic contingency: What will happen if what the Jews desire cannot be conceded by Great Britain? I wish I could omit mentioning that contingency for many reasons, personal reasons, Jewish national reasons, but to omit it is impossible. We are asked very often: "Whatever is meant by the Balfour Declaration was promised in 1917, but since then perhaps the British people have honestly come to the conclusion that they cannot do it." I deny it. I affirm they can; but when I am asked, when any Jew is asked: "What, are the Jews going to pin us down to the promise and to say—you have promised the pound of flesh, pay us the pound of flesh?" Gentlemen, here I answer you in the name of the most extreme of Zionist parties: "No!" If Great Britain really is unable to do it (not unwilling, but unable) we will bow to her decision, but we then shall expect Great Britain to act as any Mandatory who feels he cannot carry out the Mandate: give back the Mandate. . . .

SIR LAURIE HAMMOND: To whom?

ANSWER: And do it in a way which will not harm the safety of the Jews who trusted you and came to Palestine on the chances of a Zionist future. This means letting a certain time elapse while the Mandatory together with the Jews will look for the alternative. I hope that time will never come. I am fully convinced that it will not be necessary. I believe in England just as I believed in England twenty years ago when I went, against nearly all Jewish opinion, and said: "Give soldiers to Great Britain!" because I believed in her. I still believe. But if Great Britain really *cannot* live up to the Mandate— well—we shall be the losers; and we will sit down together and think what can be done; but not that Great Britain should go on holding the Mandate and pretend it is "fulfilled" while my people are still suffering in the Diaspora and still only a minority in Palestine. No, that cannot be done. That is not cricket. Therefore, Gentlemen, I submit it cannot be done, and it shall not be done.

I thank the Commission very much for their kindness and attention. I beg your forgiveness for having kept you for an hour and a half.

CHAIM WEIZMANN 1874-1952

TO WRITE A BRIEF biographical notice of Chaim Weizmann is manifestly impossible, for his was the central career of Jewish history in the first half of the twentieth century. We must content ourselves with the barest listing of dates and places, leaving it to the reader to find the rounded account in Weizmann's not unbiased, but always fascinating autobiography, *Trial and Error* (New York, 1949). As he reminded a thousand audiences, Weizmann's roots were in the old ghetto of the Russian Pale of Settlement. He was born in the village of Motol, near the city of Pinsk, and received the usual pious early training. After completing his high school education in Pinsk, Weizmann taught for a season in a Jewish private school near Darmstadt, Germany. He soon returned home, but in 1895 the family finances were sufficiently improved to enable him to enroll at the Berlin Polytechnicum. Three years of scientific studies there were followed by further work at Freiburg and Geneva. He received his doctorate from the University of Geneva in 1900 and remained to teach chemistry there for the next four years.

Weizmann decided to move to England in 1904. After some months in Manchester, he was appointed to the faculty of the university and he retained this association until 1916. Then, in the middle of the First World War, he transferred to London to direct a special laboratory that the British Government had created for his important work on the production of acetone, a vital ingredient of naval gunpowder. Weizmann remained at this post until after the war, when he became almost totally involved in Zionism. Nonetheless, throughout his life, he continued, with some fraction of his time, to work as a research chemist. During the Second World War he again pursued chemical research of military importance, both in England and the United States.

Weizmann's Zionism was a natural outgrowth of his early upbringing. He adhered to the movement announced by Herzl at the very beginning and was already a delegate to the Second Zionist Congress in 1898. Weizmann was never in complete sympathy with Herzl, as his speech in Paris (the first excerpt, below) shows. Together with Martin Buber and a number of others who are less well-known, he helped found the "Democratic fraction" within Zionism at the Congress of 1901. This oppositionist group was for cultural work and colonization as the program of Zionism as against Herzl's emphasis on diplomacy. When the Uganda controversy flared up in 1903, Weizmann was at the very head of the group who opposed even considering this territory as the place for Zionist effort.

From the beginning of his days in England, Weizmann was busy, as a Zionist, making contacts and converts in the highest political circles. He was the leader in the complex negotiations in London which led to the issuance of the Balfour Declaration. After the occupation of southern Palestine by General Allenby, Weizmann headed the Zionist Commission which went out to advise the British military government in behalf of the Jewish national interest in the country. During that stay Weizmann laid the foundation stone for the Hebrew University, though the institution did not open its doors until seven years later. It is not as well remembered that he met with Emir Feisal, in the presence of the famous Lawrence of Arabia, and came to an understanding with him about Arab-Jewish peace and co-operation.

In the next year, Weizmann was one of the leaders of the delegation which appeared before the Versailles Peace Conference to present the case for Zionist aspirations in Palestine. Soon, in 1920, he came into conflict with Brandeis (see the biographical sketch of Brandeis, Part 9) and was constrained to carry the fight to the United States. At the London Zionist Conference of 1920, when that controversy first came to a head, Weizmann was elected president of the World Zionist Organization, and he was to retain this office, with an interruption from 1931 to 1935, until 1946. As the responsible leader of Zionism he had to deal with many internal rows, including the most important, the towering fight with Jabotinsky (the second selection below is a statement of his counter-arguments). In political crisis after crisis he had to defend the Zionist position before the world and often he had to induce his followers to swallow very bitter pills, e.g., the partition proposal of the Peel Commission, which he asked them, in an emotion-packed speech, to accept as at least a beginning for negotiation (parts of this speech are the third selection below).

At the first Zionist Congress after the Second World War, Weizmann was not re-elected to the presidency of the organization. Abba Hillel Silver and Ben-Gurion both stood against him in favor of a more active policy of resistance to the British. Nonetheless, his personal eminence was unchallenged. When the state was declared, Weizmann was immediately invited to be the president of its Provisional Government Council. From 1949 to his death in 1952 he was the first President of Israel.

ZIONISM NEEDS A LIVING CONTENT (1914)

At a Zionist Meeting in Paris, April, 1914

IN ITS INITIAL STAGE, Zionism was conceived by its pioneers as a movement wholly depending on mechanical factors: there is a country which happens to be called Palestine, a country without a people, and, on the other hand, there exists the Jewish people, and it has no country. What else is necessary, then, than to fit the gem into the ring, to unite this people with this country? The owners of the country must, therefore, be persuaded and convinced that this marriage is advantageous, not only for the people and for the country, but also for themselves. On this basis grew Zionism. First, we must sell many *shekalim*[1] to show the Turks how strong we are; in the meantime, the leaders will discuss the question of the marriage. Congress upon Congress has been waiting for the result of these discussions. How is it now? Have the Turks consented, have they yet said "Yes?" And when it appeared that Congress had waited in vain for the pleasant news, consternation arose. And when, after six years of work, the answer of the Turks turned out not to be "Yes," but "No"—well, we all remember the depression which this created among Zionists.

Some, however, said, a marriage is a marriage, and if the father does not consent to give us the bride, we'll find another one; meanwhile, while gathering strength, reinforcing our armies, and getting ready to return to Palestine—let us show to the whole world that we are as fit as any people to live as an independent political community. Maybe England will chance upon an empty piece of land in need of a white population, and perhaps the Jews will happen to be these whites—three cheers for the new match! Thus Uganda was brought about. And when this match did not come off either, the search started again. This is the history of the mechanical movement in Zionism, which did not realize that a long Galut, two thousand years' sufferings, cannot be healed in a day and not in a few years. We cannot take Palestine yet, even if it were given to us. Even if the great miracle had happened and we had obtained the Charter, we should have had to wait for the greater miracle—for the Jews to know how to make use of this Charter.

After the Uganda crisis, most Jews realized that a people's movement cannot be created and kept in being mechanically. A great man has compared Zionism to a barrel composed of boards and hoops which, remaining empty, dries up, contracts, and breaks. To abide by, and to fulfill its task, Zionism needs a living content. Far be it from me to underrate the achievements of the first seven years of Zionism, when all our institutions were created—the Congress, the Jewish Colonial Trust,[2] the Keren Kayemet,[3] etc. They are all instruments of the Movement; but if the whole activity of the Movement consists in collecting money, in attending to the instruments, then the object which the instruments have been made for will never be attained. During the first years of the Movement, this method was well and good; but if we do not learn by experience, if everything remains as it was, then the whole Movement will soon become paralyzed and petrified. Money alone cannot stir the Jewish heart. Did the ICA's[4] millions arouse enthusiasm in Israel? Did they inspire the masses? If we had money only, we could not stir the Jewish heart. But the fact that we have invested the money of the Keren Kayemet in Palestinian soil—that is what makes the Jewish heart beat faster, that is the great Bank in which he has put and will put his trust.

I think of bygone days. There came into our town a fire insurance agent. For us, of course, this was something new. Who has the money to insure his possessions and pay the premium? The agent sees the wealthiest man of the town. The wealthy man inquires what premium he would have to pay. The agent replies: a hundred rubles per year. Upon this the rich man gathers the poor of the town and tells them: I will give you a hundred rubles each year if you guard my house from fire. Our town was burned down several times, but the house of the rich man is standing on the hill, for he has living guards, a living insurance.

We have not trusted our money to the treasury of some great nation, but to the living soil and into the hands of people who live in Palestine, and they who have drenched the soil with their sweat and blood will defend our possessions, should anything happen in Palestine. For this is the bond which ties together man and soil into a living unity. There we live in houses we have built ourselves, we eat the fruit of the garden we have planted with our own hands; their sound instinct tells the people what life-value is inherent in such an investment, and they do not mind those who bewail the loss of gold that has found such living investment.

This is not only economic but also political activity. Politics is life and movement, not standstill and apathy. A policy of wait and see is like a messianic belief of a new kind. Once we put our trust in Israel's hope, it was living in every heart as a religious faith, it gave the Jew the strength to bear the sufferings of the Galut. But the new, the modern, belief has not grown from hope and faith, but from despair, and there is something weary and feeble in such a belief. Only through our activities and our work in Eretz Israel do we get closer and closer to our political task. And he who does not believe in this has not rid his mind yet from the ideas of assimilation.

Perhaps much of what we do now will have to perish. I do not wish to conceal the truth, and I admit it is possible that this structure will be imperiled. But is there any other, absolutely safe, way, or do we really think that we will be led into Palestine with beating of drums and sounding of trumpets, cheered from all sides? If this were at all possible, the people who live in the Rue Renner in Paris would be Zionists like you. It is the Zionists' good fortune that they are considered mad; if we were normal, we would not think of going to Palestine, but stay put, like all normal people. Who does not believe in taking a hard road and thinks that a dangerous road should not be taken had better stay at home. With fear and timidity the permanent home of the nation cannot be established. Never has a people freed itself by profitable investments, but by energy and sacrifice. And we Jews have not made many sacrifices yet, and that is why we own only 2 per cent of the Palestinian soil.

What value there is in real sacrifice, the example of a Jew from Kiev will show you; his name is Barski. One of his sons, a worker, was killed on Palestinian soil, at Degania; the bereaved father writes a

letter of comfort to the workers in Palestine and sends his second
son into this most dangerous life to take the place of the fallen one.
This is the continuation, writes the bereaved father. And it is this
Jew who is the greatest political Zionist after Herzl.

REMINISCENCES (1927)

At a Banquet at Czernowitz
December 12, 1927

MY STAY HERE has impressed me deeply. My life and work
have mostly led me to the dispersed Jewish communities in the West
which have not the same close cohesion, the same mental strength,
you have here, and, therefore, this visit may mean more to me than
to you.

Long years of life in the West cannot remain without consequences;
and the British climate is so cold. I have, in one of my speeches,
declared geography as the greatest enemy of Zionism. To overcome
geography is one of the greatest difficulties; but just because we want
to create out of innumerable different forms of life and cultures a
new national organism, we must be extremely careful to harmonize
them into a symphony. I know very little about music; I am a one-
sided man. For Herzl things were easier; he did not know the worka-
day reality. First he thought of a Jewish State; and when the Jewish
State did not come off, it was the Charter; and when the Charter
did not come off, it was Uganda. It was a quick way. Herzl came from
the West and worked with western conceptions and views. I, unfortunately, hail from Lithuania. I know the Jewish people only too
well, and they know me better still. And that is why I lack the wings
which were given to Herzl. He came from a strange world we did not
know, and we bent our knees before the eagle who had come from
that world. Had Herzl been to a *heder*, never would the Jews have
followed him. He charmed the Jews because he came to them from
the European culture. I was able to achieve my task through hard and
sorrowful work only. Always to have the Jews before me and always

to stand before them has taught me to draw in my wings, if ever I had any, and to remain on the ground.

Herzl became a Palestine Zionist the moment the Kishinev delegates said "No" at the Uganda Congress. The vote was by name. My late father voted "Yes." I voted after him with "No." Then the names of the two delegates from Kishinev were called, and both said: "Lo" ("No"). Poor Herzl grew pale, and then he became a true Zionist. He understood the depth of the tragedy and the depth of the idea, and then he resolved upon beginning practical work in the country, even if slowly, even if only symbolically, with a few hundred pounds. I can remember Herzl saying after the vote: "I do not understand; the rope is round their necks, and still they say: 'No.'" Yes, the rope was (and still is) round our necks, and yet we said: "No." For we knew very well: That same British Government would make us another offer—and they, in fact, have made that offer.

Another reminiscence: A week after the vote I traveled to London fourth class (because there was no fifth). I went to Downing Street (I was living in Whitechapel) and I saw there the Director of the Department for the African Colonies, Percy by name. In my broken French, I tried to find out his opinion about the Uganda plan. This Englishman, of one of the noblest families in the country, and a religious Christian, said: "If I were a Jew, I would not give one sou nor one man for this cause. For you cannot exchange Palestine for some other country." I wrote about this to Herzl—I still have a copy of the letter—and the realization of this truth was for Herzl the greatest tragedy, but also his highest experience. Thus he became an adherent of Palestine. It was no longer a question of a mechanical process—of the transfer of a people into an allegedly empty country— but of an organic process. Then I learned what I have told you already: that the way does not come to meet you. Nordau's conception of Uganda was that the way would come to meet us. We young ones rebelled against it, we young ones who had traveled into the remotest corners of the ghetto. On a journey through Russia I was at least seven times in prison, where I sold a thousand shares of the Colonial Trust to a thousand Jewish families, who paid them off with ten kopecks a month. We, who had to execute Herzl's orders as his faithful servants, had to rise against our master when it was Herzl or Palestine. What came afterward has remained a lesson to me up to the present.

I do not believe that our work can be accomplished by technical and mechanical means borrowed from European technology and culture. It cannot be done; and I say that in deep earnest to my friends of the Opposition after all the painful experiences of the last years. Other peoples enforce successes for themselves by pressure and demonstrations, by showing off their power; but in our Movement these things count very little. To put it plainly: We cannot force the British Government; we can only convince it. And we can only convince it through an example of apostolic devotion to our cause. Easy gains you will not keep, but what you achieve with difficulties will be of permanent value. Those are optimists who believe that we shall gain anything by parades and demonstrations in which hundreds of thousands of New York Jews make a noise and demonstrate against Britain. I am deeply convinced that this is the wrong way. It is un-Jewish in its conception, for it works with means which cannot be applied to our Movement, calculated to grow slowly and organically. Before Herzl came to us poor, he knocked at the doors of the rich. Only when he found their doors closed he came to us and he found us ready. Read him about his impressions after the First Congress. He did not think that we would be leading in Zionism; he thought we would be an object for the Western Zionist Movement. From the combination of the antagonistic aspects of the Movement arose what we call today "synthetic Zionism."

I remember having heard Nordau saying four years ago—I refer to this without the intention to polemize—500,000 Jews shall go to Palestine, 200,000 will fail, but 300,000 will remain in the country. I have always opposed such an attitude; it may be an heroic gesture from Germanic or Greek mythology, but it is not Jewish. First of all, it is impossible, and, second, the Jewish people would never agree to pay this price. I have also learned something about sun rays which sometimes throw a sudden light on our way. Believe me, when I had the Balfour Declaration in my hand, I felt as if a sun ray had struck me; and I thought I heard the steps of the Messiah. But I remembered that the true Redeemer is said to come silently like a thief in the night. I had to hold myself back and to put restraint upon me and, moreover, I had to fulfill the bitter task of bringing back to reality the Jewish masses struck by a sun ray. It is not a pleasant part, and I can sing a bitter song about it. If you would come to the Colonial Office to negotiate, you would speak more meekly and perhaps be more modest than he who had to negotiate up till now.

I said at the last Congress that I would not lead the Organization for more than another two years; the place now becomes vacant. May he who will come after me be able, after ten years, to look back on a progress equal to that which has been made in these last ten years. I wish it from the depth of my heart. May he do more and better things, but at least as much as that.

We Jews got the Balfour Declaration quite unexpectedly; or, in other words, we are the greatest war profiteers. We never dreamed of the Balfour Declaration; to be quite frank, it came to us overnight. But— "What you have inherited from your father you must earn it anew really to possess it!" (Goethe). The Balfour Declaration of 1917 was built on air, and a foundation had to be laid for it through years of exacting work; every day and every hour of these last ten years, when opening the newspapers, I thought: Whence will the next blow come? I trembled lest the British Government would call me and ask: "Tell us, what is this Zionist Organization? Where are they, your Zionists?" For these people think in terms different from ours. The Jews, they knew, were against us; we stood alone on a little island, a tiny group of Jews with a foreign past.

This period has passed now. Now we have an address, a name, and, above all, great moral credit. Now we can build and now we can demand, now is the time. The time is approaching for greater activity on the part of the British Government, because it has been convinced that we mean business. Although many Jewish notables are not with us, the British Government knows that we have the necessary strength for the work of reconstruction. A great deal of educational work was necessary for that. One day, last June, there were at least fifty million pounds gathered at a breakfast in London. I was among them, but I contributed less than the others toward the fifty million. An eminent official of the Colonial Office was present, and we talked in great detail about the difficulties in Palestine, about the crisis, the deficit, and our worries. After the breakfast, the official, a simple, unsophisticated man, came up to me and said: "Every one of these men could remove with a stroke of the pen the whole crisis, the whole unemployment, without suffering in his pocket." I was hurt by this remark, and it did not contribute to the strengthening of my political position. Such things happen every day. Whether you come to Paris or to London, you continually meet with such difficulties in your daily work. If you, ladies and gentlemen, believe that we can make light of these things in an optimistic elation, and if you say there are Arabs, but we must get rid of them, there is Britain, but we must force it, then you may be playing the part of a contrabass in an orchestra, but it will never make a song. Of this I am firmly convinced. I do not accuse the Opposition of insincerity, nor do I think that they wish to do harm. But I am convinced they do not know this world and—forgive the simile—they remind me of the classical example of a *maggid*[5] who used to tell the story of a poor *bocher*[6] who went into the wide world, came to a king, and said: "Give me your daughter for my wife"; and the king replied: "Take her!" But the princess for whom we fight is like a beautiful woman, for whom one must strive very hard, and the *maggid* and the *moshel*[7] will remain a *maggid* and a *moshel*.

I have perhaps said more than I usually do, but it was only to give you a glimpse of all these struggles and worries and of the world in which we have to work, and to tell you that it is the greatest miracle that we have gone so far. I believe in dispensation by a Power which watches over us—may this hand rest lightly upon us. For there is something supernatural about it. A thousand times already we might have broken our neck. You see, the Arabs emerged from this war with three States in their hands, with a kingdom that stretches almost from the Euphrates to the Indian Ocean, and they demanded more and more—and today their king is an exile in Cyprus. And then it occurred to me, a Lithuanian *heder* boy, that, if one grasps too much, one seizes nothing—and according to this maxim I have acted.

You have reminded me of a certain Warsaw speech which would better not have been made. I also know the Czernowitz speech which was less extremist; but don't forget that our enemies will quote only the Warsaw speech. I can understand opposition well; I belonged to the Opposition myself. Yet remember this: We live in the middle of a great world, where every word we say might get us into a snare; every Arab paper is quoting the Warsaw speech and not the Czernowitz one. And now something else: When I came to Paris in 1918, we faced an iron wall. The military administration of Palestine and Downing Street were at least five hundred years apart. Against this iron wall we had to run our heads. We had either to convince Allenby[8] or to quarrel with him, and today Allenby is a sincere friend of our Movement. Things have moved slowly, the cost has been great; it is difficult to be a *Rebbe* (teacher) from the first, but the work has to be done. And if there is today a pleiad of people, from Balfour to some unknown British Member of Parliament, who are devoted to our cause, this is the result of our slow, systematic, lengthy, always difficult work, which has been putting stone upon stone.

The story of our work among the Jews I need not tell you: You know it just as well as I do. We have convinced everybody, except the Jews. But we shall finally convince them, too, through our educational work. This is why I speak to you with an aching heart about the slowness of our work. Don't you think that I should like it just as much as anybody else to see a great Jewish Palestine in my day? I have staked something on that Palestine, but I cannot overlook the realities of life. Mine is no easygoing optimism, but a deep-rooted belief in a fate which will fulfill itself in spite of all difficulties. Therefore, I am not afraid of Palestine's smallness, and I am not afraid of the fact that Palestine has mountains and no valleys, and has no Nile, but the Jordan. For it is *our* Palestine that we must strive for, work and suffer for. That is how things are, thus and no other. When I was a boy of twelve I wrote to my *Rebbe* (the *Rebbe* has kept the letter) that there will be a day when Britain will give us Palestine, the Britain of Disraeli and Montefiore. When the Balfour Declaration was given to us, I said to Lord Balfour: "I do not know what a wonderful, great man you are that it was granted to you to give us this present and to associate such a pre-eminent work with your life."

I have no more to tell you, and so I thank you again and wish you that your work may be easy to you. May God's hand rest lightly upon you, and may your way not be so hard and grievous as mine sometimes has been.

ON THE REPORT OF THE PALESTINE COMMISSION

Twentieth Zionist Congress
Zurich, August 4, 1937

IT IS NOT EASY to present a complete and systematic report upon the political situation. Months may have to pass before it is possible to take an objective view of the kaleidoscopic changes in events, or to place them in proper perspective. The task is especially hard for those of us who are in the thick of the fight. I must refer you to the printed report which the Executive will lay before you, and to the relevant documents which many delegates will have opportunity to study in commission, and I shall confine myself to giving a general review of the situation, which I shall try to make as impartial as possible. But no man can entirely prevent his human feelings from coloring such a report. Otherwise a gramophone record would do as well.

We are told that the Mandate is a complicated document. But we are not its authors. British statesmen, not the Jewish Agency, are its authors. The practice of many years has proved it complicated; what Jewish affairs are not complicated? Nevertheless, on the basis of this document remarkable things have been achieved, as is confirmed by the Report of the Royal Commission.

The blame lies not on the Mandate, now made a scapegoat; it lies with those who should have carried out a Mandate calmly, with strength and dignity, and who showed instead halfheartedness, weakness, and doubt.

The Royal Commission itself suggests that it might have been easier at the outset to proclaim the Jewish State than to carry on in the twilight of these twenty years. The thing might then have been carried through with a swing. There was no lack of understanding for it in the world at that time, not even among the Arabs. At that time the Emir Feisal was held to be able to speak for the Arabs, but now it is the Mufti.

With Feisal, who fully understood our aims, we were able to reach an agreement. In 1919 and 1920 there were other Arabs as well as Feisal with whom we could negotiate. But when they saw infirmity of purpose, obstacles perpetually placed in our path, a principle of balance adopted by which the Administration merely tolerated our work, and reduced its own contribution to maintaining order, with less and less determination, till in 1936 it very nearly relinquished even that attempt, the Arab extremists saw their chance: Press on, and the English will give in.

And now concession has reached such a pitch that after the economic complaints had been rejected by the Royal Commission, the political aspect is suddenly brought to the fore: Immigration must no longer be regulated by the economic absorptive capacity of Palestine, but according to some psychological principle. Whoever heard that the immigration officer must be a psychologist? And whose psychology is to be the criterion? Evidently the Mufti's. There can be no doubt about his psychology. Not one Jew is to enter the gates of Palestine. For him there is only one Jewish gate, and it is marked "Exit," not "Entrance." Where is the psychological limit which could satisfy the enemies of the National Home?

This proposal and the other "palliatives" which you will find in the Report spell the destruction of the National Home. We shall resist these proposals before the eyes of the world, openly and honestly, with every means at our disposal. This is a breach of the promise made to us in a solemn hour, at an hour of crisis for the British Empire, and the blow is the more cruel because it falls upon us in the hour of our own supreme crisis.

I say this, I, who for twenty years have made it my lifework to explain the Jewish people to the British, and the British people to the Jews. And I say it to you, who have so often girded at me, and attacked me, just because I had taken that task upon myself. But the limit has been reached. We cannot even discuss such proposals; there is no psychological criterion for immigration. Gates are opened or closed on definite principles.

I say to the Mandatory Power: You shall not outrage the Jewish nation. You shall not play fast and loose with the Jewish people. Say to us frankly that the National Home is closed, and we shall know where we stand. But this trifling with a nation bleeding from a thousand wounds must not be done by the British whose Empire is built on moral principles—that mighty Empire must not commit this sin against the People of the Book. Tell us the truth. This at least we have deserved.

[Here Weizmann broke down and wept, and then continued after a pause.]

Among the many things which we fail to understand is the latest decree of H. M. Government to restrict our immigration to 8,000 for the next eight months. Why this hurried decision, in advance of the meeting of the Mandates Commission, and while nothing is yet settled? We look upon the decree as an infringement of the Mandate, and public opinion will likewise condemn it.

I have now finished with criticisms. If I have expressed them more sharply than is my wont, it is because through me speaks the pain of one who has held his peace for twenty years. But even in this solemn moment of responsibility I would bid this Congress and all Jews remember, in the midst of their disappointment and despite the bitter injustice they have suffered, that the Palestine Administration and England are not identical. As to that there must be no mistake.

There is another England, and let us thank God for it. The voice of this England was heard in the two Houses of Parliament. That a Jew, Lord Melchett, should have said what he has said we expected from the son of Alfred Mond, and we expect yet more from him in the future. That the newly created Lord Samuel should have said what he has said did not take us by surprise. But there were other speakers, leaders of the British nation, drawn from all parties and all classes, lords and commoners; among them the head of the Anglican Church raised his powerful voice, *"Lema'an Zion lo ehesheh"* ("For the sake of Zion I cannot be silent").

Further, remember that England, although beset by anxious cares, has yet been the only Power which has made a serious attempt to contribute to the solution of the Jewish problem. The present difficulties must not for a moment blind us to this fact.

Permit me, at this historic juncture, to say a word to the Arab people. We know that the Mufti and Kawkaji are not the Arab nation. In the present world those who have bombs and revolvers at command wield political power. But in the history of a nation their life is like one day, even if it extends over years.

There is an Arab nation with a glorious past. To that nation we have stretched out our hand, and do so even now—but on one condition. Just as we wish them to overcome their crisis and to revert to the great tradition of a mighty and civilized Arab people, so must they know that we have the right to build our home in Eretz Israel, harming no one, helping all. When they acknowledge this we shall reach common ground, and I hope for the time when we shall once more recognize each other.

The Arabs will recall that in the greatest period of their history, whether in Baghdad or in Cordova, we have co-operated in preserving the treasures of European culture. Now, as ever, we are in all seriousness and sincerity prepared to negotiate; but this must be done by us, who are entrusted with the responsibility, not by self-appointed mediators in time of crisis.

I have now reached the most important part of my speech. The Report of the Royal Commission contains a revolutionary proposal which has deeply moved all Jewry: the proposal to found a Jewish State in a reduced area within the bounds of Eretz Israel. There are two tests whereby such a proposal must be judged. But I will say at once that I do not discuss the scheme contained in the Report. This particular scheme is inacceptable. I speak of the idea, the principle, the perspectives which the proposal opens out; "if long views are taken," to use the words of the Colonial Secretary in the letter I read out last night.

As I am not discussing the scheme of the Royal Commission, I need not enter into details. We shall discuss them in commission. Furthermore, you must remember that the British Government itself has not declared its acceptance of this scheme but only of the principle.

I consider that two criteria have to be applied in appraising such a principle. The first—does it offer a basis for a genuine growth of Jewish life? I mean both in quality and in volume; does it offer a basis for the development of our young Palestinian culture, of which the Report speaks with true respect? Does this principle afford a basis for building up such a Jewish life as we picture, for rearing true men and women, for creating a Jewish agriculture, industry, literature, etc. —in short, all that the ideal of Zionism comprises?

This is one test. For our great teacher, Ahad Ha-Am, who is with us no longer, it might have been the only one. But times have changed, and Jewish history, which, alas! for the most part, is not ours to mold, faces us with a tragic problem. We must, therefore, apply yet another test. Does the proposal contribute to the solution of the Jewish problem, a problem pregnant with danger to ourselves and to the world?

Does the proposal stand the two tests? It is the duty of the Congress to give a clear answer. The answer is awaited in Warsaw, in Bucharest, and in Berlin. And those who have the luck to be under the protection of a liberal regime must bethink themselves before they offer a reply.

The point here is not to calculate in percentages what part of Eretz Israel is being offered to us. We can all count. But our task is to forecast the answer which life will give to the two tests. Is it possible to do this, or is it not? I believe it is. I believe an answer can be given. Nay, more, I believe it must be given. The choice lies between a Jewish minority in the whole of Palestine or a compact Jewish State in a part.

I now address myself to those with whom I have not always been politically at one. I speak not as a Mizrahi, but as a deeply religious man, although not a strict observer of the religious ritual. I make a sharp distinction between the present realities and the messianic hope, which is part of our very selves, a hope embedded in our traditions and sanctified by the martyrdom of thousands of years, a hope which the nation cannot forget without ceasing to be a nation. A time will come when there shall be neither enemies nor frontiers, when war shall be no more, and men will be secure in the dignity of man. Then Eretz Israel will be ours.

I told the Commission: God has promised Eretz Israel to the Jews. This is our charter. But we are men of our own time, with limited horizons, heavily laden with responsibility toward the generations to come. I told the Royal Commission that the hopes of 6,000,000 Jews are centred on emigration. Then I was asked: "But can you bring

6,000,000 to Palestine?" I replied: "No. I am acquainted with the laws of physics and chemistry, and I know the force of material factors. In our generation I divide the figure by three, and you can see in that the depth of the Jewish tragedy—2,000,000 of youth, with their lives before them, who have lost the most elementary of rights, the right to work."

The old ones will pass, they will bear their fate or they will not. They are dust, economic and moral dust in a cruel world. And again I thought of our tradition. What is tradition? It is telescoped memory. We remember. Thousands of years ago we heard the words of Isaiah and Jeremiah, and my words are but a weak echo of what was said by our Judges, our Singers, and our Prophets. Two millions, and perhaps less; *She'erith Hapletah*—"only a remnant shall survive." We have to accept it. The rest we must leave to the future, to our youth. If they feel and suffer as we do, they will find the way, *Beaharith Hayamim*—"in the fullness of time."

I say to my orthodox friends: Bethink you on what ground you stand. Never in two thousand years has the responsibility been so great as now. We have neither the wisdom nor the strength to bear the responsibility. But Fate has laid it upon us, and Fate does not disclose her secrets. We can only do the possible. If the proposal opens a way, then I, who for some forty years have done all that in me lies, who have given my all to the Movement, then I shall say "Yes," and I trust that you will do likewise.

We shall request you, at one stage of our deliberations, to accept a resolution, authorizing the Executive to negotiate a scheme which will meet the two tests. Then the Executive will bring it back to you, and you will decide. I pray that sacred strength may be given to us all to find a way, and that, in advancing, we may preserve intact our national unity, for it is all we have.

RABBI ABBA HILLEL SILVER born 1893

BOTH ABBA HILLEL SILVER and David Ben-Gurion, the two men with whom this reader concludes, are still at the height of their powers. In the last rounds of the struggle for the state of Israel, after Weizmann was voted out of office in 1946 as president of the World Zionist Organization, they were, in reality, the active leaders of the movement. Not always in agreement, they came to a parting of the ways soon after Israel arose, and since then Silver has been retired from any top role in Zionism while Ben-Gurion has, of course, been the prime minister of the new state during almost all of the first decade of its existence. Obviously their careers are too much part of the present for any thumbnail historical assessment to be possible (though there are some analytic comments on the ideas—not, be it noted, the political careers—of both of them in the introduction to this volume). We must here limit ourselves to a brief account of some of the objective facts of their lives.

Silver was born in Lithuania in 1893 and brought to New York by his parents nine years later. He was a Zionist from boyhood and remained firm in these convictions even in anti-Zionist atmosphere which dominated his rabbinical seminary, the Hebrew Union College in Cincinnati, when he was a student there. Silver was ordained in 1915 and, after a brief stay in Wheeling, West Virginia, he came two years later to the post he still holds, that of rabbi of The Temple in Cleveland. Silver's brilliance, scholarship, and oratorical powers were recognized early, and he has held many of the major offices in the organized American Jewish community. The essential aspect of Silver's public career, however, has been his Zionist work. During the Weizmann-Brandeis battle of 1920–1921 he was on the side of Brandeis, but he soon returned to the fold of the Zionist Organization of America. In 1937, when Weizmann pleaded for consideration of the Peel Commission's plan to partition Palestine, Silver was vehemently opposed. He was increasingly identified with a policy of Zionist political activism, both in international affairs and on the American scene.

At the height of the Second World War, in 1943, Silver was asked by Weizmann to assume the political leadership of Zionism in America. His first major act was to lead in carrying the American Jewish Conference of that year (it was the first representative body of all American Jews since the days of the First World War) toward endorsing a Jewish Commonwealth in Palestine, and not something less, as a proper "war aim" of Jewry. In his political role Silver fought many battles for a declaration by the Congress of the United States in support of a future Jewish state, and he used every political and public relations method he could devise to bend the policies of both the major parties to this purpose. Other leaders in American Zionism regarded this activism as ill-advised and Silver, having failed to win his battle in Congress because the Roosevelt administration was opposed to such a declaration, resigned in 1944. After a year of heated internal Zionist controversy, he returned to leadership and continued in this role for the several years which were marked by the Anglo-American Committee of Inquiry of 1946, the fight against Ernest Bevin in those years, and the debates in the United Nations. He appeared both before the General Assembly and the Security Council, as spokesman of the Jewish Agency for Palestine, in the discussions which ended with the resolution of November 29, 1947, the legal basis for the state of Israel.

Silver is represented here by the speech he gave in 1943 to the American Jewish Conference, which amounts to a statement of his Zionist position, and by part of an address in the next year in which he partially defined the views he then held about the future relationship between the Jewish state and American Jewry.

TOWARD AMERICAN JEWISH UNITY (1943)

MY DEAR FRIENDS, the Jewish people is in danger of coming out of this war the most ravaged of peoples and the least healed and restored. The stark tragedy of our ravage has been abundantly told here and elsewhere—tragic, ghastly, unredeemed. To rehearse it again is only to flagellate oneself and to gash our souls again and again. But what of the healing? What is beyond the rim of blood and tears? Frankly, to some of us, nothing. We are being comforted at the moment with the hope that the Atlantic Charter and the Four Freedoms and victory will begin the healing of our people.

I am afraid that we are again sacrificing cool, albeit bitter reasoning and logic to beguiling romancing in the void. We are again turning away from history to dreams and to apocalypses which some of us amazingly enough choose to call realism and statesmanship.

The last World War made the world safe for democracy and granted the Jews of central and eastern Europe not only the rights of citizenship, but even minority rights. But you remember, or have you forgotten? It brought also in its wake the most thoroughgoing, brutal, and annihilationist anti-Semitism that our people have ever experienced.

Have you already forgotten the story of the First World War? Dare you forget it? And now again, in the Second World War, many Jews are hoping to achieve through another Allied victory what an Allied victory failed to give them after the last war, what a whole century of enlightenment, liberalism, and progress failed to give them—peace and security. They are again confusing formal political equality with immunity from economic and social pressures.

The immemorial problem of our national homelessness, which is the principal source of our millennial tragedy, remains as stark and as menacing today as it ever was. Yet some Jews are again trying to circumvent it with wishful thinking and to hide the real problem, the nettling, perplexing, insistent problem, crying for expression and solution, under the thick blanket of appeals to Jewish unity and Jewish affability.

There is a tragic fact which seems to escape so many students of anti-Semitism. The story of Jewish emancipation in Europe from the day after the French Revolution to the day before the Nazi revolution is the story of political positions captured in the face of stubborn and sullen opposition, which left our emancipated minority in each country encamped within an unbeaten and unreconciled opposition, so that at the slightest provocation, as soon as things got out of order, the opposition returned to the attack and inflicted grievous wounds.

And in our day, stirred by the political and economic struggles which have torn nations apart, this never-failing, never-reconciled opposition swept over the Jewish political and economic positions in

Europe and completely demolished them. There is a stout black cord which connects the era of Fichte[1] in Germany with its feral cry of "*hep, hep,*" and the era of Hitler with its cry of "*Jude verrecke.*" The Damascus affair of 1840 links up with the widespread reaction after the Revolution of 1848—the Mortara affair of Italy;[2] the Christian Socialist Movement in the era of Bismarck; the Tisza-Eszlar affair in Hungary;[3] the revival of blood accusations in Bohemia; the pogroms in the eighties in Russia; *La France Juive*[4] and the Dreyfus affair in France; the pogroms of 1903; the Ukrainian blood baths after the last war, and the human slaughter houses of Poland in this war.

This, my friends, is our persistent problem. This is our immediate emergency—immediate almost to every generation of our people in almost every country. What we are confronted with today is the frightful aggravation of a situation which has continuously darkened the pages of our history since the beginning of our dispersion.

Now, what is the solution for this persistent emergency in Jewish life? There is but one solution for that national homelessness which is the source, I repeat, of our millennial tragedy. There is but one solution for national homelessness. That is a national home! Not new immigration opportunities in other countries for fleeing refugees; not new colonization schemes in other parts of the world, many of which were so hopefully attempted in the last few decades, down to our very own day, and with such little success. The only solution is to normalize the political status of the Jewish people in the world by giving it a national basis in its national and historic home.

The world finally came to acknowledge the validity of this solution. In 1917, Great Britain issued the Balfour Declaration. This Declaration was not intended to be an immigrant aid scheme, an effort to open up a new avenue for Jewish immigration. Shortly before its issuance, and for many years prior thereto, Jews in very large numbers were finding opportunities for immigration in many parts of the world, especially in the Western Hemisphere. The Balfour Declaration was a political national act designed to rebuild the national life of the Jewish people in its homeland.

Now, is this my interpretation or that of Zionists only? Not at all. It was the universally accepted interpretation of the statesmen of the world and of those who were responsible in the first place for the issuance of this Declaration: Lloyd George, President Wilson, Jan Smuts, Winston Churchill. They were thinking in terms of a Jewish Commonwealth or, as many of them called it, the Jewish State, which was to be the natural outgrowth and evolution of the Jewish National Home.

And how did our American Jews in those days interpret that document? When the first American Jewish Congress met in Philadelphia in 1918, a Congress in which Zionists and non-Zionists participated, as in this Conference, it elected a delegation to represent American Jewry at the Peace Conference, and the delegation was given instructions formulated as follows:

They were to co-operate with the representatives of other Jewish organizations, specifically with the World Zionist Organization, to the end that the Peace Conference might recognize the aspirations and historic claims of the Jewish people in regard to Palestine and might declare, that in accordance with the British Government's Declaration, there shall be established such political, administrative and economic conditions in Palestine as would assure, under the trusteeship of Great Britain, acting on behalf of such a League of Nations as might be formed, the development of Palestine into a Jewish Commonwealth.

Why has there arisen among us today this mortal fear of the term "Jewish Commonwealth" which both British and American statesmen took in their stride, as it were, and which our own fellow Jews of both camps endorsed a quarter of a century ago? Why are anti-Zionists, or non-Zionists, or neutrals, determined to excise that phrase—and I suspect, in some instances, at least, that hope?

Why are they asking us, on the plea of unity, to surrender a basic political concept which was so much a part of the whole pattern of the Balfour Declaration? I suspect it is because they, or some of them, or most them, have never really reconciled themselves to the fact both of the Declaration and of the Mandate. They would like to forget about them or have the world forget about them or wish them out of existence. Of course, they have no objection to Jews going to Palestine any more than they would have any objections to Jews going to New Zealand, to Australia, or any other part of the world.

It is amazing to me, I frankly confess, that Jews are moved to applaud a fellow Jew when he consents that Jews should have the right to go to Palestine. Once having made this monumental concession that Jews have a right to go to Palestine and that that right should not be restricted, they feel justified in asking the Zionists to make a little concession of their own—just a little concession—namely, to surrender that for which they and their fathers hoped and prayed through the centuries and which is already in the process of fulfillment—a Jewish Commonwealth of Palestine.

We are told that our insistence on the Jewish Commonwealth is insistence on an ideology, and why, we are asked, should one create disunity in the ranks of American Israel over an ideology?

In all sincerity, friends, I ask you to think along with me—is it an ideology? Is the natural, normal instinct of a homeless people to find a home for itself after centuries of homelessness and to lead a normal, natural existence, an ideology? Is it an ideology for an Englishman to want an England, or for a Frenchman to want a France, a Free France, and, when exiled from it, to wish ardently to return to it?

Why is it an "ideology" for the people of Israel to want the Land of Israel from which it was driven centuries ago and so lost its peace and its rest and its joy of life?

Was it an ideology which kept alive the hope of national restoration among our people for nineteen centuries? Was it not rather the hard, cruel facts of our existence, exiles, massacres, pogroms, indignities, all the way along the black stout cord of disaster, never broken from 70 to 1943?

We are not insisting on ideologies; we are insisting on the faithful fulfillment of obligations internationally assumed toward our people and on the honoring of covenants made with us. We ask for nothing new. It is those who tell us to surrender the demands already acknowledged in international sanctions that are motivated by ideologies, not we. It is they who are forcing the reopening of a question which in all conscience should have been closed in 1917.

So, my good friends, we are not concerned here with ideologies. The reconstitution of the Jewish people as a nation in its homeland is not a playful political conceit of ours, a sort of intellectual pastime calculated to satisfy some national vanity of ours. It is the cry of despair of a people driven to the wall, fighting for its very life. It is the pressing urgency of instant and current suffering and of the besetting dangers and disabilities today and, I am afraid, also tomorrow.

From the infested, typhus-ridden ghetto of Warsaw, from the death-block of Nazi-occupied lands where myriads of our people are awaiting execution by the slow or the quick method, from a hundred concentration camps which befoul the map of Europe, from the pitiful ranks of our wandering hosts over the entire face of the earth, comes the cry: "Enough; there must be a final end to all this, a sure and certain end!"

How long is the crucifixion to last? Time and again we have been stretched upon the rack for other peoples' sins. Time and again we have been made the whipping boy for blundering governments, the scapegoat for defeat in war, for misery and depression, for conflict among classes.

How long is it to last? Are we forever to live a homeless people on the world's crumbs of sympathy, forever in need of defenders, forever doomed to thoughts of refugees and relief? Should not, I ask you fellow Jews, ought not, the incalculable and unspeakable suffering of our people and the oceans of blood which we have shed in this war and in all the wars of the centuries; should not the myriad martyrs of our people, as well as the magnificent heroism and the vast sacrifices of our brave soldier sons who are today fighting on all the battle fronts of the world—should not all this be compensated for finally and at long last with the re-establishment of a free Jewish Commonwealth?

Is not this historic justice, and is this world today not reaching out so desperately and so pathetically for a new world order of justice? Should we not be included in that world order of justice? Are we not deserving of it? I am for unity in Israel, but unity for what? It is strange; frequently, I am bewildered. If I agree with certain people, that's unity. If I ask them to agree with me, that is disunity.

I am for unity in Israel, for the realization of the total program of Jewish life, relief, rescue, reconstruction, and the national restoration in Palestine. I am not for unity on a fragment of the program, for a fragment of the program is a betrayal of the rest of the program and a tragic futility besides. We cannot truly rescue the Jews of Europe unless we have free immigration into Palestine. We cannot have free immigration into Palestine unless our political rights are recognized there. Our political rights cannot be recognized there unless our historic connection with the country is acknowledged and our right to rebuild our national home is reaffirmed. These are inseparable links in the chain. The whole chain breaks if one of the links is missing. Do not beguile yourselves. Do not let anyone beguile you with the thought that the Arabs in Palestine or the British Colonial Office, for that matter—and the two at the moment seem to be synonymous—will consent to large-scale immigration into Palestine as soon as we give up our idea of a Jewish Commonwealth. They are not that naïve—they are opposed both to a Jewish Commonwealth and to Jewish immigration.

If we surrender our national and historic claim to Palestine and rely solely on the refugee philanthropic appeal, we shall lose our case as well as do violence to the historic hopes of our people. On the basis of sheer philanthropy, of satisfying pressing immigration needs, Palestine has already done its full share for Jewish refugees. It has taken in more than one-half of the total Jewish refugees of the world, and the Palestine Arabs and their sympathizers in England and here have been quick to point out that Palestine has already done all that can be expected from a small country and far more than most of the larger countries have done. It is because Palestine is the Jewish Homeland that we have the right to insist upon unrestricted immigration. It is because of the historic connection of the Jewish people with that land that the Mandatory Government in the first place undertook to reconstitute it as a National Home and pledged itself to facilitate Jewish immigration and the close settlement of the Jews upon the land. In other words, it is on the national idea that the upbuilding of Palestine as a place of large-scale Jewish immigration has always rested and can alone continue to rest. Our right to immigration in the last analysis is predicated upon the right to build the Jewish Commonwealth in Palestine. They are interlinked and inseparable.

To ask, therefore, the Jewish people to abdicate the political positions which after centuries it finally acquired in Palestine, or, by remaining silent about them, to suggest to the world that we have abandoned them, on the vain assumption that this would lead to the opening of the doors of Palestine to large-scale Jewish immigration, is utterly fantastic. I am for unity, but here I must point out in all humility that unity of action in democratic organization depends not upon unanimity but upon the willingness of the minority to submit to the decisions of the majority.

It is folly to expect universal agreement among five million Jews of America, or among their chosen representatives here, on all basic problems affecting Jewish life. It is folly to expect it. It is naïve to anticipate it. However, this is no reason for avoiding these basic problems. This is no reason for preventing the majority from endorsing the program which the minority may not be inclined to endorse. If the overwhelming majority of American Jews believe in the upbuilding of a Jewish Commonwealth, they should have the right, through the medium of this solemn conclave, to say so and to make their demand upon the world. A strange thing has occurred here. We are asked not to relinquish our convictions but at the same time not to express them.

The minority, if it is wise, as I believe it is, and responsible, as I know it is, and responsive to the democratic process, will abide by the decision and accept the role of a loyal opposition. We are not a government and we have no authority to impose decisions, but there is a tremendous moral authority in a solemn conclave such as this of the chosen representatives of our people, and when after due deliberation it speaks in overwhelming endorsement of a certain program, its decision ought not to be lightly disregarded.

I close with this word, my friends. The heroic Yishuv in Palestine has prayerfully appealed to us to uphold its hands. You have read it in the public press. Our Yishuv today is fighting a desperate fight against enemies stretched all the way from Jerusalem through Cairo, through newspaper offices in the city of New York. It is fighting a desperate fight against enemies who are organizing another conspiracy to strangle its further development and to extinguish the great hope of national freedom which has sustained the faith and courage of those splendid men and women who are building the Jewish Commonwealth. They have appealed to us, their brothers and sisters in America, to approve of their struggle, to defend their rights and to appeal to the political leaders and statesmen of this great, free, and blessed land to help them now in this, the approaching hour of decision, with the same sympathy and the same understanding as the Presidents of the United States from Wilson down, and the Congress of the United States, helped them in the earlier years. I ask you, good friends, shall we let them down?

Shall we pass a Palestine resolution here which will mention nothing about the historic Balfour Declaration and its clear intent and underlying purpose—the upbuilding of the Jewish Commonwealth? Will it be perhaps our purpose to send a delegation to the Peace Conference with nothing more than an immigration aid plea to let Jews go to Palestine, as if Palestine were for us another Santo Domingo?

Are we to ask merely for the right of asylum in our historic home, the right which any people may claim in any part of the world, though, unfortunately, such claims are only infrequently recognized? Is this Jewish statesmanship? Is this Jewish vision, courage, faith? Or are we to declare in this great assembly, when the proper time comes, that we stand by those who have given their tears and their blood and their sweat to build for them and for us and the future generations, at long last, after the weary centuries, a home, a National Home, a Jewish Commonwealth, where the spirit of our entire people can finally be at rest as well as the people itself?

Are we going to take counsel here of fear of what this one or that one might say, of how our actions are likely to be misinterpreted; or are we to take counsel of our inner moral convictions, of our faith, of our history, of our achievements, and go forward in faith to build and to heal?

AMERICAN JEWRY IN WAR AND AFTER (1944)

AMERICAN JEWS are at last finding themselves under the necessity of doing that which Jews in the Old World have always had to do—consciously orienting themselves as Jews in a non-Jewish environment and realistically facing all the implications of their status as a minority group. The Nazis succeeded in their attempt to make the whole Western World Jew-conscious, but they also succeeded, and without any intention on their part, in making all Jews more Jew-conscious. While some Jews are rather unnerved by this new experience and are unable to make an intelligent adjustment to it, the majority of our people are being helped by this keener awareness of their true position, to a fuller, franker, and more dignified life as American Jews.

These American Jews are facing the future without any illusions but certainly not without hope. The New World, for a time, made possible a pleasant sense of almost complete identification. That is no longer the case and in all probability will never be again. The Old World brand of anti-Semitism is here to stay—not forever, of course, but for a period long enough for all practical considerations. This is realism, not defeatism. This is the landscape. After the political anti-Semitism of the Nazi variety—the kind which is sanctioned and organized by governments and employed as a weapon of economic reaction and imperial aggression—will have been defeated as a result of the defeat of the Nazis in this war, the high fever-temperature of anti-Semitism will undoubtedly drop here and elsewhere, provided, of course, no disastrous economic debacle and vast unemployment follow the Armistice. But much of what we now call the "good" and temperate anti-Semitism, in contrast to the killing and annihilationist kind, that which in happier times we used to call prejudice, will remain as a constant factor in our experience. The Civil War ended slavery in the United States. It did not solve the race problem. A country may be democratic and yet its people may be bitterly anti-Semitic. Witness Poland before the war and Weimar Germany. Political equality is not yet brotherhood. It is doubtful whether the popular sentiment of most of the countries of Europe ever heartily approved of Jewish emancipation. It seems to have come rather as a by-product of new political theories and principles of human rights which had to be consistently applied and therefore had to include also the Jews.

America is not likely to go fascist, but fascistically-minded Americans, who will always be anti-Semites, will persist in large numbers until such time as our age finds its new economic and political equilibrium after the prolonged upheavals of the technological revolution. This spiritually formless period of reorientation which will continue to be fraught with much danger and unhappiness for mankind will last far beyond our present generation.

What I am trying to say is that our lives as American Jews have now fallen into the well-known pattern of Israel's millennial experience in Diaspora. For a time we were able to regard ourselves as different. But America itself has become far less different, far less removed, and far less isolated from the Old World. It is no longer a distant land on the rim of a vast ocean. It is now the center of the world. Politically, economically, and culturally it is now enmeshed in a common destiny with the rest of the world. And American Jews also have come to share, however reluctantly, the common and inescapable destiny of their fellow Jews in the rest of the world. An unfailing rule in that millennial experience of our people has been that in normal times of political and economic stability, of peace and prosperity, we are not greatly annoyed. When conditions become disturbed and unsettled, for whatever reason, we are suddenly and severely menaced.

Following the war we shall be kept busy for a time undoing the mischief which the virulent Nazi-inspired propaganda of recent years will have accomplished in this country; busy, as it were, disinfecting the human mind. This will prove a job of no mean proportions. Thereafter we shall proceed to make the necessary adjustments to the more "normal" forms of prejudice without spending too much time and thought upon the subject—a preoccupation neither satisfying nor edifying—and we shall turn our attention to the more constructive areas of Jewish life. We have long been admonished by our sages not to observe the wind too closely lest we fail to sow, nor to regard the clouds with too much concern lest we fail to reap.

We will stop trying to find a solution for anti-Semitism and we will reconcile ourselves to a condition. We will, of course, join forces with all those elements in our population which work for the preservation of the basic traditions of American democracy. We shall be a portion of all that is around us and will share as fully as we shall be permitted in the common life. We will continue to resist the forces of darkness and disruption in our country. We will not surrender the hope of a future which will achieve in practice what has been projected in declaration, but, like the Messiah idea among our people, we shall think of it with hope but also with a saving measure of skepticism. We shall act as people who have finally matured and who do not attempt to escape into delusions or self-delusions.

DAVID BEN-GURION   born 1886

DAVID BEN-GURION was born as David Green in Plonsk, Poland, in 1886. He became active in Zionism very early in his life; as a youngster of seventeen, in 1903, he was already one of the cofounders of an early Labor-Zionist group, the Poale Zion of Poland, and two years later he was part of the Jewish self-defense that was organized there and in Russia in the wake of the Kishinev pogrom of 1903 and under the threat of the convulsions which attended the unsuccessful Russian revolution of 1905. Ben-Gurion left for Palestine in the next year, to work as a farm hand, along with others we have already mentioned (e.g., Gordon and Brenner) who were laying the foundations of a Jewish labor movement in the state they hoped they were creating.

Though Ben-Gurion began in Palestine by doing simple physical labor, he soon achieved some organizational and political prominence. He was chairman of the conference which organized its Poale Zion party in 1907 and wrote considerably in the press of this small (not more than hundreds at the time) but very important group. By 1913 he was a delegate of his party to the Eleventh World Zionist Congress, and he has played an ever more prominent role since then at the successive meetings of that body. Ben-Gurion was among the many new Zionist settlers in Palestine who were exiled by the Turkish command in 1915, and he made his way to the United States. During the three years of his stay in New York he was actively involved in organizing the American wing of Labor-Zionism and, in particular, in its effort toward encouraging American Jews to settle in Palestine. Though much of his Zionist career was to be spent in a no-quarter battle with Jabotinsky, Ben-Gurion was attracted to the idea of a Jewish Legion which Jabotinsky was bringing into being (see his biography above, Part 10), and was among the organizers of its "American" branch, i.e., of the group of Russian Jews then resident in the United States who went to join the three battalions of fusiliers which wound up in Palestine in 1918 under Allenby's command. Ben-Gurion was himself one of these soldiers.

After the war, at a conference in Haifa in 1920, he was among the founders of the Histadrut, the congress of labor unions in Palestine, and from 1921 to 1935 he served as its general secretary. In this role and in the post of chairman of the executive of the Jewish Agency that he held for the next thirteen years, until the state of Israel arose, Ben-Gurion was at the very head of the affairs of the Yishuv and of the Zionist movement. He represented Palestinian labor at several international socialist gatherings in the 1920's and 1930's and spoke for it before the various commissions of inquiry into Palestine which succeeded one another in that period. Concurrently, Ben-Gurion was, as he continues to be, a prolific journalist and speaker, whose papers and addresses have been published in many volumes.

His recent career is, of course, a dramatic element in modern history. Ben-Gurion was the leader of Palestinian Jewry in the struggles of the 1940's which preceded the state and, along with Silver, he provided the impetus toward Zionist political activism in the world arena.

Once the state was declared, he led it as its prime minister and minister of defence through its early, dangerous days. As writer and party leader, Ben-Gurion once coined a slogan for Labor-Zionism: "From class to becoming the nation as a whole." Whatever may happen to that dream for his specific group, it is undoubted that Ben-Gurion is today more than merely the political leader of Israel; he is more than its prime minister by virtue of a vote in parliament.

The passage below represents most of a speech he gave in Haifa in 1944 to a gathering of youth leaders. Many of the things he has labored for since that day are foreshadowed in this sketch of his ultimate vision.

THE IMPERATIVES OF THE JEWISH
REVOLUTION (1944)

I MUST TELL YOU at the very beginning that not only you youth leaders who are assembled here today, but every boy and girl in the land of Israel has been called to the most difficult task in our history—perhaps in the history of man! The charge that has been laid upon your generation is—unconditional allegiance, for life and death. The Jewish revolution is not the first or only one in the history of the world, but it is perhaps the most difficult. There have been a number of great revolutions—it suffices to mention the English revolution in the seventeenth century, the American and French revolutions in the eighteenth century, and the Russian revolution in our own time— and there will be others, but the Jewish revolution is fundamentally of a different order and its task is, therefore, all the harder. All other revolts, both past and future, were uprisings against a *system*, against a political, social, or economic structure. Our revolution is directed not only against a system but against *destiny*, against the unique destiny of a unique people.

No parallel exists in the history of any nation to the unique fate of the Jews, to our career which has been *sui generis* not merely since the beginning of the exile but even before, when we lived in our own land. Ours was a tiny nation inhabiting a small country, and there have been many tiny nations and many small countries, but ours was a tiny nation possessed of a great spirit, an inspired people that believed in its pioneering mission to all men, in the mission that had been preached by the prophets of Israel. This people gave the world great and eternal moral truths and commandments. This people rose to prophetic visions of the unity of the Creator with His creation, of the dignity and infinite worth of the individual (because every man is created in the divine image), of social justice, universal peace, and love—"And thou shalt love thy neighbor as thyself."[1] This people was the first to prophesy about "the end of days,"[2] the first to see the vision of a new human society.

This small land, too, is unique. Its geology, topography, and geographical position have given it a special significance in human history. From the very beginning of its career our tiny nation, in its small country, has been surrounded by two great empires, by Egypt and Assyria (or Babylon). These lands were not only immensely powerful; they were also the bearers of high cultures which made fundamental contributions to the founding of civilization, for they were the inventors of mathematics, geometry, and astronomy, as well as intensive agriculture. Both empires centered in fertile valleys irrigated by great rivers, Egypt, by the Nile, and Babylon, by the Euphrates and the Tigris. These territories were the homelands of mighty states—and also of a significant and valuable literature in history, poetry, and science, whose fragmentary remains we still admire. You have no doubt read some of these writings in Tchernichowsky's[3] brilliant translation of the "Gilgamesh Epic," but this is only a small sample of the rich literary legacy left by Assyria and Babylon, as well as by Egypt.

Our small and land-poor Jewish people, therefore, lived in constant tension between the power and influence of the neighboring great empires and its own seemingly insignificant culture—a culture poor in material wealth and tangible monuments but rich and great in its human and moral concepts and in its vision of a universal "end of days." Even today, after two and a half millennia and all the progress and revolutions that have intervened, mankind has not yet begun to approach the realization of this vision.

This Jewish people preserved its values and its prophetic hopes, and these, in turn, preserved it. These intangibles were the source of the morale which enabled us to withstand the pressure of the mighty empires on our borders and to safeguard our distinctive character. The very uniqueness of the Jewish people became the power by which it has left its mark on the history of man and by which it continues even now to be a creative force in the world. The preservation of our political, national, cultural, and moral independence has required heroic efforts, and, during our prolonged struggle to maintain our identity and our values, we have suffered grievous losses.

Many Jews did capitulate. After two thousand years of exile our numbers would not be so small were it not for two factors: extermination and conversion. These have plagued us since the beginning of the Galut. Many Jews could not bear the ever-present contempt, persecutions, and expulsions; they could not withstand the fear that was forever threatening. There were many others who lacked the stamina to resist the allure of the dominant political system, civilization, and religion, with their seeming universalism and their promise of peace and good fortune for everyone except the Jews. Yes, individuals may have surrendered and left our ranks—*but the nation as a whole neither surrendered nor lost heart!*

In all the history of the world there is no more fantastic phenomenon than this centuries-long resistance of ours. Heroism is a universal quality, and examples of it are to be found in the annals of every nation, both ancient and modern. In our own time millions displayed tremendous heroism in the Second World War, but there is nothing in the history of mankind to compare to the power of resistance and the unshakable tenacity of our people over the course of centuries and millennia. The fate of being uprooted and exiled from the homeland has been suffered by other nations, as well as the Jews, but all the others, without exception, have disappeared from the stage of history after a few decades. The Jews are the only example of a small, exiled, and forever hated people that stood fast and never surrendered from the time of their revolt against persecution by Hadrian to the recent uprisings in the ghettos of Warsaw, Lublin, and Bialystok. Resistance by a small people for so many centuries to so many powerful enemies —to refuse to surrender to historic destiny—this, in short, is the essential significance of Jewish history of the Galut.

What, therefore, is the meaning of our contemporary Jewish revolution—this revolt against destiny which the vanguard of the Jewish national renaissance has been cultivating in this small country for the last three generations? Our entire history in the Galut has represented a resistance of fate—what, therefore, is new in the content of our contemporary revolution? There is one fundamental difference: In the Galut the Jewish people knew the courage of *non-surrender*, even in the face of the noose and the *auto-da-fé*, even, as in our day, in the face of being buried alive by the tens of thousands. But the makers of the contemporary Jewish revolution have asserted: Resisting fate is not enough. *We must master our fate; we must take our destiny into our own hands!* This is the doctrine of the Jewish revolution—not non-surrender to the Galut but making an end of it.

Galut means dependence—material, political, spiritual, cultural, and intellectual dependence—because we are aliens, a minority, bereft of a homeland, rootless and separated from the soil, from labor, and from basic industry. Our task is to break radically with this dependence and to become masters of our own fate—in a word, to achieve independence. To have survived in the Galut despite all odds is not enough; we must create, by our own effort, the necessary conditions for our future survival as a free and independent people.

The meaning of the Jewish revolution is contained in one word—independence! Independence for the Jewish people in its homeland! Dependence is not merely political or economic; it is also moral, cultural, and intellectual, and it affects every limb and nerve of the body, every conscious and subconscious act. Independence, too, means more than political and economic freedom; it involves also the spiritual, moral, and intellectual realms, and, in essence, it is *independence in the heart*, in sentiment, and in will. From this inner sense of freedom outer forms of independence will develop in our way of life, social organization, relations with other people, and economic structure. Our independence will be shaped further by the conquest of labor and the land, by broadening the range of our language and its culture, by perfecting the methods of self-government and self-defense, by creating the framework and conditions for national independence and creativity, and finally—by attaining political independence. This is the essence of the Jewish revolution.

What makes this revolution so different is that it bears no relation to an existing order. The tragedy of the Jews is that we are not part of any order. A revolution directed against a well-defined social structure is a one-time affair; it can succeed by seizing control of the government and wielding the newly seized power to change the existing social and economic order. The Jewish revolution against our historic destiny must be a prolonged and continuing struggle, an enlistment of our own generation and even of those to come, and its road to success is not through seizure of power but only by the gradual shaping of the forces, mentioned above, that lead to independence, by girding ourselves with unyielding tenacity for changing our national destiny. There are only two means to this end: the ingathering of the exiles and independence in the homeland.

The Jewish revolution did not come into being and is not operating in a vacuum. Both Palestine and the Jews of the world are part of a complex pattern of international relations which are beyond our control, but which continue to affect and influence our lives, despite all our efforts to master our fate and become independent. The involved pattern of the international scene bristles with dangers, both internal and external, which threaten the Jewish revolution. Some of these forces have direct bearing on the tasks that confront the younger generation, and I shall therefore discuss them.

The Jewish revolution is taking place in a revolutionary era. This is a source of danger, and the pitfalls, though perhaps not evident on the surface, are real and deep.

Does the success of our revolution depend on ourselves, on our own meager resources, or on the great general forces now revolutionizing the world? Whatever danger threatens us is not from the open and avowed enemies of the aims and purposes of the Jewish revolution, even though such relatively unimportant adversaries must nonetheless be reckoned with.

There is some danger from the Jewish agents of foreign powers, the middlemen for alien nations and cultures, who were called in ancient times "traitors to the Covenant" and are known in our day as the "Yevsektzia" (and, in our country, as the "Fraction"),[4] but their well-known dependence on foreign influences weakens their effectiveness. The very fact that they serve unashamedly as foreign agents curbs their influence within our people. *The fate of the Jewish revolution will be determined by its own inner forces.*

There is, however, a danger that threatens the protagonists of the Jewish revolution themselves—that their capacity for *independent judgment* of the forces which will determine our future may weaken, that they may lose confidence in our own ability to be the focal and decisive factors in the shaping of the tomorrow of at least our own small world. We face the danger of self-deprecation, because we are small and weak in comparison to the great powers of the world—the danger of losing respect for our own achievements and victories in comparison with the great deeds of those nations which rule over continents and oceans. This may tempt some of us to pin our hopes on "the wave of the future"—not on our own potentialities but on forces outside ourselves. In a word, there is the danger of our orienting ourselves on "the wave of the future" of others.

The issue of "orientation" is not a new one. Open the Bible and you will find such a discussion between Jeremiah (in Chapters 42–43) and the Captains Johanan, son of Kareah, and Jezaniah, son of Hoshaiah, (and, very likely, even this was not the first debate about "orientation" in Jewish history). They asked the prophet to "tell us the way wherein we should walk and the thing we should do." Jeremiah answered: "If ye will still abide in this land, then will I build you, and not pull you down, and I will plant you and not pluck you up . . . Be not afraid of the king of Babylon." And to those who said, "No, but we will go into the land of Egypt, where we shall see no war . . . nor have hunger of bread, and there will we abide," the prophet replied: "If ye wholly set your faces to enter into Egypt and go to sojourn there; then it shall come to pass that the sword, which ye fear, shall overtake you there in the land of Egypt, and the famine, whereof ye are afraid, shall follow hard after you there in Egypt, and there ye shall die. . . . And ye shall be an execration, and an astonishment, and a curse, and a reproach; and ye shall see this place no more." This was the first expression, original and bold, of the principle of Jewish self-reliance.

This debate still continues. The issue is not whether we should look to the forces of yesterday or those of tomorrow. In history both past and future are relative terms. What was regarded yesterday as the wave of the future may today seem reactionary, and what seemed of no importance yesterday may be a great force tomorrow.

The real issue, now as in the past, is whether we should rely on the power of others or on our own strength. Both sides are finding partisans even among the protagonists of the Jewish revolution; because we are a small, weak, and numerically insignificant people, the great powers and movements are enchanting and blinding us and undermining our self-confidence.

We have always been a small power and we shall never be large in numbers. Even in Isaiah's time the Jews were a weak power surrounded by great nations which were superior to us in numbers and strength, in culture and science. An intellectual living in the days of the prophets, at home in the culture of the mighty, rich nations surrounding us—and most of the prophets were such intellectuals—had to have great faith in the mission and uniqueness of Israel in order to retain his Jewishness. Our neighbors did not know Hebrew but spoke the Egyptian and Babylonian languages. In spite of this Micah and Hosea wrote in Hebrew, a provincial tongue spoken only by a small people, yet their works are immortal, having been translated into hundreds of languages and enjoying a wider circulation than any other book in the world.

All those who relied on the mighty strength of Babylon and Egypt, of Greece and Rome, have been forgotten and every trace of them has disappeared. The works and prophecies of those who kept faith with Israel, poor and weak though she was, have endured down to our day and have left their imprint on all civilization. It is this "orientation" on a weak but independent power, the belief in its mission and its uniqueness, that has sustained the Jewish people and brought us to this point. Even in our times, if we have accomplished anything in our homeland —and we have accomplished something—our achievements were made possible by the faith we had in ourselves. The twenty youths who founded the first *kvutzah* more than thirty years ago on the banks of the Jordan did more for humanity and Jewish history, for the Jewish and international workers' movement, than all the Jewish socialists and revolutionaries who followed the chariots of the revolution among the great nations and mocked the "insignificant and peculiar" efforts of the pioneers in Israel. Yet the modest achievement of the pioneers of the Jewish revolution, grounded in their faith in themselves and their mission, has today become the sole anchor and beacon light for the Jewish survivors, the example for hundreds of thousands of Jewish young people everywhere. I am sure it will some day serve as a model for the workers' movement of the world.

However, as long as we are few and weak, we still face the danger of foreign influences. A poor man's wisdom has always been suspect. Unless we value our independence and see in our achievements the chief aim of our own efforts—even though it is only one link in the chain of the world revolution, but this is the link in which our destiny and our future are involved—the Jewish revolution will not be realized.

The first imperative of the Jewish revolution is, therefore—to guard jealously the independence, the inner moral and intellectual freedom, of our movement. Yes, we must not ignore or undervalue what is happening in the world without, and we must understand the great forces and the revolutionary movements in all the nations that are shaping the destiny of the world. But we cannot forget for a moment that the Jewish revolution can succeed only through our devotion to our own unique needs and destiny, only by reliance on our own strength, only if we exert the most stubborn efforts to increase its power and *to make it a wave of the future.* We dare not ever stray from this policy of self-reliance, from the will to make of ourselves a wave of the future—the wave of the future of the Jewish people and of a land of Israel so regenerated that it will attract Jews unto itself and make other peoples take account of it in their political and social calculations. If we ever deviate from this basic principle, we shall have destroyed the Jewish revolution and our future as a people.

The real danger that threatens is, as I have said, not entirely from the avowed "traitors to the Covenant" but also from some of those prime movers of the Jewish revolution who do not have an uncompromising and single-minded devotion, who do not adhere without any moral, ideological, or political qualification, to the unique requirements and demands of the Jewish revolution.[5]

The second indispensable imperative of the Jewish revolution is *the unity of its protagonists.* This sharing together in a fate, a creative process, and a struggle is what unites this vanguard—the pioneers, the builders of the homeland, the workers of the land of Israel, who are inspired by the vision of a Jewish renaissance on humanistic, Zionist, and socialist foundations. The conquest of labor and the land, self-defense, the development of the Hebrew language and culture, freedom for the individual and the nation, co-operation and social responsibility, preparation for further immigration, and the welding of the arrivals from the various Diasporas into a nation—these fundamental purposes are held in common, both in theory and in practice, by all those who are faithful to our revolution. These values make it possible, and indeed mandatory, that they be united. The Jewish revolution is incomparably difficult, and, unless there is unity and co-operation, it will fail. Without such inner unity we cannot hope for full realization of our creative potential; only such unity can give us the strength to withstand obstacles and reverses and make it possible for both the individual and the community to rise to their tasks.

Unity is the imperative of our mission and our destiny. Nonetheless, of all the values of our movement it is the one that is perhaps most honored in theory and least respected in practice. We may now be attempting to become rooted in the homeland and laboring to create an independent life, but the habits of disunity and anarchy which grew wild among us in the course of hundreds of years of exile and subservience cannot easily be corrected. Rifts are appearing not only in the Yishuv as a whole; after decades of displaying an unequaled capacity for unity even the *Halutzim* are being affected, first in Hehalutz,[6] then in the Kibbutz movement, and finally in the party itself. Once this disruptive force is let loose, it will not spare the Histadrut, the World Zionist Organization, or any of the other over-all bodies of the Yishuv and the Jewish people. Those who are willing to disrupt the Hehalutz or the party will have no compunction about destroying the unity of the Kibbutz movement and the Histadrut.[7]

Hehalutz is the creative laboratory of the Jewish revolution, of the conquest of labor, of the national renaissance. You cannot fragmentize and divide the Hehalutz without fragmentizing and dividing our movement as a whole. If there is no possibility and no need for a united Hehalutz of all labor in the land of Israel, a united Histadrut is also impossible and unnecessary. Those who cannot work together in Hehalutz will be no more capable of co-operating in the Histadrut. If Tirat Zvi and Ein Harod cannot accept one another as valid expressions of the pioneering spirit, can we be sure about Degania and Kinneret, or even about Yagur and Mishmar Ha-Emek? If every form of settlement on the land and every ideological faction requires a Hehalutz of its own, then their union in the general Histadrut is a fiction and a fraud. A separate Hehalutz for every kibbutz and faction in the Diaspora is the prelude to a separate Histadrut for every variety of agricultural settlement and ideological faction in the homeland. Those who regard such a policy as correct in the Diaspora cannot escape its consequences in the land of Israel.

The separatist tendency that has manifested itself in our land uses the empty phrase "of proletarian origin" as its slogan. This doctrine is totally foreign to the spirit and essence of the Jewish revolution. Not the *origin* but the *mission*, not "whence" but "whither," is what will decide the fate of our revolution. The Jewish people is not a proletarian people and there are no sons of the proletariat to assure the success of its revolution. The mission of the Jewish revolution is to *transform* the Jewish people into a *laboring* people, and our revolution, therefore, makes its demand not only of you of the youth leadership assembled here today but of every young person who belongs to our people. *Not our origin and our past but our mission and our future are what determines our path.* The dividing line between our past and our future is in Hehalutz, in the transition to a productive way of life. This is the workshop in which our revolutionary unity is forged, and the influence of that unity is then felt throughout our work—in the efforts for immigration and the conquest of labor, for resettling the land and adding to our labor force in the harbors and factories, and for spreading the knowledge of Hebrew; in the struggle for decent working conditions, national rights, and security; in the building of a new economy and a new society; and, ultimately, in attaining freedom, equality, dignity, and independence. Only together, in one Hehalutz and in one Socialist-Zionist party, in a united Jewish community and an undivided World Zionist Organization, can we assure Jewish immigration, (by whatever means), redeem and rebuild the land, and fight our way through to victory.

The Jewish revolution requires not only an undivided and organic partnership of all the workers in Israel but also the mutual co-operation of labor and the nation. Whatever we have accomplished to date—the creation of the beginnings of strength for our people and for the labor movement, of a beginning toward the conquest of labor and a return to the soil and the sea—has been hard and costly. We have succeeded in these tasks only because the revolutionary pioneers in Israel and the Jewish people as a whole have gone forward loyally arm in arm. This co-operation is based on a two-way historical tie, the bond of the Jewish people to its pioneer-workers and the bond of the worker-pioneer to the people. Whoever harms the cause of the working class, in the supposed name of the general interests of the people, is false to the historical will of the people and to its needs. And anyone who questions the ultimate authority of the nation as a whole, in the supposed name of the class-independence of labor, negates the historic mission of Jewish labor and undermines its dynamic potential. The historic strength of the Jewish worker is not rooted in his present setting and achievements—this is only the first layer—but in the hidden storehouses of our scattered nation and in its untapped abilities. Only when a way can be found to harness the latent resources of our people will we really gain the necessary strength to carry out our revolutionary tasks.

Another kind of co-operation is required from those who are loyal to our revolution: the comradeship of Jewish labor with international labor. This co-operation must be based on mutual aid and the equality of free men. We will not achieve the aims of our revolution by slavery and dependence, by estrangement and individualism, or by isolating ourselves. The difficult task we are performing on the Jewish scene is part of a tremendous movement which involves all of humanity—the world revolution, whose aims are the redemption of man from every form of enslavement, discrimination, and exploitation, no matter whether the victims are nations, races, religions, or one of the sexes. Our revolution differs from all others because our destiny is different, but the difference serves to unite us with others and not to estrange us. Though our task is unique, our revolution does have points of contact with others, and we must learn to see both the differences and the similarities. While guarding our moral and intellectual individuality, we must cultivate our international partnership with the makers of the world revolution, with the workers of all nations, but this must be an equal partnership—not equal in strength, but in rights and in dignity. We are few, our achievements are picayune, our nation is weak, and our land is small. Among the other peoples there are great, mighty, and awesome nations, ruling vast parts of the world. Nevertheless we are equal to them in rights and dignity, because we, too, have a share in the world revolution, and this share—and we will have no part of any other kind of association—is valueless without equal rights and dignity. Let us not underestimate the value of quantity—in numbers there is strength—but this is not the whole story. Little Judah certainly contributed no less to the world than mighty Egypt, Babylon, and Rome. Nor has the source of our creativity evaporated. Who knows, perhaps a regenerated Judah is still destined for great and significant accomplishment in the world of tomorrow. What Israel gave the world when it lived in its own land was achieved not by those Jews who served Egypt, Babylon, and Rome, but by those who remained faithful to our own identity. If we are destined to make a contribution once more to the totality of human civilization, that will be done only by those who keep faith with the Jewish revolution and the Jewish spirit. One Degania is worth more than all the "Yevsektzias" and assimilationists in the world.

The third—and perhaps the most important—imperative of the Jewish revolution is: Halutziut.[8]

We are nearing the end of the war. City after city and country after country are being liberated—but we Jews are not sharing in this joy, for almost the entire Jewish population of the newly liberated lands has been wiped out. The wellspring from which the Jewish revolution drew its strength has been destroyed. The Jewish masses on which our effort depended—they are obliterated. The Jewries of Poland, Lithuania, and Galicia—these no longer exist.

Now, more than ever before, we need a strong and devoted pioneering force. The desert area of our land is calling us, and the destruction of our people is crying out to us. In order to save the remnant—and all of us now constitute a remnant, including our own communities here in the land of Israel—our work must proceed at forced draft. The tasks that lie ahead will require pioneering efforts the likes of which we have never known, for we must conquer and fructify the waste places (in the mountains of Galilee, the plains of the Negev, the valley of the Jordan, the sand dunes of the seashore, and the mountains of Judea) and we must prepare the way for new immigrants from Yemen, Persia, Turkey, Egypt, Syria, Iraq, Romania, Greece, France, and Belgium— in short, from every country in which some remnant is still alive. We must look toward immigration from England, America, and North and South Africa, too, and we are not giving up the hope that even the Jews of Soviet Russia will eventually join this stream. First of all, we must conquer the sea and the desert, for these will provide us with room for new settlers and will serve as a laboratory for the development of new forms of economic and agricultural endeavor. We need men of the sea—sailors, fishermen, dock workers, and shipbuilders of our own —who will make the sea a source of economic and political strength; we need men of the desert who will know it in all its secrets and will lead us in transforming the wasteland into a blessing, a place in which to work and live. Unless we conquer both the sea and the desert—by creating Jewish sailors and even Jewish Bedouin tribes—we cannot succeed in the tasks of immigration and resettlement that we must shoulder after the war. Yes, we have made a small beginning in the sea, but we have as yet done nothing in the desert, even though it must be remembered that the bulk of our country is desert. Our desert is not a Sahara or a hopelessly arid wilderness. The deserts of Israel were once inhabited in ancient times and, even today, they are not entirely unpopulated. A beginning toward reclamation should be made by Jewish desert-dwellers, Bedouins, who will know how to live and work in tents and will be able to support themselves like the Arab, but who along with possessing primitive Bedouin skills, will also be familiar with modern cultural, scientific, and technical knowledge. This combination will enable them to find a way of making the wilderness bloom and turning the desert into a place of settled habitation.

The conquest of the desert requires bold and adventurous pioneers who will not shrink back in the face of any obstacle or hardship.

The absorption of immigration will be a more difficult task than ever before and will require of us new and unprecedented efforts. The new immigrants will be coming to us from misery and poverty and will need prolonged care and intensive help from the pioneer vanguard. Where can we get such pioneering leadership, now that the great reserves in Poland, Lithuania, Galicia, and Czechoslovakia have been done to death? *The youth of the homeland must now assume these pioneering tasks.*

It is impossible to fill the terrible void left by the destruction of European Jewry. This dreadful loss is irreplaceable—and a greater obligation is therefore placed on Israeli youth.

In my opinion no greater or more urgent task awaits our youth leadership than the work of ingathering and resettlement. But even a decision for personal commitment is not enough; you must be the nucleus for enlisting Jewish youth throughout the country, in the cities and on the farms, whatever their background. It is not enough for the children to continue the work of their fathers in Degania, Nahalal, Ein Harod, Kfar Yehezkel, Tel Yosef, and Ein Ganim. They are now called elsewhere to new works of daring, for the wastelands of both the land and the sea are beckoning.

The youth leadership must, in the first place, activate the young people now at school or in the labor force, and even those who neither work nor study, for in this all too large element, too, there are important untapped possibilities for pioneering. Destiny has chosen this generation of our young people for difficult and desperate tasks. There is a pioneering potential in every one of these young men and women, and our youth leadership can assume no greater mission than *to make pioneers of the youth of our country!* This is the greatest and most urgent need of the Jewish revolution.

Since I called, at the beginning of my remarks, for absolute allegiance to the Jewish revolution, I shall now make a few concluding remarks about the goal of our revolution: *It is the complete ingathering of the exiles into a socialist Jewish state.*

Even this is not our ultimate goal, for there is no ultimate goal in history. The ingathering of the exiles into a socialist Jewish state is in fact only a precondition for the fulfillment of the real mission of our people. We must first break the constricting chains of national and class oppression and become free men, enjoying complete individual and national independence on the soil of a redeemed homeland. After that we can address ourselves to the great mission of man on this earth —to master the forces of nature and to develop his unique creative genius to the highest degree.

I do not know how many of us will live to see that great day, but I believe that not only you of the youth leadership but all of us of the second and third Aliyot assembled here, and all our comrades from far and near, can have high hope of seeing the Jewish revolution realized in our day. This consummation does not depend only on ourselves. Outside forces beyond our control and unforeseen circumstances which we cannot now even imagine will play their parts in tipping the scales one way or another. Nonetheless, despite all that, *it does depend on us:* on the Jewish people, the Yishuv in the homeland, the labor movement, and the pioneer youth. Let us all remain faithful without any reservation, faithful in thought and deed, in emotion and will, to the demands and the mission of the Jewish revolution; let us preserve our inner dignity and unity and our continuing solidarity with both the Jewish people as a whole and the international labor movement; and let us transform the beaten and downtrodden into the pioneers of a work of immigration and resettlement equal to the grave crisis and the redemptive vision of our people. If such be our program, there is hope that many of us will live to see the consummation of the Jewish revolution—the concentration of the majority of our people in a homeland transformed into a socialist Jewish state.

Notes

ALKALAI

1. Numbers 10:36.
2. Yebamoth 64a.
3. From the Amidah (silent devotion) prescribed to be said three times a day.
4. Genesis 33:18–19.
5. Joel 2:28.

KALISCHER

1. The Five Books of Moses, and, in a larger sense, the Scriptures. The reference here is to Leviticus 11.
2. In Hebrew, *Shevilei Emunah,* a devotional book written in 1360 by the Spanish Jew, Rabbi Meir Ibn Al-Dabi. This treatise on philosophical, scientific, and theological subjects was a perennial favorite of the learned.
3. The dispersion of Jews in the countries outside of Palestine.
4. The reference is to the laws contained in the Bible prescribing the manner by which the Jews in the Holy Land were to cultivate the soil—e.g., the commandment that the land should lie fallow on the seventh year (Leviticus 25:3–4).

HESS

1. In an incident famous in its day, the Jews of Damascus were accused in 1840 of the death of a Capuchin friar, Father Thomas, who had disappeared. The other members of his order in the city spread the tale that the Jews had slain him in order to use his blood in baking the matzoth (unleavened bread) for Passover. The investigations into this "blood libel" were conducted by the local Turkish authorities with great cruelty. Jews all over the world took action, which finally forced the Turkish Government to free the accused.
2. The publisher Otto Wigand refused the book, writing Hess: "I do not want my firm to be identified with your assertions or beliefs. The book as a whole stands opposed to my pure human nature." (Theodor Zlocisti,

Moses Hess, Berlin, 1921, p. 281.)

3. Berthold Auerbach (1812–1882), well-known German Jewish novelist and short story writer, who portrayed Jewish life in Germany.

4. Reform Judaism made its formal appearance in the 1840's in Germany (there were stirrings for a generation earlier). Its extreme element believed in the elimination of all traces of national feeling from Judaism, including changing the language of worship services from Hebrew to the vernacular, and the excision from the prayers of any mention of Zion and Jerusalem.

5. "Wherever it is good, that is the homeland."

6. In Hess's lifetime the process of the unification of Italy was a major event. The first practical results of the Italian *Risorgimento* were felt in the revolutionary year of 1848, when Piedmont received a modern liberal constitution (including equality for the Jews). It culminated in 1870, after the fall of Napoleon III in the Franco-Prussian war, with the conquest of Rome, which brought the Papal State to an end.

7. Moses Mendelssohn (1729–1786), famous German Jewish philosopher and writer of the Enlightenment. In translating the Pentateuch into German, Mendelssohn hoped the Jews would learn the language and adapt themselves culturally to the modern world. He was himself a practicing orthodox Jew, but his "enlightening" influence made him one of the archetypes for religious reform.

8. Gotthold Ephraim Lessing (1729–1781), German writer, whose passion for religious tolerance led him to write his highly successful play *Nathan the Wise* (1779). He gave currency to the well-known "three ring" parable, which he used to make the point that Judaism, Christianity, and Islam were all equally valid approaches to God. He was a friend of Moses Mendelssohn and his writing had a large influence in developing a more positive regard for the Jew in Christian circles.

9. Moritz August von Bethmann-Hollweg (1795–1877) was a Prussian jurist and statesman and leader of the Liberal-Conservation party. At the time of Hess's writing he was (1858–1862) the minister of religions in the Prussian cabinet. (His grandson, Theobald, was Chancellor of Germany 1909–1917).

10. Isaiah 40:1–5.

11. "And saviors shall come up on Mount Zion to judge the mount of Esau, and the kingdom shall be the Lord's."

12. See Note 1.

13. Ernst Laharanne, was the private secretary of Napoleon III of France during the period of the growing influence of that

country in Syria. His "Zionist" book was published in Paris in 1860, under the title *La nouvelle question d'Orient: Reconstitution de la Nation Juife*. Except for Hess, no one seems to have taken it seriously, at the time. Laharanne himself is a semimysterious personality about whose life little is recorded.

14. That is, the biblical practice of offering animal sacrifices to God in the Temple in Jerusalem. See the opening chapters of the Book of Leviticus.

15. Hess is ironizing at a contemporary situation. The years 1859–1862 marked the beginning of the rule of Wilhelm I of Prussia, who broke with reaction to institute a liberal regime. These years of conflict ended in 1862 with the return of the conservative royalist-military forces to power.

SMOLENSKIN

1. The reference is probably to certain Jewish figures of the Renaissance, and especially the Venetian Rabbi Leon de Modena (1571–1648), who were reported to have been lax in their obedience to the rules of Jewish religion.

2. A Russian word meaning riot; it was used as a technical term to denote the attacks perpetrated against Jewish communities in Russia.

3. The Jewish Enlightenment, a movement of writers and intellectuals aimed at breaking down the ghettolike mentality of the Jews and getting them to adopt western ways and outlook. It traced its ancestry to Moses Mendelssohn. See Hess, Note 7.

4. In 1881 the tsarist regime embarked upon a program of terror whose purpose was to "solve" the Jewish problem by murder, emigration, and conversion to Christianity.

5. In the first half of the nineteenth century, Tsars Alexander I and Nicholas I had promulgated decrees which encouraged and even forced Jews to forsake "unproductive" occupations and to take up farming.

6. Eretz Israel=the Land of Israel.

7. A charismatic leader, who was venerated by his followers (the Hasidim) and generally credited by them with the ability to perform wondrous deeds. This pietistic movement was initiated by Rabbi Israel Baal Shem-Tov in the eighteenth century and was a major force for at least a hundred years. Its momentum is still felt today.

8. The classic text of Jewish civil and canon law. The Talmud is second only to the Bible in religous authority in Judaism; indeed the Bible can be interpreted authoritatively, in the framework of Jewish religous tradition, only in the light of the Talmud.

BEN-YEHUDAH

1. Hashahar=The Dawn; a Hebrew monthly published by Peretz Smolenskin in Vienna from 1868 to 1885.
2. The "enlighteners," the bearers of the ideas of the Jewish Enlightenment (the Haskalah). See Smolenskin, Note 3.
3. Jeremiah 29:5.
4. Talmud, Ketuboth 110b.

LILIENBLUM

1. The policy of successive tsars was to restrict the Jews to residence only in Russia's western provinces.
2. The European secondary school.
3. Lilienblum is responding to an important article by Yehudah Leib Gordon(1830–1892) that was published in the same year under the title (in full) of "Our Redemption and the Saving of Our Life." Gordon was the chief literary spokesman of the Russian Jewish Enlightenment (see Smolenskin, Note 3). The pogroms of 1881 had brought that era to an end, but in this essay Gordon, while accepting in qualified fashion the new idea of a Jewish restoration in Palestine, remained true to the main theme of the "enlighteners" that a reform and modernization of the Jewish religion and way of life remained the prime need of the age.

4. See Smolenskin, Note 7.
5. The phylacteries worn by Jews during the weekday morning prayers.
6. The prayer expressing the concept of the oneness of God. The text is, "Hear, O Israel, the Lord our God, the Lord is One." (Deuteronomy 6:4).
7. Religious elementary schools.
8. See Ben-Yehudah, Note 2.
9. Foods which the law of the Bible forbids Jews to eat, e.g., pig, and milk and meat together (Leviticus 11:1–47 and Exodus 23:19).
10. The practice whereby a woman immerses herself in a special bath prior to her marriage, a ritual that she continues every month after her marriage.
11. These were two of the three leading sects within Jewry (the third was the Essenes) between the time of the Maccabees in the second century B.C. and the destruction of the Temple in Jerusalem in the year 70 C.E. The Sadducees were adherents of the priestly caste and believed in strict and literal construction of the text of the Bible. The Pharisees were the progenitors of talmudic and rabbinic Judaism. They concentrated on further elucidation and application of the biblical text according to elaborate canons of exegesis which they created.
12. A Jewish sect that originated in the eighth century C.E. that accepted only the authority of

the Scriptures and rejected the rabbinic tradition (i.e., the Talmud and its literature) as the authoritative interpretation of the Bible.

13. Those Jews who championed the intellectual rigors of the Talmud and therefore bitterly opposed the Hasidim, in the eighteenth and nineteenth centuries, because they emphasized piety and ritual rather than learning.

14. Marr, Wilhelm (1819–1904), the father of anti-Semitism as an organized "ideological" movement in the third quarter of the nineteenth century in Germany. It is possible that he is the coiner of the word "anti-Semitism."

15. Kopek=a Russian penny.

PINSKER

1. A cry first used against the Jews during the anti-Semite excesses 1819 in Germany. It is usually, though perhaps fancifully, explained as the abbreviation of the Latin sentence *Hierosolyma est perdita*=Jerusalem is lost.

2. The allusions are to the rise of organized anti-Semitism in Germany and the recent birth (1879) of a political party avowedly based on it, led by the royal court preacher, Adolf Stöcker; to comparable, though at the moment less effective, agitation in Hungary; to the pogroms of the 1860's in Romania and the reneges of

its government on the promises it made at the Congress of Berlin (1878) to grant equal citizenship to the Jews; and, of course, to the pogroms in Russia which were the immediate cause of Pinsker's writing.

HERZL

1. The Feast of Weeks occurred that year (1895) on May 29–30. The use of the Hebrew date is in itself revealing of the revolution that was taking place in Herzl's soul.

2. *Freiland*, by Theodor Hertzka (1845–1921), was a widely read novel published in 1890 describing a communistic utopia located in Central Africa. Its author was an Austro-Hungarian writer on economics and social problems.

3. See Hess, Note 8.

4. The reference is to the efforts of Baron Maurice de Hirsch (1831–1896), the financier and railroad builder. He had founded the Jewish Colonization Society (it was known colloquially as ICA, the initials of its name in Yiddish) in 1891, and given it a princely endowment, to resettle impoverished emigrants from eastern Europe in North and South America. Its most important single endeavor was in Argentina, where a large tract of land had been purchased for agricultural settlement.

NORDAU

1. The writers of the great French Encyclopedia of the eighteenth century, which was edited by Diderot and D'Alembert. It was a summary of the outlook and values of the Enlightenment.
2. Nordau's date is wrong. The final decree emancipating the Jews was passed by the French National Assembly on September 27, 1791.
3. The word was first applied to those Jews in Spain who were forced to convert to Christianity in the fourteenth and fifteenth centuries, but who clandestinely practiced Judaism.

AHAD HA-AM

1. Hillel lived in the first century B.C.E. This formulation of the "golden rule" is to be found in the Talmud, Shabbat 31a.
2. Vofsi is the protagonist of strict rabbinic law in Yehudah Leib Gordon's poem here being discussed (see also Lilienblum, Note 3—the essay by Gordon discussed there is later than the poem referred to here, which appeared in 1876). Gordon expressed the attitude of the Haskalah at its zenith in spinning this tale in which the lack of the small dot, the Hebrew letter *yod*, is adjudged to render a religious bill of divorce invalid and hence results in condemning a woman to being for all her days neither married nor free to remarry. *The Point of a Yod*, the title and central issue of this poem, means "trifle" in idiomatic Hebrew.

3. Israel Zangwill (1864–1926), prominent Anglo-Jewish novelist and essayist. He joined Herzl as one of the early leaders of political Zionism, but he broke with the movement after the Seventh Zionist Congress of 1905 (the first after Herzl's death) voted finally to reject the British offer (made in 1902) of land in Uganda for Jewish national development. Zangwill founded the Jewish Territorial Organization, a group which believed that Palestine was not necessarily the land on which a national solution of the Jewish question could be effected.
4. Love of Zion, the name given to the movement that sprang up in Russia immediately after the events of 1881 to urge the persecuted Jews of Russia to go to Palestine and create a national life of their own there. Its leader was Leo Pinsker, and it included all the pre-Herzlian Russian Zionists mentioned in this volume.
5. The period dating from the reign of King Solomon to the destruction of the Temple in 586 B.C.E.
6. Sennacherib (705–681 B.C.E.), the Assyrian king who subdued the Kingdom of Judah but whose armies were decimated by a plague before Jerusalem.

For the context, see Isaiah 10: 5–23.

7. The period from 520 B.C.E., when the Second Temple was built, until its destruction in the year 70 by the Romans under Titus.

8. Yavneh=Jammia, an old Palestinian city on the Mediterranean in which Rabbi Johanan ben Zakkai founded a famous academy during the siege of Jerusalem by the Romans. See also Introduction, section VI.

9. On Magnes, see the biography given as introduction to his essay reproduced in this volume, Part 7.

10. *Ain Jacob (Well of Jacob)*, one of the best known works of rabbinic literature, is a collection of the moralistic, historical, and folkloristic passages of the Talmud. It was edited at the end of the fifteenth century by a recent exile from Spain, Rabbi Jacob ben Solomon ibn Habib.

11. Rashi is the abbreviation of the name of Rabbi Solomon ben Isaac (1040–1105), of the Rhineland, who wrote the classical commentaries on both the Bible and the Talmud.

12. *Menorat Hamaor (Candelabrum of the Light)*, written by Isaac Aboab, who lived in Spain in the fifteenth century, was intended to serve as a moral guide.

13. A gardening and agricultural school to train Jews to work the land of Palestine, set up in 1870 by the predominantly Franco-Jewish Alliance Israelite Universelle, near Jaffa. It was named Mikveh Israel.

14. Hovevei Zion=Lovers of Zion, i.e., the adherents of the Hibbat Zion movement, for which see above, Note 4.

15. *Galut*=exile, i.e., the status of Jewry as a dispersed people living in many lands among gentile majorities.

16. See Part 2, Lilienblum's "The Future of Our People."

17. The reference is to Simon Dubnov (1860–1941), the celebrated Jewish historian, who is best known for his synthetic *World History of the Jewish People*, in ten volumes, which has appeared in Russian, German, Spanish, Hebrew, and Yiddish. He was the founder of the school of thought here being discussed. Some of Dubnov's own writings on Jewish nationalism are now available in English in Koppel Pinson (editor), *Nationalism and History*, Philadelphia, 1958.

BIALIK

1. Lord Balfour, Arthur James (1848–1930), Foreign Secretary in the British War Cabinet, who wrote the famous letter to Lord Rothschild on November 2, 1917, which pledged the Government to "view with favor the establishment in Palestine of a national

home for the Jewish people . . ."

2. This is the ascending order of schools in the traditional system of Jewish education. *Heder* is the elementary school; *yeshivah*, the formally organized higher academy of talmudic studies; *bet-midrash* is the house of study in which already trained individuals pursued their independent studies in the sacred literature. The last two are not necessarily mutually exclusive.

3. This paragraph is a summary of the view of the Talmud and the quotations are all from it and from parallel sources.

4. Based on I Kings, 3:9–11.

5. Shammai and Hillel were the leaders of the two major schools of thought within the Pharisaic order at the end of the first century B.C. Rabbinic literature records many disagreements between the two schools. This specific discussion is to be found in the Talmud, Hagigah 12a.

6. A quota system imposed at various times and places on Jews wishing to enter schools of higher education.

7. Baraitha=a report of a tradition or judgment out of the work of the *tannaim* (the earliest masters of rabbinic law) which was not included in the Mishnah, the code compiled by Rabbi Judah the Prince in the second century.

8. Zechariah 4:10.

BERDICHEVSKI

1. *Sifrei*, Ekeb, 40. Berdichevski's farther comment on this quotation makes it obvious that his memory is at fault, for the text goes on to make this very point: "If you observe what is written in the Book, the sword will not destroy you." Here he is, of course, the protagonist of the reverse, "Nietzschean," morality.

2. Rabbi Eliezer ben Hyrkanos was the greatest of the immediate disciples of Rabbi Johanan ben Zakkai, at the end of the first century C.E. The passages quoted and discussed here are from the Mishnah, Shabbat 6:4.

3. He is quoting Rashi's comment (for Rashi, see Ahad Ha-Am, Note 11) on Genesis 1:1, which is itself based on talmudic sources.

4. Mishnah, Aboth (Ethics of the Fathers) 3:8.

5. Exodus 34:5.

6. Leviticus 20:7.

BRENNER

1. Mendele is the pen name of Shalom Jacob Abramowitz, whose collected works in Hebrew Brenner reviewed in this essay (see biographical introduction to Brenner). "Kislon" and "Kabtziel" are two of the names Mendele gave to his locale, the impoverished and benighted small towns of the

Russian Jewish ghetto; in Hebrew, the first means "foolishness" and the second, "poverty."

2. Reb Leib the *Melamed* (i.e., the teacher in the ghetto school) is the hero of Mendele's short story *Be-Yemei ha-Raash* (The Stampede), written in 1892, which gives his satirical reactions to the early days of the Hibbat Zion movement. Impelled by rosy tales of the immediate joys to be had in Palestine, all kinds of people then rushed to Odessa, the center of the movement, to offer themselves as would-be settlers. Reb Leib is such a one, an impractical dabbler in many semi-useless trades, who, having failed in all of them, now dreamed of glory in Palestine.

3. The Golden Age in Spain refers, technically, to the tenth century when, at the height of the Moorish state in Spain, Jews enjoyed a status of freedom and opportunity not paralleled elsewhere in the Middle Ages. The phrase is used, loosely, to mean the cultural symbiosis with their neighbors and the interest by Jews in all branches of learning and literature, which distinguished Spanish Jewry, even as its lot continued to worsen, until its complete expulsion by Ferdinand and Isabella in 1492.

4. Sephardim are Jews who trace their descent from those exiled from Spain.

SYRKIN

1. Shylock is Shakespeare's *Merchant of Venice;* for *Nathan the Wise,* see Hess, Note 8.

2. For *"Hep! Hep!"* see Pinsker, Note 1.

3. Hermann Ahlwardt (1846–1914), an extremist among German anti-Semitic propagandists; he was a member of the Reichstag and used its platform for denunciation of the Jews.

4. Eugen Dühring (1833–1921), a German "philosopher" of anti-Semitism who published an attack on the Jews as racially inferior under the title *Die Judenfrage als Rassen-Sitten-und Culturfrage* (1881). Friedrich Engles, Karl Marx's collaborator, answered him in his well-known book *Anti-Dühring.*

5. Ludwig Börne (1786–1837), German writer of Jewish origin; he fought for the emancipation of the Jews in Germany through novels, sketches, and polemics.

6. Arthur Schopenhauer (1788–1860), German philosopher of pessimism.

7. *Lumpen-proletariat*=the lowest class of workers.

8. In 1894 Captain Alfred Dreyfus, a Jewish officer in the French army, was falsely accused and convicted of treason. The affair, which convulsed France and rocked Europe, dragged on for twelve years until Dreyfus was exonerated

and restored to full rank. (See also introductory biographical note to Herzl, Part 3.) As Syrkin remarks, the French Left, not wanting to seem lacking in patriotism, joined the outcry against Dreyfus.

BOROCHOV

1. *The Essentials of Marx*, Algernon Lee (editor), New York, 1931, p. 176.
2. Engels, Friedrich (1820–1895), German socialist theoretician and close collaborator of Marx. (See also above, Syrkin, Note 4.)

GORDON

1. Hermann Struck (1876–1944), Berlin-born Jewish artist and etcher.
2. Rabbi Isaac Jacob Reines (1839–1915): scholar and Zionist, Reines founded the Mizrahi, the organization of those who combined Zionist nationalism with an orthodox religious outlook, in 1901.
3. These are two cities in Babylonia, in which two famous talmudical academies were founded in the third century.

KATZENELSON

1. Maxim Gorky (1868–1936), the famous Russian writer.

2. The reference is to the thought of Vladimir Jabotinsky. For a summary of his life and outlook, see the introduction to the excerpt from him in this volume, Part 10.
3. Heinrich Graetz (1817–1891), was a German-Jewish scholar who wrote the most famous and influential modern history of the Jews. It has appeared in many languages including English (in an incomplete version entitled A *History of the Jews*, Philadelphia, 1891–1898).
4. Rabbi Akiba (about 50–136 C.E.), celebrated rabbi and scholar, who, according to tradition, was put to death by the Romans.
5. The Rambam=Maimonides (the form Rambam is the Hebrew abbreviation of his name, Rabbi Moses ben Maimon). He was born in Cordova, Moorish Spain, in 1135 and died in Fostat, Egypt, in 1204. His summary of talmudic law, entitled *Yad ha-Chazakah* (*The Strong Hand*), is the classic of medieval Jewish studies in the field and his philosophical work, *The Guide of the Perplexed*, is the most important volume of Jewish philosophy.
6. Ninth day of the Hebrew month of Ab. It is an important day of fasting, commemorating the destruction of the Temple.

MOHILEVER

1. See Ahad Ha-Am, Notes 4 and 14.
2. These were the traditional alms collected throughout the Jewish world for the support of the pious in the Holy Land.
3. See Herzl, Note 4.
4. Baron Edmond de Rothschild (1845–1934), the head of the French branch of the house of Rothschild. He was motivated by religious allegiance to Zion and Jerusalem to lend large support to the early and faltering colonies in Palestine in the 1880's and 1890's. Despite obstacles, including rebellions by the colonists themselves against his paternalist regime, Rothschild persevered to remain, throughout his life, the greatest single benefactor of Zionism's practical efforts in colonization.

PINES

1. Rabbi Yehudah Halevi is the celebrated Hebrew poet who lived in Spain in the late eleventh and early twelfth centuries.
2. Rabbi Moshe ben Nahman, or Nahmanides (1195–1270), Spanish-born Talmudist and philosopher who was banished from Gerona in 1267 on trumped-up charges of blasphemy and went to Palestine, where he died.

KOOK

1. Sabbath 31. The reference is to the first section of the Mishnah, the second-century code of Jewish law, which deals with rules governing agriculture.

BUBER

1. Simon Bar Kokba, the leader of the Jewish insurrection against the Romans (132–135) which ended in failure.
2. See Nordau, Note 3.
3. By David Ben-Gurion, first Prime Minister of Israel.

FLEG

1. August 15–17, 1899.

LEWISOHN

1. Leopold Zunz (1794–1886), Famous Jewish historian, who was the founder of the *Wissenschaft des Judentums*, the modern scientific study of Jewish history and literature.

GOTTHEIL

1. Impelled by the Russian pogroms, Jewish migration to England had been growing in the 1880's and 1890's. In 1898 limitation of this immigration was proposed for the second

time (an earlier effort had been made in 1894) by the Conservative Party. Ultimately there was a Royal Commission on this subject in 1902, before which Theodor Herzl testified, and a restrictive law was enacted in 1906.

2. The reference is to Benjamin Disraeli, Lord Beaconsfield (1804–1881).

3. For Drumont, see Silver, Note 4; Adolf Stöcker (1835–1909) was the court preacher of Wilhelm II of Germany and a notorious, and very active, anti-Semite; Karl Lüger (1844–1910) was the mayor of Vienna at the turn of the century and the founder, earlier (1878), of the Austrian Christian Socialists (i.e., anti-Semites). The adolescent Adolf Hitler was one of Lüger's adherents.

SCHECHTER

1. Ludwig Philippson (1811–1889) founded the *Allgemeine Zeitung des Judentums,* which served as the organ for German Reform Jewry. The mention of synods is an allusion to the rabbinic meetings of the nineteenth century in which the doctrines of Reform Judaism were announced.

2. Julius Wellhausen (1844–1918), a German Protestant biblical scholar whose name is identified with the theory that the Pentateuch is of multiple and of relatively late author-

ship. Schechter had often repeated his bon mot, addressed at the biblical critics as headed by Wellhausen, that "the higher criticism is the higher anti-Semitism."

3. Isaiah 2:3; Micah 4:2.

BRANDEIS

1. Robert W. Seton-Watson (1879–1951), a British historian who specialized in the multinational regions of the Austro-Hungarian monarchy and the Balkans.

2. Aaron Aaronson (1875–1919), agronomist and Zionist leader; he headed a secret information center which was of great service to the British campaign in Palestine during the First World War.

3. David Yellin (1864–1941), Jerusalem-born writer, educator, and philologist; he was the son-in-law of I. M. Pines and, in his own right, a leader of Palestinian Jewry, of particular prominence in its practical affairs in the first quarter of this century.

4. Boris Schatz (1886–1932), sculptor, painter, and art educator, who founded the Bezalel School of Art in Jerusalem.

5. *Shomrim*=Guardsmen, a self-defense corps, founded in Palestine in 1907 to protect Jewish settlements against Arab marauders.

6. Henry Wickham Steed (1871–1956), English journalist and

author, who was correspondent of the London *Times* in Vienna, 1902–1913. Out of this experience he wrote a book, *The Hapsburg Monarchy* (London, 1913) from which the passage is being quoted.

KALLEN

1. Morris R. Cohen (1880–1947), prominent American philosopher and teacher.
2. Houston Stewart Chamberlain (1855–1927), an English expatriate to Germany, published his *Die Grundlagen des Neunzehnten Jahrhunderts* in 1899, in which he maintained that only the "Nordic-Aryan" race is the bearer of true civilization. He is a direct ancestor of Nazism.
3. Mikhail Nikiforovich Katkov (1818–1887), a Russian publicist and editor who began as a liberal but turned Slavophile after the Polish insurrection of 1883. In the concluding decades of his life Katkov was the leading apologist for the most ruthless Russian nationalism and tsarist absolutism.
4. David Lloyd George (1863–1945), British statesman and head of the War Cabinet during the latter years of the First World War; it was in his regime that the Balfour Declaration was issued.
5. Arthur Ruppin (1876–1943), agronomist and sociologist, was a leader among the pioneers in the building of the Zionist settlement in Palestine.
6. Ignaz Zollschan (1877–1948), Austrian-born physician, anthropologist, and writer on Zionism.
7. A famous Hasidic rabbi; his name is here invoked, of course, to stand for the ultra-orthodox in religion.
8. Benjamin L. Leonard (born 1896), well-known New York pugilist and sports figure.
9. Stephen Wise (1874–1949) was one of the leading American Zionists throughout his life.
10. Leon D. Trotsky (originally Lev Bronstein) 1877–1940, a leader in the Bolshevik Revolution in Russia and organizer of the Red Army.
11. Cyrus Adler (1863–1940), prominent educator and lay leader of American Conservative Judaism and the American Jewish Committee. Adler was one of the most important non-Zionists in American Jewry.

BAR-ILAN

1. Ecclesiastes 1:18.

CHAIM WEIZMANN

1. The shekel was a biblical coin; in modern times the name was used to denote a contribution to the World Zionist Organization, which permitted the contributor to cast a vote in the

elections to the Zionist Congress.

2. The Jewish Colonial Trust was formally organized in 1899, following out an idea of Herzl's that a bank should be created, through selling shares widely among the adherents of Zionism, to be the mainstay of future colonization efforts in Palestine. Both the initial stock sale and the ultimate business future of the Trust were disappointing.

3. The Jewish National Fund was created by resolution of the Fifth Zionist Congress, December 1901. Its purpose was to acquire soil in Palestine as the inalienable property of the Jewish people. Successful from the start in enlisting wide practical support, this agency has been a principal instrument of the practical work of the Zionist movement.

4. See Herzl, Note 4.

5. An itinerant preacher, skilled as a narrator of stories.

6. Young man.

7. Allegory.

8. Edmund Allenby (1861–1936), British general whose armies wrested Palestine from the Turks in 1917; he then revealed himself as unsympathetic toward Zionism.

SILVER

1. Johann Gottlieb Fichte (1762–1814). His *Reden an die Deutsche Nation* (1807) helped launch German nationalism and conservative romanticism. He is Hegel's predecessor in the notion that history is to end in a German era.

2. The six-year-old child Edgar Mortara of Bologna, Italy, was abducted in 1858 by Papal Guards after his governess revealed that she had secretly baptized the child. The incident had international repercussions and led to the formation of the Alliance Israelite Universelle, in 1860 in Paris, for the defense of Jewish rights.

3. This Hungarian town was the scene of a blood accusation in which several Jews were falsely accused in 1882 of murdering a Christian child. The accused were subsequently acquitted.

4. An anti-Semitic book published in France in 1886 by the notorious Jew-baiter Edouard Adolphe Drumont (1844–1917). This, the first of many such works from his pen, sold in many editions both in France and all over the world. It became a "classic text" for international anti-Semitism.

BEN-GURION

1. Leviticus 19:18.

2. E.g., Isaiah 2:1–4.

3. Saul Tchernichowsky (1875–1943), distinguished Hebrew poet, whose views resembled those of Berdichevski (Part 5). He translated a number of epics

from various classic literatures into Hebrew.

4. Yevsektzia=the bureau of Jewish affairs created within the People's Commissariat of Nationalities after the Bolshevik revolution in Russia. In that form, it was dissolved in 1930, but the reference is to the policy which it represented and which continued, i.e., the forcible imposition of Communist thought on Russian Jewry and the repression of religion, Hebrew, and Zionism. "Fraction" is an early term for the Communist Party in Palestine.

5. This comment is an obvious, though somewhat veiled, attack on the socialists to the left of him, as spearheaded by the Hashomer Hatzair, the organization of those living in the collective colonies (the *kibbutzim*) whose political orientation was at once Zionist and pro-Soviet Russia.

6. Hehalutz, a nonpolitical, worldwide agency to develop pioneers for Palestine. It was organized in 1924, at a meeting in Danzig, Poland.

7. Histadrut is the general trade union organization of Palestine. This body was created in 1920 and is, to this day, the largest nongovernmental force in Israel. It is dominated by Mapai, the Social-Democratic Party of David Ben-Gurion, though it includes a substantial minority belonging to more leftist groups of Mapam and Achdut Avodah.

8. The pioneering movement in Palestine. The term, as here used, has overtones both of the need to return to physical labor on the land and the fostering of mass immigration as the imperative task of the Zionist movement.

ACKNOWLEDGMENTS

MANY OF THE SOURCES of the reader are either in the public domain or were published by various constituents of the World Zionist Organization, and were, therefore, freely available for use in this book. Other material is being used with permission, which is herewith acknowledged with thanks:

Bloch Publishing Company, the quotations from Horace Kallen's *Judaism at Bay* and the translation of Moses Hess done by Meyer Waxman; Behrman House, the present copyright owners, the passage from Ludwig Lewisohn; Schocken Books, the excerpts from Martin Buber and Bernard Lazare; Victor Gollancz, the publisher, and Paul Goodman, the editor, the passages from Chaim Weizmann's speeches; Mr. Gollancz, the translation of material by Edmond Fleg, which is being used by permission of the copyright owner, Libraire Gallimard; East and West Library and R. and K. Paul, the Simon translations of Ahad Ha-Am; the Macmillan Company, the quotations from *The Future of the American Jew*, by M. M. Kaplan; and Miss Marie Syrkin, the excerpts from the writings of her father, Nahman Syrkin.

SOURCES

RABBI YEHUDAH ALKALAI: *Kitbe*, Vol. 1, Jerusalem, 1945, pp. 178–238 (a collection of paragraphs culled from various places in the text). Translated from the Hebrew by the editor.

RABBI ZVI HIRSCH KALISCHER: *Derishat Tsiyyon* (2nd ed.), Thorn, 1866, pp. 10–12, 21, 6–8. Translated from the Hebrew by the editor.

MOSES HESS: *Rom und Jerusalem*, Leipsic, 1862 (an arrangement of passages culled from all parts of the volume). Retranslated from the German by the editor, on the basis of an earlier translation by Meyer Waxman.

PERETZ SMOLENSKIN: *Maamarim*, Jerusalem, 1925–26, Vol. II, pp. 141–47; Vol. III, pp. 94–125; idem, pp. 37–52 (with cuts in all three selections). Translated from the Hebrew by the editor.

ELIEZER BEN-YEHUDAH: *Hashahar*, Vol. X, Vienna, 1880, pp. 241–45. Translated from the Hebrew by the editor.

MOSHE LEIB LILIENBLUM: *Derekh Tshuvah*, Warsaw, 1899, p. 282; *Kol Kitbe*, Odessa, 1913, Vol. IV, pp. 13–17; idem, pp. 57–73. Translated from the Hebrew by the editor.

LEO PINSKER: *Road to Freedom*, edited by B. Netanyahu, New York, 1944, pp. 74–95, 105–6. Translated from the German by David Blondheim.

THEODOR HERZL: *Theodor Herzl*, edited by Ludwig Lewisohn, New York, 1955, pp. 221, 233–55, 300–3, 307–12, 231. Translated from the German by Sylvie D'Avigdor (*The Jewish State*) and Maurice Samuel (the passages from the diaries); revised by Ben Halpern and Moshe Kohn.

MAX NORDAU: *Zionistische Schriften*, Berlin, 1923, pp. 39–57, 18–38 (with cuts in both selections). Translated from the German by the editor.

AHAD HA-AM: *Pardes*, Vol. II, Odessa, 1894, pp. 1–8; *Hashiloah*, Vol. XIII, Krakau, 1904, pp. 387–95 (with cuts); *Igrot Ahad Ha-Am*, Vol. IV, Tel-Aviv, 1924, pp. 148–49; *Hashiloah*, Vol. II, Berlin, 1897, pp. 568–70; idem, Vol. XX, Odessa, 1909, pp. 467–73.

Translated from the Hebrew by Sir Leon Simon; *The Jewish State and the Jewish Problem*, retranslated by the editor.

HAYYIM NAHMAN BIALIK: *Bialik al ha-Universitah ha-Ivrit* (pamphlet), Jerusalem, 1935, pp. 3–15. Translated from the Hebrew by the editor.

MICAH JOSEPH BERDICHEVSKI: *Ba-Derekh*, Vol. I, Lipsiah, 1922, p. 68; idem, Vol. II, pp. 18–20, 55–57, 45–47, 48–52. Translated from the Hebrew by Ben Halpern and the editor.

JOSEPH HAYYIM BRENNER: *Revivim*, Vol. V, Jerusalem, 1914, pp. 111–19 (with cuts). Translated from the Hebrew by the editor.

JACOB KLATZKIN: *Tehumim*, Berlin, 1925, pp. 45–48, 76–78, 81–82, 103–5. Translated from the Hebrew by the editor.

NAHMAN SYRKIN: *Die Judenfrage und der sozialistische Judenstaat*, von Ben Elieser (his pseudonym), Bern, 1898 (pamphlet, with cuts). Translated from the German by the editor.

BER BOROCHOV: *Nationalism and the Class Struggle*, New York, 1935, pp. 135–36, 183–205 (with cuts in both selections). Translated from Yiddish for that volume by Jacob Katzman and Ben Yitzhaki.

AARON DAVID GORDON: *Kitbe*, Tel-Aviv, 1927–30, Vol. I, pp. 51, 91–102, 85–90; Vol. V, pp. 214–16, 226–30. Translated from the Hebrew by the editor.

BERL KATZENELSON: *Ba-Mivhan* (pamphlet), Tel-Aviv, 1935, pp. 67–70. Translated from the Hebrew by the editor.

RABBI SAMUEL MOHILEVER: *Sefer Shmuel*, edited by J. L. Fishman, Jerusalem, 1923, pp. 67–70. Translated from the Hebrew by the editor.

YEHIEL MICHAEL PINES: *Yalde Ruhi*, Mainz, 1872, Vol. II, pp. 5–6, 42; *Emet me-Erez Tizmah*, Jerusalem, 1895, Vol. III, pp. 23–25; idem, Vol. II, pp. 16–18; *Binyan ha-Arez*, Tel-Aviv, 1939, Vol. II, pp. 112–13. Translated from the Hebrew by the editor.

RABBI ABRAHAM ISAAC KOOK: *Orot* (2nd ed.), Jerusalem, 1950: *Erez Yisrael*, paragraphs 1, 3, 4, 5, 8; *Ha-Milhamah*, paragraphs 3 and 9; *Yisrael U-Thiyato*, paragraphs 5, 28, 31; *Orot ha-Thiyah*, paragraphs 5, 8, 9, 26, 33. Translated from the Hebrew by the editor.

SAMUEL HAYYIM LANDAU: *Kitbe*, Warsaw, 1935, pp. 36–43. Translated from the Hebrew by the editor.

JUDAH LEON MAGNES: *Like All the Nations?*, Jerusalem, 1930, pp. 22–32.

MARTIN BUBER: *Israel and the World*, New York, 1948, pp. 167–72, 245–52, 231–33. The first two selections, translated from German for that volume by Olga Marx.

BERNARD LAZARE: *Job's Dungheap*, New York, 1948, pp. 62–66, 71–75, 85–86. Translated from the French for that volume by Harry Lorrin Binsse.

EDMOND FLEG: *Pourquoi je suis Juif*, Paris, 1927, selected paragraphs from the whole book. Translated from the French by Victor Gollancz.

LUDWIG LEWISOHN: *Rebirth* (editor), New York, 1935, pp. 290–96.

RICHARD J. H. GOTTHEIL: *The Aims of Zionism* (pamphlet), New York, 1899 (with cuts).

SOLOMON SCHECHTER: *Seminary Addresses and Other Papers*, New York, 1915, pp. 91–104.

LOUIS D. BRANDEIS: *Brandeis on Zionism*, New York, 1942, pp. 24–35.

HORACE M. KALLEN: *Judaism at Bay*, New York, 1932, pp. 107–10, 111–15; *The Struggle for Jewish Unity* (pamphlet), Washington, 1933, pp. 10–12.

MORDECAI M. KAPLAN: *The Future of the American Jew*, New York, 1948, pp. 128–30, 433–36, 437–40.

RABBI MEIR BAR-ILAN (BERLIN): *Kitbe*, Vol. I, Jerusalem, 1950, pp. 5–16. Translated from the Hebrew by the editor.

VLADIMIR JABOTINSKY: *Evidence Submitted to the Palestine Royal Commission* (pamphlet), London, 1937, pp. 10–29 (with cuts).

CHAIM WEIZMANN: *Chaim Weizmann*, edited by Paul Goodman, London, 1945, pp. 153–55, 196–201, 268–77 (with cuts).

ABBA HILLEL SILVER: *Vision and Victory*, New York, 1949, pp. 14–21, 211–13.

DAVID BEN-GURION: *Ba-Maarachah*, Vol. III, Tel-Aviv, 1948, pp. 197–98, 200–11. Translated from the Hebrew by the editor.

ARTHUR HERTZBERG is a historian, an Associate in the Seminar in Interreligious Relations at Columbia University, and rabbi of Temple Emanu-El in Englewood, New Jersey. He received his general education at Johns Hopkins, Harvard, and Columbia, and his rabbinic degree from the Jewish Theological Seminary of America. A frequent contributor to periodicals, he is the author of *Religion in Crisis* and co-editor of *Essays in Jewish Life and Thought*.